Marketing

Marketing

Fourth Edition

C. Shane Hunt
Idaho State University

John E. Mello
Arkansas State University

George D. Deitz
University of Memphis

MARKETING, FOURTH EDITION

Published by McGraw Hill LLC, 1325 Avenue of the Americas, New York, NY 10019. Copyright ©2024 by McGraw Hill LLC. All rights reserved. Printed in the United States of America. Previous editions ©2021, 2018, and 2015. No part of this publication may be reproduced or distributed in any form or by any means, or stored in a database or retrieval system, without the prior written consent of McGraw Hill LLC, including, but not limited to, in any network or other electronic storage or transmission, or broadcast for distance learning.

Some ancillaries, including electronic and print components, may not be available to customers outside the United States.

This book is printed on acid-free paper.

1 2 3 4 5 6 7 8 9 LWI 28 27 26 25 24 23

ISBN 978-1-265-27108-4 (bound edition)
MHID 1-265-27108-9 (bound edition)
ISBN 978-1-266-34073-4 (loose-leaf edition)
MHID 1-266-34073-4 (loose-leaf edition)

Portfolio Manager: *Jessica Dimitrijevic*
Lead Product Developer: *Kelly Pekelder*
Product Developer: *Allison Marker*
Marketing Manager: *Michelle Sweeden*
Lead Content Project Manager: *Christine Vaughan*
Senior Content Project Manager: *Emily Windelborn*
Buyer: *Rachel Hirschfield*
Senior Content Licensing Specialist: *Beth Cray*
Cover Image: *Rawpixel/Stock/Getty Images*
Compositor: *Aptara®, Inc*

All credits appearing on page or at the end of the book are considered to be an extension of the copyright page.

Library of Congress Cataloging-in-Publication Data

Names: Hunt, C. Shane, author. | Mello, John E., author. | Deitz, George, author.
Title: Marketing / C. Shane Hunt, Idaho State University, John E. Mello, Arkansas State University, George D. Deitz, University of Memphis.
Description: Fourth edition. | New York, NY : McGraw Hill LLC, [2024] | Includes bibliographical references and index.
Identifiers: LCCN 2022038269 (print) | LCCN 2022038270 (ebook) | ISBN 9781265271084 (hardback) | ISBN 9781266340734 (spiral bound) | ISBN 9781266337673 (ebook) | ISBN 9781266347535 (ebook other)
Classification: LCC HF5415 .H872 2024 (print) | LCC HF5415 (ebook) | DDC 658.8—dc23/eng/20220817
LC record available at https://lccn.loc.gov/2022038269
LC ebook record available at https://lccn.loc.gov/2022038270

The Internet addresses listed in the text were accurate at the time of publication. The inclusion of a website does not indicate an endorsement by the authors or McGraw Hill LLC, and McGraw Hill LLC does not guarantee the accuracy of the information presented at these sites.

BRIEF CONTENTS

C. Shane Hunt

Shane Hunt

Dr. C. Shane Hunt received his PhD in marketing from Oklahoma State University. Shane has won numerous awards for his teaching, including the 2010 National Inspire Integrity Award from the National Society of Collegiate Scholars, the 2010 Lt. Col. Barney Smith Award as Professor of the Year at Arkansas State University, the 2011 Excellence in Undergraduate Teaching Award, the 2015 Honors Professor of the Year Award, and the 2019 National Teaching Innovation Award presented by the Association of Collegiate Marketing Educators.

Shane's research has appeared in the *Journal of Personal Selling and Sales Management,* the *Journal of Business Logistics,* and other leading marketing journals. He has presented to numerous organizations including the American Marketing Association and the National Conference in Sales Management.

After completing his MBA degree, Shane went to work for a Fortune 500 company in Tulsa, Oklahoma, and spent eight years working as a pricing analyst, product manager, and business development manager overseeing numerous strategic initiatives. In addition to his role as a professor, Shane also serves as a consultant, speaker, and board member for businesses and nonprofit organizations across the country.

Shane is now the Dean of the College of Business and Michael C. Ruettgers Professor of Marketing at Idaho State University. He lives in Pocatello, ID, with his wife, Jenifer, and their two children, Andrew and Sarah.

John E. Mello

John E. Mello

John E. Mello (PhD Tennessee) is a Professor of Supply Chain Management and Director, Center for Supply Chain Management, Arkansas State University. Prior to entering academia, he spent 28 years in the consumer packaged goods industry in various supply chain management positions. He is the Neil Griffin College of Business Excellence in Graduate Teaching award winner for 2012 and 2018, and Excellence in Research for 2014. His research has been published in *Foresight: The International Journal of Applied Forecasting, Journal of Business Forecasting, Journal of Business Logistics, Journal of Supply Chain Management, International Journal of Physical Distribution and Logistics Management, International Journal of Logistics Management,* and *Transportation Journal, Transportation Research Part E.*

George D. Deitz

George D. Deitz

Dr. George D. Deitz completed his PhD in marketing at the University of Alabama. He is currently the George Johnson Professor in Marketing at the University of Memphis. George has enjoyed the opportunity to teach a wide variety of face-to-face and online courses at the undergraduate, MBA, and doctoral levels.

In 2013, George helped found the Consumer Neuroscience Research Laboratory (C-NRL) at Memphis, with the mission of advancing the use of physiological and neurological measurement systems to the study of marketing research questions. His research has been published in *Journal of Service Research, Journal of Business Venturing, Journal of Public Policy and Marketing,* the *Journal of Advertising Research, Journal of Business Logistics,* and other leading marketing journals. He has presented at a number of different conferences, including the American Marketing Association and the Academy of Marketing Science.

After obtaining his master's degree at West Virginia University, George began his professional career working in college athletic administration at the United States Military Academy at West Point, New York. Following that, he spent nearly a decade working in a variety of sales and sales management roles with several start-up ventures in the software industry.

George currently lives in Germantown, Tennessee, with his wife, Kristine. They have three children, Luke, Mark, and Koren.

DEDICATION

To Rodney Loren Pilgrim, our incredible Dad and Papa whose love, sacrifice, and dedication made every part of our lives better. We love you forever.

Shane

To my dear friend, Dr. Shane Hunt, who is an inspiration to us all.

John

To my brother Alex, sister-in-law Sangeeta, and the two little rays of joyous sunshine otherwise known as our nieces Surabhi and Maya.

George

Hello and welcome to Hunt, Mello, and Deitz's *Marketing* 4e. Students, particularly non-marketing majors, want to know, *"Why does this course matter to me?"* We designed our product to emphasize the universal importance of marketing . . . *because everyone is a marketer.*

We designed this product with an emphasis on student engagement and relevance, a focus embodied in these four key benefits:

- A **career focus,** to help students understand how marketing will support whatever career path they choose and how to develop their own *personal brand.*
- **Integration of key topics** that are part of the daily fabric of marketing—globalization, social media, ethics, and marketing analytics.
- Seamlessly integrated **results-driven technology.**
- The **right content** for a semester-long course.

Career Focus

The goal of higher education for most students, whatever their major, is to develop knowledge that can be put to use in productive careers. We've included features that focus on careers:

- *Executive Perspective interviews* illustrate the need for successful leaders in any organization to be effective marketers. These interviews represent a wide range of undergraduate majors, including finance, engineering, operations, and accounting.
- *Today's Professional interviews* highlight young marketing professionals who describe how developing their personal brand has helped advance their careers.
- *Career Tips* offer chapter-related ideas that can help students develop their own *personal brand*—a theme carried throughout.
- In the *Marketing Plan Exercise* threaded throughout, students apply the elements of a marketing plan in the context of *marketing themselves.* This project brings a marketing plan to life in a way that personally engages students.
- *Marketing Insights* Podcast Series featuring content from the authors and executives profiles throughout the textbook.

Integration of Key Topics

Students won't find "Ethics Tuesdays," "Global Thursdays," or "Social Media Fridays" in their careers. Therefore, we chose to integrate the key topics of *ethics, globalization, social media,* and *marketing analytics* into chapter discussions where relevant. Integration of these four key topics efficiently delivers a fully rounded, three-dimensional view of each chapter topic, to help ensure that students are gaining sufficient knowledge and skills in these essential aspects of marketing.

Results-Driven Technology

This product is "digital-first," built from the ground up to integrate digital content seamlessly. We wrote the narrative and the digital content simultaneously, dovetailing print and digital delivery in McGraw Hill's *results-driven technology* platform. The close linkage of chapter content and *Connect* assignments allows students to practice how to use classroom content to inform marketing decisions.

The Right Content

We designed our chapters to include the most valuable content for a Principles of Marketing course. Chapters are direct, concise, and approachable in length. We don't overburden students (or instructors) with content that is more appropriate in advanced marketing courses. The chapters allow a bit of classroom "breathing time" for the discussions and activities that bring marketing alive for you and your students.

In addition, we've used market feedback to revise the existing chapters, as outlined in the section Chapter-by-Chapter Changes in the Fourth Edition. Content changes in the fourth edition add increased depth or breadth—more rigor where requested or fresh coverage of emerging areas of importance to marketing theory and practice.

"Because Everyone Is a Marketer . . ."

Our goal is to build the best-possible principles of marketing product—one that captures the importance of marketing in a way that is relevant and adaptable to today's business students. Understanding and utilizing marketing to improve for-profit businesses, nonprofit organizations, and students' career prospects are critical educational activities. These activities are relevant to *any student,* regardless of his or her area of focus. We have worked to produce an integrated print and digital experience that will inspire students to explore and apply the marketing experiences they need in order to leave your course prepared for future coursework and for careers.

It is our sincere hope that *Marketing* 4e will engage your students and demonstrate the universal importance of marketing . . . *because everyone is a marketer!*

C. Shane Hunt
Idaho State University

John E. Mello
Arkansas State University

George D. Deitz
The University of Memphis

Students
Get Learning that Fits You

Effective tools for efficient studying

Connect is designed to help you be more productive with simple, flexible, intuitive tools that maximize your study time and meet your individual learning needs. Get learning that works for you with Connect.

Study anytime, anywhere

Download the free ReadAnywhere® app and access your online eBook, SmartBook® 2.0, or Adaptive Learning Assignments when it's convenient, even if you're offline. And since the app automatically syncs with your Connect account, all of your work is available every time you open it. Find out more at **mheducation.com/readanywhere**

"I really liked this app—it made it easy to study when you don't have your text-book in front of you."

- Jordan Cunningham,
  Eastern Washington University

Everything you need in one place

Your Connect course has everything you need—whether reading your digital eBook or completing assignments for class—Connect makes it easy to get your work done.

Learning for everyone

McGraw Hill works directly with Accessibility Services Departments and faculty to meet the learning needs of all students. Please contact your Accessibility Services Office and ask them to email accessibility@mheducation.com, or visit **mheducation.com/about/accessibility** for more information.

Take Students Higher

McGraw Hill supports you in moving students from foundational cognitive skills to higher-order thinking and application with a variety of digital content and assignable assets. Within Connect, each asset's alignment to the levels of Bloom's Taxonomy is identified so you can easily assign and receive reporting on student progress. The chart below outlines the asset type and how it aligns to Bloom's Taxonomy.

LOWER ——————▶ HIGHER

ASSET	DESCRIPTION	REMEMBER	UNDERSTAND	APPLY	ANALYZE	EVALUATE	CREATE
SmartBook® 2.0	Our adaptive reading experience has been made more personal, accessible, productive and mobile.	■	■				
NEW! iSeeit! Videos	Short, contemporary videos provide engaging, animated introductions to key course concepts. Available and assignable at the topic level, these videos are perfect for launching lectures or to check for understanding.	■	■				
Click and Drag	Click and Drag exercises challenge students to apply business communication concepts to a variety of scenarios critically thinking about concepts and apply them to real world scenarios.	■	■	■			
NEW! Video Case	Live-action videos with accompanying multiple-choice questions challenge students to apply business concepts to everyday situations, real products, and companies.	■	■	■	■		
Case Analysis	Mini-cases and scenarios of real-world firms accompanied by questions that help students analyze and apply core business concepts.	■	■	■	■		
Marketing Analytics	These auto-graded, marketing analytics activities challenge students to make decisions using metrics commonly seen across marketing professions. The goal of these activities is to give students practice analyzing and using marketing data to make decisions.	■	■	■	■		
Marketing Plan Prep Exercises	These exercises use guided activities and examples to help students understand and differentiate the various elements of a marketing plan.	■	■	■	■		
NEW! Application-based Activities	These highly interactive, automatically graded exercises provide students a safe space to practice using problem-solving skills to apply their knowledge to realistic scenarios. Each scenario addresses key concepts and skills that students must use to work through and solve course specific problems, resulting in improved critical thinking and relevant workplace skills.	■	■	■	■	■	
Writing Assignment PLUS	Writing Assignment Plus delivers a learning experience that helps students improve their written communication skills and conceptual understanding. Faculty can assign, monitor, grade, and provide feedback on writing projects efficiently. Built-in grammar and writing review helps students improve writing quality while an originality check helps students correct potential plagiarism before submission. End result? Improved workplace skills of writing and critical thinking.	■	■	■	■	■	■

OLC-Aligned Courses

Implementing High-Quality Instruction and Assessment through Preconfigured Courseware

In consultation with the Online Learning Consortium (OLC) and our certified Faculty Consultants, McGraw Hill has created pre-configured courseware using OLC's quality scorecard to align with best practices in online course delivery. This turnkey courseware contains a combination of formative assessments, summative assessments, homework, and application activities, and can easily be customized to meet an individual instructor's needs and desired course outcomes. For more information, visit https://www.mheducation.com/highered/olc.

Test Builder in Connect

Available within Connect, Test Builder is a cloud-based tool that enables instructors to format tests that can be printed, administered within a Learning Management System, or exported as a Word document. Test Builder offers a modern, streamlined interface for easy content configuration that matches course needs, without requiring a download.

Test Builder allows you to:

- access all test bank content from a particular title.
- easily pinpoint the most relevant content through robust filtering options.
- manipulate the order of questions or scramble questions and/or answers.
- pin questions to a specific location within a test.
- determine your preferred treatment of algorithmic questions.
- choose the layout and spacing.
- add instructions and configure default settings.

Test Builder provides a secure interface for better protection of content and allows for just-in-time updates to flow directly into assessments.

Proctorio

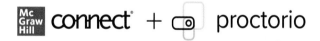

Remote Proctoring & Browser-Locking Capabilities

Remote proctoring and browser-locking capabilities, hosted by Proctorio within Connect, provide control of the assessment environment by enabling security options and verifying the identity of the student.

Seamlessly integrated within Connect, these services allow instructors to control the assessment experience by verifying identification, restricting browser activity, and monitoring student actions.

Instant and detailed reporting gives instructors an at-a-glance view of potential academic integrity concerns, thereby avoiding personal bias and supporting evidence-based claims.

CHAPTER-BY-CHAPTER CHANGES IN THE FOURTH EDITION

The fourth edition's revisions are driven by feedback from instructors and students.

Overall

- The content and examples in *Marketing* 4e were revised and added with a keen eye toward diversity, equity, and inclusion in an effort to ensure it is reflecting the diverse marketing environment around us.
- New executive perspectives and today's professional profiles throughout that will help students understand how everyone is a marketer.
- New examples of organizations across industries that utilized marketing strategy to successfully navigate the challenges of the COVID-19 pandemic.
- New examples highlighting the role of marketing in a rapidly changing world.
- Four NEW video cases featuring how marketing is impacting dynamic organizations in industries ranging from credit unions to minor league baseball to commercial real estate.

Chapter 1: Why Marketing Matters to You

- New examples and discussion on the impact of social media on modern marketing.
- New figures and exhibits highlighting the rapidly changing marketing landscape
- Updated global business/trade statistics.
- New Executive Perspective profile.
- New Today's Professional profile.

Chapter 2: Strategic Planning

- New Executive Perspective profile.
- New Social Media in Action Exercise featuring Little Caesars Pizza and TikTok.
- Updated data throughout the chapter including new presentation of auto manufacturers' market share.
- New Today's Professional profile.

Chapter 3: The Global Environment

- New discussion on the marketing impact of COVID-19.
- New Figure 3.2 on changes to income distribution and Figure 3.3 on the relationship between consumer confidence and consumption.
- New Executive Perspective and New Today's Professional profiles.
- New examples and discussion about inflation, trade agreements, and external environmental factors.

Chapter 4: Consumer Behavior

- Deeper discussion of situational influences on decision making, with new subsections and corresponding examples relating how consumers' physical surroundings, social surroundings, time, and task definition impact decisions.
- Revised section on cultural influences, including new subsections on consumptions subcultures, brand communities, and consumer tribes.

- New examples throughout the chapter, including model and lifestyle social media influencer Karlee Kloss and discussion of how consumer demand for electric vehicle batteries creates derived demand for the mineral cobalt.
- New Executive Perspective and Today's Professional profiles.

Chapter 5: Marketing Research and Analytics

- Enriched discussion of Big Data and the use of predictive analytics models in marketing decision making.
- More types and examples of secondary data sources.
- Much broader coverage and deeper elaboration on qualitative research methods, including examples of their application in marketing contexts.
- New discussion of the emergence of customer journey mapping as an important marketing research application trend.

Chapter 6: Product Development

- Discussion of the positive impact of new product development in fighting COVID-19.
- New examples and discussion of services, differentiating them from products, and why this is important to the subject of NPD.
- New Today's Professional profile.

Chapter 7: Segmentation, Targeting, and Positioning

- New Executive Perspective profile.
- Discussion of how COVID-19 impacted market targeting including examples of consumers dramatically increasing spending on their pets.
- New examples and updated figures throughout.

Chapter 8: Promotional Strategies

- Expanded coverage of changes in advertising and product placement.
- New discussion on using video games as a promotional tool.
- New Today's Professional profile.
- New examples throughout, including the expanding impact of social media on organizations' promotional strategies.

Chapter 9: Personal Selling

- Revised section on sales technology, including enhanced discussion of CRM in sales, a new post-COVID-19 section on the rise of virtual selling, and updates on best practices in social selling.
- Introduced new content on the role of the psychological trait "grit" in preserving a salesperson's positive self concept.
- Revised overview on the various types of sales roles, including new sections on customer success managers and sales operations support roles.
- New Executive Perspective profile.

Chapter 10: Supply Chain and Logistics Management

- Discussion of supply chain disruptions due to COVID-19.
- New examples and organization of supply chain management section around the topics of supply chain integration, resilience of supply chains, and logistics operations.

- Explanation of the importance of internal and external collaboration to supply chain management.
- New Executive Perspective.

Chapter 11: Pricing

- New Executive Perspective.
- Expanded discussion on the marketing impact of recent tariffs.
- New examples, including a discussion of pricing strategy for streaming services.

Chapter 12: Retailing

- Streamlined discussion of retailer types, with new examples and details on the impact of COVID-19 on selected retail categories.
- New and improved section on key trends in modern retail, with new content and examples on retail analytics, competing on customer experience, and retail technology applications, including artificial intelligence (AI), voice-activated search, geofencing, and VR/AR.
- Revised discussion of omnichannel retailing, including retailer response to the pandemic via introduction of buy-online-purchase-in-store (BOPIS) and curbside delivery services.
- New Today's Professional profile.

Chapter 13: Digital and Social Media Marketing

- Digital and social media marketing practices are fast-paced and constantly changing. We've updated content and examples throughout the chapter.
- Expanded social media marketing section, including discussion of marketers increased use of niche "SoMe" social media platforms.
- Enriched discussion of digital and social media analytics, detailing common KPIs for measuring search, content, website, and social media marketing performance.
- New Marketing Plan exercise designed to help students incorporate experts' best practices into their personal LinkedIn profiles.

Chapter 14: Branding

- Expanded discussion of the role of social media in branding.
- New Video Case featuring Idaho Central Credit Union.
- Updated Table 14.2, the top 10 most valuable global brands.

Chapter 15: Customer Relationship Management

- Updated list of companies that enjoy the highest customer experience ratings.
- Addition of the concept of a "breakpoint" in customer service as an unethical CRM practice.
- New Today's Professional profile.

Chapter 16: Social Responsibility and Sustainability

- Expanded "Ethical Dimensions" section that focuses on the goals of designing and producing new products ethically.
- New examples discussing sustainability issues with supply chain management.
- Addition of ethical and sustainability issues in new product development.

ACKNOWLEDGMENTS

We are deeply indebted to the many marketing scholars and instructors, business leaders and professionals, and colleagues and friends who have contributed their time, ideas, and insights to the development of this product. We appreciate your help and your shared passion for maximizing the educational experience of our students and future leaders.

Special Thanks to Our Reviewers

Reviewers who provided feedback that was essential to the development of the fourth edition and previous editions include:

Praveen Aggarwal,
University of Minnesota, Duluth

Raj Agnihotri,
University of Texas at Arlington

Bob Ahuja,
Xavier University

Mary Albrecht,
Maryville University

Keanon Alderson,
California Baptist University

Elizabeth C. Alexander,
Marshall University

Charlotte Allen,
Stephen F. Austin State University

Daniel Allen,
Utah State University

Elsa Anaya,
Alamo Colleges, Palo Alto College

Cynthia Anderson,
Youngstown State University

Christopher Anicich,
California State University, Fullerton

Maria Aria,
Camden County College

Timothy W. Aurand,
Northern Illinois University

Joe K. Ballenger,
Stephen F. Austin State University

Soumava Bandyopadhyay,
Lamar University

Christine Barnes,
Lakeland Community College

Jennifer Barr,
Richard Stockton College of New Jersey

Arne Baruca,
Sacred Heart University

George Bass,
Kennesaw State University

Charles Beem,
Bucks County Community College

Robert Belenger,
Bristol Community College

Frank Benna,
Raritan Valley Community College

George H. Bernard,
Seminole State College of Florida

Stephen Berry,
Anne Arundel Community College

Tom Bilyeu,
Southwestern Illinois College

Nicholas Bosco,
Suffolk County Community College

David Bourff,
Boise State University

Michael Brady,
Florida State University

Cheryl O'Meara Brown,
University of West Georgia

Kendrick Brunson,
Liberty University

Gary Brunswick,
Northern Michigan University

Kent Byus,
Texas A&M University, Corpus Christi

Kimberly Cade,
Houston Community College, Central

Kerri M. Camp,
University of Texas at Tyler

Amy Caponetti,
Pellissippi State Community College

Carla Cardellio,
Schoolcraft College

Deborah Carter,
Coahoma Community College

Eric Carter,
California State University, Bakersfield

Debi Cartwright,
Truman State University

Elisabeth Cason,
Bossier Parish Community College

Gerald Cavallo,
Fairfield University

Anindya Chatterjee,
Slippery Rock University

Ruth Chavez,
Metropolitan State University of Denver

Piotr Chelminski,
Providence College

Haozhe Chen,
East Carolina University

Lisa Cherivtch,
Oakton Community College

Jerome Christia,
Coastal Carolina University

Christina Chung,
Ramapo College of New Jersey

Janet Ciccarelli,
Herkimer County Community College

Dorene Ciletti,
Duquesne University

Paul Clark,
Coastal Carolina University

Reid Claxton,
East Carolina University

Steven Clinton,
Robert Morris University

Kyle Coble,
Lindenwood University

Gloria Cockerell,
Collin College

Kesha Coker,
Eastern Illinois University

Margy Conchar,
East Carolina University

Francisco Conejo,
University of Colorado, Denver

Mary Conran,
Temple University

Barbara T. Conte,
Florida Atlantic University

Laurel Cook,
West Virginia University

Richard Cooper,
Lindenwood University

Tracy Cosenza,
University of Memphis

Ian Cross,
Bentley University

Anna Crowe,
University of San Diego

Brent J. Cunningham,
Jacksonville State University

Mayukh Dass,
Texas Tech University

De'Amo De'Armond,
West Texas A&M University

Larry Degaris,
University of Indianapolis

Beth Deinert,
Southeast Community College

George Deitz,
University of Memphis

Duleep Delpechitre,
University of Louisiana, Lafayette

John Depies,
University of Wisconsin, Oshkosh

Chandan DeSarkar,
SUNY, University of Albany

Paul Dion,
Susquehanna University

Kim Donahue,
Indiana University Kelley School of Business, Indianapolis

Beibei Dong,
Lehigh University

Mary Anne Doty,
Texas A&M Commerce

Kathy Dougherty,
Maryville University

Howard Dover,
Salisbury University

Lawrence Duke,
Drexel University

Gregory Dumont,
University of Akron

Stu Dunlop,
Missouri Southern State University

Jill Dybus,
Oakton Community College

Judy Eberhart,
Lindenwood University

Diane Edmondson,
Middle Tennessee State University

Karen A. Evans,
Herkimer College

David J. Faulds,
University of Louisville

Ronald Feinberg,
Suffolk Community College

Janice M. Feldbauer,
Schoolcraft College

Kathleen Ferris-Costa,
Bridgewater State University

Troy Festervand,
Middle Tennessee State University

Monica Fine,
Coastal Carolina University

David Fleming,
Eastern Illinois University

Richard Flight,
Eastern Illinois University

Paul Fombele,
Northeastern University

Angel Fonseca,
Jackson College

Kendra Fowler,
Youngstown State University

Michael Fowler,
Brookdale Community College

Alexa Fox,
Ohio University

Thomas F. Frizzell, Sr.,
Massasoit Community College

Anthony R. Fruzzetti,
Johnson & Wales University

Venessa Funches,
Auburn University, Montgomery

Pat Galitz,
Southeast Community College

Carol Gaumer,
Frostburg State University

Stephanie Gillison,
University of Tennessee at Chattanooga

John T. Gironda,
Nova Southeastern University

Karl Giulian,
Atlantic Cape Community College

Connie Golden,
Lakeland Community College

Edward Gonsalves,
Boston College

Kimberly Grantham,
University of Georgia

Arlene Green,
Indian River State College

Mike Grier,
Central Piedmont Community College

Melodi Guilbault,
New Jersey Institute of Technology

Audrey Guskey,
Duquesne University

Jamey R. Halleck,
Marshall University

Richard Hanna,
Northeastern University

John T. Hansen,
University of Alabama at Birmingham

Ivan Franklin Harber Jr.,
Indian River State College

Robert Harrison,
Western Michigan University

Kelli Hatin,
Adirondack Community College

Adrienne Hinds,
Northern Virginia Community College

Bryan Hochstein,
University of Alabama

Nasim Hosein,
Northwood University

Tarique Hossain,
California State Polytechnic University, Pomona

Robert Hucks,
Bob Jones University

Gail Hudson,
Arkansas State University

Janet Huetteman,
Fairfield University

Steven Huff,
Utah Valley University

Doug Hughes,
Michigan State University

Jing Hu,
California State Polytechnic University, Pomona

Wade Hyde,
El Centro College

James Jarrard,
University of Wisconsin, Platteville

Sean Jasso,
University of California, Riverside

Keith Jones,
Saint Leo University

Michael Jones,
Southeastern Louisiana University

Stephen Juma,
Southern Arkansas University

Sungwoo Jung,
Columbus State University

Marla Kameny,
Baton Rouge Community College

Tommy Karam,
Louisiana State University

Vishal Kashyap,
Xavier University

Bruce Keillor,
Youngstown State University

Sylvia Keyes,
Bridgewater State University

Tina Kiesler,
California State University, Northridge

Nancy Kimble,
Carroll Community College

Taewan Kim,
Lehigh University

Rose Klimovich,
Manhattan College

George B. Krueger,
University of Wisconsin, Platteville

Mike Krush,
North Dakota State University

Ann Kuzma,
Minnesota State University, Mankato

Jane Lang,
East Carolina University

Nikki Lee-Wingate,
Fairfield University

Marilyn Liebrenz-Himes,
George Washington University

Fuan Li,
William Paterson University

Noah Lim,
University of Wisconsin, Madison

Guy Lochiatto,
MassBay Community College

Subhash Lonial,
University of Louisville

Pat Lupino,
Nassau Community College

A. Maamoun,
University of Minnesota, Duluth

Lisa Machado,
Southeast Community College, Lincoln

Deanna Mader,
Marshall University

Cesar Maloles,
California State University, East Bay

Gayle Marco,
Robert Morris University

Peter Maresco,
Sacred Heart University

Melissa M. Martirano,
New Jersey City University

Anil Mathur,
Hofstra University

William Matthews,
William Paterson University

Brian Mazur,
Schoolcraft College

Enda McGovern,
Sacred Heart University

Rajiv Mehta,
New Jersey Institute of Technology

Havva Meric,
East Carolina University

William Merkle,
Bob Jones University

Deborah Merrigan,
Rockland Community College

Bob Meyer,
Parkland College

Marty Meyers,
University of Wisconsin, Stevens Point

Mark Mitchell,
Coastal Carolina University

Iris Mohr,
St. John's University

Risto Moisio,
Cal State Long Beach

Detra Montoya,
University of Washington

Melissa Moore,
Mississippi State University

Paula T. Morris,
Salisbury University

Jay Mulki,
D'Amore McKim School of Business, Northeastern University

Jun Myers,
California State Polytechnic University, Pomona

Thomas Myers,
Virginia Commonwealth University

Gergana Nenkov,
Boston College

Mary Norman,
University of North Georgia

Hudson Nwakanma,
Florida A&M University

Louis Nzegwu,
University of Wisconsin, Platteville

Matt O'Hern,
University of Oregon

Carlton O'Neal,
University of San Diego

Joanne Orabone,
Community College of Rhode Island

Judy Orfao,
Middlesex Community College

Karen Overton,
Houston Community College, Southwest

Thomas J. Passero,
Owens Community College

Kirsten Passyn,
Salisbury University

Debra Perosio,
Cornell University

Edward Petkus,
Ramapo College of New Jersey

Maria Petrescu,
Nova Southeastern University

Julie Pharr,
Tennessee Tech University

Carly Pierson,
Missouri State University

Warren Purdy,
University of Southern Maine

Sekar Raju,
Iowa State University

Bruce Ramsey,
Franklin University

Sampath Kumar Ranganathan,
University of Wisconsin, Green Bay

Mohammed Y. A. Rawwas,
University of Northern Iowa

Kristen Regine,
Johnson & Wales University

Timothy Reisenwitz,
Valdosta State University

Eddie Rhee,
Stonehill College

William E. Rice,
California State University, Fresno

Brent Richard,
North Central Michigan College

Michael A. Richarme,
University of Texas at Arlington

Ralph J. Rich,
Marian University

David Robinson,
University of California, Berkeley

Jessica Rogers,
Texas A&M University, Commerce

Joseph Roman,
New Jersey Institute of Technology

Ann Root,
Florida Atlantic University

Emily Rosenzweig,
Tulane University

Christopher Ross,
Trident Technical College

Doug Ross,
Franklin University

Carol Rowey,
Community College of Rhode Island

Donald Roy,
Middle Tennessee State University

Catherine Ruggieri,
St. John's University

David Rylander,
Texas Woman's College

Ritesh Saini,
University of Texas at Arlington

Alan Sandomir,
University of Utah

Kumar Sarangee,
Santa Clara University

Fritz Scherz,
Morrisville State College

Roberta Schultz,
Western Michigan University

Eric Schulz,
Utah State University

Joe Schwartz,
Georgia College and State University

Ronald Scott,
Trident Technical College

Sandipan Sen,
Southeast Missouri State University

Ravi Shanmugam,
Santa Clara University

J. Richard Shannon,
Western Kentucky University

Lisa Siegal,
Texas A&M University, San Antonio

Rob Simon,
University of Nebraska, Lincoln

Shweta Singh,
Kean University

Ian Skurnik,
Eccles School of Business, University of Utah

Rudy Soliz,
Houston Community College

Karen L. Stewart,
Stockton University

Pete Stone,
Spartanburg Community College

Randy Stuart,
Kennesaw State University

Ramendra Thakur,
University of Louisiana, Lafayette

Kin Thompson,
Northeastern State University

Willie Frank Thompson,
Troy University

Scott Thorne,
Southeast Missouri State University

Patricia Todd,
Western Kentucky University

Deborah Toomey,
Northwest Missouri State University

Dennis Tootelian,
California State University, Sacramento

Hope K. Torkornoo,
Kennesaw State University

Philip Trocchia,
University of South Florida, St. Petersburg

Lisa Troy,
Texas A&M University

Patricia Turnbull,
California State University, Fresno

Ed Valenski,
Long Island University

Laura Lott Valenti,
Nicholls State University

Sal Veas,
Santa Monica College

Ann Veeck,
Western Michigan University

Franck Vigneron,
California State University, Northridge

Jorge Villa,
Park University

Mary Kay Wachter,
Pittsburg State University

Del Wakley,
Milwaukee Area Technical College

Mary Walker,
Xavier University

Michael Walsh,
West Virginia University

Wakiuru Wamwara,
Wright State University

Ursula Wefers,
Plymouth State University

Diane Whitney,
University of Maryland, College Park

Debbora Whitson,
California State Polytechnic University, Pomona

Natalie Winter,
California Baptist University

Jefrey Woodall,
York College of Pennsylvania

Van Wood,
Virginia Commonwealth University

Barbara Ross Wooldridge,
University of Texas at Tyler

Poh-Lin Yeoh,
Bentley University

Mark Yi-Cheon Yim,
Canisius College

Albert Yu,
Santa Rosa Junior College

James E. Zemanek
Jr., East Carolina University

This product would not have been possible without the effort and expertise of many people. First and foremost, we would like to recognize and thank the entire editorial and marketing teams at McGraw Hill Education who have made this product possible. We are very thankful to Meredith Fossel and Jessica Dimitrijevic who surrounded us with the best team in all of higher education publishing. We are thankful for our development editors, Allison Marker and Kelly Pekelder, for keeping us on track and focused on all of the integrated aspects of the product. We are thankful for Michelle Sweeden, a truly amazing marketing manager, whose vision was instrumental in communicating the message of our product.

In addition, we are thankful for Christine Vaughan, Kelly Luchtman, Jacob Sullivan, Keri Johnson, and all of the talented people McGraw Hill assembled whose guidance and feedback made the product much better. It has been our pleasure and privilege to work with these incredibly talented and skilled professionals who have shaped the final product that you are about to read.

We are thankful for Cortney Kieffer, who was Shane's and John's McGraw Hill field representative at Arkansas State University. Cortney was our first exposure to McGraw Hill, and her professionalism, dedication to our students, and friendship made us want to be part of the McGraw Hill family.

We thank Mohammed Rawwas, University of Northern Iowa, for his work in helping develop our new marketing analytics exercises in *Connect*. We also want to thank our colleagues at Idaho State University, Arkansas State University, and the University of Memphis. It is an honor every day to get to work with brilliant people who genuinely and passionately care about the education of our students. In particular, our work on this edition was greatly enhanced by feedback from Sandra Smith, Alex Rose, Nicole Hanson, John Ney, Gail Hudson, Emin Babakus, Dan Sherrell, Mike Peasley, Jennifer Tatara, and Subhash Jha. Their support and friendship is priceless, and we feel very thankful to be part of these truly world-class institutions.

We want to thank our families for their love, support, and patience while we developed this edition. We want to thank the great faculty members at Oklahoma State University, the University of Tennessee, and The University of Alabama for the training and knowledge they gave us during our doctoral programs. We want to thank our many great colleagues in the private sector, at companies including Williams, MediFAX EDI, Citynet, Playtex, and Unilever, who provided us with experiences that sharpened our focus on the practical applications of marketing and preparing our students for today's competitive job market.

Finally, we want to thank our students. Being a marketing professor is the best job in the world because of the students we get to teach, help, and learn from. The great students at Idaho State University, Arkansas State University, the University of Memphis, and throughout the country and the world drove our decision to create this product. Marketing is an extremely important topic for their careers and their lives, and we hope we have developed a product to help them succeed and achieve their dreams.

Shane Hunt, John Mello, and George Deitz

Rafael Henrique/SOPA Images/LightRocket/Getty Images

Tinnaporn Sathapornnanont/Shutterstock

Fly View Productions/Getty Images

Jeff Gilbert/Alamy Stock Photo

Marmaduke St. John/Alamy Stock Photo

Richard Newstead/Flickr/Getty Images

Steve Schaack

Erik Isakson/Blend Images

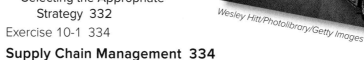

Wesley Hitt/Photolibrary/Getty Images

supparsorn/Shutterstock

TY Lim/Shutterstock

Anatolii Babii/Alamy Stock Photo

Kostic Dusan/fotokostic/123RF

Rob Wilson/Shutterstock

Rawpixel.com/Shutterstock

Part **ONE**

Marketing in the Twenty-First Century

Rafael Henrique/SOPA Images/LightRocket/Getty Images

Tinnaporn Sathapornnanont/Shutterstock

COVID-19 and travel:
Help protect yourself and others

Please maintain
a safe distance
from others whenever
possible.

6'
2m

Fly View Productions/Getty Images

Chapter **1**

Why Marketing Matters to You

Rafael Henrique/SOPA Images/LightRocket/Getty Images

At the beginning of each chapter, you'll see a list of learning objectives that identify the key topics you need to master. You can also use the list as an outline for taking notes as you read through the chapter.

Learning Objectives

After reading this chapter, you should be able to

LO 1-1 Describe a marketer's role in creating, communicating, and delivering value.

LO 1-2 Differentiate among the various eras in the history of marketing.

LO 1-3 Distinguish between consumer needs and consumer wants.

LO 1-4 Explain the four elements in the marketing mix.

LO 1-5 Discuss the importance of globalization in the field of marketing.

LO 1-6 Explain the role of analytics in marketing.

LO 1-7 Demonstrate the relationship between ethical business practices and marketplace success.

LO 1-8 Analyze the functions of marketing beyond the for-profit firm.

Executive **Perspective** ... because everyone is a marketer

Jaime Gaudet
Market Director
Aflac

Jaime Gaudet

Jaime Gaudet majored in chemistry and then developed leadership skills as a high school teacher and coach. She joined Aflac as a sales manager in Louisiana and found a company that shared her value system.

At Aflac now for over 18 years, Gaudet oversees sales for the company in Idaho, Oregon, Montana, and Wyoming, working with business owners, providing insurance products that help strengthen the benefits packages they offer, and educating and enrolling their employees.

What has been the most important thing in making you successful at your job?

I would say it comes down to (4) main things:

- My ability to take care of people.
- Self-awareness is key; learning to read people and situations, and then react intentionally and appropriately has gotten me a long way.
- Continually growing and forever being a student of leadership helps me to learn something new every week. I'm okay being a little uncomfortable, in a good way, because it leads to growth.
- Being passionate about my work. My team and I get to make a difference in people's lives.

What advice would you give soon-to-be graduates?

Take risks at the beginning of your career. This is a unique time in your life because risk-taking often becomes more difficult as we age. Make a big leap as a new graduate. I wish people had said that to me at that point in my life.

Make your passion pay you. Find something that makes you happy and makes you a living rather than try to be happy making a living. When you're passionate about your work, when it's more to you than clocking in and out, you'll naturally be more successful. A lot of people think they've "arrived" at their job or success, but they may not make it in the long term because they stop growing and improving.

How is marketing relevant to your role at the Aflac?

You can't sell an intangible product without marketing. Marketing is *vital* to our selling process. Almost everyone knows the Aflac Duck—we have over 80 percent brand recognition—and with that comes a greater responsibility to protect the brand.

From there, through a variety of mass and micro tactics, communications funnel customers through knowledge of and connection to the brand. Eventually this lands with a specific value for their business at a 1:1 level through our expert sales force. That's how sales and marketing intersect and complement one another. It's why marketing professionals should learn about sales best practices and salespeople should learn about marketing best practices.

What do you consider your personal brand to be?

I started with Aflac in 2003 because we share the same value system. It's summed up in Aflac's seven commitments:

1. Communicate regularly.
2. Respond immediately.
3. Know your stuff.
4. Treat everyone with respect and care.
5. Your problem is my problem.
6. Shoot straight.
7. Cover your customer, not your behind.

I get to impact lives and help change the world by leading a sales organization for a Fortune 500 company. I seek people who share that purpose and passion to join my team. We start with helping to change our communities with the claims we pay; it makes a difference in people's lives when they're sick or hurt. They are our "why," and they are why I've been with Aflac so long. Over time, helping people and making a difference has just become more and more important to me.

LO 1-1

Describe a marketer's role in creating, communicating, and delivering value.

marketing

The activity, set of institutions, and processes for creating, communicating, delivering, and exchanging offerings that have value for customers, clients, partners, and society at large.

THE VALUE OF MARKETING

Welcome to marketing. Wherever your life and career take you after this course, you can be assured that knowing how to implement marketing principles will be an important part of your professional success.

In fact, if you've ever had a job in retail sales or customer service, there is a good chance you have already used marketing principles. **Marketing** is the activity, set of institutions, and processes for creating, communicating, delivering, and exchanging offerings that have value for customers, clients, partners, and society at large. Marketers manage customer relationships in ways that benefit the organization and its employees, its customers, its investors, and society as a whole. This is a fairly lengthy definition, and it is important to understand three main components—creating, communicating, and delivering value—before we proceed.

Creating Value

customer value

The perceived benefits, both monetary and nonmonetary, that a customer receives from a product compared with the cost of obtaining it.

Organizations today are constantly looking for new ways to create value for customers. This is true whether we are talking about a consumer product such as the Apple Watch, social networking applications like Instagram, or educational software like the McGraw Hill *Connect* package that accompanies this text. **Customer value** refers to the perceived benefits, both monetary and nonmonetary, that customers receive from a product, compared with the cost associated with obtaining the product. Examples of perceived benefits might be making customers safer (ADT home security), saving them money (GEICO), or making their lives easier (Samsung Galaxy smartphone). If the benefit of the product or service equals or exceeds its cost, the organization has *created value.*

The key ingredient for creating value is providing consumers with benefits that meet their needs and wants. Merely creating a new product does not guarantee success. Over

Apple can charge higher prices than its competitors without fear of losing sales because of the value customers place on Apple products. *Canadapanda/Shutterstock*

80 percent of all new products fail, a percentage that remains consistent in both good and bad economic conditions.[1] To create value, a new good, service, or idea must satisfy a perceived marketplace demand. Understanding marketplace demands before competitors do is one of the secrets of great marketing.

In later chapters, we will explore specific strategies that support the effort of value creation. These strategies include analysis of the market environment, effective marketing research, and an understanding of customer behavior. Once a company has created a valuable product, it must communicate that value to potential customers.

Communicating Value

Business history is littered with failed companies that had a valuable offering but failed to get that message out to potential customers. For example, there may be a restaurant in the city where you live that serves great food; however, if the restaurant doesn't market itself well, you may never even know it exists. A firm must communicate not only what its product is but what value that product brings to potential customers. A new Subway restaurant near your college campus, for example, might use online advertisements to communicate its convenient location, healthy alternatives, and monthly student specials.

Communicating value also will be critical for you on a personal level as you begin looking for a job. Imagine a human resource manager looking at a stack of 400 resumes, all from applicants with a college degree similar to yours. If your resume looks like every other resume in the stack, odds are your value will not be communicated. Job applicants who are better at marketing themselves will get more interviews and opportunities.

This book will help you learn to communicate your professional value. It includes various features, like the Career Tips section at the end of each chapter, that will help you learn to market yourself. In this chapter, the Career Tips feature focuses on moving your resume out of the stack and getting you into an interview. Once you've landed a job, delivering on the value you communicated will be key, not only to keeping your job but also to moving up in your organization. In the same way, to be successful, firms must deliver on the value of the goods, services, and ideas they offer.

Many of the most successful firms in the world, including Coca-Cola, Walmart, and UPS, excel at managing their supply chains efficiently and have made delivering value a competitive advantage in their industries. *Justin Sullivan/ Getty Images*

Delivering Value

Isn't it remarkable to think that you can buy Diet Coke at a grocery store in Chicago, a mall in San Francisco, a restaurant in Miami, a gas station in rural Idaho, and practically everywhere in between? Millions of people throughout the world buy and enjoy Diet Coke. That phenomenon is made possible by Coca-Cola's ability to deliver its product to countless places. Coca-Cola's *supply chain* is critical in delivering value.

A firm's **supply chain** is a set of multiple companies directly linked by one or more of the upstream and downstream flows of products, services, finances, and information

supply chain

The linked set of companies that perform or support the delivery of a company's goods or services to customers.

logistics
That part of supply chain management that plans, implements, and controls the flow of goods, services, and information between the point of origin and the final customer.

from a source to a customer.[2] Members of the supply chain can include manufacturers, wholesalers, retailers, transportation companies, and other groups, depending on the specific industry. The part of supply chain management that plans, implements, and controls the flow of goods, services, and information between the point of origin and the final customer is called **logistics**. We will examine the challenges and strategies associated with logistics and supply chain management in a later chapter.

HISTORY OF MARKETING

LO 1-2

Differentiate among the various eras in the history of marketing.

Before we consider modern marketing, let's briefly discuss how marketing has evolved to its current state.

Production Orientation

production orientation
A marketing strategy in which the firm focused on efficient processes and production to create quality products and reduce unit costs.

Prior to the 1920s, most firms in the United States and the rest of the developed world had a **production orientation**: They focused on efficient processes and production in order to create quality products and reduce unit costs. Firms with a production orientation believed that quality products would simply sell themselves. The production orientation is summarized in the old saying, "Build a better mousetrap, and the world will beat a path to your door."

In the mid-1920s, the growth in production outpaced consumer demand. To sell what they were able to produce, companies needed new strategies. In an effort to increase demand, firms sought to develop effective sales forces that could find customers for their growing production capacity.

Henry Ford's production line innovation and success manufacturing the Model A automobile represents the production-orientation era, during which firms believed that quality products would sell themselves. *Hulton Archive/Archive Photos/Getty Images*

Sales Orientation

As the size and impact of sales forces grew, many firms shifted to a **sales orientation**: They used personal selling and advertising to persuade consumers to buy new products and more of existing products. This strategy was especially important during the Great Depression: Consumers had little money, so firms competed intensely for customers' dollars. Firms such as Ford could no longer sell all of their products, even though mass production had reduced manufacturing costs. Ford increasingly had to rely on personal selling and advertising to get consumers to buy its products instead of the products of competitors such as General Motors. The sales-orientation era continued until the end of World War II.

sales orientation
A marketing strategy in which personal selling and advertising are used to persuade consumers to buy new products and more of existing products.

Marketing Concept

After two decades of economic depression and world war, the United States entered an era of expansion beginning in the early 1950s. Demand for goods and services increased significantly. Products that had been in limited supply during the war flooded the market, forcing firms to develop new strategies to compete. As a result, a strategy focused on the consumer began to emerge. That strategy, the **marketing concept**, is the idea that a firm's long-term success must include a companywide effort to satisfy customer needs.

The marketing concept is characterized by a *customer orientation,* which stresses the idea that everyone in a firm should assess, then satisfy, a consumer's needs. Walmart's focus on customer satisfaction is an example of the marketing concept in action: Employees in every department are expected to meet customer needs: the cashier checking out customers, the logistics department holding down costs, and a customer service representative handling product returns. The customer orientation has helped Walmart succeed in a competitive environment, even though very few of the products it sells are unique to its stores. Rather than offering unique products, Walmart has focused on satisfying consumers' desire for lower prices, friendly service, and convenience.

The marketing concept continues to evolve. Technology now enables marketers to tailor offerings in a way that has never before been possible. Dell provides a historical example: It became a market leader in the 1990s by allowing individual consumers to customize computers to purchase exactly what they wanted. Customers now have come to like and look for options to customize.

Organizations today also focus on establishing relationships with customers. **Relationship marketing**, a strategy that focuses on attracting, maintaining, and enhancing customer relationships,[3] is of primary importance for today's most successful firms. Amazon, the largest e-retailer in the United States, uses technology and large amounts of data to develop a relationship with its customers. It provides personalized product recommendations and multiple delivery options to meet the individual needs of customers. This type of custom outreach helps marketers sell products. More importantly, it also helps the firm develop relationships with the customers who are most likely to buy its products.

marketing concept
The idea that a firm's long-term success must include a companywide effort to satisfy customer needs and wants.

relationship marketing
A marketing strategy that focuses on attracting, maintaining, and enhancing customer relationships.

The Future of Marketing

More exciting than the history of marketing is thinking about how marketing will develop in the years ahead. As technology and other changes affect the business world, firms will need to explore new models that address what customers want and how they prefer to receive information. For example, consider how these data might affect the way firms reach customers:

- By 2021, less than half of all Americans primarily watched television through cable and satellite providers.[4]
- At the same time, the number of Americans using the Internet or online streaming services such as Netflix, Disney+, and Peacock reached an all-time high.

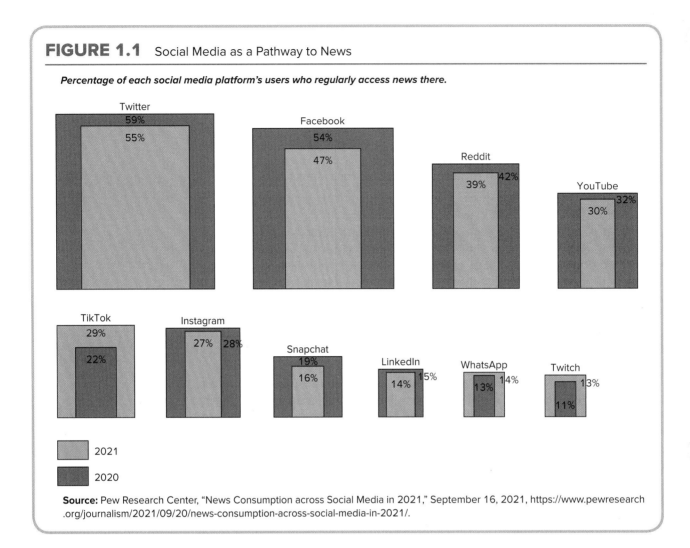

FIGURE 1.1 Social Media as a Pathway to News

Percentage of each social media platform's users who regularly access news there.

Twitter 59% / 55%
Facebook 54% / 47%
Reddit 42% / 39%
YouTube 32% / 30%
TikTok 29% / 22%
Instagram 28% / 27%
Snapchat 19% / 16%
LinkedIn 15% / 14%
WhatsApp 14% / 13%
Twitch 13% / 11%

2021
2020

Source: Pew Research Center, "News Consumption across Social Media in 2021," September 16, 2021, https://www.pewresearch.org/journalism/2021/09/20/news-consumption-across-social-media-in-2021/.

- Newspaper circulation has decreased significantly over the past two decades.
- The amount of news consumers get through social media platforms is at an all-time high. Products like Facebook, Instagram, TikTok, and Twitter are changing how firms interact with customers.

Figure 1.1 details the percentage of users who get their news from various social media sites. In the coming years, marketers will no longer automatically think of television, newspaper, or magazine advertising as the first choice for reaching customers.

exchange

An activity that occurs when a buyer and seller trade things of value so that each is better off as a result.

Regardless of how marketing evolves in the years ahead, remember that the basic goal of marketing—to create, communicate, and deliver value—doesn't change. To achieve this goal, marketers must use all the tools and strategies at their disposal to satisfy the needs and wants of customers.

LO 1-3 NEEDS VERSUS WANTS

Distinguish between consumer needs and consumer wants.

Marketers create value for customers when they develop products that allow consumers to satisfy their needs and wants through exchange relationships. **Exchange** happens when a buyer and seller trade things of value, so that each is better off as a result. For example, Microsoft initiates its part of the exchange by *creating* a product like the Xbox game console. It then *communicates* the value and enjoyment of owning an Xbox through television ads and online content. Finally, it *delivers* the Xbox consoles to retailers like Best Buy and Amazon, from whom consumers can purchase them. Consumers complete their side of the exchange by providing the money necessary to purchase the Xbox. In addition to the financial exchange that has taken place, consumers have also likely exchanged information, such as their e-mail address or phone number.

Perhaps the most basic concept in marketing is the difference between consumer needs and wants. **Needs** are states of felt deprivation. Consumers feel deprivation when they lack something essential like food, clothing, shelter, transportation, or safety. Notice that marketers do not *create* needs; needs are a basic part of our human makeup. Regardless of whether you ever view an ad, talk to a salesperson, or receive an e-mail from an online retailer, you still need food, water, shelter, and transportation.

Marketing's role is to match your need with a want. **Wants** are the form that human needs take as they are shaped by personality, culture, and buying situation. Marketers seek to turn your need for food into a want or desire for, say, an In-N-Out hamburger or a salad from Panera. Likewise, consumers need shelter. Marketers work to turn that need into a want, perhaps for an apartment on a bus route near campus or a condo where someone else takes care of the yard.

Wants are influenced by numerous things, including a consumer's family, job, and background. For example, a college student might want a shirt from a specific store or shoes that reflect his personality and make him feel good about how he looks. The wants of that student may well differ from those of the person who sits next to him in class, if they have different backgrounds and interests.

Satisfying needs and wants can prove challenging for firms that do not fully appreciate the difference between the two. Distinguishing between needs and wants affects the way firms market their products to customers.

needs
States of felt deprivation. Consumers feel that deprivation when they lack something useful or desirable like food, clothing, shelter, transportation, or safety.

wants
The form that human needs take as they are shaped by personality, culture, and buying situation.

Distinguishing Needs from Wants

The distinction between needs and wants is not always clear. For example, people need transportation to go to work, or to attend school, or to pick up their children. Consumers can meet their *need* for transportation in many ways—by driving a car, riding a bike, or taking a bus or some other form of mass transit. A luxury-car marketer bets on the fact that you *want* to fulfill your need for transportation to work by sitting on heated seats while listening to satellite radio.

The better a firm understands the difference between customers' needs and wants, the more effectively it can target its message to convince customers to buy its good or service. The marketer seeks to convince customers that the firm's offering will meet their needs and wants better than any competing good or service.

The Ethical Implications of Needs versus Wants

To avoid potential problems for the firm, and sometimes for society as a whole, evaluating customer needs and wants must be done through an ethical framework.

For example: The global economic recession that began in December 2007 was, in part, the result of a housing crisis in which the United States experienced the largest increase in home foreclosures and drop in

Most people need transportation of one kind or another; it's marketing's job to satisfy that need in a way that also meets the customer's wants, perhaps for a luxury car. *Don Mason/Getty Images*

home prices in over half a century.[5] The housing crisis was triggered by marketers who took consumers' basic *need* for a house and encouraged their *want* to buy a house that was more than they could afford. At the time, the exchange appeared to be a win–win proposition: Consumers got the house of their dreams, and the firms that sold, financed, and securitized the real estate made hefty profits for years.

Ultimately, however, this strategy led to billions of dollars in financial losses and millions of lost jobs. Marketers were using several of the sound marketing approaches we will discuss throughout this book. However, the problem stemmed from the fact that many were doing so in an unethical manner, such as ignoring the level of income needed to support the cost of the house. Later in this chapter, you will read about an ethical decision-making framework that you can use as you develop your marketing knowledge.

First, though, we'll discuss the four basic elements that make up the *marketing mix,* a concept that provides a foundation for much of modern marketing.

LO 1-4

Explain the four elements in the marketing mix.

marketing mix

A combination of activities that represent everything a firm can do to influence demand for its good, service, or idea; often referred to as the four Ps of marketing (product, price, place, and promotion).

THE MARKETING MIX: THE FOUR PS

One thing most business graduates remember from their first marketing class is the "four Ps"—product, price, place (distribution), and promotion—more formally known as the *marketing mix.* The **marketing mix** represents everything that a firm can do to influence demand for its good, service, or idea. The four Ps of the marketing mix provide marketers with the tools to increase customer awareness, sales, and profitability.

Successful marketing managers can make strategic decisions focusing on a specific element of the marketing mix, such as discounting prices or changing the product's packaging, to gain advantages over competitors and achieve long-term success. Figure 1.2 highlights some of the strategic decisions that can affect each of the marketing-mix elements. To develop such strategies, you must first understand each element in more detail.

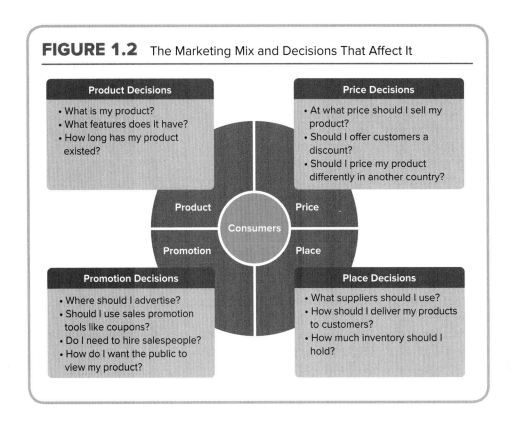

FIGURE 1.2   The Marketing Mix and Decisions That Affect It

Product Decisions
- What is my product?
- What features does it have?
- How long has my product existed?

Price Decisions
- At what price should I sell my product?
- Should I offer customers a discount?
- Should I price my product differently in another country?

Product   Price
Consumers
Promotion   Place

Promotion Decisions
- Where should I advertise?
- Should I use sales promotion tools like coupons?
- Do I need to hire salespeople?
- How do I want the public to view my product?

Place Decisions
- What suppliers should I use?
- How should I deliver my products to customers?
- How much inventory should I hold?

Product

The discussion of the marketing mix typically begins with the product. Without the product, a firm has few, if any, decisions to make about price, place, or promotion. **Product** is a specific combination of goods, services, or ideas that a firm offers to consumers.

Consider a good like the Chevrolet Camaro. The Camaro product consists of an engine, tires, seats, transmission, and other parts. Beyond this, a new Camaro also comes with a warranty and service guarantee. Those features, while not physical attributes like an engine, make up part of the car's basic product offering. In addition, the design of the car, the Chevy name, and features like satellite radio or the navigation system are all part of the product offering. Finally, consumers buy cars not just for the benefit of getting from place to place (the *need* for transportation) but also for what cars represent, for example, status, freedom, and youth (the *want*). All of these tangible and intangible characteristics are components of the Camaro product.

In addition to goods such as automobiles, products can also take the form of services or ideas. Examples of services are those provided by an attorney, electrician, or piano teacher. Ideas might be those offered by a management consultant or an architect. We will discuss product types in greater detail in Chapter 6 on product development.

product
The specific combination of goods, services, or ideas that a firm offers to consumers.

Price

Price is the amount of something—money, time, or effort—that a buyer exchanges with a seller to obtain a product. Setting a price is one of the most important strategic decisions a firm faces because it relates to the value consumers place on the product.

How many firms can you think of that are affected by the price they charge for their products? Your list could include nearly every firm you know! Pricing's power is a result of the signal it can send about product quality. If we put three jars of peanut butter in front of you with no labels except price tags of $1, $5, and $10, which jar would you say is of the highest quality? Without tasting the product, you might say the $10 jar, simply because of the higher price.

In addition, pricing is typically the easiest marketing-mix element to change. That fact makes price a powerful tool for firms looking to quickly adjust their market share or revenue. *Revenue* is the amount earned from selling products to customers. It is a function of the price of a product multiplied by the number of units sold.

If the firm sets the price too high, it will sell fewer units, thus reducing revenue. If the firm sets the price too low, it may sell more units, but it could see a reduction in overall revenue if the money earned from the additional units sold isn't enough to offset the lower price. Suppose you sell someone an NFL football game ticket for $50 but find out later that the buyer would gladly have paid $100. Yes, you sold the ticket, but you also lost $50 of potential revenue.

We will discuss pricing and how pricing strategy is changing in Chapter 11 on pricing.

price
The amount of something—money, time, or effort—that a buyer exchanges with a seller to obtain a product.

Technology like smartphone barcode scanners makes pricing a complicated and influential component of the marketing mix because consumers can quickly compare prices from firm to firm and from store to store. *javitrapero.com/Shutterstock*

Place

Place is one of the most remarkable parts of marketing. Consider this: You can travel to some of the most remote towns in the world and find McDonald's products close by. This is possible because McDonald's focuses heavily on the place element of its marketing mix.

place

As one of the "four Ps," includes the activities the firm undertakes to make its product available to potential customers. Also known as *distribution.*

Place includes the activities a firm undertakes to make its product available to potential consumers.

Companies must be able to distribute products to customers where they can buy and consume them without difficulty. Even if you have the right product at the right price, if customers cannot easily purchase the product, they will likely find a substitute. For example, let's say that a consumer in Oklahoma City loves Minute Maid Orange Juice, but due to distribution problems, the closest place they can buy it is Dallas, Texas, some 200 miles away. Chances are the consumer in Oklahoma City will begin drinking Tropicana or some other orange juice that's available closer to home. Minute Maid will have lost business because it couldn't deliver its product to its customer.

Place decisions relate to locations, transportation, logistics, and supply chain management. It's a broad and interesting topic, which we address in more detail in Chapter 10 on supply chain and logistics management.

Promotion

promotion

All the activities that communicate the value of a product and persuade customers to buy it.

The promotion element of the marketing mix is what most people think of when asked what marketing is. **Promotion** is all the activities that communicate the value of a product and persuade customers to buy it. Promotion includes advertising, sales promotion, personal selling, and public relations. You've been on the receiving end of a promotional activity if you've ever:

- Seen television commercials for car insurance, restaurants, resorts, or thousands of other products (*advertising*).
- Used a coupon to purchase some product (*sales promotion*).
- Talked with a salesperson (*personal selling*).
- Attended an event sponsored by a company (*public relations*).

Icons throughout the chapter highlight social media–related content.

As you read, keep an eye out for tie-back features in which the executive profiled at the start of the chapter comments on how the chapter concepts relate to his or her professional experience.

As is the case with every element of the marketing mix, successful promotion involves the firm's ability to integrate these activities in a way that maximizes the value of each. You have probably heard the saying "the whole is greater than the sum of its parts," perhaps said about a successful sports team. It means that the players might be good by themselves but are great when they work together as a team. The same can be said of a firm's successful promotional strategy: When well done, the whole strategy is better than the sum of its parts. It effectively integrates advertising, sales promotion, personal selling, and public relations to communicate a product's value to potential customers.

Recently, promotional activities have been undergoing a transformation. Today, firms of all sizes and from all industries can communicate quickly and directly with their customers using a variety of online and digital tools, such as smartphone apps and social media. The term **social media** refers to Internet-based applications that enable users to create their own content and share it with others who access the sites.

Firms that use social media for promotion try to create content that attracts attention and encourages readers to share the content with their social networks. In this way, a corporate message spreads from user to user. A company that uses social media hopes its message resonates with consumers because it appears to come from a trusted, third-party source, as opposed to from the company itself.

Use of social media has become easily accessible to anyone with Internet access. Because the communication

Executive Perspective ...
because everyone is a marketer

Jaime Gaudet
Market Director
Aflac

Jaime Gaudet

How has promotion impacted your role at Aflac?

Aflac has an advantage over our competition because of our promotional efforts. It's easier to get in the door of a business because most already know who Aflac is, whereas many competitors have to provide more information about their companies and make their cases before they can get to a sales opportunity.

is driven by word of mouth, promotion through social media results in free, rather than paid, messages. As a result, social media serve as a relatively inexpensive platform for smaller firms and nonprofit organizations to implement promotional strategies.[6]

Marketers expect the use of social media to continue to explode in coming years. Those who understand and can use them in effective and creative ways will benefit. Because of the growing importance of social media in marketing, throughout this book we highlight coverage of topics related to social media in various ways.

social media
Internet-based applications that enable users to create their own content and share it with others who access these sites.

Mc Graw Hill connect Exercise **1-1**

Social Media in Action ←

The role of social media in marketing entered a new phase as organizations across the world responded to the COVID-19 pandemic. Global ad spending across Facebook and Instagram soared 43 percent in 2021 in the wake of the pandemic, while TikTok came out on top for global app downloads in the first quarter of 2021. As many consumers remained under full or partial lockdown restrictions across the world, it was clear that people of all ages were continuing to flock to social media for entertainment and a bit of escapism.

They were also increasingly going to social media to shop. In the United Kingdom for example, one in four online purchases in 2020 were made as a result of interacting with a social media platform. Furthermore, close to one-fifth of consumers specifically went to social apps for shopping. Of those that do, 35 percent cited convenience as a key purchase driver, while 26 percent also said they liked how quick it is to check out.

While these increases helped brands navigate sales during the pandemic, there are warning signs for marketers. For example, 58 percent of respondents claimed they were dissatisfied with their social media purchases and 38 percent were in the process of trying to process a refund or return of such items. Even more concerning, from a customer service standpoint, is that just 20 percent of the consumers who attempted to return an item said they have received a full refund via the method with which they first paid and 88 percent said they have been left out of pocket for at least one purchase. As social media becomes increasingly more important for consumer purchases across the world, marketers will have to constantly assess how best to balance potential sales with meeting the demands of buyer expectations.

Source: See eConsultancy, "Stats Roundup: How Social Media Marketing Has Changed after COVID-19" December 6, 2021 https://econsultancy.com/stats-roundup-how-social-media-marketing-has-changed-after-covid-19/

Social Media in Action features discuss how companies use social media to market their products. The Application Exercise that accompanies this feature, which is available in McGraw Hill Connect, asks you to make decisions about the best use of social media in specific marketing scenarios.

TRENDS AFFECTING MARKETING

The social media trend will increasingly influence how marketers promote their products to customers, but it isn't the only trend affecting modern marketing. Firms today must take a broader focus than they have in the past. While marketers want to expand their reach to international consumers, they face new challenges resulting from global competition. Meanwhile, more and more consumers seek out firms that emphasize social responsibility and ethical practices.

In the sections that follow, we'll discuss three additional trends affecting marketing: globalization, marketing analytics, and ethics. In each chapter, you will examine how these trends affect core marketing principles.

Globalization affects almost every aspect of marketing. Icons within each chapter highlight discussions of the concepts in a global context.

LO 1-5

Discuss the importance of globalization in the field of marketing.

Global Marketing

Modern marketers must not only create, communicate, and deliver value but also do so in a truly global marketplace. Global forces affect everything we do in marketing, from pricing to product development to supply chain management. For example, the devaluation of the Chinese currency in 2015 or the tariffs imposed by the United States in 2018 on Chinese goods had an impact on the price of products across the globe.[7] Much of the growth in U.S. firms, ranging from Walmart to General Motors, comes from their expansion into international markets.

Events of the past two decades have clearly illustrated how connected the global economy is. When the United States entered a significant recession starting in December 2007, manufacturing at Chinese plants of products targeted to American consumers declined significantly, increasing unemployment and slowing growth in China.[8] Also, as the European Union dealt with a continent-wide banking crisis, U.S. firms saw their stock prices drop as investors feared possible exposure to the problems in Europe. More than at any time in history, businesses today are affected by developments across the globe. Consider these facts:

- Nearly 39 million jobs in the United States are supported by exports.[9]
- In 2020, total U.S. exports were worth more than $2.1 trillion even with the impact of the COVID-19 pandemic.[10]
- The United States is the world's leading exporter of services.[11]
- Exports account for around 12 percent of the total U.S. economy.[12]

The Interconnected World The idea of *globalization,* the increasingly interconnected nature of the world economy, evokes different reactions from different people. International trade agreements, such as the North American Free Trade Agreement (NAFTA), relaxed trade restrictions between the United States, Canada, and Mexico. These agreements are viewed both positively and negatively, depending on an individual's circumstances.

For U.S. farmers who have been able to ship and sell their produce to Canada and Mexico, NAFTA has expanded their business and increased profits. Canada and Mexico have accounted for 37 percent of the total growth of U.S. agricultural exports since 1993.[13] The share of total U.S. agricultural exports destined for Canada or Mexico grew from 22 percent at the time NAFTA was passed in 1993 to over 30 percent less than 15 years later.

However, in the view of employees from some manufacturing firms, NAFTA has made it easier for companies to move jobs to lower-wage areas on the continent, endangering local job prospects and threatening the existence of entire communities.

In 2018, the three countries reached agreement on the United States–Mexico–Canada Agreement, or USMCA, which is a successor to NAFTA and makes several small changes to the original agreement in areas ranging from cars to dairy to dispute resolutions.[14]

The importance of globalization grows with each passing year. Marketers must develop a global vision by proactively recognizing and responding to international marketing opportunities.

Marketing on a Global Scale Less than 5 percent of the world's population lives in the United States. That fact leads marketers to seek ways to promote and sell their products to the billions of potential consumers living outside the United

States. **Global marketing** is a marketing strategy that consciously addresses customers, markets, and competition throughout the world.[15]

Coca-Cola is one of the most globally active companies. It sells over 3,500 different beverages in over 200 countries worldwide.[16] Over 40 percent of the firm's sales come from international markets.[17] Coca-Cola's marketers have developed products to meet the unique tastes of international customers. The firm actively promotes its **brand**—the name, term, symbol, design, or any combination of these that identifies and differentiates a firm's products—through advertising and social media. It also makes pricing decisions based on economic and competitive factors in each region of the world in which it does business. Coca-Cola is at the cutting edge of delivering its products to places where global customers can buy them, whether that means moving bottling operations to Turkey or coordinating deliveries to remote places in Africa.

Throughout this book, we will embed many examples of firms doing global marketing in text discussions. In addition, many chapters include a separate section on global marketing as it relates to the chapter topic. Both types of global coverage are identified by a globe icon in the margin.

Firms that want to market on a global scale must pay particular attention to whether the benefits exceed the costs. Marketing analytics is therefore emerging as another trend that will increasingly affect the practice of marketing in the coming years.

global marketing

A marketing strategy that consciously addresses customers, markets, and competition throughout the world.

brand

The name, term, symbol, design, or any combination of these that identifies and differentiates a firm's products.

Coca-Cola has demonstrated a commitment to using each of the four Ps—product, price, place, and promotion—to drive global success. *Dave Moyer*

Marketing Analytics

Marketing analytics is the practice of measuring, managing, and analyzing market performance. Broadly, it is the processes and technologies that enable marketers to evaluate the success of marketing initiatives by measuring performance using business metrics.[18] Marketing analytics is an essential tool for helping organizations make better decisions. Marketing analytics can be used for issues ranging from justifying how advertising dollars get spent to what to do with large amounts of consumer data that are now available.

marketing analytics

The practice of measuring, managing, and analyzing market performance.

Companies are using business metrics and big data to help make marketing decisions. The "MA" icons in chapters identify text discussions relating to marketing analytics.

LO 1-6

Explain the role of analytics in marketing.

Marketers can use analytics whether they are selling products, services, or ideas. During the 2016 presidential campaign, for example, candidates in both major political parties sought a marketing advantage using analytics. Analytics suggested that political strategists should seek out bargains when placing advertisements to promote their candidates, such as skipping *Sunday Night Football* and instead buying airtime during *Law & Order* reruns, which cost a quarter as much but still deliver large numbers of likely voters.[19] Whether in politics or business, marketers who do not use analytics are likely wasting resources: They either are not reaching people or are reaching people who will not be receptive to the message.

Business executives are facing rising pressure to be more data-driven, with marketing receiving particular scrutiny.[20] The percentage of marketing budgets allocated for marketing analytics is expected to almost double in the next three years. Because of the growing use of marketing analytics, we will present the most popular marketing analytics tools throughout the book, with opportunities for you to apply them in homework activities.

LO 1-7 Ethics in Marketing

Demonstrate the relationship between ethical business practices and marketplace success.

ethics
The moral standards expected by a society.

Like social media, globalization, and marketing analytics, ethical decision making should be a key component of a successful marketing approach. **Ethics** are moral standards expected by a society. Marketers should clearly understand the norms and values expected of them and act in a way that puts their company, their profession, and themselves in a positive, ethical light.

The American Marketing Association has published a thorough Code of Ethics, which marketers should read and adhere to. We encourage you to read the AMA Code of Ethics in Figure 1.3 and use it as a guide as you develop your marketing knowledge throughout this text.

The Impact of Ethics on Business
The consequences of not adhering to an ethical code can be serious. In 2016, Wells Fargo employees secretly created millions of unauthorized bank and credit card accounts without their customers knowing it. The bank was hit with a $185 million fine and thousands of Wells Fargo employees lost their jobs.[21] Ignoring ethical considerations has destroyed some of the largest companies in the world over the past 20 years:

- Enron (No. 18 on the Fortune 500 list of the world's largest corporations in 2000).
- Telecommunications giant WorldCom.
- Arthur Andersen (the largest accounting firm in the United States in 2000).
- AIG (the largest insurance company in the world in 2008).[22]

Each of you, as a college graduate, will face a more challenging job market, partly because of unethical behavior by firms. For example, Arthur Andersen was a leading recruiter of college graduates throughout the 1990s until a series of unethical decisions by a limited number of employees led to its demise. Now out of business, Arthur Andersen, WorldCom, Enron, Bear Stearns, and a host of other large firms that fell victim to ethical lapses and closed their doors have no jobs to offer college graduates. As you can see, unethical marketing practices harm customers, employees, and society as a whole.

Making ethical decisions not only makes good business sense, it can also generate profits, even during a recession. Figure 1.4 illustrates the relationship between ethical business practices and marketplace success. The WME Index measures the stock returns of all publicly traded World's Most Ethical Company honorees. Figure 1.4 compares the WME Index to the U.S. Large-Cap Index, which offers a comprehensive view of equity returns in the United States. As you can see, firms that were identified as ethical outperformed the mix of companies included in the U.S. Large-Cap Index through different political, regulatory, and economic circumstances.

FIGURE 1.3   American Marketing Association Code of Ethics

PREAMBLE

The American Marketing Association commits itself to promoting the highest standard of professional ethical norms and values for its members (practitioners, academics and students). Norms are established standards of conduct that are expected and maintained by society and/or professional organizations. Values represent the collective conception of what communities find desirable, important and morally proper. Values also serve as the criteria for evaluating our own personal actions and the actions of others. As marketers, we recognize that we not only serve our organizations but also act as stewards of society in creating, facilitating and executing the transactions that are part of the greater economy. In this role, marketers are expected to embrace the highest professional ethical norms and the ethical values implied by our responsibility toward multiple stakeholders (e.g., customers, employees, investors, peers, channel members, regulators and the host community).

ETHICAL NORMS

As Marketers, we must:

1. **Do no harm.** This means consciously avoiding harmful actions or omissions by embodying high ethical standards and adhering to all applicable laws and regulations in the choices we make.
2. **Foster trust in the marketing system.** This means striving for good faith and fair dealing so as to contribute toward the efficacy of the exchange process as well as avoiding deception in product design, pricing, communication, and delivery of distribution.
3. **Embrace ethical values.** This means building relationships and enhancing consumer confidence in the integrity of marketing by affirming these core values: honesty, responsibility, fairness, respect, transparency and citizenship.

ETHICAL VALUES

Honesty—to be forthright in dealings with customers and stakeholders. To this end, we will:
- Strive to be truthful in all situations and at all times.
- Offer products of value that do what we claim in our communications.
- Stand behind our products if they fail to deliver their claimed benefits.
- Honor our explicit and implicit commitments and promises.

Responsibility—to accept the consequences of our marketing decisions and strategies. To this end, we will:
- Strive to serve the needs of customers.
- Avoid using coercion with all stakeholders.
- Acknowledge the social obligations to stakeholders that come with increased marketing and economic power.
- Recognize our special commitments to vulnerable market segments such as children, seniors, the economically impoverished, market illiterates and others who may be substantially disadvantaged.
- Consider environmental stewardship in our decision-making.

Fairness—to balance justly the needs of the buyer with the interests of the seller. To this end, we will:
- Represent products in a clear way in selling, advertising and other forms of communication; this includes the avoidance of false, misleading and deceptive promotion.
- Reject manipulations and sales tactics that harm customer trust.
- Refuse to engage in price fixing, predatory pricing, price gouging or "bait-and-switch" tactics.
- Avoid knowing participation in conflicts of interest.
- Seek to protect the private information of customers, employees and partners.

Respect—to acknowledge the basic human dignity of all stakeholders. To this end, we will:
- Value individual differences and avoid stereotyping customers or depicting demographic groups (e.g., gender, race, sexual orientation) in a negative or dehumanizing way.
- Listen to the needs of customers and make all reasonable efforts to monitor and improve their satisfaction on an ongoing basis.
- Make every effort to understand and respectfully treat buyers, suppliers, intermediaries and distributors from all cultures.
- Acknowledge the contributions of others, such as consultants, employees and coworkers, to marketing endeavors.
- Treat everyone, including our competitors, as we would wish to be treated.

Transparency—to create a spirit of openness in marketing operations. To this end, we will:
- Strive to communicate clearly with all constituencies.
- Accept constructive criticism from customers and other stakeholders.
- Explain and take appropriate action regarding significant product or service risks, component substitutions or other foreseeable eventualities that could affect customers or their perception of the purchase decision.
- Disclose list prices and terms of financing as well as available price deals and adjustments.

Citizenship—to fulfill the economic, legal, philanthropic and societal responsibilities that serve stakeholders. To this end, we will:
- Strive to protect the ecological environment in the execution of marketing campaigns.
- Give back to the community through volunteerism and charitable donations.
- Contribute to the overall betterment of marketing and its reputation.
- Urge supply chain members to ensure that trade is fair for all participants, including producers in developing countries.

IMPLEMENTATION

We expect AMA members to be courageous and proactive in leading and/or aiding their organizations in the fulfillment of the explicit and implicit promises made to those stakeholders. We recognize that every industry sector and marketing sub-discipline (e.g., marketing research, e-commerce, Internet selling, direct marketing, and advertising) has its own specific ethical issues that require policies and commentary. An array of such codes can be accessed through links on the AMA Web site. Consistent with the principle of subsidiarity (solving issues at the level where the expertise resides), we encourage all such groups to develop and/or refine their industry and discipline-specific codes of ethics to supplement these guiding ethical norms and values.

Source: American Marketing Association, "Statement of Ethics," n.d., http://www.marketingpower.com/aboutama/pages/statement%20of%20ethics.aspx.

FIGURE 1.4   Performance Comparison of the 2021 World's Most Ethical Companies and the U.S. Large-Cap Index

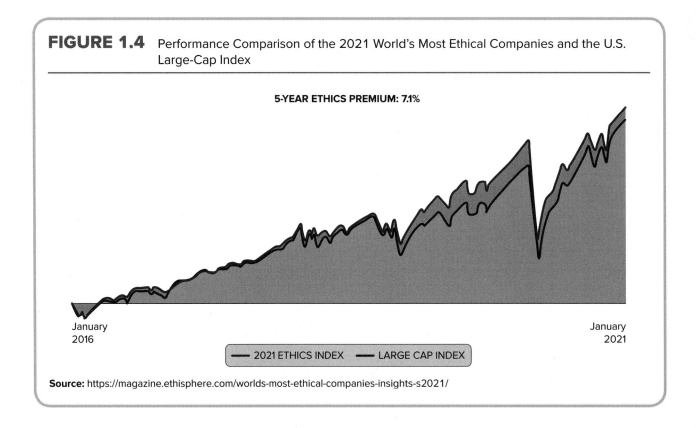

5-YEAR ETHICS PREMIUM: 7.1%

January 2016

January 2021

— 2021 ETHICS INDEX   — LARGE CAP INDEX

Source: https://magazine.ethisphere.com/worlds-most-ethical-companies-insights-s2021/

Ethical Decision-Making Framework   Despite the positive impact ethical decision making can have on a firm, the ethical choice is not always clear. Figure 1.5 illustrates an ethical decision-making framework that you can use in your future career and in almost any marketing challenge you will encounter, in this class and beyond.[23] You can apply this systematic framework to the ethical problems discussed throughout this course.

1. **Determine the facts in an unbiased manner.** First, determine the factual elements of a specific problem without letting any potential bias influence the decision. We are all products of our environment, and each of us brings our background, history, and experiences to any ethical problem. These fundamental factors can influence how we review and interpret the facts at hand, especially if we don't make a conscious effort to determine the relevant information in an unbiased way.
2. **Identify the ethical issue at hand.** It's possible to avoid ethical problems if you can clearly identify the ethical issue. The rest of the ethical decision-making framework will be valuable only if you clearly understand the issue itself.
3. **Identify the stakeholders affected by the decision.** Remember, stakeholders can be both external and internal. They include the firm's employees, both current and retired; customers; suppliers; shareholders; and the community in which the firm operates. Identify and consider each group as part of the ethical decision-making framework.
4. **Consider all available alternatives.** After identifying the relevant stakeholders, all parties should brainstorm alternatives. Different groups often view issues through different perspectives. Group brainstorming can lead to creative and useful solutions.

5. **Consider how the decision will affect the stakeholders.** Managers sometimes refer to this step as "seeing through a problem to the other side." This means considering ahead of time how the decision will affect all stakeholders. For example, mortgage companies that engaged in subprime lending in the years leading up to 2008 should have considered how lax lending standards might affect stakeholders over the long term, rather than waiting until foreclosures and unemployment increased during the recession.
6. **Discuss the pending decision with the stakeholders.** Seek feedback from stakeholders about potential decisions. It is often impossible to fully appreciate all of the dynamics of an ethical decision without getting input from those who will be affected. Many business problems can be avoided if a thoughtful discussion occurs when the decision is still pending.
7. **Make the decision.** Once the issue has been discussed with the relevant parties, make a final decision based on the stated criteria. Making decisions that affect others can be a stressful and challenging task, but using this decision-making framework can ensure thoroughness in arriving at the decision.
8. **Monitor and assess the quality of the decision.** The economy, regulatory environment, and consumer opinions are always changing and developing. A generation or two ago, smoking cigarettes on planes and in office buildings was considered perfectly ethical. Today, because we have more information about the dangers of secondhand smoke, laws prevent people from smoking in many public places. Firms will face many ethical challenges in the years ahead—online privacy regulations, environmental concerns, sustainability, and childhood obesity, to name a few. It will be incumbent upon all business professionals, including marketers, to monitor and assess whether the decisions they've made still represent the right and ethical choice for the firm, their consumers, and society as a whole.

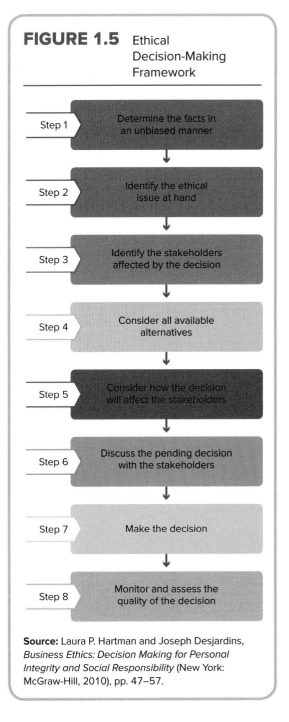

FIGURE 1.5   Ethical Decision-Making Framework

Step 1 — Determine the facts in an unbiased manner

Step 2 — Identify the ethical issue at hand

Step 3 — Identify the stakeholders affected by the decision

Step 4 — Consider all available alternatives

Step 5 — Consider how the decision will affect the stakeholders

Step 6 — Discuss the pending decision with the stakeholders

Step 7 — Make the decision

Step 8 — Monitor and assess the quality of the decision

Source: Laura P. Hartman and Joseph Desjardins, *Business Ethics: Decision Making for Personal Integrity and Social Responsibility* (New York: McGraw-Hill, 2010), pp. 47–57.

Marketers may confront decisions that will boost short-term sales at the expense of the long-term reputation of the company. For example, employees may have to choose between the short-term benefit of a sales commission and the potential long-term relationship with the customer if they don't adhere to ethical standards. The list that follows contains some common ethical questions that marketers may face within each element of the marketing mix during their careers. As you read each item, think about how you might respond, using the ethical decision-making framework as a guide.

Product

- What default privacy settings should be built into a website?
- What safety risks, especially for children and older people, might a product pose?
- Should environmentally friendly packaging be used even if it costs more?

Place

- Should jobs be outsourced to other members of the supply chain?
- Are the relationships between wholesalers and retailers inappropriate?
- What opportunities for personal gain might tempt a firm's suppliers?

Price

- Should the firm charge customers different prices based on their ability to pay?
- Should the firm increase prices due to a lack of local competition?
- Should the firm lower prices on soft drinks and fast food to attract a greater customer following, even if those products present potential health risks?

Promotion

- Does the advertising message represent the product's benefits honestly?
- Does the promotional strategy incorporate violence, sex, or profanity that may be inappropriate for some members of society?
- Does the advertising message attack competing products rather than highlight the benefits of the firm's product?

Ethics is an essential element in marketing and in your entire business curriculum. Most students find that though they may have a basic grasp of ethics in their personal lives, they are not sure how to apply ethics in business situations. Therefore, throughout this book we will embed real-world examples in text discussions of ethical issues in marketing decisions. Also, every chapter includes an Ethical Challenge in the homework section.

McGraw Hill connect Exercise **1-2**

Please complete the *Connect* exercise for Chapter 1 that focuses on ethics. Applying the ethical decision-making framework to an actual scenario will provide insight into how to evaluate ethical challenges and the potential risks involved when an ethical approach is not selected.

LO 1-8

Analyze the functions of marketing beyond the for-profit firm.

MARKETING FOR NONPROFIT ORGANIZATIONS

So far in this chapter, we've focused on for-profit firms. However, nonprofit organizations are a big part of the U.S. economy. *Nonprofit organizations* are those whose motive is something *other than* to make a profit for owners. Nonprofits generally are organized to serve the general public in some way. They include hospitals, charities, universities, zoos, and churches.

Nonprofit organizations employ approximately 11 million people and represent the third-largest employment sector in the United States.[24] Nonprofit organizations have increased employment more than private-sector firms during the past decade. A Johns Hopkins University study found that between 2000 and 2010, the nonprofit sector grew at an average annual rate of 2.1 percent. During the same time period, for-profit jobs were declining by 0.6 percent a year.

As with for-profit firms, marketing efforts are an essential part of the success of nonprofit organizations. The economic turmoil of the recession left many nonprofits

Austin Sandy

Brand Manager
KLTV 7, Tyler, TX

Describe your job. I'm the Brand Manager for two local ABC affiliates in East Texas. As the stations' Brand Manager, I oversee the brand development and implementation of over a dozen subsidiaries and niche mobile apps owned by KLTV and KTRE. From a local recipe app to regional sports, we have a brand for nearly every kind of content consumer. It is my team's job to build and retain an audience for each of our products by maintaining a unique brand strategy for each property. I'm fortunate to work for a company who lets the job form to fit the person (I'd suggest asking about this kind of flexibility in a job interview). In my current role, I'm able to coordinate projects between my marketing content producers and myself using each of our strongest skills. Managing brands with a small staff is a team effort. You may become a copywriter, designer, project manager, and so much more under your job title. I hope hats look good on you, because as a marketing professional, you're about to wear a lot of them.

Austin Sandy

How did you get your job? As a student I interned at Oan advertising agency with locations in St. Louis and Kansas City, Missouri and Nashville, Tennessee. Upon my return, I took a part-time camera operator job at the local television station to afford rent during my last semester of college. While employed part-time at that station, I attended the American Advertising Awards as a student and sat with my classmates. A few tables over sat the TV station executives with whom I worked. I knew their faces, but as a part-time employee, hadn't had many opportunities to interact with them. That night, I received three awards and much to my surprise, I was called in for a meeting with the station manager a week later. They knew that my college graduation was approaching and that I'd been interviewing for full-time employment around the country. The station management knew me as a part-time camera operator . . . until they saw my work at the American Advertising Awards. They offered me their Digital Marketing Manager role . . . on the spot! I was later nominated for the parent company's marketing leadership program which opened the door for me to be promoted to KLTV and KTRE's Brand Manager.

What has been the most important thing in making you successful at your job? As a young professional, I have become unashamed of three things: questions, failures, and weird ideas. I took a class in college where the professor had us write down every idea that came to mind. We'd be given a

prompt and then set free to think of 100 different iterations of that prompt. We'd branch off and be digging 40 feet deep for that hundredth idea. About 78 of those 100 ideas were strange and many of them may not fit a client's desire. But I learned in that class that even if 99 of my ideas didn't work, at least I had 100 to choose from! That class has helped me be outspoken among business professionals with decades of experience. I've had grumpy old executives laugh at my ideas and even say "that's crazy". But there have been many more instances where I've heard "that might be crazy enough to work". I believe being comfortable in your own creativity is the one thing that can make you most successful in marketing.

What advice would you give soon-to-be graduates? You're about to enter a world of professionals, some who have been doing this for decades. That can be intimidating, but you're young and full of fresh ideas. Even though some of your future colleagues have 30 years on you, that's also 30 years of milking the same idea udder. Your vision hasn't been seen yet. You'll sit down in a meeting with these well-established pros, you'll mention an idea, and they'll run with it. All the validation you've ever needed is just one idea away. So speak up and surprise yourself.

What do you consider your personal brand to be? Similar to code-switching to fit the atmosphere of conversation, I think we all have multiple personal brands. Am I the Emmy-nominated Broadcast Marketer or am I the camping, hiking, Jeeping outdoorsman? It depends on who I'm around or what I'm doing. Both are true and both are developed in different environments for different audiences. I think of a personal brand as an eight-point umbrella with eight buckets below. Everyone sees your umbrella brand, but a smaller portion of your audience sees the depth of what's inside each little brand bucket. Some of your buckets may be larger than others. Some of your buckets may go away and some of your buckets may need to be replaced with a larger trough as time goes on. The key is remembering your buckets and developing them when they need it. Just as a company may need a brand refresh, your personal and career life can be refreshed and changed as well. Make sure your brand lives and breathes just as you do. Don't be afraid of a personal brand shift. Your personal brand now won't look anything like your personal brand when you retire and that's okay.

Pictured is the St. Jude Children's Research Hospital cafeteria, named "Kay Kafe" in honor of Kay Jewelers' support of the hospital. By participating in St. Jude Children's Research Hospital *Thanks and Giving* campaign, Kay Jewelers has raised over $70 million in donations from employees and customers since 1999. *Kay Kafe at St. Jude Children's Research Hospital, Courtesy of St. Jude Children's Research Hospital*

facing increased competition for support, membership, and donations. Successful marketing helps nonprofit organizations attract membership and much-needed funds. For example, St. Jude Children's Research Hospital in Memphis, Tennessee, focuses much of its marketing efforts on raising funds to support pediatric cancer research and treatment. St. Jude partners with more than 70 corporate supporters, such as Chili's and Best Buy, to raise money for research and care. Kay Jewelers supports the St. Jude *Thanks and Giving* holiday campaign through the sale of exclusive products that benefit St. Jude. In addition, Kay supports the *My St. Jude Family* campaign by offering in-store products in the month leading up to Mother's Day.[25] Such marketing efforts help enable St. Jude to fund the more than $2 million per day it takes to operate one of the leading children's research hospitals in the world, a place where families never receive a bill for treatment, travel, housing, or food.[26]

As you continue through this course, you'll see how the marketing principles that apply to for-profit firms also can be applied to nonprofit organizations.

MARKETING YOURSELF

Some of you reading this text will become marketing majors and take more courses in marketing such as consumer behavior, professional selling, marketing research, and advertising. Some of you will major in another subject. Either way, your ability to use the principles in this book to *market yourself* will be critical to your success after you leave college.

Don't consider the information in this book as a collection of random concepts that you can forget about once you take your final exam. Instead, think about how the principles you're learning will help you position yourself relative to others competing for the same job. As you prepare your resume, think about how to communicate your value so that you get an interview over hundreds of other candidates.

The era of mass marketing has passed. So, too, has the day when simply putting your name and college degree on a resume guaranteed you a great job for life, or even an interview. Some of you will work for firms looking to increase profits. Your job will be to successfully market the firm's goods and services through a minefield of competitors, global economic uncertainty, and new advertising media. Some of you will work for nonprofit organizations. In the nonprofit environment, you will have to successfully market your organization to prospective donors, possibly competing for a shrinking pool of dollars.

Ultimately, wherever your career leads you, you will need to market yourself effectively to reach the professional goals you have set. This book will prepare you with the marketing knowledge to answer challenging questions in the future, perhaps most relevantly, "Why should I hire *you*?"

Mc Graw Hill connect   Exercise 1-3

Please complete the *Connect* exercise for Chapter 1 that focuses on careers in marketing. Match personal and job characteristics to specific marketing careers to better understand how your passion may be best served through a career in marketing.

SUMMARY

LO 1-1 Describe a marketer's role in creating, communicating, and delivering value.

Canadapanda/ Shutterstock

Marketing is an organizational function and set of processes for creating, communicating, and delivering value to customers. Marketers manage customer relationships in ways that benefit the organization and its stakeholders. To *create* value, a new good or service must satisfy a perceived marketplace demand. The marketer then *communicates* this value to potential customers. A company's supply chain is critical in *delivering* value. Members of the supply chain can include suppliers, manufacturers, wholesalers, distributors, retailers, transportation companies, and other groups, depending on the industry.

LO 1-2 Differentiate among the various eras in the history of marketing.

Hulton Archive/ Archive Photos/ Getty Images

Prior to the 1920s, most firms were *production-oriented;* they believed that quality products would simply sell themselves. In the mid-1920s, as production outpaced demand, many firms shifted to a *sales orientation:* The task of personal selling and advertising was to persuade consumers to buy products.

After two decades of economic depression and world war, the economy entered an era of expansion, in which the demand for goods and services increased significantly. The *marketing concept* was developed during this period. It reflects a company-wide consumer orientation, with a focus on establishing, maintaining, and growing relationships with customers. ·

LO 1-3 Distinguish between consumer needs and consumer wants.

Don Mason/Getty Images

Perhaps the most basic concept underlying marketing is that of needs versus wants. Human *needs* are states of felt deprivation. They include the need for food, clothing, shelter, transportation, and safety.

Wants are the form that human needs take as they are shaped by personality, culture, and buying situation. The better a firm understands the difference between customers' needs and wants, the more effectively it can target its message and convince customers to buy its good or service.

LO 1-4 Explain the four elements in the marketing mix.

javitrapero.com/ Shutterstock

The marketing mix is made up of the four Ps—product, price, place, and promotion. It represents everything that a firm can do to influence demand for its good or service.

Product is the specific combination of goods or services that a firm offers to consumers. *Price* is the amount of something that a buyer must exchange with a seller to obtain a product. *Place* includes the activities that make the product available to potential consumers. *Promotion* is all the activities that communicate the value of the product and persuade customers to buy it, including advertising, sales promotion, personal selling, and public relations.

LO 1-5 Discuss the importance of globalization in the field of marketing.

Dave Moyer

Global marketing is a marketing strategy that consciously addresses customers, markets, and competition throughout the world. Global forces affect everything we do in marketing, from product development to pricing to supply chain management. As the importance of globalization grows, marketers must develop a global vision by proactively recognizing and responding to international marketing opportunities.

LO 1-6 Explain the role of analytics in marketing.

Marketing analytics is the practice of measuring, managing, and analyzing marketing performance. It consists of processes and technologies that monitor important business metrics. Marketing analytics are an essential tool for helping organizations make better marketing decisions. They shed light on issues ranging from how advertising dollars get spent to what to do with large amounts of consumer data that are now available. Business executives are facing rising pressure to be more data-driven, with marketing receiving particular scrutiny.

LO 1-7 Demonstrate the relationship between ethical business practices and marketplace success.

Ethics are moral standards expected by a society. Unethical marketing practices can harm both customers and society as a whole. Marketers are sometimes faced with decisions that will boost short-term sales at the expense of the long-term reputation of the company. Using an ethical decision-making framework to make decisions is important because the right choice will not always be clear.

LO 1-8 Analyze the functions of marketing beyond the for-profit firm.

Kay Kafe at St. Jude Children's Research Hospital, Courtesy of St. Jude Children's Research Hospital

Nonprofit organizations are organizations whose motive is something other than to make a profit for owners. They rely on marketing to raise money and support, particularly in economically difficult times.

Many marketing principles apply to both for-profit and nonprofit organizations. Whether you eventually work in a for-profit firm or a nonprofit organization, ultimately you will need to be able to market yourself effectively to reach the professional goals you have set.

KEY TERMS

brand (p. 15)
customer value (p. 4)
ethics (p. 16)
exchange (p. 8)
global marketing (p. 15)
logistics (p. 6)
marketing (p. 4)

marketing analytics (p. 15)
marketing concept (p. 7)
marketing mix (p. 10)
needs (p. 9)
place (distribution) (p. 12)
price (p. 11)
product (p. 11)

production orientation (p. 6)
promotion (p. 12)
relationship marketing (p. 7)
sales orientation (p. 7)
social media (p. 13)
supply chain (p. 5)
wants (p. 9)

A Marketing Plan Exercise in each chapter helps you learn the elements of the marketing plan in the context of marketing the most important product or brand of your life: yourself.

MARKETING PLAN EXERCISE • Marketing Yourself

As a professional in any field, it is important to have a comprehensive understanding of what a marketing plan is and why it is there. A marketing plan is an action-oriented document or playbook that guides the analysis, implementation, and control of all marketing activities. Throughout this book, you will develop a professional marketing plan. The twist is that your marketing plan will focus on how to *market yourself* to achieve your career goals.

Many businesses fail to execute on their marketing plans because they did not spend adequate time clearly identifying what they wanted or expected to do. As a first step in developing your personal marketing plan, you will need to identify the specific objectives that you want to achieve. In developing these objectives, you should ask yourself several questions, such as:

- Do I want to attend graduate school? If so, where and what program?
- Where do I want to work?
- Where do I want to live?
- What kind of life do I want to have?
- How much will I need to earn to have that life?

Such questions will help you focus on what specific things you need to do to achieve your goals. The more clearly you define your objectives, the more likely you are to realize them.

Your Task: Clearly state three to five specific objectives for your future, and include a brief one- to two-sentence description of each objective.

DISCUSSION QUESTIONS

1. Identify a firm that you think effectively markets its goods, services, or ideas, and describe how the firm creates, communicates, and delivers value.
2. Reflect on the evolution of marketing over the past century. Then describe three major changes that you think will affect the field of marketing over the next decade.
3. Ask five people you know to list their needs and wants. Are their lists accurate reflections of the definition of each? Are there any differences due to age or gender?

4. Illustrate each step of the ethical decision-making framework by examining whether the state you live in should use a lottery to help pay for part of your college tuition. What are the ethical issues? Who are the relevant stakeholders? How are those stakeholders affected by potential outcomes? What decision would you make?
5. Describe three examples of promotion that caught your attention in your hometown. Why do you think each worked well?

The Social Media Application asks you to analyze the social media activities of the organizations with which you are most familiar, including your school, your favorite restaurant, or the company you'd like to work for after obtaining your degree.

 # SOCIAL MEDIA APPLICATION

Choose three products that you currently use—for example, clothes that you wear, restaurants where you eat, or the car that you drive. Analyze the social media presence of these products using the following questions and activities as a guide:

1. What is being done to market each product on social media?
2. What are people saying about each product on social media?

3. Give each of the three products a grade (A–F) based on how effective you feel its social media presence is.
4. Describe why you gave each the grade that you did, and make recommendations for how the product's firm could improve its social media marketing activities (e.g., modifying content or utilizing a different social media platform).

The Marketing Analytics Exercise engages you with analytics tools and techniques for practice analyzing and using data that inform marketing decisions related to the chapter topic.

MARKETING ANALYTICS EXERCISE

Please complete the *Connect* exercise in Chapter 1 that introduces the topic of marketing analytics. The exercise gives you a basic overview of an Excel model used in marketing analytics activities.

Ethical Challenges in each chapter ask you to consider how ethical issues permeate every marketing decision.

ETHICAL CHALLENGE

Marketing decisions are driven increasingly by analytics produced from massive amounts of consumer data. Every time you shop online or post something on a social media platform like Instagram, marketers capture lots of information about you that can be helpful but also can create potential problems.

Facebook faced significant backlash from consumers and legislators in 2021, but ethical questions had been raised much earlier. For example, a Facebook study in 2012 sparked criticism from consumers when researchers from Facebook and Cornell University manipulated the news feeds of nearly 700,000 Facebook users for a week to gauge whether emotions spread on social media. The research found that users who saw more positive posts tended to write more positive posts themselves. The results were interesting for marketers who are increasingly trying to engage with and persuade consumers through social media. However, Facebook admitted that the study may have included users younger than 18. Facebook said it had changed its guidelines since the research was conducted, and new studies now are vetted through three internal reviews, including one focused on privacy for user data.

The incident highlights how marketers can utilize the massive amount of data created online. A variety of companies, including Facebook and Google, routinely test adjustments to their sites to examine different effects. These changes include prompts to users to click on more links, or view more advertisements, which are the companies' main source of revenue.

The trade-offs between marketing information and consumer privacy are likely to be a strongly debated issue in the decade ahead. Use the ethical decision-making framework to answer the following questions:

1. What are the major ethical issues surrounding Facebook's study? Who are the affected stakeholders? How will those stakeholders be affected?
2. Reviewing this case years later, monitor and assess the quality of Facebook's decision.
3. As a consumer, how do you personally feel about the information that is captured about you and used to market products to you? Do your feelings affect your online buying behavior?

Source: See Reed Albergotti and Elizabeth Dwoskin, "Facebook Study Sparks Soul-Searching and Ethical Questions," *The Wall Street Journal*, June 30, 2014, http://www.wsj.com/articles/facebook-study-sparks-ethical-questions-1404172292.

Video Cases with each chapter, available in McGraw Hill Connect, often feature the executive you've learned about throughout the chapter.

VIDEO CASE

Please go to *Connect* to access the video case featuring April Slayton from the National Park Service that accompanies this chapter.

Go beyond the text! Our **Marketing Insights Podcast Series** connects you to marketing content intended to inform, educate, entertain, and inspire. Updated regularly with timely topics, these 7–10 minute podcasts were created by marketing professionals and educators with you in mind. Available on iTunes, Spotify, Google Play, and Stitcher to *go with you wherever you go.* Go to **http://bit.ly/mktinsightspodcasts** to listen now.

PODCAST

Please go to Connect to access the podcast that accompanies this chapter.

Photo provided by Steve DeVore

CAREER **TIPS**

Landing the Job of Your Dreams

You have read in this chapter about the importance of marketing yourself. As you get closer to finishing your degree, two major elements of this include developing a resume that will catch the attention of potential employers and giving an effective interview. Steve DeVore, president of Twin Oaks Integrated Marketing, has hired large numbers of new college graduates. He offers 10 marketing tips for landing the job of your dreams.

STEP 1. Realize what a resume is and isn't.

- Like a marketing plan, a resume's objective is to generate interest (not follow a formula).
- Your resume immediately gives employers a sense of who you are.
- If your resume looks and feels like all of the others, it will stay with the others in the pile.
- Although an interesting resume is important, understand that a majority of new hires come from referrals, not incoming resumes. Work on both your resume and a network for referrals.

STEP 2. Break all the rules . . . in a smart way.

- Great resume building is about creativity, not conventional thinking.
- Don't think of your resume as a list of accomplishments; think of it as a story.

STEP 3. Customize your approach.

- Don't approach different companies with a copy-and-paste mentality.
- Consider what skills each company values most and highlight them appropriately by customizing your resume for each company.

STEP 4. Be concise, but be meaningful.

- Don't go into too much depth about your previous experience. For example, make the description of the company and your role at the company each one sentence. You can use some of the saved space to tell three things you accomplished at each company or job.
- When you are beginning your career, what you learned is more important than where you learned it. Consider adding a box to your resume that lists the knowledge you've gained through volunteering, internships, and group memberships.

STEP 5. Make your resume visually appealing. (Consider adding color, for example.)

STEP 6. Know what you want.

- Don't be indifferent.
- Make the interviewer feel your passion.
- Have a career goal that exceeds what you are interviewing for.

STEP 7. Go beyond Google.

- Be resourceful. Find out something unique about the company you are applying to and what it does.
- Just like your resume, your content and responses to application and interview questions should be tailored to fit.

STEP 8. Understand as much as you can about the people interviewing you.

- Ask whom you will be meeting with and what their roles are.
- Leverage social media tools to find out more.

STEP 9. Be prepared with unobvious answers.

- Have a compelling answer about what the company does.
- Go beyond the surface. Be prepared with answers that not every candidate will give.

STEP 10. Know what message you want to leave behind.

- Prepare so that your responses are sharp and differentiated.
- Find your balance between humility and confidence.
- Chemistry and cultural fit are as important as talent.

CHAPTER NOTES

1. Ravi Sawhney and Deepa Prahalad, "The Role of Design in Business," *Bloomberg Businessweek,* February 1, 2010, http://www.businessweek.com/stories/2010-02-01/the-role-of-design-in-businessweek-business-news-stock-market-and-financial-advice.

2. John T. Mentzer (ed.), *Supply Chain Management* (Thousand Oaks, CA: Sage Publications, 2001), p.14.

3. Leonard L. Berry, "Relationship Marketing of Services—Perspectives from 1983 and 2000," *Journal of Relationship Marketing* 1, no. 1 (2002), http://www.uni-kl.de/icrm/jrm/pages/jrm_01.pdf#page=62.

4. Fred Backus, "More Americans Say They Are 'Cutting the Cord'," *CBS News,* April 23, 2021 https://www.cbsnews.com/news/cord-cutting-americans-rising/.

5. Peter Coy, "The Great Recession: An Affair to Remember," *Bloomberg Businessweek,* October 11, 2012, http://www.businessweek.com/articles/2012-10-11/the-great-recession-an-affair-to-remember.

6. Mikaela Louve, "Social Media Marketing: Not a Magic Bean, but a Very Inexpensive One," *Technorati,* September 20, 2011, http://technorati.com/business/small-business/article/social-media-marketing-not-a-magic/page-2/.

7. Jon Hilsenrath and Brian Blackstone, "Cheaper Chinese Currency Has Global Impact," *The Wall Street Journal,* August 22, 2015, http://www.wsj.com/articles/cheaper-chinese-currency-has-global-impact-1439336422; *CNBC,* "Walmart Warns Trump's Tariffs May Force It to Hike Prices," September 21, 2018, https://www.cnbc.com/2018/09/21/walmart-warns-trumps-tariffs-may-force-it-to-hike-prices.html.

8. Barry Peterson, "China Feeling Impact of U.S. Recession," *CBS News,* July 9, 2009, http://www.cbsnews.com/8301-18563_162-5059809.html.

9. Business Roundtable, "New Study: International Trade Supports Nearly 39 Million American Jobs," March 18, 2019, https://www.businessroundtable.org/new-study-international-trade-supports-nearly-39-million-american-jobs.

10. U.S. Census Bureau, "Annual Trade Highlights," https://www.census.gov/foreign-trade/statistics/highlights/AnnualPressHighlights.pdf.

11. United States International Trade Commission, "United States Was the World's Largest Exporter and Importer of Services in 2018, Reports USITC," July 28, 2020. USITChttps://www.usitc.gov/press_room/news_release/2020/er0728ll1612.htm.

12. World Bank, "Country Snapshot," n.d., https://wits.worldbank.org/CountrySnapshot/en/USA/textview.

13. Office of the United States Trade Representative, "NAFTA Facts," n.d., http://www.ustr.gov/sites/default/files/NAFTA-Myth-versus-Fact.pdf.

14. Shawn Donnan, Andrew Mayeda, Jenny Leonard, and Jeremy C. F. Lin, "Trump's 'Historic' Trade Deal: How Different Is It from NAFTA?," Bloomberg, October 2, 2018, https://www.bloomberg.com/graphics/2018-nafta-vs-usmca/.

15. American Marketing Association, "AMA Dictionary," n.d., http://www.marketingpower.com/_layouts/Dictionary.aspx?dLetter=G.

16. Coca-Cola, "Coca-Cola Beverages and Products," n.d., http://www.worldofcoca-cola.com/coca-colaproducts.htm.

17. Reem Nasr, "Coca-Cola Posts Earnings of 63 Cents per Share vs. 60 Cents Estimate," *CNBC,* July 22, 2015, http://www.cnbc.com/2015/07/22/.

18. SAS, "Marketing Analytics," http://www.sas.com/en_us/insights/marketing/marketing-analytics.html.

19. Sasha Issenberg, "How Analytics Has Reshaped Political Campaigning Forever," *Bloomberg Businessweek,* November 5, 2015, http://www.bloomberg.com/news/articles/2015-11-05/how-analytics-has-reshaped-political-campaigning-forever.

20. Nathalie Tedina, "Social Media Spending Is on the Rise but Impact Is Hard to Measure," *The Wall Street Journal,* September 3, 2014, http://blogs.wsj.com/cmo/2014/09/03/social-media-spending-is-on-the-rise-but-impact-is-hard-to-measure/.

21. Jackie Wattles, Ben Geier, Matt Egan, and Danielle Wiener-Bronner, "Wells Fargo's 20-Month Nightmare," *CNNMoney,* April 24, 2018, https://money.cnn.com/2018/04/24/news/companies/wells-fargo-timeline-shareholders/index.html.

22. *CNNMoney,* "Fortune 500 2012," n.d., http://money.cnn.com/magazines/fortune/fortune500/.

23. Laura P. Hartman and Joseph Desjardins, *Business Ethics: Decision Making for Personal Integrity & Social Responsibility,* 2nd ed. (New York: McGraw-Hill, 2010).

24. Nonprofit Employment Practices Survey, "Nonprofits Project Growth in 2015 That Could Outpace the Corporate Sector," http://www.prnewswire.com/news-releases/study-nonprofits-project-growth-in-2015-that-could-outpace-the-corporate-sector-300044776.html.

25. St. Jude Children's Research Hospital, n.d., https://www.stjude.org/get-involved/other-ways/partner-with-st-jude/corporate-partners/signet-jewelers.html.

26. St. Jude Children's Research Hospital, *Facts for Media,* https://www.stjude.org/media-resources/media-tools/facts.html#6cfb38b83fde9b8e59bde2275f78101c38537ffed31c1bfcd50790aaae276750=6.

Chapter 2

Strategic Planning

Tinnaporn Sathapornnanont/Shutterstock

Learning Objectives

After reading this chapter, you should be able to

LO 2-1 Discuss the importance of strategic planning for marketing.

LO 2-2 Analyze the characteristics of an effective mission statement.

LO 2-3 Outline the five main components of the marketing plan.

LO 2-4 Explain three tools and techniques for the situation analysis: market summary, SWOT analysis, and competition analysis.

LO 2-5 Explain the basic tools and techniques of marketing strategy: segmentation, strategic direction, and the marketing mix.

LO 2-6 Discuss the strategic decisions involved in reaching international consumers.

LO 2-7 Describe the use of four key marketing analytics: return on marketing investment (ROMI), revenue analysis, market share analysis, and profitability analysis.

Executive **Perspective** ... because everyone is a marketer

Melissa Lowry
Chief Marketing Officer
Zelle

Melissa Lowry

A finance major and volleyball player in college, Melissa launched here career working for some of the leading investment banks in the world. After completing her MBA, she moved to California and took on several leadership roles in product strategy and innovation.

In 2016, Melissa became Vice President for Marketing and Branding at Zelle and was responsible for strategy, messaging, and execution across owned, paid, earned, and social channels. Today, Melissa serves as the Chief Marketing Officer for the Zelle brand and leads their marketing and communications strategy, execution, and results. Melissa manages a world-class marketing organization responsible for functions including brand strategy, B2B marketing, internal and external communications, digital operations, and integrated consumer-facing campaigns.

What has been the most important thing in making you successful at your job?

Listening! I make time to chat with team members across the company, customers, and partners on an informal and regular basis. You learn a lot about what's really going on when you talk to folks outside of scheduled meetings or research sessions. Not only do I get incredible insights on trends or potential issues, but it's also given me opportunities to help coworkers in different groups and build strong relationships across the company.

What advice would you give soon-to-be graduates?

Be open to opportunities. You may not know your passion yet or exactly what you want to be doing in 10 years. That's OK. Try new things, pay attention to what excites you, and be open to learning from each opportunity that will help you take the next step. My own career was not a linear path; I worked in investment banking, business strategy, and product management before finding my way to marketing. Each role taught me something new that has helped me to be successful in what I do today.

How is marketing relevant to your role at Zelle?

Marketing is central to my role as Chief Marketing Officer, but in order to lead marketing effectively, I'm involved in a number of different functional areas. On any given day, I may be reviewing budget spreadsheets with finance, digging into research with my analytics team for new, actionable insights, listening to customer support calls, or reviewing potential pain points in our user experience. Whether it's a technical update to Zelle or a strategic decision for our business, I think about what it means for the customer and their end-to-end experience.

What do you consider your personal brand to be?

What I hope people see in me is that I am curious, supportive, and empathetic. I bring a lot of positivity to every project and interaction, and I genuinely care about my team.

THE IMPORTANCE OF STRATEGIC PLANNING

Strategic planning is essential to meeting both professional and personal objectives. In the same way that a strategic plan will help you accomplish your goal of earning a college degree, a firm's strategic plan helps guide it to success. *Robert Churchill/the Agency Collection/Getty Images*

Imagine starting college and just randomly taking classes because they seem interesting or easy, or because your friends are taking them. You could be a full-time student each semester and get good grades, and at the end of four years, what would you have? Not much, except student loan debt. Instead, most of you have a checklist of courses you must complete to graduate in your selected field. Selecting your major and then determining when you will take the required courses is a *strategic plan* you set for yourself. Unless you have the specific objectives of your degree program and a strategy for balancing your classes with the other demands on your time, it will be hard to succeed in achieving your desired result: a college diploma.

Strategic planning can greatly increase the likelihood of success. This is true whether you are marketing yourself for a job or whether a company is marketing a product or service. **Strategic planning** is the process of thoughtfully defining a firm's objectives and developing a method for achieving those objectives. A **strategic plan** typically includes an organization's plans for key functional areas, such as marketing, human resources, finance, and risk management. Figure 2.1 shows the component areas of a sample strategic plan.

strategic planning
The process of thoughtfully defining a firm's objectives and developing a method for achieving those objectives.

strategic plan
An organization's plans for key functional areas, such as marketing, human resources, finance, and risk management.

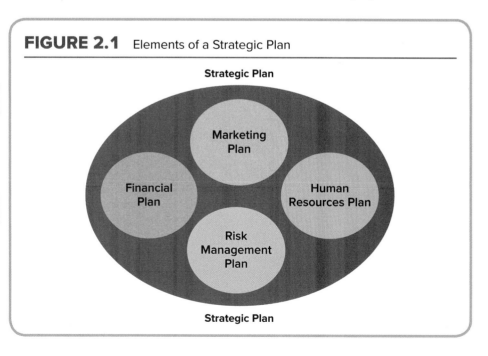

FIGURE 2.1 Elements of a Strategic Plan

Strategic Plan

- Marketing Plan
- Financial Plan
- Human Resources Plan
- Risk Management Plan

Strategic Plan

Firms must continually undertake strategic planning. Because customer needs change and competitive threats pop up, what worked in the past will not always work in the future. Firms must continually modify their strategies as conditions shift. Strategic planning helps ensure that the organization will have the needed resources—financial, human, and operational—to succeed. Such planning helps marketers select and execute the right marketing-mix strategies to maximize success. The strategic plan is shaped by the organization's mission.

Executive Perspective . . .
because everyone is a marketer

Melissa Lowry
Chief Marketing Officer
Melissa Lowry   **Zelle**

What is something you think is critical to marketing strategy today?

A "customer-first" mindset is foundational to marketing—without it, you can't develop a deep understanding of your customers' needs; and if you don't understand their needs and wants, you can't authentically connect with them.

MISSION STATEMENT

Before it can do its strategic planning, an organization must know what it wants to accomplish. The first step in creating a quality strategic plan is to develop an effective mission statement. A **mission statement** is a concise affirmation of the firm's long-term purpose. It describes the markets in which the firm will compete and the goods or services it will provide.[1] An effective mission statement provides employees with a shared sense of ambition, direction, and opportunity.

LO 2-2

Analyze the characteristics of an effective mission statement.

mission statement
A concise affirmation of the firm's long-term purpose.

A firm should begin the process of developing a mission statement by considering the following questions:[2]

- What is our business?
- Who is our customer?
- What is our value to the customer?
- What *should* our business be?

These basic questions are often the most challenging and important that a firm will ever answer. From there, the firm should focus on developing the three primary characteristics of a good mission statement.[3] The mission statement should:

1. **Be focused on a limited number of goals.** Companies whose mission statements contain 10 or more goals are typically focusing on small, less-meaningful objectives. Instead, companies should create a broad statement that provides purpose and direction to the entire organization. Avon's mission statement had multiple goals and was over 230 words long. Although each goal was positive, the overall length distracted employees from the truly important things that define success for the organization.[4]
2. **Be customer-oriented and focused on satisfying basic customer needs and wants.** Specific goods and services change over time; customer needs and wants are longer-lasting. For example, advanced technological products of just a generation ago, such as the VCR or Blackberry phones, are outdated technologies today. Still, consumers' desire to watch movies in their home and to take and share pictures with friends and family is stronger than ever. Apple has very successfully designed and marketed innovative new products like the iPod, iPhone, and iPad. It is quite possible, though, that consumers 20 years from now will think of these products the same way you think about VCRs and Atari game systems today. Thus, Apple's mission statement should reflect the firm's customer orientation and focus on meeting customer needs (rather than specific products).
3. **Capture a shared purpose and provide motivation for the employees of the firm.** Effective mission statements should emphasize the firm's strengths, as Google's

Nordstrom focuses their marketing and customer service efforts in pursuit of its mission statement to give customers the most compelling shopping experience possible. *Andrew Francis Wallace/Toronto Star/Getty Images*

does: "Google's mission is to organize the world's information and make it universally accessible and useful."[5]

The mission statements of some well-known, market-leading companies illustrate these three characteristics:

Amazon: We seek to be Earth's most customer-centric company for four primary customer sets: consumers, sellers, enterprises, and content creators.[6]

American Express: At American Express, we have a mission to be the world's most respected service brand. To do this, we have established a culture that supports our team members, so they can provide exceptional service to our customers.[7]

Nordstrom: To give customers the most compelling shopping experience possible.[8]

Panda Express: To deliver exceptional Asian dining experiences by building an organization where people are inspired to better their lives.[9]

Urban One: Our mission is to be the most trusted source in the African-American community that informs, entertains and inspires our audience by providing culturally relevant integrated content through our radio, television, and digital platforms.[10]

Tesla: To accelerate the world's transition to sustainable energy.[11]

A firm's mission statement drives many of the other decisions it makes, including how best to market its goods and services to consumers. The mission statement provides a standard to ensure that the business never strays too far from its core goals and values through changing times. A sound mission statement provides a basis for developing the marketing plan.

marketing plan

An action-oriented document or playbook that guides the analysis, implementation, and control of the firm's marketing strategy.

> **LO 2-3**
>
> Outline the five main components of the marketing plan.

THE MARKETING PLAN

A primary strategic planning tool is the organization's marketing plan. The **marketing plan** is an action-oriented document that guides the firm's marketing strategy. It must be consistent with the overall strategic plan of the organization, grounded in the firm's mission statement.

Creating a marketing plan requires the input, guidance, and review of employees throughout various departments of a firm, not just the marketing department. Therefore, it is important that every future business professional understand the components of the marketing plan.

The specific format of the marketing plan differs from organization to organization. Most marketing plans include five components: executive summary, situation analysis, marketing strategy, financials section, and controls section. These five components communicate what the organization desires to accomplish and how it plans to achieve its goals. Figure 2.2 gives a brief description of each component, which we discuss in the following sections.

Executive Summary

At some point in your career, you will likely run into senior-level executives in casual places, such as the elevator or break room. When they ask what you are working on, you won't have 20 minutes to discuss your projects. More likely, you will have time for only a short *elevator pitch,* which is a one- to two-minute opportunity to market yourself and share the main points of your work. The executive summary in an organization's marketing plan serves as the plan's elevator pitch. It provides a one- to two-page synopsis of the marketing plan's main points.

Just as every second of your elevator pitch to a senior manager counts, so too does every line of an executive summary. It should convey the most valuable information of the marketing plan. The marketing plan may be viewed by dozens or even hundreds of people. Some will take the time to read each line, but most are looking to quickly understand the basic ideas and strategies behind the plan. The executive summary provides this resource. Although the executive summary comes first in the marketing plan, most firms complete this part of the plan last.

situation analysis
The systematic collection of data to identify the trends, conditions, and competitive forces that have the potential to influence the performance of the firm and the choice of appropriate strategies.

Situation Analysis

A **situation analysis** is a systematic collection of data to identify market trends, conditions, and competitive forces. Its purpose is to identify factors that have the potential to influence the firm's performance and the choice of appropriate strategies.

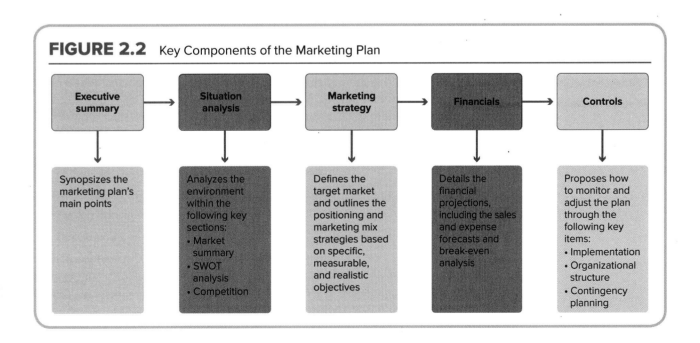

FIGURE 2.2 Key Components of the Marketing Plan

Executive summary	Situation analysis	Marketing strategy	Financials	Controls
Synopsizes the marketing plan's main points	Analyzes the environment within the following key sections: • Market summary • SWOT analysis • Competition	Defines the target market and outlines the positioning and marketing mix strategies based on specific, measurable, and realistic objectives	Details the financial projections, including the sales and expense forecasts and break-even analysis	Proposes how to monitor and adjust the plan through the following key items: • Implementation • Organizational structure • Contingency planning

Organizations must clearly understand their current situation to make strategic decisions about how best to move forward.

The situation analysis has three subsections:

- *Market summary:* A *market* is the group of consumers or organizations that is interested in and able to buy a particular product. The **market summary** describes the current state of the market. Understanding where a market is and where it might be going gives organizations a view of what resources to invest where.
- *SWOT analysis:* A *SWOT analysis* is an evaluation of a firm's strengths (S), weaknesses (W), opportunities (O), and threats (T).
- *Competition analysis:* The *competition analysis* subsection lists the firm's direct competitors. This list should include both direct and indirect competitors. *Indirect competitors* are those that can take market share as macro trends or consumer preferences change. It is often easier to identify direct competitors than it is to understand who might be indirect competitors.

We will examine the tools and techniques used for the market summary, SWOT analysis, and competition analysis a bit later in the chapter.

Marketing Strategy

Once the situation analysis is complete in the marketing plan, marketers focus on defining the firm's marketing strategy. A **strategy** is the set of actions taken to accomplish organizational objectives. The *marketing strategy* component lists the actions the firm must take to accomplish the marketing objectives it established in its mission statement and strategic planning. A successful marketing strategy can lead to higher profits, stronger brands, and larger market share. We'll explore the basic tools and techniques of marketing strategy later in the chapter.

Financials

The fourth section of the marketing plan is the *financials* section. It details the overall profitability of both the firm and its individual units. **Financial projections** provide those reading the plan with a bottom-line numerical estimate of the organization's profitability. Financial projections can include numerous items; all should contain a sales forecast, an expense forecast, and a break-even analysis:

- *Sales forecast.* A *sales forecast* projects how many units of a product the company expects to sell during a specific time period. Sales forecasts must be as accurate as possible. A sales forecast that is too low can lead a company to run out of product to sell. A forecast that is too high can leave a firm with unused inventory, which can severely strain a firm's financial resources.
- *Expense forecast.* The *expense forecast* is an estimate of the costs the company will incur to create, communicate, and deliver the product. Without an expense forecast, the firm will have a difficult time allocating resources and predicting profits.
- *Break-even analysis.* *Break-even analysis* combines the data from the sales and expense forecasts. The result is an estimate of how much the company needs to sell to cover its expenses—that is, to break even.

Controls

The final section in most marketing plans outlines the *controls* the firm will put in place to monitor performance and adjust the plan over time. Good strategy planning alone does not guarantee marketing success. Evaluation and control is a critical link between an organization and its environment. Such activities help a firm determine how well it is able to respond to ever-changing environmental constraints.[12]

The controls section includes the following three items:

1. *Implementation.* No matter how good the marketing plan is, it is of little value unless the company implements it successfully. The *implementation* section provides a detailed account of *how* the specific actions of the marketing plan will be carried out and *who* will be responsible for doing so. Should the company buy advertising on a specific television channel? Should it utilize a new Twitter hashtag? Answers to questions like these should tie back to the marketing strategy and the specific objectives laid out during the strategic planning process. Marketers should carefully monitor each marketing strategy and expect to make adjustments depending on results or as market conditions change over time.

2. *Organizational structure.* An outline of the organizational structure assigns specific responsibility for the parts of the marketing plan. By clearly outlining who is accountable for which tasks, the marketing plan can help drive positive results. One organizational structure trend is the increasing number of chief marketing officers (CMOs) within organizations. Recent research suggests that organizations benefit by having a CMO as part of an organization's top management team.[13]

3. *Contingency planning.* Contingency planning defines the actions the company will take if the initial marketing strategy falls short of expected results. For example, Coca-Cola famously changed direction after its New Coke product failed to meet company objectives. The firm reintroduced the old Coke formula as Coca-Cola Classic and began to add profits and market share again.

Throughout this text and the course, you will have the opportunity to prepare marketing plans that include the five components just discussed. Depending on how your instructor structures the course, the marketing plan you prepare may be for products or services, real or imagined. Or you might use the Marketing Plan Exercise at the end of each chapter. It will help you learn the elements of the marketing plan in the context of the most important product or brand of your life: *yourself.*

We next turn our attention to the tools and techniques marketers use to prepare a situation analysis.

TOOLS AND TECHNIQUES FOR THE SITUATION ANALYSIS

LO 2-4

Explain three tools and techniques for the situation analysis: market summary, SWOT analysis, and competition analysis.

As discussed earlier, the situation analysis in the marketing plan includes a market summary, a SWOT analysis, and an analysis of the competition. Here, we review those tools in more detail.

Market Summary

The market summary sets the stage for the situation analysis section by focusing on the current state of the market to which the firm will sell its products. For example, a market summary for McDonald's might look at the size of the fast-food market in the United States and how rapidly its numbers are growing or declining.

A quality market summary should provide a perspective on important marketplace trends. For example, a market summary for McDonald's might look at the eating habits of two large demographic groups, Baby Boomers and Millennials. A market summary for the residential home phone market would point out that the number of traditional landline customers for AT&T, Verizon, and other carriers shrinks every year as more people decide to use only a cell phone. Market summaries for both markets would also consider the growth opportunities internationally and potential sales through international expansion.

BCG Matrix One of the most popular analysis tools to describe the current market is the Boston Consulting Group (BCG) matrix. The tool is a two-by-two matrix that graphically describes the strength and attractiveness of a market. Figure 2.3 illustrates the BCG matrix. The vertical axis measures market growth; the horizontal axis measures relative market share. (*Relative market share* is defined as the sales volume of a product divided by the sales volume of the largest competitor.) The BCG matrix combines those two elements—market growth and relative market share—to produce four unique product categories. Each of those four product categories—stars, cash cows, question marks, and dogs—requires a different marketing strategy.

- *Star* products combine large market share in an industry with a high growth rate. The Apple Watch falls in this category. Marketing efforts around star products focus on maintaining the product's market position for as long as possible. Firms with star products generally have to invest heavily in marketing to communicate value as the industry continues to grow.
- *Cash cows* are products that have a large market share in an industry with low growth rates. A recent example of a cash cow is the Apple iPod. The market growth rate for MP3-type players has slowed in recent years, but the iPod still retains a large share of the market. As a result, Apple marketers may decide to allocate only enough marketing resources (e.g., television commercials, special pricing discounts) to keep sales strong without increasing product development costs or negatively affecting profits. Marketers might also make the decision to reallocate resources from cash cows to drive additional growth in future star products, similar to what Apple did when it discontinued the iPod in 2022.
- *Question marks* have small market share in a high-growth industry. Products in this quadrant are typically new to the market. They require significant marketing investment in promotion, product management, and distribution. Apple TV+ is a question-mark product. Marketers for the new streaming service must move quickly and creatively to reach potential users before competitors develop comparable products. Question marks have an uncertain future. As a result, marketers must monitor the product's position to determine whether to continue allocating resources to it.
- *Dogs* are products that have small market share in industries with low growth rates. An example of a dog product might be compact discs, an industry in which no firm has large market share and the growth rate is declining. Products that fall into this category typically should be discontinued. Doing so frees up resources for products with more profit potential.

As part of the market summary, the BCG matrix allows a company to determine where its product will fall in the marketplace. Such knowledge serves as a starting point for developing marketing strategies to address that market position.

SWOT Analysis

A second situation analysis technique is a SWOT analysis—evaluation of a firm's strengths, weaknesses, opportunities, and threats. A SWOT analysis can be a valuable tool in the development of a marketing plan. Perhaps the most common mistake a firm makes when conducting a SWOT analysis is failing to separate internal issues from external issues. The strengths and the weaknesses aspects of the analysis focus on

SWOT analysis

An evaluation of a firm's strengths, weaknesses, opportunities, and threats.

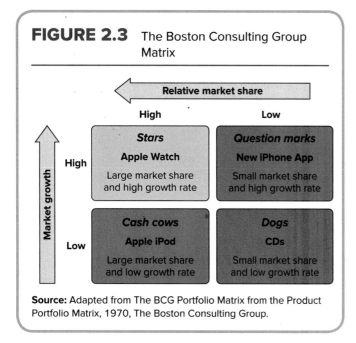

FIGURE 2.3 The Boston Consulting Group Matrix

Source: Adapted from The BCG Portfolio Matrix from the Product Portfolio Matrix, 1970, The Boston Consulting Group.

internal characteristics of the firm. The opportunities and threats aspects of the SWOT analysis focus on the *external* environment. As we discuss these internal and external aspects, we'll consider how a firm like McDonald's might conduct a SWOT analysis.

Internal Considerations The internal considerations in a SWOT analysis are the firm's strengths and weaknesses. **Strengths** are internal capabilities that help the company achieve its objectives. McDonald's strengths include:

Companies like McDonald's often complete a SWOT analysis to identify and evaluate their strengths, weakness, opportunities, and threats. *David Paul Morris/Getty Images*

- Strong brand recognition with consumers of all ages and backgrounds.
- Long-term profitability and a franchise system that ties individual store owners' profits to company profits. The company has the financial strength to consistently develop new products, promote its brand, and make strategic acquisitions.
- McDonald's continuing reputation as the most popular breakfast restaurant in the United States.[14]

Weaknesses are internal limitations that may prevent or disrupt the firm's ability to meet its stated objectives. Marketers must be honest with themselves when identifying weaknesses. The firm cannot develop strategies to overcome weaknesses if it doesn't recognize them as problems. For McDonald's, weaknesses might be:

- The challenge of finding and keeping quality employees.
- Traditional menu filled with high-calorie items.
- Longer wait times. Since 2007, the company has expanded its menus by 70 percent.[15] The longer menu has complicated food preparation and slowed food delivery.

External Considerations The external considerations in a SWOT analysis are the opportunities and threats the firm faces. **Opportunities** are external factors that the firm may be able to capitalize on to meet its stated objectives. Opportunities for McDonald's in the years ahead include:

- Increased international expansion. McDonald's currently serves approximately 69 million customers each day in over 100 countries.[16] International growth, especially in Europe and Asia, has exceeded earnings growth at domestic McDonald's restaurants in recent years.[17]
- Expanded service menu.
- Public interest in ethical and sustainable business practices.

Threats are current or potential external factors that may challenge the firm's short- and long-term performance. McDonald's faces a number of potential threats, including:

- A declining global economy.
- The U.S. consumer trend of eating healthier and consuming less fast food.
- Increasing production costs due to inflation.
- Difficulty finding enough workers to staff restaurants.

External factors can be both threats and opportunities. For example, during the recent sluggish economy, consumers have tried to rein in their budgets by eating out less often. This reality threatens the restaurant industry, including McDonald's. However, factors such as inflation have also prompted consumers to look for cheaper

strengths (in SWOT analysis)
Internal capabilities that help the company achieve its objectives.

weaknesses (in SWOT analysis)
Internal limitations that may prevent or disrupt the firm's ability to meet its stated objectives.

opportunities (in SWOT analysis)
External factors that the firm may be able to capitalize on to meet or exceed its stated objectives.

threats (in SWOT analysis)
Current and potential external factors that may challenge the firm's short- and long-term performance.

TABLE 2.1　Example SWOT Analysis for McDonald's

Internal Considerations	
Strengths	**Weaknesses**
• Strong brand recognition • Long-term profitability and franchise system • Breakfast reputation	• Difficulty finding and retaining quality employees • Traditional menu filled with high-calorie items • Longer wait times
External Considerations	
Opportunities	**Threats**
• International expansion • Menu or service expansions • Public interest in ethical and sustainable business practices	• Weak economy that cuts dining-out budgets • Increasing production costs • Health consciousness of U.S. population

food alternatives; as the world's leading choice for discounted dining, McDonald's has an opportunity to take advantage of this trend.

When a company has a filled-in SWOT diagram (see Table 2.1 for McDonald's), what happens next? The SWOT analysis enables managers to look for ideas and strategies that might produce a competitive advantage. By focusing on the various SWOT factors, the firm can ask questions such as:[18]

- *How can the firm use its strengths to take advantage of opportunities?* Given the popularity of its breakfast menu, McDonald's began offering breakfast service after 10:30 a.m. in 2015. While they stopped offering the all-day breakfast menu in 2021, perhaps it could also consider offering popular regular menu items such as hamburgers, chicken nuggets, or french fries during traditional breakfast hours.
- *How can the firm overcome weaknesses that keep it from taking advantage of opportunities?* Change employee incentives to encourage workers to stay with the company, perhaps by expanding training opportunities for international postings.
- *How can the firm use its strengths to reduce the impact of threats?* Launch an ad campaign showing consumers spending their dining dollars on McDonald's food—for example, a family with excited kids picking up a drive-through order featuring healthier side items, which then are eaten at a local park where the kids are playing.
- *How can the firm overcome weaknesses that will make threats a reality?* Find ways to speed up production times, possibly through new technologies or elimination of unprofitable menu items.

In short, firms must understand and analyze environmental factors—both internal and external—to develop quality strategic and marketing plans.

connect Exercise 2-1

Please complete the *Connect* exercise for Chapter 2 that focuses on conducting a SWOT analysis. By identifying which elements of a fictional company's situation analysis fall into each category, you will understand the differences among the four SWOT components.

Competition Analysis

A third tool in the situation analysis is an analysis of the competition. The competition analysis section should begin by clearly stating the organization's *direct competitors.* For McDonald's, direct competitors include Burger King and Wendy's. The direct-competitors section should briefly describe how Burger King and Wendy's position their products relative to McDonald's. It should also indicate where McDonald's is most vulnerable to Burger King and Wendy's on important customer metrics such as taste, value, pricing, convenience, and customer satisfaction. Marketing research can provide key data for this section of the analysis.

When completing a situation analysis, it's just as important for a firm like McDonald's to analyze indirect competitors, such as Panera Bread, as it is to analyze direct competitors, such as Burger King. *Scott Eells/Getty Images*

Most marketing plans are able to identify and examine direct competitors. *Indirect competitors,* though, typically receive far less attention or are overlooked entirely. For example, McDonald's must worry not only about other burger chains but also about the consumer trend of eating healthier. That trend has translated into massive expansion for chains like Subway and Chipotle. In 2015, Subway surpassed McDonald's as the largest restaurant chain in the world, with almost 45,000 stores worldwide, compared with fewer than 37,000 for McDonald's.[19] Similarly, fast-casual restaurants like Chipotle are becoming indirect competitors as they emphasize a healthier and more sustainable menu and make their service lines faster.[20] McDonald's responded in 2018 by removing cheeseburgers from its Happy Meal menu and furthering its plans to cut the sugar content of chocolate milk and adding bottled water to the menu. By the end of 2022, McDonald's goal is that at least 50 percent or more of the Happy Meals listed on menus will be 600 calories or less.[21] Also, consumers choosing to eat at home rather than purchase fast food in a weak economy compete indirectly with McDonald's as well. A good study of the competition provides a thoughtful analysis of both the direct and indirect competitors.

BASIC TOOLS AND TECHNIQUES OF MARKETING STRATEGY

LO 2-5

Explain the basic tools and techniques of marketing strategy: segmentation, strategic direction, and the marketing mix.

The next component of the marketing plan is the *marketing strategy.* It lists the specific actions the firm must take to accomplish the marketing objectives it has established. The basic tools and techniques of marketing strategy include decisions about (1) segmentation, target markets, and positioning; (2) strategic directions; and (3) the marketing mix. This section gives an overview of these topics. They are important marketing concepts that we will continue to use and elaborate on throughout the course.

The effectiveness of the marketing strategy depends, in part, on the clarity of the short- and medium-term objectives the firm has defined. Quality marketing objectives have three basic characteristics:

1. ***They are specific.*** Objectives are of little value if they are not specific. If Facebook identified an objective to increase ad revenues, how would it formulate a strategy around that? Would it be happy with $1 of revenue growth over the next 10 years? How could Facebook develop a strategy without more detail? Vague marketing objectives lead to a lack of focus and accountability. A more specific objective, such as Facebook plans to "increase ad revenues 14 percent in the next 12 months," provides much better direction to the marketing decisions that will be made.

2. *They are measurable.* Objectives must be measurable so that marketers know if their strategies are working. A common phrase used in offices around the globe is, "If it can't be measured, it can't be managed." Firms want to see a specific return on their marketing investment. Marketers aren't often fired for having a bad idea (we all have bad ideas from time to time). They might lose a job, though, if they make the same mistake over and over again because, due to a lack of measurable metrics, they don't realize their strategy isn't working.

3. *They are realistic.* Objectives need to be realistic so that marketers do not demotivate their organizations with unattainable goals. Imagine if your professor said that to get an A in this marketing course, you had to score 100 percent. You might be demotivated to try your best and might decide that a B in marketing is good enough.

Objectives also should be realistic in order to show those reading the marketing plan that it is a serious, thoughtful document. Consider a professional sports organization that sets an objective to increase ticket revenue by 300 percent, even though the team continues to lose. Someone reading the document might well doubt the reliability of the other parts of the marketing plan, too.

Based on these criteria for marketing objectives, McDonald's marketers might set objectives to sell 5 percent more premium coffee or 3 percent more chicken nuggets in existing U.S. stores. Either of these hypothetical objectives would be specific, measurable, and realistic. Before McDonald's can establish strategies to meet either objective, it must clearly identify which customers are most likely to buy premium coffee or chicken nuggets. Only then can it decide how best to position each product in the minds of those customers. The need to identify customers by their purchase patterns takes us to the first of the basic marketing strategy tools and techniques: segmentation, target markets, and positioning.

Segmentation, Target Markets, and Positioning

Marketers must identify who their intended customers are. That knowledge enables them to segment the market, identify a target market, and correctly position their product for that market.

market segmentation

The process of dividing a larger market into smaller groups, or market segments, based on meaningfully shared characteristics.

Segmentation
Market segmentation is the process of dividing a large market into smaller groups. Those smaller groups are **market segments**, the groups of consumers who have shared characteristics and similar product needs. Market segmentation plays an important role in the success of almost every organization in the United States and throughout the world. Without it, marketing efforts are often unfocused and largely wasted.

market segments

The groups of consumers who have shared characteristics and similar product needs.

Target Markets
A **target market** is the group of customers toward which an organization directs its marketing efforts. Small firms may have only one target market. Large organizations might enter multiple target markets. McDonald's has multiple target markets: adults, teenagers, and families with small children. In recent years, McDonald's has targeted gourmet coffee drinkers in an effort to win them away from companies like Starbucks. Regardless of size, firms tend to enter multiple markets by first serving one group and then expanding based on success with that group.

target market

The group of customers toward which an organization has decided to direct its marketing efforts.

Positioning
Success within the target market depends, to some degree, on how the firm *positions* its product. **Positioning** refers to the activities a firm undertakes to create a certain perception of its product in the eyes of the target market. The firm has total control over this element of its marketing efforts, and the concept is critical to how it develops the rest of its marketing strategy.

positioning

The activities a firm undertakes to create a certain perception of its product in the eyes of the target market.

To position its product, the firm must take into consideration various issues. These include the competition, the needs and wants of the target market, and the element of mystique or drama that the good or service naturally has. When McDonald's entered the gourmet coffee market, it had to overcome the perception that it was simply a place to get Big Macs and Happy Meals. McDonald's marketers launched an advertising campaign called "Unsnobby Coffee." It put espresso machines in thousands of its stores and aggressively positioned itself as a place for consumers to get great coffee for a lower price than Starbucks.

Another example of successful positioning is the Ford Fusion Hybrid. Ford marketers positioned the Fusion as a more stylish, youthful hybrid car than competitors like the Toyota Camry Hybrid. The Fusion's Aston Martin–like design helped build excitement among younger buyers, including many who had never before purchased a Ford. The positioning helped the Ford Fusion set record hybrid sales numbers for the company and introduced the Ford brand to a new generation of car buyers.

FIGURE 2.4 The Four Basic Categories of Marketing Growth Strategies

Strategic Direction

Another technique used in the marketing strategy section of the marketing plan relates to strategic direction. A company's marketing strategy can follow various paths, which depend on the product and industry. As Figure 2.4 shows, most marketing strategies seek to move the product in one of four directions:[22]

- *Market penetration:* selling more of existing goods and services to existing customers.
- *Product development:* creating new goods and services for existing markets.
- *Market development:* selling existing goods and services to new customers.
- *Diversification:* offering new goods and services to attract new customers.

Each of these categories represents the intersection of a strategy related to products and another related to markets.

Market Penetration
Market penetration strategies emphasize selling more of the firm's existing goods and services to existing customers. This growth strategy often involves encouraging current customers to buy more each time they patronize a store or to buy from the store on a more frequent basis. For example, marketers at Pizza Hut try to get existing consumers to buy one more pizza each month or add an order of breadsticks to their normal pizza order. They found success during the 2021 holiday season by offering the "Triple Threat Box," which includes 2 medium pizzas, 5 breadsticks, and 10 Cinnabon Mini Rolls. The product introduced consumers to side dishes such as cinnamon rolls or breadsticks that they might not have thought to buy from Pizza Hut. For a market penetration strategy to succeed, firms often must increase advertising expenses, develop new distribution frameworks, or enhance their social media offerings.

market penetration
A marketing strategy that emphasizes selling more of existing goods and services to existing customers.

Product Development
Product development strategies involve creating new goods and services for existing markets. Dr Pepper used such a strategy when it introduced Dr Pepper Ten, a 10-calorie soft drink, using a male-targeted marketing campaign with the slogan, "It's not for women." The strategy focused on male consumers who enjoyed Dr Pepper but wanted a beverage with fewer calories.[23] Dr Pepper

product development
A marketing strategy that involves creating new goods and services for existing markets.

marketed Ten as a better-tasting, "manlier" product in an effort to reach its target market in a new way.

A new product can also be an improved product or one with a new feature or innovation. Apple successfully uses this strategy: It has successfully developed multiple new iPhone products with additional features and functionality for its consumers. Long lines of customers and strong initial sales have welcomed each new iPhone.

Market Development
Market development strategies focus on selling existing goods and services to new customers. The targeted new customers could be of a different gender, age group, or education level.

market development

A marketing strategy that focuses on selling existing goods and services to new customers.

For virtually any company or industry, globalization is an increasingly critical market development strategy. Most of the 100 largest U.S.-based companies are aggressively implementing market development strategies by increasing their international presence. Arkansas-based retail giant Walmart has recently seen its international division grow to account for over 23 percent ($118 billion) of total company revenue.[24] In 2022, Walmart International operated in 23 countries, including China, Japan, Brazil, and Mexico, where it had over 5,100 international stores.[25]

A company maximizes its chances for success by having a clear strategy for implementation as it expands into foreign markets. Later in the chapter, we'll discuss the various strategies firms can use to enter international markets.

diversification

A marketing strategy that seeks to attract new customers by offering new products that are unrelated to the existing products produced by the organization.

Diversification
Diversification strategies seek to attract new customers by offering new products that are unrelated to the firm's existing products. Disney has used this strategy over the past few decades: It used to be a company that produced animated movies and ran theme parks; it now has diversified into an international family entertainment and media enterprise. Disney owns television channels like ABC and ESPN as well as independent movie-production companies like Lucasfilm. It sells vacation properties, books, apparel, and international consumer products. Diversification enables companies like Disney to hedge against decreasing sales in some product lines due to economic conditions.

International expansion is an increasingly necessary part of a successful market development strategy for small firms as well as large retailers like Walmart.
Heorshe/Alamy Stock Photo

Mc Graw Hill connect Exercise 2-2

Please complete the *Connect* exercise for Chapter 2 that focuses on the four strategic directions a firm can take. By matching particular strategies with companies that used those strategies, you will better understand how different marketing strategies may affect your future employer.

Marketing Mix

Recall that the *marketing mix* is the combination of activities that a firm can do to influence demand for its good or service. It is often referred to as the *four Ps of marketing:* product, price, place, and promotion. The final tool used in the marketing strategy section of the marketing plan focuses on determining how each element of the marketing mix will support the chosen strategy.

Product
The *product* section of the marketing plan consists of a detailed description of the product being offered. This description includes not only the good or service itself, but also any related services like warranties and guarantees that accompany the good or service. The product description should clearly state what *value* the product

holds for the customer. It also should build on the competition section, to explain what competitive advantage the firm's product offers.

A product possesses a **competitive advantage** when customers perceive that it has more value than other products in its category. Competitive advantage can be short-lived if competitors are quickly able to offer the same or better features. The firm's real goal is to develop products that achieve *sustainable competitive advantage*—that outperform competitors over a long period of time.

One way to achieve sustainable competitive advantage is to focus on the complete product rather than solely on the good or service itself. By doing so, the firm can satisfy the unmet needs and wants of potential customers and differentiate itself from its competitors. For example, McDonald's provides food and beverage products, but so do many other restaurant chains. McDonald's competitive advantage relates to its ability to provide these items in a fast, low-cost way in a clean restaurant. Thinking of the product as a *combination* of goods, services, and ideas allows McDonald's to consider what the consumer is actually buying beyond just burgers, fries, and chicken nuggets. For a family stopping at McDonald's on a vacation, the value might be the combination of clean restrooms, free wireless Internet access, and the comfort of choosing a familiar place to eat. The marketing plan should clearly address how the firm communicates what its product is and what value the product holds for the consumer.

> **competitive advantage**
>
> The superior position a product enjoys over competing products if consumers believe it has more value than other products in its category.

Promotion

Promotion The *promotion* section of the marketing plan details *how* the firm will communicate the value of its product. This section builds on the strengths of the product section. It references the specific promotional tools—advertising, sales promotion, personal selling, or public relations—the firm will use to reach its target market. McDonald's might plan to increase advertising spending to promote its Filet-o-Fish sandwiches during Lent, when many religious consumers stop eating meat on Fridays. McDonald's could also use part of its approximately $2.0 billion annual advertising budget to promote the quality of its food across social media, in an effort to encourage Millennials to dine there more often.[26]

Distribution

Distribution Distribution strategies fall within the *place* marketing-mix element. The distribution section of the marketing plan describes where and when the firm will deliver value to its customers. The distribution section should outline all the different companies, people, and technologies that will be involved in the process of delivering the product to customers.

McDonald's has a number of distribution decisions to make: How will it get products to more than 30,000 stores in a fresh and safe manner? Should it partner with gas stations and travel centers to offer its products at facilities beyond McDonald's restaurants? In 2021, McDonald's negotiated new deals with two of its third-party delivery platforms, DoorDash and Uber Eats, and will be integrating McDelivery into its mobile smartphone app. McDonald's said McDelivery has provided significant business and profit growth since it was launched in 2017 with 3,000 restaurants. Now, more than 32,000 restaurants in 100 countries have partnerships with local and global delivery platforms.[27] Another distribution decision was McDonald's announcement that it will use only cage-free eggs in its North American restaurants.[28]

McDonald's made the strategic decision in 2015 to shift toward using only cage-free eggs. The company faces a distribution challenge because fewer than 10 percent of the nation's laying hens were categorized as "cage-free" at the time of the announcement. It could take McDonald's up to a decade to reach its goal of having 100 percent cage-free eggs in its products.[29] *Gary Friedman/Getty Images*

Pricing The *pricing* section of the marketing plan specifies how much money customers must pay for the product and explains why the firm selected that price. For example, McDonald's increased menu prices by 1 percent in 2011 because of an increase in the price of commodities like hamburger meat and buns. However, those commodity prices rose several percentage points more than 1 percent. McDonald's didn't increase its prices by the same amount because the firm's marketers understood that consumers remained concerned about overspending in a weak economy.[30] McDonald's marketers believed that keeping price increases small was essential to keeping customer volume up. The pricing section of the marketing plan should include this type of information.

---

connect Exercise 2-3

Social Media in Action

In 2021, several social media influencers found out how they would look with some extra stuffing thanks to a unique activation strategy that embraces the fun nature of Little Caesars marketing.

As part of the company's Extra Stuffed pizza launch, Little Caesars delivered "stuffed people"—life-sized dolls with nine feet of cheese and pepperoni stuffed inside of them. Little Caesars based several of these "stuffed people" off of popular TikTokers, including Spencer X, Adam Waheed, The McFarlands, and Brooke Averick. The TikTok stars then shared a series of videos on their accounts featuring their stuffed versions doing a variety of mundane tasks.

Little Caesars marketers are focused on their brand voice and how they connect to consumers. Little Caesars marketers identified TikTok as a platform where they could get in early and express this fun personality in a new way to young, highly engaged audiences. TikTok users have embraced Little Caesars, which is now the most-followed pizza brand.

The Social Media in Action Connect exercise for Chapter 2 asks you to decide how social media strategies fit into a marketing plan. By understanding the role social media can play in achieving your objectives, you will be able to apply social media strategies to successfully implement a marketing plan for your organization in the years ahead.

Source: Larissa Faw, "Little Caesars Drops Mini Dopplegangers," Adweek.com, July 22, 2021.

Discuss the strategic decisions involved in reaching international consumers.

MARKETING STRATEGY IN A GLOBAL CONTEXT

The marketing plan elements we've discussed assume the firm's activities are directed only to the domestic market. However, globalization is the new reality. As a result, a firm's strategic planning process must consider what, if any, international presence the firm wants to pursue. One of the most critical strategic decisions involves how to enter foreign markets. As part of a global marketing plan that involves global marketing, the firm has five major strategic options: exporting, licensing, franchising, joint venture, or direct ownership. Each of these options, illustrated in Figure 2.5 and discussed in the following sections, offers a unique mix of risk and reward.

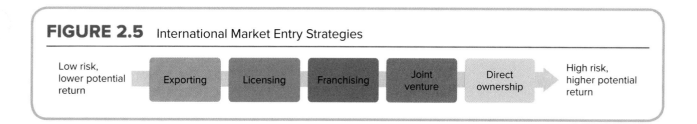

FIGURE 2.5 International Market Entry Strategies

Low risk, lower potential return → Exporting — Licensing — Franchising — Joint venture — Direct ownership → High risk, higher potential return

Exporting

Exporting is selling domestically produced products to foreign markets. It typically is the least risky option for entering international markets. Increasingly, firms of all sizes export their products to other countries. Large firms like Cargill (producer of food, agricultural, financial, and industrial goods and services) and ExxonMobil (oil and gas) are exporters. They ship tens of thousands of products annually in support of their various business units. But exporting is popular not just among the companies that make up the Fortune 500. Small companies, like those that many of you will work for after college, account for 98 percent of all U.S. exporters.[31]

Social media tools enable small businesses to engage global customers in a way that was not possible a decade ago. Logistics firms like FedEx and UPS also help increase export opportunities; they provide small businesses with a quick, efficient way to deliver products almost anywhere in the world. These tools provide almost any small business in the United States with the opportunity to become an exporter.

exporting
Selling domestically produced products to foreign markets.

Licensing

Licensing is a legal process in which one firm pays to use or distribute another firm's resources. The resources being licensed might include products, trademarks, patents, intellectual property, or other proprietary knowledge. Through such arrangements, the domestic licensor allows a foreign company to use its resources. For example, with mounting interest from overseas markets, Major League Baseball (MLB) continues to enjoy strong licensing revenues. MLB licensees operate Clubhouse stores in Puerto Rico and sell MLB-licensed apparel at Harrods department store in London.[32] Revenue from global retail sales of licensed sports merchandise reached $34 billion in 2020.[33]

In recent years, the use of licensing to enter international markets has increased significantly. More regulation, rising research and development (R&D) costs, and shortened product life cycles have increased domestic development costs. Licensing helps overcome some of these barriers because the licensee is typically locally owned and brings unique insight about its local consumers, Licensing offers marketers the advantages of expanding the reach of their products quickly in a low-cost way.

Despite its growing popularity, licensing is typically a riskier option than exporting. Major risks include:

licensing
A legal process in which one firm pays to use or distribute another firm's resources, including products, trademarks, patents, intellectual property, or other proprietary knowledge.

- The licensor may be inadvertently creating a future competitor in the form of the licensee.
- The licensor shares information and the right to use its proprietary technology with the licensee, who might use that knowledge in the future.
- The licensee could potentially misuse trademarks.

However, the short-term benefits of licensing often outweigh the potential longer-term risks facing marketers.

Burger King allows franchisees to offer specific products in Japan, such as the "Aka Samurai Chicken" and "Aka Samurai Beef," to better satisfy local customer tastes. *Koji Sasahara/AP Images*

franchising

A contractual arrangement in which the franchisor provides a franchisee the right to use its name and marketing and operational support in exchange for a fee and, typically, a share of the profits.

joint venture

An arrangement in which a domestic firm partners with a foreign company to create a new entity, thus allowing the domestic firm to enter the foreign company's market.

Franchising

You may already be familiar with franchising at U.S. companies like McDonald's. **Franchising** is a contractual arrangement in which the franchisor (McDonald's) provides a franchisee (local owner-operator) the right to use its name and marketing and operational support; in return, the franchisee pays the franchisor a fee and, typically, a share of the profits. International franchise agreements are essentially the same as domestic agreements. The obvious difference is that they must meet the commercial laws of the country in which the franchise exists.

Franchising is an attractive method of entering foreign markets. The franchisee assumes the majority of the capital costs and human resource issues. The franchisor provides knowledge and information about running the business. That division of responsibility increases the likelihood of success. Franchisors typically allow companies to offer new products for consumers in specific international markets, adding further product appeal. For example, in Japan, Burger King offers the "Aka Samurai Chicken" sandwich and "Aka Samurai Beef" burger, complete with red buns, red cheese, and red hot sauce.[34]

The disadvantages of franchising include the risks of granting your name to a franchisee in a faraway place where direct oversight is difficult. If a Burger King in Asia were involved in a negative public event, it could damage the Burger King name throughout the world. Franchisors also run the risk of providing such detailed information that a franchisee could potentially have a competitive advantage if they chose to open a competing business.

Joint Venture

A riskier option than exporting, licensing, or franchising is a joint venture. In an international **joint venture**, a domestic firm partners with a foreign company to create a new entity; through this partnership, the domestic firm enters the foreign company's market. The local partner shares equity (ownership) in the new entity and thus claims some portion of the profits. In return, the local partner provides the foreign entrant with valuable information about local consumers, suppliers, and the regulatory environment.

Joint ventures work best when:

- The partners' strategic goals align.
- Their competitive goals diverge.
- They are able to learn from one another without infringing on each other's proprietary skills.

For example, Italian coffee company Lavazza formed a joint venture with Yum China Holdings Inc. in 2020 in hopes of increasing revenue and adding hundreds of stores in China. Yum China is a local operator with exclusive rights in mainland China to popular restaurant brands including KFC and Pizza Hut. Lavazza will benefit from access to Yum's supply chain and logistics infrastructure, as well as its knowledge of the local market. Yum owns 65 percent of the partnership, and Lavazza holds the rest. By 2021, Lavazza had already opened 20 cafes across Shanghai, Hangzhou, Beijing, and Guangzhou.[35]

Joint ventures come with inherent risk. Domestic and international firms often operate differently, which can lead to culture clashes. Joint ventures also can result in mistrust over proprietary knowledge, conflict over new investments, and disagreements about how to share revenue and profits. AT&T entered into a joint venture with Philips NV, an Amsterdam-based electronics company, to produce telecommunications equipment in

Europe. The venture was ultimately unsuccessful due to Philips NV's inability to help AT&T penetrate the French telecom market.[36] The success of an international joint venture also depends on the local economy. The success of Macy's joint venture with Fung Retailing, for example, will depend in part on the continued growth of the Chinese economy.

Direct Ownership

The riskiest strategy for entering an international market is direct ownership. In **direct ownership**, a domestic firm actively manages a foreign company or overseas facilities. Direct ownership is a good strategic option under certain conditions:

- The firm sees substantial sales potential in the international market.
- There is very little political risk (the risk of local government unrest).
- Similarities exist between the foreign and domestic cultures.

Still, maintaining 100 percent ownership of offices, plants, and facilities in a foreign country exposes the domestic firm to significant risks. Even in the best of conditions, direct ownership can be risky, as illustrated by Target, which announced in 2015 it was liquidating all 133 stores it owned in Canada, due to their lack of success. The international direct ownership strategy cost Target over $2 billion since its start in 2011, sucking up resources from other strategic initiatives the company could have pursued.[37]

Direct ownership requires far more resources and commitment than any of the other options. It can be difficult to manage local resources from afar. However, direct ownership provides the firm with more control over its intellectual property, advertising, pricing, and product distribution. Marketers should thoroughly analyze the risks and rewards of each type of foreign entry as they develop their marketing plan. The strategy for entering international markets must align with the firm's objectives, as defined in its mission statement and strategic planning.

direct ownership

A method of entering an international market in which a domestic firm actively manages a foreign company or overseas facilities.

Mc Graw Hill connect Exercise **2-4**

Please complete the *Connect* exercise for Chapter 2 that focuses on the approaches to entering an international market. By identifying an example of each strategy and its risk level, you will better understand the potential risks and rewards of marketing your products globally.

MARKETING ANALYTICS

Marketing is one of the biggest expenditures for most organizations. But many organizations have performed marketing activities without knowing what value they add to the firm. Such scattered efforts have frustrated executives, and sometimes even led them to question the value of marketing investments.[38] **Marketing analytics** is the practice of measuring, managing, and analyzing marketing performance. Its goal is to maximize marketing effectiveness and optimize return on investment. Use of marketing analytics enables organizations to measure and evaluate marketing outcomes. Marketing strategy becomes more accountable when organizations base decisions on analytics.[39]

Throughout this text, we will present various marketing analytics tools. We'll show how organizations use these tools. Also, we'll give you opportunities to practice using them so that when you have an opportunity to use them "on the job," they'll be familiar to you. In this chapter, we look at four key analytical tools that many marketers use, starting with return on marketing investment.

LO 2-7

Describe the use of four key marketing analytics: return on marketing investment (ROMI), revenue analysis, market share analysis, and profitability analysis.

marketing analytics

The practice of measuring, managing, and analyzing market performance.

Return on Marketing Investment

Organizations calculate *return on investment* to ensure that their expenditures produce results. **Return on marketing investment (ROMI)** is a measure of the firm's effectiveness in using the resources allocated to its marketing effort. Specifically, it indicates the rate at which spending on marketing contributes to profits.[40] ROMI is calculated as follows:

$$\text{Return on marketing investment } (ROMI) = \frac{(Sales \times Gross\ margin\ \%) - Marketing\ expenditures}{Marketing\ expenditures}$$

In the calculation:

- *Sales* include all of the revenue generated by core and noncore business activities.
- *Gross margin* equals the difference between price (the amount paid by the customer) and cost (the amount required to produce the good or service), which is expressed as a percentage. Gross margin is calculated by subtracting the cost of goods sold per unit from the selling price of the item, divided by the selling price.
- *Marketing expenditures* is the amount of money spent on all marketing activities during a specified period of time.

For example, let's suppose that Best Buy sells large flat-screen televisions for $1,000; the cost of goods sold is $500 per TV. Best Buy's gross margin on each TV is:

$$Gross\ margin = \frac{\$1,000 - \$500}{\$1,000} = 0.50 = 50\%$$

Continuing with our Best Buy example, assume that the company has sales of $200,000 and total marketing expenditures of $70,000. Given this information, we can calculate the return on marketing investment as follows:

$$ROMI = \frac{(\$200,000 \times 0.50) - \$70,000}{\$70,000}$$
$$= \frac{\$30,000}{\$70,000} = 0.429 = 42.9\%$$

The return on marketing investment in this scenario means that every dollar invested in marketing activities returned about 43 cents in revenue. That is a good number for most industries, indicating that Best Buy has put its marketing resources to good use. Usually, marketing spending will be considered justified if the return is positive.[41]

Return on marketing investment tells only part of the story, however. Companies often need to do further analysis to measure the success of specific aspects of their marketing strategy. We discuss three additional tools—revenue analysis, market share analysis, and profitability analysis—in the sections that follow.

Revenue Analysis

Firms that look only at ROMI may fall into the common trap of thinking all is well. In fact, one successful product line may have masked failures in other parts of the company. For a fuller picture, it is useful to quantify the various sources of revenue. Doing so can result in a more targeted and more efficient deployment of resources, ultimately increasing return on marketing investment.

Revenue analysis measures and evaluates revenue from *specific* products or regions. Its goal is to pinpoint what is working and what is not, relative to the objectives of the organization. For example, Kohl's revenue analysis might find that a new line of children's clothing is meeting the firm's objectives at midwestern stores but falling short of objectives in the southeast. This information can help the firm's marketers select what merchandise to sell and how to allocate promotional resources.

Revenue analysis pinpoints the *specific sources* of revenue. The firm also will want to keep an eye on the size of revenue and its growth over time, to monitor whether revenues are keeping pace with the goals set in the strategic plan. Marketing professionals must understand the limitations of simply measuring revenue. They must combine this analysis with an evaluation of market share and profitability before making decisions.

Market Share Analysis

Market share analysis indicates *market share,* which is the percentage of the total market sales captured by a brand, product, or firm. Market share provides marketers with a quick look at how they are performing relative to their competitors. For example, Apple has captured substantial market share across its product lines. In 2021, the iPad accounted for over 34 percent of global tablet shipments, while the iPhone accounted for 14 percent of global smartphone sales.[42]

It is important to understand what market share does and does not show. It does measure the firm's sales as a *percentage* of total market sales. It does not indicate the *size* of the market sales. Let's say your product has achieved 25 percent market share. Is that 25 percent of market sales of $500,000, or 25 percent of market sales of $5,000,000? Market share is especially important to industries in which total market share can change significantly. Auto manufacturing is one such industry: In 2009, during the recession, total U.S. sales of new cars, trucks, and SUVs were 10.4 million vehicles.[43]

Market share is typically depicted using a pie graph, and auto manufacturers were facing a shrinking pie in 2009. As the economy began to recover, the pie grew again: By 2017, vehicle sales were up to over 17.2 million.[44] Figure 2.6 illustrates market share

market share analysis
Marketing analytics tool that measures the percentage of total market sales captured by a brand, product, or firm.

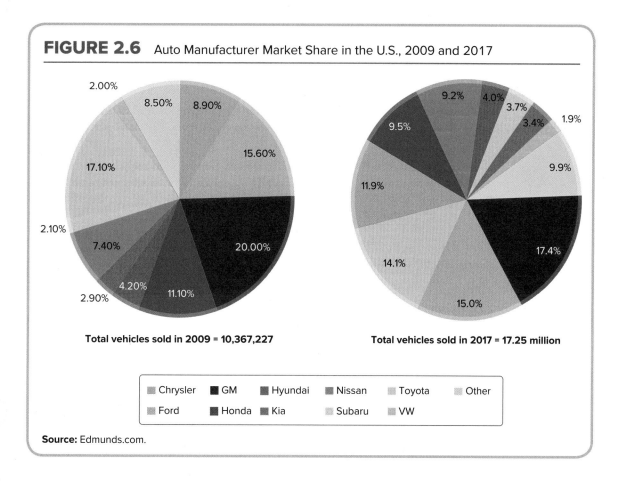

FIGURE 2.6   Auto Manufacturer Market Share in the U.S., 2009 and 2017

Total vehicles sold in 2009 = 10,367,227

Total vehicles sold in 2017 = 17.25 million

Chrysler   ■ GM   ■ Hyundai   ■ Nissan   Toyota   Other
■ Ford   ■ Honda   ■ Kia   ■ Subaru   ■ VW

Source: Edmunds.com.

graphs for automobile sales in the United States for 2009 and 2017. You can see that although percentages for the various manufacturers are similar, each represents more vehicles sold in 2017 than in 2009. For example, Hyundai's 4.2 percent market share in 2009 represented 435,064 vehicles sold. Its 4.0 percent market share in 2017 represented 685,555 vehicles sold.[45]

As with revenue, firms should not analyze market share data in isolation. Rather, they should look at market share data relative to revenue and profitability. A firm can gain market share by drastically reducing prices, but such action will likely lead to decreased revenue and profitability. Ultimately, firms should seek revenue and market share levels that maximize profits for the firm.

Profitability Analysis

Profits are the positive gain from a business operation after subtracting all expenses. **Profitability analysis** measures how much profit the firm generates. It can also be broken down to measure the profit contribution of regions, channels, or customer segments.

Marketers often use two important metrics to evaluate profitability: customer acquisition and customer profitability.

profitability analysis

Marketing analytics tool that measures how much profit the firm generates, as well as how much profit certain aspects of the firm, including regions, channels, and customer segments, contribute.

- *Customer acquisition* measures how much the firm spent to gain new customers. Customer-acquisition costs typically include spending on marketing advertising, public relations, and sales. Why measure customer-acquisition costs? Because sometimes additional customers don't equal additional profit. The firm's goal should be to allocate marketing resources to obtain additional customers at a low cost.

  However, a firm's marketing strategy sometimes makes this goal impossible. For example, Netflix increased its customer-acquisition costs 59 percent in 2015.[46] Netflix marketers made a strategic choice to accept the higher acquisition costs in the short term; they believed that those customers would become profitable repeat subscribers in the months and years ahead.

- Marketers also measure *individual customer profitability,* which is the profit a firm makes from a customer over a specified period of time. Netflix marketers found that profitability per customer was lower internationally than in the United States.[47] That analysis spurred Netflix marketers to allocate additional resources to international markets to try to increase customer profitability in its international segment.

Netflix/Entertainment Pictures/Alamy Stock Photo

Kylle Scott

Marketing Director
Greenway Equipment

Describe your job. I serve as the Marketing Director for Greenway Equipment, a John Deere Equipment Dealer with 32 locations across Arkansas and Southeast Missouri. In this capacity, I manage a team of marketing professionals with whom I develop and implement large-scale marketing campaigns, manage and promote our company brand, facilitate and oversee digital and traditional advertising across our entire territory, coordinate and execute major events like tradeshows and grand openings, and have most recently spearheaded the launch of our new e-commerce website aimed at creating a "virtual dealership."

Kylle Scott

How did you get your job? Upon seeing the job post for my position, I reached out to an individual I knew who was employed by the company to get a better understanding of both the business and the position. On his own volition, he reached out to the entire leadership team on my behalf. To this day, I credit him with playing a significant role in me landing an interview. While prepping for my interview, I learned more about the agriculture industry than ever but also knew it was only the tip of the iceberg. I approached the interview with a humble confidence—I vividly remember being completely transparent about my unfamiliarity with the industry. I believe my exact words were "if you're looking for someone who can rattle off tractor specs, I'm not your person. But I know marketing, I'm a quick learner, and I can tell a good story." I knew I would be a gamble for them, but I'm so grateful they saw enough potential to bet on me.

What has been the most important thing in making you successful at your job? One of the most prominent impacts on my success in this role are the mentors who have helped me learn and grow throughout my time at Greenway. Whether it was directing me to educational content, offering the opportunity to experience and operate the machines we sell, or providing me with the tangible resources and opportunities I needed to progress, I would not be where I am today without their willingness to invest time and effort into developing me as a professional. Surprisingly, my lack of baseline knowledge about the agriculture industry became one of my strengths. It allowed me to have a fresh perspective on the company's brand presence and rethink the promotional outlets being used to reach our target audience. This also worked to my advantage as we worked toward building our new e-commerce website.

What advice would you give soon-to-be graduates? My two major pieces of advice would be to keep an open mind and always be adaptable. Keeping an open mind during your job hunt can lead you to possibilities you may not have considered previously. As I mentioned earlier, I never would have thought a career in agriculture would have been a fit for me, but now I cannot imagine doing anything else. If I had kept a closed mind and scrolled right past that job listing, I might not be where I am today!

Being adaptable is also an undervalued asset. Change is inevitable: processes will change; your team will change; your business and industry will change. When change occurs, you have two options: fight it or embrace it. While learning to embrace change can be challenging, the results are remarkable. Complacency breeds mediocrity, and mediocrity in business yields stagnation. Being able to adapt to fluctuations in supply and demand, technological advancements, emerging industry trends, and organizational adjustments will keep your finger on the pulse of your industry and help you grow as a professional.

What do you consider your personal brand to be? Throughout my time in the workplace, I have worked toward developing and maintaining a personal brand that reflects my dedication to being a champion in all aspects of my professional life. I've always been a competitor. Whether it was on a sports team, playing a board game, or finishing my multiplication tables first in elementary, I have always had an intrinsic motivation to be the best—average was never an option. In the workplace, both my team members and managers know that I make a conscious effort to do my absolute best work in completing any task handed to me. As a manager myself, I also expect the best possible work out of my team members. Because of this expectation, I am constantly checking in to make sure that I'm providing my team with all the resources and coaching necessary for them to meet those expectations. At the end of the day, I want to be a champion, but I also want to enable others to be their own champion, too.

SUMMARY

LO 2-1 Discuss the importance of strategic planning for marketing.

Robert Churchill/ the Agency Collection/Getty Images

Strategic planning helps ensure that marketers will select and execute the right marketing-mix strategies to maximize success. Strategic planning is the process of thoughtfully defining a firm's objectives and developing a method for achieving those objectives.

LO 2-2 Analyze the characteristics of an effective mission statement.

Andrew Francis Wallace/Toronto Star/Getty Images

A mission statement is a concise affirmation of the firm's long-term purpose. A quality mission statement provides employees with a shared sense of purpose, direction, and opportunity. Effective mission statements share three key characteristics: (1) They focus on a limited number of goals. (2) They are customer-oriented and focused on satisfying basic customer needs and wants. (3) They should capture a shared purpose and provide motivation for the employees of the firm.

LO 2-3 Outline the five main components of the marketing plan.

A marketing plan should be an action-oriented document that guides the firm's marketing strategy. A typical marketing plan includes five sections: an executive summary, a situation analysis, the marketing strategy, financials, and controls.

LO 2-4 Explain three tools and techniques for the situation analysis: market summary, SWOT analysis, and competition analysis.

David Paul Morris/ Getty Images

The *market summary* focuses on the current state of the market, including current marketplace trends. One popular market summary tool is the *BCG matrix*. It uses market growth and relative market share to produce four unique product categories (stars, cash cows, question marks, and dogs), each of which requires a different marketing strategy.

A *SWOT analysis* is an evaluation of a firm's strengths, weaknesses, opportunities, and threats. Strengths are internal capabilities that help the company achieve its objectives. Weaknesses are internal limitations that may prevent or disrupt the firm's ability to meet its stated objectives and goals. Opportunities are external factors that the firm may be able to capitalize on to meet its stated objectives. Threats are current and potential external factors that may challenge the firm's short- and long-term performance.

A *competition analysis* identifies both direct and indirect competitors, some of which are obvious and some of which may not be.

LO 2-5 Explain the basic tools and techniques of marketing strategy: segmentation, strategic direction, and the marketing mix.

Heorshe/ Alamy Stock Photo

One marketing strategy technique is segmentation. Market segmentation involves dividing a large market into smaller groups, or segments, each of which has shared characteristics and similar product needs. Knowing those segments, the firm can decide which target market(s) to aim at and how to position its product to create a certain perception in the eyes of the target market.

Most marketing strategies fall under four basic strategic directions: *Market penetration* strategies emphasize selling more of existing products to existing customers. *Product development* strategies involve creating new products or services for existing markets. *Market development* strategies involve selling existing products to new customers. *Diversification* strategies seek to attract new customers by offering new products that are unrelated to the organization's existing products.

The *marketing mix* is the combination of activities that a firm can do to influence demand for its good or service, often referred to as the four Ps of marketing: product, price, place, and promotion. The marketing strategy section of the marketing plan focuses on determining how each element of the marketing mix will support the organization's chosen strategy.

LO 2-6 Discuss the strategic decisions involved in reaching international consumers.

Koji Sasahara/ AP Images

A company can enter the global marketplace using one of five major approaches: exporting, licensing, franchising, joint venture, and direct ownership. *Exporting* is selling domestically produced products to foreign markets; it is typically the least-risky option for entering international markets. *Licensing* is a legal process in which one firm pays to use or distribute another firm's resources. *Franchising* is a contractual arrangement in which the franchisor provides a franchisee the right to use its name and marketing and operational support in exchange for a fee and, typically, a share of the profits. In an *international joint venture,* a domestic firm partners with a foreign company to create a new entity. *Direct ownership,* typically the riskiest method, requires a domestic firm to actively manage a foreign company or overseas facilities.

LO 2-7 Describe the use of four key marketing analytics: return on marketing investment (ROMI), revenue analysis, market share analysis, and profitability analysis.

The need to measure and evaluate the success of marketing activities is essential to building a great organization. Marketing strategy becomes more accountable when organizations base decisions on analytics.

Return on marketing investment (ROMI) measures the firm's effectiveness in using the resources allocated to its marketing effort. *Revenue analysis* measures and evaluates source of revenue to pinpoint what is working and what is not in terms of specific products and regions. *Market share analysis* indicates the percentage of the total market sales captured by a brand, product, or firm. It provides a quick look at how the firm is performing relative to competitors. *Profitability analysis* measures how much profit the organization generates as well as the profit contribution from specific regions, channels, and customer segments.

None of these measures should be viewed in isolation; one measure alone may not give an accurate picture of the health of an organization.

KEY TERMS

competitive advantage (p. 43)
direct ownership (p. 47)
diversification (p. 42)
exporting (p. 45)
financial projections (p. 34)
franchising (p. 46)
joint venture (p. 46)
licensing (p. 45)
market development (p. 42)
market penetration (p. 41)
market segmentation (p. 40)
market segments (p. 40)

market share analysis (p. 49)
market summary (p. 34)
marketing analytics (p. 47)
marketing plan (p. 32)
mission statement (p. 31)
opportunities (in SWOT analysis) (p. 37)
positioning (p. 40)
product development (p. 41)
profitability analysis (p. 50)
return on marketing investment
   (ROMI) (p. 48)
revenue analysis (p. 48)

situation analysis (p. 33)
strategic plan (p. 30)
strategic planning (p. 30)
strategy (p. 34)
strengths (in SWOT analysis) (p. 37)
SWOT analysis (p. 36)
target market (p. 40)
threats (in SWOT analysis) (p. 37)
weaknesses (in SWOT analysis)
   (p. 37)

MARKETING PLAN EXERCISE • Marketing Yourself

In this chapter we discussed the elements and importance of the situation analysis. The next step in developing a full marketing plan for yourself is to conduct a SWOT analysis on yourself. It should tie back to the objectives you developed at the end of Chapter 1. Be sure to think through each element and honestly assess where you are today. This will help you focus on what you need to accomplish over the rest of your college career.

Strengths. Most people have some notion of their strengths—maybe you're an effective public speaker, pay a great deal of attention to detail, or work well with others, for example. It's likely that you've had those strengths reinforced by those around you over the course of your life.

To effectively complete the strengths part of your personal SWOT analysis, list three to five strengths that you possess that will most affect your ability to achieve the objectives you identified in Chapter 1.

Weaknesses. Most people are very honest about their strengths but are typically far less likely to be aware of, or to acknowledge, their weaknesses. Corporate recruiters often tell humorous stories about the responses they receive when asking new college graduates about their biggest weaknesses. Answers range from "I care too much," or "I am too smart for my group members," to "I am too attractive to have many friends." (Any of these responses might produce a negative impression in a job interview, by the way.)

Give serious consideration to your personal weaknesses, and then list three to five weaknesses that will affect your ability to achieve your objectives. By properly identifying your weaknesses, you can begin to plan strategically how to overcome them or, at the very least, minimize their influence on your career objectives.

Opportunities. As the global economy changes, you will enter a job market very different from the one faced by previous generations. It is important to honestly assess your opportunities. Ask yourself questions: What jobs in my major are most in demand? What internship openings are there, and how might those put me in a better position to find my dream job? If your goal is to attend graduate school, what kinds of scholarships, assistantships, or enrollment opportunities are out there for you?

For this part of the SWOT analysis, identify three to five external opportunities that could potentially benefit you in your professional development.

Threats. Assessing threats is an essential part of developing a strategic plan for your professional future. If the economy goes into a recession at the same time you graduate, for example, your earnings growth could be reduced for years to come. By examining what potential threats could affect your professional development and creating contingency plans, you will be in a better position to succeed in your pursuit of a job.

Describe three to five threats that could affect your ability to achieve your objectives.

Your Task: You've now listed three to five strengths, weaknesses, opportunities, and threats that could affect your professional development. For each weakness and threat you identify, include a brief one- to two-sentence description of how you might overcome the challenge associated with it.

DISCUSSION QUESTIONS

1. Find mission statements from five Fortune 500 companies, then rank them from best (1) to worst (5). Discuss why you ranked them in that order. Which mission statement(s) did you like best, and why? How would you modify the mission statement you ranked last to make it better?

2. Conduct a SWOT analysis for your college or university. List three to five strengths, weaknesses, opportunities, and threats for your school.

3. Select a marketing strategy implemented by a large firm or nonprofit organization that you think was effective. Describe why you liked the strategy. Identify which of the strategic directions discussed in this chapter best reflects the strategy you chose.

4. Select two businesses you frequent (e.g., restaurants, clothing stores, grocery stores, etc.). Who is their target market? Then identify at least two competitors (either direct or indirect) for each business. Describe how the two businesses you selected position themselves in the market relative to their competitors. Which one of the two businesses does a better job positioning its products to its target market? Explain your answer.

5. Is marketing a firm's products globally always a good decision? Discuss your answer and provide examples of firms that have both succeeded and failed in international markets.

6. Select a company from which you have made a purchase in the past month. Search online to conduct a market share analysis and a profitability analysis about that company. Based on that analysis, give the organization a marketing grade based on performance. Explain your grade.

 SOCIAL MEDIA APPLICATION

Review your entire social media profile and consider how each of the social media platforms you use personally can affect your career positively or negatively as you move forward. Analyze your efforts to build your brand via social media using the following questions and activities as a guide:

1. List the social media platforms on which you have any type of presence. How many of those platforms do you check or use at least once per week?

2. Is the content you provide across the platforms consistent? Do you have the same image across platforms? What grade would you give your overall social media profile? Explain your answer.

3. In the chapter we discussed some traditional marketing analytics (also called *metrics*) used to measure marketing effectiveness. People use all sorts of metrics for all sorts of things. Here, use metrics to justify the overall social media grade you gave yourself. You can use any type of analytical tools (for example, number of friends, followers, likes, Klout score) to support your overall grade.

 MARKETING ANALYTICS EXERCISE

Please complete the *Connect* exercise in Chapter 2 that focuses on a key marketing analytics measure: return on marketing investment (ROMI).

ETHICAL CHALLENGE

Sports marketers in the United States have wondered for years if legalized gambling would lead to more people watching games, leading to increasing numbers of consumers seeing ads and engaging with brands in a variety of different ways. Betting on sports is legal in many parts of the world including Australia and western Europe, but flourishes globally even when it's outlawed. Annual illegal sports wagers are estimated at $50 billion to $150 billion compared with Nevada's record $4.8 billion of legal sports bets in 2017. In May 2018, the Supreme Court struck down the 1992 law that made sports gambling legal only in Nevada, freeing New Jersey to legalize sports gambling and other states to follow. Professional U.S. sports leagues, which had been traditionally concerned how betting would encourage corruption, have now become increasingly supportive. The National Basketball Association and Major League Baseball are seeking a 1 percent fee on all bets placed on their games.

One case for legalization is that sports betting goes on regardless of whether the law permits it, so why not generate taxes that benefit communities? Legalization also gives bettors greater assurance their wagers will be honored and raises government funding that otherwise went into the pockets of illegal bookmakers. Some marketers highlight data that suggest higher television ratings and increased social media activity occur for heavily wagered games. However, those who oppose the issue say that the benefits don't justify the costs of gambling, including potential indebtedness of a larger number of citizens. Some stakeholders want marketers to have similar limits on ads promoting gambling to younger people that currently exist for tobacco and alcohol. Athletes and academics also warn of a growing gambling culture around sports, in which the point spread becomes the focus of fans rather than cheering for a favorite team and simply following the action. This loss of fan identification with a favorite team might also reduce the ability of sports marketers to develop lifelong fans that might buy jerseys, tickets, and merchandise for generations to come.

1. Analyze the reasons for the success of legalized sports gambling from a marketing perspective. Explain how legalized sports gambling may benefit a company in your home state?
2. Use the ethical decision-making framework to analyze Major League Baseball's decision to support legalized gambling and its request to receive a 1 percent fee on all bets made on the sport.
3. If you were a marketer for the National Collegiate Athletic Association, would you look to develop partnerships to profit off of legalized gambling on collegiate sports? Explain your answer.

Source: Ira Boudway and Grant Clark, "Sports Betting," Bloomberg.com, May 17, 2018, https://www.bloomberg.com/quicktake/sports-betting.

VIDEO CASE

Please go to *Connect* to access the video cases featuring Potbelly Sandwich Shop that accompanies this chapter.

PODCAST

Please go to Connect to access the podcast that accompanies this chapter.

Photo provided by
Michael Friloux

CAREER **TIPS**

The Power of Questions and People Skills

You have read in this chapter about the importance of planning for your career and future. As you strategically plan for your career, Michael Friloux, Senior Vice President and Chief Technology Officer at Uniti, a strategic capital partner to communications network operators, encourages you to spend time considering two things that many college graduates don't fully appreciate: the power of questions and the importance of people skills.

THE POWER OF QUESTIONS

I have found that certain habits influence the opportunities and careers of individuals, some more so than others. I would venture to say that the most influential habit to adopt is what I call the power of questions. I have seen many employees, interviewees, colleagues, and superiors shy away from asking questions for fear of sounding dumb, looking ridiculous, or giving the appearance of weakness.

In practice, I have found the exact opposite to be true. Individuals who seek out information and clarity by asking lots of questions, no matter how basic or mundane, not only perform their jobs better, but can also empower those around them, thus indirectly freeing the flow and quality of communications. Many times people perform tasks incorrectly because they failed to ask the right questions. This is harmful not only to the individual but also to the business enterprise.

My advice would be to develop the habit of asking questions, to always listen attentively, and to continually seek to improve the quality of the questions you ask. When in doubt, always ask the question. You'll be glad you did.

THE IMPORTANCE OF PEOPLE SKILLS

Take a minute to inventory all of the most successful people you know. My guess is they all have one trait in common: superior people skills. Many people, myself included, begin their careers with the belief that they will create the most value for themselves by being the best at what they do. However, highly focused individuals who overlook the importance of building relationships inhibit their ability to grow and prosper in their careers.

You could be the best marketer, engineer, teacher, chemist, or fill-in-the-blank in the world, but if people don't like you or, for whatever reason, can't relate to you, they aren't going to want to work with you either. Conversely, if you have average technical skills but possess superior people skills, all sorts of opportunities, including promotions, will open up to you.

Of course, you should always seek to be the best at whatever trade or course you choose, but recognize that it's equally important to cultivate positive and productive interactions with everyone you work with.

CHAPTER NOTES

1. Frank T. Rothaermel, *Strategic Management,* 3rd ed. (Burr Ridge, IL: McGraw-Hill Education, 2017).
2. These are the classic questions suggested by Peter Drucker, considered the "father of modern management," in his book *Management: Tasks, Responsibilities, Practices* (New York: Truman Talley Books, 1986), pp. 58–69.
3. Frank T. Rothaermel, *Strategic Management,* 3rd ed. (Burr Ridge, IL: McGraw-Hill Education, 2017).
4. Minda Zetlin, "The 9 Worst Mission Statements of All Time," *Inc.,* November 15, 2013, https://www.inc.com/minda-zetlin/9-worst-mission-statements-all-time.html.
5. Google, "Company," n.d., http://www.google.com/about/company/.
6. Amazon, "Amazon Investor Relations," n.d., http://phx.corporate-ir.net/phoenix.zhtml?c=97664&p=irol-irhome.
7. American Express, n.d., https://www.americanexpress.com/au/content/careers/culture.html.
8. Nordstrom, "History, Mission, and Vision," n.d., https://nordstromcompanyanalysis.weebly.com/vission-and-mission.html.
9. Panda Express, https://www.pandarg.com/about-us.
10. Urban One. https://urban1.com/company/.
11. Tesla, "About Tesla," n.d., https://www.tesla.com/about.
12. B. Ramaseshan, Asmai Ishak, and Russel P. J. Kingshott, "Interactive Effects of Marketing Strategy Formulation and Implementation upon Firm Performance," *Journal of Marketing Management* 29, nos. 11–12 (2013): 1224–1250, http://dx.doi.org/10.1080/0267257X.2013.796319.
13. Frank Germann, Peter Ebbes, and Rajdeep Grewal, "The Chief Marketing Officer Matters!," *Journal of Marketing* 79, no. 3 (May 2015): 1–22, https://doi.org/10.1509/jm.14.0244.
14. Khushbu Shah, "McDonald's Is America's Favorite Breakfast Spot, according to a New Report," *Eater,* August 18,

2015, http://www.eater.com/2015/8/18/9171735/american-breakfast-eating-habits-mcdonalds-burger-king.

15. Ashley Lutz, "McDonald's Could Start Cutting a Lot of Menu Items," *Business Insider,* May 17, 2013, http://www.businessinsider.com/mcdonalds-to-start-cutting-menu-items-2013-5.

16. McDonald's, "Our Story," n.d., http://www.mcdonalds.com/us/en/our_story.html.

17. Dan Burrows, "McDonald's Stock Hits Record High on Global Growth," *MoneyWatch,* October 21, 2011, http://www.cbsnews.com/8301-505123_162-49043138/mcdonalds-stock-hits-record-high-on-global-growth/.

18. Frank T. Rothaermel, *Strategic Management,* 2nd ed. (Burr Ridge, IL: McGraw-Hill Education), p.118.

19. Subway, n.d., http://www.subway.com/subwayroot/exploreourworld.aspx/.

20. Ashley Lutz, "Three Reasons Chipotle Is Destroying McDonald's," *Business Insider,* February 13, 2014, http://www.businessinsider.com/reasons-chipotle-is-killing-mcdonalds-2014-2.

21. Sam Chambers, "McDonald's Cuts Cheeseburgers from Happy Meals," Bloomberg, February 15, 2018, https://www.bloomberg.com/news/articles/2018-02-15/mcdonald-s-puts-happy-meal-on-a-diet-saying-hold-the-cheese.

22. H. Igor Ansoff, "Strategies for Diversification," *Harvard Business Review* 35, no. 5 (September–October 1957): 113–124.

23. Mae Anderson, "Dr Pepper's New Brand Is a Manly Man's Soda," Associated Press, October 10, 2011, http://www.msnbc.msn.com/id/44849414/ns/business-us_business/t/dr-peppers-new-brand-manly-mans-soda/.

24. Walmart, 2018 *Annual Report,* (n.d.) http://s2.q4cdn.com/056532643/files/doc_financials/2018/annual/WMT-2018_Annual-Report.pdf.

25. Walmart, "About," (n.d.). https://corporate.walmart.com/about.

26. Giovanni Bruno, "McDonald's Rethinks Its $2 Billion Ad Budget," *The Street,* October 26, 2017, https://www.thestreet.com/story/14362329/1/mcdonald-s-to-examine-how-its-spending-its-ad-dollars.html.

27. Ron Ruggless, "McDonald's Signs New Deals with Door-Dash, Uber Eats," *Nation's Restaurant News,* November 16, 2021. https://www.nrn.com/quick-service/mcdonald-s-signs-new-deals-doordash-uber-eats.

28. Julie Jargon and Lisa Beilfuss, "McDonald's Continues Image Shift with Move to Cage-Free Eggs in North America," *The Wall Street Journal,* September 9, 2015, http://www.wsj.com/articles/mcdonalds-to-source-cage-free-eggs-in-u-s-canada-1441798121.

29. Stephanie Strom, "McDonald's Plans a Shift to Eggs from Only Cage-Free Hens," *The New York Times,* September 9, 2015, http://www.nytimes.com/2015/09/10/business/mcdonalds-to-use-eggs-from-only-cage-free-hens.html?_r=0.

30. Convenience Store News, "McDonald's Reveals Pricing Strategy," *CSNews Foodservice,* April 22, 2011, http://foodservice.csnews.com/top-story-mcdonald_s_reveals_pricing_strategy_-838.html.

31. U.S. Small Business Administration, "Export Business Planner for Your Small Business," n.d., https://www.sba.gov/sites/default/files/FAQ_Sept_2012.pdf.

32. Major League Baseball International, "Licensing and Sponsorship," n.d., http://www.mlbinternational.com/?p=articles&art_cat_id=66.

33. Research and Markets, "Global Licensed Sports Merchandise Market Report 2021: Market to Reach a Revised Size of $49.8 Billion by 2027," *PRNewswire,* June 18, 2021. https://www.prnewswire.com/news-releases/global-licensed-sports-merchandise-market-report-2021-market-to-reach-a-revised-size-of-49-8-billion-by-2027—301315552.html.

34. Katie Little, "Burger King Has New Burger Coming Out . . . That's Red," *CNBC,* June 17, 2015, http://www.cnbc.com/2015/06/17/burger-king-has-new-burger-coming-outthats-red.html.

35. Flavia Rotondi and Daniela Wei, "Italy's Lavazza Espresso Brand Takes On Starbucks in China," *Bloomberg Businessweek,* October 27, 2021, https://www.bloomberg.com/news/articles/2021-10-27/lavazza-takes-on-starbucks-sbux-in-china-with-yum-china-espresso-partnership.

36. Aimin Yan and Yadong Luo, International Joint Ventures: *Theory and Practice* (Armonk, NY: M.E. Sharpe, 2001).

37. Matthew Townsend, "Why Target Is Raking Up Its Maple Leaves," Bloomberg, January 22, 2015, http://www.bloomberg.com/news/articles/2015-01-22/why-target-is-closing-up-shop-in-canada#r=hpt-fs.

38. Frank Germann, Peter Ebbes, and Rajdeep Grewal, "The Chief Marketing Officer Matters!," *Journal of Marketing* 79, no. 3 (May 2015): 1–22, https://doi.org/10.1509/jm.14.0244.

39. Koen Pauwels, "Truly Accountable Marketing: The Right Metrics for the Right Results," *GfK-Marketing Intelligence Review,* 2015, 9–15, https://doi.org/10.1509/jm.14.024415.

40. Common Language Marketing Dictionary, "Return on marketing investment" entry, https://marketing-dictionary.org/m/marketing-return-on-investment/.

41. Common Language Marketing Dictionary, "Return on marketing investment" entry, https://marketing-dictionary.org/m/marketing-return-on-investment/.

42. Federica Laricchia, "Global Market Share Held by Apple's iPad of Global Tablet Shipments 2012–2022," *Statista,* May 19, 2022, https://www.statista.com/statistics/268711/global-market-share-of-the-apple-ipad-since-2010/; S. O'Dea, "Apple iPhone Smartphone Market Share Worldwide 2007–2022," *Statista,* May 4, 2022, https://www.statista.com/statistics/216459/global-market-share-of-apple-iphone/.

43. Bill Vlasic and Nick Bunkley, "Sales Fell in August for Carmakers," The New York Times, September 1, 2010, http://www.nytimes.com/2010/09/02/business/02auto.html.

44. Todd Lassa, "U.S. Auto Sales Totaled 17.25 Million in 2017," *Automobile,* January 4, 2018, https://www.automobilemag.com/news/u-s-auto-sales-totaled-17-25-million-calendar-2017/.

45. Todd Lassa, "U.S. Auto Sales Totaled 17.25 Million in 2017," Automobile, January 4, 2018, https://www.automobilemag.com/news/u-s-auto-sales-totaled-17-25-million-calendar-2017/.

46. Tim Peterson, "Netflix's Subscriber Numbers Beat Estimates as It Spends More on Marketing" *AdAge,* January 20, 2015, http://adage.com/article/digital/netflix-s-marketing-costs-grow-subscriber-numbers/296670/.

47. Tim Peterson, "Netflix's Subscriber Numbers Beat Estimates as It Spends More on Marketing" *AdAge,* January 20, 2015, http://adage.com/article/digital/netflix-s-marketing-costs-grow-subscriber-numbers/296670/.

Cuisine Masters Restaurant Supply

TABLE OF CONTENTS

EXECUTIVE SUMMARY

Cuisine Masters Restaurant Supply, Inc. (CMRS) is offering the Automated Salad Maker (ASM), which is a technologically advanced salad maker that can supply any type of salad within seconds of order entry. The capacity of the Automated Salad Maker will be to produce 60 to 120 salads per hour, depending on size and ingredients used. This salad maker is a one-of-a-kind piece of equipment with no direct competition; however, CMRS has existing competition within the southeastern and south-central portions of the United States for other restaurant supply products. The targeted market segment will be restaurants that provide house and custom salads to consumers in a high-volume, sit-down-style setting in the southeastern and south-central United States. Total market size consists of both chain and privately owned restaurants. The ASM will reduce labor needs and costs for the establishment while producing quality-controlled salads in a quick, efficient manner.

The executive summary provides a one- to two-page synopsis of the marketing plan's main points. While the executive summary is listed first, firms typically complete it last. Every line of an executive summary should convey the most valuable information of the marketing plan.

The primary marketing objective is to reach a 3 percent share of the market within the first year with volume unit sales of 184 units. Additionally, a 5 percent share of the market will be met in the second year with volume unit sales of 306 units. The final goal is to reach a 10 percent share of the market in the fifth year with volume unit sales of 613 units.

SITUATION ANALYSIS

Cuisine Masters Restaurant Supply, Inc. was founded in 2012 by three entrepreneurs to satisfy the needs of restaurants across the southeastern and south-central United States. Our vision is to supply technologically advanced restaurant equipment to high-volume, sit-down restaurants so they can reduce kitchen support staff while still providing high-quality meals and services to their customers. The business is set up as a limited liability corporation and has distribution rights to several innovative product lines. We offer research and development (R&D) and engineering services to several manufacturing firms and create these strategic alliances based on market trend and market demand needs. We own the patents and intellectual capital for most of these products.

CMRS competes against several large restaurant supply businesses in our area. To successfully compete in our chosen markets, we employ four salespeople to cover the target regions and one additional salesperson for corporate chain accounts. We also partner with manufacturing facilities that are strategically sourced based on engineering and cost support. We employ several full-time R&D engineers to create new, innovative product lines.

Market Summary

Overall restaurant industry sales are expected to post positive growth and reach $604 billion in 2019, which would stop a three-year trend of decreasing sales. The final expectation for 2018 is sales growth of 3.6 percent over and above 2017 sales. There are currently 960,000 restaurant locations that employ 12.8 million people in the United States. Sales at full-service restaurants are projected to reach $194.6 billion in 2019, an increase of 3.1 percent over 2018. The south-Atlantic area of the country is expected to post the strongest restaurant sales growth at 3.9 percent, totaling $93.9 billion among its eight states, which include Delaware, Florida, Georgia, Maryland, North Carolina, South Carolina, Virginia, and West Virginia.

CMRS's target market for the Automated Salad Maker consists of three of the six primary restaurant sectors: family dining, casual dining, and upscale or fine dining. The geographic segmentation for these three sectors is broken down into two service and sales territories: the southeastern United States and the south-central United States.

The situation analysis identifies the trends, conditions, and competitive forces that have the potential to influence the performance of the firm and the choice of appropriate strategies. In many ways, this section serves as the foundation of the marketing plan. The situation analysis typically comprises three areas: market summary, SWOT analysis, and competition.

The market summary describes the current state of the market, including how large the market is and how quickly it's growing or declining. The market summary also provides a perspective on important marketplace trends.

The three sectors that CMRS will avoid are fast food, high-end fast food, and specialty beverage shops.

The target market is made up of restaurants that provide house and custom salads to consumers in a high-volume, sit-down-style setting. Total market size consists of both chain and privately owned restaurants. To gain market share in this expansive market, we will specifically target nationally branded chain restaurants such as Applebee's, Chili's, Cracker Barrel, Denny's, IHOP, Panera Bread, and Ruby Tuesday. The southeastern U.S. market offers 4,127 chain restaurants and the south-central U.S. market offers 2,098 chain restaurants.

The potential market sales size for the Automated Salad Maker in the southeastern territory is $14,444,500, which is based on 4,127 chain restaurants multiplied by the $3,500 price per automated salad maker. The potential market sales size for the Automated Salad Maker in the south-central territory is $7,343,000, which is based on 2,098 chain restaurants multiplied by $3,500 per Automated Salad Maker. Together, the annual sales potential for the ASM product line is $21.7 million.

Strengths, Weaknesses, Opportunities, and Threats (SWOT) Analysis

Strengths CMRS can build on three important strengths:

1. **Owns patents and intellectual capital for products**—We own the patents and intellectual capital for our products so that they cannot be imitated.
2. **Excellent quality product**—We take great pride in providing a high-quality and durable product, free of defects.
3. **Excellent management team**—The entrepreneurs that own CMRS are three young and highly talented managers with new ideas and determination.

Weaknesses CMRS has three main weaknesses:

1. **Lack of recognition with consumers because CMRS is a start-up organization**—We have no established brand or image whereas other manufacturers do. We will address this with aggressive marketing.
2. **The need to take on debt to get the business off the ground**—We have access to a limited amount of cash. Initial financing will not be difficult due to solid credit and the low inventory depreciation rate, but ongoing financing will be more difficult to obtain. It is not the receivable days that will wreak havoc on the cash plan because sales are 100 percent cash; it is the operating and marketing expenses.
3. **CMRS's new and innovative products do not have a lot of visibility in the United States yet**—Our products are relatively new to the market and are still unnoticed by many valuable customers.

> The SWOT analysis evaluates a firm's strengths, weaknesses, opportunities, and threats. The strengths and the weaknesses aspects of the analysis focus on the firm's internal characteristics, while the opportunities and threats sections focus on the external factors a firm must consider.

Opportunities CMRS can take advantage of three major market opportunities:

1. **No focused, well-marketed competition**—The market for new and innovative restaurant equipment is not very strong or well established. This gives us the opportunity to develop the market and establish ourselves as the market "original."

2. **The cost of Internet and other direct marketing opportunities has decreased in recent years**—The cost of selling via e-commerce and through mail order has decreased tremendously in recent years. Internet domain names (www.your-name.com) cost $35 a year, and e-commerce servers may be set up for only $30 a month. Certain high-circulation catalog companies will develop custom catalogs for vendors and mail them for a fixed fee. This is incredibly cost-effective for companies that do not have relationships with printers, graphic artists, and the like. Both direct mail and Internet sales are growing segments of our business.

3. **Participation in a growing market with a significant percentage of the target market still not aware that CMRS and its products exist**—We are a relatively new company with many opportunities to market ourselves and gain business as we build name recognition.

Threats CMRS faces two main threats:

1. **High capital costs**—The high cost of capital limits us from investing money in other activities, such as marketing, that would enable the business to gain a larger customer base.

2. **Future/potential competition from national companies**—Established companies will soon begin to imitate our products and produce replicas.

Competition

Competition within the restaurant supply industry has been negatively affected since 2008 with the economic downturn and the lack of extra income for nonessential spending. Fortunately, this situation is beginning to improve. The geographic region that CMRS will focus on is served by local, national, and even international suppliers; however, local suppliers can be more reactive to individual customer needs. The key competitors include local suppliers that provide quality customer service, training, and maintenance. Key local competitors are

> **Burr Ridge Fixture and Sales Company Inc.**—Located in Burr Ridge, Illinois, and serving the midwestern United States, which includes Illinois, Michigan, Iowa, Missouri, and Wisconsin. Burr Ridge Fixture and Sales Company has 70 years of experience and provides over 9,000 in-stock items and products

The competition section should address both the direct and indirect competition the firm will face. It should include a brief summary of the most relevant competitors and highlight any major differences between what they offer and what the firm will offer.

from over 10,000 manufacturers. It provides next-day shipping for virtually all items in stock.

Hall Brothers Restaurant Equipment–Located in Moore, Oklahoma, and serving Oklahoma and southern Kansas, Hall Brothers has over 25 years of experience and provides quality restaurant equipment, as well as delivery, installation, and service.

Marcy's Restaurant Supply–Located in both San Diego and Anaheim, California, and serving over 20 states, Marcy's Restaurant Supply has almost 30 years of experience and provides quality restaurant equipment to over 5,000 customers. Marcy's offers goods and services to enable customers to solve business problems and create cost-effective solutions for their business.

Irwin Restaurant Supply–Located in Oxford, Alabama, and Memphis, Tennessee, Irwin serves these states and provides service for nationwide customers. Irwin Restaurant Supply provides sales and delivery of quality restaurant equipment; however, it does not provide service and installation.

In our effort to supply national chain restaurants, national suppliers will be relevant competition. Key national suppliers include:

Southern Restaurant Products–Located in Little Rock, Arkansas, Southern Restaurant Products has been a national supplier of restaurant products for over 20 years. Southern has over 250,000 customers and offers more than 450,000 items from over 1,000 quality brands. It offers e-commerce and technical support services.

The Pilgrim Company–Headquartered in Lancaster, Pennsylvania, Pilgrim has been in business since 1902 and bills itself as "America's leading supplier and distributor of food service supplies and equipment." Pilgrim has distribution centers in Ohio, Pennsylvania, Texas, Florida, and Arizona to make 48-hour delivery possible for its customers.

Competition will be strong; however, CMRS can achieve success in the restaurant supply industry with high-quality equipment offerings and by controlling the patents for innovative equipment, such as the Automated Salad Maker. By offering products that streamline restaurant activities, CMRS will help restaurants achieve greater customer satisfaction and save money.

MARKETING STRATEGY

CMRS's primary marketing strategy will be an extensive promotion to create knowledge and demand in an untapped market. Our primary consumers are chain restaurants, but we are also targeting family dining, casual dining, and upscale or fine dining.

CMRS is able to address many different segments of the market because, although each segment is different, CMRS's product is useful to all of the different segments.

Objectives

Mission Statement The vision of Cuisine Masters Restaurant Supply, Inc. is to supply technologically advanced restaurant equipment to high-volume, sit-down restaurants to allow them to reduce kitchen support staff while still providing high-quality meals and services to their customers.

We have set modest but practical and attainable goals for the first, second, and fifth years of market entry. These sales goals are based off historical sales levels achieved for similar product offerings and similar new-product launches:

- **First-Year Unit Sales Objective**—We are aiming for a 3 percent share of the salad makers market through volume unit sales of 184 individual units.
- **Second-Year Unit Sales Objective**—Our second-year objective is to capture a 5 percent share of the salad makers market through volume unit sales of 306 individual units.
- **Fifth-Year Unit Sales Objective**—Our fifth-year objective is to achieve 10 percent share of the market through volume unit sales of 613 individual units. We plan to reach this goal by expanding our business and offering additional products for the kitchen.

Target Markets

CMRS is focusing on a positioning strategy of product differentiation. Our primary targets are privately owned and chain restaurants in three different restaurant sectors: family dining, casual dining, and upscale or fine dining. The restaurants in these target markets produce high-volume, high-quality food and offer standardized service across all their locations. The restaurant industry grew by 3 percent in 2015 and is expected to grow by 3.6 percent in 2016. With these expected growth rates, the competition between restaurants should escalate, driving the need for highly specialized restaurant equipment. This equipment will not only help reduce operating costs but should also help produce excellent quality food and improve service times to the customer.

CMRS is specifically targeting chain restaurants because these restaurants are expanding more quickly than privately owned restaurants and they use standardized food preparation products in each individual location. We can increase market share quickly by focusing on these major chain restaurants. Geographic segmentation has produced two territories—the southeastern and south-central regions of the United States, which now encompass more than 6,000 restaurants. As the business expands, CMRS will seek to reach other markets in the United States.

A mission statement is a concise affirmation of the firm's long-term purpose. Creating an effective mission statement is the first step in developing a quality marketing plan. Once a mission statement is in place, the firm will have an easier time establishing quality objectives for the short and medium terms.

Quality objectives must be specific, measurable, and realistic. They state the goal or intention of the firm over a certain period of time, usually 1–5 years. The remaining sections of the marketing strategy should be designed to help the firm meet these objectives.

The target markets and positioning sections give a detailed description of the groups of customers toward which the firm has decided to direct its marketing efforts and define how the firm would like customers to perceive the product.

The product element of the marketing-mix section consists of a detailed description of the product being offered, not only the good or service itself, but also any related services like warranties and guarantees that accompany the product (as CMRS does with its Automated Salad Maker and training and extended warranty service products). This section should build on the competition section to explain what competitive advantage the firm's product offers.

Positioning

CMRS will position the Automated Salad Maker to our target markets as a high-tech, high-quality, high-performance, and innovative piece of equipment that can be integrated into any kitchen to reduce cost while improving service time and food quality to the customer. The selling points we will leverage are greater customer satisfaction due to improved food delivery times and expanded menu choices, increased menu flexibility as a result of computerized salad recipes, five-year parts and labor coverage from highly trained technical representatives located in each sales territory, and on-site training for all restaurant personnel to coincide with the delivery of each Automated Salad Maker.

Marketing Mix

Product CMRS's newest product is the Automated Salad Maker, which is a technologically advanced salad maker that can supply any type of salad within seconds of order entry. The piece of equipment is a little larger than a large bread-making oven and measures 44″ wide × 55.5″ deep × 92″ high. It has 15 different styles of stainless-steel cutting instruments that are paired with a patented array of size, shape, color, and chemical analyzers. The analyzers allow it to choose from a refrigerated supply of vegetables and other toppings to create either a custom ordered or traditional house salad derived from recipes programmed by the individual restaurant. Its standard features include bins for plate storage and products, dressings and oils, and wireless capability between the Automated Salad Maker and the wait staff's handheld order pads. It also comes fully equipped with a self-cleaning function that can be run nightly to sterilize and fully clean the equipment to governmental standards.

The sales potential for the Automated Salad Maker product line is $21.7 million based on the potential market size (south-central territory of 2,098 and southeastern territory of 4,127 restaurants) and a sales price of $3,500. The initial goal for CMRS is to achieve a 10 percent share of the target market within five years. Additional products that can be packaged and sold with each Automated Salad Maker include products from the categories of refrigeration, furniture, concessions, food preparation, shelving and carts, dishwashing and sanitation, cooking equipment, and dining room service products. A wide selection of products that range from manual operation to technologically advanced options are offered in each category and provide cost-reducing, service-enhancing options to our end customers.

CMRS is also going to market a service product as part of this offering. CMRS will offer training packages in which members of our team will go to a customer site and demonstrate the best practices for using the product to management and employees. In addition, we will be selling an extended warranty package, which specifies that our expert technicians will continue to provide on-site repairs and maintenance for as long as the customer pays for the service. Our technical service support will be the best trained and most customer-friendly team in the industry.

Promotion An internally trained sales force will make cold calls to all potential customers and franchises operating in each of our three targeted restaurant markets. The salespeople will each be equipped with a full web-based application running off a tablet device that will showcase CMRS's full line of innovative equipment. These tablets will be used to offer each customer a tailored presentation that is created based off information gathered from industry statistics related to that customer's operating market (demographics, price points, traffic analysis, and restaurant capacity). These presentations will showcase the Automated Salad Maker and all other peripheral equipment that could reduce cost and improve delivery to the restaurant's end customer in the targeted market segment. Salespeople will also have an annual budget that will allow them to attend and present at trade shows specifically tailored to our market segments.

Place/Distribution CMRS operates as the supplier and will distribute products by direct sales to create a variety of purchase options for the customer. The purchasing options will include the following:

- Sales representatives are assigned to cover the south-central and southeastern portions of the United States; two will operate in each region and one additional sales representative will be assigned to the corporate chain accounts. Sales representatives will make cold calls to local and chain restaurants within their service area. They will provide individualized customer service throughout the entire process, from the initial sales call, to the setup, to the installation and training for the purchased item.
- Web purchases are available for standard stock items. Purchases of specialized items that require installation and training may be initiated online but will require contact with a salesperson before the purchase is final.
- Chain restaurant sales may require sales and services to be provided outside the targeted supply area due to the purchasing requirements of the franchise. These needs will be met as if in the targeted supply area.
- Catalogs will include all products while featuring the Automated Salad Maker and other innovative products for which we retain the patents. Purchase requests may be sent via phone, fax, or e-mail and will be processed through the assigned sales representative to ensure that appropriate customer service is available.

Delivery of the products will depend on the items purchased. Smaller, nonspecialized items will be shipped via UPS or FedEx, while larger orders will require scheduled

The promotion section should outline the key strategies for communicating the value of the product to targeted customers. It will likely include a discussion of one or more of the following promotional tools: personal selling, advertising, sales promotion, or public relations.

The distribution section explains in detail how a firm plans to make its products available to targeted consumers. It should summarize the various distribution methods, including the key transportation partners that will be used (e.g., FedEx or UPS).

deliveries by hired freight companies. Future delivery plans may include an in-house freight delivery system.

Pricing The Automated Salad Maker will be offered for the initial price of $3,500 per unit, with a five-year warranty that includes free maintenance and repairs. CMRS will work to hold this price constant every year as we make manufacturing and engineering improvements to drive down production costs and improve production efficiencies.

For the service aspects of our plan, we will charge $1,000 per one day of training at a customer site plus expenses. If a customer buys 10 or more units within a six-month time period, it is entitled to one free day of training, with the only charge being the expenses of our trainer getting to the customer location. The extended service warranty will be priced at $395 per year and begins after the initial five-year warranty expires. The extended service warranty provides continued basic service, maintenance, and repair for as long as the customer pays for the service.

FINANCIALS

Total first-year sales revenue for the Automated Salad Maker is projected to reach $644,000. This represents 3 percent of the market at a sales level of 184 individual units. The Automated Salad Maker's product line revenues and associated costs are shown in Table 1. Based on the first year's forecast costs, this product line is projected to lose $69,000 in its first year of sales.

TABLE 1 Sales and Expense Forecast

	Cuisine Masters Restaurant Supply Forecast Income Statement (In thousands) Automated Salad Maker				
	2022	2021	2020	2019	2018
Sales	$2,146	$1,608	$1,340	$1,071	$644
Cost of Goods Sold	1,073	804	670	536	322
Gross Profit	*$1,073*	*$804*	*$670*	*$536*	*$322*
Warranty & Training	215	161	134	107	64
Production & Engineering Fees	107	80	67	54	32
Marketing Expenses	64	48	40	32	19
Selling, General, and Administrative Expenses	275	275	275	275	275
EBIT	*$412*	*$240*	*$154*	*$68*	*$(69)*
EBIT%	*19.2%*	*14.9%*	*11.5%*	*6.3%*	*(10.7)%*

Break-even sales in the first year of production are shown in Table 2. Break-even sales in units for the first year are 240 units, based on monthly sales of 20 units at a sales price of $3,500 per unit.

TABLE 2 Break-Even Analysis

	2018
Monthly Units Breakeven	20
Monthly Sales Breakeven	$70,000
Assumptions	
Average Per-Unit Revenue	$ 3,500
Average Per-Unit Variable Cost	$ 1,400
Estimated Monthly Fixed Cost	$41,432

The marketing expenses are forecast to be 3 percent of product line revenue and are shown in Table 3. The individual expense line items are forecast as an estimated percentage of total spending based on historical spending patterns for other product lines. The marketing manager is responsible for tracking and managing the marketing expense budget.

TABLE 3 Marketing Expense Budget

	Cuisine Masters Restaurant Supply Forecast Marketing Expense Automated Salad Maker				
	2022	2021	2020	2019	2018
	$64,365	$48,248	$40,189	$32,130	$19,320
Advertisements	$25,746	$19,299	$16,076	$12,852	$7,728
Website Charges	16,091	12,062	10,047	8,033	4,830
Printed Material	12,873	9,650	8,038	6,426	3,864
Entertainment	9,655	7,237	6,028	4,820	2,898
Total Expenses	$64,365	$48,248	$40,189	$32,130	$19,320

CONTROLS

The purpose of CMRS's marketing plan is to enable senior management to guide the organization in the correct and most profitable way. The following areas will be monitored continuously to help maintain efficiency and gauge performance:

- Revenue: monthly and annually
- Expenses: monthly and annually

Financial projections provide a bottom-line estimate of the organization's profitability. Financial projections can include numerous items, but all should contain a sales forecast (or fundraising projections for a nonprofit), an expense forecast, and a break-even analysis.

The controls section is the final section in most marketing plans. It outlines the systems that will be put in place to monitor and adjust the plan as the firm executes on the marketing strategy. The controls section should discuss implementation, organizational structure, and contingency planning.

The implementation section should provide a detailed list of specific items that must be executed to achieve the objectives set by the firm. This section should act as a playbook for the firm's activities for the first six months after the product launch.

The organizational structure section should clarify who is accountable for the marketing activities for the specific project.

Finally, the contingency planning section should outline potential threats that might derail the success of the marketing plan.

- Customer satisfaction: continuous
- New-product development: continuous

Implementation

CMRS will use our interactive sales representatives to track customer response to all equipment purchased and to determine additional needs of the customer. Additionally, tight quality control measures are in place to ensure products delivered to customers are of high quality and defect free. Sales representatives oversee the installation and training needed for major equipment, providing on-site assistance to avoid potential issues with purchases. Sales numbers will be monitored monthly to ensure we are on track to reach our objectives. Owners will meet with the sales representatives monthly to discuss any issues with sales and the success of the marketing plan. If any issues are found, immediate action will be taken to improve the situation.

In order to have a successful product launch and to begin realizing targeted first year sales of 184 units, we have created a series of actions and programs that will be implemented in sequential, campaign order:

1. December 2017—Product literature is printed and distributed. This includes electronic distribution from our internal website and print brochures for direct mailings and face-to-face sales calls.
2. December 2017—Salespeople are provided computer tablets with product applications and marketing campaign literature.
3. December 2017—Salespeople are given sales routes and first product meetings are scheduled and completed with top 20 targeted customers.
4. January 2018—Invite representatives from targeted top five restaurant chains to tour the Automated Salad Maker's production facility and to discuss new opportunities.
5. February 2018—Chosen company representatives attend and present at the Southeastern Restaurant Supply Conference and Trade Show to provide information and demonstration of CMRS's products. This is a shared action item across all product lines with cost support to come from the general marketing fund. All new company products will be displayed at the CMRS booth.
6. March 2018—Advertise in two trade magazines: *Chain Leader* and *Restaurant Report*.
7. April 2018—Host internal sales conference to provide salespeople with Quarter 1, 2018, statistics, solicit feedback on the level of success of the marketing plan, and make adjustments to the plan accordingly.

Organizational Structure

CMRS owners work as a team to manage the marketing activities of the company. Initial plans are discussed and decisions are approved before implementation, which is the responsibility of the vice president of marketing. A catalog publication firm will be hired to provide customized catalogs for the different target segments, and a consultant will be retained to build a website for customer communication and purchasing.

Contingency Planning

Difficulties and Risks

- Problems generating visibility.
- An entry into the market that adopts similar products.

Worst Case Risks May Include

- Determining that the business cannot support itself on an ongoing basis.
- Having to liquidate equipment to cover liabilities.

Chapter **3**

The Global Environment

COVID-19 and travel:
Help protect yourself and others

Please maintain a safe distance from others whenever possible.

6′
2 m

Fly View Productions/Getty Images

Learning Objectives

After reading this chapter, you should be able to

LO 3-1 Differentiate between direct and indirect competition.

LO 3-2 Summarize the major external factors that influence the marketing environment.

LO 3-3 Extend the analysis of the marketing environment beyond the borders of the United States.

LO 3-4 Identify the major trade agreements, monetary unions, and organizations that affect the international marketing environment.

LO 3-5 Describe the emerging factors that influence the nonprofit marketing environment.

Executive **Perspective** ... because everyone is a marketer

Matt Slick
Senior Principal, Global Pricing and Price to Win
DXC Technology

Photo by Shannon Kaye Portrait Design

As a college student, Matt Slick majored in finance not knowing how marketing would become a significant part of his professional journey. Early in his career, Matt worked in business development then took his first leadership position in a marketing organization by managing the pricing administration team at WilTel Communications.

Over the past 15 years, Matt has led global sales operations and global deal structuring for some of the leading technology companies in the world. Today, Matt serves as Senior Principal for Global Pricing and Price to Win at DXC Technology where he works with sales teams on IT outsourcing contracts with values greater than $100 million. His role on these teams is to build a client business case with a target price, and the actual price with a supporting P&L for internal governance approvals. He also work with sales teams to refine the client value proposition "Value Story" and ensure the pricing structure supports the story.

What has been the most important thing in making you successful at your job?

I would say there are three main things. Initially, develop a first draft as soon as possible with placeholders for unknown elements and iterate as many times as possible to the finished product. Next, determine the questions people are likely to ask, and answer those questions in your work product. Finally, realize everyone has shortcomings and bad days, be patient and flexible and they will do the same with you.

What advice would you give soon-to-be graduates?

You don't have to be an expert on everything. You can make an impact if you can quickly determine the levers in any situation or problem. Identify the levers and understand if the change will be good or bad, big or small when you pull them. Also, you may not use everything you were taught in school, but you will utilize your experiences, thought processes, your problem-solving skills, people skills, and concepts learned every day. Your education has helped you understand why things happen, the how may differ from one situation to another.

How is marketing relevant to your role at DXC?

Marketing helps the business build playbooks with value stories that help sales teams tell consistent sales stories that play to the client's value perception. For example, our company will do this for you using these people, processes, and tools, and it will provide cost savings of x% while increasing business performance by y% with an improved customer experience resulting from z.

What do you consider your personal brand to be?

In baseball, there is a concept of a utility player who can play several different positions. My role is to determine pricing but also to help other roles as necessary with my experience. Sometimes I might help to make sure the costs from engineers look correct, the sales story is convincing, the contract doesn't feel too tight or too loose, or the revenue recognition and accounting treatment seems reasonable.

LO 3-1

COMPETITIVE ENVIRONMENT

Differentiate between direct and indirect competition.

SiriusXM was launched a little less than two decades ago. It is the largest satellite radio provider in North America, offering hundreds of channels of commercial-free music, sports, and talk. Today, over 34 million subscribers pay a monthly fee for the service.[1] Companies like SiriusXM compete in a dynamic and changing environment. The **marketing environment** consists of the outside factors and forces that affect a company's ability to meet its marketing goals. Those forces include political, economic, demographic, sociocultural, technological, and legal factors.

To be successful, marketers must understand the marketing environment, including both the competition and the domestic and international factors that affect the company. The competitive environment includes both direct and indirect competitors seeking to acquire market share.

marketing environment

The outside factors and forces that affect a company's ability to meet its marketing goals. Those forces include political, economic, demographic, sociocultural, technological, and legal factors.

direct competition

A situation in which products that perform the same function compete against one another. Also called *category competition or brand competition.*

substitute products

Goods and services that perform very similar functions and can be used in place of one another.

indirect competition

A process in which products provide alternative solutions to the same market.

Direct Competition

The most obvious form of competition is **direct competition** (also called *category competition* or *brand competition*), in which products that perform the same function compete against one another. For example, Wendy's competes directly with hamburger chains McDonald's and Burger King for customers and market share. In 2012, Wendy's passed Burger King in sales volume for the first time, to become the second-largest U.S. hamburger chain behind McDonald's. Wendy's revenue growth continued into 2018, led by its popular "4 for $4 meal."[2] However, sales at Wendy's were dwarfed by its other major direct competitor—McDonald's. During the same period, its total sales volume rose to $37.4 billion, more than four times Wendy's annual sales of $9.2 billion.[3]

The direct competition for SiriusXM includes traditional radio stations as well as Internet radio services like Spotify that stream across broadband connections. Traditional and Internet radio are examples of substitute products. **Substitute products** are goods and services that perform very similar functions and can be used in place of one another. For SiriusXM to succeed, it must differentiate its product from substitutes in ways that add value to the customer's listening experience. SiriusXM does this by forgoing commercials and offering specific content that is not available on any substitute product.

Marketing professionals at SiriusXM and every organization must recognize the challenges both direct and indirect competition present and develop strategies to protect and expand their organization in light of those challenges.
Cindy Ord/Getty Images Entertainment/Getty Images

Indirect Competition

Companies also face indirect competition. **Indirect competition** occurs when products provide alternative solutions to the same market. For SiriusXM, indirect competition would include products such as Apple's iPhone, which allows consumers to download and listen to their favorite music, audiobooks, and podcasts in their home or car.

Indirect competition also affects the fast-food industry. Despite reaching the number-two position among U.S. hamburger chains, Wendy's overall growth was relatively small due to increased indirect competition. As U.S. consumers looked for healthier dining choices, Subway jumped past both Wendy's and Burger King to become the third-largest restaurant chain in the United States, with approximately $10.2 billion in sales.[4] While Wendy's products were able to make gains relative to Burger King's Whopper, they lost ground to healthier sandwiches and Subway's cleverly marketed "$5 Footlong" and "Eat Fresh Refresh" campaigns.

The beverage category offers another example of indirect competition. Direct competitors Coca-Cola and Pepsi have battled over soft-drink market share for decades. However, as consumers seek healthier drinks, soft-drink sales have begun to decline. Coca-Cola and Pepsi have seen indirect competitors gain market share selling juices, teas, energy drinks, and different types of water. Faced with this marketing trend, Coca-Cola and Pepsi aggressively expanded their offerings by acquiring brands (e.g., Coca-Cola with Dasani and Pepsi with Gatorade and Tropicana) in these emerging drink categories.

The shift in consumers' desire to eat, drink, and live healthier is one of several external factors currently affecting the marketing environment. To be successful, a firm must understand and adjust to the external environment, both domestic and international. In the next section, we'll discuss the major external factors firms should consider.

Firms that closely monitor indirect competition can take steps to reduce its impact by expanding their offerings, as Coca-Cola did in response to competition from firms promoting healthy alternatives to soft drinks. *Nicolas Asfouri/AFP/Getty Images*

EXTERNAL MARKETING ENVIRONMENT

Marketing does not occur in a vacuum. Unforeseen developments external to the firm can directly affect the success of its marketing strategy. For this reason, marketers continually scan the external environment. **Environmental scanning** involves monitoring developments outside the firm's control. The goal is to detect and respond to threats and opportunities that might affect the firm.

Historically, environmental scanning at U.S. companies focused almost exclusively on the domestic environment. American auto giants Ford, General Motors, and Chrysler spent much of the twentieth century concerned mostly with competition from each other, for example. However, with increasing globalization, firms have expanded their scanning activities to include the environment beyond U.S. borders. Today international car manufacturers such as Toyota and Honda affect General Motors just as much as Ford.

In subsequent sections, we'll discuss the six major external factors that influence the firm's marketing environment—economic, demographic, sociocultural, political, legal, and technological—shown in Figure 3.1. All of these factors occur on both a domestic and global scale. In this chapter, we'll first focus on how they occur in the domestic environment before we expand the discussion to include the global environment as well.

Economic Factors

Economic factors influence almost every marketing decision a firm makes. Economic conditions affect consumers' willingness and ability to buy products. As a result, firms must create, communicate, and deliver value in a way that's appropriate for the current economic climate.

Four economic elements influence marketers: gross domestic product (GDP), income distribution, inflation, and consumer confidence.

LO 3-2

Summarize the major external factors that influence the marketing environment.

environmental scanning

The act of monitoring developments outside the firm's control with the goal of detecting and responding to threats and opportunities.

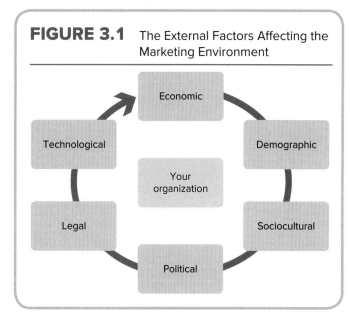

FIGURE 3.1   The External Factors Affecting the Marketing Environment

gross domestic product (GDP)

A measure of the market value of all officially recognized final goods and services produced within a country in a given period.

Gross Domestic Product
Gross domestic product paints a simple picture of the economic health of a nation. **Gross domestic product (GDP)** refers to the market value of all officially recognized final goods and services produced within a country in a given period. A country's GDP is a function of both the quantity of goods and services produced and their market values.

Overall GDP measures the overall size and health of an economy. The United States has the largest gross domestic product in the world for a single country, with almost $21 trillion in 2020.[5] However, in recent years China, India, and other developing nations have seen the highest GDP growth rates. While the United States grew 2.16 percent in 2019 (the last full year before COVID-19), China's economy grew almost three times faster, at 5.95 percent.[6] Higher GDP growth often drives lower unemployment rates, higher consumer confidence, and increased wealth across most income levels. All of this leaves customers with more money to spend. However, lower GDP growth can also open up opportunities for marketers who anticipate the trend and modify their marketing-mix strategy accordingly.

The overall GDP number doesn't give a full picture of a country's economic health, though. Marketers also find it useful to know the average productivity or income per person. *GDP per capita* is often considered an indicator of a country's standard of living.[7] It is calculated by dividing a country's overall GDP by its population. For example, the GDP per capita in the United States was $59,531 in 2017 compared with $8,902 in Mexico and $8,827 in China.[8]

Meanwhile, overall GDP is the most common gauge of the overall expansion or contraction of an economy. A **recession** occurs when overall GDP declines for two or more consecutive quarters. The most recent U.S. recession began in 2020 when the COVID-19 pandemic led to a 31.4 percent drop in GDP in the second quarter of the year.[9] Recessions can have a powerful negative effect on marketing. They typically involve layoffs, increased unemployment, and reduced consumer confidence. These factors influence consumers' ability and willingness to buy products and to contribute to nonprofit organizations.

recession

A period of time during which overall gross domestic product (GDP) declines for two or more consecutive quarters.

Income Distribution
Distribution of income across the U.S. population has shifted over the past several decades. This shift has forced marketers to develop new strategies to satisfy consumers at different ends of the spectrum. For example in 2017, the top 5 percent of the U.S. population earned approximately 36 percent of the country's adjusted gross income. Meanwhile, the bottom 50 percent earned less than 12 percent of the country's income.[10] Figure 3.2 illustrates the change in mean household income in the United States for various household segments over the past few decades in current dollar values. As the figure shows, though income for all household segments increased, income for the highest wage earners grew at a much quicker pace than it did for households in the bottom quintile.

Shifting income distribution offers marketers new opportunities to satisfy consumer needs and wants at various income levels. Many companies, such as Dollar General, have thrived by targeting consumers with modest incomes. Dollar General's marketing strategy includes offering low-income families quality food, health, and beauty products at reduced prices. This approach turned the company into a retailing bright spot over the past decade. While other firms struggled during the recession that began in December 2007, Dollar General opened new stores. Beyond this, it gained customers who have stayed loyal even as the economy began to rebound.[11]

On the other end of the spectrum is luxury brand Louis Vuitton, which makes shoes, watches, accessories, and other premium items. Catering to high-income consumers, the company has consistently increased its brand value. During the most recent recession, Louis Vuitton's marketing strategy involved raising prices and heightening its focus on quality. The result was additional sales to its wealthiest clients, and thus higher profits.[12]

FIGURE 3.2   Change in Average U.S. Household Income

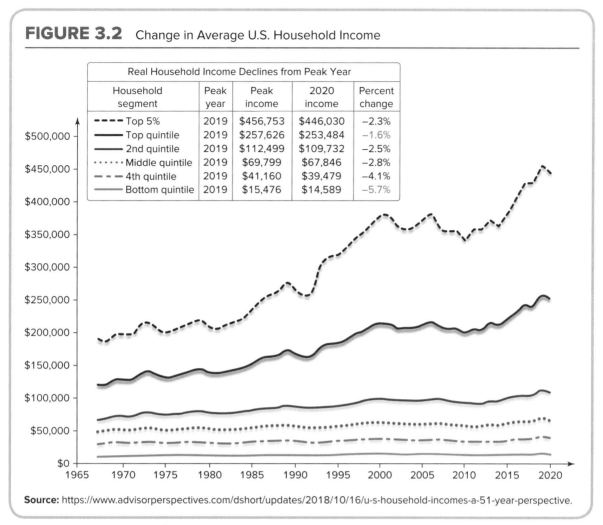

Real Household Income Declines from Peak Year				
Household segment	Peak year	Peak income	2020 income	Percent change
Top 5%	2019	$456,753	$446,030	−2.3%
Top quintile	2019	$257,626	$253,484	−1.6%
2nd quintile	2019	$112,499	$109,732	−2.5%
Middle quintile	2019	$69,799	$67,846	−2.8%
4th quintile	2019	$41,160	$39,479	−4.1%
Bottom quintile	2019	$15,476	$14,589	−5.7%

Source: https://www.advisorperspectives.com/dshort/updates/2018/10/16/u-s-household-incomes-a-51-year-perspective.

Inflation   You may have heard older friends and relatives talk about how, back in their day, a gallon of milk cost less than $2. The fact that the same gallon of milk costs over $4 today is the result of inflation. **Inflation** is an increase in the general level of prices of products in an economy over a period of time. When the general price level rises, each

inflation

An increase in the general level of prices of products in an economy over a period of time.

Brian Killian/Getty Images Enertainment/Getty Images

A. Astes/Alamy Stock Photo

Though they pursued markedly different strategies, both Louis Vuitton and Dollar General had success marketing to a U.S. population characterized by shifting income distribution.

unit of currency (e.g., each U.S. dollar) buys fewer goods and services. In 2021, prices rose by 7 percent compared to the previous year, which was the fastest rate in almost four decades causing challenges for marketers and consumers across the economy.[13]

Consequently, inflation also reflects erosion in the purchasing power of money. **Purchasing power** is the amount of goods and services that can be purchased for a specific amount of money. For example, if the price of gasoline goes up 10 percent this year, the amount of gasoline you can purchase for $20 decreases by that same 10 percent. Three decades ago, $10 might have filled up your tank as average gas prices in the late 1980s were below $1 per gallon.[14]

Inflation can affect marketing significantly if prices rise faster than consumer incomes. In the last decade, U.S. consumers have seen significant increases in the cost of gasoline and food. During the same period, they've experienced a comparable decrease in the amount left to spend on all other goods and services. Each of you may be experiencing the impact of inflation as you read these words. College tuition and fees have increased 440 percent since 1980. Meanwhile the average family's income has risen less than 150 percent.[15] Because the cost of college has outpaced average family income, more students have been forced to take out additional student loans and families must spend a greater percentage of their household budgets to send children to college. Consequently, university marketing professionals are increasingly tasked with providing evidence of the value of higher education to current and future students. Their strategy includes increasing career service staffs, offering more integrated course programs, and spending more time educating people about the financial benefits of a college degree.

purchasing power

A measure of the amount of goods and services that can be purchased for a specific amount of money.

consumer confidence

A measure of how optimistic consumers are about the overall state of the economy and their own personal finances.

Consumer Confidence   Consumer spending accounts for more than two-thirds of U.S. economic activity. The amount consumers are willing and able to spend is often based on their confidence in the stability of their future income. As a result, consumer confidence can provide an effective measure of the health of the economy. **Consumer confidence** measures how optimistic consumers are about the overall state of the economy and their own personal finances.

Consumers purchase more when consumer confidence is high. If the economy contracts and people lose jobs, consumer confidence decreases, leading to more saving and less spending. The effects of decreasing consumer confidence were seen in the United States during the most recent recession. Figure 3.3 illustrates the changes in consumer confidence and the subsequent change in real consumer spending over the past couple of decades. The green line reflects consumer confidence; the red line illustrates the change in real consumer spending over the same time period. As you can see, these measures often trend together, though there isn't an exact correlation between the two.

Marketers who can find strategic ways to help consumers feel confident about their purchases can improve performance during challenging times. For example, in 2009 Hyundai recognized that U.S. consumers were not confident in buying a new car because they feared

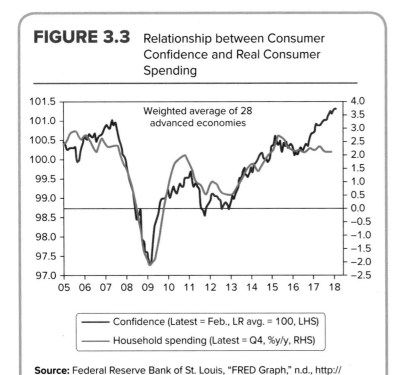

FIGURE 3.3   Relationship between Consumer Confidence and Real Consumer Spending

Weighted average of 28 advanced economies

Confidence (Latest = Feb., LR avg. = 100, LHS)
Household spending (Latest = Q4, %y/y, RHS)

Source: Federal Reserve Bank of St. Louis, "FRED Graph," n.d., http://research.stlouisfed.org/fred2/graph/?utm_source=research&utm_medium=website&utm_campaign=data-tools.

Hyundai's Buyer Assurance program, which focused on addressing low consumer confidence due to a weak economy, allowed the car company to increase domestic sales, profits, and market share during an economic recession. *Jonathan Weiss/Shutterstock*

losing their jobs. In response, Hyundai launched the Buyer Assurance program. The program allowed Hyundai buyers to return their car within 12 months, no questions asked, if they lost their job.[16] Hyundai identified and tapped into basic and powerful consumer fears to develop a strategy that sought to help consumers feel more confident in purchasing. This strategy helped Hyundai increase market share significantly; its sales increased by 22 percent while the rest of the auto industry saw declining sales in the year after the promotion launched.[17]

Marketers cannot dictate the state of the economic environment. Instead, they must develop marketing strategies to position their firm for success, regardless of economic factors. From 2008 to 2010, with consumer confidence low due to the recession, Subway was looking for a value offering to compete against other restaurant chains that were expanding their low-price menus. A local Subway franchise in Miami first offered footlong sandwiches for only $5 on the weekends.[18] When the stores offering the promotion had lines out the doors, Subway knew it had a winning marketing strategy. Subway worked with its ad agency to develop the now famous "$5 Footlong" jingle. More customers upgraded their orders from 6-inch subs to footlongs; others bought a footlong sandwich, ate half, and saved the rest for lunch the next day. The $5 footlong helped Subway expand domestic sales by 17 percent at a time when virtually all other restaurant chains were watching sales decrease.[19] Just three years after the introduction of the $5 footlong, Subway surpassed McDonald's; it now operates the most locations of any restaurant chain in the world.[20]

Executive Perspective . . .

because everyone is a marketer

Matt Slick
Senior Principal
DXC Technology

Photo by Shannon Kaye Portrait Design

What is a way you see marketing impacting profitability each day?

Marketing is immensely important because value is perceived, and marketing creates that perception. Any company can obtain a higher price and improved profit when the marketplace perceives value. If you must battle on price between two perceived equals, it's tougher to win and profit will certainly be less.

Demographic Factors

demographics

The characteristics of human populations that can be used to identify consumer markets.

Economic factors provide a macro framework for understanding consumer purchase patterns. At the same time, marketers are equally concerned with identifying consumers' demographic characteristics. **Demographics** are the characteristics of human populations that can be used to identify consumer markets. They include things such as age, gender, ethnicity, and education level, all of which influence the products consumers buy. Typical demographic information is readily available from the U.S. Census Bureau and research firms such as Nielsen. Access to demographic information is essential to identifying and characterizing a firm's target markets.

Age Do you consume information in the same way as your parents? Do you consume information the same way you did five years ago? The likely answer to both of these questions is no. Age plays an important role in how consumers process information. This in turn affects what marketing strategy firms should use to reach them.

Baby Boomers

The generation born between 1946 and 1964.

disposable income

The amount of spending money available to households after paying taxes.

Millennials

The generation born between 1978 and the late twentieth century. Also known as *Generation Y.*

Each year, the average age of the population of the United States rises. The median age of the U.S. population is expected to grow from age 38 today to age 43 by 2060.[21] Seniors are the fastest-growing demographic group. As illustrated in Figure 3.4, it is projected that by 2035 the older adults will outnumber children in the United States for the first time in history. There are 74 million **Baby Boomers**[22]—the generation of children born between 1946 and 1964. They are retiring from the workforce at a rate of 10,000 per day.[23] Members of this generation typically possess two things that marketing professionals seek: disposable income and free time. **Disposable income** is the amount of spending money available to households after paying taxes.

Baby Boomers represent the wealthiest generation in U.S. history; when they retire, they have free time to spend some of their wealth. Rapidly retiring Baby Boomers make up only a quarter of the U.S. population but account for 50 percent of all domestic consumer spending.[24] In an effort to reach this demographic, firms are making changes to encourage older Americans to shop at their stores. Paint retailer Sherwin-Williams has redesigned its 3,400 stores by adding more lighting and seating, to make them more comfortable for older shoppers. Pharmacy CVS Caremark has retrofitted its stores to appeal to older shoppers by lowering shelves and adding carpeting to reduce slipping.[25] However, the news is not all positive for marketers looking to target Boomers. Older adults are more likely to complain and often require more special attention and resources than their younger counterparts.

Some of you reading this belong to a generational cohort known as **Millennials**, the generation of children born between 1981 and the late twentieth century. Also known as *Generation Y,* Millennials comprise over 75 million members in the United States.[26] They are the second-largest generational group behind the Baby Boomers. Millennials generally have the greatest familiarity with and most use for digital communication, social media, and other forms of technology.

FIGURE 3.4   Projected Number of Children and Older Adults

For the First Time in U.S. History Older Adults Are Projected to Outnumber Children by 2035

Projected percentage of population

22.8%   Adults 65+   23.5%

Children under 18   19.8%

15.2%

Projected number (millions)

49.2   73.6   78.0 76.4   94.7 79.8

2016 '20 '25 '30 2035 '40 '45 '50 '55 2060

Source: U.S. Census Bureau https://www.census.gov/newsroom/press-releases/2018/cb18-41-population-projections.html, March 13, 2018.

Marketers trying to reach this large consumer group increasingly deliver their messages using channels, like the Internet, that are most likely to be used by this market. For example, Gap targeted Millennials by promoting its brand on the Internet and participating in design collaborations with fashion blogs that are popular with younger consumers.[27] In 2015, Millennials became the largest share of the U.S. workforce, and their importance to marketers will only grow in the decades ahead.[28]

Many of you reading this belong to a generational cohort known as *Generation Z,* the generation of children born between 1997 and 2012. Gen Zers are more diverse, more highly educated, and less likely to move than previous generations.[29] The typical Gen Z consumer uses 1 to 10 apps per day and a majority are willing to pay for music apps. Music app providers like Spotify focus on providing additional content and perks for younger consumers to stay on one platform, by tapping into Gen Z consumers' desire to connect by offering features that recommend local concerts to users based on their music preferences. Spotify's partnership with Songkick and Pandora's acquisition of Ticketfly provide additional evidence of how important nondigital experiences remain in today's digital age.[30]

Mc Graw Hill connect Exercise **3-1**

Social Media in Action

Financial advisers across the globe, including independent advisers running their own small businesses, are increasingly recognizing the importance of marketing themselves on social media. Financial advisers are using social media to win business at the highest rate in their history. An annual survey from Putnam Investments found that 97 percent of financial advisers use social media for business. The share of advisers acquiring clients through social media jumped from 49 percent in 2013 to 86 percent in 2018. Indeed, regardless of industry, social media are increasingly important to winning the business of fast-paced, tech-savvy consumers.

Financial advisers of all ages are adjusting to their changing marketing environment. LinkedIn is the network of choice of advisers for their business, with 73 percent reporting they use it, compared with 56 percent who use Facebook and 46 percent who report using Twitter for business. Use of other platforms for business is also growing: 42 percent of advisers indicate they use Yelp, 39 percent use YouTube, and 34 percent use Instagram for business. Advisers are using different social networks for different business reasons. For example, they may use LinkedIn to get more referrals and connect with other financial professionals. They may try to develop closer relationships with small business clients and prospects by, say, sharing a Facebook article about cycling with clients who are cycling enthusiasts.

The Social Media in Action Connect exercise in Chapter 3 asks you to develop different social media marketing strategies for a small business. By understanding how social media can help small businesses in different industries, you will be able to apply these strategies in the service of a small business you might work for or own in the years ahead.

Source: https://www.businesswire.com/news/home/20180403006208/en/ Financial-Advisors-Broadly-View-Social-Media-Disruptive.

Gender   One of the most important changes in the United States in recent decades has been the roles, attitudes, and buying habits of people in the marketplace. Historically, female consumers were targeted for a much less diverse set of goods and services than men. Today women take on the role of decision maker across a large and expanding variety of products. Female consumers now account for 85 percent of all consumer purchase decisions in the United States, including everything from cars to groceries to health care.[31] Women are responsible for more than half of the new-car purchases in the United States. Seventy-five percent of women identify themselves as the primary shopper in their household.[32]

Their control over the majority of consumer spending makes women a target market across products. Marketers at Toyota targeted their promotional activities for the Sienna minivan toward female buyers with a marketing campaign titled "Swagger Wagon." The campaign appealed emotionally to female consumers who did not want parenthood to take away from their ability to drive a cool car. Delivered via television and over two dozen YouTube videos, the ads featured a woman and her family describing how the Sienna fit their lifestyle rather than a list of features. "Swagger Wagon" generated over 5 million YouTube hits and was named one of the top marketing campaigns of the year.[33]

Education   Historically, highly educated consumers are more likely to be employed than are those with less education. As Figure 3.5 shows, even during the height of the recession that began in December 2007 or the COVID-19 recession in 2020, the unemployment rate for college-educated workers was approximately half that of the nation as a whole.[34] Though the trend in the unemployment rate for college-educated consumers mirrors the trend for the rest of the population, their overall unemployment numbers remain low in comparison.

The United States has been pushing over the past decade to lead the world in college graduation rates.[35] As a result, the number of professional workers with college degrees is expected to increase significantly in the coming years. Educated consumers

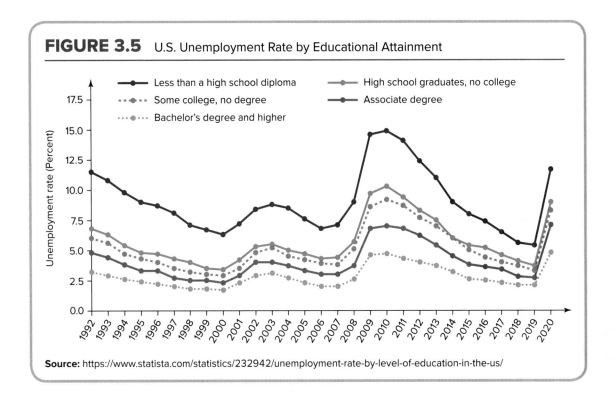

FIGURE 3.5   U.S. Unemployment Rate by Educational Attainment

Source: https://www.statista.com/statistics/232942/unemployment-rate-by-level-of-education-in-the-us/

are likely to earn significantly more money throughout the course of their lifetimes and also may more readily comprehend an advertiser's message. These factors make highly educated consumers prime targets for marketing strategies. The increase in the average education level of the country will continue to give marketers new opportunities.

Ethnicity The ethnic composition of the U.S. population is changing rapidly. Projections indicate that by 2050 the Hispanic population in the United States will almost double to more than 127 million, representing over 30 percent of the entire U.S. population.[36] The African American population in the United States grew at rate that outpaced the 12 percent population growth for the country as a whole.[37] Asian Americans now represent the highest-income, best-educated, and fastest-growing racial group in the United States, thereby increasing their purchasing power and importance to marketers.[38] Figure 3.6 illustrates changes in the ethnic breakdown of the United States over the past decade and changes projected for the decades ahead.

The United States is moving rapidly toward greater multiculturalism. Ethnic minorities' purchasing power was $3.8 trillion in 2018 and expected to grow significantly over the next decade.[39] Marketers already have taken basic steps to reach out to different ethnic groups. Advertising in multiple languages is one such step. Food company General Mills's research showed that consumers of Hispanic ethnicity prefer to buy the brands of goods and services they see advertised on television. The company significantly increased the number of ads it ran on Spanish-language media. When it did so, it saw sales of popular General Mills products like Progresso

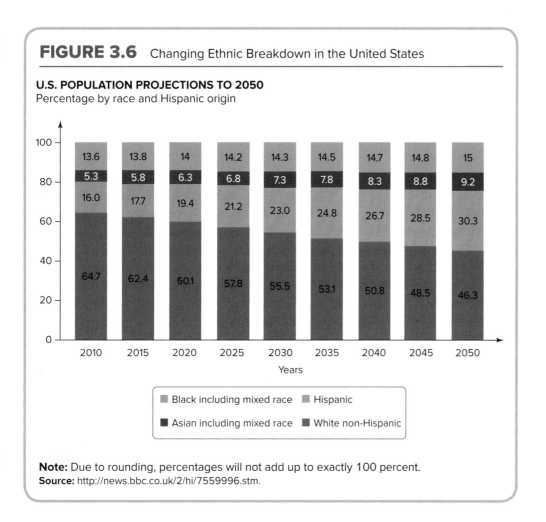

FIGURE 3.6 Changing Ethnic Breakdown in the United States

U.S. POPULATION PROJECTIONS TO 2050
Percentage by race and Hispanic origin

Year	Black including mixed race	Asian including mixed race	Hispanic	White non-Hispanic
2010	13.6	5.3	16.0	64.7
2015	13.8	5.8	17.7	62.4
2020	14	6.3	19.4	60.1
2025	14.2	6.8	21.2	57.8
2030	14.3	7.3	23.0	55.5
2035	14.5	7.8	24.8	53.1
2040	14.7	8.3	26.7	50.8
2045	14.8	8.8	28.5	48.5
2050	15	9.2	30.3	46.3

Legend:
- Black including mixed race
- Hispanic
- Asian including mixed race
- White non-Hispanic

Note: Due to rounding, percentages will not add up to exactly 100 percent.
Source: http://news.bbc.co.uk/2/hi/7559996.stm.

soup and Honey Nut Cheerios soar.[40] As the ethnic makeup of the United States continues to change, marketing professionals will need to keep studying different ethnic groups and their buying behavior.

Sociocultural Factors

sociocultural

The combination of social and cultural factors that affect individual development.

Our society and culture help shape our beliefs, values, and norms, which, in turn, define our tastes and purchasing habits. **Sociocultural** factors are the combination of social and cultural factors that affect individual development.

One of the biggest sociocultural changes in the United States over the past half century has been the shift from a nation of primarily one-income families, in which one spouse stayed home to raise children. Today, two-income families and single-parent households predominate. Less than 15 percent of U.S. households consist of a working parent and a stay-at-home parent.[41]

The new sociocultural reality of busy families has created opportunities for firms to offer new kinds of value. Banks, for example, have expanded their offerings to include later evening hours and more services through ATMs. They've also launched additional online banking options, like online check depositing, that give busy consumers more opportunities to use the bank's services.

Other sociocultural changes are taking place in the United States—an increasing number of single adults, rising concerns about protecting consumer privacy, and the growth in environmentally conscious consumers. Such changes provide firms with many reasons to market products in new and better ways. For example, in response to the increase in consumer demand for environmentally friendly goods and services, car manufacturers have increased their hybrid and electric-car offerings. Marketers of personal care products have introduced a wider selection of natural and organic items.

Cultural differences can also influence how consumers respond to advertisements and other marketing messages. For example, Asian American participants in one research study heavily favored preventive messages, such as the suggestion that a product can reduce the risk of cancer.[42] Anglo American participants preferred messages for that same product that are more promotional, that highlight the potential benefits, such as that it can produce higher energy levels. Such cultural differences provide marketers important insights into how to most effectively reach different consumers.

Political Factors

Firms must understand how the changing political climate affects them. They then can develop marketing strategies that will lead to success under various conditions. The political climate in the United States can change the direction of government policy quickly. Such change also can affect how marketers position their products. For example, video game marketers were very concerned about legislation proposed in Pennsylvania in 2018 that would add a 10 percent tax on the purchase of all mature-rated video games in the state.[43] The proposed tax would raise the cost of purchasing these types of video games and could force marketers to reconsider their target market and positioning strategies. They might need to replace lost revenue from consumers who could no longer afford to buy as many products with sales to other market segments or develop more new products that will not carry the mature label. Pennsylvania and many other states continue to deal with political pressure to reduce youth violence.

Firms need not be completely passive when it comes to the political decisions that affect their businesses. It's becoming increasingly possible for firms to affect politics. For example, the number and influence of *political action committees (PACs)* have increased dramatically in the past two decades. PACs

Oscar Mayer's Lunchables, which typically include crackers, cheese, and meat slices, appeal to busier families looking for a convenient way to prepare their children's lunch. *Michael Neelon(misc)/Alamy Stock Photo*

raise money to help elect individuals who regard their organization positively or to promote a particular issue related to their industry. Some PACs lobby government officials on issues that affect marketing, such as restrictions on certain types of advertising or protection of consumers' rights. For example, in 2015 the American Medical Association (AMA) announced it would seek curbs on the ability of pharmaceutical companies to market prescription drugs like Eli Lilly's Cialis, Pfizer's Viagra, and AstraZeneca's Crestor on television. The pharmaceutical lobby, which is one of the top 10 spenders among all lobbyists, pledged to fight this curb; it wants to protect the ability for pharmaceutical companies to advertise directly to consumers. If the AMA is successful, the curb could decrease marketers' ability to generate revenue from consumers and change the legal environment within the pharmaceutical industry.[44]

Legal Factors

The legal system is another factor of the external environment that affects how firms market their products. Marketing professionals need to know and work within the laws that affect marketing. Table 3.1 highlights some of the U.S. laws that are most important to understanding the marketing environment.

Federal, state, and local governments enact regulations for two main purposes:

1. *To ensure businesses compete fairly with each other.* For example, the Sherman Antitrust Act (1890) was passed to eliminate monopolies and guarantee competition. The Robinson–Patman Act (1936) refined prohibitions on selling the same product at different prices. The Wheeler–Lea Act (1938) made deceptive and misleading advertising illegal. These laws are among those enforced by the **Federal Trade Commission (FTC)**, which serves as the consumer protection agency for the

Federal Trade Commission (FTC)

The consumer protection agency for the United States.

TABLE 3.1   U.S. Laws That Affect Marketers

Legislation (Year Enacted)	Importance to Marketing
Sherman Antitrust Act (1890)	Combats anticompetitive practices, reduces market domination by individual corporations, and preserves unfettered competition as the rule of trade.
Robinson–Patman Act (1936)	Prohibits firms from selling the same product at different prices in interstate commerce unless based on a cost difference or if the goods are not of similar quality.
Wheeler–Lea Amendment (1938)	Authorizes the Federal Trade Commission to restrict unfair or deceptive acts; also called the *Advertising Act*. Broadened the Federal Trade Commission's powers to include protection of consumers from false advertising practices.
Fair Packaging and Labeling Act (1966)	Applies to labels on many consumer products. It requires the label to state the identity of the product; the name and place of business of the manufacturer, packer, or distributor; and the net quantity of contents.
Telephone Consumer Protection Act (1991)	Limits commercial solicitation calls to between 8 a.m. and 9 p.m. Requires telemarketers to maintain a do-not-call list and honor any request to not be called again.
Credit Card Accountability, Responsibility, and Disclosure Act (2009)	Protects consumer rights and abolishes deceptive lending practices.

United States. The FTC collects complaints about organizations that violate regulations; those complaints lead to investigations and possible prosecutions.

2. *To ensure businesses don't take advantage of consumers.* For example, the Fair Packaging and Labeling Act (1966) guarantees that product packages are labeled correctly. The Telephone Consumer Protection Act of 1991 has reduced the use of *telemarketing,* or selling products directly to consumers over the telephone. The act allows consumers to limit the number of telemarketing calls they receive and opt out of being called by some companies.[45]

In addition, banks and other financial institutions were required to change how they dealt with consumers following passage of the Credit Card Accountability, Responsibility, and Disclosure (CARD) Act of 2009. The law banned unfair credit card rate increases. It also required that disclosures regarding minimum payments and interest rates be made in plain English, to better protect consumers.[46]

Companies often spend significantly through their PACs to protect their legal position and make sure that new laws are as favorable to them as possible. In 2018, Amazon spent more than $3 million per quarter lobbying for laws impacting government procurement and cloud modernization. Facebook spent almost $3.5 million during one three-month period lobbying for a variety of legal changes on issues ranging from trade to high-skilled immigration.[47]

Technological Factors

Of all the external factors, rapidly evolving technology represents one of the most significant challenges, and one of the most significant opportunities, for marketing professionals. Technology influences how consumers satisfy their needs and wants, the basic concept underlying all marketing activities. For example, if you had been at college in the early 1990s and heard a song on the radio you wanted to buy, you had a couple of options: You could buy the song as a single on compact disc (CD) for $3 to $5. Or you could buy the artist's entire album on CD for $15 to $20, even though the album was filled with nine other songs you didn't care about. Technology changed the market: Apple's iPod and iTunes Store now allow consumers to purchase only the specific songs they like, for as little as $0.99. This technological advancement has forever changed the way consumers purchase music.

Technology also changes how firms promote their products. In recent years, a growing number of consumers have abandoned the traditional landline telephone in favor of smartphones. This technology-driven change gives marketers new ways to reach consumers: Applications track consumer locations, making it possible for marketers to know where a customer is. Marketers can then send electronic coupons, such as those provided by Groupon, to the customer's smartphone, with an offer for that moment and location. Imagine walking through downtown Chicago around dinner time and receiving an electronic coupon for a deep-dish pizza restaurant less than a block from where you are. In fact, we don't have to imagine such a scenario. These tools are available today, and they illustrate how technology can change the way firms market to consumers. Walt Disney World Resort uses technology to provide a more hassle-free experience at its theme parks. In 2013, Disney introduced MagicBands, which are wristbands enabled with a radio-frequency identification device (RFID) chip. MagicBands function as a room key and park entry pass for guests at Disney's parks.[48] The MagicBand can also be linked to a Walt Disney World Resort hotel guest's hotel bill, making purchases within the parks easier and quicker. Beyond the added value of improving the guest experience, MagicBands also provide marketers with useful information. By tracking consumers' ride and purchasing patterns, Disney can design attractions to best meet customer needs and wants.

New technology, such as Disney's MagicBands, not only delivers convenience to consumers but also provides marketers with valuable information about a customer's purchasing patterns and habits. *Gregg Matthews/The New York Times/Redux Pictures*

McGraw Hill connect Exercise **3-2**

Please complete the *Connect* exercise in Chapter 3 that focuses on the external factors that affect marketers. The exercise asks you to identify how external factors affect large organizations. By doing this exercise, you will better understand how forces outside the marketing department's control can influence decisions the firm must make.

INTERNATIONAL MARKETING ENVIRONMENT

LO 3-3

Extend the analysis of the marketing environment beyond the borders of the United States.

Recent estimates put the world's population at almost 8 billion people. Experts predict that it will grow to almost 10 billion people by the year 2050.[49] For some firms, analyzing external factors as they occur in the United States is sufficient. Increasingly, though, even small businesses and firms that sell primarily to U.S. customers are affected by global trends, events, and competitors. The process of environmental scanning must take into account the international marketing environment as well.

In theory, the key external factors that affect a firm in the international space don't differ substantially from those in the domestic space. Consumers' age, education level, and gender still matter. The political and legal systems within a given country often dictate how easy it will be to sell and distribute products there. And a country's level of technological advancement has important implications for how the firm promotes its product to the local population. In practice, though, environmental scanning on a global scale often has added layers of complexity. In this section, we'll discuss some of the factors that marketers should be aware of when analyzing the international marketing environment.

Currency Fluctuation

currency exchange rate

The price of one country's currency in terms of another country's currency.

Currency fluctuation refers to how the value of one country's currency changes in relation to the value of other currencies. Currency fluctuation can affect either positively or negatively how firms market products internationally. The outcome depends on one's perspective: Consider, for example, the currency exchange rate between the U.S. dollar ($) and the European Union's currency, the euro (€). The **currency exchange rate** is the price of one country's currency in terms of another country's currency. In December 2020, €1 was worth $1.22. One year later, in December 2021, the same €1 was worth $1.14.[50] As the value of the euro depreciated relative to the dollar, it increased the spending power of American consumers seeking to buy European products. In contrast, as the dollar appreciated, American goods and services became more expensive to consumers in Europe.

The world's largest country in terms of population, China, has been criticized for undervaluing its currency, that is, pricing the yuan lower than it is actually worth. Many nations believe this tactic gives China an advantage in selling exports because it can price its products cheaper than other countries' products. Financial experts and government officials believe the yuan could appreciate in the years ahead.[51] U.S. marketers ranging from Coca-Cola to General Motors are stepping up advertising and distribution efforts in China, to entice consumers in China to buy more of their products. Due to the stronger yuan-to-dollar exchange rate, the U.S. products now cost Chinese consumers less.

Whether a currency is appreciating or depreciating, currency fluctuations can provide marketing opportunities. For example, let's say the value of the euro increases relative to the dollar. That change may encourage more families from Europe to travel to Walt Disney World in Orlando, Florida, because they could do so cheaply. Disney marketers could target these families with advertisements promoting the idea that there has never been a better time to go to a theme park in the United States. It's important for marketers working in the international environment to understand the effect of currency fluctuations on product value.

Income Distribution

A country's income distribution often provides the most reliable picture of its purchasing power. Marketers are particularly attracted to countries with a growing middle class because a nation's purchasing capability tends to increase as the proportion of middle-income households increases. For example, income growth in developing nations in Asia and Latin America is likely to stimulate world trade as more of their residents move into the middle class.

Figure 3.7 illustrates how the percentage of middle-class consumption in key Asian countries is projected to change in comparison to the United States over the next few decades. As you can see, the percentage of middle-class consumption in India may outstrip that of the United States by the year 2050. Even countries that don't have a rapidly increasing middle class may have higher purchasing power than may be apparent from initial statistics, due to government subsidies for food, transportation, or health care.

Continuously scanning the global economic environment is an important aspect of doing business in international markets. In addition, marketers are increasingly using metrics to analyze international markets.

Using Metrics to Analyze International Markets

Evaluating the international marketing environment is a complex process. It requires marketers to interpret a significant amount of information in order to make the best decisions. Marketers have a variety of tools that can help them analyze the international marketing environment. For example, Google Analytics allows you to quickly see what countries visitors to your website are from, how many pages they visited, and how long they stayed on the site. Google Analytics can also help marketers evaluate what consumers from different countries are searching for on their sites. Such search data help provide insight into the external international environment and evolving consumer preferences.

Using analytics tools like these, combined with information about income distribution and currency fluctuation, provides marketers with a clearer picture of the international environment affecting their organization.

Major Trade Agreements and Organizations

In addition to scanning the international economic environment, marketing professionals must possess a working knowledge of major trade

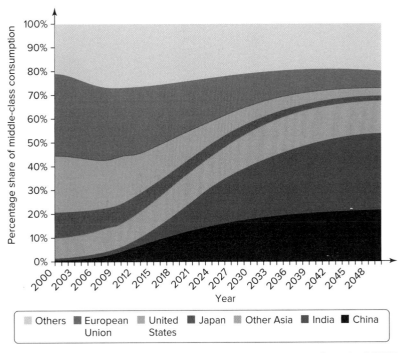

FIGURE 3.7 Projected Changes in Global Middle-Class Consumption

Source: Kharas, H. (2010), "The Emerging Middle Class in Developing Countries," OECD Development Centre, Working Papers, No. 285, OECD Publishing, http://dx.doi.org/10.1787/5kmmp8lncrns-en.

agreements and international organizations. These could govern their firm's interaction with international markets. Whether you work for a firm such as Bank of America that is planning to expand in China or a small rice farm hoping to sell more products to European countries, you will need a basic understanding of each of these agreements and organizations to successfully navigate the international marketplace.

International trade agreements, monetary unions, and organizations can have substantial impact on the environment in which a firm operates. They can affect how easy it is for firms to enter a foreign market, what the currency exchange rate is between countries, and even what competition firms will encounter in the domestic market. Trade agreements and monetary unions facilitate the exchange of money and products across borders. International organizations provide regulatory oversight to economic activity. In the sections that follow, we'll discuss the key entities you should be aware of.

North American Free Trade Agreement Perhaps the most familiar U.S. trade agreement is the North American Free Trade Agreement (NAFTA). The **North American Free Trade Agreement (NAFTA)** established a free-trade zone among the United States, Canada, and Mexico. Its goal was to eliminate barriers to trade and investment among the three countries. As Figure 3.8 shows, the United States exports more products to Canada and Mexico than to any other individual country. This is largely because NAFTA made exchange among the three countries so easy.

One of the key barriers to international trade is **tariffs,** which are taxes on imports and exports between countries. NAFTA's implementation on January 1, 1994, brought the immediate elimination of tariffs on more than one-half of U.S. imports from Mexico and

LO 3-4

Identify the major trade agreements, monetary unions, and organizations that affect the international marketing environment.

North American Free Trade Agreement (NAFTA)

An international agreement that established a free-trade zone among the United States, Canada, and Mexico.

tariffs

Taxes on imports and exports between countries.

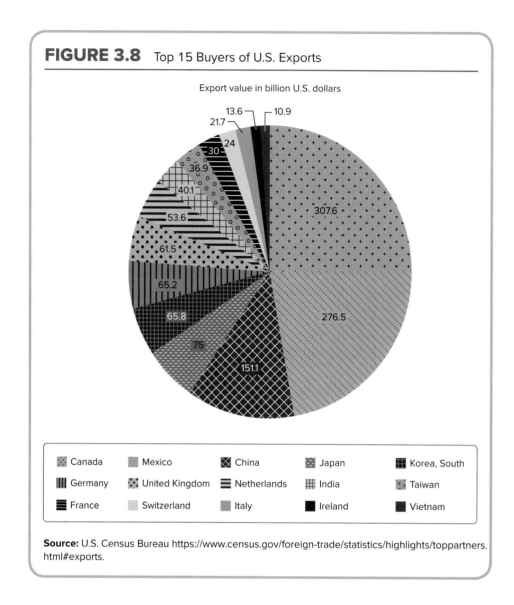

FIGURE 3.8 Top 15 Buyers of U.S. Exports

Export value in billion U.S. dollars

Legend:
- Canada
- Mexico
- China
- Japan
- Korea, South
- Germany
- United Kingdom
- Netherlands
- India
- Taiwan
- France
- Switzerland
- Italy
- Ireland
- Vietnam

Source: U.S. Census Bureau https://www.census.gov/foreign-trade/statistics/highlights/toppartners.html#exports.

more than one-third of U.S. exports to Mexico. Within 10 years of implementation, all U.S.–Mexico tariffs were eliminated, except for some on U.S. agricultural exports to Mexico that were to be phased out within 15 years. Most U.S.–Canada trade was already free of tariffs. NAFTA also sought to eliminate nontariff trade barriers such as embargoes or sanctions.

In 2018, the three countries reached a new deal to replace NAFTA, which will be known as the **United States–Mexico–Canada Agreement (USMCA)**. One goal of the new deal is to have more cars and truck parts made in North America. Starting in 2020, to qualify for zero tariffs, a car or truck has to have 75 percent of its components manufactured in Canada, Mexico, or the United States. The agreement also makes significant upgrades to environmental and labor regulations, opens up Canadian dairy markets for farmers in the United States, and provides more-stringent protections for patents and trademarks.[52]

United States–Mexico–Canada Agreement (USMCA)

A trade agreement between the United States, Mexico, and Canada passed in 2018 that supports free trade among those countries.

Dominican Republic–Central America Free Trade Agreement

A decade after NAFTA was implemented, the United States entered discussions about a new agreement with the Central American countries of Costa Rica, El Salvador, Guatemala, Honduras, and Nicaragua. This agreement was called the *Central America Free Trade Agreement (CAFTA)*. In 2004, the Dominican Republic joined the negotiations, and the agreement was renamed Dominican Republic–Central America Free Trade Agreement. Like NAFTA, the **Dominican Republic–Central America Free Trade Agreement (DR-CAFTA)** focuses on eliminating tariffs, reducing nontariff barriers, and facilitating investment among the member states.

With the addition of the Dominican Republic, the trade group's largest economy, the region covered by DR-CAFTA is the second-largest Latin American export market for U.S. producers behind Mexico. It buys over $31 billion worth of goods from the United States a year.[53] Trade between the United States and countries covered under this agreement amounts to about $60 billion annually.

European Union

Agreements like NAFTA and DR-CAFTA are designed to ease trade between nations. Entities like the European Union go further, integrating countries to a much larger degree. The **European Union (EU)** is an economic, political, and monetary union of 27 European nations as of 2022. It was formed to create a single European market by reducing barriers to the free trade of goods, services, and finances among member countries.

In 2021, the EU generated approximately 15 percent of the global gross domestic product, making it one of the largest economies in the world.[54] It is the largest exporter, the largest importer, and the biggest trading partner for several large countries, including China, India, and the United States. However, EU nations such as Greece, Spain, Portugal, and Italy have faced significant economic challenges in recent years. These challenges have had a negative impact on their domestic markets and also make it more difficult for U.S. marketers to sell their products to consumers in those countries.

In 2016, the United Kingdom voted to leave the European Union, which set the stage for years of negotiations between the UK and the other 27 EU nations. The decision was made that Great Britain would leave the EU in 2019, which will continue to impact marketers across the globe in the years ahead.

World Trade Organization

The World Trade Organization was officially formed on January 1, 1995, under the Marrakech Agreement. The **World Trade Organization (WTO)** regulates trade among participating countries and helps importers and exporters conduct their business. It is the only international organization dealing with the rules of trade between nations.

In addition, the WTO provides a framework for negotiating and formalizing trade agreements and a dispute-resolution process aimed at enforcing participants' adherence to WTO agreements. The WTO, headquartered in Geneva, Switzerland, has 162 members, representing more than 97 percent of the world's population, and over 20 observer nations, most of which are seeking membership.

International Monetary Fund

Soon after the end of World War II, 29 countries signed an agreement to form the International Monetary Fund. Headquartered in Washington, D.C., the **International Monetary Fund (IMF)** "works to foster international monetary cooperation, secure financial stability, facilitate international trade, promote high employment and sustainable economic growth, and reduce poverty around the world."[55] It was formed to promote international economic cooperation, trade, employment, and currency exchange rate stability. The IMF is governed by the 188 countries that make up its near-global membership.

One of the IMF's important activities is to make resources available to member countries to help them manage their debts. Each country contributes to a pool of financial resources. Countries with debt obligations they can't meet can borrow from this pool, on a temporary basis. When it was first created in 1945, the IMF helped stabilize the world's economic system after World War II. To this day, the IMF works to improve the economies of its member countries.

Dominican Republic–Central America Free Trade Agreement (DR-CAFTA)

An international agreement that eliminated tariffs, reduced nontariff barriers, and facilitated investment among the United States, Costa Rica, El Salvador, Guatemala, Honduras, Nicaragua, and the Dominican Republic.

European Union (EU)

An economic, political, and monetary union among 27 European nations that created a single European market by reducing barriers to the free trade of goods, services, and finances.

World Trade Organization (WTO)

An international organization that regulates trade among participating countries and helps importers and exporters conduct their business.

International Monetary Fund (IMF)

An international organization that works to foster international monetary cooperation, secure financial stability, facilitate international trade, promote high employment and sustainable economic growth, and reduce poverty around the world.

connect   Exercise 3-3

Please complete the *Connect* exercise for Chapter 3 that focuses on international trade agreements. By identifying the major aspects of critical trade agreements, you will better understand the international marketing environment and be prepared to develop effective global marketing strategies.

Technology

Once marketers understand the economic factors and trade agreements and organizations that affect their global activities, they must look more specifically at how best to reach their international audience. Today, technology enables even small businesses to reach consumers around the globe. Websites act as a front door to billions of potential consumers. Social media help companies develop relationships with customers anywhere, for very little cost. Tools such as Google Translate allow customers to view websites in their own language, making it easier to promote products in different countries.

In addition, global shipping firms like FedEx and UPS enable small manufacturers to ship their products to customers around the world. Technology enables both the buyer and the seller to track those shipments. Understanding how technology affects the international marketing environment benefits marketers as they attempt to meet the needs and wants of consumers in global markets.

Cultural Fit

consumer ethnocentrism

A belief by residents of a country that it is inappropriate or immoral to purchase foreign-made goods and services.

One of the biggest mistakes domestic firms make when they attempt to take their business global is to believe that what works "at home" will work abroad. It's often a mistake to think that consumers abroad want exactly the same products that are sold in the United States and want them marketed in the same way. Burger King was widely criticized when it created an in-store ad for some European stores that showed a Hindu goddess atop a ham sandwich with the caption, "A snack that is sacred."[56] Many of the nearly 1 billion Hindus throughout the world, most of whom are vegetarian, were offended and protested the use of the ad. Burger King eventually pulled it. The negative attention and the potential long-term damage to Burger King's goal of expanding its market illustrate the importance of understanding cultural fit.

A growing concern for firms with overseas operations is consumer ethnocentrism. **Consumer ethnocentrism** refers to a belief by residents of a country that it is inappropriate or immoral to purchase foreign-made goods and services.[57] This belief is on the rise in many developed nations, including the United States, France, Germany, and China. Consumer ethnocentrism is rarely grounded in fact, but the belief makes the marketer's job even more difficult. For example, in 2003, following France's refusal to join the U.S. military operation in Iraq, many U.S. consumers refused to eat french fries, even though there was nothing French about the product. Proactive marketers across the country looked for a clever way to resolve the issue and, for a brief time, renamed their product "freedom fries."

Consumer ethnocentrism sometimes presents a challenge to marketers with international operations. Promoting a product in a different way can overcome such challenges. *Nicolas Khayat/Newscom*

Obinna Okechukwu

Senior Product Consultant
Docusign

Obinna Okechukwu

Describe your job. I am a Sr. Product Consultant at DocuSign Inc. I work with enterprises and nonprofit organizations assisting them in their digital transformation projects as they transition from legacy contract systems to a more integrated ecosystem that enables them to align with their strategic goals of operating more seamlessly, efficiently, and effectively in their contract agreement lifecycle processes.

How did you get your job? I was contacted by a recruiter on LinkedIn (a networking website) who reached out to me asking if I was available for a quick chat on an opening the company had. The recruiter told me that while looking up my profile on LinkedIn, she felt I was the right fit for the role. I made an appointment with the recruiter and discussed further about the role and felt it was an exciting opportunity. I had seven interviews with individuals and teams, discussing the role and the responsibilities and how it aligns with my personal goals. After the lengthy interview process, I was offered the position and I will say, I am really glad I accepted the role, it has been an exciting process so far!

What has been the most important thing in making you successful at your job? Willingness to learn and a positive attitude. The learning curve for me in my current role has been rather steep. There are a lot of things I learned in the process and a lot I am still learning. However, without a doubt, the most important tool in my toolbox that has been very effective in making me successful at my job has been a willingness to learn and approaching each day with a positive attitude. Reaching out to colleagues and asking for assistance where needed while helping others and learning from the experience. Seizing every opportunity as a learning opportunity has definitely made me grow in my career.

What advice would you give soon-to-be graduates? Be hungry. I have noticed over the course of my career experience, that most people who rise to the top and excel at what they do are those who always seek opportunities to learn and grow. Once an individual no longer realizes opportunities to learn, stagnancy sets in and that becomes a huge disadvantage. Always set higher goals and seek ways to learn as you move toward those goals. Learn to course-correct when you realize you may be heading in the wrong direction. Get feedback from others but always be focused on going one step further than your current step.

What do you consider your personal brand to be? I am very passionate about finding creative solutions to real world problems. I strongly believe almost all problems and challenges can be solved if approached with a creative, pragmatic, and determined solution—not discounting the power of working with smart, motivated individuals. Developing products and or solutions requires an open mind and creative lenses to problem solving and that is a core strength of mine.

Analyzing cultural fit and overcoming consumer ethnocentrism are essential aspects of environmental scanning on a global scale that help firms create value for international consumers.

McGraw Hill connect Exercise **3-4**

Please complete the *Connect* exercise in Chapter 3 that focuses on how cultural fit affects the international marketing environment. By understanding which domestic firms and products are more likely to fit with the culture in specific foreign countries, you will be able to develop a more effective global marketing strategy.

LO 3-5

Describe the emerging factors that influence the nonprofit marketing environment.

NONPROFIT MARKETING ENVIRONMENT

Environmental scanning for a nonprofit organization presents challenges that for-profit businesses do not face. Those who donate money to a nonprofit such as a hospital, university, or faith-based institution do not walk away with a tangible product or benefit directly from any service. Instead, nonprofit marketers must convince donors to support the mission of the organization without receiving any direct benefit. Nonprofits primarily rely on three sources of funding—grants, special events, and individual donations. Marketing generally plays an important role in securing each.

The competitive environment for nonprofit funding has increased dramatically in recent years. In 1995, there were only 600,000 nonprofits in the United States. Today, that number is over 1.8 million and growing rapidly.[58] A 300 percent increase in the number of nonprofit organizations isn't the only hurdle. In addition, the total donations to nonprofit organizations dipped from 2007 to 2009 as the recession worsened. Figure 3.9 illustrates total giving to nonprofit organizations since 1974, including the dip during the recession.

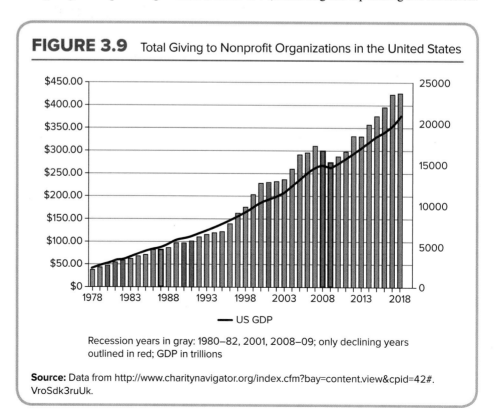

FIGURE 3.9   Total Giving to Nonprofit Organizations in the United States

— US GDP

Recession years in gray: 1980–82, 2001, 2008–09; only declining years outlined in red; GDP in trillions

Source: Data from http://www.charitynavigator.org/index.cfm?bay=content.view&cpid=42#. VroSdk3ruUk.

For nonprofit marketers to be successful in this type of competitive environment, they must understand the external environment in which they operate. They are affected by many of the same external factors discussed earlier in the chapter: economic, legal, political, and technological factors. However, due to their mission and chronic lack of funds, the impact can be quite different.

Economic Factors

During the recession that began in December 2007, Americans reduced their overall charitable giving by over 20 percent from levels prior to the recession.[59] The decline was far sharper than in previous economic recessions.

One strategy nonprofit marketers are using to combat that change is to develop new ways to recognize existing donors for their contributions. For example, a hospital might display a digital recognition system in its front lobby, listing donors of all sizes. These new methods foster pride and enthusiasm in donors about how their efforts improve the lives of others.

Political Factors

In addition to its economic impact, the recession led to political pressure to reduce federal, state, and municipal budgets. This, in turn, has forced many nonprofit organizations to fund basic programs in innovative ways. Public universities, which receive a substantial portion of their funding from their respective state legislatures, have been hit especially hard. Figure 3.10 highlights the decrease in state funding as a percentage of total projected revenues at Temple University in the last decade. This trend is consistent across many public universities throughout the United States.

In order to increase student financial aid and faculty retention, universities must raise more money from alumni and other supporters. The marketing department at the University of Colorado had success by increasing the campus profile of *planned gifts.* These are bequests, given to the nonprofit upon the death of the donor. Planned gifts became a major part of the University of Colorado's increased fundraising success. The university developed new packets of information for planned giving and promoted the program at all types of university events. This form of giving delivered value to donors: It did not require them to sacrifice financially during their lives but helped them leave a legacy at the university they loved. In the first year after the marketing program began, the University of Colorado saw a 700 percent increase in bequests that will help students and the university for generations to come.[60]

Legal Factors

In addition to the economic and political factors that have challenged nonprofits, several new laws and regulations have had an impact as well. The benefit that nonprofit marketers offer to potential donors typically includes some combination of information about how the donation will be used, how the donor will be recognized, and the tax incentives (e.g., the tax deductibility of charitable gifts) that will accompany the donation.

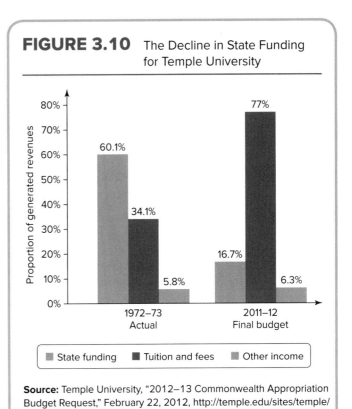

FIGURE 3.10 The Decline in State Funding for Temple University

State funding Tuition and fees Other income

Source: Temple University, "2012–13 Commonwealth Appropriation Budget Request," February 22, 2012, http://temple.edu/sites/temple/files/uploads/documents/Attachment_9-2012-Table_5-Generated_Revenue.pdf.

Legal changes to the tax-incentive element can alter the way marketing professionals communicate the organization's value to potential donors. For example, wealthy contributors—those making over $10 million per year—are the largest donors to numerous charities throughout the state of New York. The state proposed a law that restricts the amount of charitable contributions that very wealthy people can deduct from their taxes.[61] Nonprofit marketing professionals worry that such changes in the tax law, whether in New York or other states, or on federal tax returns, will act as a disincentive, further challenging fundraising efforts in a difficult economy. They fear that, without tax incentives, charitable giving may decline. Such legal changes have made it increasingly necessary for nonprofit firms to develop programs that generate more first-time contributors, to make up for potential reductions from high-income donors.

Technology Factors

Many nonprofit organizations utilize new technology to increase awareness and enhance relationships with donors. The rise of social media has changed the nonprofit landscape in important ways. Organizations such as Greenpeace, Amnesty International, and the Sierra Club have benefited from the appeal of social media. Social media sites let them engage interested parties through more personal connections than through more mainstream platforms.

When it comes to organizing activists, conducting charity campaigns, or simply influencing communities and stakeholders, social media offer nonprofit organizations substantial advantages. For example, in 2013 Big Brothers Big Sisters of America used Facebook to reunite program participants with their big brother or big sister from childhood. This use of social media deepened engagement among new members and increased loyalty, interest, and volunteer retention. The project was successful in reengaging many individuals who had prior contact with the organization and retaining them as volunteers in the future.

Many nonprofit organizations, such as Big Brothers Big Sisters, use social media to deepen engagement with stakeholders as part of their marketing strategy. *Source: Big Brothers Big Sisters of America*

SUMMARY

Cindy Ord/Getty Images Entertainment/Getty Images

Brian Killian/Getty Images Enertainment/Getty Images

LO 3-1 Differentiate between direct and indirect competition.

The competitive environment includes the direct competitors a firm faces and the indirect competitors seeking to take market share and profits. The most commonly discussed form of competition is direct competition. Direct competition occurs when products performing the same function compete against each other. Indirect competition occurs when products provide an alternative solution to the same market.

LO 3-2 Summarize the major external factors that influence the marketing environment.

Six major external factors influence the marketing environment: economic, demographic, sociocultural, political, legal, and technological. Economic factors like GDP, consumer confidence, and income distribution influence almost every marketing decision a firm makes. Demographics, including age, gender, education level, and ethnicity, indicate the characteristics of human populations and groups that are used to identify consumer markets. Sociocultural refers to the combination of social and cultural factors that affect individual development and help shape consumers' tastes and purchasing habits.

Political factors result from actions of federal, state, and local governments. These entities enact regulations to promote two key objectives: that businesses compete fairly with each other and that they don't take advantage of consumers. Legal changes, such as new laws that protect consumers against unfair practices related to credit cards, continue to refine the way marketers promote their goods and services. Technological change affects how consumers use products and the way firms promote their products.

LO 3-3 Extend the analysis of the marketing environment beyond the borders of the United States.

The currency exchange rate, which is the price of one country's currency in terms of another country's currency, affects how firms market products internationally. A country's income distribution often gives the most reliable picture of a country's purchasing power. Marketers are particularly attracted to countries with a growing middle class; a nation's purchasing capability tends to increase as the proportion of middle-income households increases. Marketers also must understand how technology can facilitate communicating and delivering value to consumers around the world and how the firm's goods and services fit with different cultures.

Nicolas Khayat/ Newscom

LO 3-4 Identify the major trade agreements, monetary unions, and organizations that affect the international marketing environment.

The North American Free Trade Agreement (NAFTA) established a free-trade zone among the United States, Canada, and Mexico. NAFTA was replaced in 2018 by the United States–Mexico–Canada Agreement (USMCA). The Dominican Republic–Central America Free

Trade Agreement (DR-CAFTA) is a free-trade agreement among the United States, Costa Rica, El Salvador, Guatemala, Honduras, Nicaragua, and the Dominican Republic.

The European Union (EU) is a single European market, created to reduce barriers to the free trade of products, services, and finances among member countries. The World Trade Organization (WTO) supervises international trade. The International Monetary Fund (IMF) is an intergovernmental organization that promotes international economic cooperation and offers a pool of funds that can be borrowed on a short-term basis.

Source: Big Brothers Big Sisters of America

LO 3-5 Describe the emerging factors that influence the nonprofit marketing environment.

The competitive environment for nonprofit funding has increased dramatically in recent years. The number of nonprofits in the United States has tripled since 1995 and now stands at more than 1.8 million. For nonprofit marketers to successfully compete for funding, they must understand the external environment in which their organization operates. Changes to external economic, political, legal, and technological factors can affect nonprofit marketers' strategies, restrictions, and resources.

KEY TERMS

Baby Boomers (p. 78)
consumer confidence (p. 76)
consumer ethnocentrism (p. 90)
currency exchange rate (p. 86)
demographics (p. 78)
direct competition (p. 72)
disposable income (p. 78)
Dominican Republic–Central America
 Free Trade Agreement
 (DR-CAFTA) (p. 89)

environmental scanning (p. 73)
European Union (EU) (p. 89)
Federal Trade Commission (FTC) (p. 83)
gross domestic product (GDP) (p. 74)
indirect competition (p. 72)
inflation (p. 75)
International Monetary Fund (IMF)
 (p. 89)
marketing environment (p. 72)
Millennials (p. 78)

North American Free Trade
 Agreement (NAFTA) (p. 87)
purchasing power (p. 76)
recession (p. 74)
sociocultural (p. 82)
substitute products (p. 72)
tariffs (p. 87)
United States–Mexico–Canada
 Agreement (USMCA) (p. 88)
World Trade Organization (WTO) (p. 89)

MARKETING PLAN EXERCISE • Marketing Yourself

In this chapter we discussed the importance of analyzing the marketing environment. In the next section of the marketing plan exercise, you will analyze the environment you will be entering upon graduation. Your assignment is to prepare a market summary for the job or graduate school program you discussed as your objective in Chapter 1. If your

objective is a specific job or career, you need to answer questions like:

- What is the average salary?
- What are the companies that are best positioned to offer the kind of job you want?

- Are there jobs in this field located where you want to live?
- What is the total size and growth rate of the industry you are planning to enter?
- What is the current unemployment rate in that field, and what percentage of jobs are filled by new college graduates?
- If your objective is graduate school, you need to answer questions like:
- What schools offer this program?
- What are those schools' admission statistics (percentage accepted, tuition and fees, financial aid available, etc.)?
- What are the average Grade Point Average (GPA) and entrance exam (LSAT, GMAT, MCAT, etc.) scores?

- What is the average starting salary for graduates of these programs?

It is important to conduct an honest environmental assessment. Students sometimes have unrealistic expectations of what their first job out of school or a graduate program may be like. The better you understand the environment you are entering, the better you will be able to market yourself and your skills to succeed in it.

Your Task: Write at least a two-paragraph marketing summary describing the environment you will face after graduation.

DISCUSSION QUESTIONS

1. With your current university or college in mind, develop a list of the direct and indirect competitors it will face in the next decade.
2. Assume you are going to open a new pizza restaurant in the town in which you live. What external factors will affect your business decisions? What types of technology would you use to market your pizza business, and how would you use them?
3. Assume you work in marketing for Dr Pepper, and you are looking to expand the brand internationally. You narrow the international target market to three choices: Mexico, Australia, and India. Using the global environmental factors discussed in this chapter—currency fluctuations, income distribution, cultural fit, and technology—rank the countries based on which would provide the best opportunity for

Dr Pepper's expansion. Explain your ranking for each country.
4. Choose a firm that you are familiar with that is located in the same state as your university. Next, decide if the North American Free Trade Agreement (NAFTA) and the United States–Mexico–Canada Agreement (USMCA) have been good or bad for that business. Explain your answer. Has NAFTA and/or USMCA been good or bad for all of that firm's stakeholders (investors, employees, communities, etc.), or has it been good for some and bad for others? Explain your answers.
5. Choose a nonprofit organization that you think markets itself effectively. Why did you pick that organization? What external factors do you think the organization should be most concerned about?

 # SOCIAL MEDIA APPLICATION

Choose a charity that you support. It could be anything from Make-A-Wish to the United Way to your local faith-based institution. Analyze the charity's efforts to market itself through social media, using the following questions and activities as a guide:

1. What is the charity doing to market itself through social media?

2. What grade would you give the organization on its social media efforts and why?
3. Provide at least two recommendations for how the charity could improve its social media marketing activities. In addition, provide an example of a charity that you think is doing a great job marketing itself using social media, and describe what it does.

 # MARKETING ANALYTICS EXERCISE

Please complete the *Connect* exercise for Chapter 3 that focuses on analyzing website traffic from international shoppers.

ETHICAL CHALLENGE

The economic environment has changed in the past decade due to stock market losses, rising health-care costs, and declining property values. As a result, many older adults were forced to look for new ways to generate income after their working careers ended. One of the primary beneficiaries of this shift was firms marketing reverse mortgages.

Reverse mortgages allow older homeowners to tap into the equity of their home and receive payments against its value. Typically, when the homeowners die, their heirs must repay the loan, including interest and fees. These repayments often come from the heirs' sale of the home.

For the past two decades, the vast majority of reverse mortgages have been offered under the federally insured Home Equity Conversion Mortgages program, which applies to people aged 62 and older.[62] Market factors, including the rising number of seniors in the United States, have led to an increase in advertisements promoting the benefits of these programs. As traditional real estate sales struggled since the collapse of the housing market in

2007, reverse-mortgage loans have become more attractive to lenders.

Like many other industries, the reverse-mortgage business contains two sides of an ethical dilemma. On one side are those marketers who are increasing profits by helping older people access the equity in their home. On the other are those who are potentially taking advantage of desperate seniors who may not fully understand what a reverse mortgage is.

Use the ethical decision-making framework to answer the following questions:

1. Which parties are affected by reverse-mortgage marketing strategies?
2. If you are a bank hoping to increase profits, would you try to expand your marketing of reverse mortgages to older adults?
3. If you are a marketing manager at a bank that has made the strategic decision to grow its reverse-mortgage business, how would you go about promoting the product?

VIDEO CASE

Please go to *Connect* to access the video case featuring Task Rabbit that accompanies this chapter.

Photo provided by
Erin Brewer

CAREER **TIPS**

A Career in the Nonprofit Sector

You have read in this chapter about the marketing environment and how external factors influence that environment for both for-profit and nonprofit organizations. As you think about your future, you may be considering a career in the nonprofit sector. Erin Brewer has spent over

a decade working for various nonprofit organizations. She offers some tips for securing a nonprofit position.

- **Gain experience.** Before you start interviewing for full-time positions, get some experience in charity work as a volunteer or an intern. The majority of nonprofits utilize both volunteers and interns, so plenty of opportunities are available. A combination of volunteerism and internships provides the biggest advantage to a job seeker. It shows the hiring nonprofit that you're passionate about helping and that you know how similar organizations function. Some people begin their careers in the nonprofit world to gain significant hands-on experience before making the leap to the corporate world. Others go the reverse route, getting their feet wet on the corporate side, and then taking on positions of greater responsibility in the charitable realm. The same principles of marketing apply to both sides of the spectrum, and the smart professional can readily adapt.

- **Craft an effective resume.** Communicating who you are on a single piece of paper is a daunting task! Make sure that your resume conveys the right things about you. Be succinct, be compelling, be professional, and show a bit of personality. Highlight your unique accomplishments rather than simply listing your responsibilities. Tailor your resume for each job you apply for. Always run spell check!

- **Put your intangibles to work.** Let your charm, gift for the spoken word, and passion for service shine. Once you have secured an interview, be prepared. Anticipate questions you may be asked and prepare a brief description of yourself and your goals. Be ready to ask some questions of your own. (To this day, I won't hire a candidate who doesn't ask a question.) Use your marketing coursework to your advantage by "spinning" your experience to suit the position you hope to attain. Be polite, be punctual, be honest, and most importantly, be yourself. And always send a thank-you note.

CHAPTER NOTES

1. Marie Charlotte Götting, "Number of Sirius XM Subscribers in the U.S. 2011–2021," *Statista,* April 26, 2022, https://www.statista.com/statistics/252812/number-of-sirius-xms-subscribers/#:~:text=In%20the%20third%20quarter%20of,the%20final%20quarter%20of%202019.

2. Julie Jargon and Joshua Jamerson, "Wendy's Profit, Revenue Top Expectations," *The Wall Street Journal,* February 9, 2016, http://www.wsj.com/articles/wendys-profit-revenue-tops-expectations-1455018972.

3. "The QSR 50," QSR, n.d., https://www.qsrmagazine.com/content/qsr50-2018-top-50-chart.

4. S. Lock, "Sales of Subway Restaurants in the U.S. 2015–2020," *Statista,* March 7, 2022, https://www.statista.com/statistics/464277/subway-us-sales/#:~:text=Global%20quick%20service%20restaurant%20(QSR,million%20from%20the%20previous%20year.&text=Subway%20is%20the%20leading%20sandwich,of%20its%20closest%20competitor%20Arby's.

5. News Release, "Gross Domestic Product, 4th Quarter and Year 2020 (Advance Estimate)," January 28, 2021, https://www.bea.gov/news/2021/gross-domestic-product-4th-quarter-and-year-2020-advance-estimate.

6. "U.S. GDP Growth Rate 1961–2022," (n.d.), https://www.macrotrends.net/countries/USA/united-states/gdp-growth-rate#:~:text=U.S.%20gdp%20growth%20rate%20for,a%200.62%25%20increase%20from%202016.

7. Tim Callen, "Gross Domestic Product: An Economy's All," March 28, 2012, http://www.imf.org/external/pubs/ft/fandd/basics/gdp.htm.

8. World Bank, "GDP per Capita (Current US$)," n.d., https://data.worldbank.org/indicator/NY.GDP.PCAP.CD.

9. Jeff Cox, "It's Official: The COVID Recession Lasted just Two Months, the Shortest in U.S. History," *CNBC,* July 19, 2021, https://www.cnbc.com/2021/07/19/its-official-the-covid-recession-lasted-just-two-months-the-shortest-in-us-history.html.

10. Rocky Mengle and Kevin McCormally, "Where You Rank as a Taxpayer," *Kiplinger,* January 31, 2019, https://www.kiplinger.com/article/taxes/T056-C000-S001-where-you-rank-as-a-taxpayer.html.

11. Gene Marchial, "Discount Retailer Dollar General Taking Away Market Share from No. 1 Wal-Mart," *Forbes,* December 29, 2011, http://www.forbes.com/sites/genemarcial/2011/12/29/discount-retailer-dollar-general-taking-away-market-share-from-no-1-wal-mart/.

12. "The Substance of Style," *The Economist,* September 17, 2009, http://www.economist.com/node/14447276.

13. Rachel Siegel and Andrew Van Dam, "December Prices Rise 7 Percent Compared with a Year Ago, as 2021 Inflation Reaches Highest in 40 Years," *The Washington Post,* January 12, 2022, https://www.washingtonpost.com/business/2022/01/12/december-cpi-inflation/.

14. Energy.Gov, http://energy.gov/eere/vehicles/fact-835-august-25-average-historical-annual-gasoline-pump-price-1929-2013.

15. Louis Lataif, "Universities on the Brink," *Forbes,* February 1, 2011, http://www.forbes.com/2011/02/01/college-education-bubble-opinions-contributors-louis-lataif.html.

16. Stephanie Startz, "Hyundai Formula: Inconspicuous Luxury Plus Empathy," *BrandChannel,* September 22, 2009, http://www.brandchannel.com/home/post/2009/09/22/Hyundai-Formula-Inconspicuous-Luxury-Plus-Empathy.aspx#.

17. Jean Halliday, "Marketer of the Year: Hyundai," *Ad Age,* November 9, 2009, http://adage.com/article/special-report-marketer-of-the-year-2009/hyundai-marketer-year-2009/140380/.

18. Mathew Boyle, "The Accidental Hero," *Bloomberg Businessweek,* November 5, 2009, http://www.businessweek.com/magazine/content/09_46/b4155058815908.htm.

19. Mathew Boyle, "The Accidental Hero," *Bloomberg Businessweek,* November 5, 2009, http://www.businessweek.com/magazine/content/09_46/b4155058815908.htm.

20. Julianne Pepitone, "Subway Beats McDonald's to Become Top Restaurant Chain," *CNNMoney,* March 8, 2011, http://money.cnn.com/2011/03/07/news/companies/subway_mcdonalds/index.htm.

21. U.S. Census Bureau, "Older People Projected to Outnumber Children for First Time in U.S. History," September 6, 2018, https://www.census.gov/newsroom/press-releases/2018/cb18-41-population-projections.html.

22. Richard Fry, "Millennials Projected to Overtake Baby Boomers as America's Largest Generation," Pew Research Center, March 1, 2018, http://www.pewresearch.org/fact-tank/2018/03/01/millennials-overtake-baby-boomers/.

23. Glen Kessler, "Do 10,000 Baby Boomers Retire Every Day?" *The Washington Post,* July 24, 2014, https://www.washingtonpost.com/news/fact-checker/wp/2014/07/24/do-10000-baby-boomers-retire-every-day/.

24. Immersion Active, "50+ Facts and Fiction," n.d., http://www.immersionactive.com/resources/50-plus-facts-and-fiction/.

25. Ellen Byron, "From Diapers to 'Depends': Marketers Discreetly Retool for Aging Boomers," *The Wall Street Journal,* February 5, 2011, http://online.wsj.com/article/SB10001424052748704013604576104394209062996.html.

26. Danielle Sacks, "Scenes from the Culture Clash," *Fast Company,* January 1, 2006, http://www.fastcompany.com/54444/scenes-culture-clash.

27. Matt Townsend, "Young Consumers Pinch Their Pennies," *Bloomberg Businessweek,* March 22, 2012, http://www.businessweek.com/articles/2012-03-22/young-consumers-pinch-their-pennies.

28. Richard Fry, "Millennials Are the Largest Generation in the U.S. Labor Force," Pew Research Center, April 11, 2018, http://www.pewresearch.org/fact-tank/2015/05/11/millennials-surpass-gen-xers-as-the-largest-generation-in-u-s-labor-force/.

29. Richard Fry and Kim Parker, "Early Benchmarks Show 'Post-Millennials' on Track to Be Most Diverse, Best-Educated Generation Yet," Pew Research Center, November 15, 2018, http://www.pewsocialtrends.org/2018/11/15/early-benchmarks-show-post-millennials-on-track-to-be-most-diverse-best-educated-generation-yet/.

30. "Marketing Lifehacks for Engaging Generation Z," *Marketing Week,* September 24, 2018, https://www.marketingweek.com/2018/09/24/unidays-generation-z/.

31. Elizabeth Segran, "Female Shoppers No Longer Trust Ads or Endorsements," *Fast Company,* September 28, 2015, http://www.fastcompany.com/3051491/most-creative-people/female-shoppers-no-longer-trust-ads-or-celebrity-endorsements.

32. Elizabeth Segran, "Female Shoppers No Longer Trust Ads or Endorsements," *Fast Company,* September 28, 2015, http://www.fastcompany.com/3051491/most-creative-people/female-shoppers-no-longer-trust-ads-or-celebrity-endorsements.

33. Greg Bardsley, "This Year's Top 4 Integrated Campaigns," *iMedia Connection,* September 2, 2010, http://www.imediaconnection.com/content/27503.asp.

34. Statista Research Department, "U.S. Unemployment Rate, by Education 1992–2020," *Statista,* May 2, 2022, https://www.statista.com/statistics/232942/unemployment-rate-by-level-of-education-in-the-us/.

35. Tamar Lewin, "Once a Leader, U.S. Lags in College Degrees," *The New York Times,* July 23, 2010, http://www.nytimes.com/2010/07/23/education/23college.html?_r=0.

36. Haya El Nasser, "U.S. Hispanic Population to Triple by 2050," *USA Today,* February 12, 2008, http://usatoday30.usatoday.com/news/nation/2008-02-11-population-study_N.htm.

37. Jeffrey Humphreys, "The Multicultural Economy 2013," *Terry College of Business Selig Center for Economic Growth* (2013), http://www.latinocollaborative.com/wp-content/uploads/2013/10/Multicultural-Economy-2013-SELIG-Center.pdf.

38. "Asian Americans," Pew Research Center, n.d., http://www.pewsocialtrends.org/asianamericans-graphics/.

39. Jeff Humphreys, "UGA Report Breaks Down 'Buying Power' by Demographic," *Atlanta Business Chronicle,* April 9, 2018, https://www.bizjournals.com/atlanta/news/2018/04/09/uga-report-breaks-down-buying-power-by-demographic.html.

40. *Adweek,* "Are You Winning with Hispanics?" April 27, 2011, http://www.adweek.com/sa-article/are-you-winning-hispanics-131093.

41. Hunter Schwarz, "Most American Households Today Are Unmarried, and Only 15 Percent of Children Have a Stay-at-Home Parent," *The Washington Post,* January 28, 2015, https://www.washingtonpost.com/blogs/govbeat/wp/2015/01/28/most-american-households-today-are-unmarried-and-only-15-percent-of-children-have-a-stay-at-home-parent/.

42. Alice LaPlante, "When Does Culture Matter in Marketing?" *Insights by Stanford Business,* November 1, 2005, https://www.gsb.stanford.edu/insights/when-does-culture-matter-marketing.

43. Adam Hermann, "Legislation Proposed by Delco State Representative Would Tax Mature Video Games in Pennsylvania," *Philly Voice,* October 25, 2018, https://www.phillyvoice.com/mature-violent-video-game-tax-pennsylvania-legislation-christopher-quinn-red-dead-redemption-2/.

44. Christina Wilkie, "Top Lobbying Groups Spent $64 Million to Influence Congress, White House," *The Huffington Post,* April 23, 2015, http://www.huffingtonpost.com/2015/04/23/lobbying-groups-gop_n_7130040.html; Tobias Burns, "Here's How Much TV Networks Would Miss All Those Viagra Ads," *TheStreet,* November 20, 2015, http://www.thestreet.com/story/13373304/1/pharmaceutical-advertising-ban-could-infect-media-stocks-too.html.

45. Federal Communications Commission, "Unwanted Telephone Marketing Calls," n.d., http://www.fcc.gov/guides/unwanted-telephone-marketing-calls.

46. Ron Lieber, "Consumers Are Dealt a New Hand in Credit Cards," *The New York Times,* May 19, 2009, http://www.nytimes.com/2009/05/20/your-money/20money.html.

47. Ali Breland, "Facebook, Amazon Hit Record Spending in Last Lobbying Quarter," *The Hill,* July 23, 2018, https://thehill.com/policy/technology/398373-facebook-amazon-hit-new-capitol-hill-lobbying-records-amid-heightened.

48. Ben Weitzenkorn, "Disney World to Track Visitors with Wireless Wristbands," *NBC News,* January 8, 2013, http://www.nbcnews.com/travel/travelkit/disney-world-track-visitors-wireless-wristbands-1B7874882.

49. Rakesh Kochhar, "10 Projections for the Global Population in 2050," Pew Research Center, February 3, 2014, http://www.pewresearch.org/fact-tank/2014/02/03/10-projections-for-the-global-population-in-2050/.

50. Raynor de Best, "EUR/USD FX Rate, Up until April 29, 2022," *Statista*, May 2, 2022, https://www.statista.com/statistics/412794/euro-to-u-s-dollar-annual-average-exchange-rate/.

51. Kasia Klimasinska, "U.S.'s Lew Says There's Still Room for China's Yuan to Increase," Bloomberg, October 19, 2015, http://www.bloomberg.com/news/articles/2015-10-19/u-s-s-lew-says-there-s-still-room-for-china-s-yuan-to-increase.

52. Heather Long, "U.S., Canada and Mexico Just Reached a Sweeping New NAFTA Deal. Here's What's in It," *The Washington Post,* October 1, 2018, https://www.washingtonpost.com/business/2018/10/01/us-canada-mexico-just-reached-sweeping-new-nafta-deal-heres-whats-it/?utm_term=.8908113a240b.

53. Export.Gov, http://www.export.gov/fta/cafta-dr/.

54. Aaron O'Neill, "Share of the EU in the Global Gross Domestic Product Adjusted for Purchasing Power," *Statista,* November 24, 2021, https://www.statista.com/statistics/253512/share-of-the-eu-in-the-inflation-adjusted-global-gross-domestic-product/.

55. International Monetary Fund, "The IMF at a Glance," August 22, 2012, http://www.imf.org/external/np/exr/facts/glance.htm.

56. *ABC News,* "Burger King Ad Outrages Hindus," July 7, 2009, http://abclocal.go.com/kgo/story?section=news/national_world&id=6904129.

57. Terence A. Shimp and Subhash Sharma, "Consumer Ethnocentrism: Construction and Validation of the CETSCALE," *Journal of Marketing Research* 24 (August 1987): 280–289.

58. F. Duke Haddad, "Are There Too Many Nonprofit Organizations in the US?" *NonProfit PRO,* October 20, 2017, https://www.nonprofitpro.com/post/many-nonprofit-organizations-us/.

59. Holly Hall, "Americans Gave a Lot Less in the Recession Than Experts Predicted," *The Chronicle of Philanthropy,* April 22, 2011, http://philanthropy.com/article/Americans-Gave-a-Lot-Less-in/127244/.

60. Kristen L. Dugdale, "University of Colorado Foundation," *Crescendo,* n.d., http://cals.giftlegacy.com/egifts.jsp.

61. Grant Williams, "Nonprofit Groups Try to Block New York Charitable-Deduction Limit," *The Chronicle of Philanthropy,* June 29, 2010, http://philanthropy.com/article/Nonprofit-Groups-Try-to-Block/66085/.

62. David Bogoslaw, "Boomers' Shrunken 401(k)s Spark Interest in Reverse Mortgages," *Bloomberg Businessweek,* October 7, 2010, http://www.businessweek.com/investor/content/oct2010/pi2010107_409429.htm.

Part **TWO**

Understanding Your Customer

Jeff Gilbert/Alamy Stock Photo

Chapter **4**

Consumer Behavior

Marmaduke St. John/Alamy Stock Photo

Chapter **5**

Marketing Research and Analytics

Richard Newstead/Flickr/Getty Images

Chapter **6**

Product Development

Steve Schaack

Chapter **7**

Segmentation, Targeting, and Positioning

Chapter **4**

Consumer Behavior

Jeff Gilbert/Alamy Stock Photo

Learning Objectives

After reading this chapter, you should be able to

LO 4-1 Discuss traditional and emerging perspectives on consumer decision-making processes.

LO 4-2 Explain consumer decision-making processes.

LO 4-3 Describe the cultural and social influences on consumer behavior.

LO 4-4 Describe the individual differences that influence consumer behavior.

LO 4-5 Describe the psychological processes that influence consumer behavior.

LO 4-6 Summarize how situational factors and involvement influence consumer decisions.

LO 4-7 Compare business-to-business marketing to business-to-consumer marketing.

LO 4-8 Discuss the different types of B2B customers.

LO 4-9 Compare the different buying situations in business-to-business marketing.

Executive **Perspective** . . . because everyone is a marketer

Knowing her customer has always been part of MaKinzie Foos success. After graduating with a degree in management, Foos spent her early career working in sports marketing and sales at both the collegiate and professional levels. As she progressed from an account executive to a ticket sales manager, understanding what mattered to her customers was an essential component in meeting the customers needs. In her current role, MaKinzie works for the Memphis Grizzlies' NBA G-League franchise, the Memphis Hustle. As the director of business operations for the Memphis Hustle, she is largely responsible for the overall business strategy.

MaKinzie Foos
Director of Business Operations
Memphis Hustle

MaKinzie Foos

What has been the most important thing in making you successful at your job?

Although many factors go into being successful, one of the most important things for me has been being open to learning. I know I still have so much more to learn, but my desire to gain as much knowledge about every aspect of the business is really why I'm in this position. Knowing more than I may need to about a department—even if it's an area that doesn't directly apply to my job—helps me to put the best processes in place and to make more informed decisions. Always be curious and ask questions.

What advice would you give soon-to-be graduates?

Get comfortable being uncomfortable and don't be afraid to fail. When you get your first sales job after college, you are going to find yourself in situations that are new to you. Embrace those moments and don't be afraid to step up to the challenge, even if it's your first time to do it. Be confident in yourself. Regardless of the outcome, there is always something to be learned, and ultimately those are the moments when growth happens. Having a career in marketing and sales is both challenging and rewarding. Be yourself and build good relationships with people. Focus on controlling the things that you can control such as attitude, effort, and being open to learning.

How is marketing relevant to your role with the Memphis Hustle?

Marketing is at the core of everything we do. I'm tasked with launching and overseeing the day-to-day business operations of the team, including all of the sales functions, from ticket sales and corporate partnerships to marketing and the fan experience. I'm pretty much responsible for everything except the basketball.

What do you consider your personal brand to be?

In my career, I've had the pleasure of working with many great professionals, and there is one thing that I have seen that sets the best ones apart from the rest: attitude. Your attitude is one of the few things you have complete control over, and it's crucial because sales is tough. You are going to deal with rejection more often than not, and although you can't control the outcome, you can control how you react to every situation. Having the right attitude and responding positively to a variety of situations is at the core of my personal brand.

Forecast

This chapter explores the importance of knowing your customers and how they make decisions. If you understand why the people and firms buying your product behave, you will be able to develop effective marketing strategies that appeal specifically to them. This chapter outlines the consumer decision-making process, describes how situational and psychological factors influence consumers, and discusses the differences between marketing to individual consumers and marketing to other firms.

LO 4-1
Discuss traditional and emerging perspectives on consumer decision-making processes.

UNDERSTANDING CONSUMER BEHAVIOR

It is often said that people are defined by their choices. If this is true, few aspects of our daily lives have a more profound impact in shaping who we are than the decisions we make as consumers. This statement applies equally to each of us as individuals, as well as collectively, as a society.

Every second, billions of people across the world make decisions. By some estimates, the average U.S. adult makes as many as 35,000 remotely conscious decisions each day.[1] In fact, the average American makes approximately 227 choices each day on food alone.[2] Many decisions—such as what to eat for breakfast or watch on TV—are fairly simple. They carry few, if any, long-term consequences. Others—such as choosing a school, career, or city to live in—are more complex and can have a deep impact over a lifetime.

consumer behavior

The study of individuals, groups, or organizations and the processes they use to select, secure, use, and dispose of products, services, experiences, or ideas to satisfy needs, and the impacts that these processes have on the consumer and society.

To develop successful marketing campaigns, organizations strive to understand how individuals arrive at the choices they make with respect to goods and services. Over the years, researchers have drawn from areas such as psychology, sociology, anthropology, economics, cognitive neuroscience, and marketing to gain knowledge of the mechanisms underlying consumption decisions and behaviors. The field of **consumer behavior** involves the study of individuals, groups, or organizations and the processes they use to select, secure, use, and dispose of products, services, experiences, or ideas to satisfy needs. Importantly, consumer behavior also entails study of how these processes impact individuals and society.[3]

This chapter includes a discussion of consumer behavior as it relates to two markets:

business-to-consumer (B2C) marketing

Selling goods and services to end-user customers.

- **Business-to-consumer (B2C) marketing** involves selling goods and services to end-user customers. Examples of B2C businesses include restaurants, car dealerships, and barber shops, each of which market to individual consumers like you who might use their products.
- **Business-to-business (B2B) marketing** involves marketing to organizations that acquire goods and services in the production of other goods and services that are then sold or supplied to others.

business-to-business (B2B) marketing

Marketing to organizations that acquire goods and services in the production of other goods and services that are then sold or supplied to others.

We will begin with B2C marketing and will look at B2B marketing later in the chapter.

Traditional Perspectives on Consumer Decision Making

The buying decision is the focal point of all marketing efforts. Traditional views of decision making portray a fully informed consumer following a logical, step-by-step deliberation. In this sequence, a person would:

1. Identify an unmet need.
2. Carefully collect information about competing products.
3. Consciously weigh the relative importance of key product attributes.
4. Create a choice set.
5. Compute the optimal purchase decision, taking into account relative price and performance on each attribute.
6. After purchase, compare product performance to expectations and hold those data in memory to guide future action.

Now, think about this process in terms of your weekly grocery shopping trip. If your decision-making process were fully conscious and you were to verbalize it, a visit down the peanut butter aisle might go something like this:

Hmm . . . I associate Skippy with childhood. It's been around forever, so it must be trustworthy. But isn't it loaded with sugar and other preservatives I shouldn't be eating?

Same goes for Peter Pan. Plus the name and logo is a little silly. I am definitely not buying that generic brand. It costs 40 cents less, but in my experience you get what you pay for. What about the organic stuff? Runny and tasteless the few times I've had it. Also, it's almost double the price. OK, Jif. What's that old advertising slogan? "Choosy Mothers Choose Jif." Well, I have pretty discriminating tastes, so maybe that's the one for me.

Your shopping trip would take hours as you cross-referenced all the variables of brand, price, ingredients, and volume for each item. People may adopt some form of this über-rational decision-making process when making their most important purchases. It is unrealistic, though, to expect people to perform such exhaustive mental analyses for each buying decision.

Inside Buyers' Brains

Psychologists and neuroscientists have learned more about how the brain works during the past 25 years than during all previous recorded history.[4] It turns out that the mind of the modern consumer diverges in important ways from earlier models of how people make decisions.

The human brain contains about 10 billion neurons that are wired together in enormously complex ways.[5] In order to gain an initial grasp of human behavior, psychologists and economists of the last century sought to simplify this complexity by focusing tightly on cognition and rationality. As a result, dominant perspectives within these fields have largely ignored the impact of nonconscious forces, such as emotion, on decision making.

However, today it is widely accepted that roughly 90 percent of mental activity occurs below the level of conscious awareness.[6] As a result, many scientists now view emotions as closely interwoven with reasoning processes. Behavioral economist George Loewenstein, who uses brain-imaging tools to study decision making, suggests much of what happens in the brain is actually dominated by automatic processes. Rather than guiding or controlling behavior, he suggests, consciousness seems mainly to make sense of behavior after it has been executed.[7]

Thinking, Fast and Slow
In his book *Thinking, Fast and Slow,* Nobel Prize winner Daniel Kahneman metaphorically describes these emotional and cognitive modes of thought as System 1 and System 2.[8] System 1 is an automatic, nonconscious way of thinking. It is capable of making quick decisions based on very little information. Also, it is good at recognizing patterns, able to answer many questions based on resemblances and associations. System 1 is what leads us to go with our "gut" instinct. Examples of activities associated with System 1 processing include:

- Knowing the answer to $2 + 2$.
- Completing the phrase "bread and. . . ."
- Detecting hostility in a voice.
- Driving a car on an empty road.

In contrast, System 2 is an effortful, slow, and controlled way of thinking. It allocates attention to the effortful mental activities that demand it, like complex computations. System 2 also has the task of monitoring, and if necessary, overriding System 1. Yet System 2 is a "lazy" controller; energy is required to engage it. Once activated, however, it can filter the sometimes-faulty instincts of System 1. Examples of activities associated with System 2 processing include:

- Calculating the answer to 17×24.
- Focusing on the voice of a particular person in a crowded room.

Marketers are utilizing new tools and emerging research techniques to better understand how consumers think and make decisions. Such information provides insights as marketers work to develop more effective marketing strategies. *ARTQU/iStock/Getty Images*

- Maintaining a faster than normal walking pace.
- Parking in a narrow space.

Though System 1 requires little energy to operate, it is prone to biases and systematic errors in judgment. On the other hand, while reason dominates System 2, its heavy-footed, analytical style makes its use impractical in many social settings. While we typically identify our sense of "who we are" with the rational System 2, System 1 is actually more influential, guiding and steering System 2 to a large extent.[9]

How do the two modes of thought influence consumer decision making? Research has shown that consumers' use of Systems 1 and 2 in decision making, as well as the quality of their decisions, are greatly affected by external factors. Such factors include the way in which a choice is framed as well as cues within the external environment. For instance, one famous behavioral economics study showed thirsty beachgoers were willing to pay nearly twice as much for a beer from a resort than for the same brew from a small, rundown bodega.[10]

In the sections that follow, we explain consumer decision making, highlighting the impact of conscious and nonconscious mental processing. We then discuss important individual differences and external factors that can influence this process.

LO 4-2

Explain consumer decision-making processes.

CONSUMER DECISION-MAKING PROCESSES

Modern marketing thought recognizes consumers may employ a variety of decision styles. These approaches range from sudden impulse purchases of a candy bar to spreadsheet-driven deliberations in buying a new car or home. Also, consumers may pass slowly or quickly through each phase of the decision process. In some cases, they may even skip, reverse, or repeat steps. For instance, a harried parent on their way home from work may recognize the need to pick up a gallon of milk and go straight to the closest convenience store. They won't spend time evaluating information about the product or considering alterative retail locations.

For more complex or newer purchases, consumers tend to increase the corresponding level of effort they are willing to put into making a good decision. This "effort" continuum is anchored by habitual decision making on one end and extended problem solving on the other:

habitual decision making

Consumer decisions made out of "habit," without much deliberation or product comparison.

limited problem solving

Refers to situations in which the consumer has established basic criteria for evaluating the product category, but is unfamiliar with suppliers, product options, prices, and so on.

extended problem solving

Consumer decisions requiring considerable cognitive activity, thought, and behavioral effort.

- **Habitual decision making** refers to consumer decisions made out of "habit," without much deliberation or product comparison. An example is buying a pack of gum.
- **Limited problem solving** refers to situations in which the consumer has established basic criteria for evaluating the product category, but is unfamiliar with suppliers, product options, prices, and so on.
- **Extended problem solving** refers to consumer decisions requiring considerable cognitive activity, thought, and effort. An example is deciding to purchase a new automobile.

When consumers engage in extended problem solving, many proceed through each of the steps outlined in Figure 4.1.

Problem Recognition

Consumers "hire" goods and services to help them solve problems. Marketers must remember that without recognition of a problem, there is no need for customer action. **Problem recognition** occurs when consumers identify a gap between their current status and a desired end state. The recognized gap must be sufficient to arouse action on the part of the individual. Their desire to address this imbalance depends on:

- The relative importance or urgency of the problem.
- The magnitude of the discrepancy between their actual and desired states.

Promotional activities like advertisements, product placements, billboards, and social media serve as external triggers that heighten awareness of a problem and differences between actual and desired states. Many marketing campaigns will emphasize how a product or service will improve an individual's life by resolving these discrepancies. Marketers may use either rational or emotional appeals to elevate concerns or alter perceptions of the consumer's existing or potential end state.

In order to better understand consumers problem recognition, companies often conduct market research. The aim of such research is to flesh out consumers' daily challenges and learn the processes that led the consumer to a particular solution or brand to satisfy their need. Social media and online forums are also increasingly used as sources to track customer trends and views of current solutions to various problems.

Information Search

Once consumers recognize a problem, they seek out information that will help them identify and sort available alternatives. Basically, consumers try and find answers to the following questions:

1. What alternative solutions exist?
2. What are the appropriate criteria for evaluating solutions?
3. How well does each solution perform on each evaluative criteria?

Suppose you were in the market for a new mobile phone. Your first thought might be, "What features do I want in a smartphone?" You would then search your memory to identify product attributes you have enjoyed in past smartphones as well as new breakthroughs that you've seen or heard about from others. If you haven't purchased or upgraded your phone in several years, you might also seek out information from outside sources, like friends or review websites, to learn about the capabilities of newer phones and available service options.

On the basis of information identified in your information search process, you would then narrow down your choices. Your list of possibilities shrinks from all phone models you know of to a shorter list of options you will actually consider. That shorter list of brands or products evaluated as potential solutions to a recognized consumer problem is known as an **evoked set** (also called a *consideration set*).

The amount of effort spent by a consumer during the information-search phase can vary based on several factors. For instance, more expensive purchases, like buying a new truck, can require a great deal of information gathering. However, even relatively lower-cost purchases, such as a birthday card for a new romantic partner, can involve extensive information searches because of their importance to the consumer.

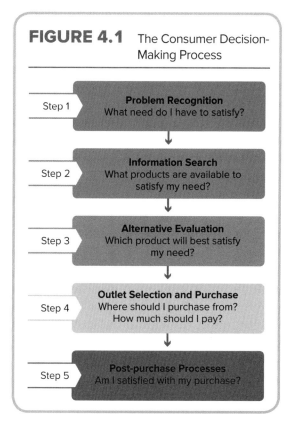

FIGURE 4.1 The Consumer Decision-Making Process

Step 1 — **Problem Recognition** What need do I have to satisfy?

Step 2 — **Information Search** What products are available to satisfy my need?

Step 3 — **Alternative Evaluation** Which product will best satisfy my need?

Step 4 — **Outlet Selection and Purchase** Where should I purchase from? How much should I pay?

Step 5 — **Post-purchase Processes** Am I satisfied with my purchase?

problem recognition

The stage of the buying process in which consumers recognize a gap between their current situation and a desired end-state.

evoked set

The brands or products a person will evaluate as options for the solution of a particular consumer problem. Also known as a *consideration set*.

internal information search

Consumers' use of past experiences with items from the same brand or product class as sources of information.

external information search

Consumers' search for information beyond their personal knowledge and experience, to support them in their buying decision.

search marketing

A form of Internet marketing that promotes websites by increasing their visibility in search engine results pages.

Sources of Information Information searches fall into two broad categories: internal and external search. With **internal information search**, consumers draw from prior searches or past experiences with the same brand or product class. In the case of a frequently purchased item, internal information is often a sufficient basis for making a decision. For instance, you can easily bring to mind the Netflix series you are in the middle of binge-watching; that information will likely influence what you watch for entertainment tonight.

In contrast, when consumers seek information beyond their personal knowledge and experience to support a buying decision, they engage in **external information search**. External search may include any of the following:

- Personal sources (e.g., family, friends).
- Independent sources (e.g., Yelp reviews).
- Experiential sources (e.g., product trial).
- Company-originated sources (e.g., websites, sales personnel, advertisements).

Some individuals find the process of learning about goods and services to be pleasurable. They routinely acquire information for potential later use. For instance, an avid musician may enjoy researching different guitars and music accessories even in the absence of an explicit need or desire to upgrade their existing equipment.

The Internet, Social Media Marketing, and Information Search Whether people are shopping for new snow tires or a trip to the beach for spring break, the Internet has changed how they decide what to buy. Using smartphones, tablets, and other connected devices, consumers have easy and cheap access to product information, virtually anytime and anywhere.

According to a recent survey, more than 80 percent of shoppers research products online before purchasing. Further, 60 percent begin their research on a search engine before going to a specific e-commerce website.[11] Since most customers are unlikely to visit more than a handful of sites prior to making a decision, the order in which a brand or retailer appears in the search results can have a disproportionate impact on the likelihood of purchase.

This "race to the top" of the search engine results page has led to the growth of search marketing. **Search marketing** is a form of Internet marketing that promotes websites by increasing their visibility in search engine results pages. In 2021, global advertisers were projected to spend $171.6 billion on search marketing efforts.[12] These efforts generally fall into two categories: search engine marketing (SEM) and search engine optimization (SEO). SEM broadly involves buying website traffic via paid search listings. SEO improves search engine page rankings "organically" by continuously updating site content and making it easier to navigate.

Many firms also use social media to empower consumers' information search. Social media feeds the discovery of new content, helping brands build links that in turn elevate search page rankings. For instance, online furniture and home goods retailer Wayfair uses tagged images in its Instagram posts to improve traffic to product pages and increase sales.

Social media marketing is not limited to e-commerce retailers or tech-savvy start-up firms. Mainstream brands make wide use of tools like Facebook, Twitter, YouTube, and Instagram to strengthen brand awareness and interest. Ford Motors is widely seen as a social media pioneer, dating back to its 2011 #FiestaMovement campaign.

⬥ wayfair

Juna 28" Table Lamp
$183.99

Eleta Cotton 1
Pillow
$56.99

Camire End Table
$78.00

Acevedo Coffee Table
with Tray Top
$166.00

♡ ◯ ⊲   ⧠

1,727 likes

wayfair Add energy to a cool-toned room with bright red accent furniture. These tables are just the right touch!

Through Instagram shopping, brands have the ability to tag specific products within a picture so users can go directly to a landing page and buy it.

Source: *Wayfair*

Seeking to attract grassroots buzz from Millennial car buyers, Ford placed Fiestas in the hands of 100 social "influencers" ahead of its U.S. introduction. In exchange for free use of the car, fuel, and insurance for 6 months, the influencers agreed to compete in various challenges that promoted Ford's new vehicle via Twitter, blogs, videos, and events. The campaign generated nearly 8 million YouTube views and Twitter impressions within 6 months, resulting in expressed interest from 50,000 potential customers, all at the fraction of the cost of traditional new product advertising.[13]

Mc Graw Hill connect Exercise **4-1**

Social Media in Action

In the early days of social media marketing, many brands focused on attracting as many followers as they could, as quickly as possible. Today, however, more and more brands are aiming to grow brand advocates authentically, by adding real people—not bots—who love the brand and are seeking to engage.

Why this change in approach? Marketers have discovered that growing social media engagement can have a snowball effect on customer loyalty and sales. In part, this is due to the algorithms used by social media platforms that determine which content is shown to users. When one person interacts with a post by liking, sharing, replying, or commenting, that person is telling the platform's algorithm that the content is valuable. As more people engage with the post, endorsing its value, the algorithm will deliver it to more news feeds. Higher levels of engagement also increase the likelihood that others will be inclined to interact with the post. Therefore, building a core group of highly engaged fans can be more valuable than being able to claim millions of disengaged followers.

So how do social media marketers identify and mobilize these brand champions?

A good start is for social media brand managers to always respond to followers on social platforms. Consistent interactions on social media help to create a human voice for the brand and make its audience feel valued. For instance, Wendy's Twitter account has received wide attention and notoriety for its distinctive brand voice, one that includes constant zingers in response to users and competitors alike. In the past, social media managers of the account have picked and won fights with rivals like Burger King, and several of their posts have gone viral owing to their quick wit. In so doing, the brand has created a personality that is well-defined and unique.[14]

Brands may also evaluate their social media audience to identify their most engaged and influential fans. Using free tools like SocialRank enables marketers to sort their Twitter and Instagram audiences into

Source: *Wendy's*

categories like "most valuable" (followers with the most clout) and "most engaged" (followers who interact most frequently). Once potential champions have been identified, marketers can encourage greater engagement by featuring fan-generated content on the brand's pages. For instance, in 2017 Apple launched its official Instagram account to showcase iPhone photography. The company invited iPhone users to submit photos and videos using the hashtag #ShotoniPhone. The account features the best submissions, including quotes and voiceovers by the photographers, as well as the photographers' Instagram handles.

The Social Media in Action Connect *exercise in Chapter 4 will let you develop social media strategies to maximize the engagement between your brand and the consumer. As social media become important influences on consumer behavior, it's important to consider ways to maximize their full potential.*

Source: https://www.socialmediaexaminer.com/brand-champions-social-media/

evaluative criteria

The attributes a consumer considers important about a certain product.

attribute-based choice

Process in which consumers select a product based on attribute-by-attribute comparisons across brands.

affective choice

Process in which consumers make a choice based on how they think the product will make them feel.

attitude-based choice

Process that involves the use of general attitudes and summary impressions.

Evaluating Alternatives

Once consumers have obtained information, they can more closely evaluate alternatives within their evoked set. In this process, consumers use a set of **evaluative criteria**: the attributes they consider most important. For example, when considering a car purchase, you would likely rank certain attributes (such as price, warranty, safety features, or fuel economy) ahead of others (such as headlight design). The type of evaluative criteria a consumer uses in a decision varies from *tangible* features, like cost and performance, to *intangible* factors such as style, feelings generated, and brand image. Evaluative criteria can differ from consumer to consumer.

Consumers make choices among their evoked-set alternatives in various ways:

- Using **attribute-based choice**, consumers select a product via attribute-by-attribute brand comparisons. Attribute-based choice relies heavily on System 2 mental processing. Consumers must know products' specific attributes at the time of choice in order to make meaningful comparisons. Since it is time-consuming and mentally effortful, consumers tend to reserve it for their most important purchases.
  - Using **affective choice**, consumers make a decision based on their feelings about owning the product. Affective choice relies on the immediate emotional response to the offering, based on a "How do I feel about it?" decision rule.[15]
  - **Attitude-based choice** is a selection process that involves the use of general attitudes and summary impressions. For instance, many Mac computer users were favorably inclined to purchase the original iPhone when it came out because they already held such positive attitudes toward other Apple products.

These processes are not necessarily used in isolation. For instance, consumers may adopt a phased approach, in which they use feelings and attitudes to help form an evoked set, then make a final decision based on a detailed comparison of product features.

Subaru has made safety a key selling feature of its various models, including the Outback and the Tribeca. *Sebastien Feval/ AFP/Getty Images*

Marketing Tactics for Influencing Buyer Evaluations In

order to influence buyer evaluations of alternatives, marketers emphasize key benefits of their offering. In addition, they use strategies to ensure potential buyers view those benefits as the most relevant in resolving the problem the purchase is intended to satisfy. For example, a company marketing an extremely fuel-efficient car might explain that you can use the several thousand dollars a year you will save on gas to pay off credit card debt or fund a family vacation. In contrast, a company marketing a giant sport-utility vehicle (SUV) with poor fuel efficiency might tell you how the vehicle's safety features can protect your family or talk about the flexibility it will give you to take more family members on trips.

Hiring managers go through a similar process as they consider applicants for internships and jobs. When you interview for a new position, it is beneficial to keep in mind the importance of this stage of the decision-making process: Employers are likely to evaluate you (the "product") relative to other job applicants (competing "products") on various attributes: college major, GPA, work experience, achievements, skills, and potential for development within the organization. Your resume and interview should convey that the benefits you would bring to the organization match criteria that matter most to the prospective employer. For example:

- If your GPA is a little lower relative to others, highlight your work experience or leadership in student organizations. Emphasize that the employer needs someone with a proven track record of delivering results and leading others.
- If your work experience is limited, highlight other benefits you bring to the table. Stress the idea that your high GPA shows discipline, focus, and high intellectual ability that will help you bring fresh ideas to your role with the company.

Your ability to match your accomplishments to the attributes most important to the hiring firm will directly benefit your search for a fulfilling career.

Outlet Selection and Purchase

After selecting the brand, the consumer must next choose a retail outlet. (Remember that we're discussing the B2C market here.) Selecting a retail outlet involves comparing options based on a consumer's evaluative criteria. Commonly considered factors include store location or convenience, price, merchandise quality and selection, service levels, attractiveness of physical facilities (or website), shopping atmosphere, return policies, marketing promotions, and retailer reputation.

Once the consumer has selected a specific brand of product and a retail outlet, it is time to complete the transaction. To the extent possible, smart retailers simplify this final phase. If transactions aren't crisp or if the checkout process is not clear at a glance, shoppers may feel frustrated and walk away. Many customers won't even enter a store if the line to pay looks long or chaotic. Brick-and-mortar retailers try to use technology to speed up checkout as much as possible: Some invest in self-service kiosks. Since the pandemic, many are now offering curbside pickup and home delivery for items purchased online.

Streamlining checkout and payment is perhaps even more essential for online retailers. By some estimates, three-quarters of all e-commerce shopping carts are abandoned before the purchase is complete. That percentage translates to over $4.6 trillion in lost retail sales each year.[16] If the checkout page looks overly complex, shoppers may not be willing to devote the cognitive resources to figure it out. Also, no one likes unexpected shipping costs tacked on at the end, nor does anyone like to wait a long time for the purchase to be delivered. Offering free and quick delivery eliminates potential friction and helps convert shoppers into customers.

We next look at two other factors that can greatly affect consumer decision making at the outlet selection and purchase stage: unplanned purchases and credit card and mobile payment systems.

unplanned purchases

Purchases made in a retail outlet that are different from those the consumer planned prior to entering the store.

reminder purchases

Purchases that occur due to retailers' prompts to consumers while consumers are in the store.

impulse purchases

Purchases that occur when a consumer sees an item in-store and purchases it, with little or no deliberation, as the result of a sudden, powerful urge to have it.

Unplanned Purchases

Have you ever gone to the grocery store—perhaps close to dinner time—and left with more items than you originally planned? If so, you are far from alone. **Unplanned purchases** are purchases made in a retail outlet that are different from those the consumer planned prior to entering the store.

Unplanned purchases may result from in-store reminders or impulsive shopper behavior:

- **Reminder purchases** are those that occur due to retailers' prompts to consumers while consumers are in the store. For instance, reminder purchases occur when a consumer notices an end-of-aisle display for tortilla chips and remembers that they are almost out at home.
- **Impulse purchases** occur when a consumer sees an item in-store and purchases it, with little or no deliberation, as the result of a sudden, powerful urge to have it. This type of purchase behavior typically results from additional information processing that occurs within the retail outlet or e-commerce website.

The incidence of unplanned purchases may be influenced by a number of shopper-related differences.[17] For example:

- People who consider themselves very "fast and efficient" shoppers are far less likely to make impulse buys; they buy 82 percent less than the average.
- Young, unmarried adult households with higher incomes do 45 percent more unplanned buying.
- If a shopping trip includes stops at multiple stores, 9 percent less unplanned buying occurs at the second or third store.
- The amount of unplanned buying goes up with the total number of categories.

Unplanned purchases actually may not be completely unplanned. Even if shoppers have a list of items when they walk into a store, they often leave room in their mental budget for additional non-list items (sometimes called "in-store slack"). Slack is usually spent on fun, self-indulgent items—things like ice cream or cookies. Decisions to buy those items usually come toward the end of the shopping trip, when consumers are tired and want to reward themselves.[18]

With consumers increasingly able to tune out or avoid advertising in traditional media, the impact of shopper marketing on in-store decision making is a growing area of interest. For retailers in lower-margin retail sectors, such as grocery, reminder and impulse purchases often mean the difference between profits and losses. Stores aiming to grow profits through increased impulse purchasing need to carefully weigh strategic options. They might choose to invest in marketing tactics aimed at attracting new customers who fit particular impulse-buying profiles. Or they might instead opt for in-store marketing tactics (e.g., store signage, displays, changes in layout) designed to increase impulse purchases by existing customers.

Credit Cards and Mobile Payment Systems

Mainstream economic theory suggests that the decision to purchase is independent of how the transaction is paid. However, studies have shown the ability to pay electronically rather than with cash increases both the amount consumers are willing to pay and the number of items they purchase. This behavior is not simply a matter of greater convenience. Rather, brain scans show that having to shell out cash for something actually activates centers within the brain associated with physical pain. Use of credit cards effectively anesthetizes the "pain of paying." Buying on credit separates the consumption experience from payment for that same experience.[19]

The rapid growth of mobile payment systems reduces the "pain of paying" even further. **Mobile payment**, also referred to as *digital wallets,* refers broadly to payment services performed from or via a mobile device, and operated under financial regulation. For instance, mobile payment networks like Apple Pay and Samsung Pay offer consumers the ability to make secure payments for in-store and online purchases using a smartphone or other connected device. Companies are exploring ways to enhance the security and privacy of mobile payments. One promising approach involves the addition of biometric payment authentication tools—typically, using a customer's fingerprint, voice, or facial features, along with a PIN or password.

The advent of mobile payment technologies has also lowered competitive barriers for small retailers. For instance, many students are likely familiar with Square, a service that enables small retailers, like their favorite food-truck operators, to take credit card payments using a mobile device. The rise of mobile payments also has important implications in lifting people around the world out of poverty. It is estimated that around 2 billion people worldwide, including more than 9 million American households, are "unbanked"—that is, they don't have bank accounts or access to financial institutions.[20] Today, wide use of inexpensive cell phones to make and receive payments in sub-Saharan Africa and Asia has helped spur economic development and is making these regions leaders in the use of mobile financial services.

Use of mobile payment systems, such as Kenya's M-Pesa, have helped fuel small business growth in poverty-stricken areas of sub-Saharan Africa that lack established banking institutions and infrastructure. *Sven Torfinn/Panos Pictures/Redux Pictures*

mobile payment
Payment services performed from or via a mobile device, and operated under financial regulation. Also called *digital wallets.*

Post-Purchase Evaluation

Consumers' post-purchase evaluations are critical in driving future behaviors: Their thoughts and feelings about the purchase will likely affect whether they become repeat buyers of a good or service. Post-purchase evaluation is even more important today because of the power of online customer reviews. Such reviews can become critical factors in the firm's ability to win over new customers.

Marketers seeking to influence consumers' post-purchase evaluation often focus on reducing buyers' feelings of unease or remorse associated with the purchase. This phenomenon, known as **cognitive dissonance**, refers to the mental conflict that people undergo when they acquire new information

Whether buying a car, booking a hotel, or choosing a restaurant, consumers increasingly use sites like Yelp and TripAdvisor to read other consumers' evaluations prior to making a purchase. *ronstik/Alamy Stock Photo*

cognitive dissonance
The mental conflict that people undergo when they acquire new information that contradicts their beliefs or assumptions.

that contradicts their beliefs or assumptions.[21] In marketing, cognitive dissonance is sometimes referred to as *buyer's remorse*. It often arises when consumers begin to wonder if they made the right purchase decision.

Feelings of cognitive dissonance following a purchase can arise for numerous reasons. Perhaps you discover that the gas mileage of the car you just bought isn't as good as you'd expected. Or you find out a member of your extended family bought the same car for a lower price. Or you hear a friend talking about how much they enjoy another make of car that you also considered.

Marketers can use various tactics to reduce buyer's remorse. For example, a car company might offer an extended warranty or provide a toll-free number for you to call with any issues about your new car. It might enhance your early experience with your new car by offering free trials of features like the OnStar system or SiriusXM satellite radio. These additional free features typically extend through the first 6 to 12 months after your new car purchase, the time during which consumers are most likely to experience cognitive dissonance. By making consumers feel better about their car purchase, marketers increase the likelihood that those consumers will provide positive external information about the car to other people and ultimately consider returning for their next purchase.

connect Exercise **4-2**

Please complete the *Connect* exercise for Chapter 4 that focuses on the consumer decision-making process. By understanding the dynamics of each stage, you should gain insight into how marketers can affect consumer decisions and help their organizations succeed.

LO 4-3

Describe the cultural and social influences on consumer behavior.

CULTURAL AND SOCIAL INFLUENCES ON CONSUMER BEHAVIOR

Group-based differences and influence can affect the consumer decision-making process; an effective marketing strategy takes these factors into account. We begin by looking at the effect of culture and social factors on consumer behavior.

culture

The broad set of knowledge, beliefs, laws, morals, customs, and any other capabilities or habits acquired by humans as members of society.

Culture

Culture is the broad set of knowledge, beliefs, laws, morals, customs, and any other capabilities or habits acquired by humans as members of society. Although culture is ever-present in nearly everything we do, we are seldom aware of its influence. We behave, think, and feel in a way that is consistent with other members of society because it feels "natural" to do so.

Culture supplies boundaries within which most individuals think and act. These boundaries are sometimes called **norms**. They are formal or informal societal rules that specify or prohibit certain behaviors in specific situations. Violations of cultural norms can results in sanctions, or penalties, by other members of society. These sanctions range from mild social disapproval to banishment from the group.

norms

Formal or informal societal rules that specify or prohibit certain behaviors in specific situations.

Differences in National Cultures Cultural differences can present a significant challenge to firms and marketers seeking a global presence. Marketers must understand existing and emerging cultural values within the markets that they serve.

Perhaps the most pervasive difference at a national level relates to individualism versus collectivism. Some cultures emphasize and reward individual initiative. Others tend to more heavily value cooperation and group conformity. Individualism is a defining characteristic of many Western cultures, such as the United States, Australia, the

United Kingdom, Canada, and Sweden. People in countries such as China, Korea, Mexico, India, and Russia tend to be more collective in their orientation. Another key difference is in family orientation. For example, the needs or interests of a consumer's extended family have a greater impact on consumer behavior in China than in the United States and western Europe.[22]

It is important for marketers to remember that culture is multifaceted and dynamic. It typically evolves slowly. However, current events and global changes can lead to more rapid changes among key subpopulations. For instance, the behavior of young Chinese consumers appears to be increasingly driven by a spirit of individualism, or "what fits me." The behavior of young U.S. consumers, in contrast, is often driven by a desire to make a social statement.[23] As more firms market to international consumers, they must be aware of the unique patterns of consumer behavior around the world.

Subcultures of Consumption, Brand Communities, and Consumer Tribes

A **subculture** is a segment of a larger culture whose members share distinguishing values and patterns of behavior. Identifying the subcultures to which a specific product will appeal is a key task for marketing managers. *Ethnic subcultures,* which are based on shared race, language, or national background, are the most commonly described subcultures. In the United States, religions, geographic regions, and generations are also bases for strong subcultures.

It is possible to be part of several different subcultures at once, each one influencing a different aspect of your lifestyle. For instance, food preferences may be strongly influenced by your ethnic subculture. while your taste in music and clothing may be more closely defined by your generational subculture.

A subculture of consumption is a distinctive subgroup of society that self-selects on the basis of a shared commitment to a particular product class, brand, or consumption activity.[24] The focus of subcultures of consumption range from interests like Harley-Davidson motorcycles to surfing to extreme fanaticism of certain movie franchises, like *Star Wars.* Being part of a consumption subculture requires deeper commitment than simply being a casual fan or participant. These collectives are characterized by a hierarchical social structure that emphasizes authenticity and commitment to a shared ideology that precludes other social affiliations. New members enter the subculture via a lengthy socialization processes through which they acquire legitimacy and experience varying degrees of identity transformation.

Researchers have identified other types of socially embedded marketplace communities that also influence consumer behavior. A **brand community** is a specialized, non-geographically bound community that is based on a structured set of social relations among admirers of a brand.[25] Brand communities generate shared rituals and ways of doing things, a sense of moral responsibility toward other members, and a religious zeal toward the focal brand. These characteristics enhance the co-creation of value by consumers and firms by upholding brand values, increasing members' affiliation and commitment to the brand, and offering managers opportunity for dialogue with loyal consumers.

Some consumption communities do not center their socialization around a singular brand or activity. **Consumer tribes** exist when consumers identify with one another and share experiences *through a variety* of brands, products, activities, and services. Consumer tribes differ from consumption subcultures and brand communities in several important ways. First, while consumers may identify with multiple tribes, they rarely dominate consumers' lives in the same way as subcultures of consumption and brand communities. Second, tribes are playful, devoid of the moral responsibility felt by members of a brand community or respect engendered by the social hierarchies exhibited in subcultures of consumption. Finally, tribes are transient, they emerge and disappear as combinations of people and products change.

subculture
A segment of a larger culture whose members share distinguishing values and patterns of behavior.

brand community
A specialized, non-geographically bound community based on a structured set of social relationships among admirers of a brand.

consumer tribe
A consumption collective that exists when consumers identify with one another and share experiences through a variety of brands, products, activities, and services.

Country-of-Origin Effects

Marketers should also be aware of how unique factors in different nations can influence consumer behavior. The image that global consumers have of other countries can lead to what are called country-of-origin effects. Country-of-origin effects are the beliefs and associations people in one country have about goods and services produced in another country. They can reflect an overall positive or negative feeling about that country or be specific to certain products.[26] Germany, for example, has a reputation for excellence in engineering. Marketers at BMW and Mercedes have capitalized on this perception by focusing on the German precision of their automobiles to appeal to consumers in other countries.

country-of-origin effects
The beliefs and associations people in one country have about goods and services produced in another country.

Social Factors

Did you know that the biggest predictor of the grades of students enrolled at U.S. universities is the grades of the other students living in the same dormitory?[27] Germs are not the only things that can spread; behaviors can spread as well. Sociologists have shown that we are subtly, and often unconsciously, influenced by the people around us—by social networks. A social network is a set of social actors (such as individuals or organizations) along with the set of ties between each pair of actors. By studying the properties of the social networks within which each of us interacts, scientists—and marketers—are gaining new understanding of the social roots underlying our behavior.

social network
A set of social actors (such as individuals or organizations) along with the set of ties between each pair of actors.

Perhaps you are familiar with the *six-degrees-of-separation concept* (sometimes referred to as the *Kevin Bacon game*). The main idea is that the average number of interpersonal connections separating any random pair of individuals—such as Hollywood actors—is around six. Moreover, the power of our influence within a network extends out by three degrees (our friends' friends' friends). Even as personal influence weakens with each ripple, the geometric number of our influence points grows exponentially. As a result, the behaviors of the people near us tend to influence our own actions, much like a flock of geese has no leader but flies in formation in a common direction.

Research on social networks has demonstrated their impact on many parts of our lives. These impacts include our beliefs, our health, our career success, and even our personal happiness. In this section, we examine a number of social factors that help shape our social networks and consumption behaviors: family, reference groups, and opinion leaders.

Family Influences

Family members are one of the greatest influences on consumer behavior. Think about buying a new car and what those in your life might say about different brands or types of vehicles. You might be impressed by the salespeople and commercials for a certain type of car. But if your parents or other relatives tell you about a bad experience they had with that brand, their opinions may carry more weight than your impressions.

The level of influence varies across families. It also evolves as a family ages and as new members join the family through marriage or birth. Family influences are particularly important in some cultures: Family is of primary importance in the Hispanic culture, for example. It therefore should be a central theme when developing targeted messages for Hispanic populations in the United States and throughout the world.

In addition, the composition of families has changed greatly in recent decades to include more single parents and same-sex households. Such changes can affect consumer decisions in different ways important to marketers.

The power of family as personal external information sources highlights why marketers must establish good relationships with all customers. It's impossible to predict how one consumer's experience might influence the buying decision and information of another potential customer.

Children's Influence on Family Purchases   Children often influence family purchases during the middles stages of the family life cycle, particularly in food-related sectors. Marketers at McDonald's, Sonic, and Burger King spend a significant amount of money advertising to young consumers and giving away toys and books with their kids' meals. McDonald's has dedicated an entire website, www.happymeal.com, to marketing to kids through games and technology. These successful promotions aimed at children can enhance restaurant traffic and revenues. However, marketing food to children has become a controversial topic for firms. You can examine the growing concern over the relationship between marketing food to kids and childhood obesity in the Ethical Challenge at the end of this chapter.

In addition to family, consumers typically belong to or come into contact with various other social groups—reference groups and opinion leaders—that can influence their purchase decisions.

Reference Groups   Reference groups can provide consumers with perspective on how to live their lives. A **reference group** is the collection of people to whom a consumer compares themselves. For example, when you start your first job after graduation, how will you know what to wear on your first day at work? You might recall what you saw people around the office wearing when you interviewed. Or you might make a guess on that first day and then ask your new coworkers what they wear to work. In such a case, your coworkers serve as your reference group. Marketers recognize that the more public the purchase decision, the more impact reference groups are likely to have. For example, reference groups tend to significantly influence a consumer's clothing purchases.

reference group
A collection of people to whom a consumer compares himself or herself.

Firms typically focus on three consumer reference groups when developing a marketing strategy:

1. A **membership reference group** is the group to which a consumer actually belongs. Membership groups could include school clubs, fraternities and sororities, and the workplace. Marketers who understand the influence members of these groups have on consumers can target products aimed at group members. For example, a local bank near your university might offer free checks for students or a debit card featuring the school's logo. Purchasing such products might be seen by new students as a way to assimilate to their new reference group.

membership reference group
The group to which a consumer actually belongs.

2. An **aspirational reference group** refers to the individuals a consumer would like to emulate. For example, in terms of physical fitness, world-class athletes represent an ideal for many people. Subway made use of this reference group in its marketing campaign in the weeks leading up to the 2012 Summer Olympics in London. Subway commercials showed athletes, such as swimmer Michael Phelps, talking about Subway products as an important part of their training regimen.

aspirational reference group
The individuals a consumer would like to emulate.

3. **Dissociative reference groups** include people that the individual would *not* like to be like. Teenagers and young adults provide perhaps the most notable example of dissociative reference groups: They actively seek to dissociate themselves from groups they view as "uncool" or as something their parents might be interested in. But dissociative reference groups can play a role in marketing to all consumers. DirecTV has run a series of marketing campaigns to encourage consumers not to be like those who have traditional cable television.

dissociative reference groups
The people that the individual would not like to be like.

Outerwear is you.

Retro AdArchives/Alamy Stock Photo

Model and lifestyle social influencer Karlee Kloss leverages her celebrity as a platform for encouraging young girls to pursue their interests in science and technology.
George Etheredge/The New York Times/Redux Pictures

opinion leaders

Individuals who exert an unequal amount of influence on the decisions of others because they are considered knowledgeable about particular products.

Opinion Leaders Individuals who exert an unequal amount of influence on the decisions of others because they are considered knowledgeable about particular products are **opinion leaders**.[28] Opinion leadership ranges from Stephen Curry endorsing Under Armour basketball sneakers to Rachael Ray promoting a specific type of cooking utensil.

Opinion leaders are not just celebrities. Research suggests that 1 in 10 Americans has a disproportionate influence on the attitudes, beliefs, and behaviors of the other nine. However, the active lifestyles and eclectic media habits of opinion leaders make them hard to reach by marketers. Building affinity through cause-related marketing and community sponsorship is a more effective strategy to reach opinion leaders than traditional one-way marketing communications.[29]

Social media have fueled the opinion-leader trend, enabling everyday people and celebrities alike to become powerful sources of influence. A social media influencer is an individual who has gained popularity and trust among a growing audience of online followers by becoming an early adopter, innovator, or niche expert in a specific area of interest such as fashion, health, or technology. For example, Karlee Kloss is a model and top lifestyle influencer with more than 7 million Instagram followers. She is also a big influence when it comes to getting girls involved with science and tech. She is founder of the nonprofit "Kode with Klossy" program and has appeared on *Bill Nye Saves the World*.[30]

Marketers are seeking to tap into the power of social media influencers through perks and other benefits. For example, credit card companies offer special rewards to customers they deem to be possible opinion leaders; airlines, too, give influencers free flights in an effort to encourage them to use their influence on behalf of the company's products.[31] We will learn more about influencer marketing later in the text in the chapter on digital and social media marketing.

LO 4-4

Describe the individual differences that influence consumer behavior.

INDIVIDUAL INFLUENCES ON CONSUMER BEHAVIOR

Consumers also of course make decisions based on their individual differences. A consumer's personality, lifestyle, and values directly affect their behavior. Firms should understand these influences in order to tailor their marketing strategies accordingly.

Personality

personality

The set of distinctive characteristics that lead an individual to respond in a consistent way to certain situations.

A consumer's personality might include traits that make them confident, personable, deferential, adaptable, or dominant. **Personality** is the set of distinctive characteristics in thinking, feeling, and behaving that lead an individual to respond in a consistent way to certain situations. Around 25 years ago, psychologists converged on an accepted view of personality, which simplified dozens of personality traits into five core factors. Called the "Big 5" model, the factors—openness, conscientiousness, extraversion, agreeableness, and neuroticism—form an easy to remember acronym. OCEAN. An individual can be mapped on a sliding scale of high to low on each factor (see Figure 4.2).

For marketers, understanding dominant consumer personality profiles can help brands better engage consumers with personalized messages, ads, and content in ways

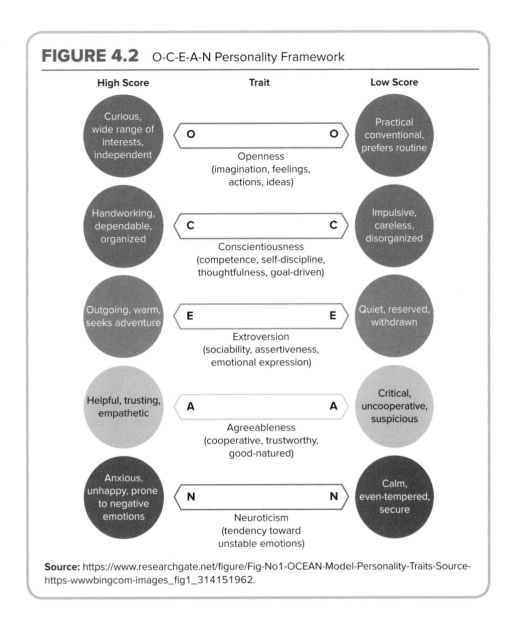

FIGURE 4.2 O-C-E-A-N Personality Framework

High Score	Trait	Low Score
Curious, wide range of interests, independent	**O** O **O** Openness (imagination, feelings, actions, ideas)	Practical conventional, prefers routine
Handworking, dependable, organized	**C** C **C** Conscientiousness (competence, self-discipline, thoughtfulness, goal-driven)	Impulsive, careless, disorganized
Outgoing, warm, seeks adventure	**E** E **E** Extroversion (sociability, assertiveness, emotional expression)	Quiet, reserved, withdrawn
Helpful, trusting, empathetic	**A** A **A** Agreeableness (cooperative, trustworthy, good-natured)	Critical, uncooperative, suspicious
Anxious, unhappy, prone to negative emotions	**N** N **N** Neuroticism (tendency toward unstable emotions)	Calm, even-tempered, secure

Source: https://www.researchgate.net/figure/Fig-No1-OCEAN-Model-Personality-Traits-Source-https-wwwbingcom-images_fig1_314151962.

that are more likely to resonate. This use of personality-based marketing has implications beyond the sale of consumer goods. Studies of health communications have shown personalized messaging positively impacts patient compliance. For instance, we know that matching reminder advertising to individuals' personality profiles helps promote cancer-prevention behaviors, including smoking cessation, dieting, exercising, and regular cancer screenings.

Lifestyle

Lifestyle characteristics are often easier for a firm to understand and measure than personality traits. Lifestyle is a person's typical way of life as expressed by their activities, interests, and opinions.

Fashion and apparel makers, such as Patagonia and J.Crew, have long emphasized lifestyle in their branding efforts. Such approaches have been less common in more mundane categories, like personal health—until now. In 2016, Johnson & Johnson's Listerine mouthwash brand launched a global "Bring Out the Bold" campaign in

lifestyle

A person's typical way of life as expressed by their activities, interests, and opinions.

LISTERINE KILLS 99.9% OF BAD BREATH GERMS IN A SINGLE SWISH. A SUPERPOWER FOR 100% OF MANKIND.

BRING OUT THE BOLD
KILLS 99.9% OF BAD BREATH GERMS

Lifestyle marketing campaigns, like the one initiated by Listerine, enable brands to build distinct positions around global trends as well as the unique interests of their target customers. *Source: Listerine*

values
A consumer's belief that specific behaviors are socially or personally preferable to other behaviors.

Companies that focus on eco-friendly goods and services are emphasizing values to affect consumers' decision making. *Rich Pedroncelli/AP Images*

more than 80 countries, around the idea that people who use its products most are more adventurous than nonusers. A video ad in Asia, for example, shows a woman who "fears no food" tearing into crab legs, dried squid, and crushed ice as terrified fish look on from an adjacent aquarium, awaiting their fate. Another "Bring Out the Bold" ad shows a man who impresses women by cracking walnuts in his mouth.

The insight behind the campaign came from what J&J calls its Spotlight process, a 16-week deep dive into "a brand's core consumers, character, assets, promises, and purpose," said Dave Crutchfield, president, Global Oral Care and Compromised Skin.[32] It included talking with 6,000 consumers in six countries, split evenly among brand users and nonusers. Researchers offered both groups odder, more challenging, or spicier foods. Listerine users were more likely to choose them than were nonusers. Listerine users proved to "have a little more edge than non-Listerine users," Crutchfield said.

Values

Values reflect a consumer's belief that a specific behavior is socially or personally preferable to another behavior. Personal values include everything from a consumer's religious beliefs to a belief in self-responsibility. It is likely that your value system also corresponds to your buying behavior for many goods and services.

By demonstrating the firm's alignment with a customer's values and ethics, values-based branding shifts marketing from a product-centric approach to a customer-centric one. For example, many consumers hold strongly held beliefs about environmental sustainability and various social issues; they favor businesses and brands that promote products and business practices that are consistent with those value. In turn, marketers can design appeals and messaging aimed at demonstrating the brand's compatibility with these consumer values. For instance, Toyota rolled out its "Start Your Impossible" campaign during the 2018 Winter Olympics in South Korea, which highlighted real-life mobility stories of Olympic and Paralympic athletes as well as everyday athletes. The global campaign signaled Toyota's long-term commitment to creating a more inclusive and sustainable society in which everyone can challenge their impossible through stories of determination as well as through Toyota technologies.

Increasingly, many consumers look for goods and services that embrace *sustainability,* that is, products produced in a way that meets the needs of the present without compromising future generations. Nielsen's 2016 Global Survey on Corporate Social Responsibility of 30,000 individuals across 60 countries showed that 66 percent of global online consumers were willing to pay more for goods and services from companies that are committed to positive social and environmental impact. This trend in consumer behavior was especially prevalent (73 percent) among Millennials and Generation Z consumers.[33] As consumers place more value on sustainability, its impact on marketing will continue to grow.

PSYCHOLOGICAL INFLUENCES ON CONSUMER BEHAVIOR

When making a purchase decision, consumers engage in certain psychological processes that can prompt or influence consumer behavior. These include perception, motivation, attitudes, and learning. Understanding these psychological processes can help marketers develop more effective product and communication strategies.

Perception

We experience practically our entire understanding of the world via our senses. **Sensation** is the *physical* process during which our sensory organs—those involved with hearing, vision, touch, smell, and taste—respond to external stimuli. In turn, **perception** is the *psychological* process by which people select, organize, and interpret sensory information to form a meaningful picture of the world. In essence, perception is the way we see the world around us.

The perception process begins when a consumer is exposed to either an internal or external **stimulus**, which is any input affecting one of the five senses: sight, sound, smell, touch, or taste. From a marketing perspective, consumer action arises in response to internal or external stimuli. *Internal stimuli* can be thought of those that originate within an individual. For example, imagine studying for an exam, but you are finding it hard to concentrate due to a grumbling stomach. You would rather not feel hungry, so you think about taking a snack break at the student union. *External stimuli* arise from an outside source, such as a distinctive ringtone, the innovative package design of the tablet you have been eyeing, or an online review about that new tapas restaurant you've heard about.

Consumers today are bombarded with external stimuli every day, including brand messaging. It is practically impossible for them to process each and every input received from their environment. Therefore, they use *selective attention* to decide which stimuli to notice and which ones to ignore. Two concepts closely related to selective exposure are selective distortion and selective retention:

- *Selective distortion* is the tendency to interpret information in a way that fits our preconceptions. Consumers often distort new information to be consistent with prior brand and product beliefs.
- *Selective retention* relates to the tendency for people to more easily recall information that is consistent with their feeling and beliefs. Because of selective retention, we are prone to remember good points about brands and products we like and forget good points about competing offerings.

Sensory Marketing Have you ever entered the lobby of a DoubleTree hotel after a long day of travel, to be immediately greeted by the smell of fresh-baked chocolate chip cookies? If you are like many of its test consumers, this scent evokes strong, subconscious feelings of warmth, comfort, and luxury.

In the face of increasingly fragmented and competitive markets, some firms are seeking to use sensation and perception to influence consumer preferences and choice. **Sensory marketing** is marketing that engages consumers' senses and affects their behaviors. Through use of sensory marketing, brands can create subconscious triggers. These triggers define consumer perceptions of the product (e.g., its sophistication, quality, innovativeness) as well as its unique attributes (e.g., color, taste, smell, shape).

LO 4-5

Describe the psychological processes that influence consumer behavior.

sensation

The physical process during which our sensory organs—those involved with hearing, smell, sight, touch, and taste—respond to external stimuli.

perception

The psychological process by which people select, organize, and interpret sensory information to form a meaningful picture of the world.

stimulus

A detectable change in the internal or external environment that can elicit or evoke a physiological response from an organism.

sensory marketing

Marketing that engages consumers' senses and affects their behaviors.

Shape is an instantaneously recognizable element of any brand. Theodore Tobler, inspired by his native Swiss Alps, designed a triangular shape for his chocolate bar. In 1906, Toblerone became the first chocolate product in the world to be patented. Seventeen years later, Milton S. Hershey registered his Hershey Kisses and turned his plume-wrapped chocolates into a cultural icon. *David J. Green/Alamy Stock Photo*

Two-thirds of our sensory input is received through our eyes. So, it is not surprising that visual stimuli have long dominated branding efforts. Many consumers today, however, are overloaded with visual information. In 2021, it was estimated that the average American adult is exposed to between 6,000 and 10,000 ads each day.[34] In response to visual clutter, companies are seeking to incorporate scent, sound, taste, and textures into their branding efforts. By appealing to senses other than sight, marketers seek to garner attention and build stronger connections with consumers.

Scientific evidence backs up the benefits of brands engaging with consumers through multiple senses. For instance, research has found that different characteristics of ambient sound, such as music heard in restaurants and hotels, can influence consumer mood, time spent in a location, and even spending.[35] In a study that took place in a wine store, the type of music played affected purchases: Shoppers bought more French wine when French music played and more German wine when German music played.[36] Responses to a post-purchase questionnaire indicated that the shoppers were unaware of the effects of music on their purchase decisions.

Olfactory branding is also becoming more common. Smell is the one sense we can't turn off. (We smell with every breath we take.) In one study, the presence of "warm" scents, like peppermint, increased consumer perceptions of power, leading to greater purchases of premium products.[37] Due to the way our brains are wired, smell is also the sense that is most closely related to our memory and emotions. A study led by Aradhna Krishna, a leader in the field of sensory marketing research, provided subjects with a 10-point list of selling points for a pencil that was either unscented or pine-scented. When the subjects returned to the testing lab two weeks later, those in the pine-scented group were able to recall four times as many product attributes.[38]

Motivation

motivation

The inward drive we have to get what we need or want.

A second psychological process that affects consumer behavior is motivation. **Motivation** is our inward drive to get what we need or want. Marketers spend billions of dollars on research to understand how they can motivate people to buy a full range of consumer products.

One of the most well-known models for understanding consumer motivation was developed by Abraham Maslow in the mid-1900s. He theorized that humans have various types of needs; these range from simple needs like water, food, and sleep to more complex needs like love and self-esteem.[40] Maslow's *hierarchy of needs model,* shown in Figure 4.3, illustrates the needs Maslow identified. His theory is that people seek to meet their basic needs (those at the bottom of the pyramid) before fulfilling higher-level needs.

Physiological Needs
For the most part, *physiological needs* are the simple requirements for human survival. These form the base of Maslow's hierarchy. According to Maslow, a consumer who lacks food, safety, love, and esteem would consider food their greatest need and would seek to fulfill that need before any of the others. Many marketers of food products, beverages, and mattresses are often focused primarily on meeting the basic physiological needs of their target customers.

Due to COVID-19-related conditions, many people experienced strong motivations to ensure their physiological needs were met. One of the first issues many came across during the early weeks and months of pandemic was the fear of lack of food and other basic necessities. This led to panic buying and hording of certain supplies. When supermarkets and other

Hyatt Place's scent brand Seamless is now featured in over 300 hotels across the United States. This blend of warm vanilla, musk, light florals, and fresh blueberries has proven to be an integral aspect of Hyatt Place's brand strategy.[39] *Dietmar Denger/laif/Redux Pictures*

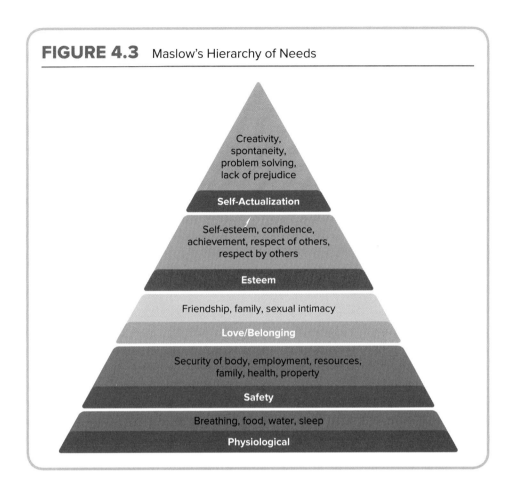

FIGURE 4.3   Maslow's Hierarchy of Needs

retailers were unable to keep up with the sudden increase in demand, the shelves eventually emptied, which led to even more fear. Public policy responses to COVID-19 have also elevated concerns over meeting physiological needs. For example, stay-at-home orders have inadvertently had an adverse impact on individuals' ability to exercise and stay physically fit. Experts have also raised concerns that stay-at-home orders and virus fears are causing individuals to skip routine doctor visits and treatments, leading to increased deaths from heart attacks, strokes, cancer, and other chronic illnesses.

Safety Needs   Once the physical needs have been satisfied, consumers' *safety needs* take precedence and begin to dominate behavior. Safety can take different forms, including physical safety, health, and economic safety. The absence of physical safety—due to natural disaster, family violence, or war, for example—can lead people to experience post-traumatic stress disorder or other emotional conditions. A sudden concern over health safety, for instance owing to a troubling doctor's visit, can likewise be emotionally or physically disabling. The absence of economic safety—due to economic crisis or lack of job opportunities—leads consumers to seek out greater job security, reduce discretionary spending, and, increase savings.

Depending on the infection and mortality rates and trends in their cities, individuals have placed greater emphasis on meeting physical, health, and economic safety needs during the COVID-19 pandemic. This has impacted consumers in a variety of ways:

- During the early days of the pandemic, sales of hygiene-related products such as hand-sanitizer, masks, and cleaning products skyrocketed.
- Many businesses subjected to extended lockdowns closed or laid off workers. As a result, individuals lost their positions or were anxious over their job security.

- According to Mastercard, there were nearly 1 billion more contactless payments in the first quarter of 2021 compared to the same period in 2020.
- Heath-conscious consumers loaded up on vitamins and supplements.
- Due to stay-at-home and travel restrictions, remote work arrangements became the norm at many companies. This led to the emergence of new video-conferencing solutions like Zoom.

Need for Love and Belonging Love and belonging needs involve feelings of intimacy, family, friendships, and the strength of those relationships. Smart marketers recognize that the need to connect with others is a basic human motivation and proactively incorporate it into their products, customer experiences, and brand messaging. Just think of all the advertising you encounter for engagement rings, floral arrangements, chocolate-covered berries, and gigantic stuffed teddy bears for loved ones around Valentine's Day! The dating site eHarmony made its mark in the online dating landscape by establishing its brand as the site for the serious relationship seeker, particularly women. Because the perception of finding a soulmate provides more value to the user than just finding a date, eHarmony was able to charge customers a premium of up to $60 per month for matches.[41]

During the COVID-19 pandemic, observers have warned about the potential adverse effects of social distancing and mandatory masking on loneliness and mental health. But how has the pandemic impacted the world of online dating? With bars closed and private group gatherings off the table due to stay-at-home orders, dating apps like Tinder and OkCupid attracted millions of new users. On a single day in late March 2020, Tinder broke its record for most activity in a single day with 3 billion swipes!

Not only are people spending more time on dating apps, the pandemic in some ways has changed the nature of dating itself. Rather than taking physical risk to meet in-person for a first date, many users now prefer to chat over video first to test out chemistry. Beyond simple video chat, couples are leveraging technology and creatively bridging several apps to create entirely virtual dating experiences. For example, instead of going on an in-person date, a couple might take a virtual tour of an art museum before sharing a DoorDash meal together over Zoom.

esteem

The need all humans have to be respected by others as well as by themselves.

Esteem The fourth level in Maslow's hierarchy of needs is *esteem*. **Esteem** is the need all humans have to be respected by others and by themselves. Maslow described two kinds of esteem needs: lower and higher:

- *Lower esteem needs* include the need for the respect of others, status, recognition, fame, prestige, and attention. Jewelry stores and luxury car makers like Lexus often target their marketing at consumers looking to increase their status or prestige. Lexus commercials often focus on all of the neighbors admiring the new Lexus.
- *Higher esteem needs* include the need for self-respect, strength, competence, mastery, self-confidence, independence, and freedom. For example, makers of foreign language education software market their products as a way for consumers to fulfill a lifelong dream of speaking another language. Their commercials show happy customers who say that learning a new language has helped them excel at their job, increased their mental dexterity, or enhanced their vacations in foreign countries. Rosetta Stone has used this marketing strategy to become the top-selling language learning software company in the world.[42]

To be certain, the pandemic has led individuals to place relatively greater focus on lower-order needs compared to higher-order esteem and self-actualization needs. This trend is clearly evident in both offline and online consumer behaviors. Microsoft researchers examined over 35 billion Bing web searches over 14 months, finding that the expression of basic needs increased "exponentially" during this time while higher-level aspirations declined.[43] This pattern is consistent with consumer offline spending in categories like food: at-home food consumption has sharply increased while restaurant spending has dropped off the cliff.

Despite an overall shift in lifestyles and needs emphasis, however, many individuals have found new ways to satisfy esteem needs. For example, home hair color products have proven to be especially popular as regular salon visits were cancelled due to lockdowns. Gourmet coffee was another popular choice for lockdown consumers working from home; sales of Starbucks at-home products grew at a double digit rate in 2021.

Self-Actualization The top tier of Maslow's hierarchy is the aspiration to become everything that one is capable of becoming. **Self-actualization** pertains to a person's full potential and the need to realize that potential.

When applied to individual consumers, the need for self-actualization is specific. For example, one individual may have a strong desire to become an ideal parent; another may want to become a superior athlete; another may want to excel at painting, photography, or inventing. Professional basketball player Dwyane Wade targeted consumers' self-actualization needs by establishing a basketball fantasy camp. The camp was promoted as a way for successful adults to realize their dream of playing basketball against an NBA star.[44]

Even for people who have secured lower-order needs during the COVID-19 pandemic, many simply re-shaped the ways they went about fulfilling self-actualization needs. For instance, many individuals took up new hobbies, like learning yoga, baking sourdough bread, or smoking meat. A recent survey of homeowners found that 89 percent made some type of improvement to their home during the pandemic, on average spending more than $3,500.[45] Still others sought to make improvements to their own bodies by investing in home-fitness equipment. Exercise bike maker Peloton experienced a 172 percent surge in sales in 2020, with more than 1 million people subscribing to its streaming classes.[46]

self-actualization

A person's full potential and the need to realize that potential.

attitude

A relatively enduring organization of beliefs, feelings, and behavioral tendencies toward socially significant objects, groups, events, or symbols, typically expressed through general liking or disliking of the attitude target.

Attitudes

Another psychological factor in consumer behavior is attitudes. An **attitude** is a relatively enduring organization of beliefs, feelings, and behavioral tendencies toward socially significant objects, groups, events, or symbols.[47] Individuals express these tendencies by indicating some degree of favor or disfavor toward particular individuals or objects. Attitudes are widely thought to be one of the most significant topics within social psychology and can greatly influence consumer behavior.

Of the various ways psychologists think about attitudes and attitude change, the most influential is the *ABC model*. It suggests that the structure of the way we feel about something (i.e., an *attitude object*), is comprised of three dimensions:[48]

- **Affective:** The affective component of attitudes refers to *feelings or emotions* linked to an attitude object, such as, "I am afraid of snakes."
- **Behavioral:** The behavioral component of attitudes refers to *past experiences and future intentions* regarding an attitude object, such as, "If I see a snake, I will try to avoid it."
- **Cognitive:** The cognitive component of attitudes relates to *beliefs and thoughts* we associate with an object, such as, "Snakes are dangerous and gross."

Throughout the pandemic, social media has been overflowing with photos of frothy sourdough starters—many of them named, like a family pet—and the fresh-baked loaves that resulted. *ilian photo/Stockimo/ Alamy Stock Photo*

Advertisers have long tried to influence consumer liking toward their brands through the affective dimensions with tactics such as use of infectious commercial jingles. Nationwide is well known for using celebrity talent, such as Leslie Odom Jr. from the Broadway hit *Hamilton,* to promote its brand using the familiar "Nationwide is on your side" jingle. *Source: Nationwide*

Affective Dimension of Attitudes

The *affective component* is made up of feelings or emotional reactions to the attitude object. It is a classic System 1–type response; it often exists as nothing more than a vague, general feeling. Despite its seeming ambiguous nature, affective attitudes can have a powerful impact on actual behavior. For instance, studies have shown affective attitudes more strongly influence health intentions and behaviors than do cognitive attitudes. Further, individuals may need only to anticipate the experience of affect for it to play a role in shaping overall attitudes.

Think about your favorite Super Bowl advertisements from last year. Odds are that the ones that you remember most favorably offered little in the way of product information. Instead, they sought to improve your liking of the brand through use of humor or by tugging at your heartstrings. Firms increasingly attempt to influence consumers' liking of their brands with little thought toward influencing beliefs or behaviors. Marketers adopting this approach presume that liking will influence brand awareness. They're betting that approach will result in the likelihood of the brand being included in a consumer's evoked set, leading to eventual purchase.

Behavioral Dimension of Attitudes

The *behavioral component* of an attitude relates to someone's tendencies to respond in a certain manner toward an attitude object based on past experiences or future intentions. While actual behaviors largely reflect these intentions, they may be modified by the situation in which the behavior occurs.

Marketers seeking to influence consumer behaviors should be on the lookout for factors that may keep someone from acting on favorable attitudes. For instance, an advertising campaign may be well received by consumers, but if it's not widely distributed or viewed, it may not have the desired financial impact. The relationship may also work the opposite way: Past experiences might serve as the basis of consumer's future affective or cognitive attitudinal components.

Cognitive Dimension of Attitudes

The *cognitive component* of consumer attitudes rests largely upon a person's beliefs about a product, brand, or other attitude object. A **belief** is an organized pattern of knowledge that an individual holds to be true about their world. For most attitude objects, individuals can simultaneously hold a number of beliefs. For instance, with respect to Taco Bell, an individual may believe that:

belief

An organized pattern of knowledge that an individual holds to be true about his or her world.

- Taco Bell offers fast service.
- Taco Bell has low prices for its food items.
- Taco Bell does not offer authentic Mexican food.
- Taco Bell's food is not healthy.

Influencing the cognitive component of someone's attitude depends on altering these underlying beliefs. When multiple beliefs are held about a brand, some are likely to be more strongly held than others. Beliefs that are weakly held are more susceptible to persuasion attempts. Strengthening the cognitive component of consumer attitudes often involves providing consumers with facts or statements about functional capabilities; those facts or statement are intended to change existing beliefs or provide the basis for new beliefs.

While attitudes tend to be consistent across the three components, this is not always the case. For instance, it is possible that someone may hold highly favorable beliefs and feelings about Rolex watches, but not be able to purchase one due to their high price. Conversely, behaviors can occur in contrast to negative cognitive and emotional components. For instance, rather than appear rude, you may choose to go out with friends to a bar or restaurant that you don't like.

⚏ connect Exercise **4-3**

Please complete the *Connect* exercise for Chapter 4 that focuses on Maslow's hierarchy of needs. By understanding the dynamics of each stage of Maslow's hierarchy, you should gain insight into how marketers can affect consumer decisions and help their organizations be more successful.

SITUATIONAL INFLUENCES AND INVOLVEMENT

Situational Influences

LO 4-6

Summarize how situational factors and involvement influence consumer decisions.

Situational influences describe factors particular to a time and place that have a demonstrable and systematic effect on buyer behaiors.[49] These factors can temporarily alter customers' preferences, attitudes, or intentions, leading them to replace their typical perspective with one that is situational. By accounting for characteristics specific to time and place, one is able to more fully understand consumer motivations and behaviors. We briefly elaborate on four situational variables: physical surroundings, social surroundings, time, and task definition.

situational influences

Factors like time and involvement that serve as an interface between consumers and their decision-making process.

Physical Surroundings The physical environment is the most readily apparent feature of a situation. While traditional views have focused on aspects of in-store environments, more recent work has extended consideration of the physical environment to include online consumer experiences.

Design of the physical setting pertain to visual elements, which might include the particular layout and style of a retail store or website. Aesthetic features relate to ambient background conditions, such as lighting, scent, and music or other sounds. Research indicates that it is the overall configuration of these cues that combine to influence consumer response. For instance, one recent study found that "warm" ambient scents (e.g., cinnamon) affected spatial perceptions of the retail setting, ultimately impacting brand preferences.[50]

Social Surroundings Social surroundings offer a distinct set of situational considerations. The presence of others, there apparent roles within the environment, and the occurrence and nature of interpersonal interactions are all potentially relevant features.

The influence of social surroundings is not limited to direct interactions with employees or other shoppers. Crowded environments are common in daily life—think about your last visit to Costco on a Saturday afternoon or Black Friday shopping! When someone perceives their personal space is invaded, they feel less in control and become motivated to protect themselves from potential threats. Research in cognitive neuroscience has shown feelings of crowdedness induce stress and lead to avoidance behavior.[51] On its face, it would seem clear that retail managers would desire to take steps to maximize foot traffic in their store locations; however, consumer perceptions of crowdedness have been shown to have negative consequences on store performance, resulting in reduced average time spent shopping, lower willingness to pay for products, and diminished customer satisfaction.

Time People today feel more pressure on their time today than they did a generation or two ago. Companies throughout the world understand consumers' time pressures, and they design goods and services to alleviate those pressures. For example, many banks have expanded their hours to offer financial services to people whose time commitments prevent them from banking during traditional daytime hours.

Perceptions of time available affect consumer decision making and behaviors in two key ways. First, time limitations restrict the extent to which consumers are willing or able to process information relevant to their purchases. Second, time pressures increase stress, which in turn interferes with memory retrieval.[52] It follows that many consumers will narrow their information search and consideration of alternatives in order to save time and reduce feelings of discomfort.

As a result, consumers are often willing to pay more for products if the placement of those products saves them time. For example, a consumer shopping for a last-minute get together with friends may realize that soft drinks, beer, potato chips, and salsa are significantly more expensive at a local convenience store than at a supermarket. Yet they may be willing to pay a premium for the time savings of parking close, shopping in a smaller store, and checking out quickly. By placing products in a more convenient location, marketers can often increase their profits on individual items while still providing great value to their customers.

involvement
The personal, financial, and social significance of the decision being made.

Task Definition Customer perceptions, attitudes, and behaviors may also be situationally influenced by the nature of the task they are seeking to fulfill and the intended use of the item. One customer may visit Best Buy with the intent to purchase a specific HD television, while a second customer may be browsing in the same section to gather more information for a later purchase.

Task definition may also reflect differences in buyer and user roles. For instance, someone shopping for a small appliance as a wedding gift is in a different situation than a person buying the same item for personal use. Research in this area has shown that the nature of the defined task can greatly impact customers' variety-seeking behaviors, choice of retailer, and product selection.[53]

Involvement

How consumers make choices is influenced by their level of involvement in the decision process. **Involvement** is the personal, financial, and social significance of the decision being made.[54] The study of involvement focuses on how consumers choose which alternative to purchase. Involvement may be high or low. Figure 4.4 compares the characteristics of low-involvement buying decisions with those of high-involvement buying decisions. Understanding the degree of consumer involvement is important as firms develop strategies to sell their products.

Executive Perspective . . .
because everyone is a marketer

MaKinzie Foos
Director of Business Operations
Memphis Hustle

MaKinzie Foos

What advice would you give on building a career in B2C marketing?

Being open to new opportunities and stepping out of my comfort zone is the best advice I can give for building a career in B2C marketing. For instance, I had worked my way up to senior ticket sales manager for the Memphis Grizzlies when they acquired the expansion G-League franchise. When the Hustle launched, I took on the additional responsibility of building and managing the ticket sales staff for the new team. After completing two seasons in that role, I was given the opportunity to take on greater responsibilities for the entire business operation and expand my skill set beyond just ticket sales.

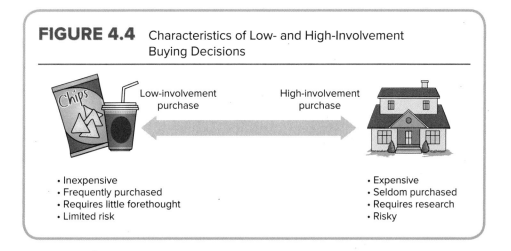

FIGURE 4.4 Characteristics of Low- and High-Involvement Buying Decisions

Low-involvement purchase ⟷ High-involvement purchase

- Inexpensive
- Frequently purchased
- Requires little forethought
- Limited risk

- Expensive
- Seldom purchased
- Requires research
- Risky

Low-Involvement Buying Decisions

Most likely, you have made an impulse purchase sometime in the past month. As described earlier in the chapter, *impulse buying* occurs when a consumer purchases a product with no planning or forethought. Buying gum in a grocery store checkout line or a new cap that you notice as you walk through a mall are examples of impulse buying. Impulse purchases usually occur with low-involvement products. **Low-involvement products** are inexpensive products that can be purchased without much forethought and that are purchased with some frequency.

Consumers often do not recognize their desire for a low-involvement product until they are in the store. That behavior influences the strategic decisions for marketing these items. In-store promotion, for example, is a very useful tool for marketing low-involvement products. Unique packaging or special displays capture the consumer's attention and quickly explain the product's purpose and benefits. Examples of marketing strategies for low-involvement products include:

- Colorful packaging that highlights newly released DVDs for sale at Target.
- Kellogg's signage at Walmart stores explaining the relatively low cost of eating breakfast at home versus at a restaurant.
- A promotional display in a supermarket aisle that features a promotional tie-in between Kraft's Macaroni and Cheese dinners and the DreamWorks movie *Minions.*

Tactics like low-tech cardboard displays found at the end of aisles can drive more impulse purchases than temporary price reductions.

High-Involvement Buying Decisions

High-involvement products are significant purchases that carry a greater risk to consumers if they fail. The two most common examples of high-involvement purchases are a car and a house. Companies that market high-involvement products must provide potential consumers with extensive and helpful information as they go through the decision-making process. An informative advertisement can outline to the consumer the major benefits of a specific product purchase. Residential brokerage firm Coldwell Banker provides a wealth of information about the homes it is

low-involvement products
Inexpensive products that can be purchased without much forethought and that are purchased with some frequency.

high-involvement products
Significant purchases that carry a greater risk to consumers if they fail.

The spring 2019 release of *Avengers: Endgame* generated more than $200 million in promotional revenue, a record for the genre.[55] Much of this total came from manufacturers of low-involvement products, such as fast food and soft drinks. *Sarunyu L/Shutterstock*

Whether a purchase decision is high or low involvement often depends on the individual consumer. For some, purchasing sunglasses is a low-involvement purchase that involves only a few minutes at a gas station convenience store to buy a new $10 pair. For others, the decision is a high-involvement fashion statement that requires greater investment of time and money. *Roger Kisby/Getty Images Entertainment/Getty Images*

attempting to sell. The goal is to help potential buyers understand more, not just about the house itself but also about local schools, financing options, and moving services.

The difference between low-involvement and high-involvement products is not always absolute. It depends on the priorities of the individual making the purchase. A consumer who considers their appearance to be extremely important might view shampoo as a high-involvement item; they might spend considerable time searching for information and evaluating alternatives. If they are pleased with their post-purchase evaluation of the shampoo, they will likely continue to buy it on a regular basis, with far less involvement. If marketers can effectively remove doubts about the efficacy of the product, they can transition certain high-involvement products to low-involvement products for satisfied consumers.

BUSINESS-TO-BUSINESS MARKETING

LO 4-7

Compare business-to-business marketing to business-to-consumer marketing.

business-to-business (B2B) marketing

Marketing to organizations that acquire goods and services in the production of other goods and services that are then sold or supplied to others.

Up to this point in the chapter, we've focused on the decision-making process of individual consumers. Firms also sell and market their goods and services to other businesses, of course. **Business-to-business (B2B) marketing** consists of marketing to organizations that acquire goods and services in the production of other goods and services that are then sold or supplied to others. For example, American Tower builds cell phone towers that it sells to companies like AT&T and Sprint to help those businesses provide service to consumers like you.

You might be surprised to know that more dollars change hands in sales to business buyers than in sales to end consumers. An increasing number of college graduates are working for organizations focused on business-to-business marketing. If you pursue a career in marketing, it's very possible that at some point you will work in a B2B setting. Table 4.1 illustrates key differences between B2C and B2B marketing contexts.

TABLE 4.1   Comparison of Consumer and Organizational Buying

Business-to-Consumer (B2C) Buying	Business-to-Business (B2B) Buying
Purchases made for individual or household consumption.	Purchases made for some purpose other than personal consumption.
Decisions usually made by individuals.	Decisions usually made by a committee.
Purchases frequently made on impulse.	Purchasers often engage in lengthy decision processes.
Many individual buyers geographically dispersed across the entire population.	Limited number of large buyers, often geographically concentrated in a specific area.
Demand based on consumer needs and preferences.	Demand derived from demand for other goods and services.
Buyers engage in limited-term or one-time-only relationships with many different sellers.	Interdependencies between buyers and sellers lead to establishment of long-term relationships.
Most purchases made at "list price" with cash or credit cards.	Purchases may involve competitive bidding, price negotiations, and complex financial arrangements.

The stereotype of organizational buying behavior is that it is a cold, efficient, economically driven process. But business buyers are human beings, too. It follows that B2B purchasers and purchasing processes can be subject to some of the same types of cultural, social, individual, psychological, and situational influences as B2C buying. Several factors, though, are certainly unique to business markets and we look at these in the sections that follow.

Professional Purchasing

The procurement of B2B products often impacts many functions and individuals across the enterprise. In some instances, the purchases involve technologically complex products that require extensive customization or retrofitting prior to implementation. As a result, organizational purchasing processes are typically more formalized. For instance, prior to most major purchases, business organizations publish a **request for proposal (RFP)** document. The RFP specifies what the customer is looking for and describes each evaluation criterion on which a vendor's proposal will be assessed. This helps business buyers weed out unqualified suppliers and simplifies evaluation of competing bids.

In many organizations, purchases will involve professionally trained purchasing agents, managers who are experienced in the policies and procedures necessary to make a large deal. In fact, in addition to a college degree, many professional purchasing agents will complete a rigorous certification program to earn the designation of Certified Purchasing Manager (CPM). In some large organizations, purchasing managers may spend a large portion of their careers purchasing a limited number of items and even become known as industry experts on these items. For example, a professional buyer at Nordstrom or Dillard's might specialize in purchasing the shoes and clothes eventually featured in those store departments.

request for proposal (RFP) Specifies what the customer is looking for and describes each evaluation criterion on which a vendor's proposal will be assessed.

Derived Demand

Businesses buy goods and services in order to produce goods and services to sell to consumers. Thus, we say that the need for business goods is *derived from* demand for consumer goods. **Derived demand** refers to demand for one product that occurs because of demand for a related product. For example, B2B telecommunications companies such as Level 3 Communications provide fiber-optic bandwidth for

derived demand Demand for one product that occurs because of demand for a related product.

Amnesty International says human rights abuses, including the use of child labor, in the extraction of minerals used to make the batteries that power electric vehicles is undermining ethical claims about the cars. *Left: Travelerpix/Shutterstock; Right: JB Russell/Panos Pictures/Redux Pictures*

wireless companies like AT&T, Verizon Wireless, and Sprint. The demand that AT&T, Verizon, and Sprint have for Level 3's services is derived from the demand of their wireless customers. While Level 3 does not directly provide wireless goods and services to individual consumers, the success of its business depends on the buying patterns of individual consumers.

In order to stimulate derived demand, many B2B suppliers seek to actively manage relationships with not only their direct customers but also with indirect customers—that is, their customer's customers.[56] Such efforts can provide marketers with valuable information on downstream market characteristics and preferences, helping them create improved value propositions for their own buyers. For example, network equipment manufacturer Cisco delivers its systems to service providers, but also approaches the service providers' customers to learn about their needs and requirements. In many instances, B2B suppliers work cooperatively with their direct customers in meeting with downstream buyers, helping strengthen trust and commitment toward the supplier firm.

The presence of derived demand can make it more difficult for corporate leaders and policy makers to accurately gauge the social and environmental costs of products and services. For example, the rising popularity of electronic vehicles has created greater derived demand for rare minerals used in the production of EV batteries. But the raw materials needed for batteries are extracted at a high human and environmental toll. For instance, more than half of the global supply of cobalt comes from the Democratic Republic of the Congo, which has a poor record for child labor, workplace safety, and human rights. In addition, a significant recycling challenge looms ahead as over 11 million tons of spent lithium-ion batteries are forecast to be discarded by 2030, with few systems in place to enable reuse and recycling.[57]

Fewer Buyers, Larger Purchases

Another unique factor for business markets relates to size: Business marketers typically deal with far fewer buyers than consumer marketers. However, business buyers usually buy in much larger order quantities. As a result, each individual customer tends to be more essential to a B2B firm's success.

For example, the potential demand for pizza is almost unlimited in the United States. However, the demand for large-sized pizza ovens is confined to medium- and large-sized pizza businesses; many of these belong to major national chains like Pizza

Hut and Little Caesars. Because there are only a few buyers for the large-sized ovens, the souring of a relationship with Pizza Hut might cost a pizza oven maker its entire annual profit. In contrast, a bad relationship with an individual pizza consumer might cost the local Pizza Hut only $20 per week. Thus, B2B marketers feel pressure to offer high-quality products to their business customers and maintain good relationships with customers.

TYPES OF BUSINESS CUSTOMERS

Business-to-business marketing professionals focus on several major categories of business customers, including producers, resellers, government markets, and institutional markets.

LO 4-8

Discuss the different types of B2B customers.

Producers

Producers are profit-oriented individuals and organizations that use purchased goods and services to produce other products or to facilitate their daily operations. They include both manufacturers and service providers, totaling more than 13 million U.S. firms. Producers range in size from large, multinational companies like American Airlines and IBM down to your locally owned dental practice and hardware store.

One particular type of producer is known as an **original equipment manufacturer (OEM)**. An OEM is a producer whose products are used as components or subsystems in another firm's products. For instance, in technology contexts, OEM software is the third-party software that might come bundled with your new laptop, printer, or digital camera. An OEM will typically work very closely with the company that sells the finished product to customize designs based on that company's needs.

original equipment manufacturer (OEM)

A producer whose products are used as components or subsystems in another firm's products.

North American Industry Classification System

Producers in the United States, Canada, and Mexico are categorized according to the **North American Industry Classification System (NAICS)**. This industry-classification system was introduced with the passage of the North American Free Trade Agreement (NAFTA) in 1993. It is used to generate comparable statistics for businesses and industries across the three countries. NAICS divides industrial activity into 20 sectors, from construction and retail to education services. While the NAFTA agreement was replaced by the USMCA in 2020, the new trade agreement maintains the NAICS industry classification schema.

Since each member country uses a common criteria in categorizing businesses, NAICS is a valued tool that helps marketers assess business markets and select attractive target market segments. Each category is fairly similar in terms of its needs and market served. The number, size, and geographic dispersion of businesses within each category can be readily identified. This information helps knowledgeable marketing researchers estimate market potential, market shares, and sales forecasts.

The first two numbers in the code represent the two-digit sector designation—manufacturing, for example. The third digit reflects the subsector, the fourth digit reflects the industry group, and the fifth digit represents the industry. The first five digits of the NAICS codes are fixed for each country. However, the sixth digit can vary among USMCA countries. Figure 4.5 shows the NAICS code for a mechanical pulp mill in Canada. In this example, the sixth digit reflects specific data from Canada.

North American Industry Classification System (NAICS)

An industry-classification system used by the members of NAFTA (the United States, Canada, and Mexico) to generate comparable statistics for businesses and industries across the three countries.

Reseller Markets

Resellers include retailers and wholesalers that buy finished goods and resell them for a profit. A retailer is any organization that sells directly to end-user consumers, like you. Walmart, Kroger, Target, The Home Depot, and Best Buy, for example, are retailers.

resellers

Retailers and wholesalers that buy finished goods and resell them for a profit.

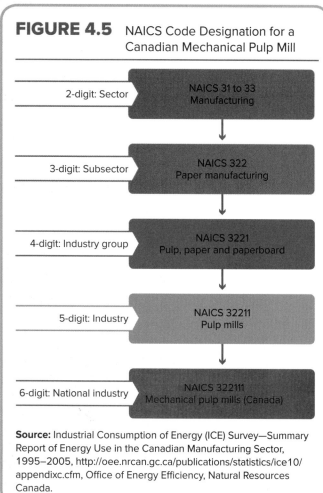

FIGURE 4.5 NAICS Code Designation for a Canadian Mechanical Pulp Mill

2-digit: Sector → NAICS 31 to 33 Manufacturing

3-digit: Subsector → NAICS 322 Paper manufacturing

4-digit: Industry group → NAICS 3221 Pulp, paper and paperboard

5-digit: Industry → NAICS 32211 Pulp mills

6-digit: National industry → NAICS 322111 Mechanical pulp mills (Canada)

Source: Industrial Consumption of Energy (ICE) Survey—Summary Report of Energy Use in the Canadian Manufacturing Sector, 1995–2005, http://oee.nrcan.gc.ca/publications/statistics/ice10/appendixc.cfm, Office of Energy Efficiency, Natural Resources Canada.

wholesaling

The sale of goods to retailers, to industrial, commercial, institutional, or other professional business users, or to other wholesalers.

wholesaler

A company that sells to other businesses, such as retailers and other industrial companies.

There are over 1 million different retailers in the United States. Retailing is such an important topic for marketing professionals that we have devoted an entire chapter of this book to it.

Wholesaling is the sale of goods to retailers, to industrial, commercial, institutional, or other professional business users, or to other wholesalers. A **wholesaler** is a company that buys large quantities of products from manufacturers and then sells those products to retailers. Wholesalers frequently purchase a large quantity of a good (e.g., hamburger meat) at a low cost and then sell off smaller quantities of the good (e.g., hamburger meat packaged for an individual family) at a higher per-unit price.

Traditionally, wholesalers were physically closer to the markets they supplied than the source from which they got the products. However, technology advances in developing nations have increased the number of wholesalers located near manufacturing bases in, among other places, China, Taiwan, and Southeast Asia.

Government Markets

Government markets include thousands of federal, state, and local entities. They purchase everything from heavy equipment used to clear snowy roads to paperclips used to keep office records organized. The federal government is one of the world's largest customers, spending hundreds of billions of dollars a year. Marketing goods and services to the U.S. government requires strict adherence to certain policies, procedures, and documentation obligations.

In addition to the federal government, there are 50 state governments and approximately 90,000 local governments, all of which must purchase goods and services. As the number of services they provide has expanded, their spending has also increased. Budget pressures have forced state and local governments to focus on increasing the value of their purchases.

Because the public holds the government accountable for its expenditures, the buying procedures are often complex. These procedures are in place to ensure that purchases meet the necessary requirements. To succeed at marketing to federal agencies and departments, such as the Department of Defense, for example, firms must complete extensive documentation. For example, Mississippi-based Gulf Coast Produce spent considerable time and resources winning a government contract to provide millions of dollars in fruits and vegetables to the military.[58]

The complex process involved in selling to governments has made some marketers, especially in small businesses, reluctant to bid on government business. Of the 20 million small businesses in the United States, only about 500,000 have completed the documentation necessary to be eligible to sell to the federal government.[59] However, smart marketers and organizations have found government markets highly lucrative.

Institutional Markets

Institutional markets represent organizations such as hospitals, schools, and faith-based and secular nonprofit organizations. Institutional markets can vary widely in their buying practices. For example, a large 600-bed university medical center will likely have a director of procurement and a whole team of purchasing agents. In contrast, when offering services to a small rural clinic, a marketer or salesperson may simply need to meet with a general business office manager or the physician-owner.

These diverse buying situations pose unique challenges for institutional marketers. They must develop flexible, customized solutions that meet the specific needs of differently sized organizations. Educating institutional customers about how specific goods and services can make their organizations more efficient or effective is a firm's best tool for selling products in this type of B2B market. For

Boeing is one of the largest U.S. Department of Defense contractors because of its ability to meet the complex requirements of selling to a large government entity. *Source: U.S. Navy photo by Mass Communication Specialist 2nd Class John P. Curtis*

example, marketers for a medical technology firm could show a hospital how the company's customized technology solutions can reduce costs for the hospital while also improving patient care. All of these different business markets—producers, resellers, governments, and institutions—present unique challenges to firms engaged in B2B marketing. In the next section, we'll discuss several features of business buying behavior that affect how a B2B firm markets its product to various types of business customers.

BUSINESS BUYING BEHAVIOR

Modern B2B buyers expect their enterprise buying experiences to match the ease and comfort of their consumer buying experiences. As a result, B2B purchases may be influenced by many of the same factors described in discussing B2C. However, there are two key concepts that make organizational buying unique: First, decision making can differ greatly based on the type of B2B buying decision. Second, many significant B2B purchase decisions entail the use of a committee, often referred to as the buying center. Next, we discuss each of these characteristics in greater detail.

LO 4-9

Compare the different buying situations in business-to-business marketing.

B2B Buying Situations

While the types of B2B customers can vary, the buying situations for each are often quite similar. Marketers can classify business-to-business buying situations into three general categories—new buy, straight rebuy, and modified rebuy—as explained below.

marketing analytics

New Buy A **new buy** involves a business customer purchasing a product for the very first time. For example, let's say that Dell is looking to market its personal computers to a college that has not previously bought from the company. Since the college has little or no experience with Dell, its decision process will likely be extensive; it may require a significant amount of information and negotiation. From a marketing standpoint, Dell's reputation for meeting specifications and providing high-quality service to its current business and college customers could prove to be a critical factor in selling to the college for the first time.

new buy

A buying situation in which a business customer is purchasing a product for the very first time.

straight rebuy

A buying situation in which a business customer signals its satisfaction by agreeing to purchase the same product at the same price.

Straight Rebuy

A **straight rebuy** occurs when a business customer signals its satisfaction by agreeing to purchase the same product at the same price. B2B marketers prefer the straight rebuy outcome to any other. Straight rebuys normally do not require any additional design modifications or contract negotiations.

Another major advantage of a straight rebuy is that the customer typically does not look for competing bids from other companies. To revisit our Dell example, in a straight rebuy scenario, Dell would work hard to produce high-quality computers at a competitive price with great service. That set of benefits would make the college feel good about its purchase decision. In addition, Dell marketers might also look for ways to make ordering additional PCs easier: Dell might initiate simple online or automated reordering systems through which the college can order new computers without delays or hassle. Marketers who make it as easy as possible for customers to do business with their firm increase the likelihood that the customers will perceive value and develop loyalty.

modified rebuy

A buying situation in which the customer's needs change slightly or they are not completely satisfied with the product they purchased.

Modified Rebuy

A **modified rebuy** occurs when the customer's needs change slightly or the customer is not completely satisfied with the product it purchased. In our Dell example, the college might want Dell to modify its computers to add additional features, lower its prices, or reduce delivery times.

Modified rebuys provide marketers with both positive and negative feedback. By wanting to buy from Dell again, the college signals that it is pleased with at least certain parts of its purchase experience. However, modified rebuys can also be negative if the college asks Dell to reduce its price or modify design characteristics to a point where the agreement no longer earns Dell a profit.

The ability of a supplier to walk away from a modified rebuy provides marketers with an important negotiation tactic. If Dell consistently agrees to terms that cause the company to lose money in order gain new business, its long-term health as an organization could be jeopardized. There are many instances in which top executives, as well as mid-tier marketing and sales managers, are financially rewarded for pursuing short-term gains in market share by reducing prices—and sacrificing profitability. Although there may be times in which this is a viable approach, it is one that should be exercised with caution.

Lowering prices, even temporarily, can permanently change buyers' brand perceptions and their price expectations in the future. Lowering prices to attract new customers also has the potential to negatively affect the level of a company's customer satisfaction and retention, as well as the profits derived from its existing client base. Companies must take care to:

- Incentivize top managers to act in the best long-term interests of the company and brand.
- Negotiate prices in a manner that is consistent with the broader marketing plan and marketing-mix tactics.

With the release of Office 365, Microsoft has made the straight rebuy even easier by offering subscription access to its Office Suite. *Mario Tama/Getty Images News/Getty Images*

Regardless of the type of business customer or buying situation, B2B marketing should seek to create,

Katie Chikonde

Director of Capital Markets
Go Mortgage

Describe your job. I monitor market conditions and oversee our company's secondary department. I work closely with executive and leadership teams on planning and strategy, and make recommendations to improve the business, minimize risk, and maximize profit.

How did you get your job? One of my favorite clients at my old job recognized my talent and offered me the position.

What has been the most important thing in making you successful at your job? Taking action—executing on plans and strategy. Action must meet intention, you can plan all you want but if you don't take action you're in the same place you started.

Jay Cupcake Photography

What advice would you give soon-to-be graduates? Find what interests you, get started somewhere, work hard, don't be afraid of looking dumb or failing, know your worth, be authentic, trust yourself!

What do you consider your personal brand to be? Business professional specializing in data analytics, secondary marketing, and pipeline risk management. I can implement effective strategies at any level. I like to focus on simplification and efficiency to streamline activities and achieve goals.

communicate, and deliver value to customers in a way that is ultimately profitable, just as marketers would with individual consumers.

Buying Centers

buying center

The group of people within an organization who are involved in a purchase decision.

A **buying center** is the group of people within an organization who are involved in a purchase decision. In most instances, the buying center will consist of individuals from various areas of the firm, such as accounting, engineering, operations, and marketing. They will meet specifically to evaluate options and make a purchase decision. The size and makeup of the buying center will depend on the magnitude, complexity, and importance of the purchase decision. As the level of each increases, the buying center will involve more personnel from a wider variety of functional areas and organizational levels.

Within the buying center, individuals perform one or more informally prescribed roles:[60]

- The *initiator* is the individual who first suggests making the purchase.
- *Influencers* are people who influence the decision. They often define technical specifications and provide information for evaluating options.
- *Gatekeepers* regulate the flow of information and access to other members of the buying center. Purchasing agents derive much of their power within the buying center through the gatekeeping role.
- The *decider* is the person who has the formal or informal power to approve selection of the supplier or brand.
- The *purchaser* is the person who actually negotiates the terms of the purchase.
- *Users* are members of the organization who will actually end up using the product.

B2B marketers and salespeople should identify the roles of the buying center's members. With that information, marketers can determine each member's relative influence and be able to craft more effective marketing strategies. Be aware that in some instances, the buying process can be drawn out. In such cases, the influence of buying center members may grow or decrease over time. For instance, senior executives may drop out during the middle stages, only to reemerge later to oversee the deal closing.

SUMMARY

ARTQU/
iStock/Getty
Images

LO 4-1 Discuss traditional and emerging perspectives on consumer decision-making processes.

Consumer behavior is the study of individuals, groups, or organizations and the processes they use to select, secure, use, and dispose of products, services, experiences, or ideas to satisfy needs. Traditional views of consumer decision making portray a highly informed, logically minded consumer following a deliberate, step-by-step sequence. Research has shown, though, that the decision-making process of the modern consumer does not strictly conform to that traditional model of how people make (or *should* make) decisions. Rather, much of what guides decision-making processes is dominated by fairly automatic processes.

Source:
Wayfair

LO 4-2 Explain consumer decision-making processes.

The consumer decision-making process has five stages: (1) the consumer recognizes a need to satisfy or a problem to solve; (2) he or she seeks information; (3) the consumer evaluates the alternatives; (4) the consumer selects the purchase outlet and buys a product; and (5) the consumer evaluates his or her purchase.

The process does not always occur in the orderly stages discussed. Marketers should not assume that success at one stage of the process guarantees success at the next. Numerous situational influences can occur at various points in the process to change the path taken by any customer.

Retro AdArchives/Alamy Stock Photo

LO 4-3 Describe the cultural and social influences on consumer behavior.

Culture is the broad set of knowledge, beliefs, laws, morals, customs, and any other capabilities or habits acquired by humans as members of society. Culture supplies boundaries, called *norms,* within which most individuals think and act. Marketers must understand both the existing and emerging cultural values within the societies that they serve. Those values differ by *subcultures* within countries and by nations. The image that global consumers have of other countries can lead to *country-of-origin effects* for products from other countries.

Social factors develop from a consumer's relationships with others and have a significant impact on consumer behavior. These social factors include family influences, reference groups, and opinion leaders. Different family members can deeply influence various consumption choices. *Reference groups,* the people to whom consumers compare themselves, can influence purchasing behavior. Likewise, *opinion leaders* exert broad public influence on people's decisions.

Rich Pedroncelli/ AP Images

LO 4-4 Describe the individual differences that influence consumer behavior.

Consumers also make decisions based on personal factors, such as personality, lifestyle, and values. *Lifestyle characteristic*s are often easier for a firm to understand and measure than *personality traits. Values* reflect a consumer's very personal beliefs about socially or personally preferable behaviors, and are often seen in a person's buying behavior. *Sustainability* is one such value.

David J. Green/ Alamy Stock Photo

LO 4-5 Describe the psychological processes that influence consumer behavior.

Psychological processes that influence consumer behavior include perception, motivation, attitude, and learning. *Perception* is the psychological process by which people select, organize, and interpret sensory information to form a meaningful picture of the world. *Sensory marketing* attempts to affect consumer behavior by engaging consumers' senses.

Motivation is the inward drive we have to get what we need. One useful model in understanding consumer motivation is Abraham Maslow's hierarchy of needs model. It theorizes that consumers will seek to meet their lower-level needs (e.g., physiological and safety) before they begin fulfilling higher-level needs (e.g., belonging, esteem, and self-actualization).

Attitude is a person's overall evaluation of an object involving general feelings of like or dislike. The *ABC model* suggests three dimensions of attitude: affective, behavioral, and

cognitive. *Learning* refers to behavior modifications that result from repeated experiences.

Sarunyu L/Shutterstock

LO 4-6 Summarize how situational factors influence consumer decisions.

Time considerations, especially in today's time-starved society, often affect what consumers buy. The amount of time involved in a purchase can also affect what a consumer is willing to pay.

Involvement is the personal, financial, and social significance of the decision being made. *Impulse buying* is the purchase of a product with no planning or forethought. It usually occurs with *low-involvement products;* they are typically inexpensive, purchased with some frequency, and with little forethought. *High-involvement products* include more significant purchases that carry a greater risk to consumers if they fail. The difference between low-involvement and high-involvement products is not always absolute and depends on the priorities of the individual consumer.

Travelerpix/ Shutterstock

LO 4-7 Compare business-to-business marketing to business-to-consumer marketing.

Business-to-business (B2B) marketing consists of marketing to organizations that acquire goods and services in the production of other goods and services that are then sold or supplied to others. Business-to-business marketers face many of the same challenges as marketers to individual consumers. B2B marketers are affected by several factors unique to business markets: professional purchasing, *derived demand,* and fewer buyers.

Source: U.S. Navy photo by Mass Communication Specialist 2nd Class John P. Curtis

LO 4-8 Discuss the different types of B2B customers.

There are several major categories of B2B customers: *Producers* are profit-oriented individuals and organizations that use purchased goods and services to produce other products or to facilitate their daily operations. They include both manufacturers and service providers. One particular type of producer is known as an *original equipment manufacturer (OEM),* whose products are used as components or subsystems in another firm's products. Producers In North America are categorized according to the *North American Industry Classification System (NAICS),* an industry-classification system used by the members of USMCA trade agreement.

Another type of B2B customer is *resellers,* which includes retailers and wholesalers that buy finished goods and resell them for a profit. A *retailer* is a company that sells mainly to end-user consumers. A *wholesaler* is a company that buys large quantities of products from manufacturers and then sells those products to retailers.

A third category of B2B customers is *government markets,* consisting of the federal government, 50 state governments, and approximately 90,000 local governments, all of which must purchase goods and services. Buying procedures in government markets are often complex because of the need for accountability to the public.

A fourth category of B2B customers is institutional markets. *Institutional markets* represent organizations such as hospitals, schools, churches, and other nonprofit organizations. Institutional markets can vary widely in their buying practices, depending on the size of the institution.

Mario Tama/Getty Images News/Getty Images

LO 4-9 Compare the different buying situations in business-to-business marketing.

Marketers can classify B2B buying situations into three general categories: A *new buy* involves a business customer purchasing a product for the very first time. A *straight rebuy* occurs when a business customer signals its satisfaction by agreeing to purchase the same product at the same price. A *modified rebuy* occurs when the customer's needs change slightly or they are not completely satisfied with the product they purchased.

KEY TERMS

affective choice (p. 110)
aspirational reference group (p. 117)
attitude (p. 125)
attitude-based choice (p. 110)
attribute-based choice (p. 110)
belief (p. 126)
brand community (p. 115)
business-to-business (B2B)
    marketing (p. 104, 130)
business-to-consumer (B2C)
    marketing (p. 104)
buying center (p. 138)
cognitive dissonance (p. 113)
consumer behavior (p. 104)
consumer tribe (p. 115)
country-of-origin effects (p. 116)
culture (p. 114)
derived demand (p. 131)
dissociative reference
    groups (p. 117)
esteem (p. 124)
evaluative criteria (p. 110)

evoked set (p. 107)
extended problem solving (p. 106)
external information search (p. 108)
habitual decision making (p. 106)
high-involvement products (p. 129)
impulse purchases (p. 112)
internal information search (p. 108)
involvement (p. 128)
lifestyle (p. 119)
limited problem solving (p. 106)
low-involvement products (p. 129)
membership reference group (p. 117)
mobile payment (p. 113)
modified rebuy (p. 136)
motivation (p. 122)
new buy (p. 135)
norms (p. 114)
North American Industry Classification
    System (NAICS) (p. 133)
opinion leaders (p. 118)
original equipment manufacturer
    (OEM) (p. 133)

perception (p. 121)
personality (p. 118)
problem recognition (p. 107)
reference group (p. 117)
reminder purchases (p. 112)
request for proposal (RFP) (p. 131)
resellers (p. 133)
search marketing (p. 108)
self-actualization (p. 125)
sensation (p. 121)
sensory marketing (p. 121)
situational influences (p. 127)
social network (p. 116)
stimulus (p. 121)
straight rebuy (p. 136)
subculture (p. 115)
unplanned purchases (p. 112)
values (p. 120)
wholesaler (p. 134)
wholesaling (p. 134)

MARKETING PLAN EXERCISE • Marketing Yourself

In this chapter we discussed the differences between consumer and business markets. In the next section of the marketing plan exercise, you will evaluate the characteristics of each and decide which may be better for you as a career choice.

Your assignment for this chapter is to decide whether you would prefer to have a career in a B2B or a B2C organization. Think through each type of organization carefully, and assess which better fits your personality. Finding a good fit will affect your ability to excel at and enjoy your career after college. Also, this knowledge will help you focus your job search, whether you want to work in marketing, finance, human resources, or any other area of the organization.

Many professionals end up working in both B2B and B2C organizations over the course of their careers. You too will likely have many opportunities to move from one to the other in the future. However, the additional focus will help you build a career that can put you ahead of your fellow graduates.

Your Task: Write a one-paragraph summary explaining whether you would prefer to work in a B2C or B2B organization. Discuss what organizational characteristics affected your decision. Conclude your paragraph with the names of three potential employers in the area where you would most want to live that focus on your chosen market.

DISCUSSION QUESTIONS

1. Think of a recent purchase you have made and describe the actions you took at each stage of the consumer decision-making process. Did you skip any of the stages? Which stage do you think should be most important to marketers? Does it depend on what type of product is being marketed?

2. Which of the situational influences described in this chapter influence your buying decisions most? Explain your answer.

3. List two high-involvement purchases you have made in the past year. What made them high involvement to you?

4. Describe how derived demand might affect a college campus bookstore.

5. Pick a company that you or someone in your family has worked for. Then go to the NAICS website at http://www.census.gov/naics/ and figure out the full six-figure NAICS code for that company. What are two other companies with the same code? How can this information be valuable to a small business marketer?

 # SOCIAL MEDIA APPLICATION

Pick a company that you would like to work for after graduation and assume that you have been asked to interview there for a job next month. Analyze how social media can help you prepare for your interview using the following questions and activities as a guide:

1. Go onto the firm's social media platforms and find at least two helpful pieces of information that you can use in your interview that cannot be found on the organization's general website.

2. In addition to the organization's social media platforms, do the executives or managers of the firm actively engage through social media? If so, are there useful pieces of information (such as Facebook posts or tweets) that can help give you an advantage over others competing for the same job?

3. What are two things you can do with your own social media presence to better position yourself for the interview?

 # MARKETING ANALYTICS EXERCISE

Please complete the *Connect* exercise for Chapter 4 that focuses on using marketing analytics to calculate profits of different B2B buying situations.

ETHICAL CHALLENGE

For parents trying to promote healthy eating habits, online sales pitches are potentially leading to problems for their families, according to a study by the Center for Digital Democracy and American University. The center released a report detailing how companies market low-nutrient foods online to young consumers. These campaigns market to kids using everything from avatars in virtual worlds to web sweepstakes and interactive games. The report's authors suggest that marketing to kids that are spending larger chunks of time online encourages them to make poor food choices, contributing to childhood obesity and diet-related health problems.

Thanks to advertisements, many kids and their friends see fast-food restaurants as a fantastic place. They know about the toys and the characters associated with each, making it difficult to explain why parents won't let the family eat there more than once a month.

Food advertising is a central part of many of the free, ad-supported online services offered to kids. Part of the reason is that advertisers know that food, like toys, is an area where kids have both purchasing power and sway over their parents' decisions. Kids between ages 4 and 12 directly impact over $30 billion annually in sales, according to Juliet Schor, coauthor of *Born to Buy: The Commercialized Child and the New Consumer Culture.*

Brands are also implanting their logos where kids spend most of their time, such as with items in virtual worlds. Companies are drawing kids to their heavily branded sites in a variety of ways from interactive games to music competitions. The report cites Kellogg's promotion of its Pop-Tarts pastries on Habbo Hotel, an online virtual community aimed at kids and teens. In exchange for answering a poll asking kids 13 and over to pick the Pop-Tart flavor most like them, respondents were entered to receive virtual furniture for their avatars. There is a law, the Children's Online Privacy Protection Act, that prevents companies from collecting information on kids in order to target ads more directly to them.

Many companies cite additional internal practices they have adopted in order to address concerns about marketing to kids. Kraft includes logos on web pages to encourage kids to go offline and do something active. Both McDonald's and Kellogg's say they are working on industry self-regulation initiatives. The General Mills Foundation has provided $7.5 million in Champions for Healthy Kids grants to 650 nonprofit organizations across the United States to support grassroots projects promoting healthy eating and active lifestyles for children and their families.

The FTC could decide that more brands have to promote vegetables and other healthy foods on their sites, regardless of whether they sell them or not. Or it could leave the industry to regulate itself, in the hope that brands, wary of angering parents, will limit ads for less-healthy alternatives.

Please use the ethical decision-making framework to complete the following activities:

1. Analyze McDonald's efforts to market Happy Meals that contain free toys to children.
2. Find a company or organization that you think is using online marketing tools to reduce the trend in childhood obesity. List the website and describe what the company is doing to lessen childhood obesity in the United States.
3. Can online marketers promote healthy choices and still be profitable? Explain your reasoning and provide examples for why or why not.

Source: Catherine Holahan, "Is Online Marketing Making Kids Obese?" *Bloomberg Businessweek,* May 17, 2007, http://www.businessweek.com/stories/2007-05-17/is-online-marketing-making-kids-obese-businessweek-business-news-stock-market-and-financial-advice.

VIDEO CASE

Please go to *Connect* to access the video case that accompanies this chapter.

PODCAST

Please go to Connect to access the podcast that accompanies this chapter.

Photo provided by Tracey Rogers

CAREER **TIPS**

Media Marketing

You have read in this chapter about the importance of understanding what drives purchase decisions for both individual consumers and organizations. Whether your passion is working in a B2C or B2B world, media marketing can be a very rewarding career. As you consider your future, Tracey Rogers, General Manager for television station WKRN in Nashville, TN, offers some tips that have helped her achieve success in the field of media marketing.

- **Love what you do.** If you do not have passion for a job, it is doubtful that the money you get paid will ever be enough to make you happy. I have found consistently that the best people I hire are people who truly want to be here and enjoy what they do. You have your whole lives ahead of you to work, so make sure you pursue something you are passionate about.
- **Know your audience.** When you are on the job hunt, you should know who your target audience is. You are typically trying to impress people who are older than you and established in their careers. They will often expect certain things from you

during the interview process. These range from large things, like a demonstration of what you know about the company, to small things, like whether your attire is suitable. The better you understand what potential employers expect, the better you will be able to position yourself to win the job.

- **Learn every aspect of media marketing.** The more versatile you are, the more attractive you will be as a team member. Look to develop different skills. If you want to work on the more creative aspects of media marketing, a job in sales is often a great way to get your foot in the door.
- **Pay your dues.** Take on all the tasks that are offered and view every one as an opportunity. Too many young professionals want to stay within the box of their job description. In media marketing,

there is always a new challenge or emerging technology that offers opportunities for those who are not afraid to take them on. Some of the best moves of my career occurred when I took on challenges that others did not want and made an impact that my managers noticed. Look for ways to expand your job and you can impress more people.

- **Be a cheerleader for those around you.** This is a lost art in most media companies. We have way too many people who want to take all of the credit and deflect the blame to others. As a manager, I can tell you that this act gets old very fast. A positive person who is great at what he or she does and can also help and support others will increase the odds of being noticed, respected, and promoted to higher levels of the organization.

CHAPTER NOTES

1. Richard Feenstra, "How Many Decisions Does a Person Make in an Average Day?" *Quora,* October 12, 2017, https://www.quora.com/How-many-decisions-does-a-person-make-in-an-average-day.
2. Brian Wansink and Jeffrey Sobal, "Mindless Eating: The 200 Daily Food Decisions We Overlook," *Environment and Behavior* 39, no. 1 (2007): 106–123.
3. D. I. Hawkins and D. L. Mothersbaugh, *Consumer Behavior: Building Marketing Strategy,* 12th ed. (New York: McGraw-Hill, 2013).
4. Antonio Damasio, "How the Brain Creates the Mind," *Scientific American* 12, no. 1 (2002): 4.
5. J. LeDoux, *The Emotional Brain: The Mysterious Underpinnings of Emotional Life* (New York: Simon & Schuster, 1998).
6. J. LeDoux, *The Emotional Brain: The Mysterious Underpinnings of Emotional Life* (New York: Simon & Schuster, 1998); S. Pinker, How the Mind Works (New York: Norton, 1997).
7. George Loewenstein, "The Creative Destruction of Decision Research," *Journal of Consumer Research* 28, no. 3 (2001): 499–505.
8. Daniel Kahneman, *Thinking, Fast and Slow* (New York: Farrar, Straus and Giroux, 2011).
9. Daniel Kahneman, *Thinking, Fast and Slow* (New York: Farrar, Straus and Giroux, 2011).
10. Richard Thaler, "Toward a Positive Theory of Consumer Choice," *Journal of Economic Behavior and Organization* 1, no. 1 (1980): 39–60.
11. SalesLion, "81% of Shoppers Research Their Product Online Before Purchasing," (n.d.), https://transaction.agency/ecommerce-statistics/81-of-shoppers-research-their-product-online-before-purchasing/#:~:text=Statistic%20Info&text=According%20to%20the%20study%2C%2081,before%20making%20a%20major%20purchase.
12. Greg Sterling, "IAB: Search, the Largest Category of Digital Ad Spending, Generated $40.6B in 2017," *SearchEngineLand.com,* 2018, https://searchengine-land.com/iab-search-the-largest-category-of-digital-ad-spending-generated-40-6b-in-2017-298010.
13. Bradford Wernle, "Scott Monty, Ford's Social Media Pioneer, Leaves Company," *Ad Age,* published on May 20, 2014. https://adage.com/article/cmo-strategy/scott-monty-ford-s-social-media-pioneer-leaves-company/293298/.
14. Ana Gotter, "What Wendy's Twitter Account Can Teach Us about 'Doing Social'," *Agora Pulse,* April 12, 2017, https://www.agorapulse.com/blog/wendys-twitter-account/.
15. M. T. Pham, "Representativeness, Relevance, and the Use of Feelings in Decision Making," *Journal of Consumer Research* 25, no. 2 (1998): 144–159.
16. FinancesOnline, "88 Relevant Shopping Cart Abandonment Statistics: 2021 Value, Causes, Analysis & Data," (n.d.), https://financesonline.com/shopping-cart-abandonment-statistics/.
17. D. R. Bell, D. Corsten, and G. Knox, "From Point of Purchase to Path to Purchase: How Preshopping Factors Drive Unplanned Buying," *Journal of Marketing* 75, no. 1 (2011): 31–45.
18. K. M. Stilley, J. J. Inman, and K. L. Wakefield, "Planning to Make Unplanned Purchases? The Role of In-Store Slack in Budget Deviation," *Journal of Consumer Research* 37, no. 2 (2010): 264–278; K. M. Stilley, J. J. Inman, and K. L. Wakefield, "Spending on the Fly: Mental Budgets, Promotions, and Spending Behavior," *Journal of Marketing* 74, no. 3 (2010): 34–47.
19. D. Prelec and G. Loewenstein, "The Red and the Black: Mental Accounting of Savings and Debt," *Marketing Science* 17, no. 1 (1998): 4–28.
20. Federal Deposit Insurance Corporation, "2017 FDIC National Survey of Unbanked and Underbanked

Households," October 22, 2018, https://www.fdic.gov/householdsurvey/.

21. James Montier, *Behavioral Finance: Insights into Irrational Minds and Markets* (Hoboken, NJ: Wiley, 2002).

22. McKinsey and Company, "2010 Annual Chinese Consumer Study," August 2010, https://solutions.mckinsey.com/insightchina/_SiteNote/WWW/GetFile.aspx?uri=/insightschina/default/en-us/aboutus/news/Files/wp2055036759/McKinsey%20Insights%20China%20-%202010%20Annual%20Consumer%20Study%20-%20EN_d81cb1d7-3a47-4d27-953f-ede02b28da7a.pdf.

23. McKinsey and Company, "2010 Annual Chinese Consumer Study," August 2010, https://solutions.mckinsey.com/insightchina/_SiteNote/WWW/GetFile.aspx?uri=/insightschina/default/en-us/aboutus/news/Files/wp2055036759/McKinsey%20Insights%20China%20-%202010%20Annual%20Consumer%20Study%20-%20EN_d81cb1d7-3a47-4d27-953f-ede02b28da7a.pdf.

24. J. W. Schouten and J. H. McAlexander, "Subcultures of Consumption: An Ethnography of the New Bikers," *Journal of Consumer Research* 22, no. 1 (1995): 43–61.

25. A. M. Muniz and T. C. O'Guinn, "Brand Community," *Journal of Consumer Research* 27, no. 4 (2001): 412–432.

26. G. M. Erickson, J. K. Johansson, and P. Chao, "Image Variables in Multi-Attribute Product Evaluations: Country-of-Origin Effects," *Journal of Consumer Research* 11, no. 2 (1984): 694–699.

27. N. A. Christakis and J. H. Fowler, *Connected: The Surprising Power of Our Social Networks and How They Shape Our Lives* (New York: Little, Brown, 2009).

28. Leisa Reinecke Flynn, Ronald E. Goldsmith, and Jacqueline K. Eastman, "Opinion Leaders and Opinion Seekers: Two New Measurement Scales," *Journal of the Academy of Marketing Science* 24, no. 2 (1996): 137–147.

29. Ed Keller and Jon Berry, *The Influentials* (New York: Free Press, 2003).

30. Izea, "Top Female Social Media Influencers," March 27, 2018, https://izea.com/resources/top-female-social-media-influencers/.

31. Zsolt Katona, "How to Identify Influence Leaders in Social Media," *Bloomberg,* February 26, 2012, http://www.bloomberg.com/news/2012-02-27/how-to-identify-influence-leaders-in-social-media-zsolt-katona.html.

32. Jack Neff, "Listerine Looks to Become a Lifestyle Brand," *Ad Age,* April 5, 2016. https://adage.com/article/cmo-strategy/bold-move-listerine-a-lifestyle-brand/303379/.

33. Douglas Miller, "Nielsen Global Corporate Sustainability Report by Doug Miller, Founder and President, ManagInc," *Everyone Can Win,* November 4, 2016, https://www.everyonecanwin.com/news/2016/11/4/nielsen-global-corporate-sustainability-report-by-doug-miller-founder-and-president-managinc.

34. Sam Carr, "How Many Ads Do We See a Day in 2022," *PPC Protect,* February 15, 2021, https://ppcprotect.com/blog/strategy/how-many-ads-do-we-see-a-day/.

35. A. Krishna, "An Integrative Review of Sensory Marketing: Engaging the Senses to Affect Perception, Judgment and Behavior," *Journal of Consumer Psychology* 22, no. 3 (2012): 332–351.

36. A. C. North, D. J. Hargreaves, and J. McKendrick, "The Influence of In-Store Music on Wine Selections," *Journal of Applied Psychology* 84, no. 2 (1999): 271.

37. A. V. Madzharov, L. G. Block, and M. Morrin, "The Cool Scent of Power: Effects of Ambient Scent on Consumer Preferences and Choice Behavior," *Journal of Marketing* 79, no. 1 (2015): 83–96.

38. Aradhna Krishna, May Lwin, and Maureen Morrin, "Product Scent and Memory," *Journal of Consumer Research* 37 (June 2010): 57–67.

39. Peter Rubin, "The Future of Travel Has Arrived: Virtual-Reality Beach Locations," *Wired,* September 2014.

40. Abraham Maslow, *Motivation and Personality* (New York: Harper, 1954), 236.

41. John Tierney, "A Match Made in the Code," *The New York Times,* February 11, 2013, http://www.nytimes.com/2013/02/12/science/skepticism-as-eharmony-defends-its-matchmaking-algorithm.html?pagewanted=all&_r=0.

42. Andrew Adam Newman, "An Emphasis on Fun for Language Learners," *The New York Times,* June 19, 2012, http://www.nytimes.com/2012/06/20/business/media/rosetta-stone-ads-emphasize-fun-not-efficiency.html.

43. Kyle Wiggers, "Microsoft Researchers Use Bing Data to Track Shifting Human Needs During the Pandemic," *Venture Beat,* August 21, 2020, https://venturebeat.com/2020/08/21/microsoft-researchers-use-bing-data-to-track-shifting-human-needs-during-the-pandemic/.

44. Ira Winderman, "Dwyane Wade Miami Beach Fantasy Camp Carries $12,500 Tab," *South Florida Sun Sentinel,* May 11, 2011, http://articles.sun-sentinel.com/2011-05-11/sports/sfl-miami-heat-dwyane-wade-s051111_1_fantasy-camp-youth-camps-website.

45. Gabrielle Olya, "The 11 Most Popular Pandemic Home Improvement Projects—Plus, How Much They Cost," MSN.com, October 4, 2021, https://www.msn.com/en-us/money/realestate/the-11-most-popular-pandemic-home-improvement-projects-%E2%80%93-plus-how-much-they-cost/ss-AAKk9O1.

46. Jordan Valinsky, "Peloton Sales Surge 172% as Pandemic Bolsters Home Fitness Industry," *CNN Business,* September 11, 2020, https://www.cnn.com/2020/09/11/business/peloton-stock-earnings/index.html.

47. Gordon Allport, "Attitudes," in *A Handbook of Social Psychology,* ed. C. Murchison (Worcester, MA: Clark University Press, 1935), pp.789–844.

48. T. M. Ostrom, "The Relationship between the Affective, Behavioral, and Cognitive Components of Attitude," *Journal of Experimental Social Psychology* 5, no. 1 (1969): 12–30; and R. P. Bagozzi, "The Construct Validity of the Affective, Behavioral, and Cognitive Components of Attitude by Analysis of Covariance Structures," *Multivariate Behavioral Research* 13, no. 1 (1978): 9–31.

49. R. W. Belk, "Situational Variables and Consumer Behaviour," *Journal of Consumer Research,* December 1975, 157–164.

50. A. V. Madzharov, L. G. Block, and M. Morrin, "The Cool Scent of Power: Effects of Ambient Scent on Consumer Preferences and Choice Behavior," *Journal of Marketing* 79, no. 1 (2015): 83–96.

51. C. K. Cain and J. E. LeDoux, "Emotional Processing and Motivation: In Search of Brain Mechanisms," in AJ Elliot (ed.) *Handbook of Approach and Avoidance Motivation,* (2008), pp. 17–34, Psychology Press, London, UK.

52. P. A. Dabholkar and R. P. Bagozzi, "An Attitudinal Model of Technology-Based Self-Service: Moderating Effects of Consumer Traits and Situational Factors," *Journal of the Academy of Marketing Science* 30, no. 3 (2002): 184–201.

53. I. Simonson, "The Effect of Purchase Quantity and Timing on Variety-Seeking Behavior," *Journal of Marketing Research* 27, no. 2 (1990): 150–162.

54. John C. Mowen and Michael Minor, *Consumer Behavior: A Framework* (Upper Saddle River, NJ: Pearson Prentice-Hall, 2001).

55. Anthony D'Alessandro, "*Avengers: Endgame* $200M+ Promo Campaign Is Marvel's Biggest Ever, Surpassing Infinity Wars & More," *Deadline,* April 17. 2019, https://deadline.com/2019/04/avengers-endgame-mcdonalds-google-coca-cola-ultra-beauty-audi-all-time-record-marketing-campaign-videos-1202595738/.

56. Christian Homburg, Halina Wiliczek, and Alexander Hahn, "Looking beyond the Horizon: How to Approach the Customer's Customer in Business to Business Markets," *Journal of Marketing* 78 (September 2014): 58–77.

57. Douglas Broom, "The Dirty Secret of Electric Vehicles," World Economic Forum, March 27, 2019, https://www.weforum.org/agenda/2019/03/the-dirty-secret-of-electric-vehicles/.

58. AP News, "Miss. Producer Distributor Has Military Contract," *Bloomberg Businessweek,* March 29, 2013, http://www.businessweek.com/ap/2013-03-29/miss-dot-produce-distributor-has-military-contract.

59. Sharon McLoone, "Getting Government Contracts," *The New York Times,* October 7, 2009, http://www.nytimes.com/2009/10/08/business/smallbusiness/08contracts.html?_r=0.

60. F. E. Webster Jr. and Y. Wind, "A General Model for Understanding Organizational Buying Behavior," *Journal of Marketing* (1972): 12–19.

Chapter 5

Marketing Research and Analytics

Marmaduke St. John/Alamy Stock Photo

Learning Objectives

After reading this chapter, you should be able to

LO 5-1 Explain the importance of marketing research and explain the marketing research process.

LO 5-2 Describe the various types of secondary data sources and explain the importance of predictive analytics.

LO 5-3 Discuss the need for primary research and describe qualitative and quantitative research approaches.

LO 5-4 Explain the importance of research to firms marketing products globally.

LO 5-5 Understand several of the latest trends in marketing research, including customer journey mapping, mobile marketing research, and neuromarketing.

LO 5-6 Discuss the main ethical issues in conducting marketing research.

A.J. Fernández
*Owner and Executive
Director*
Phocus

Alejandro Fernández

A.J. Fernández is the owner and executive director of Phocus, a brand consulting firm based in Panama City, Panama. He began his career in advertising but changed course to brand consulting 12 years ago after participating in his first brand consulting project for a FutureBrand–affiliated firm. A few years later he became one of the first members of the NMSBA, a global neuromarketing association, headquartered in the Netherlands. Combining this scientific knowledge with his many years of experience, Fernández is now tackling the potential of brands through neuroscience and choice architecture.

He has a bachelor's degree from New York University and a master of science in integrated marketing communications from Northwestern University.

What has been the most important thing in making you successful at your job?

That is the easiest question ever—it's my curiosity.

You might be familiar with the fable "The Hedgehog and the Fox." I maintain focus on a key area of expertise—in my case, strategic brand work. This is the "hedgehog." But I have continuously sought to complement that knowledge from other areas, like neuroscience, genetics, and behavioral economics. These are "foxes." So I am able to differentiate what I have to offer to clients by surrounding something that may be a bit more common—that is, the hedgehog; in my case brand strategy—with a lot of "foxy" ideas.

My curiosity is what drives me to continuously discover and learn about these new things. If I have had any sort of success in my career, I owe it to that.

What advice would you give soon-to-be graduates?

Follow your passion. Looking back on my life and career, the best things that have happened to me ultimately have come from devoting myself to something that I feel very passionate about. It doesn't matter if it means more or less money at the beginning. If you're truly passionate about something, you will probably find a way to earn a living doing it. A horrible thing would be to get to the end of your career and realize that you've wasted your time doing things you didn't like, just to make a little more money. I know it sounds pretty idealistic, but it has been 100 percent true in my case.

How is marketing relevant to your role at Phocus?

As CEO of a brand consultancy, I need to constantly sell myself and my company to potential clients in order for my business to grow. Obviously, since the company is focused on strategic branding, marketing is also critical to the clients. This drives me to keep up with emerging ideas that are constantly reshaping marketing thought and practice. Right now, I'm really interested in genetics and marketing. I think in the near future, companies will have access to DNA information that could enable them to market products and services based on an individual's genes, not his or her brains.

What do you consider your personal brand to be?

I would like to be known for always going the extra mile to understand what the needs and the wants of my clients and of my clients' customers *really* are. I believe very few people in the industry are truly committed to pursuing this goal to the same extent that I do. I am constantly learning about advances in scientific knowledge—be it neuroscience, genetics, or economics—and translating that understanding into practical insights that will be useful for my clients. For me, it's not about science for science's sake. Being a theorist—someone who loves academics—but at the same time, being a pragmatist—someone grounded in the need to make sure my clients are successful—is a combination that I think makes me unique.

Explain the importance of marketing research and explain the marketing research process.

MARKETING RESEARCH PROCESS

As we learned in Chapter 4, consumers and business buyers can differ widely in terms of the processes they use in buying situations. Their preferences and behaviors can change over time and are constantly reshaped by purchase contexts and social influences. In addition, many industries have been rocked by the COVID-19 pandemic, disruptive new technologies, and increased global competition.

Good decision making in today's complex and dynamic business setting does not happen by chance. By employing modern marketing research processes and tools, managers are equipped to help their organizations improve marketing outcomes and financial performance.

What Is Marketing Research

marketing research

Organizational activity that links the consumer, customer, and public to the marketer through information. The organization uses that information to identify and define marketing opportunities and problems; generate, refine, and evaluate marketing actions; monitor marketing performance; and improve understanding of marketing as a process.

Marketing research is an organizational activity that links the consumer, customer, and public to the marketer through information. The organization uses that information to identify and define marketing opportunities and problems; generate, refine, and evaluate marketing actions; monitor marketing performance; and improve understanding of marketing as a process.

Market research can inform almost every aspect of a company's business. We can see this impact clearly in terms of the four Ps—product, price, place, and promotion.

1. *Products* should be developed based on real customer needs and wants, not just the whims of engineers or marketing executives. The success of a new product often rests on iterative market research across multiple stages of the NPD process.

2. *Pricing* decisions are often shaped by **demand analysis**, which estimates the level of demand for a particular product as well as how changes in price and other factors influence customer purchases.[1]

3. Decisions regarding the *place* or distribution function often rely on sales forecasts. **Sales forecasting** predicts the number of units sold in a market over a given time period. Using this research, firms know how much product to hold in inventory at various points in the distribution network or where to locate new retail locations.

4. *Promotional* activities, such as advertising, must be evaluated based on their effectiveness. For example, **advertising effectiveness studies** measure how well an advertising campaign meets marketing objectives (such as increasing brand awareness or market share).[2]

demand analysis

A type of research used to estimate how much customer demand there is for a particular product and understand the factors driving that demand.

sales forecasting

A form of research that estimates how much of a product will sell over a given period of time.

advertising effectiveness studies

A type of research that measures how well an advertising campaign meets marketing objectives.

Marketing research is increasingly important to understanding consumer preferences and is a key driver of the marketing strategy for organizations of all sizes. *ESB Professional/Shutterstock*

When done properly, marketing research activities help companies better understand and satisfy the needs and wants of customers. However, with global competition and fast-paced changes in technology, the need for accurate and timely market insights has never been greater. In 2019, companies worldwide spent more than $73 billion with external marketing research agencies.[3] In addition, firms are investing heavily in business analytics technologies to help them derive improved and more timely insights from internal and external data sources.

Marketing Research Process

A systematic approach to marketing research follows a five-step process: (1) define the problem, (2) develop a research plan, (3) collect data, (4) analyze the data, and (5) present results and take action. Figure 5.1 shows this process for a hypothetical product sold by beverage company Fuze. Although Figure 5.1 shows the process as a linear progression, sometimes marketers skip steps if they get an early solution to the problem. Or they may go back to an earlier step to gather additional information or reanalyze data as needed.

Step 1: Define the Problem
Defining the problem is the first step in the marketing research process. Often firms know that they have a problem but cannot precisely pinpoint or clearly define the issue. By clarifying the exact nature of the problem, the firm avoids wasting time, money, and human resources chasing the wrong data—and coming up with the wrong solutions.

Defining the problem has three components:

1. *Specify the research objectives:* What questions will the research aim to answer?
2. *Define the population of interest:* Who do we wish to study or learn more about?
3. *Identify relevant environmental factors:* What aspects of the organization's internal or external environment are relevant to answering the research questions?

As with overall marketing objectives, the firm should set research objectives that are specific and measurable. They represent what the firm seeks to gain by conducting the research. Next, the marketer will determine a set of procedures for addressing these research needs, which we will discuss in the next section.

Step 2: Develop a Research Plan
The next step is to develop a research plan. In this step, the firm identifies the best approach to acquiring the information needed. Research plan development, sometimes called *research design,* involves:

- Specifying what information is needed.
- Determining what type of research techniques may be used to acquire it.
- Presenting this research plan to management.

As part of this effort, the research plan outlines sources of relevant existing data and details the research approach, sampling plans, materials, and instruments the research team will need to gather new data.

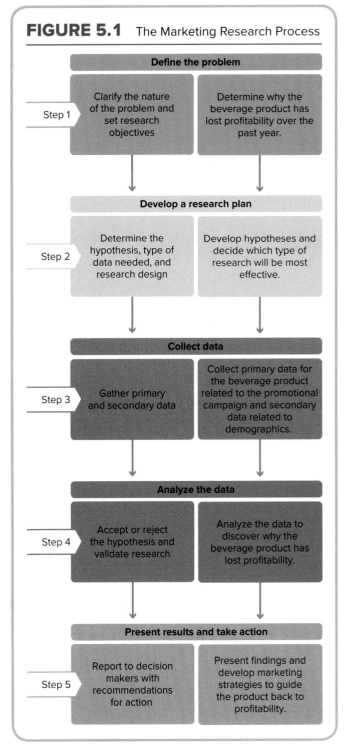

FIGURE 5.1 The Marketing Research Process

Define the problem

Step 1 — Clarify the nature of the problem and set research objectives | Determine why the beverage product has lost profitability over the past year.

Develop a research plan

Step 2 — Determine the hypothesis, type of data needed, and research design | Develop hypotheses and decide which type of research will be most effective.

Collect data

Step 3 — Gather primary and secondary data | Collect primary data for the beverage product related to the promotional campaign and secondary data related to demographics.

Analyze the data

Step 4 — Accept or reject the hypothesis and validate research | Analyze the data to discover why the beverage product has lost profitability.

Present results and take action

Step 5 — Report to decision makers with recommendations for action | Present findings and develop marketing strategies to guide the product back to profitability.

Types of Research The nature of the research objectives will dictate what approach is most appropriate, Managers can choose from among the following three types of research:

1. **Exploratory research** seeks to discover new insights that help the firm better understand and define the research problem and suggest testable hypotheses. Exploratory research usually involves some type of face-to-face interaction, such as a focus group.

2. **Descriptive research** seeks to describe consumer behavior by answering the questions who, what, when, where, and how.[4] Examples of descriptive information include estimating market potential for a good or service; evaluating consumers' attitudes toward a product or company; identifying individual steps in customers' journey toward purchase; uncovering ways that consumers behave (do they prefer to shop online or in-person); and gathering demographic information.

3. **Causal research** is used to test hypotheses in order to understand the cause-and-effect relationships among variables. Causal research often involves manipulating *independent variables* (the cause or source) to see how they affect a particular *dependent variable* (the effect or outcome). For example, Fuze could conduct an experiment that manipulates the packaging of its beverages (the independent variable) to see how different package styles affect sales (the dependent variable). Figure 5.2 shows the relationships among research objectives and the collection methods and types.

Companies need not limit themselves to one type of research. Findings from an exploratory or descriptive study can inform research hypotheses tested in follow-up causal research. For example, Fuze may use exploratory methods to get a deeper understanding of what factors motivate or prevent individuals from trying out new beverage products. Subsequently, Fuze could employ a causal study to test how different packaging concepts may lead consumers currently drinking another brand to try a new flavored tea drink.

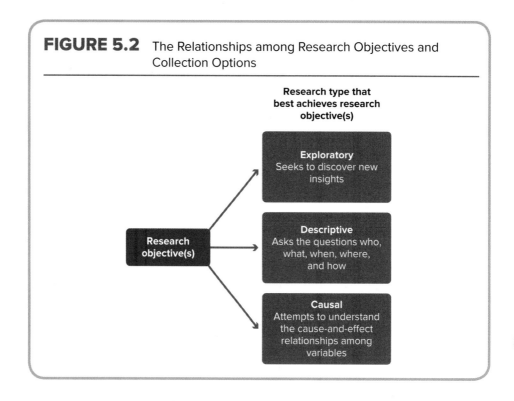

FIGURE 5.2   The Relationships among Research Objectives and Collection Options

Research type that best achieves research objective(s)

Research objective(s)

Exploratory
Seeks to discover new insights

Descriptive
Asks the questions who, what, when, where, and how

Causal
Attempts to understand the cause-and-effect relationships among variables

Sampling   It would be impossible—from both a budget and time perspective—for marketing professionals to obtain feedback from all the members of its target market. Instead, they must rely on sampling. **Sampling** is the process of selecting a subset of the population that is representative of the population as a whole.

Sampling can be broken down into two basic types: probability and nonprobability. **Probability sampling** ensures every person in the target population has a chance of being selected, and the probability of each person being selected is known. To conduct probability sampling, Fuze would need to structure its study so that it could calculate each beverage drinker's probability of being included. The most common example of probability sampling is **simple random sampling**, in which everyone in the target population has an *equal* chance of being selected. **Nonprobability sampling**, on the other hand, does not attempt to ensure that every member of the target population has a chance of being selected. Nonprobability sampling contains an element of judgment, in which the researcher narrows the target population by some criteria before selecting participants. Perhaps the most common nonprobability sampling approach is a **convenience sample**, in which the researcher invites responses from people who are easily accessible—for example, relatives, friends, or employees.

Which sampling approach to use depends upon the research objective. Probability sampling enables researchers to generalize findings from a portion of a target population. Nonprobability sampling, though, can generate findings that may be more appropriate to the research question.

Step 3: Collect Data

The third step of the marketing research process is to collect the data. Data collection begins with the firm's decision to use secondary or primary data. **Secondary data** are information collected for alternative purposes prior to the study, typically by another entity or person. In the context of Fuze, an external secondary data source may be an industry report that summarizes nonalcoholic beverage consumption trends amongst Millennial consumers.

In contrast, **primary data** are collected *specifically* for the research problem at hand. Primary data collection methods may either be qualitative or quantitative. For example, Fuze may hold a series of focus groups in various markets to obtain detailed qualitative feedback on a new drink concept. Alternatively, the brand's research team might conduct a quantitative survey that assess consumers attitudes toward its brand or perceptions of its beverage products. Table 5.1 outlines differences between primary and secondary data.

The Marketing Information System   Primary and secondary data are acquired, processed, and stored by the firm's marketing information system. A **marketing information system** consists of the people, technologies, and procedures aimed at supplying an organization's marketing information needs. It assesses those needs, develops the needed information, and helps managers use information to create, validate, and apply actionable customer insights. Figure 5.3 illustrates the marketing information system (MIS) concept. The process begins with an assessment of the information needs of key users aligned with the firm's interests: marketing managers, strategic partners, suppliers, compliance officers, public relations, senior decision makers, and others. Based on these criteria, the marketing information system acts as a filter. It systematically captures desired information from the data streams that flow through the organization and screens out unneeded clutter and noise.

Decision Support Systems   A **decision support system (DSS)** is software that enables timely access and use of the information the company collects. Information for the DSS can come from internal records (e.g., sales data, customer satisfaction studies).

---

sampling

The process of selecting a subset of the population that is representative of the population as a whole.

probability sampling

A type of sampling in which every person in the target population has a chance of being selected, and the probability of each person being selected is known.

simple random sampling

A type of sampling in which everyone in the target population has an equal chance of being selected.

nonprobability sampling

A type of sampling that does not attempt to ensure that every member of the target population has a chance of being selected.

convenience sample

A research sample drawn from respondents who are easily accessible to the researcher—for example, relatives, friends, or employees.

secondary data

Information collected for alternative purposes prior to the study.

primary data

Data collected specifically for the research problem at hand.

marketing information system

Consists of the people, technologies, and procedures aimed at supplying an organization's marketing information needs.

decision support system (DSS)

A computer program that enables access and use of the information stored in the data warehouse.

TABLE 5.1 Differences between Primary and Secondary Data

	Primary Data	Secondary Data
Collection Method Examples	Focus groups Surveys Observations In-depth personal interviews Neuromarketing techniques (e.g., EEG, eye-tracking)	Literature reviews Online electronic searches Company records Marketing information systems Private research companies Boundary spanners (e.g., salespersons)
Advantages	Pertain only to firm's research	Less expensive (often free)
	May provide insight into why and how consumers make choices	Information typically readily accessible
Disadvantages	More expensive	Data may not be relevant
	May be difficult to enlist customer participation	Data may not be accurate
	May take excessive amount of time to collect	Data may have been altered
		Data may contain bias
Examples of Use	To understand what motivates consumers	To gather macroeconomic data
	To determine the effect of variables (e.g., price) on product choice	To gather socioeconomic data
	To gain feedback on company's existing and proposed products	To obtain information about competitors
		To gain insight into international cultures and markets

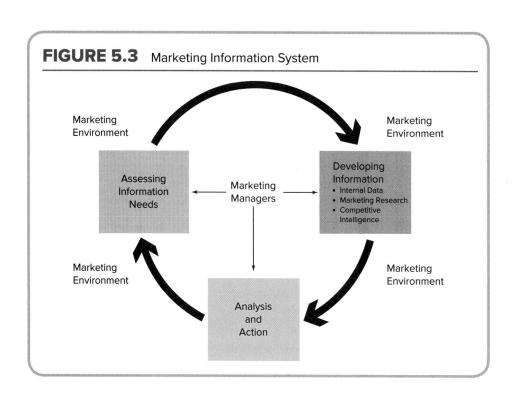

FIGURE 5.3 Marketing Information System

It also can include external information that's entered or imported into the database (e.g., competitor information). Many companies today have augmented their DSS with analytics tools, graphics, and real-time performance dashboards. This enables marketers to:

- Manipulate and organize data in more useful ways.
- Explore sales trends for specific product and markets.
- Identify problems with elements of the marketing mix.
- Provide quick feedback to managers concerning proposed marketing plans.

Step 4: Analyze the Data The purpose of data analysis is to convert the data collected in Step 3 into information. Data can be defined as raw numbers, statistics, or text that on its own has very limited value to marketing. The raw data becomes usable information that the firm can use to solve a marketing problem only after it has been organized, analyzed, and interpreted.

It is important that researchers apply the appropriate analytic techniques for the data and research questions at hand. For simple questions involving descriptive accounts of quantitative data, researchers may take advantage of one-way frequency counts or cross-tabulations. One-way frequency tables simply tally the number of unique responses to a question. For instance, coding answers to the question "What brand of cereal do you buy most often?" would provide a one-way frequency distribution. A **cross-tabulation** enables the analyst to examine responses to one question in relation to responses from one or more other questions. Figure 5.4 provides a visual depiction of cross-tabulated output from a satisfaction study.

For causal research, more powerful and sophisticated statistical techniques are typically required, such as measures of association, analysis of variance (ANOVA), and regression analysis. A detailed explanation of these techniques is beyond the scope of this chapter but can readily be obtained from an introductory statistics or marketing research text.

Ideally, the information obtained from the research process will enable marketers to address the research objective. If it does not satisfy this requirement, additional research might be necessary.

cross-tabulation

A data analysis technique that enables someone to examine responses to one question in relation to responses from one or more other questions.

Step 5: Present Results and Take Action The culmination of the marketing research process is a formal, written report to decision makers. The report typically includes a summary of the findings and a set of recommendations. Research findings should be presented in a clear, concise, and understandable language and include appropriate visual data, such as figures and tables, to support conclusions. Often an oral presentation is delivered along with a written report.

The research report should provide sufficient information to support managerial action. For example, let's say that the results of Fuze's research indicated that its consumers are spending more time on their smartphones watching short videos or a streaming new series on Netflix rather than watching cable television. This finding might prompt the marketing department to revise their advertising budgets, develop new promotional campaigns that target mobile users, or introduce customized content via their TikTok channel.

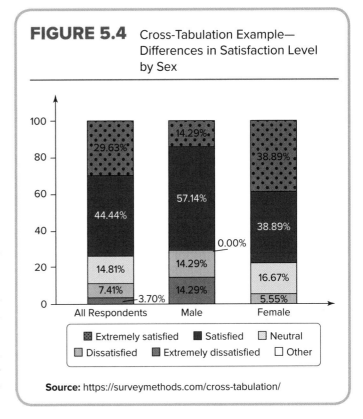

FIGURE 5.4 Cross-Tabulation Example—Differences in Satisfaction Level by Sex

Legend: Extremely satisfied, Satisfied, Neutral, Dissatisfied, Extremely dissatisfied, Other

Source: https://surveymethods.com/cross-tabulation/

data visualization

The presentation of data and research results in pictorial or graphical format.

Data Visualization Data visualization is the presentation of data and research results in pictorial or graphical format. By presenting data and analytics visually, decision makers can more easily uncover new patterns in data and grasp difficult-to-understand concepts. Many marketers today are supplementing classic forms of data visualization, such as charts and graphs, with new techniques that offer greater visual appeal. *Infographics* are graphic visual representations of information, data, or knowledge intended to present information quickly and clearly.[5] Many popular online tools and templates are available for easily creating professional looking infographics.

Marketing Research and You

You may find the marketing research concepts and techniques discussed in this chapter to be especially useful as you plan your career path (and later, as you evaluate different firms and positions). Interviewing individuals who are currently working in a field or industry you are considering is a great approach to learning whether it is right for you. By thoughtfully developing a sequence of questions (an interview guide), before the meeting, you can gain insights into what skills and experiences to focus on developing prior to graduation. You also may apply many of the online and social media research techniques in identifying career opportunities. Some employment websites, like Glassdoor.com, include job-specific reviews of a company from current and former employees as well as feedback from recent job applicants on the interview scheduling and questioning process.

McGraw Hill connect Exercise 5-1

Please complete the *Connect* exercise for Chapter 5 that focuses on the steps of the marketing research process. By understanding the decisions at each step, you will be able to conduct better marketing research and thus improve the quality of your marketing strategy going forward.

LO 5-2

Describe the various types of secondary data sources and explain the importance of predictive analytics.

SECONDARY DATA AND PREDICTIVE ANALYTICS

Research investigating such topics often begin with a review of secondary data; that is, data that are gathered and recorded by someone else prior to (and for purposes other than) the current project. Secondary data is particularly useful at the problem identification stage; However, there are certainly situations in which these data are sufficiently robust to support meaningful tests of research hypotheses. Next, we discuss the uses of secondary data for business researchers as well as key advantages and limitations of working with secondary data.

Use of Secondary Data for Business Research

What types of secondary data do marketers need? Clearly, any data that provides deeper understanding of customer differences and market trends ranks very high. In addition, as we know from earlier chapters, marketing performance is affected by environmental factors outside the company's control. So, maintaining a close watch on the actions on rival firms, a process known as *competitive intelligence,* is another focal area. In addition *environmental scanning* research involves monitoring the firm's macroenvironment for the emergence of new technologies, changes in supply markets, and shifts in the political and economic landscape.

Customer and Market Trends Data

Business researchers are constantly on the lookout for research on changes in consumption patterns and market trends. Information on emerging consumer trends and behaviors is often available from panel data providers. **Panel data** are gathered from a group (or panel) of consumers over a period of time. The NPD Group's *National Eating Trends* (NET) study monitors the eating and drinking habits of thousands of families. This data is based on records of meals and diaries kept by a set of households that agree to record their dining behaviors over time. The service enables NPD's clients to stay on top of food and beverage consumption trends and better understand when, where, why, and how food is consumed.

Marketers must also be aware of broad market-level trends. For instance, nearly all major consumer goods manufacturers routinely assess changes in product category sales and brand market share over time. Market tracking research is the observation of industry trends and sales volume over time. Data from such studies are available on a subscription basis from research services organizations. Such information can include longitudinal comparisons with competing brands as well as brand performance across geographic regions.

panel data
Information collected from a group (or panel) of consumers over a period of time.

Competitive Intelligence

Until now, we have focused on secondary data related to the firm and its customers. But another important component of marketing research involves gathering data about what competitors are doing. **Competitive intelligence** is the systematic gathering of data about strategies that direct and indirect competitors are pursuing. Such information can provide a firm with advance knowledge of a competitor's upcoming promotions or new products. With that information, the firm can respond in a way that blunts the effects of the competitor's actions.

A company can obtain information about another company's activities and plans in a number of ways. Government agencies, such as the U.S. Patent and Trademark Office (USPTO) offer important information regarding competitors innovation activities and upcoming new products. Regular attendance at conferences and trade shows provide opportunities to network and converse with customers about industry developments. By monitoring rivals' websites and social media accounts, researchers can identify subtle changes in a competitor's market positioning and value propositions. In some instances, rival firms may share common suppliers, distributors, retailers, and even customers. Routine interactions with individuals at these organizations often produce important takeaways that may not be otherwise available.

competitive intelligence
The systematic gathering of data about strategies that direct and indirect competitors are pursuing in terms of new-product development and the marketing mix.

Social media sites like Glassdoor, Monster, and Indeed, which give employees an opportunity to rate and review the companies they work for, allow firms to collect information about their competitors in new ways. *Glassdoor*

While the approaches mentioned above are legitimate, it should be noted that there are *unethical* ways of obtaining competitive intelligence. Bribing competitors' employees or customers for information is an unethical and illegal way of getting competitive information. Firms should scrupulously avoid such activities for legal reasons as well as for the damage they can do to a company's image and reputation. We discuss ethical considerations of marketing research in detail later in the chapter.

Environmental Scanning Firms also rely on secondary data to stay abreast of how changes in the broader macroenvironment are likely to impact the firm or its stakeholders. Environmental scanning research refers to the collection and utilization of information regarding events, relationships, and trends that impact an organization's industry. While this type of fact-finding is inherently backward looking, its aim is to identify and if need be respond to significant environmental shifts in their earliest stages of development.

Where do companies turn to keep up with societal shifts in public attitudes, lifestyles, and values? There are several major syndicated research data services that report findings from public opinion polls. For instance, the PR firm Yankelovich offers a variety of public opinion surveys on a regular basis pertaining to political issues of the day, generational changes in cultural values, and consumption behaviors.

Advantages and Disadvantages of Secondary Data There are several advantages to consider when working with secondary data. The first advantage is availability. With the rise of internal ERP and CRM information systems, managers are able to easily access customer records and make ad hoc queries using internal information systems. Many external secondary databases are available for immediate download from government sources and other data aggregators. Websites and social media likewise offer managers and researchers with readily available data.

The second main advantage is cost. Since it does not require access to human respondents or subjects, secondary data is almost always less expensive than acquiring primary data. A third plus is that secondary sources sometimes provides data that is not readily available via primary data sources. For instance, the U.S. Bureau of Transportation Statistics provides monthly updates on airlines' on-time performance for each route flown into or from all major American airports. Such data would be exceedingly difficult for any individual airline or air service provider to collect and distribute.

The most significant disadvantage to working with secondary data is that because the data was acquired by someone else for other purposes, it often fails to meet the researcher's specific needs. For instance, a secondary data source may be inadequate due to: (1) data being outdated; (2) data being too general or aggregated at too high or low of a level; (3) data comes from a population that is not an appropriate match to the researcher's target market, or; (4) an inability to verify data accuracy or the methods used to acquire the data.

Next, we discuss several secondary data sources commonly used in business research.

Secondary Data Sources

Secondary data sources differ in several important ways. But the most fundamental is whether it is housed within the organization's information systems or if it resides with an external party. We begin our discussion of secondary data sources by examining internal company data.

Internal Company Data Perhaps the largest source of useful data flowing through any organization is that which it generates, or co-generates, itself in the course of its daily operations. *Internal company data* would include any or all of the following:

- *A company's sales records:* details on consumer characteristics, what they ordered, how much they ordered, when they ordered, whether they used coupons, and so forth.
- *Customer support records:* details relating to the nature of reported service failures and other problems, how quickly the company responded, and whether the issue was resolved to the satisfaction of affected customers.
- *Accounting and finance information:* detailed records of costs, payments, and cash flow.
- *Sales force reports:* records of sales activities, including details relating to customer and prospect interactions, competitive activities, and expectations of future sales revenue.
- *Operation and supply chain management information:* timely information about production and shipments, inventory levels, and product returns.

Internal data sources are comparatively easy to access using modern corporate information systems. But integrating data from disparate sources is never without problems. For one thing, valuable information can reside in separate functional areas or even different strategic business units. It is not at all uncommon for information from various parts of the firm to be managed using different database systems. Also, some have conflicting protocols for access rights, distribution, and usage. For large organizations with multiple lines of business, making sure that all useful data are accessible to information users across the organization may involve as much political skill as technological expertise. Further, some data, like purchase transactions, may be collected in real time; other data, such as sales call reports and expense records, are more likely to be generated on a weekly or even monthly basis. In such an environment, it is a special challenge to make sure customer-facing portions of the company are consistently updated with the most relevant and timely information.

External Secondary Data Sources External secondary data can come
from many sources. We briefly review several major categories and provide examples of how companies utilize such data to help improve their marketing decision making.

Government Sources U.S. government agencies are prolific producers of data,
much of it available to the public for free or at very low cost. Many students are familiar with the *U.S. Census of Population* (www.census.gov), which provides a wealth of information on a wide variety of demographic and socioeconomic trends across major cities, counties, and states. But there are other useful governmental data sources. Banks and other financial services providers rely heavily on the *Federal Reserve Bulletin.* Builders and contractors use information published in the *American Housing Survey* and *American Community Survey* published by the Department of Housing and Urban Development (HUD). Detailed information about the operations of a publicly held competitor can be found in the company's financial reports on the U.S. Securities and Exchange Commission website (www.sec.gov).

Trade Associations In certain large industries, trade associations gather data on a
range of topics of interest to members. Examples include the American Hospital Association (hospitals) and Food Marketing Institute (grocery stores). By virtue of their participation in these trade associations, organizations often receive exclusive access premium data and research reports. For instance, to help retailers safely operate during the pandemic, the National Retail Federation provided members with a variety of useful resources, including benchmarking surveys, daily updates, and webinars.

Media Sources   Broadcast, print, and online media sources regularly collect and distribute data on a wide variety of subjects. For example, *Fortune* magazine commissions research and publishes company ratings, including corporate reputation (Most Admired Companies) and workplace quality (100 Best Companies to Work For). For marketers in the nonprofit sector, *The Chronicle of Philanthropy* offers subscribers access to research and data on the U.S. charitable organizations and large donors. While some media sources offer only limited details with respect to the research methods and analysis used in developing their data and reports, they nonetheless offer interesting insights and are generally available for free or at low cost.

Commercial Sources   Companies known as *syndicated market research providers* compile secondary data and provide access to other businesses on a paid basis. Some providers may specialize in distributing specific types of data, such as scanner data, surveys, or product launch analysis. These firms can also differ by virtue of the scope of their coverage. For instance, some might focus their research on a single industry, while others cover a broader range of industries. In addition, some syndicated data companies differ in terms of offering global coverage versus featuring distinct geographic markets.

scanner data

Data obtained from scanner readings of UPC codes at checkout counters.

Companies like Nielsen Corporation and Information Resources, Inc. (IRI) acquire point-of-sale (POS) retail data from grocery and pharmacy chains, which they in turn offer to researchers on a subscription basis. **Scanner data** are obtained from scanner readings of UPC codes at checkout counters. This type of data is particularly valuable for clients in the consumer packaged-goods industry; these companies often lack the resources to obtain data directly from end users or from the thousands of retail outlets in which their products are sold. Several syndicated data providers offer information to help advertisers optimize their media mix and ensure they are reaching their intended target markets. For instance, Nielsen Corporation (formerly ACNielsen) is also well known for using consumer panels to provide advertisers with audience ratings for television and radio programming.

With more than 5,000 business clients, Euromonitor International is the world's leading provider of global business intelligence, market analysis, and consumer insights. Passport, its award-winning syndicated market research database provides detailed data and analysis on industries and consumers, across 1,200 cities and 210 countries. Annual forecasts for key industries are updated on a quarterly basis to better reflect fast-changing economic conditions. On the other end of the spectrum, ISR Reports offers research products and services that are exclusively focused on the needs of the pharmaceutical industry.

Big Data and Predictive Analytics

Big Data

A term that describes both the growth in information that inundates businesses each day and the complex tools used to analyze the data and derive meaningful insights.

No conversation today about the use of secondary data by businesses would be complete without discussing the implications of Big Data and predictive analytics on marketing decision making. **Big Data** is a term that describes both the growth in information that inundates businesses each day and the complex tools used to analyze the data and derive meaningful insights. **Predictive analytics** is a an umbrella term for a set of statistical techniques and algorithms that enable organizations to recognize patterns within data. By analyzing patterns of past behaviors, these statistical models can be used to help companies predict future events, such as buying behavior or customer switching.[6]

predictive analytics

Is an umbrella term for a set of statistical tools, techniques and algorithms that enable organizations to recognize patterns in their data and make predictions about the future.

By 2025, it is estimated that humanity will create 463 exabytes of data each day.[7] To put that statistic into perspective, all of the words ever spoken by a human would fit onto 5 exabytes. These data come from everywhere: sensors used to gather climate information, posts on social media, digital pictures, online videos, purchase-transaction records, and cell phone GPS signals, to name a few. The *volume, velocity,* and *variety* of structured and unstructured information available to marketers and business managers continues to grow at an exponential basis. These features of Big Data are exemplified below:

- The lower costs associated with e-commerce make it feasible to do business with more and more customers and trading partners, increasing the overall *volume* of data to be managed.
- Likewise, e-commerce has increased the *velocity* with which data enter the organization.
- Data management has been made more complex by the growing *variety* in data formats, often unstructured in form and possessing incompatible data structures (e.g., images, videos, text, numbers).

Meeting the business challenges presented by Big Data is not simply a matter of increasing cloud storage capacity or database management capabilities. It's what the organization *does with the data* that truly matters. Next, we delve more deeply into world of predictive analytics and discuss how marketers are using these tools to augment their traditional decision-making processes.

Predictive Analytics

With the emergence of Web 2.0, companies have ready access to mountains of consumer-generated content from various sources: Twitter, Facebook, Pinterest, Google search trends, YouTube videos, and more. Many marketers are leveraging Big Data sources by applying predictive analytics tools to help create more relevant, personalized brand experiences and better anticipate changing customer preferences. Figure 5.5 illustrates the development of predictive analytics over the past 40 years.

Predictive analytic applications can be broadly grouped into two general classes of models.

1. *Unsupervised learning (or clustering) models:* Unsupervised learning involves teaching an algorithm to look for hidden patterns in data and group things together without being taught what to look for. For example, streaming media platforms, such as Netflix and Amazon Prime, use unsupervised learning to group users together based on similarities in past viewing behavior. The streaming service can then use these clusters or segments to provide a recommendation on what to watch next.

2. *Supervised learning (or propensity) models:* Supervised learning involves teaching an algorithm to come to a specific conclusion based on historical data. For example, if the question is "Will this customer churn?" an analyst can look at historical data to determine the qualities of past customers that have left. Using this information, the model will train an algorithm to determine which existing customers are most likely to leave in the future.[8]

Data Generated Every Minute	
Google	Conducts 5.7M searches
Discord	Users send 668k messages
iMessage	12M people send an iMessage
Clubhouse	Creates 208 rooms
Snapchat	Users send 2M snapchats
Amazon	Customers spend $283k
Online	6M people shop online
Strava	Athletes share 1.5k activities
Instacart	Users spend $67k
Venmo	Users send $304k
Slack	Users send 148k messages
Zoom	Hosts 856 minutes of webinars
Teams	Connects 100k users
Netflix	Users stream 452k hours
YouTube	Users stream 694k hours
Facebook	Live receives 44M views
Facebook	Users share 240k photos
Instagram	Users share 65k photos
Twitter	Users post 575k tweets
TikTok	Users watch 167M videos

Data Never Sleeps: The amount of digital data generated every minute is astounding.

Source: *https://www.businesswire.com/news/home/20210929005835/en/.*

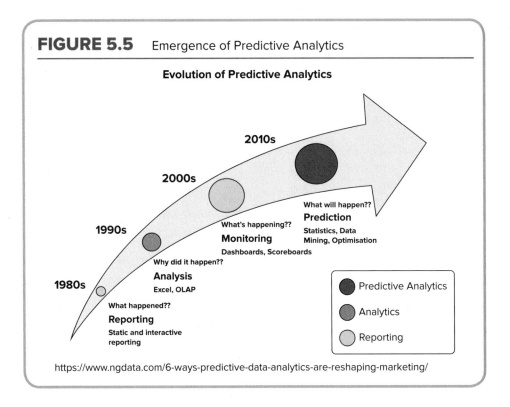

FIGURE 5.5   Emergence of Predictive Analytics

https://www.ngdata.com/6-ways-predictive-data-analytics-are-reshaping-marketing/

Companies in many industries offer similar products and use comparable technology. Insights generated from predictive analytics models offer a means of improving the quality, speed, and precision of decision making in ways that can help firms gain strategic advantage. Table 5.2 describes several of the ways that marketers use predictive models to help improve performance. For instance, one big challenge marketers face is how to personalize communications and promotional offers to individuals so that they resonate with the recipient. Predictive analytics models applications can take a great deal of the guesswork out of this task: They crunch large amounts of structured and unstructured data, to identify messaging and offers that are more likely to be well received.

Limitations of Predictive Analytics Models   Despite the immense usefulness of predictive analytics in many marketing contexts, it is not a fool-proof, fail-safe technique. Predictive models require a specific set of conditions to work well. If these criteria are unmet, the value of these tools for decision makers may be greatly diminished.

1. **Need for Massive Training Data:** Predictive analytics models typically require large-scale training data sets in order to perform well. Models derived from smaller training data can be unduly influenced by anomalies and outliers, which can distort findings.
2. **Apples versus Oranges:** The characteristics of the population used for the training data must be representative of the targeted population in the test data set.
3. **Present Must Look Like the Past:** The current (or future) market conditions that the model is being applied to must be similar to the conditions under which the training data were collected.
4. **Garbage In, Garbage Out:** The algorithms used in both unsupervised and supervised learning models are heavily dependent upon the quality of input data. Data is ultimately a human creation. As such, it can be prone to error; input data may be incomplete, inaccurate, contain duplicate entries, or be labelled in an inconsistent manner. In such instances, the algorithms will be unable to produce managerially useful results.[9]

TABLE 5.2 Marketing Applications of Predictive Modeling

Research Question	How Predictive Models Can Help
1. Which customers and customer segments generate the most lifetime value?	Predictive models can enable marketers to more accurately predict CLV for individual customers and segments. Managers can then direct marketing investments toward attracting and retaining the company's most valuable customers.
2. How do I find more new customers who look like my existing best customers?	Predictive models can help marketers to develop more effective segmentation criteria using real-world behavioral data, identify the most attractive target markets, and even identify new potential markets for the company's product and services.
3. Which prospects are most likely to buy?	Predictive models can help managers better forecast which customers are most likely to purchase as well as what channels are most likely to reach those customers.
4. What other products or content might this customer be interested in?	Based on previous purchasing behaviors by similar customers, predictive analytics can provide suggestions for additional products and services that might appeal to existing customers, thereby increasing customer loyalty and generating new revenue.
5. How do I reduce customer defections?	Predictive analytics can help reduce customer churn by identifying signs of customer dissatisfaction and point out customers or customer segments that are at the most risk for leaving.

"Big Data hubris" is the often implicit assumption that Big Data and predictive analytics are a substitute for, rather than a supplement to, traditional data collection and analysis.[10] When the conditions mentioned above are met, predictive models excel in letting managers known "when" they should consider taking action. But they are not necessarily very good at telling you "why" you must take action or "what" action it is that you should take.

When secondary data sources are not able to satisfy the desired research objectives, managers will seek to address these questions through primary marketing research studies. In the next section, we take a closer look at qualitative and quantitative primary research methods.

PRIMARY DATA RESEARCH METHODS

LO 5-3

When secondary data are insufficient for addressing identified research objectives, firms collect primary data to address their more specific research needs. Depending on the aims of the research (exploratory, descriptive, or causal), the company may select from a variety of primary data-collection methods. Qualitative research includes techniques like focus groups, depth interviews, semi-structured interviews, and ethnographic research. Quantitative research methods include surveys, experiments, and observational studies. Next, we review several of these methods in greater detail.

Discuss the need for primary research and describe qualitative and quantitative research approaches.

qualitative research

Research approaches that address business questions through techniques that permit researchers to offer detailed interpretations of market phenomena without depending on numerical measurement.

Qualitative Methods for Business Research

Qualitative research seeks to address business questions through techniques that permit the research team to offer detailed interpretations of market phenomena without depending on numerical measurement. These methods may be employed in studying consumers, executives, or organizations. Its focus is on discovery, rather than testing preconceived hypotheses.

Qualitative research approaches are much less structured compared to quantitative methods. The goal of the research team is to extract meaning from unstructured data generated from the study, such as text from a recorded interview or pictures selected by a customer to represent their brand experiences. Using established guidelines and procedures, trained qualitative researchers are able to effectively code and organize the data to identify key themes and insights.

Focus Group Interviews
A **focus group** is an unstructured interview typically conducted with a small group of between 6 and 10 participants who interact with each other in a spontaneous way as they discuss a particular topic or concept. Focus group sessions are led by trained moderators and tend to follow a flexible outline that encourages participant dialogue. The moderator may start things off with some sort of opening statement that steers the conversation in a broad direction. From that point, they will strive to avoid direct questioning and allow topics to emerge from the group conversation.

Successful focus group studies rely heavily on the skill and experience of the moderator. This individual must be able to quickly build rapport with the group in order to promote discussion. Listening skills are essential. While they may at times need to redirect the conversation to keep the group on-point, they cannot do so in an over-bearing way. Most importantly, they must always reject the temptation to interject their personal opinions into the discussion.

Organizations conducting focus groups must also closely consider the size and composition of their focus groups. If the group is too small, one or two individuals with a strong personality may intimidate the others and dominate the conversation. On the other hand, groups that are too large may not permit adequate participation from all members. In addition, some businesses or research organizations may seek to reduce costs by including different types of individuals—perhaps representing diverse market segments—in the same focus group. This is a big mistake! If researchers wish to collect information from different types of people, it is typically more productive to conduct separate sessions for each group.

Depth and Semi-Structured Interviews
In a **depth interview**, a trained researcher, working with one participant at a time, asks open-ended questions about how the individual perceives and uses various products or brands. The interviewer may follow up answers by asking probing questions that require deeper elaboration. Similar to the focus group, a trained interviewer is critical to obtaining useful insights from depth interview research projects. The interviewer must be skilled at gaining the respondent's confidence, encouraging them to speak openly and frankly without unduly influencing the direction or tone of the conversation.

Semi-structured interviews usually ask respondents for a short essay response to specific open-ended questions. Respondents are free to write as little or as much as they would like. Similar to the depth interview process, the questioning begins with an opening question followed by a series of probing questions. A sentence-completion task is a similar approach, by which respondents are asked to complete a few partial sentences with the first word or phrase that comes to mind. While this free-association does not allow for probing questions, it is cost-effective and is commonly used in association with other approaches. For instance, researchers at Fuze might start their focus group by asking respondents to complete statements such as:

- *People who drink nonalcoholic fruit-flavored drinks are* _____.
- *The woman drinking the ice tea in the commercial was* _____.
- *Ice tea is best enjoyed* _____.

focus group

An unstructured interview typically conducted with a small group of between 6 and 10 participants who interact with each other in a spontaneous way as they discuss a particular topic or concept.

depth interview

A data-collection tool in which the researcher, working with one participant at a time, asks open-ended questions about how the individual perceives and uses various products or brands.

semi-structured interview

Interview technique that asks respondents for a short essay response to a series of specific open-ended questions.

Focus groups, depth interviews, and semi-structured interviews can all be conducted online; there may even be advantages for doing so in certain contexts. However, even if the online approach effectively replicates many of the same features of the traditional face-to-face method, there are always trade-offs that should be thought about in advance. For instance, it is not uncommon for online studies to be less expensive. There is also added benefit that it allows researchers to more easily investigate individuals from geographically dispersed markets. At the same time, it is much harder to generate interaction between online focus group participants. Further, in online focus groups and depth interviews, the moderator may find it more difficult to build rapport, and they lose much of their ability to monitor and react to nonverbal cues. These factors can limit the openness of the discussion and hinder the ability of interviewers to ask the types of probing questions that reveal meaningful new information.

A market researcher conducting a depth interview
Aleksandr Davydov/123RF

Ethnographic Research
Drawing techniques from the field of anthropology, **ethnographic research** sends trained participant-observers to watch and interact with a subject population in their natural environment. The participant-observer becomes immersed with the culture or subculture they are studying and draws data via their direct observations.

ethnographic research

A data-collection method that sends trained observers to watch and interact with a subject population in their natural environment.

Many companies and marketing research firms have adapted ethnographic research approaches to the study of online consumer groups. This approach, sometimes referred to as *netnography,* involves observing the behavior of online communities that have been organized around a particular consumer interest. Often the members of such communities are *first movers,* that is, consumers who take the lead in adopting new products and often are dedicated to the product. The researcher enters the online forums to gather data and then uses the community members to verify their findings.

Pros and Cons of Qualitative Research Methods
There are many benefits as well as drawbacks to qualitative research. One limitation is that interpretations of qualitative data are inherently subjective, even when using trained experts. While this type of research does not lend itself to hypothesis testing, it is very effective for uncovering topic areas and research questions that merit additional investigation. Therefore, analysis of qualitative data provides researchers with useful information about subjects and research questions that can later be tested using quantitative methods.

While qualitative research commonly requires professional research personnel to collect and (especially) analyze the unstructured data, findings from the analysis often provides much richer detail than what would be feasible using quantitative methods. Since there are no predetermined sets of responses (e.g., no multiple-choice answers), participants may bring up novel ideas that the researcher did not previously consider. Finally, even though qualitative studies can be time-consuming and expensive to conduct, they often allow the researcher greater flexibility to probe emerging topics during the course of the study.

Each of the data-collection methods discussed so far can provide a great deal of insight. They don't necessarily allow researchers to draw generalized conclusions about the larger consumer population. It is difficult to demonstrate causal patterns between variables in such studies. As a result, to collect the necessary data to achieve certain research objectives, companies turn to quantitative-based techniques, such as surveys, experiments, and observational research.

Quantitative Methods for Primary Business Research

When companies are more interested in gathering descriptive statistical information or testing hypothesized causal relationships, they often engage in quantitative primary research studies. In this section, we briefly discuss three common techniques: survey research, experiments, and observation studies.

Survey Research   Survey research is amongst the most common approaches to obtaining primary data in applied business settings. A **survey** is defined as a method of collecting primary data based on communication with a representative sample of individuals, who provide responses to a sequence of questions. Survey are a snapshot in time. Surveys are used to collect a wide variety of data.[11] In marketing contexts, they are often used to help determine consumer attitudes, intended behavior, and the motivations behind those behavior. While surveys are typically thought of as quantifying opinions or factual information, they can also be utilized to obtain qualitative data. Owing to the ease with which surveys can be delivered and completed, they are particularly useful in gathering feedback from a large number of respondents.

Online surveys have replaced telephone interviews, mail, and mall-intercept techniques as the predominant approach to collecting quantitative survey data. An online survey is a questionnaire accessed via a web browser. Companies like Qualtrics and SurveyMonkey offer platforms that help organizations to create, distribute, and record responses to online surveys. Increasingly, online surveys are completed on smartphones and tablets, which raises potential formatting challenges. *Mobile-optimized surveys* are online surveys that have been adapted to fit smaller mobile device screens. Mobile optimized surveys also take advantage of touchscreens and other smartphone features, like cameras and microphones. Use of mobile surveys provides respondents with a more convenient and improved survey experience. This helps researchers by promoting more timely feedback and higher response rates.

As more survey research has moved online, there has been corresponding growth in the use of paid online panels. Researchers provide the panel company with a link to the survey and sample specifications, things like the desired number of respondents, demographic characteristics, education, and professional profile. The online panel companies charge per-subject rates; these vary, depending mainly on the level of specificity required by the company for whom the research is being done. Once the rate is set, the panel company then invites its members to take part in the survey, for which they receive a small payment.

survey

A method of collecting primary data based on communication with a representative sample of individuals.

Design of the Research Instrument   The research team is responsible for creating the *research instrument,* a generic term used to describe a measurement device such as a survey, test, or questionnaire. If possible, the team will try to identify established measures and adapt them to their needs. If no established measures are available, the team may need to write new research items.

In designing studies, marketing researchers try to ensure that the selected measures exhibit adequate *reliability* and *validity:*

- A measurement instrument exhibits **reliability** if it produces almost identical results over repeated trials.
- **Validity** broadly references the extent to which an instrument measures what it is supposed to measure, and not something else.

reliability (of research)

The ability of a measurement instrument to produce almost identical results over repeated trials.

validity

The extent to which a research instrument measures what it is intended to measure.

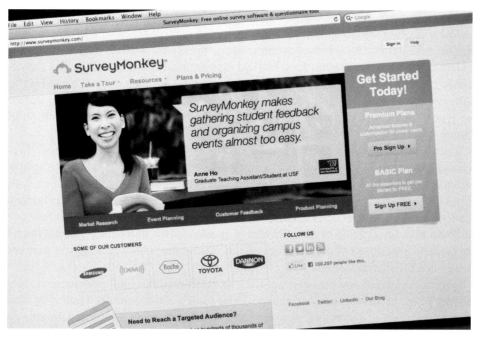

Web-based survey software, such as SurveyMonkey, has made the delivery and analysis of online surveys much easier for researchers. *NetPhotos/Alamy Stock Photo*

In most cases it makes sense to share the draft of the research instrument with colleagues to obtain feedback on the item content and wording. It also may be wise to pretest the instrument with a small group of customers in order to ensure reliability and validity of measures. These extra steps allows researchers to catch potential problems at an early stage. After analyzing peer feedback and sample data, researchers may choose to make small modifications prior to final deployment of the survey.

Experiments *Experiments* are a type of quantitative research study in which the researcher systematically manipulates one or more variables to determine which variables most affect a given outcome. By randomizing subjects into treatment and control groups, experimental researchers can tightly control for the effects of confounding external factors, particularly in laboratory settings. As a result, experimental research is a powerful tool in demonstrating causality. Experiments can be conducted in either a tightly controlled research lab or in field settings.

The most significant distinction between laboratory and fields tests is the environment in which the research is conducted. The big advantage of laboratory experiments is that the lab setting provides researchers with greater control over outside influences that might confound the study results. These extraneous variables leave open the possibility of alternative explanations and can invalidate the experiment. Because of the controlled setting, laboratory experiments are also easier to administer and less expensive than field tests.[12]

In contrast to lab research, a **field experiment** is a study that examines the impact of an intervention in the real

field experiment

A study that examines the impact of an intervention in the real world.

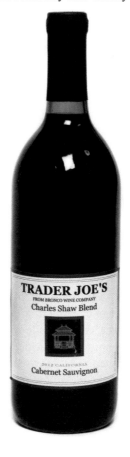

Firms like Trader Joe's use causal research to analyze the effect of a potential price increase on products such as Charles Shaw brand wine, which was known as "Two-Buck Chuck" during its first 11 years at Trader Joe's stores. *Ed Endicott/Alamy Stock Photo*

A/B testing

Involves directly comparing two versions of a product to see which one performs better with customers. Also known as *split testing*.

world. Just as in lab experiments, field experiments generally seek to randomize subjects or other sampling units into treatment and control groups. Field experiments enable researchers to observe outcomes in a real-world setting, which increases external validity. One popular form of field experiment, known as **A/B testing** (sometimes called *split testing*), involves directly comparing two versions of a product or advertisement—a control and test version—to see which generates stronger customer response. The better performing version typically becomes the control condition in future A/B tests.

Returning to our example, Fuze might develop an experiment in which researchers change the color of the product's packaging (an independent variable) and observe how often consumers look at the product (the dependent variable) on a simulated store shelf in a laboratory. Or, taking a field experiment approach, the research team might introduce two different label designs (keeping price and other features the same) into test markets for a brief period of time. By analyzing sales for the competing designs, results of the field experiment might help the company determine which package will perform better in a full-market release.

Some companies are now also applying research methods and measurement techniques from the field of neuroscience in order to gain a better understanding of consumer response to marketing stimuli. Sometimes referred to as *neuromarketing* or *consumer neuroscience,* this exciting area of experimental research is gaining greater attention in recent years from brands and marketing research firms alike. One well-known study used brain-imaging technology in a twist on the famous Pepsi Challenge taste test from the 1970s. Based on the part of the brain activated during the tasting session, the researchers concluded that participants' preference for Coke had less to do with the soft drink's taste than with the lifetime of positive associations the subjects had experienced with the Coca-Cola brand.[13] We will discuss neuromarketing research techniques in greater detail later in the chapter.

observation research

A data-collection tool that involves watching how people behave and recording anything about that behavior that might be relevant to the research objective.

Observation Studies

Observation research is a systematic process that involves watching how people behave and recording anything about that behavior that might be relevant to the research objective. Companies often find such information useful, but participants may subconsciously try to please researchers and act as they think researchers expect them to. While observation allows researchers to see *how* people behave, it is not useful in determining *why* they behave that way. Firms often use observation in conjunction with other techniques that help them identify the motivation behind particular behaviors.

mystery shoppers

Trained researchers hired to pose as customers in order to gather information about the physical appearance or customer service attributes of a store.

A form of observation research commonly used by service firms is the use of mystery shoppers. **Mystery shoppers** are trained researchers hired to pose as customers in order to gather information about the physical appearance or customer service attributes of a store. A mystery shopper might report on the neatness of the shelves, cleanliness of bathrooms, and amount of time it takes to receive service. For instance, *QSR* magazine publishes an annual study (see Table 5.3) that rates the speed and quality of various customer service attributes of national fast-food chains; these data come from responses of dozens of mystery shoppers for each chain.[14]

behavioral targeting

A data-collection method that utilizes a variety of technologies to anonymously track and compile individual consumer behaviors.

Another form of observation-based marketing research is behavioral targeting. Using **behavioral targeting**, companies utilize a variety of technologies to anonymously track and compile individual consumer behaviors. For instance, many website and e-commerce providers place cookies on visitors' browsers to trace which websites they visited, what they searched for, how long they lingered on a specific page, and whether they made a purchase. Collection and use of this passive data, acquired without user awareness or in some cases explicit consent, raises interesting questions about

TABLE 5.3 *QSR* Magazine Results of Drive-Through Study

Chain	Eye Contact	"Please"	Pleasant Demeanor	Smile	"Thank You"
Arby's	90.2	38.7	87.7	73.0	93.3
Burger King	87.2	39.6	86.6	75.6	94.5
Carl's Jr.	91.3	55.0	86.3	76.3	91.3
Chick-fil-A	92.4	67.6	94.6	91.4	94.1
Dunkin' Donuts	90.6	38.8	83.1	75.0	86.3
Hardee's	84.9	40.7	79.1	60.5	87.2
KFC	89.9	44.9	82.9	78.5	89.2
McDonald's	85.3	41.7	76.1	73.6	89.6
Taco Bell	89.0	41.1	85.3	77.3	89.0
Wendy's	78.9	41.6	82.0	68.9	90.7

Source: *https://www.qsrmagazine.com/reports/2018-qsr-drive-thru-study.*

consumer privacy and marketing research ethics. We will discuss these issue in greater detail later in this chapter.

Behavioral targeting is not an online-only activity: Retailers also track shopping behaviors in brick-and-mortar stores. For instance, Kroger's has implemented a sensor-based technology, known as the QueVision system, to help reduce wait times in check-out lines and improve employee scheduling. By installing a network of infrared motion detectors above its entry doors and cash registers, Kroger's is able to automatically determine precisely when it needs to open additional checkout lanes. During the COVID-19 pandemic, QueVision was credited in helping to monitor customer capacity, enabling the grocery chain to better maintain a safe shopping environment for customers.[15]

Customer Insights from Social Media Data Many brands today actively engage consumers on social media and use it to gain deeper insights on their customers wants and needs, gauge product and service quality through online reviews, and track response to brands' advertising and promotions. Brand managers track a variety of social media metrics on a weekly or even daily basis, including: number of brand mentions, sentiment (e.g., ratio of positive to negative, and engagement (number of likes, dislikes, and comments).

Blog mining involves using automated tools to find and extract information found on the web about a brand and then using specialized software to analyze and make sense of these large amounts of text-based data. Many powerful tools are freely available on the web for this purpose: For instance, Google Insights (http://www.google.com/insights/search/) can be configured to search within a specified region or over a specified date range. Similarly, a number of Twitter-related search tools and services, such as Search, Twitter, and TweetDeck, enable marketers to search and analyze brand-related tweets from microbloggers across the world.

blog mining

A research technique that uses automated tools to find and extract information on the web about a brand and then uses specialized software to analyze these large amounts of text-based data.

connect Exercise 5-2

Social Media in Action

Social media are changing the way organizations conduct marketing research. For example, Dr Pepper uses marketing insights from over 8 million Facebook fans to figure out which marketing messages might work best. Dr Pepper sends out multiple messages each day and then tracks and monitors fan reactions. Social media allow Dr Pepper to measure how many times a message is viewed, how many times it is shared with other users, and what people are saying about it. One of the insights the company captured from this research is that loyal Dr Pepper customers like "edgy" one-line messages such as, "If liking you is wrong, we don't want to be right." These types of messages were more likely to be passed along to other users.

Other firms, including language-learning company Rosetta Stone, use social media's research and targeting capabilities to find new markets for their products. Social media marketing research suggested that some consumers want to learn a new language for the mental challenge rather than for reasons such as their job or an upcoming trip. Based on this marketing research, Rosetta Stone targeted social media ads to people interested in mental fitness. The marketing campaign based on social media research was well received, performing better than previous campaigns.

The Social Media in Action Connect exercise in Chapter 5 will let you decide how to utilize social media to improve marketing research and then how to develop strategies from those findings. By understanding the role social media can play in helping your organization gain insights from consumers, you will be able to apply these strategies to successfully target current and potential customers.

Source: See Geoffrey A. Fowler, "Are You Talking to Me?" *The Wall Street Journal,* June 18, 2012, http://online.wsj.com/article/SB1000142405274870411640457626308397 0961862.html.

Pros and Cons of Quantitative Research Quantitative methods for collecting and analyzing data can often be done quickly, at low cost, and may help better researchers understand cause-and-effect patterns in consumer behaviors. As with qualitative research, there are trade-offs and occasional drawbacks to relying on these techniques. For instance, statistical analysis of quantitative data can give marketing professionals descriptive or predictive insight into buyer behavior. However, the validity of inferences drawn from statistical tests is dependent upon the quality of the data and representativeness of the sample.

Further, the degree to which statistical results are generalizable beyond the sample data may be questioned absent evidence that the individuals studied are truly representative of that broader population. Table 5.4 summarizes several key advantages and disadvantages of qualitative and quantitative research methods.

Thus far, we have explained the marketing research process and explored various ways companies utilize primary and secondary data to help formulate and address research questions in both B2C and B2B settings. While these frameworks and approaches translate across national borders, cultural differences may still need to be considered when undertaking international research studies. In the next section, we take a closer look at some of the most important issues facing global marketing researchers.

TABLE 5.4 Advantages and Disadvantages of Qualitative and Quantitative Research

Research Method Type	Advantages	Disadvantages
Qualitative	Uncovers details concerning the motivations behind behaviors	Results may be difficult to measure objectively
	Is not limited to a predetermined set of responses	Research can take longer than quantitative methods
	Can be a good way to start research into a marketing problem	Potential for researcher bias
	Can be very flexible in approach	Individual participants may not represent general target market
	Can be used to generate marketing ideas	Small sample size
Quantitative	Results may be generalizable to a larger population	May be limited by researchers' questions
	Some methods can be conducted quickly and inexpensively	Response rates can be very low
	Analysis of data can be faster than in qualitative research	Difficult to determine nonresponse bias
	Can conduct causal studies that indicate why behaviors occur	Possible respondent self-selection bias
	Can be cost-effective	Participant resistance to giving sensitive information
	Often convenient for respondent	

GLOBAL MARKETING RESEARCH

LO 5-4

Explain the importance of research to firms marketing products globally.

Misunderstanding differences in customer needs and wants in other regions often presents difficulties for firms seeking to market products globally. As a result, firms doing business in foreign countries typically engage in international marketing research. Global marketing research is the systematic design, collection, recording, analysis, interpretation, and reporting of information pertinent to a particular marketing decision facing a company operating internationally. As Frans van Houten, chief executive officer of the Dutch health and well-being company Royal Philips Electronics, says: "In a very diverse world with customers in China, Brazil, and in the U.S., we cannot generalize that they [customers] have the same needs. Innovation is only really meaningful when it is relevant to the local market."[16] The answer, obviously, is for firms to do global marketing research.

Consider China, the most populous country on the planet. The rise of China as an economic powerhouse makes companies want to sell their products there. But consumer culture in China is unique to that country. Chinese consumers are very conscientious about saving money, extremely price-sensitive, and do not like to pay by credit card.[17] However, consumers from China want luxury products. They are willing to pay more for products consumed in public than those consumed in private. Consequently, they seek luxury items more as status symbols than for their intrinsic value. In the absence of research into Chinese consumer culture, Western companies might not have a complete picture of the cultural differences that make marketing in China considerably different from marketing in the United States or Europe.

global

Challenges Unique to International Marketing Research

When research objectives require marketing researchers to venture across borders and cultures, potential problems can quickly multiply. In many foreign markets, primary data are vital due to the questionable validity and comparability of secondary data sources.[18] However, a range of factors including language; culture; technology; and social, legal, and political environments can complicate the collection and analysis of primary data.

Language Language is perhaps the most obvious obstacle. Many idioms and phrases hold different meanings across languages; some words simply don't exist. Before the study begins, questionnaires or interview guides must be translated into the language of each country being studied. To ensure the interpretations are equivalent, the study materials should be back-translated into the original language by a second translator. Similarly, qualitative responses from study subjects must be translated back into the original language prior to analysis. Each of these steps increase costs and potential errors.

Culture Cultural differences must also be considered. For instance, the willingness and ability of respondents to provide a free-form response can vary considerably based upon broad cultural norms and beliefs. Within some cultures, questions dealing with certain topics (e.g., sex) or product categories (e.g., feminine hygiene) may be considered rude or inappropriate. The use of mixed-gender focus groups involving nonmarried individuals may even violate religious laws in some national cultures or subcultures. The culture of the region being studied will impact how the study is conducted, what is asked, and the length and form of information received in response.

Technology When designing an international marketing research study, it's important that you select the right technology solution to reach your target audience. While digital surveys have become a primary means of data collection in many countries, there remains vast differences worldwide in terms of access to and adoption of computing platforms. In many developing economies, for instance, the mobile phone has become the most frequently used computing device for consumers and businesspeople alike. Technology preferences are also important to know. In certain countries, research is more often done using SMS text messaging, while online surveys using a mobile browser or branded app are more common in others.

Social, Legal, and Political Environment A lack of stability in the social, legal, and political environment in some parts of the world can represent another distinct set of marketing research problems. For instance, high levels of crime in working-class neighborhoods in Brazil and other parts of Latin America can make door-to-door interviewing dangerous.[19]

Laws pertaining to marketing and marketing research can also differ by country. Businesses conducting research in EU countries must comply with newly enacted data privacy protocols or risk hefty fines. In China, foreign companies are allowed to conduct surveys but only by hiring domestic research companies licensed by the National Bureau of Statistics. While these legal restrictions certainly can create obstacles, the consequences of not conducting research prior to implementing changes in pricing or new promotions can cause great harm to a brand. In early 2022, Starbucks found itself in hot water in China after announcing a 30 percent increase in prices to offset rising inflation and supply chain costs. The announcement, which came on the heels of a recent product safety controversy at some Chinese stores, fueled nationalist sentiment amongst many consumers. Users on

Weibo, a Chinese social media platform, urged consumers to boycott the chain, with others claiming they'd instead opt for cheaper local brands.[20]

Whether a company conducts its own research or hires an international research firm to do it, the research tasks remain the same:

Starbucks caused an outcry amongst Chinese consumers following an announced pricing increase. The incident highlights the importance of conducting high-quality marketing research in global markets. *Imaginechina Limited/Alamy Stock Photo*

1. Analyze the global market to understand the following: the fastest-growing markets overall, the largest markets for the firm's products, trends in the various global markets that relate to the firm's products, and any restrictions on the importing of the firm's products such as quotas or tariffs.[21] This type of information may be obtained through secondary sources, such as trade reports and websites, specific to the country being researched.

2. Acquire specific information about the products the firm wants to sell globally. This information should include: the names of the competitors, what market share they hold, what promotional activities they engage in, and at what prices they sell their products.

3. Estimate the potential market share and sales of products at particular price points to ensure that the venture will be a profitable one.

MARKETING RESEARCH TRENDS

LO 5-5

Understand several of the latest trends in marketing research, including customer journey mapping, mobile marketing research, and neuromarketing.

Several key innovations and technological advances are altering the face of marketing research. These are occurring in areas such as mobile communications, the rise of social media, and methods from the field of neuroscience. In some cases, they have led to only small modifications of traditional research design and measurement. In others, they have resulted in novel research methods. We briefly discuss three important marketing research trends: the growing use of customer journey mapping, mobile marketing research, and neuromarketing.

Customer Journey Maps

As businesses seek to differentiate themselves around superior customer experiences, customer journey mapping has emerged as an important marketing research exercise. A **customer journey map** is a visual depiction of the steps customers go through when engaging with a company in order to achieve a particular goal.[22] From an operational standpoint, the journey map highlights major firm-customer touchpoints. However, it should also highlight customer pre- and post-engagement actions, emotions, and expectations that define the entire customer experience. Outlining a full customer journey map in such detail requires extensive market research, often involving multiple data sources and research methods.

Creating a customer journey map begins with developing a customer persona for each of the company's most important customer segments. A **persona** is a semi-fictional customer profile that represents the key traits of a large segment of a company's audience.[23] It commonly consists of demographic data along with other behavioral and

customer journey map

A diagram that illustrates the physical and emotional steps customers go through when engaging with a company's touchpoint in order to achieve a particular goal.

persona

A semi-fictional profile representing the key traits and motivations of a key segment of a brand's customer base.

psychographic details like the customer's goals, time frame, interests, lifestyle, and challenges. Figure 5.6 provides an example of a customer persona profile.

Development of the customer profile is informed by primary market research, social media monitoring, web analytics, customer service interactions, and identifiable buyer behaviors. Elements of a persona include answers to questions like:

- What does a typical customer do? What does their typical day look like?
- What are their frustrations and pain points?
- What are they seeking to accomplish via their brand engagements?
- What mental images come to mind when you think about them?

Customers go through multiple steps as they interact with the brand. For example, locating a product in the store or reaching out to support with a technical issue. Each of these steps constitute a distinct touchpoint. A touchpoint refers to any moment in their journey when a customer comes into contact with a brand (website, social media, online review, advertisements, purchase, customer service).[24] The research team would establish the sequence of touchpoints a customer encounters as they seek to accomplish a task along with the emotions (delight, frustration) they experience at each point of the journey. In so doing, the journey map should highlight touchpoints that are a **moment of truth**; a critical point in a customer journey when a key event occurs and a lasting impression about the brand is formed. These are touchpoints when the customer either falls in love with the brand or turns away and leaves.

In order to develop personas, establish customer touchpoints for achieving various goals, and identify moments of truth, researchers will utilize a variety of research methods. Table 5.5 describes how data from various primary research approaches may be used to support customer journey mapping exercises.

moment of truth

A critical touchpoint within a customer journey when a key event occurs and a lasting impression about the brand is formed.

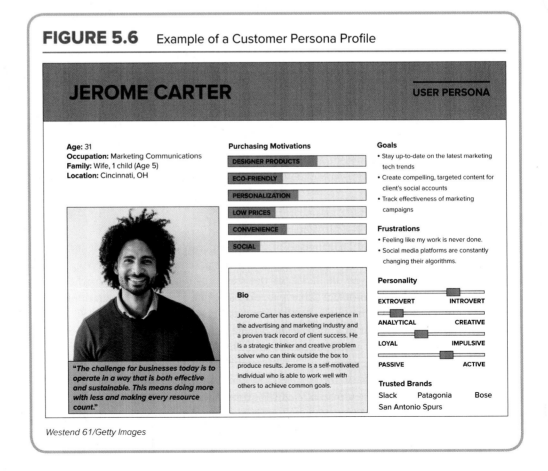

FIGURE 5.6   Example of a Customer Persona Profile

Westend 61/Getty Images

TABLE 5.5 Research Methods used to Create Customer Journey Maps

Research Method	Why It's Used for Customer Journey Mapping
Customer depth interviews or focus groups	One-on-one or group conversations with customers to uncover first-hand stories, frustrations, and needs.
Observation study	Observing users perform actions in their natural environments enables the research team to better understand the actual flow of user interactions and uncover mindsets that interviewees were not able to recall.
Contextual observation studies	Observe users perform tasks while researchers maintain the ability to ask clarifying questions and provoke open-ended conversation.
Diary studies	Long-term studies that allow customers to document their behaviors, thoughts, and emotions over time so that the researcher can understand a variety of customer experiences and journeys.
Competitive analysis	Competitive evaluations allow managers to benchmark their customer' experiences with their competitors to identify strengths and areas for potential improvement.

Mobile Marketing Research

Nearly 85 percent of the world's population today owns a smartphone, with more than 6.63 billion unique mobile subscribers.[25] There are actually more connected devices than there are people on the planet! Not surprisingly, the ubiquity of devices such as smartphones and tablet computers has made mobile marketing research a fast-growing field. The term **mobile marketing research** refers to participants taking part in marketing research via mobile devices.[26]

mobile marketing research
Research that involves participants taking part in marketing research via mobile devices.

Mobile marketing research can take a variety of forms. For instance:

- Quantitative research in which participants complete surveys on their mobile devices.
- Quantitative research in which participants allow applications on their mobile devices to gather information about them or their environment. This is referred to as *passive data collection.*
- Qualitative research in which the mobile device either facilitates communication (e.g., taking part in an online focus group using a tablet) or facilitates data collection (e.g., collecting photos, recordings) by the research subject.
- Qualitative or quantitative research in which the researcher uses a mobile device to collect data.

Mobile marketing research offers several key advantages. First, it enables researchers to reach audiences through the channel that they are most comfortable. People tend to have their smartphones with them all the time. Second, the advent of mobile market research has introduced respondent location to the market research process. Taking advantage of GPS-enabled smartphones and mobile apps, research firms are able to push short, targeted "smart" surveys to respondent's devices based on their location. This facilitates the type of "in the moment" research that enables companies to more effectively map customer journeys and gain insights into customers' emotional experiences at key touchpoints and lessens reliance on consumers' memories. Third, almost all mobile devices come standard with a keyboard, camera, and microphone. This offers the opportunity for researchers to obtain rich, multimedia data from consumers in the form of texts, photos, videos, and voice recordings. These smartphone features offer a complement to traditional qualitative methods, such as ethnography or focus groups, by allowing individuals to capture their personal experiences with a brand or product via their mobile device as they are occurring.

Finally, GPS receivers and other instrumentation in smartphones and tablets enable researchers to gather information about what people actually do, without even asking survey questions. For example, retailers of all types, including well-known stores like Family Dollar, Cabela's, and Kroger's, have installed systems that track signals transmitted from shoppers' smartphones as they continuously seek to identify available Wi-Fi networks.[27] Using these constant-probe requests, stores can actually track how often the customer (or more exactly, the customer's phone) visits the store, and they can track the phone's location, within a few feet, during any given visit. Retailers can use these technologies and the resulting data to decide on matters like changing store layouts, merchandise selection, and offering customized coupons.

Neuromarketing

Traditional research methods rely heavily on the use of self-reported measures of attitudes, intentions, and behaviors. However, there are several drawbacks:

- Certain research topics may be embarrassing or uncomfortable, and some research participants cannot or do not answer honestly.
- In some cases, a chosen measurement instrument may not allow the subject to express the true degree of feeling about an evaluated item.
- In other cases, subjects may not be consciously aware of their attitudes or have difficulty articulating their thinking or feeling into a reported response.

neuromarketing

The use of insights and tools from neuroscience to better understand consumer responses to different kinds of marketing stimuli.

In such cases, neuromarketing techniques are useful in addressing such "can't say" or "won't say" limitations. **Neuromarketing** is the use of neuroscientific methods to better understand consumer decision making and responses to different kinds of marketing stimuli. The term also covers a variety of methods for measuring behavioral and physiological responses to marketing stimuli. These methods include fMRI, EEG, eye-tracking, facial expression coding, and core biometrics (e.g., heart rate, respiration, skin conductance).

Brain-Imaging Techniques
A number of brain-imaging techniques have been developed by medical researchers. The two most widely used by marketing researchers today are *functional magnetic resonance imaging (fMRI)* and *electroencephalography (EEG)*.

Functional Magnetic Resonance Imaging (fMRI) Neuroscientists have established certain regions of the brain are closely associated with specific functions, such as planning and emotions. Brain activation consumes energy. This activity triggers a biological response aimed at replenishing spent glucose and oxygen supplies from the activated area. fMRI machines emit an electromagnetic pulse that measures the amount of this oxygenated blood flow. fMRI can pinpoint activation in even the deepest parts of the brain down to the nearest millimeter.

During an fMRI study, the participant will lie down, face-up within a narrow cylinder. Marketing stimuli are then projected onto a small reflective surface, somewhat resembling a car's rear-view mirror. The subject may be given a button-box, with which they can signal a decision or action during the study. By using fMRI to monitor brain activity when individuals are exposed to marketing stimuli or make choices, researchers can draw inferences with respect to subjects' implicit attitudes and desires.

Electroencephalography (EEG) EEG measures patterns of electrical activity emanating from the cortex, the outermost part of the brain. The cortex is responsible for "higher" brain functions, such as decoding sensory information, memories, and planning. As neurons in the cortex fire up, they create small electrical fields. These currents can be captured and amplified by sensors placed around the scalp, typically embedded within an EEG cap. The brainwave signals are then sent to a computer for analysis with specialized software.

In comparison to fMRI, EEG is a much less expensive technology. Prices for some lower-end, research-grade systems start at around $1,000 (compared to $4 million for an fMRI machine). While EEG lacks the spatial resolution of fMRI testing, there is no temporal delay in EEG response. This makes it possible to match EEG data up with data from other sensors, such as eye-tracking systems. Combining data from multiple systems can be powerful, allowing researchers to track not only where an individual was looking but also how he or she was reacting while looking there.

Eye-Tracking

In the past 15 years, commercial application of eye-tracking technology to assess the effectiveness of visual marketing efforts has quickly grown. This trend has been driven in large measure by technology advances that have led to increased ease of use of eye-tracking devices and a sharp decline in their cost. Companies like P&G, Unilever, Pepsi, Google, and Nestlé are avid users of eye-tracking, especially in areas like advertising, product development, user experience (UX) testing, and packaging.

Eye-tracking technologies use infrared light and specialized cameras to non-intrusively track individual's visual attention. Results from eye-tracking studies provide researchers with direct measures of how consumers allocate their attention to marketing and nonmarketing stimuli in their environment. Because there is no meaningful lag between where someone is looking and what they are thinking, eye-tracking research can also provide clues into consumers' mental processes.

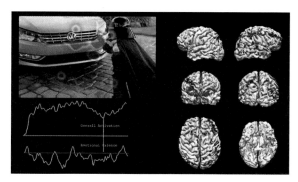

EEG study shows brain activation as subjects view Super Bowl advertisements. *Sands Research*

Executive Perspective...
because everyone is a marketer

A.J. Fernández
Alejandro Fernández   Owner, Executive Director of Phocus
Panama City, Panama

What are some key insights you've discovered when conducting cross-cultural research?

One take-away has been the importance of using multiple research methods to triangulate study results.

A few years ago, we were helping a Colombian coffee brand that was looking to introduce a premium coffee in the Guangdong province of China. While China is still very much a tea-oriented culture, coffee is gaining popularity throughout China, particularly amongst the affluent and in larger cities. There are 120 million people in Guangdong alone—that is the size of Mexico in a single state. So, the opportunity is significant.

We worked with a business partner, MindMetrics, in setting up a series of eye-tracking and EEG studies to measure Chinese consumers' response to various packaging concepts. Observing participants in real-time, we noticed they seemed to be spending a lot of time focused on an area of the package containing Chinese characters indicating the coffee was from Colombia. The level of attention was too high, but we didn't know why. Were the Chinese characters right? Should we phrase it in a different way? Perhaps we should take the characters out altogether?

We decided to add an item to our post-study questionnaire that asked participants an open-ended question about this particular element of the packaging. And the answers we got back were amazing. It turns out that there was nothing wrong with the characters or the grammar. In case after case, what we found were subjects commenting that "if this is real Colombian coffee, how come it has Chinese characters in front? Shouldn't this package have more Spanish letters or something that is more related to Colombia, like the Juan Valdez symbol?" By virtue of placing the Chinese symbols directly on the packaging, it raised consumers' suspicions that the coffee was not authentically Colombian. By printing the product's provenance in Chinese, it actually lowered trust in the quality of the product. Even though it was less aesthetically pleasing, consumers preferred a sticker with the Chinese symbols placed near the Spanish words on the packaging that indicated the product's origin.

This is an insight we never would have obtained using neuro-methods alone. And we would not have known to even ask about it in a survey without the eye-tracking and EEG study.

FIGURE 5.7   Example of a Heat Map for a Print Advertisement

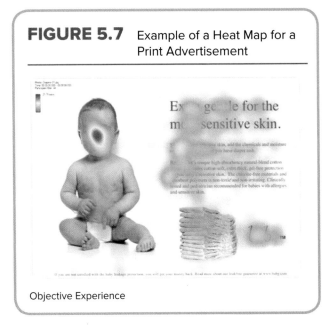

Objective Experience

How can you tell if someone is smiling for real? The only true indicator of happiness is when the muscles along the sides of the eyes are activated and pulled up (crow's feet). However, only 1 in 10 people can consciously activate that muscle. This is why when people are smiling during holiday cards or photo shoots, it doesn't look real. *Science of People*

Eye-tracking studies are particularly useful for answering questions in marketing situations such as:

- *Print advertising:* What elements of a magazine ad "pop out" visually?
- *User experience:* What steps, such as identifying product availability in nearby stores, do consumers take in trying to find information using a web page or mobile app?
- *Promotions:* How do colors, shapes, and spacing affect attention to products displayed within in-store circulars?
- *Packaging and retail store layout:* How can we change packaging or item display to increase the probability that our consumers consider our more-profitable store-brand items?
- *Television advertising:* Does the television advertising campaign for our new product visually engage viewers, such that it leads to greater brand awareness and recall?

Eye-tracking data are often visualized in a number of interesting ways. **Heat maps** are colored regions overlaid on an image; they are the most frequently offered eye-tracking output. The maps are usually color-coded so that the warmer the color, the higher the levels of attention to that area. (For example, red indicates the highest attention, blue the lowest.) Figure 5.7 shows a sample heat map.

Eye-tracking offers a number of key advantages: It is relatively inexpensive; it is rather easy to set up studies; and it requires little complex knowledge to generate useful output. The fundamental challenge is that while eye-tracking does a good job of showing precisely where someone looked, it does not necessarily tell you *why*. For this reason, eye-tracking experts often suggest the additional use of other research methods, such as open-ended questioning, during or after eye-tracking studies in order to gain deeper insights into consumers' attention processes.

Automated Facial Coding   Quick, make a happy face and hold it. Which facial muscles were activated when you smiled? How about when you frown? Or are angry? Disgusted?

According to body language expert Vanessa Van Edwards, CEO of the consulting firm Science of People, the face is the best indicator of a person's emotions. Understanding how to read and interpret microexpressions is an essential part of understanding nonverbal behavior and reading people. A **microexpression** is a brief, involuntary facial expression that appears on a person's face according to the emotions being experienced. Unlike regular, prolonged facial expressions, it is difficult to fake a microexpression. **Facial coding** is the categorization of facial microexpressions to reveal the emotional response of an individual while processing content.

It is thought that the communication of emotion through facial expressions precedes the development of language. In fact, the idea that facial expressions are universally linked to emotions dates back to Darwin's work on evolution. However, it was not until the 1970s that psychologist Dr. Paul Ekman demonstrated that certain facial muscle movements are consistently associated with discrete affective states across human cultures. The basic emotions identified through Ekman's cross-cultural research on facial microexpressions are joy, surprise, sadness, anger, fear, contempt, and disgust.

Dr. Ekman and his associates have since trained thousands of psychologists, researchers, and law-enforcement, military, and national security professionals to detect deception by recognizing split-second changes in an individual's facial microexpressions. However, reliance on human expert coders makes it costly and difficult to scale this methodology for use in larger research projects. However, thanks to advances in imaging technology and artificial intelligence, new systems allow for automated facial coding. There is even a free smartphone app available (Affectiva's *Affdexme*) for Apple IOS and Android users. Try it out!

Whether using state-of-the-art neuromarketing techniques or traditional research methods, marketing researchers must remain cognizant of ethical issues involving the treatment of their participants and the use of study findings. We discuss these issues in the following section.

heat map

Colored regions overlaid on an image; the most frequently offered eye-tracking output.

microexpression

A brief, involuntary facial expression that appears on a person's face according to the emotions being experienced.

facial coding

The categorization of facial expressions to reveal the emotional response of an individual while processing content.

▥ connect Exercise **5-3**

Please complete the *Connect* exercise for Chapter 5 that focuses on how marketers can utilize neuromarketing tools to better understand consumer responses to different kinds of marketing stimuli. By understanding the insights that neuromarketing can provide, you will be able to choose the most effective tactics to successfully execute your organization's marketing strategy.

MARKETING RESEARCH ETHICS

LO 5-6

Discuss the main ethical issues in conducting marketing research.

High-profile scandals involving questionable research practices and the misuse of customer data have placed ethical concerns over marketing research squarely in the public spotlight. A few notable examples include:

- Amazon was fined $887 million by EU regulators for making it difficult for users to reject web-tracking cookies that enable the company to collect and share customers' personal data.[28]
- The online dating site OkCupid admitted it conducted experiments in which it skewed couples compatibility percentiles to manipulate users into thinking they were a better match than they really were—and vice versa.[29]
- Facebook conducted a secret study in which it sought to manipulate the emotions of nearly 700,000 unwitting users by showing them either more positive or negative posts on their news feeds.[30]
- Google settled with the DOJ and paid a $500 million criminal penalty for knowingly abetting the illegal importation of prescription drugs into the United States with geo-targeted advertising facilitated by misuse of users' private data.[31]

In each instance, the companies insisted their actions were *legally* permittable as part of their user terms of service agreements. But ethics experts question whether the research and use of customer data represented ethical research practices. Given the wide availability of customer data, understanding the need to conduct marketing research in an above-the-board manner has never been greater.

Electronic toy manufacturer VTech Electronics Limited agreed to settle charges by the Federal Trade Commission (FTC) that the company violated a U.S. children's privacy law by collecting personal information from children without providing direct notice and obtaining their parents' consent. VTech paid $650,000 as part of its settlement with the FTC.[32] *John Phillips/AP Images*

Respecting Customer Data Privacy

Increasingly powerful computer capabilities allow for the collection, storage, and analysis of data from millions of consumers. In many instances, passive data is gathered automatically, without the end user's explicit knowledge as they navigate the Internet or peruse a social media platform. Tech companies like Twitter, Facebook, and Google leverage their customers' personal data to increase advertising revenues. Online retailers, like Amazon, can readily access customers' product search and purchase histories to prompt customer purchases through specialized offers.

At issue here is the willful intrusion on individuals' privacy and use of customers' personal data without their consent. Companies must be mindful about what types of information they are collecting, how they are using it, who they share it with, and how they are storing and securing it. There is enough concern about consumer privacy in some industries that many companies have named C-level executives, who are charged with protecting customer interest and serving as internal watchdogs, guarding against unethical practices in their company's collection and use of customer data.

Standards for Ethical Marketing Research

Marketing research professionals must guard against potential abuses and conflicts of interest, particularly in sponsored research. For instance, it is not uncommon for a market research firm to be compelled by their client to arrive at a predetermined conclusion that is favorable to the client's interest.[33] While such work can be lucrative in the short term, the researcher must keep in mind that placing their name on such research risks long-term reputational damage. If findings from a study are made public, the research should be published with a statement disclosing any interest by sponsors funding the research, so that the results can be understood in context. For example if a survey into the effects of a certain mattress technology on sleep quality was paid for by a mattress manufacturer, this relationship should be clearly identified wherever the results are published.

Marketing researchers must also be aware of their obligations to participants and prospective participants of their studies. For instance, participation in market research should be completely voluntary. Consider the case of a retail business planning to study how it might improve frontline employee productivity and retention. If workers were unduly pressured, cajoled, or coerced by supervisors to complete this survey, this would raise serious ethical concerns (and likely bias the results). In addition, all individuals should be fully informed of all benefits and potential risks of study participation, including psychological risks, before agreeing to participate in the study. Once the study has been completed, the researcher is responsible for upholding assurances of participant anonymity and data confidentiality that were represented at the outset of the study. Compromise of personally identifying data from a research study is a serious breach that in some contexts can carry serious legal consequences.

Another significant research ethics issue involves the use of deception in marketing research. For example, tactics such as misrepresenting the purpose of a study or not disclosing the length of an interview because of a concern that respondents will not cooperate otherwise are clearly unethical. In certain instances, however, deception may be acceptable provided it serves a legitimate purpose and does not encourage participation from people who would otherwise not participate. For instance, consider a survey about consumer attitudes toward electric vehicles done on behalf of Tesla. If respondents were told Tesla was the research sponsor, they might respond differently than if the research was presented as a general interest survey. One could reasonably argue that this would be a valid reason not to disclose the research sponsor.[34]

Organizations like the American Marketing Association, the Marketing Research Association (MRA), the International Chamber of Commerce (ICC), and ESOMAR, have established ethical standards for conducting research. Table 5.6 lists the key components of the Insights Association's Code of Standards.[35] Such standards are important to the industry because they help maintain public trust. Without that trust, individuals will be less likely to participate in future marketing research.

Consumer distrust of how companies use information will have negative consequences: Consumers may refuse to participate in research studies or may be unwilling to provide personal information either online or face-to-face. At the extreme, consumers will hesitate to visit company websites or order products online. Additionally, ethical behavior on the part of companies will make it unnecessary for the government to increase regulation of marketing research practices. Clearly, it is in the best interests of companies to conduct marketing research in the most ethical manner possible.

TABLE 5.6   Marketing Research Association's *Code of Marketing Research Standards*

MRA members will . . .

1. Treat respondents with respect and in a professional manner.
2. Protect the rights of respondents, including the right to refuse to participate in all or some of the research process.
3. Influence no respondent's opinion or attitude through direct or indirect attempts, including the framing or order of questions.
4. Protect the privacy of respondents. Keep confidential all information/data that could identify respondents to third parties without the respondents' consent. If such permission is given, it must be documented and the data may be used only for the purpose to which the respondent has agreed.
5. Proactively or upon request identify by name the research organization collecting data.
6. Obtain consent from respondents prior to utilizing their data in a manner materially different than that to which the respondent has agreed.
7. Ensure that respondent information collected during any study will not be used for sales, solicitations, push-polling or any other non-research purpose.
8. Make factually correct statements to secure cooperation, including for database/sample development, and honor all promises made to respondents including but not limited to the use of data.
9. Ensure that respondents are informed at the outset if an interview or discussion is being audio or video recorded and obtain written consent if the recorded interview or discussion will be viewed by a third party or reproduced for outside use.
10. Not represent non-research activity as research.
11. Provide respondents with clear notice and choice about participation when passively collecting data for research purposes from non-public sources or places, where the respondent would not reasonably expect information to be collected.
12. When collecting data, maintain an internal do-not-collect database as a complement to requests made by respondents for future communications and participation in marketing research projects.
13. Collect personally identifiable information (PII), including email addresses, whether actively or passively, only with respondents awareness and permission.
14. Collect, maintain and utilize Internet samples of only those individuals who have provided their permission to be contacted for marketing research purposes and those who have a reasonable expectation based on an existing business relationship that they will receive invitations for marketing research purposes.
15. Consider data privacy a fundamental part of planning and the research process, and maintain a clear, concise and easy to understand privacy or terms of use policy that describes the way respondents data is collected, used, disclosed and managed.
16. Take special care and adhere to applicable law when conducting research across state and national borders and when conducting research with vulnerable populations, including but not limited to children.
17. When having the responsibility of creating products and services for use by respondents, provide products and services that are safe and fit for their intended use, are labeled in accordance with all laws and regulations, and provide the means to make the respondent whole should problems arise, in part by including emergency contact information.

Source: Marketing Research Association

Amie Larum

Client Success Manager
iMotions

Describe your job. As a Client Success Manager, I am responsible for training, demoing, and consulting on the iMotions biometric research platform. I manage both academic and corporate accounts, whose departments/industries range from psychology to marketing to computer science to packaging design. My every day includes internal meetings, client phone calls, screen-sharing trainings, and an occasional trip out to see a client or attend a conference.

Describe how you got the job that you have. I got my job at iMotions through my academic adviser in college. My adviser was also my professor for several classes I took, so we built up a good relationship. I would often go to his office for career advice during my senior spring semester. He had a friend that worked at iMotions who sent him a job description. He sent me this info and encouraged me to apply. The reference from my adviser to his iMotions' friend definitely helped me as I went through the interview process.

What has been the most important thing in making you successful at your job? The most important thing in making me successful at my job has been my willingness and ability to take initiative. The day-to-day responsibilities of your job definitely give you valuable career skills, but you could be professionally growing much more if you extended yourself. These extra responsibilities not only provide you with extra skills, but they also build support with management, which is handy when looking at moving up or within a company

Amie Larum

What advice would you give soon-to-be graduates? My number one piece of advice would be to keep your heart open to all options and realize many have not presented themselves to you yet. I thought I was destined for a Ph.D. and research my senior year. Less than six months after I formulated that "destiny," I was hired in corporate America! Little did I know at the time of senior year that I would feel comfortable, successful, and happy in this role. Even to this day I am unsure what the future holds, but I know if I work hard and extend myself, exciting new opportunities will arise. Another piece of advice I have is to network as much as possible. I wouldn't be at my job right now without my network. Connect with others whose careers interest you. Reach out and ask for an informational interview. The worse thing that could happen is that they say no (and that rarely happens!)

What do you consider your personal brand to be? My personal brand is one of a specific background yet a broad expertise. It is the unique skillset that comes from years of studying and researching that has enabled me to be successful at my job and build up how people view me. What makes me unique is that I am able to take this specific field and turn it into consultative success in other academic and corporate research fields. I provide a fresh perspective for my clients that goes beyond their field. As I learn more about these contrasting fields, my brand continues to develop and envelop other fields. With this new broad expertise, my personal brand can take me down many different careers paths.

SUMMARY

LO 5-1 Explain the importance of marketing research and explain the marketing research process.

Marketing research involves collecting, interpreting, and reporting information to address a clearly defined marketing problem. The goal of marketing research is to help companies understand and satisfy the needs and wants of customers. This task has become more important, and more complicated, as markets continue to become globalized, product life cycles continue to become shorter, and markets continue to change rapidly. In addition to its impact on businesses, marketing is important to consumers as well. Consumers rely on companies to develop and market goods and services that they need and want.

LO 5-2 Describe the various types of secondary data sources and explain the importance of predictive analytics.

Meeting the challenge presented by Big Data is not simply a matter of increasing data warehousing and database management capabilities. In this information-rich age, companies want information systems that give managers access to the right information, in the right form, at the right time to help them create customer value and strengthen relationships. A *marketing information system (MIS)* consists of the people, technologies, and procedures aimed at supplying an organization's marketing information needs. Effective marketing requires knowledge about current trends in the marketplace and information about what individual consumers are buying or are interested in buying. In-house systems, such as *decision support systems (DSS)* and online systems that support social media sites, allow companies to collect and analyze huge amounts of data. From there, recommendations for marketing actions can be made. The Internet enables researchers to conduct a variety of research, such as surveys, focus groups, and social media website monitoring.

Internal company data are the largest source of data a company has. Companies need ways to organize and make sense of the data in order to make them useful for marketing purposes. In addition, companies systematically gather *competitive intelligence* about what direct and indirect competitors are doing in terms of new-product development and their marketing mix. Such information can give a firm foreknowledge of a competitor's upcoming promotions or products, so that it can respond in a way that blunts the effects of the competitor's actions.

LO 5-3 Discuss the need for primary research and describe qualitative and quantitative research approaches.

The marketing research process is a well-defined set of five steps that, if followed, should yield invaluable information concerning a firm's market and its competition. The five steps include (1) define the problem, (2) develop a plan, (3) collect data, (4) analyze the data, and (5) present results and take action. During problem definition, the firm clarifies the exact nature of the problem. Developing the research plan involves identifying what type of research to do: *exploratory, descriptive,* or *causal.* The firm designs the research instrument, making sure that the selected measures exhibit both *reliability* and *validity.*

The third step, data collection, begins with the firm's decision to use secondary or primary data. Secondary data may already reside in the company's management information system or may be obtained from outside sources like the Internet. Primary data can be collected by various qualitative techniques such as focus groups, interviews, and observation, or by quantitative techniques such as surveys and experiments. *Sampling* enables marketing researchers to obtain feedback from a subset of the population that is representative of the population as a whole.

Researchers then analyze the collected data, converting the data into information that will be useful to marketers. The culmination of the research is a formal, written report to decision makers that includes an executive summary, research objectives, methods used, findings, and recommendations about how the firm should take action. *Data visualization* enables marketing researchers to present data and research results in pictorial or graphical format, which helps uncover new patterns in data and grasp difficult-to-understand concepts.

LO 5-4 Explain the importance of research to firms marketing products globally.

Global marketing research presents a number of different challenges compared to domestic research. One is the unfamiliar nature of foreign markets. A good way for a company to learn about consumer behavior in other regions is to use local marketing research companies, where available. Political, legal, sociocultural, and technological factors influence whether a company's products can be successfully marketed in a particular country.

LO 5-5 Understand several of the latest trends in marketing research, including customer journey mapping, mobile marketing research, and neuromarketing.

Several key innovations and technological advances are altering the face of marketing research. These are occurring in areas such as mobile communications, the rise of social media, and methods from the field of neuroscience. Over the last decade, the largest change in online research has come from the ever-increasing volume of user-generated content associated with social media.

Neuromarketing is the use of insights and tools from neuroscience to better understand consumer responses to different kinds of marketing stimuli. The neuromarketing "toolbox" consists of imaging technologies, such as fMRI or EEG, that directly measure brain activity. It also includes a variety of methods for measuring behavioral and physiological responses to marketing stimuli, such as eye-tracking, facial expression coding, core biometrics (e.g., heart rate, respiration, skin conductance), and implicit response testing.

John Phillips/
AP Images

LO 5-6 Discuss the main ethical issues in conducting marketing research.

The increasingly powerful computer capabilities available to companies allow for the collection, storage, and analysis of data from millions of consumers. But companies must be careful not to go too far in collecting information of a sensitive nature.

Another ethical issue in marketing research is the misuse of research methods and findings. Marketing research firms may be compelled by their clients to return findings favorable to the client or to arrive at a conclusion predetermined by the client. Marketing organizations like the American Marketing Association, the Marketing Research Association, and ESOMAR are concerned with the reliability of research results and have set up ethical standards for conducting research.

KEY TERMS

A/B testing (p. 166)
advertising effectiveness
   studies (p. 148)
behavioral targeting (p.166)
Big Data (p. 158)
blog mining (p. 167)
causal research (p. 150)
competitive intelligence (p. 155)
convenience sample (p. 151)
cross-tabulation (p. 153)
customer journey map (p. 171)
data visualization (p. 154)
decision support system (DSS) (p. 151)
demand analysis (p. 148)
depth interview (p. 162)
descriptive research (p. 150)

ethnographic research (p. 163)
exploratory research (p. 150)
facial coding (p. 177)
field experiment (p. 165)
focus group (p. 162)
heat map (p. 177)
marketing information system (p. 151)
marketing research (p. 148)
microexpression (p. 177)
mobile marketing research (p. 173)
moment of truth (p. 172)
mystery shoppers (p. 166)
neuromarketing (p. 174)
nonprobability sampling (p. 151)
observation research (p. 166)
panel data (p. 155)

persona (p. 171)
predictive analytics (p. 158)
primary data (p. 151)
probability sampling (p. 151)
qualitative research (p. 161)
reliability (of research) (p. 164)
sales forecasting (p. 148)
sampling (p. 151)
scanner data (p. 158)
secondary data (p. 151)
semi-structured interview (p. 162)
simple random sampling (p. 151)
survey (p. 164)
validity (p. 164)

MARKETING PLAN EXERCISE • Marketing Yourself

In this chapter we focused on the importance of marketing research. The next step in developing your personal marketing plan is to conduct some research of your own to better understand the competition you will face for your dream job or graduate school program.

Your assignment is to research online the job or graduate school program you discussed as your objective in Chapter 1. Try to figure out how competitive the applicant pool is. Check with someone at the firm's human resource department or contact the graduate school's admissions office to find out the average number of applicants for each open slot. Often, you can find summary statistics on the average work experience or GPA that is common among newcomers. That information will give you an idea of where you stand relative to your competition.

For those of you targeting graduate school, you should conduct extensive research on the GPA and entrance exam (GMAT, LSAT, GRE) requirements for the programs you are targeting. The Internet and web publications such as *U.S. News and World Report* provide a wealth of data on all types of graduate school programs. You should see how

your GPA and entrance exam scores compare to the averages at targeted schools. In the same way that firms want to know what their competition is doing to better understand their potential for success, so should you.

Your Task: Prepare a one- to two-paragraph research report that summarizes your findings and describes the actions you will take based on your research. Your report should include the following information:

1. If focusing on a specific job, list the average number of applicants, the starting pay, and where these types of job openings are most commonly found.
2. If your focus is on graduate school, list what the average GPA and entrance exam score is for the program as well as the acceptance rate for that program.
3. Make an honest assessment of the likelihood that you will get your desired job or be accepted to the graduate program. Based on this assessment, what is one area that you need to improve on to increase your chances of achieving your goal?

DISCUSSION QUESTIONS

1. What are the ways that marketing research enables companies to meet their objectives? Explain the reasoning behind your answer.
2. Your company is considering relaunching its most profitable line of products: shampoo and conditioner. The manager wants to ensure that the new package will be one that consumers are drawn to. What research method do you think would be best for determining how to design the new package? Explain why you selected that method.
3. Go to your Facebook page or that of a friend. What information is available on the page that might be useful to marketing researchers? Do you feel that

using that information for marketing research purposes would be an invasion of privacy? Explain your answer.

4. You are the head of marketing research at a major retailer. You have been asked to conduct research about your competitors' products, including prices and features. What are some of the ways you could access that type of information?
5. List at least six types of information a company would need to know about an international market before the company can successfully sell its products in that market. How might an organization get that type of information? From where would it be obtained?

 # SOCIAL MEDIA APPLICATION

Pick an organization that you are familiar with and then visit that organization's social media presence. Analyze the organization's efforts to market itself through social media using the following questions and activities as a guide. Be sure to support each of your answers with specific quotes, pictures, or comments from social media users.

1. Based on what you read on the organization's various social media platforms, what information about the company can you find?

2. Who are the most frequent types of customers for the organization?
3. Which of the organization's products are well received and which ones have a more negative perception?
4. Should you visit a competitor's social media sites, and if so, what should you be looking for?

 # MARKETING ANALYTICS EXERCISE

Please complete the *Connect* exercise for Chapter 5 that focuses on making marketing investment decisions using Big Data.

ETHICAL CHALLENGE

Social media are increasingly used as a source of data for marketing research. Marketing researchers can find comments about goods and services as well as personal information. Imagine that you are the vice president of marketing for a large consumer-electronics company. The head of your marketing research department has just given a presentation on how to mine data on the Internet by electronically searching social network sites for keywords and phrases. The manager of the video games division was at the presentation and is very keen to gather data on preteen boys between 10 and 12 years old concerning their use of violent video games. They want to have the research department gather data on as many preteen boys as possible to determine who they are, where they live, who else is in their family, who their friends are, and what types of games they are interested in playing.

She is asking for your permission and funding to undertake this type of research. Please use the ethical decision-making framework to answer the following questions:

1. First, research the ICC/ESOMAR Standards for Marketing Research by going on its website (https://esomar.org), searching for and downloading its "Notes on How to Apply ICC/ESOMAR Code," and reading the code. Next, using the notes, identify at least three potential ethical problems with the manager's proposal. Explain why you think they may be an issue.
2. What might your company do to work around any ethical issues you identified?
3. Would you approve this proposal or not? Explain your answer.

VIDEO CASE

Please go to *Connect* to access the video cases featuring (1) Experian and (2) iMotions that accompany this chapter.

PODCAST

Please go to Connect to access the podcast that accompanies this chapter.

Alejandro Fernández

CAREER **TIPS**

Marketing Your Future

You have read in this chapter about the importance of marketing research. Marketing research is one of the fastest-growing areas in marketing. It can be an exciting, fulfilling, and financially rewarding direction to go with your career. As you consider your future, A.J. Fernández, who was featured in the Executive Perspective at the beginning of the chapter, has some suggestions that can help you get a marketing research job and then build a career in this industry.

1. While you are in college, challenge yourself with statistics classes, database information, and possibly some computer programming. Continued technological change will give firms access to more and more data in coming years that will need deeper analysis and broader data-organization capabilities.
2. Read to keep up with trends in your industry. The world is changing fast, so learn to skim for ideas.

Find the most valuable things to read to enhance your knowledge and maximize your value.
3. Before your job interview, learn all you can about the company and its competitors. Go online for a few hours of searching for knowledge that will enable you to talk about how you can contribute to the organization's mission and demonstrate your interest in it. You will not get a marketing research job if it is not clear that you have done significant marketing research on the company you are interviewing with.
4. My most valuable employees keep everyone up to date with new happenings in the industries in which we work. Talk to people, stay engaged, pay attention to what is happening in the industry around you. The one who knows what merger is happening by 8 a.m. and tells us all is greatly appreciated.
5. To keep up your knowledge, subscribe to the best daily print and digital information sources from your industry, and skim them in the morning or in the evening after work. Make a point of gaining additional knowledge on your own.

CHAPTER NOTES

1. Joseph R. Hair Jr., Robert P. Bush, and David J. Ortinau, *Marketing Research in a Digital Information Environment,* 4th ed. (New York: McGraw-Hill/Irwin, 2009).
2. Joseph R. Hair Jr., Robert P. Bush, and David J. Ortinau, *Marketing Research in a Digital Information Environment,* 4th ed. (New York: McGraw Hill/Irwin, 2009).
3. Statista Research Department, "Global Revenue of the Market Research Industry 2008–2021," *Statista,* April 26, 2022, https://www.statista.com/statistics/242477/global-revenue-of-market-research-companies/.
4. Joseph R. Hair Jr., Mary F. Wolfinbarger, David J. Ortinau, and Robert P. Bush, *Essentials of Marketing Research,* 2nd ed. (New York: McGraw-Hill/Irwin, 2010).
5. Doug Newsom and Jim Haynes, *Public Relations Writing: Form and Style* (Boston: Wadsworth, 2004), p. 236.
6. Wayne Eckerson, *Extending the Value of Your Data Warehousing Investment* (The Data Warehouse Institute, May 10, 2007).
7. Branka Vuleta, "How Much Data Is Created Every Day?" *SeedScientific,* October 28, 2021 https://seedscientific.com/how-much-data-is-created-every-day/.

8. Alteryx, "Predictive Analytics," (n.d.), https://www.alteryx .com/glossary/predictive-analytics?language=de.

9. Michael Dixon, "Types of Predictive Analytics Models and How They Work," *Selerity,* December 12, 2019 https:// seleritysas.com/blog/2019/12/12/types-of-predictive-analytics-models-and-how-they-work/.

10. James Williamson, "Limitations of Predictive Analytics," *WordPress,* May 14, 2018, https://jameswilliamsonhnd .wordpress.com/2018/05/14/limitations-of-predictive-analytics/.

11. Joseph R. Hair Jr., Mary F. Wolfinbarger, David J. Ortinau, and Robert P. Bush, *Essentials of Marketing Research,* 2nd ed. (New York: McGraw-Hill/Irwin, 2010).

12. https://www.simplypsychology.org/experimental-method .html.

13. S. M. McClure, J. Li, D. Tomlin, K. S. Cypert, L. M. Montague, and P. R. Montague, "Neural Correlates of Behavioral Preference for Culturally Familiar Drinks," *Neuron* 44, no. 2 (2004): 379–387.

14. Bruce Horovitz, "Drive-Thru Times Slow to a Crawl," *USA Today*, October 6, 2014, http://www.usatoday.com/story/ money/business/2014/10/06/fast-food-drive-thru-times-restaurants-mcdonalds-taco-bell-wendys/16644673/.

15. Siobhan Riley, "Mid-South Kroger Grocery Stores Use Que Vision System to Aid in Coronavirus Pandemic," FOX13Memphis.com, May 15, 2020, https://www. fox13memphis.com/news/local/mid-south-kroger-grocery-stores-use-que-vision-system-aid-coronavirus-pandemic/ 2VBOEXVDFVAM5DZVBLX67YTAOA/.

16. Kate Linebaugh, "For Philips, Matching the Product to the Market," *The Wall Street Journal*, May 30, 2012, http://online.wsj.com/article/SB1000142405270230339 56045777434171435274122.html.

17. Tom Doctoroff, "What the Chinese Want," *The Wall Street Journal,* May 18, 2012, http://online.wsj.com/article/SB1 00014240527023033605045774084937238142 10 .html.

18. Joseph R. Hair Jr., Mary F. Wolfinbarger, David J. Ortinau, and Robert P. Bush, *Essentials of Marketing Research*, 2nd ed. (New York: McGraw-Hill/Irwin, 2010).

19. John Price, "Best Practices for Market Research in Latin America," Americas Market Intelligence, December 12, 2016, https://www.slideshare.net/Americas MarketIntelligence/best-practices-for-market-research-in-latin-america-70061657.

20. Stella Yifan Xie, "Starbucks Faces Online Uproar in China after Coffee Price Hike," *Wall Street Journal,* February 17, 2022, https://www.wsj.com/articles/ starbucks-faces-online-uproar-in-china-after-coffee-price-hike-11645103944?mod=e2tw.

21. John Price, "Best Practices for Market Research in Latin America," Americas Market Intelligence, December 12, 2016, https://www.slideshare.net/AmericasMarketIntel-ligence/best-practices-for-market-research-in-latin-america-70061657.

22. Nextiva, "How to use a Customer Journey Map to Keep More Customers [+Real Examples]," November 17, 2021, https://www.nextiva.com/blog/customer-journey-map.html.

23. Caylin White, "Customer Personas: A Definitive Guide," *iThemes,* October 15, 2021, https://ithemes.com/blog/ customer-personas-guide/.

24. Creately, "The Easy Guide to Customer Journey Maps with Editable Templates," December 8, 2021, https://creately.com/blog/diagrams/what-is-a-customer-journey-map/.

25. BankMyCell, "How Many Smartphones Are in the World?" (n.d.), https://www.bankmycell.com/blog/ how-many-phones-are-in-the-world.

26. R. Poynter, N. Williams, and S. York, *The Handbook of Mobile Market Research: Tools and Techniques for Market Researchers* (Hoboken, NJ: Wiley, 2014).

27. Stephanie Clifford and Quentin Hardy, "Attention Shoppers: Store Is Tracking Your Cell," *The New York Times,* July 15, 2013, http://www.nytimes.com/ 2013/07/15/business/attention-shopper-stores-are-tracking-your-cell.html?_r=0.

28. Jonathan Greig, "Amazon Fined $887 Million for GDPR Privacy Violations," *ZDNet,* July 30, 2021, https://www .zdnet.com/article/amazon-fined-887-million-for-gdpr-privacy-violations/.

29. Michael Luca, "Were OkCupid's and Facebook's Experiments Unethical?" *Harvard Business Review,* July 29, 2014, https://hbr.org/2014/07/ were-okcupids-and-facebooks-experiments-unethical.

30. Charles Arthur, "Facebook Emotion Study Breached Ethical Guidelines, Researchers Say," *The Guardian,* June 30, 2014, https://www.theguardian.com/technology/ 2014/jun/30/facebook-emotion-study-breached-ethical-guidelines-researchers-say.

31. David Goldman, "Google Pays $500 Million to Settle DOJ Case over Illegal Drug Ads," *CNN Money,* August 24, 2011, https://money.cnn.com/2011/08/24/ technology/google_settlement/index.htm.

32. Federal Trade Commission, "Electronic Toy Maker VTech Settles FTC Allegations That It Violated Children's Privacy Law and the FTC Act," January 8, 2018, https://www.ftc.gov/news-events/press-releases/ 2018/01/electronic-toy-maker-vtech-settles-ftc-allegations-it-violated.

33. Joseph R. Hair Jr., Mary F. Wolfinbarger, David J. Ortinau, and Robert P. Bush, *Essentials of Marketing Research*, 2nd ed. (New York: McGraw-Hill/Irwin, 2010).

34. Seymour Sudman, "Survey Research and Ethics," in *NA—Advances in Consumer Research Volume 25,* eds. Joseph W. Alba & J. Wesley Hutchinson (Provo, UT : Association for Consumer Research, 1998), pp. 69–71.

35. https://www.insightsassociation.org/Tools-Resources/ Codes-of-Standards.

Chapter **6**

Product Development

Richard Newstead/Flickr/Getty Images

Learning Objectives

After reading this chapter, you should be able to

LO 6-1 Understand the different types of new products, their advantages, and their risks.

LO 6-2 Describe the various stages of new-product development.

LO 6-3 Discuss the major risks in new-product development and how to reduce those risks.

LO 6-4 Describe the categories of new-product adopters and the implications of adoption to marketers.

LO 6-5 Describe the stages and aspects of the product life cycle and how they affect the marketing mix.

Executive **Perspective** ... because everyone is a marketer

Tom Payne
Vice President of Carrier Relations
Uniti Fiber

Tom Payne

During college, Tom Payne came to realize that he had a talent for solving problems. After obtaining a degree in applied mathematics from West Point, he put those skills to use as an officer in the U.S. Army.

When he returned to civilian life, Payne took a position as a product analyst for a large telecommunications manufacturer. He quickly realized that problem solving was an essential part of product development and product management. Today, Payne is vice president of carrier relations for Uniti Fiber, a company that focuses on customizing solutions for wireless carriers through broad partnerships with numerous telecommunications firms. He manages a team of representatives from various departments that develops product solutions for the firm's customers, including large wireless companies.

What has been the most important thing in making you successful at your job?

A positive attitude. Again and again I have seen very talented people reviewed poorly and passed over for raises because of their attitude. They either felt the company owed them more than was reasonable, or they did not work well with others. Companies are just groups of people joined in a common activity. Like any group of people, they do not respond well to group members who are arrogant, ill-tempered, or depressing.

What advice would you give soon-to-be graduates?

There are a couple of areas that I always like to tell new graduates to think about when entering corporate America. The first is flexibility. When your manager comes to you with a problem no one has solved, that is opportunity knocking. Even if you are hired as a product manager, you may be asked to give presentations for products you don't actually make, or you may have to step in and take charge of a production line or process. We remember heroes; we forget crowds.

The second bit of advice I would give seems obvious, but so few seem to get it: Use your personal network. Dozens of companies are begging your university for good candidates—use these resources. Also open your eyes to what your friends and relatives do for a living. They

may work in a business you are interested in. A personal introduction or reference is better than sending 500 resumes blindly into some "job bank." Family and friends, professors, university recruiters, and private recruiters are how I would rank the best sources for a great job.

How is marketing relevant to your role at Uniti Fiber?

Marketing is relevant to every job in an organization. Marketing is the key driver to increase revenues and profits, without which it is impossible to have a viable business.

To be successful at my job, I have to make product decisions daily that help determine the satisfaction of our customers. I help our sales team develop solutions that provide a valuable service to our customers and generate profits for our company. I have worked for companies of all sizes across different industries, and marketing has been relevant to every job I have ever held.

What do you consider your personal brand to be?

Companies I've worked for have been sold, been relocated, and even gone bankrupt. I have changed jobs several times and had many different titles and responsibilities—but I have never had to look for work. My personal brand has made that possible.

People who know me and have worked with me understand that I bring two things to the job: attitude and character. No one hires me thinking they will get the smartest telecommunications professional in the business. They *do* know they will get a guy who will work hard, treat the company's money like his own, and have a positive attitude about whatever job I'm given. Develop and encourage those traits, and people will want to hire you.

LO 6-1

Understand the different types of new products, their advantages, and their risks.

product

The specific combination of goods, services, or ideas that a firm offers to consumers.

WHAT IS A NEW PRODUCT?

A **product** is the specific combination of goods, services, or ideas that a firm offers to consumers. Specifically,

- Goods are tangible products with physical dimensions, like a car. They must be manufactured, stored, and transported to customers.
- Services are intangible products; they cannot be touched, weighed, or measured. Netflix, for example, provides a service by delivering media content to devices such as televisions and personal computers.
- Ideas are also intangible and represent formulated thoughts or opinions. The perfect vacation that the state of Michigan promotes through its "Pure Michigan" marketing campaign is an example of an idea.
- An *experience* is a product with characteristics that are difficult to observe in advance, but that are realized after consumption. A trip on a cruise ship is an example of an experience.

Products enrich the lives of consumers by providing designs, features, and functions that people need and want.

For thousands of years people lived their entire lives and only rarely saw a new product. In modern times it seems we hear about a new product every day. Several factors led to this change:

1. *Faster and more economical transportation.* A millennium ago, routes were slow. At each long and dangerous stage of the journey, goods would change hands at increasingly higher prices. Today, most cargo travels vast distances with only a modest increase in price and in a dramatically shorter period of time. As late as the nineteenth century, a traveler never saw information, goods, or people travel faster than the speed of a horse. Today, it can take as few as 11 days for a product to cross the Pacific Ocean by ship, hours by aircraft, and almost no time at all if it can be digitized.

2. *Mass production.* Books, for example, used to be copied by hand, greatly limiting the number of copies available to prospective readers. Around 1439, Johannes Gutenberg was the first European to use movable-type printing, which allowed books to be mass-produced. With few exceptions, most modern products can be mass-produced. Mass production makes products available to many more customers as well as more affordable.

3. *The advent of electronic communication.* Modern communication enables news of a product to spread quickly around the globe. Consumers now become aware of new products through television advertising, company web pages, social media, and smartphone apps. Electronic communication also enables companies to create excitement about new products even before they reach the market. Consumers now hold more power because they can access information about products easily, including features, functions, and price.

New goods, services, and ideas are critical to a company's survival in today's marketing environment. That environment places an ever-increasing emphasis on new, improved, and technologically advanced product offerings. Many companies have fallen by the wayside because they failed to innovate. Atari, for example, dominated the home video game market in the early to mid-1980s but lost ground to Nintendo and Sony when they introduced superior technology.[1] Companies such as Hewlett-Packard introduce thousands of new products each year to remain leaders in industries in which products become obsolete rapidly and competition is fierce.

What, exactly, is a new product? A *new product* is one that is new to a company *in any way.* It may be functionally different from existing products in the market. Or it may be considered new because the company has not marketed it in its current form or manner. We categorize new products in four ways:

- New-to-the-market products.
- New-category entries.
- Product-line extensions.
- Revamped products.

We'll discuss each of these categories in more depth in the sections that follow.

A company's core competencies and strengths influence its strategy toward developing new products. Design-led companies, which tend to have strong research and development (R&D) departments, will focus on developing new-to-the-market products to beat the competition. Firms that have a strong brand and company image can take advantage of existing products to extend or revamp their current product lines with similar but differentiated attributes.

New-to-the-Market Products

As Nick Santhanam of McKinsey's America says: "Over time, every franchise dies." An Example is Nokia, which once held a dominant position in the hand-held devices market, but due to lack of urgency and the willingness to expend resources, eventually lost its market dominance.[2] Inventions that have never before been seen and create a new market are considered **new-to-the-market products**. They make up the smallest percentage of new products, but they carry the most potential for the company introducing them. Apple CEO Tim Cook's objective is to "give you things that you can't live without that you just don't know you need."[3] While new-to-the-market products offer the potential for tremendous sales, they also carry the most risk because of the cost to develop and market them. As Samsung Electronics Company's mobile chief D. J. Koh says, "If we are afraid of technology innovation, we will die [as a company]."[4]

New-to-the-market products often are examples of a **disruptive technology**: one that displaces an established technology and shakes up the industry, or a groundbreaking product that creates a completely new industry.[5]

The smartphone versus cell phone is an example of a disruptive technology that displaced an established technology. The introduction of the personal computer industry in the 1980s is an example of a groundbreaking product that created a new industry. New-to-the-market products can be so disruptive and offer so much value to customers that they often render existing products obsolete. For example, advances in batteries used in electric cars are extending the range of newer models beyond 300 miles; such advances make existing all-electric cars with ranges of fewer miles much less desirable.[6]

However, even new-to-the-market products such as smartphones lose their luster over time. A global slide in sales and the absence of any earth-shattering new innovations has affected the image of smartphones. Product offerings that once were state-of-the-art are now starting to look more mature. This is why companies like Apple and Samsung are experiencing encroachment into the market by Chinese companies Huawei, Xiaomi, and Oppo, which can offer consumers lower cost products that can do basically what the higher-prices brands do.[7]

Companies whose strategy is to develop new-to-the-market products must have strong R&D and marketing departments. Not only must the product or service be completely new; the company must also be able to convince consumers that they need to own the product or use the service. Apple is an example of an innovative company that has created entirely new markets by inventing new-to-the-world products and then convincing people that the product is a "must-have." Apple put significant resources into R&D, inventing new-to-the-market products that would put it ahead of competitors.

new-to-the-market products

Inventions that have never before been seen and create a new market.

disruptive technology

A technology that displaces an established technology and shakes up the industry, or a groundbreaking product that creates a completely new industry.

Even after the dot-com bubble burst in 2000, while most Silicon Valley companies cut back or stopped investing, Apple continued to invest heavily in R&D.[8] Some of the results of this emphasis on innovation were the iPhone, iPod, the iTunes store, Apple stores, and the Apple Watch. In the food industry, innovation is coming back into style. Wall Street investors are looking for growth in this industry, and innovation that can effect rapid change in consumer tastes is rewarded by the market. Food companies that want to expand their markets and market shares need to keep things changing. Conagra is an example: It revamped older products brands such as Healthy Choice and Marie Callender's by adding fashionable ingredients, such as kale, to their recipes.[9]

New-to-the-market products represent tremendous upside potential for firms. Getting to the market before competitors often means increased sales, profits, and customer loyalty. It also might produce a sustained leadership position in that market. In the global market, new-to-the-market goods and services can enable a company to capture international customers before the competition does, opening up a whole new set of customers. New-to-the-market products include those that are salable throughout the world, such as the iPhone. Or they may be designed to sell to a certain region of the world. For example, Henkel AG's Gliss Restore & Refresh shampoo and Unilever PLC's Sunsilk shampoo are region-specific products designed for Middle Eastern women who wear hijabs.[10] Such products can open the door for a company to market other products in the region.

However, new-to-the-market products can be time-consuming and expensive to develop. They often create significant risk for a firm. The majority of new products fail. Such failures leave the firm with development costs and no offsetting revenue to compensate for expenditures of financial and human resources. Certain types of products can be particularly difficult to get consumers to try. Food and beverage consumers, for example, are often creatures of habit, making it difficult to sell them something new. Examples abound: Coca-Cola rolled out New Coke in 1985, but after 79 days reverted to the original product because customers preferred the original Coke flavor. McDonald's McPizza, Cheetos flavored lip balm, Colgate frozen foods, Texco Strawberries and cream sandwiches, and Life Savers soda all proved to be ideas that should have never made it to market, but did.[11]

Perhaps the best example of a new-to-the-market product that has had a tremendous effect on the world is the development of the messenger ribonucleic acid (mRNA) versions of the COVID-19 virus vaccination. mRNA is the molecule that cells use to carry DNA's instructions to cells' protein-building machinery that produce a viral protein to help the body's immune system build an immune response. The technology used to produce the vaccines developed by Moderna and Pfizer (along with its German partner BioNTech) had never been used to fight a virus. Amazingly, the companies developed and asked for emergency FDA authorization to use mRNA-based vaccines to fight the coronavirus in just 10 months. To date, these products have saved countless lives and have helped countries revive their economies.[12]

Service Innovation
Services as well as products can be "new-to-the-market." Service innovation involves a new or considerably changed service concept. That change might occur in how the company interacts with a customer or how it delivers the service. Or the change might involve an entirely new technology altogether. Typically, the changes, alone or in combination, result in a service function that the market recognizes as new and valuable.[13] Types of service innovation include:

1. *New types of services.* Innovative services are ones that are brand new to a market or that have been considerably changed to meet customers' needs better. Netflix and Lyft are examples of innovative services; they significantly change the way people watch shows or get transportation. Amazon's addition of cloud

Thanks to the amazing work of Moderna and the partners Pfizer and BioNTech the world received a highly effect vaccine against COVID-19 in less than a year, *Mariusz Burcz/Alamy Stock Photo*

computing services with its Azure product that helps businesses with data storage, information technology, and computer applications, has helped bring the company back near the top of the world's most valuable companies.[14]

2. ***Changes to the way a service is processed or delivered.*** Innovative service processes involve new methods to perform an existing service. For example, instead of delivering all of the packages it picks up from shippers itself, UPS and FedEx now use the United States Postal Service (USPS) as a partner to deliver packages to customers. Doing so saves money, particularly in rural areas where the postal service is delivering to homes six days a week; for UPS and FedEx, such deliveries used to involve a special trip to deliver the package.[15]

New-Category Entries

New-category entries are products that are new to a company but *not* new to the marketplace.

These new products help companies compete better in an already-established market or enter a new market. Entering new markets is very important to businesses because it opens up a whole new set of customers and potentially a great deal more revenue and profits.

New-category entries are less risky than new-to-the-market products. Because other companies have sold similar products, the company introducing the new-category entry can access information on sales trends, competitor products and prices, and location of markets. Samsung, for example, released a smartphone with a display that wraps around the side of the phone and a virtual reality headset. It also introduced a standalone wristwatch that can send and receive calls without being connected to a smartphone. These products are similar to other products Samsung or one of its competitors' markets, but they may offer more advanced features than current products.[16] Their similarity to existing products makes their introduction less risky for Samsung than a new-to-the-market product. For another example, Ninja Tech recently developed Ninja Tech Nutritional Bars designed to improve memory. Their previous products have all been technology related, and therefore new products for the food market would be considered a new product line. [17]

However, there still can be considerable risk in developing a new-category entry, even if a company has experience with an older product. For example, BlackBerry (formerly known as Research in Motion Ltd.) used to dominate the cell phone market.

new-category entries
Products that are new to a company but not new to the marketplace.

The Chevy Bolt EV is an example of a product new to a company but not the market. Electric cars have been around for years. However, they are new to General Motors.
SeongJoon Cho/Bloomberg/Getty Images

product line

A group of related products marketed by the same firm.

product-line extensions

Products that extend and supplement a company's established product line.

Companies such as Apple and Samsung began to market smartphones, which were much more appealing to the market. To gain back market share, BlackBerry developed a new phone, the Z10, to compete with other companies' new smartphones. However, the Z10 failed to deliver sufficient features to differentiate itself from its competitors. The phone was not well received by the market, causing AT&T and Best Buy to cut prices in order to sell them.

Product-Line Extensions

A **product line** is a group of related products marketed by the same firm. **Product-line extensions** are products that extend and supplement a company's established product line.

Product-line extensions add new functions, flavors, or other attributes to an existing product line. FedEx, for example, started its service business by offering air shipment and home delivery of packages. Over the years, it has extended its services line and now offers FedEx Ground, SmartPost, Freight, Custom Critical, Supply Chain, and Office delivery services. All provide a number of services based on the same model: shipping packages for customers. LEGO has attempted to modernize its traditional toy line of products by developing video games based on its plastic bricks.[18]

Product-line extensions have various advantages:

- The company and brand may be easily recognized.
- Customers may already feel loyal to the product line.
- For goods, manufacturing may be easier and more efficient because the firm already produces similar goods.
- The new product can be advertised alongside existing products.

Product-line extensions are common, especially among companies hoping to offset reduced sales on other products due to seasonality or trends. For example, Dyson piggybacked on its popular line of vacuum cleaners when it introduced the Airwrap, a hairstyling tool that met with immediate success, Altar'd State introduced the A'Beautiful Soul line of fashion products offering items of the same quality and price as the Altar'd State original, but tailored specifically for women in the size 10–24 range. And Mattel marketed the Creatable World Dolls that promises to "keep labels out and invite everyone in." This proved to be a very successful and well-received product that appeals to children who "don't want their toys dictated by gender norms."[19]

cannibalization

A reduction in sales volume or market share of a company's existing product due to the introduction of a new product made by the same company.

Product-line extensions carry some risk due to uncertainty about how well the new products will be accepted by the market. Another risk is the cannibalization of current products. Product **cannibalization** refers to a reduction in sales volume or market share of a company's existing product due to the introduction of a new product made by the same company. Product-line extensions are a major source of cannibalization of a company's products because the extensions often are simply substituted for already existing products in the product line. For example, the introduction of Coke Zero (now called Coke Zero Sugar) reduced the sales of Diet Coke. Overall, though, they carry far less risk than new-to-the-market products or new-category entries.

revamped product

A product that has new packaging, different features, and updated designs and functions.

Revamped Products

A new product can sometimes take the form of a **revamped product**, which has new packaging, different features, and updated designs and functions.[20] If you have seen a label claiming a product is new and improved, it falls within this category. Legally, according to the Federal Trade Commission (FTC), a company can label a product *new* only if the product has been changed in a "functionally significant or substantial respect."[21] Also, the company can advertise a product as new and improved for only six months after it hits store shelves.

Reformulations of current products are a common type of revamped product. For example, laundry detergent companies have begun making concentrated liquids under existing brand names. The packaging uses less plastic, which has environmental as well as cost implications: Companies save money on materials and need less space to store the finished goods; the products weigh less and are therefore cheaper to ship; and consumers send less plastic to a landfill if they choose not to recycle the package.

Because firms base revamped products on existing brands, the new products carry much less risk than new-to-the-market products or new-category entries. In addition to leveraging brand recognition and customer loyalty to existing products, firms can advertise the revamped products along with existing ones and capitalize on the network that already exists to sell the products.

An important example of a revamped product is the glass vial used in medicine. Production and distribution of the COVID-19 mRNA vaccine requires many types of technologies, and since the two vaccines had to be stored and transferred at below zero Fahrenheit temperatures, several potential problems emerged. One was that the glass vials used to hold the vaccine had to be able to withstand these temperatures, and not break, from production all the way to delivery into the arm of a patient. Corning Inc., which had not produced medical vials since the 1980s, developed a glass vial, called "Valor," that was much stronger than previous ones. This proved to be an excellent product, and the company expanded production and is opening a new plant to produce the vials. This is an example of a revamped product that can have a profound effect on people's lives.[22]

Mc Graw Hill connect Exercise **6-1**

Please complete the *Connect* exercise for Chapter 6 that focuses on identifying new-product categories. By better understanding the different types of new products, you will be able to successfully develop strategies for marketing different goods and services.

THE STAGES OF NEW-PRODUCT DEVELOPMENT

Whatever new-product type a firm plans to develop, it will likely follow a formal **new-product development (NPD)** process. This process, shown in Figure 6.1, consists of seven stages: (1) new-product strategy development, (2) idea generation, (3) idea screening, (4) business analysis, (5) product development, (6) test marketing, and (7) product launch. Although this process is shown as linear, in practice companies may need to back-track to earlier stages when issues arise. For example, when a company puts a product in the test marketing stage it may find that the product can not be sold at the price determined in the business analysis stage. The company may then decide to go back to the product development stage and redesign the product to make it more affordable to the target market.

Stage 1: New-Product Strategy Development

In the first stage of the NPD process, the firm establishes a new-product strategy to align its product development with its overall marketing strategy. **New-product strategy development** involves determining the direction a company will take when

LO 6-2

Describe the various stages of new-product development.

new-product development (NPD)

The process of conceiving, testing, and launching a new product in the marketplace.

new-product strategy development

The stage of new-product development in which the company determines the direction it will take when it develops a new product.

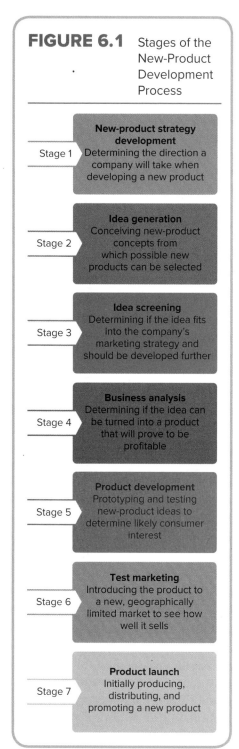

FIGURE 6.1 Stages of the New-Product Development Process

Stage 1 — **New-product strategy development** Determining the direction a company will take when developing a new product

Stage 2 — **Idea generation** Conceiving new-product concepts from which possible new products can be selected

Stage 3 — **Idea screening** Determining if the idea fits into the company's marketing strategy and should be developed further

Stage 4 — **Business analysis** Determining if the idea can be turned into a product that will prove to be profitable

Stage 5 — **Product development** Prototyping and testing new-product ideas to determine likely consumer interest

Stage 6 — **Test marketing** Introducing the product to a new, geographically limited market to see how well it sells

Stage 7 — **Product launch** Initially producing, distributing, and promoting a new product

idea generation

The stage of new-product development in which a set of product concepts is generated from which to identify potentially viable new products.

(not if) it develops a new product. A new-product strategy accomplishes the following:

- Provides general guidelines for the NPD process.
- Specifies how new products will fit into the company's marketing plan.
- Outlines the general characteristics of the types of products the firm will develop.
- Specifies the target markets to be served by new products.

As discussed in Chapter 2, some companies use a SWOT analysis and environmental scanning to determine where new products might help strengthen the firm's marketing position. Also, as you found out in Chapter 4, companies do marketing research of one sort or another. In that research, companies seek to discover what customers want and what goods and services are already serving those customers. These efforts seek to identify gaps—and opportunities—that might exist between what customers want and existing goods and services. A new-product strategy also should include financial estimates; these detail when the firm can expect the product to be profitable and the profit the company hopes to make from the product.

The same methods for new-product strategy development should be used for goods and services alike. As with goods, the strategy for developing a new service should be tied to overall marketing plans. It should also identify the type of service the company plans to develop as well as the specific target markets to be served.

A new-product strategy also should consider the potential benefits and risks of bringing new products into international markets. Some new products are standardized for global distribution. Others are individualized for specific markets. An example of individualization is Hyundai, which offers cup holders that fit travel coffee mugs in U.S. versions of its cars; its cars designed for the Korean market have cup holders only large enough to hold a Dixie cup. Coca-Cola sells region-specific products geared to the tastes in the area in Latin America, Europe, Eurasia, Africa, and the Asia-Pacific. As disposable incomes continue to rise throughout the world, companies that once found it difficult, if not impossible, to sell their products in developing countries are seeing markets open up. As a result, including international opportunities in a new-product strategy is critical for many companies.

Stage 2: Idea Generation

Once the firm establishes a new-product strategy, it moves to the second stage of the NPD process, idea generation. **Idea generation** involves generating a set of product concepts from which to identify potentially viable new products. Few of these ideas ever become marketed products. In fact, a firm must generate as many as 100 ideas to find one product that will actually make it to the marketplace.[23]

Internal Idea Generation Ideas for new products can come from a variety of sources. Some come from company employees. Perhaps the classic example is Arthur Fry, an engineer in the paper products division at 3M. Mr. Fry attended a presentation by another engineer, Sheldon Silver, who had developed a weak glue compound. Mr. Fry was not particularly impressed by the new glue. However, he was a member of his church choir, and he had a habit of using pieces of paper to mark the songs in his hymnal that would be sung during the church service. The pieces of paper often fell out of the book, leaving Mr. Fry searching for the right hymn. One day, he had an idea: apply Mr. Silver's glue to the pieces of paper. The pieces would stick well enough to hold on

New-product strategy should consider international markets. Products can be standardized for global distribution or individualized for specific markets. Here, a vendor shows the range of Coca-Cola products available in New Delhi, India. *Dinodia Photos /Alamy Stock Photo*

the book, but they could also be reused for next week's songs. Post-it Notes was born! Smart companies give their employees incentives to suggest new-product ideas.

Research and development departments within a company exist to come up with innovative product ideas for companies. An innovative technique for internally generating new-product ideas is **design thinking**. Design thinking is a process that encourages organizations to focus on the people they're creating products for. There are two steps to the idea generation part of the process. The first step is to gain an empathic understanding of the customer's needs. This involves observing and engaging with people to better understand their experiences and motivations. In the second step, the firm defines the problem in a human-centric way. For example, rather than defining the problem as "we need to develop food products to get into the new parents market," the problem would be stated in this way: "New parents need to have products that help them feel that their children are well nourished." In this way a company can focus on what the customer actually wants or needs by coming at the problem from the customer's perspective.[24]

design thinking

Design thinking is a process that encourages organizations to focus on the people they're creating products for.

External Idea Generation   Many ideas originate from external sources. Procter & Gamble, for example, gets more than half of its new-product ideas from outside the company.[25] Google uses outside developers to create different hardware modules, such as a blood-sugar monitor, which customers can select for their own personalized "modular smartphone."[26] Customers, too, can be excellent sources of ideas. Salespeople talk on a regular basis to individual customers as well as business customers like resellers; if salespeople ask the right questions, they can gather ideas about what their customers need and want.

Another source of idea generation is **crowdsourcing**. Crowdsourcing involves the process of getting ideas by asking for input from a large group of people, especially online communities, rather than getting them employees. With crowdsourcing a company can get many innovative ideas with little financial expenditure on its part. LEGO is an example of a company that allows users to design new products. Any user can submit a design; other users then can vote for the new design, which helps LEGO determine the marketability of the potential product. When a product gets 10,000 votes it

crowdsourcing

The practice of getting ideas by soliciting contributions from a large, online group of people rather than the traditional way of obtaining them from employees.

will be produced unless there is a legal or other type of problem with the design. The person who submits an accepted design gets 1 percent of the profits from its sale.[27]

Competitors' products also provide an important idea source. Many companies, such as automobile manufacturers, purchase the new products their competitors offer; they then analyze and use those products to devise similar, but better, alternatives. Similarly, companies use existing service offerings from other companies as a basis for creating new services. A number of online dating services, for example, have taken the idea developed by OkCupid of giving singles a "match percentage" to quantify compatibility with prospective dates. Blendr matches singles based on GPS proximity.

outsource

To procure goods, services, or ideas from a third-party supplier rather than from an internal source.

Firms can also **outsource** their R&D to independent laboratories that provide new-product ideas. Outsourcing occurs when a firm procures goods, services, or ideas from a third-party supplier rather than from an internal source.

Other possible sources of external inspiration include suppliers, universities, and independent inventors. Many companies use **open innovation**, a way of generating new-product ideas by gathering both external ideas and internal ideas. Procter & Gamble has a program called "Connect + Develop" that allows individuals and other companies to submit ideas to P&G developers for possible partnerships. P&G Ventures' start-up studio, P&G Ventures, works with entrepreneurs, inventors, and start-ups to create new brands and businesses outside of the categories in which it currently competes. Starbucks has a program called "MyStarbucksIdea" to generate new products from ideas submitted to its website. Facebook, Unilever, and Peperami are other examples of companies using open innovation to help their company develop new ideas.

open innovation

A way of generating new-product ideas by gathering both external ideas and internal ideas.

Companies with cultures that value all new-product ideas, whatever the source, tend to develop more blockbuster products than companies that are unwilling to search far and wide for new ideas. Some company cultures slow down innovation. Mattel, for example, requires lengthy analysis and meetings before deciding on a new-product idea.[28]

idea screening

The stage of new-product development in which the firm evaluates ideas to determine their fit within the new-product strategy.

Flexibility can be an asset as well. Sometimes ideas that start out in one direction can be *pivoted* to another, better direction. (Development of Post-it Notes is an example.) Pivoting typically occurs in the mobile and web sectors, where it is possible to quickly and inexpensively develop and change a software product.

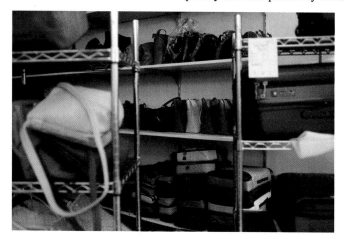

Here, bags await their "photo shoot" for images that will be posted on a mobile app named eBags Obsession. The app helps customers sort through the retailer's array of more than 12,000 handbags by swiping right if they "Love it" or left to "Leave it." The app came about in an idea-generating session aimed at increasing the speed and efficacy of mobile-device shopping on eBags.com. The company now uses a formal process for innovation and has regular "hackathon contests" that allow its engineering and product teams to build tools that might not otherwise come out of normal website development.
RJ Sangosti/The Denver Post/Getty Images

Stage 3: Idea Screening

Next, during the **idea-screening** stage, the firm evaluates ideas to determine their fit within the new-product strategy. At this stage, the company often ends up rejecting, for one reason or another, most ideas for new goods and services. Firms may reject products on a number of different bases. Potential issues with product safety may cause a firm to reject an idea for regulatory compliance, liability, and ethical reasons. Firms will also want to make sure that the potential product meets their return-on-investment (ROI) requirements.

Companies often have a minimum ROI "hurdle" that a new product must clear to be considered for further development. If the potential revenue generated by the product doesn't meet the minimum requirement, the idea goes no further. It's not unusual to attend product meetings in which the head of the finance department rejects several new-product ideas based on such an ROI hurdle.

The use of accurate data at this stage cannot be overemphasized. A company that makes a decision based on the "gut-feeling" of a high-level executive, without knowing all of the facts, can lose money on a new-product idea. This happened to Black-Berry when it went ahead with the Storm, a smartphone with a clickable screen. The company's CEO did not like the sensation of typing on glass and could not understand why customers would not want what he wanted. The phone was a marketing failure.[29]

Idea-Screening Questions   Beyond ROI requirements, firms should ask (and answer) key questions during the idea-screening stage, including the following:

- *Will the product sell?* Companies can often confirm an idea's sales potential through a concept test. In a **concept test**, marketing professionals ask consumers for their reactions to verbal descriptions and rough visual models of a potential product.
- *Can the product be developed and marketed within the time and budget constraints of the company?* Sometimes, lack of resources keeps a company from getting its new product to market first. In that case, the lost sales from being second may render the product less attractive as an investment. Also, human and financial resources are limited. New ideas must be compared based on the expenditure of these resources. A perfectly good idea may need to be rejected if another new idea that requires the same resources seems more promising.
- *Is the proposed product within the company's ability to produce?* Some new products require the company to purchase new equipment, build more space, or establish different processes. Such projects may be rejected due to the time and uncertainty these items could add to the product launch. Again, such considerations often make product-line extension and revamped product ideas more attractive than other new-product types.

concept test

A procedure in which marketing professionals ask consumers for their reactions to verbal descriptions and rough visual models of a potential product.

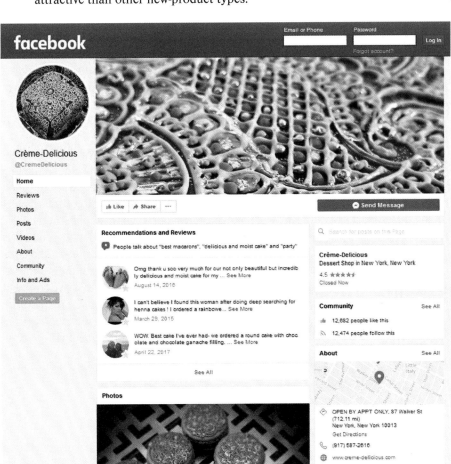

Crème-Delicious is a delicacy boutique in New York City that specializes in hand-decorated, henna-inspired delicacies. Its social media site on Facebook allows consumers to post reviews, comments, and photos of intricate designs executed by the bakery. Source: *Crème-Delicious*

The Role of Social Media in Idea Screening Organizations increasingly use social media to evaluate potential new products. Social media are especially valuable for small businesses and nonprofit organizations, which typically have less money to spend on the NPD process. Flash Purchase in Charlotte, North Carolina, deployed surveys on various social media platforms to gauge which new-product ideas would be of most interest to consumers.[30] Crème-Delicious, a dessert boutique in New York City, uploaded pictures of new cake designs to its Facebook page to obtain consumer feedback.[31] Through social media, consumers can help screen ideas to ensure only those new products that will be best received in the market move ahead in the process.

Stage 4: Business Analysis

Even if a product passes the idea-screening step, the firm cannot guarantee that it will be profitable. The first step in determining profitability is the ROI hurdle. However, ROI calculations don't take into account the changing value of money over time (due to compounding of interest). To be reasonably sure that a new product will be sufficiently profitable, firms must use additional, more complex analysis. Profitability is measured by subtracting costs (all the costs to produce and sell the good or service) from revenue (the price of the good or service multiplied by the number of units sold). That calculation can be difficult to determine: For *new* products, costs and revenues are projected (estimated) amounts; those projections are that much harder to get right if the product is new-to-the-market.

business analysis
The process of analyzing a new product to determine its profitability.

To determine profitability, a company must undertake a **business analysis**, which includes:

1. *Estimating costs.* Firms must estimate all costs related to the product. To limit costs, firms often try to achieve *economies of scale,* which allow them to spread the cost of production across a large number of goods, thereby reducing the average cost of each. They also may use less-expensive components or outsource production and distribution activities to third parties. In our global economy, many companies find offshore companies that will produce a good or perform a service for less than domestic suppliers. An **offshore** organization is one that is located or based in a foreign country.

offshore
An organization that is located or based in a foreign country.

2. *Identifying at what price the product will likely be sold.* Setting the price involves both marketing research and the cost estimates mentioned previously. Marketing research can tell the company what prices customers are willing to pay for the good or service. If customers won't pay a price high enough to cover the cost of developing the product, the company will not make any money and may abandon the idea.

3. *Estimating demand for the product.* This is the trickiest part. If the product is similar to ones the company or other companies have marketed already, the company can use an established sales baseline to estimate the sales forecast. When Starbucks came out with its Pike Place Roast coffee, it already had sales data for previous line extensions and therefore could forecast sales of the new flavor. For new-to-the-market products, firms research a number of factors to gauge potential opportunities for, or threats to, future sales of the product: the potential size of the market; what customers are willing to pay; market trends; and economic indicators.

3D printing of prototypes is one method used to develop visual models and functional prototypes because it can automate the process, saving time and labor. This process helps to reduce risk of design errors that can lead to expensive and time-consuming changes at all stages of the development process. *wir0man/iStock/Getty Images*

Stage 5: Product Development

Once a firm feels confident that the new product will generate a profit for the company, it enters the **product development stage**. In this stage, the firm determines that the good can be produced or the service can be offered in a way that meets customer needs and generates profits. The marketing department should also begin developing a marketing strategy during this stage.

Packaging design is an important part of product development. Primary packaging is the packaging the consumer sees in an ad or on a store shelf. It needs to be designed in a way that encourages a customer to buy the product by being attractive and providing information that the consumer should know about the product. It also should represent the company's and brand's image. An example of primary packaging is the box that a product sits in while it is on a store shelf. Some products also need to have tamper evident packaging so that consumers can be assured that the package has not been opened. Over-the-counter drugs such as ibuprofen are examples of such products. Secondary packaging needs to be designed to protect the product in transit and while being stored. Cardboard boxes that contain product are examples of secondary packaging.[32]

For a good, the company may create a prototype based on previous concept testing. A **prototype** is a mock-up of the good, often created individually with the materials the firm expects to use in the final product. 3D printing is one method used to develop visual models and functional prototypes because it can automate the process, saving time and labor. For example, Volvo saved thousands of dollars and 20 weeks development work by using a 3D printer to prototype a part for their construction equipment. This method proved very successful and will lead to "building mock-up engine components so the platform and manufacturing teams can provide feedback at a much earlier stage in the development process," said Jeff Hartman, Product Designer. "This should reduce risk of errors and the need for changes at all stages of the development process."[33] Visual models give companies an opportunity to test the marketability of various aspects of a new design, while functional prototypes help test the performance and manufacturability of a new product.

Prototype tests seek to ensure favorable responses to questions such as:

- Will the product be safe to users or their families?
- Can it be produced in the company's or supplier's manufacturing facilities?
- Can it be manufactured at a cost low enough to generate profits?

If the firm is developing a new service rather than a good, it may use this stage to:

- Establish protocols for training employees.
- Identify the types of equipment needed.
- Determine the staffing required to provide the service.

Lyft and Uber are examples of a service using a mobile app to connect drivers willing to use their own cars as a taxi for customers to get rides. Such an app would need extensive testing to ensure that it works to the satisfaction of both the drivers and their passengers, that payments are processed correctly, and that both drivers and passengers feel safe in using the service.

Regardless of whether the product is a good or service, the product development stage of the NPD process can be long and costly. Only a small number of ideas make it through this process. If the firm determines that it can feasibly offer the product, it moves to the next stage of the process: test marketing.

Stage 6: Test Marketing

A product that makes it past the product development stage is ready to be tested more fully with potential customers. **Test marketing** involves introducing a new product in its final form to a geographically limited market to see how well the product sells and to get reactions from potential users. The product or service being tested at this stage may be different from the prototype in the earlier stage.

The company selects test markets based on how well they mirror the overall target market in terms of demographics, income levels, and lifestyles. The selection of test

product development stage

The stage of new-product development at which a firm determines that the good can be produced or the service can be offered in a way that meets customer needs and generates profits.

prototype

A mock-up of a good, often created individually with the materials the firm expects to use in the final product.

test marketing

Introducing a new product in its final form to a geographically limited market to see how well the product sells and to get reactions from potential users.

markets is critical to ensuring that the results of the test will be representative of the sales the company can expect. An example of an inappropriate test market would be selecting an area that has a very high population of retired persons to test how well a new video game will sell. Some cities are regularly selected for test sites because they reflect the demographics of the nation or region. In the United States, these include Nashville, Tennessee; Cincinnati, Ohio; Indianapolis, Indiana; Charleston, South Carolina; Jacksonville, Florida; Greenville, South Carolina; Oklahoma City, Oklahoma; Phoenix, Arizona; Albuquerque, New Mexico; and Winston, North Carolina.[34]

During the test-marketing stage, the firm tests not only the product itself but also the marketing strategy related to it. The marketing department may simultaneously try different approaches in different test markets, to see which marketing-mix approach works best. For example, an airline might want to know which service offering generates more seat upgrades. It might offer more legroom in certain sections of the airplane at a higher price in one region. In another similar region, it might offer no luggage fees for first- and business-class customers, and it then would compare the results of the two tests.

simulated test markets
A procedure in which the firm builds a mock shopping experience for participants, in order to observe their response to marketing stimuli.

Risks of Test Marketing

Although test marketing can be valuable, there are downsides. First, the process is expensive. Second, it can be time-consuming. For example, Unilever established a test market for one of its products, a Nordic shampoo called Timotei. The test market was extensive, involving multiple test sites and thousands of samples; the test lasted more than a year. After spending a great deal of money and resources, the company determined that the product had little chance of making a profit in the United States and dropped it from the NPD process. A third risk to test marketing is that firms show their ideas and open themselves up to imitation from competitors, which can diminish the advantages of being first to market.

Economical Test-Marketing Options

Some companies use less-costly means for test marketing. New products can be introduced through **simulated test markets**, in which the firm builds a mock shopping experience for participants, in order to observe their response to marketing stimuli. Simulated test markets often show potential consumers advertisements for the new product and its competitors; they ask consumers to choose between the firm's product and competing products.

Online test marketing is another economical test-marketing tool. In an online test market, firms use their website to sell to consumers sample products that are unavailable in stores. This practice allows the firm to keep costs down while still obtaining valuable information. Test marketing can keep firms from potentially wasting money before they know what the consumer reaction to the product will be. Further, it allows them to fine-tune the marketing plan as they prepare to launch the product.

Stage 7: Product Launch

When the firm feels the product is ready for the market, it enters the final stage of the NPD process. The **product launch** involves completing all the final preparations for

Executive Perspective . . .
because everyone is a marketer

Tom Payne
Director of Access Planning
PEG Bandwidth

Tom Payne

What is the step in the product development process that companies get wrong more than any other?

I would say test marketing, for a couple of reasons. First, test marketing is expensive, so companies try to pinch pennies and reduce test-marketing times or locations, which is usually a big mistake. As a product manager, you want to be very sure that your product will be successful before you launch it across the country and throughout the world. Too many marketers end up saving a little money by reducing their test-market expenses, only to lose significantly more money by rolling out a product that fails in a larger market.

The other reason surrounds processes. It is the responsibility of product managers to make sure the processes are in place for the product during the test-marketing stage. They should have clear guidelines for how the product is packaged, billed, priced, and serviced. It should be very clear within the organization which specific people or groups are responsible for every one of these items. Unfortunately, too many companies and product managers lack the attention to detail to get this right, which causes more problems down the road.

making the fully tested product available to the market. At this stage, the firm may undertake any or all of the following activities:

- Purchasing the materials to make and package the good.
- Hiring employees, such as bank tellers, to provide the service.
- Manufacturing enough of a good to fill the distribution pipelines and to store as inventory for continuing distribution.
- Building enough capacity to provide a service for the expected level of sales.
- Strategically placing the good in warehouses in preparation for customer orders.
- Preparing internal systems for taking service orders.
- Training new employees on how best to deliver the service.

Firms must carefully plan the product launch to ensure that the product hits the market according to schedule. Still, even the best efforts to plan a product launch can be disrupted by unforeseen problems or those beyond the control of the company. Numerous product launches have been delayed because suppliers could not deliver on time, consumer demand was unexpectedly high, or goods couldn't be released due to quality problems. For example, the Boeing 787 was delayed by production and safety issues. The original development-to-delivery of the first aircraft was scheduled for four years, at a cost of $6 billion. The actual delivery took eight years, at a cost of about $32 billion. Additionally, the 787 fleet was grounded for electrical problems due to the aircraft's lithium-ion batteries, causing ill-will with its customers.[35] Delayed product launches also often cost companies a great deal of money. Companies often will incur overtime labor and shipping charges to get a product delivered as soon as possible, to keep customers happy.

The launch stage of the NPD process is usually the most expensive stage for new products. To minimize the cost implications and smooth out production levels and marketing activities, some companies release new products to geographic areas in a gradual manner. But firms take a risk by proceeding slowly with product launches. The speed with which a company launches a product (its **time to market**) can be extremely important, especially for high-tech products. Being the first company to market, a new product can mean the difference between success and failure. It is also important to meet new product shipping dates. Delays in shipment give competitors time to react to new products, can cost the company sales, and lead to customer disappointment with the company or brand.[36]

product launch

Completing all the final preparations for making the fully tested product available to the market.

time to market

The speed with which a company launches a product.

Boeing's 787 Dreamliner provides an extreme example of the price of a delayed product launch. The unexpected additional costs of a three-year delay due to design and supply chain problems seriously hurt the company's near-term sales opportunities. *Kevin P. Casey/Bloomberg/Getty Images*

Mc Graw Hill connect Exercise 6-2

Social Media in Action

Social media are becoming increasingly powerful tools for new-product launches. In just a couple of months, Unilever's Clear shampoo and conditioner went from anonymity to a product line that had consumers across the United States talking. This occurred largely because of social media. Clear's social media–heavy product launch drew hundreds of thousands of consumers into conversation about the new product. Consumers were encouraged to go to the brand's Facebook page and order a free sample of the product. Marketers created a celebrity-driven web mini-series called "Best Night Ever" that featured people using the new product. Twitter hashtags specifically for the product launch helped bridge the conversation across multiple social media platforms and spread positive opinion more quickly.

The Social Media in Action Connect exercise in Chapter 6 asks you to develop social media strategies to enhance a new-product launch. Product launches occur at practically every company, making it important for you to consider ways to utilize all of the available social media tools to make each product launch as successful as possible.

Source: See Doren Bloch, "Top 5 Product Launch Lessons from Clear Hair Care's Big Debut," *Forbes,* July 12, 2012, http://www.forbes.com/sites/yec/2012/07/12/top-5-product-launch-lessons-from-clear-hair-cares-big-debut/.

RISKS IN NEW-PRODUCT DEVELOPMENT

LO 6-3

Discuss the major risks in new-product development and how to reduce those risks.

Firms that want to maintain or improve their competitive position in the marketplace generally must develop new products. Failure to do so carries tremendous risk; that risk is greatest for companies that develop products that quickly become obsolete. Any product, for example, that is on the "cutting edge" of technology, such as phone apps or computer games, can rapidly become obsolete as new technology products enter the market.

However, NPD comes with its own sets of risks. Table 6.1 identifies some of these risks, their level of severity, and possible outcomes to firms.[37] Companies need to understand both the types and severity of risks and how to mitigate those risks in order to succeed in introducing new products to the marketplace.

Examples of risks by category include the following:

- *Very high risk: PepsiCo's change from aspartame to sucralose as a sweetener.* Pepsi's change is said to be the biggest change to a soda since New Coke's fiasco in 1985, when long-time Coke drinkers rebelled against the new product and Coke had to bring back the old formula as "Coke Classic." Changes to recipes are very risky because taste matters a great deal in food and drink products.[38] Failure to adequately test a new product can create brand image and liability issues. Some of Samsung's Galaxy Note 7 smartphones caught fire due to battery problems, causing the company to recall 2.5 million phones, costing upward of $5 billion in recall costs and lost sales.[39] As a result, Samsung took a more cautious approach to new technologies with the launch of the Galaxy 9, with fewer major changes in the product.[40]

TABLE 6.1 New-Product Development Risks and Related Outcomes

Severity of Risk	Types of Risk	Outcome
Very high	Product fails to meet needs and wants of customers.	Costs are not recouped; company loses money.
	Product proves to be dangerous or defective.	Company suffers legal liabilities and product recalls.
High	Quality is not up to customer standards.	Customers are dissatisfied; there are excessive returns.
	Supply of product is inadequate to meet demand.	Company loses orders, sales, and customers.
	New product is not accepted well in the marketplace.	Company loses revenue and profits and is stuck with obsolete goods.
	Inadequate supply of materials delays production.	Product launch is delayed; first-to-market advantage is lost.
	Target price is not accepted by the market.	Company reduces price, resulting in lost revenue and profits.
Moderate	Supplier cost savings are not achieved.	Profitability is reduced.
	Product takes sales from existing products.	Total company revenue and profits are less than expected.
	Competitors copy products and sell them at a lower price.	Company loses market share and profits.

- High risk: Ford F-150 pickup truck changes. The Ford F-150 is the a high-volume, high-profit vehicle that has been the best-selling vehicle in the United States for over 30 years; a significant change to its structure is high risk if the market concludes that it is not as desirable as previous pickups. However, according to Bill Ford, former executive chair of Ford Motor Company, "The role we are in now requires us to stick our necks out. We've got to place bets. We've got to have a point of view about the future."[41] His perspective is that unless Ford is willing to take risks, it will fall behind in the market as other companies introduce risky but successful innovations.[42] The all-electric Ford F-150 Lightning is an example of such a high-risk product. It remains to be seen if pick-up truck buyers will be interested in an all-electric vehicle. However, Ford is betting on significant adoption of its truck as the world begins to transition from gasoline and diesel to electrically powered vehicles.

- Moderate risk: The Coca-Cola K-Cup.[43] In 2015 Coca-Cola signed a 10-year partnership agreement with Green Mountain Coffee Roasters, the maker of the Keurig single-serve coffeemaker, to sell a new type of machine to make sodas. This product is a moderate risk: Countertop soda-making machines already exist, and Coca-Cola already has a very recognizable and high-selling product line. The risk will be Coca-Cola's investment to build the machines. Will consumers decide that the ability to make Coca-Cola at home warrants the cost of the machine and the pods necessary to make the soda?

The Ford F-150 Lightning is an example of an innovative product that represents a risk for a company. How well an electric version of the pickup truck will be received by consumers presents a potential issue for Ford if acceptance by the market is less-than-anticipated. *JA/Everett Collection/Alamy Stock Photo*

Categorizing Risks in New-Product Development

The highest level of risk occurs when products fail to generate sales or prove to be dangerous, defective, or deceptive. These risks can be devastating to a company if they permanently damage the firm's image or create legal liabilities. Volkswagen (VW), for example, introduced diesel automobiles in the United States that were designed to fool EPA tests regarding their emissions. News of this deception had devastating effects on VW's company image and sales, as well as billions of dollars of government fines.

Beyond legal issues, new products can fail to capture the public's imagination or prove to be poor sales performers. Such problems are costly because of significant amounts spent in development, production, advertising, and distribution. Even the best companies launch products that fail to do well:

- Juicero was a Wi-Fi-enabled juicer that cost $700 and that could only use special Juicero fruit packets which cost up to $8 each. Customers quickly dismissed the idea; they viewed it as unnecessary and extremely overpriced. The company shut down less than six months after it started.[44]
- During the COVID-19 pandemic, Singapore Airlines scrapped plans to launch three-hour scenic flights that would take off and land from Changi Airport. However, they scrapped the plans due to pressure for environmental groups.[45]
- An Under Armour project to develop an electronic shirt to monitor biometrics turned into just a heart-rate strap, which was later phased out due to production problems.[46]

Marketing new products internationally comes with significant risk. Issues with product quality, supply, or marketing mix can lead to missed launch dates, dissatisfied customers, excessive returns, and lost profits. For example, Nokia's launch of its Lumia smartphone met with poor sales in some parts of the world, such as the Middle East, Africa, and Asia. The problem was a marketing-mix issue: The prices that Nokia was charging were too high for most people in those regions.[47] As a result, Nokia had to substantially lower its prices to compete with rivals like Samsung, which sells less-expensive models.

New products and services often fail for a variety of reasons. Singapore Airline's planned three-hour scenic flights from and returning to the same airport met resistance from environmental groups as causing unnecessary pollution, and the company decided not to launch the service. *SpaceKris/Shutterstock*

Reducing Risks in New-Product Development

Companies can reduce the risk of new-product failures by doing the following:

1. *Listening to the customer carefully.* Customer needs and wants drive purchasing behavior. The voice of the customer should always help guide idea generation and screening.
2. *Making a commitment to the NPD process.* Every stage of the NPD process must be followed for the process to work correctly. Companies trying to launch a poorly conceived or executed product just to get a jump on the market or to generate quick profits are likely to damage their brand image as well as lose money.
3. *Understanding current market trends and anticipating changes in the market.* Gathering data requires a commitment to both marketing and technical research. A firm must stay on top of changing economic, demographic, cultural, and technological conditions so it can anticipate market demand over time.
4. *Asking the right questions.* Some questions a firm should ask include: What is the expected demand for the good or service over time? How much will it cost to produce and distribute the good or service at varying levels of demand? What level of quality will be required for the product to be competitive? Are there any potential environmental and safety issues? What is the best pricing strategy to apply at the launch of the product?
5. *Being willing to fail on occasion.* Companies that develop new products sometimes will fail. However, firms must learn from past failures. Learning should come not only from products that failed after launch but also from those that failed during the NPD process.

Firms that take steps to reduce risk in new-product development, particularly by analyzing and learning from mistakes, are well positioned to see their new products adopted by consumers. Later in the chapter, we'll discuss the consumer-adoption process. First, we'll discuss the ethical implications of new-product development and how ignoring ethical issues can also be risky for firms.

PRODUCT ADOPTION

LO 6-4

Describe the categories of new-product adopters and the implications of adoption to marketers.

A product has been *adopted* when a consumer purchases and uses it. The process by which a product is adopted and spreads across various types of adopters is called **diffusion**. Marketers who understand diffusion—how their new products are likely to be adopted, the rate at which they will be adopted, and the process by which they will spread into markets—will have a better chance of successfully launching and sustaining new products. Understanding diffusion enables marketers to figure out who will likely buy their product over a period of time. With that knowledge, they can plan an appropriate marketing mix and forecast potential sales.

Up to this point in the chapter, we have discussed the new-product development process. Customer adoption of new products also follows a process. The **consumer-adoption process** is the process by which customers formally accept and purchase products. It includes the following five stages:[48]

diffusion

The process by which a product is adopted and spreads across various types of adopters.

consumer-adoption process

The process by which customers formally accept and purchase products.

1. *Awareness.* The consumer has been exposed to the product and knows it is available on the market.
2. *Interest.* Interest occurs when the product registers as a potential purchase in a consumer's mind, and when someone begins to look for information about it.
3. *Evaluation.* The customer thinks about the product's value and whether to try it out. They also evaluate competing products to determine which product best satisfies his or her needs and wants.

FIGURE 6.2   Percentage of Each Type of Adopter

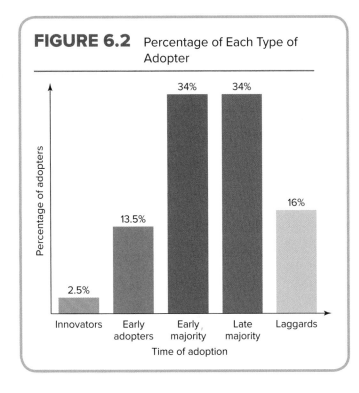

4. *Trial.* The consumer tests or uses the product to see if it meets requirements. Trials include things like test-driving an automobile, borrowing a new shampoo from a friend, or signing up for 30-day access to Hulu's online streaming services.
5. *Adoption.* The consumer buys and uses the product.

Adoption happens at different times depending on the type of adopter.

Types of Adopters

Following product launch, customers buy new goods or services at different rates. This is true for both individual and business customers. When a firm launches a new product, only a few people buy it; as word spreads, consumers purchase the product at an increasing rate for a period of time. We can group consumers into categories of adopters, based on how quickly they adopt new products. There are five categories: innovators, early adopters, early majority, late majority, and laggards. Figure 6.2 shows the approximate percentage of the population that falls into each adopter category.

innovators

A category of consumers that adopt a product almost immediately after it is launched.

early adopters

A category of consumers that purchase and use a product soon after it has been introduced, but not as quickly as innovators.

Innovators Approximately 2.5 percent of those who adopt a product do so almost immediately after the product is launched. These people are **innovators**. If you are always one of the first people you know to try a new product, you probably fall into this category. Innovators tend to be younger and more mobile than those who adopt a product later in the diffusion process. They are often obsessed with the idea of newness and unafraid to take risks when it comes to trying new products. In addition, they tend to be very knowledgeable, have higher-than-average incomes, possess self-confidence, and choose not to follow conventional norms.

Firms value innovators because they share information about the product with others, which can help promote market acceptance. Innovators are important to companies introducing new-to-the-world goods and services, particularly those based on transformative innovation. These goods and services are often a difficult sell due to the reluctance of many people to try new experiences or learn how to use new products.

Early Adopters Early adopters comprise roughly another 13.5 percent of adopters. **Early adopters** purchase a product soon after it has been introduced, but not as quickly as innovators. They tend to conform to group norms and values more closely than innovators and have closer ties to social groups and their communities. Though they adopt products earlier than the remaining categories, early adopters, unlike innovators, wait for product reviews and further information concerning new products before purchasing them.

Early adopters are typically well respected by their peers and tend to be opinion leaders. Marketers seek to gain their acceptance, in the hope that they will share their purchase experiences with others. Early adopters are therefore important to the diffusion of a new product.

Early adopters not only help marketers spread the message about a product to the rest of the population, they also provide valuable feedback to marketers about their products.
Jack Plunkett/LG Electronics USA/AP Images

Early Majority The next category of adopters, the early majority, comprises approximately 34 percent of the adopters of a new product. Adopters in the **early majority** gather more information and spend more time deciding to make a purchase than innovators and early adopters. They are careful in their approach. Typically, by the time the early majority buys a product, more competitors have entered the market; this group will have some choice as to which product to buy.

Members of the early majority generally are not opinion leaders themselves, but they often are associated with such leaders. If this group does not purchase the product, the good or service will likely fail to be profitable. The early majority also serves as a bridge to the next group of adopters: the late majority.

Late Majority The late majority also comprises about 34 percent of adopters. Members of the **late majority** rely on others for information, buying a good or service because others have already done so. They tend to be cautious about new things and ideas. They often are older than members of the previous three categories and may not act on a new product without peer pressure. When the late majority purchases a product, the product has typically achieved all it can from a market in terms of profitability and growth.

Laggards Laggards make up about 16 percent of the market. **Laggards** do not like change and may remain loyal to a product until it is no longer available for sale. Laggards are typically older and less-educated than members of the other four categories.[49] Many choose not to use the Internet. They tend to be tied to tradition and are not easily motivated by promotional strategies.

In fact, marketers may never convince laggards to buy their good or service. For example, if an individual has no access to the Internet, or has access but rarely ventures there, he or she is not likely to use Amazon as a source from which to buy products. As a result, marketers often do not expend a great deal of time or effort trying to reach this group.

Product Characteristics

Categories of adopters aren't the only thing that affects the diffusion of a new product. New-product characteristics, including the following, also affect the adoption rate:

- *Competitive advantage.* A product obtains a **competitive advantage** over competing products if consumers believe it has more value than other products in its category. If a product has a competitive advantage, consumers will quickly adopt it. The Apple iPhone had a competitive advantage over the original Black-Berry because its operating system used icons for navigation on the phone, which users were familiar and comfortable with.
- *Compatibility.* *Compatibility* refers to how well a new product fits into potential customers' needs, values, product knowledge, and past behaviors. For example, a new beer will not be a compatible product in countries that forbid alcoholic beverages due to religious taboos.
- *Observability.* When people can see others using a product and perceive value in its use, the product will diffuse quickly. Some products are naturally more visible than others. For example, people who

early majority

A category of consumers that gather more information and spend more time deciding to make a purchase than innovators and early adopters.

late majority

A category of consumers that rely on others for information, buying a good or service because others have already done so.

laggards

A category of consumers that do not like change and may remain loyal to a product until it is no longer available for sale.

competitive advantage

The superior position a product enjoys over competing products if consumers believe it has more value than other products in its category.

High-end digital cameras with a multitude of functions, like the Canon EOS R RF24 digital SLR, might not be adopted quickly by the average consumer. Instead, the firm targets camera enthusiasts willing to spend time to learn how to use the camera's features. *Oliver Berg/dpa/Alamy Stock Photo*

do not have ATM cards or smartphones can easily see the convenience that other people experience using them. Personal products such as suntan lotions, on the other hand, are not as easily observed, so how well they work can be difficult to confirm.

- *Complexity.* Typically, the easier it is to understand and use a product, the faster it will diffuse. If the market finds a new product too difficult to use, as happened with the first videocassette recording (VCR) devices, sales often will not increase until the product is simplified. In the case of the VCR, the addition of on-screen programming made it possible for the average user to follow directions for recording a television show.

  The effect of complexity may differ between regions of the world. In industrialized societies, consumers are exposed to and use more technologically complex products. They therefore may accept, and even desire, intricate products that offer additional features. In areas of the world less exposed to high-tech products, complexity will be an even bigger issue. An example is the popularity of the traditional BlackBerry phone: It continues to be popular in some parts of the world, such as a few Southeast Asian, Latin American, and African countries, although competing phones are loaded with apps and are often less expensive.[50]

trialability

The extent to which a potential customer can examine the merits of a new product without having to spend a lot of money or time doing so.

- *Trialability.* Trialability refers to the extent to which a potential customer can examine the merits of a new product without having to spend a lot of money or time doing so. Most of the time, products that consumers can try without significant expense will diffuse more quickly than others. For example, a GPS phone app that costs $0.99 or less will diffuse much faster than a stand-alone GPS device like a Garmin Drive 51 LM costing $89.95. Similarly, consumers may adopt a product they are first exposed to through trial sizes, free-sampling programs, and in-store trials (e.g., taste testing food).

 International Product-Adoption Considerations Cultural and societal issues also come into play with product adoption. At the international level, several factors can affect the adoption of a product or service.

- *Cosmopolitanism,* the extent to which a country is connected to other cultures, can play a part in adoption. The more cosmopolitan a country, the more potential customers are exposed to the adoption of a new product or service elsewhere in the world, and the easier it is for the product to be adopted.
- *Modernity* refers to the extent to which a culture values "progress." For example, in the United States, the claim of "new and improved" can be considered a selling point for many consumers. In countries with more cultural traditions, the potential for disruption to the culture can cause new products to be seen as undesirable. However, cultures may change over time, and marketers must stay aware of those changes in order to take advantage of them.
- *Homiphily,* the extent to which consumers in a society are relatively similar to each other, can help the adoption of a new product or service if it fits well with the society's culture. People who are similar usually have many of the same needs, likes and dislikes, social taboos, and culturally acceptable ways to act. This similarity can help a new product or service be adopted more readily.
- *Physical distance* can hurt the adoption of new goods and services. If consumers are not in close proximity to each other, they are less likely to interact with other users of a product. The result is less observability and trialability available, and so the adoption rate is slower.[51]

The rate at which product diffusion occurs influences the length of the product's life cycle, which we'll discuss in the next section.

THE PRODUCT LIFE CYCLE

The launch of a new product begins that product's life. Like humans, products go through various stages that mark their lifespan. This series of stages is called the **product life cycle (PLC)**.

Stages of the Product Life Cycle

Figure 6.3 illustrates the five stages of the PLC and shows the general trends of sales and profits during the life of a product. In general:

- During the *new-product development stage,* the product actually costs the company money in development costs.
- During the *introduction stage,* sales increase slowly, as the firm's marketing activities begin to raise awareness of the product. The firm may not yet be making a profit on the product because of the costs of advertising, manufacturing, and distribution.
- The *growth stage* brings a spike in sales and profits as consumers recognize the product's ability to satisfy their needs and wants.
- Sales and profits begin to drop in the *maturity stage,* as competition increases and customers begin to look for the next big thing,
- Sales and profits then fall off completely during the *decline stage.*

New-Product Development Up to this point, the chapter has focused on the new-product development stage. The ability of companies to have a full pipeline of new ideas that result in market-winning products is the difference between success and failure in the marketplace. In the sections that follow, we will discuss the remaining stages of the product life cycle: introduction through decline stages. We will show how the various aspects of a product's life cycle influence how a company markets the product (or service).

Introduction Once the firm launches the product into the marketplace and innovators begin to buy it, it has entered the **introduction stage** of the PLC. This stage is characterized by few or no competitors if the product is new to the market. Sales are typically slow because customers are not yet accustomed to the product. An example of a product in the introductory phase is home 3D printers. While 3D printers are catching on for business applications, home 3D printing has not sold as well. It remains to be seen whether technological advances making the printers work better and faster will spur consumers to begin adopting them, or whether they will not make it beyond the introductory stage.[52]

If a firm is first to market, it may be able to capture a large percentage of the market early, giving it advantages in economies of scale and brand recognition. Also, if the product is a good, the company may be able to monopolize the capacity of available suppliers. Other companies then will find it more difficult to get supplies of components from which to make competing products of their own. Competition can be fierce for first-to-market status if several companies are introducing a new product or service. Companies that have an effective and rapid new product development process can have a competitive advantage over other companies.

LO 6-5

Describe the stages and aspects of the product life cycle and how they affect the marketing mix.

product life cycle (PLC)

The series of stages a product goes through from the time it is launched into the market until the time it is removed from the market.

introduction stage

The stage of the product life cycle that occurs after the firm launches the product into the marketplace and innovators begin to buy it.

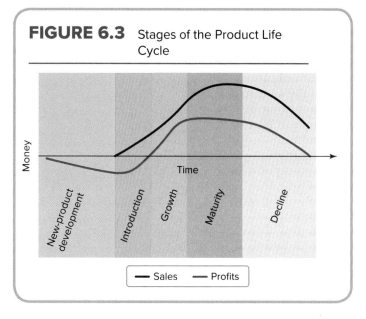

FIGURE 6.3 Stages of the Product Life Cycle

Sales typically increase slowly during the introduction stage. Companies may need to offer incentives to stores to get them to carry the product, thus limiting distribution. New services may require similar incentives. Companies might offer their customers a low introductory price to interest them in the service, for example. Due to the high cost of developing, advertising, manufacturing, and distributing a new product, profits are often low or negative at this point in the PLC. During this phase, the firm attempts few refinements. Firms tend to produce basic models until the product's sales improve to the point at which the product is profitable.

Several factors influence how long the introduction stage lasts. These include the product's relative advantage, the amount of resources the company puts into promoting the product, and the effort required to educate the market about the product's attributes. For example, high-definition TVs moved slowly through the introduction stage; smartphones, on the other hand, moved quickly.

Growth   Early adopters, followed by the early majority, begin to buy the product during the **growth stage**. when sales, profits, and competition increase. At this stage, companies begin to take advantage of economies of scale in purchasing, manufacturing, and distribution.

As competitors enter the market, the firm has to promote the differences between its brand and the competition's. It may attempt to refine aspects of the product by improving quality or adding new features. It also may focus its marketing efforts on showcasing the competitive advantage of its product over others. Although promotional costs will still be substantial due to these efforts, they generally drop from the high levels of the introduction phase. However, additional competition may force prices down. Making product changes that improve quality or add new features will enable the company to maintain initial pricing.

The firm also must concentrate on building the distribution of the product to increase market share. For goods, this is accomplished through intense efforts to enlist dealers, distributors, and retailers to carry the good. For products, it takes place by expanding the service distribution network through additional locations or personnel.

If the product satisfies the market, repeat purchases help make the product profitable, and brand loyalty begins to develop. Electric vehicles are examples of a product in the growth stage. Their sales are increasing due to their advanced technology and environmental impact.

Maturity   In the maturity stage, late majority and repeat buyers make up an increasing percentage of the customer base. The main focuses of the **maturity stage** are profitability and maintaining the firm's market share for as long as possible. As the market becomes saturated, sales level off and competition becomes fierce. Companies not doing well will drop out of the market.

During the maturity stage, marketing costs rise due to competition, as each firm tries to find ways to gain market share. The firm may need to make large promotional expenditures to show the differences between the firm's product and the competition. The firm also may feel pressure to reduce prices. As a result, profits typically begin to decline during this stage.

To prolong the product's life, the company may begin to offer more versions in different styles and with different features. It also may continue to improve its quality and performance features. To accommodate more product options, the firm may need to adjust the marketing mix. The iPhone is an example of a product at its maturity phase. Periodically, Apple comes out with a new version of the iPhone, with changes in size, memory, and capabilities such as added security; these new versions are based on the original iPhone concept. Apple is also moving into the "digital assistant" market of virtual assistants to sell more hardware to offset plateauing of its phone sales.[53] Services

growth stage

The stage of the product life cycle characterized by increases in sales, profits, and competition.

maturity stage

The stage of the product life cycle during which the firm focuses on profitability and maintaining the firm's market share for as long as possible.

Julian Jackson

Network Implementation Specialist
Laerdal Medical

Describe your job. My job as a network implementation specialist consists of traveling to hospitals, universities, and military bases to install, test, and train clients on our software, which is focused on capture, debriefing, and assessment of medical training and clinical events. Further, I recommend solutions for the best installation standards for implementing our medical simulators. This includes consulting during the pre-sales phase and recommending any enhancements regarding product, application or documentation based on information received from the customer.

Julian Jackson

How did you get your job? After graduating from college, I knew I wanted to focus on networking or security with the end goal of starting my own company. I purposely took on roles in startup companies to learn multiple roles that would help with my future goal. While working at a startup company in Denver, I was contacted by a recruiter on LinkedIn who asked if I had ever thought about working for a medical company. She continued by saying my resume and skillset aligned with an open position in the company and that a liaison was needed because the firm was in the process of acquiring a software startup company. Following a short phone call, I was invited to speak with the hiring manager. The call went great and I realized I was in a position to make a difference while also being able to continue to focus on my goals. Following this video call, I was invited to New York, where I went through a series of five interviews, talking with various people about my work experience and seeing how I would fit into the company culture. This was by far one of the most intense interviews I had been through. It showed me how genuine the company was and how passionate my potential coworkers were about our mission, "Helping Saves Lives."

What has been the most important thing in making you successful at your job? Learnability. In my field, the world of software is always changing for the better.

Processes we implement one month may change in the next two months. Because of this, it is important that I continue to adapt and build on skills by expanding my knowledge base. Success in my current field is measured by how well we can take a new concept and apply it in our software to keep up with industry trends. This skill allows me to provide even better customer service, as I am the key person to explain these changes/improvements in a way that the customer can understand and use to their benefit.

What advice would you give soon-to-be graduates? Learn from anything and everything. Go down that rabbit hole. Ask questions . . . and a lot of them. Being curious is key to how I am in the position I am. Pay attention to everything going on around you and, when you fail, pay extra close attention because this will be one of your biggest learning experiences. The world is full of problems and solutions. It's our job to figure out what works best for us and why. It will be hard and you may not understand a lot going on around you, but when you make those connections, you will see that your hard work does pay off.

What do you consider your personal brand to be? Helping people is my mission. I want to be the bridge to understanding how positive communication and working together can lead to a great and lasting relationship. When you put others before you, it allows you to understand who they are and how being connected with them can make you a better person. This also teaches you humility and shows that you understand. You understand that not everyone is perfect and people have different styles of communication. But, by coming together, we really can create great things and help make society better. In whatever way you can, be that person that someone didn't expect to meet today.

211

also attempt to differentiate themselves from competitors during this stage. For example, the airline industry promotes service quality through things like on-time arrivals, more favorable cancellation policies, and early-boarding options.

Companies may use price reductions, more effective advertising, and trade promotions to generate demand in the maturity stage. Promotion to resellers often increases during this stage, to entice them to continue to buy the company's product rather than a competitor's. Customer service and repairs begin to take on significance and can serve as a source of differentiation from competing products. The maturity stage is usually the longest stage of the PLC.

decline stage

The stage of the product life cycle characterized by decreases in sales and profits.

New material technology in fly rods made bamboo rods much less attractive due to the superior performance of graphite and boron, yet the market for bamboo rods still exists. Though an R.L. Winston bamboo rod can cost $3,000, aficionados of this type of rod continue to purchase them even though more effective rods cost less. *Gabe Souza/Portland Press Herald/Getty Images*

Decline The **decline stage** of the PLC is characterized by decreases in sales and profits. Depending on the product, the decline in sales during this stage may be rapid or could occur over a long period of time. During the decline stage, competitors drop out of the market as the product becomes unprofitable.

Personal computers (PCs) are an example of a product in the decline stage. With technology enabling consumers to use their smartphones and tablet-type devices to do more of what they did with PCs, consumers are beginning to move away from PCs to the more mobile devices. The PC market is expected to continue to decline due to size and portability issues.[54]

In the decline stage, the firm will likely cut prices to generate sales. Coupons or buy-one-get-one-free promotions may be used to prolong sales and reduce existing inventories. The firm also will look for ways to cut costs: curtail advertising, eliminate unprofitable items from the product line, and reduce or eliminate promotion to individual consumers and resellers. At this stage, little or no effort is put into changing a good's appearance or functionality; consumers have moved on to other types of products. CD players are an example of a product that went into the decline phase when technologies such as the iPod and smartphone offered similar functions in smaller and more portable devices. Other products in the decline phase include bar soap, alkaline batteries, ground coffee, powder detergent, frozen juice concentrate, and processed cheese.[55]

At this point the firm must decide whether to discontinue the product. If the product or service is deemed obsolete, the firm may be able to sell it off to discount retailers, such as Big Lots. If the firm keeps the product active, it may put little effort into selling or advertising it, happy just to have any sales it produces. Or the firm may attempt to find a niche market for the product that may be small but profitable. For example, travel agency services are in far less demand than they were a generation ago, before travelers could research and book and plan trips online. In response, many travel agencies have shifted their focus from general consumer markets to niche markets, such as horseback-riding trips in South America or wine-tasting tours in Europe. Such trips generate limited demand but can still earn profits for the agency.

McGraw Hill connect Exercise **6-3**

Please complete the *Connect* exercise for Chapter 6 that focuses on the product life cycle. By matching various products or product types to their proper category, you will sharpen your understanding of the product life cycle.

Estimating the Length of a Product's Life

Once firms understand the stages of the PLC, they can appropriately tailor the marketing mix for their new products at each stage. As a first step, marketers should estimate the length of the product's life. To do so, they will take into account marketing research and analysis of any similar competitive products. For example, an iPad has many similarities with a personal computer, and possibly many of the same customers. When developing the iPad, Apple could have used data from its personal computer products to estimate the iPad's product life.

Product life cycles can be of varying lengths, depending on the type of product. Technology-driven products like computers tend to have a short PLC because of rapid changes in computing power and features. Other products may remain viable in the marketplace for decades. For example, the Vaseline Intensive Care line of products has been around since the 1960s. However, in general, product life cycles are getting shorter. We've noted that changes in technology make products obsolete more quickly. In addition, firms now introduce new products at a faster rate, pushing existing products into the mature and decline stages faster.

Organizations can combat shortening life cycles by developing a product mix that consists of various products at different stages of the PLC. A firm's **product mix** comprises all of the products that it sells. A company's product mix is characterized by width, depth, and consistency:

- Product width is determined by the extent to which a company offers different product categories. For example, General Motors offers multiple categories (sedans, electric, performance, crossovers, SUVs, and trucks) and brands (Chevrolet, GMC, Buick, and Cadillac). Amazon.com markets Fire TV sets, cloud computing, Prime Video, and has opened grocery stores under its brand name.[56] Product width helps companies with the ever-shortening product life cycles: Some products will have longer PLCs than others, and those with longer life cycles can offset products with shorter ones.
- Product depth refers to the number of products a company offers within each category or brand. The Chevrolet brand, for example, has the Camaro, Corvette, Bolt, Blazer, Equinox, Malibu, Spark, Trax, and Trailblazer. Product depth also works to combat the trend of shorter PLCs. It makes sure that within product categories there is a variety of products, some of which will have longer PLCs than others.
- Product-mix consistency pertains to how closely related product lines are to one another in terms of use, production, and distribution. The Buick and GMC brands are closely related in terms of distribution since they are often sold at the same dealership. Product-mix consistency could work against a company if the products are closely related and exhibit similar, short PLCs. When this occurs, companies would need to develop new products at a high rate in order to offset the effects of having many products in the mature and decline stages of the PLC.

Companies offering services also have a product mix. For example, Bank of America's product mix includes a variety of services—checking and savings accounts, credit cards, student banking, and online and mobile banking. The new mobile banking service might be in the introduction stage; basic savings accounts might, at the same time, be in the decline stage. Each of these items within the product mix provides Bank of America's marketers with unique opportunities. The new mobile banking product might include features and technology that create value for busy, tech-savvy consumers. A basic savings account, though in the decline stage, still allows marketers to serve more traditional consumers; it might also enable the bank to reach young consumers who might be opening their first bank account and could develop a lifelong relationship with Bank of America.

product mix
The combination of all the products a company sells.

Sometimes companies get into trouble by diluting their markets with too many products. Unilever, for example, was forced to reduce the number of its products by 30 percent. Many of these products were introduced to sell as special offers in particular countries and, over time, proved no longer profitable.[57] Another issue is that although consumers like choice, having too much choice can hurt sales, because consumers often rebel against having too many options from which to choose.

Projecting the Shape of the PLC Curve

high-learning products

Products that take longer for consumers to see the benefits of or that do not have a good infrastructure in place to support them.

low-learning products

Products with benefits customers can easily see.

fad product

A product that is very popular for a relatively short amount of time.

fashion product

A product that comes in and out of favor with consumers.

As a second step in tailoring the marketing mix, firms should project the shape of the PLC curve for their product. Figure 6.4 shows four common PLC curves, which vary by type of product:

- Products that take longer for consumers to see the benefits of or that do not have a good infrastructure in place to support them are called **high-learning products**. Examples are the personal computer when it was introduced for home use and electric automobiles. High-learning products will have a life cycle curve with a long, flat-shaped introductory and growth phase.
- Products with benefits customers can easily see are called **low-learning products**. Concentrated laundry detergent is an example of a product in which consumers can easily see benefits. An example of a low-learning service is a free checking account at a local bank. Low-learning products have a curve that is steep through the maturity phase.
- A **fad product** is one that is very popular for a relatively short amount of time. Fidget spinners are an example of a fad product that quickly gained and then lost appeal to the market. Fad products will have a steep up-and-down curve, as consumers rapidly adopt and then abandon the product.
- A **fashion product** is one that comes in and out of favor with consumers. Men's hats were fashionable for decades but lost their appeal in the 1960s, only to recently start becoming fashionable again. Fashion life cycles typically last longer than fad products, but they are short compared with high-learning and

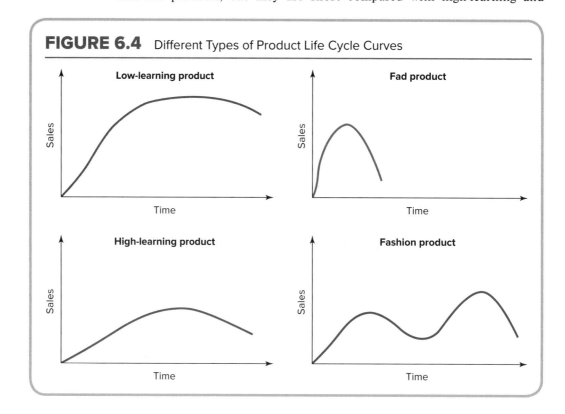

FIGURE 6.4   Different Types of Product Life Cycle Curves

low-learning product curves. Some companies, like athletic clothes manufacturer lululemon, manage their new items with a short life cycle in mind. Lululemon comes out with new colors and seasonal items that have 3-, 6-, or 12-week life cycles, to make its stores seem very up-to-date and fresh.

Marketers must understand which of these four types their product is in order to project its likely product life cycle.

Strategic Implications for the Marketing Mix

Just as our interest, activities, and abilities change as we enter various stages of life, the stage of a product's life has many implications for how a firm markets the product. Firms can modify their marketing-mix (four Ps) strategies in response to what stage of life a product is in.

- *Product strategies.* The number of products a firm offers will change over a product's life cycle. Firms will typically offer a small number of models or service offerings in the introductory stage. As adopters of the product increase in the growth stage, the firm will expand the number of products, reaching a full line of products in the maturity stage. In the decline stage, the firm will reduce the number of models or service offerings, so that only the best-selling products remain.
- *Place (distribution) strategies.* Distribution is generally limited in the introductory phase. Distribution channels increase during the growth stage and become extensive in the maturity stage. As the product loses profitability, the number of distribution channels contracts.
- *Promotional strategies.* Promotional strategies in the introductory stage usually involve making customers aware of the product and its attributes. Intensive advertising that stresses how the product differs from the competition appears in the growth stage. In the maturity stage, advertising typically reminds consumers about the product and its value to them. Minimal promotion, or none at all, takes place in the decline stage.
- *Price strategies.* Price is usually higher in the introductory phase due to lack of competition and high launch costs. It then starts to fall in the growth stage as competition becomes more intense. Price continues to fall through the maturity stage, when a firm must defend its market share. It then levels out in the decline stage.

Table 6.2 lists the typical strategies a firm undertakes for each of the four Ps, depending on where the product is in its life cycle.

TABLE 6.2 Typical Marketing-Mix Strategies during a Product's Life Cycle

Stage	Product Strategies	Place Strategies	Promotional Strategies	Price Strategies
Introduction	Offer small number of models	Limit distribution; attract channel partners	Promote to develop customer awareness	Price high
Growth	Offer variety of models and many modifications	Make intensive effort to expand distribution	Promote to build awareness; increase personal selling	Lower price gradually as competition arrives
Maturity	Offer full line of products	Make intensive effort to maintain distribution	Promote to point out brand attributes and differentiating features	Price equal to or below competitors
Decline	Reduce number of products based on profitability	Phase out unprofitable outlets	Reduce promotion to a minimum or eliminate	Price to maintain small profit; increase price if product appeals to niche market

SUMMARY

Mariusz Burcz/
Alamy Stock Photo

LO 6-1 Understand the different types of new products, their advantages, and their risks.

A new product is one that is new to a company in any way. If a product is functionally different from existing products in the market or is not marketed in its current form or manner by the company, it can be considered a new product. New products can be categorized as (1) *new-to-the-market products,* which are inventions that have never been seen before and that create a new market; (2) *new-category entries,* which involve the introduction of products new to a company but *not* new to the marketplace; (3) *product-line extensions,* which are products that extend and supplement a company's already-established product line; and (4) *revamped products,* which are existing products that have been changed in some way.

Dinodia Photos /
Alamy Stock Photo

LO 6-2 Describe the various stages of new-product development.

The new-product development process consists of seven steps: (1) *New-product strategy development* involves determining the direction a company will take when it develops a new product. (2) *Idea generation* involves coming up with a set of product concepts from which to identify potentially viable new products. (3) *Idea screening* involves evaluating the idea to determine whether it fits into the new-product strategy. (4) *Business analysis* is undertaken to determine profitability. (5) *Product development* confirms that the product can be made in a way that meets customer needs and generates profits. (6) *Test marketing* involves introducing a potential new product to a geographically limited market. (7) *Product launch* involves making the product available to the market.

JA/Everett Collection/
Alamy Stock Photo

LO 6-3 Discuss the major risks in new-product development and how to reduce those risks.

Failing to develop new products carries tremendous risk for companies, particularly those with products that quickly become obsolete. But NPD comes with its own risks: The product may prove to be dangerous or defective, or it might produce less-than-expected revenue.

Companies can reduce the risk of new-product failures by doing the following: (1) listening to the customer carefully, (2) making a commitment to the NPD process, (3) understanding current market trends and anticipating changes in the market, (4) asking the right questions, and (5) being willing to fail on occasion.

Jack Plunkett/LG
Electronics USA/AP
Images

LO 6-4 Describe the categories of new-product adopters and the implications of adoption to marketers.

Product adoption includes the following five steps: (1) awareness, (2) interest, (3) evaluation, (4) trial, and (5) adoption. Adoption happens at different times during a product's lifespan, depending on the type of adopter buying the product.

The characteristics of a new product, such as its relative advantage and complexity, affect its *diffusion* rate, or how quickly the various categories of adopters—innovators, early adopters, early majority, late majority, and laggards—will buy it.

Various new-product characteristics affect the adoption rate. These include competitive advantage, compatibility, observability, complexity, and ability of potential new consumers to try products. Those characteristics also apply when marketing products internationally, as do characteristics of international markets: cosmopolitanism, modernity, the similarity of consumers (homophily), and physical distance.

Gabe Souza/
Portland Press
Herald/Getty Images

LO 6-5 Describe the stages and aspects of the product life cycle and how they affect the marketing mix.

There are five stages in a product's life cycle: (1) product development, (2) introduction, (3) growth, (4) maturity, and (5) decline.

After the product's launch, sales increase slowly in the *introduction stage,* as the firm's marketing activities begin to raise awareness of the product. The *growth stage* brings a spike in sales and profits as consumers recognize the product's ability to satisfy their needs and wants. Sales and profits begin to decline in the *maturity stage* as competition increases and customers begin to look for the next big thing. In the *decline stage,* sales and profits completely fall off.

Organizations can combat shortening life cycles by developing a product mix that consists of various products at different stages of the PLC. A company's product mix is characterized by width, depth, and consistency.

The length of a product's life and the shape of its PLC curve also depend on whether the product is a *high-learning product* or a *low-learning product.*

The PLC affects the marketing mix: the number of products or services a company offers, the extent of their distribution, types of promotions, and the prices charged, depending on where the product or service is in its PLC.

KEY TERMS

business analysis (p. 198)
cannibalization (p. 192)
competitive advantage (p. 207)
concept test (p. 197)
consumer-adoption process (p. 205)
crowdsourcing (p. 195)
decline stage (p. 212)
design thinking (p. 195)
diffusion (p. 205)
disruptive technology (p. 189)
early adopters (p. 206)
early majority (p. 207)
fad product (p. 214)
fashion product (p. 214)
growth stage (p. 210)

high-learning products (p. 214)
idea generation (p. 194)
idea screening (p. 196)
innovators (p. 206)
introduction stage (p. 209)
laggards (p. 207)
late majority (p. 207)
low-learning products (p. 214)
maturity stage (p. 210)
new-category entries (p. 191)
new-product development (NPD) (p. 193)
new-product strategy development
    (p. 193)
new-to-the-market products (p. 189)
offshore (p. 198)

open innovation (p. 196)
outsource (p. 196)
product (p. 188)
product development stage (p. 199)
product launch (p. 201)
product life cycle (PLC) (p. 209)
product line (p. 192)
product-line extensions (p. 192)
product mix (p. 213)
prototype (p. 199)
revamped product (p. 192)
simulated test markets (p. 200)
test marketing (p. 199)
time to market (p. 201)
trialability (p. 208)

MARKETING PLAN EXERCISE • Marketing Yourself

In this chapter we talked about developing successful products. The next step in developing your personal marketing plan is to provide a concise description of the product you are offering the company or graduate school program you seek—you.

Think through the SWOT analysis you completed in Chapter 2 and think about your personal product offering. Focus on the specific value you would bring to the firm or graduate school. Think of the description as your *elevator pitch,* a 30- to 60-second description of the value you would bring to an organization. Formalizing this in your personal marketing plan will also help you identify specific jobs that match the skill sets that you offer. Your pitch might include answers to the following questions:

- What makes you different from other potential employees?

- Why is the company or graduate program better *with* you than *without* you?
- How do your skills and background fit into what the organization wants to do?

Your Task: Write a two-paragraph product description of yourself that you can read or present in less than 60 seconds. The description should highlight your value to a potential organization or graduate school. You have only a limited amount of time, so choose your words carefully to ensure they create the maximum impact.

DISCUSSION QUESTIONS

1. Assume that you are the vice president of marketing for a consumer packaged-goods company (like Procter & Gamble) that produces everyday items at a low price. Your marketing team has expressed a desire to revamp one of its brands to appeal to younger buyers. Develop a list of questions to determine the risks and rewards this revamping strategy poses for the company.

2. Select a product, either a good or service, that you consider to be in the decline phase of the PLC. Discuss some of the options the company has for dealing with this product. What do you think is the best option, and why do you think so?

3. Which product characteristics influence the length and shape of a product's PLC? What changes might a company make in its product design to lengthen its life cycle?

4. Assume you are in charge of the business analysis stage of a company's NPD process. What data will you need to collect to make an informed decision about whether product development should continue? What elements of bias might exist from the data you receive from the marketing department?

SOCIAL MEDIA APPLICATION

Pick a new product that has been launched in the past three months. This could be any type of new product, from a new menu item at a fast-food restaurant to a new video game.

Analyze how the organization has used social media to launch its new product, using the following questions and activities as a guide:

1. How has the company used social media to make customers aware of the new product?

2. Explain what you like or dislike about how the company is using social media to promote the product.
3. If you worked in marketing at the company, what two specific suggestions would you have about how the company could use social media more effectively?

MARKETING ANALYTICS EXERCISE

Please complete the *Connect* exercise for Chapter 6 that focuses on making new-product decisions using estimated cost and demand.

VIDEO CASE

Please go to *Connect* to access the video case featuring EA Sports that accompanies this chapter.

PODCAST

Please go to Connect to access the podcast that accompanies this chapter.

Tom Payne

CAREER **TIPS**

Characteristics of Good Product Managers

You have read in this chapter about the importance of developing products. Good product managers are rare—they seldom lack work, and they earn a good living. Tom Payne, who was

featured in the Executive Perspective at the beginning of the chapter, describes some of the intangible characteristics that good product managers share. Should you consider product management in your future?

1. ***A positive attitude.*** What most of us learned in grade school is true: Attitude *is* everything. No one likes to work around a naysayer. If the product manager doesn't believe in the product and

the outcome, who will? I have never known a sour, sarcastic, negative product manager—well, I have, but they don't stay in product marketing long.

2. **Responsibility.** Good product managers run toward problems, not away from them. They understand that they are responsible for making sure that every task is identified and every issue is considered and resolved. They never say, "That's not my job." That does not mean they do everything themselves. Rather, they ensure that process problems are not ignored or passed around.

3. **Financial understanding.** Why do companies hire product managers to create and manage products? To make money, of course! No matter what your product is, you will be expected to deliver it on time and on budget. As your product matures, it will be expected to produce revenue for the company; if you are a "good" product manager, it will produce profits. Yes, products need to be of good quality and they need to work, but I have seen plenty of good products fail because they did not sell.

4. **Aptitude for learning.** This is a hard one to say, but dumb people don't make good product managers (nor do lazy people). As a product manager, you are often, by definition, creating something new. If you are developing a new product, you are both creating the questions (How will we do this? What should it look like? How should we package it?) and finding the answers. There are seldom easy answers and no one person you can go ask. So how do you answer these questions? You're the product manager; go figure it out! (That's probably what your boss will say when you ask her—at least, that's what mine said to me.)

5. **Understand that software is a tool, not a solution.** Project management software is both a blessing and a curse. So many product management professionals believe that if they just put all the data into their planning software and check all the boxes, that will get the job done. Does buying MS Word write your term paper? Software organizes data, it helps track dates and budgets, but it does not create profitable products.

CHAPTER NOTES

1. Julianne Pepitone, "Atari U.S. Files for Bankruptcy but Plays On," *CNNMoney,* January 21, 2013, http://money.cnn.com/2013/01/21/technology/atari-bankrupt/index.html.
2. John D. Stoll, "Apple Needs a Next Act," *The Wall Street Journal,* January 12–13, 2019, B7.
3. Daisuke Wakabayashi and Eva Dou, "Apple Likely to Hold Off on Major iPhone Changes," *The Wall Street Journal,* June 21, 2016, p. B1.
4. Timothy W. Martin, "Crisis Shaped Latest Galaxy Note," *The Wall Street Journal,* August 24, 2017, p. B3.
5. Margaret Rouse, "Disruptive Technology," WhatIs.com, (n.d.) http://whatis.techtarget.com/definition/disruptive-technology.
6. Mike Ramsey, "Electric Cars Glide to 200-Mile Range," *The Wall Street Journal,* August 11, 2014.
7. Timothy W. Martin and Sarah Krouse, "Smartphone Overload!," *The Wall Street Journal,* January 12–13, 2019, B1, B6.
8. Justin Scheck and Paul Glader, "R&D Spending Holds Steady in Slump," *The Wall Street Journal,* April 6, 2009, http://online.wsj.com/article/SB123819035034460761.html.
9. Aaron Back and Carol Ryan, "The Lessons from Kraft's Sudden Fall," *The Wall Street Journal,* February 23–24, 2019, B14.
10. Peter Evans and Caitlan Reeg, "Personal-Care Firms Uncover New Markets," *The Wall Street Journal,* May 20, 2014, p. B7.
11. "Top Ten Failed Food Products," https://www.integrated-foodprojects.com/news/top-10-failed-food-products.
12. Anne Trafton, "Explained: Why RNA Vaccines for Covid-19 Raced to the Front of the Pack," *MIT News Office,* December 11, 2021, https://news.mit.edu/2020/rna-vaccines-explained-covid-19-1211.
13. awinsider.com/dictionary/new-service#:~:text=New%20Service%20means%20a%20service%20that%20(i)%20is%20distinguished%20from, service%20configuration%20by%20the%20Utility.
14. John D. Stoll, "Apple Needs a Next Act," *The Wall Street Journal,* January 12–13, 2019, B7.
15. https://www.wsj.com/articles/u-s-mail-does-the-trick-for-fedex-ups-1407182247.
16. Jonathan Cheng and Wilson Rothman, "Samsung Phone Seeks Edge," *The Wall Street Journal,* September 4.

17. Jennifer Lombardo, "Types of New Products: New Product Lines, Product Improvements & More," Study.com, (n.d.), https://study.com/academy/lesson/types-of-new-products-new-product-lines-product-improvements-more.html.

18. Saabira Chaudhuri, "Lego Hits Brick Wall as Digital Play Grows," *The Wall Street Journal,* September 5, 2017, p. A1.

19. "4 Innovative Product Line Extensions," *The Studio,* October 13, 2019, https://www.thestudio.com/blog/4-innovative-product-line-extension-examples-eng.

20. Lisa McQuerrey, "Objectives of Revamping a Product," *Houston Chronicle,* n.d., http://smallbusiness.chron.com/objectives-revamping-product-50406.html.

21. Federal Trade Commission, *Code of Federal Regulations,* Title 16, Volume 1, Part 500, Rev. January 1, 2000.

22. Jared S. Hopkins, "Vaccine Depends on Strong Vial," *The Wall Street Journal,* November 14–15, 2020, A7.

23. Adam Bryant, "In the Idea Kitchen, Too Many Cooks Can Spoil the Broth," *The New York Times,* November 24, 2012, http://www.nytimes.com/2012/11/25/business/nottingham-spirks-co-presidents-on-cultivating-new-ideas.html?_r=O.

24. Rikke Dam and Teo Siang, "Five Stages in the Design Thinking Process," 2018, https://www.interaction-design.org/literature/article/5-stages-in-the-design-thinking-process.

25. Lydia Dishman, "How Outsiders Get Their Products to the Innovation Big League at Procter & Gamble," *Fast Company,* July 13, 2012, http://www.fastcompany.com/1842577/how-outsiders-get-their-products-innovation-big-league-procter-gamble.

26. Alistair Barr, "Google Plans 'Modular' Smartphone," *The Wall Street Journal,* April 16, 2014.

27. Mike Shoultz, "Cloudsourcing . . . 12 Examples of How Brands Crowdsource for Ideas," September 4, 2016, https://digitalsparkmarketing.com/crowdsourcing.

28. Paul Ziobro, "Floundering Mattel Tries to Make Things Fun Again," *The Wall Street Journal,* December 23, 2014.

29. Jacquie McNish and Sean Silcoff, "The Lost Signal: BlackBerry's Fall," *The Wall Street Journal,* May 23, 2015.

30. Melinda Emerson, "Using Social Media to Test Your Idea before You Try to Sell It," *The New York Times,* August 3, 2012, http://boss.blogs.nytimes.com/2012/08/03/using-social-media-to-test-your-idea-before-you-try-to-sell-it/.

31. Melinda Emerson, "Using Social Media to Test Your Idea before You Try to Sell It," *The New York Times,* August 3, 2012, http://boss.blogs.nytimes.com/2012/08/03/using-social-media-to-test-your-idea-before-you-try-to-sell-it/.

32. Smirti, "Objectives of Packaging," November 28, 2016, https://www.managementnote.com/objectives-packaging-packaging-principles-marketing.

33. StrataSys, "Volvo Construction Equipment Digs ups Cost-Savings with 3D Printed Prototypes," January 26, 2022, https://www.stratasys.com/explore/case-study/Volvo.

34. Christpher Pilney, "Top U.S. Microcosm Cities to Test a National Product," August 28, 2014, https://smallbusiness.com/product-development/best-u-s-cities-to-test-market-a-national-product.

35. David Fickling and Susanna Ray, "Boeing Loses Qantas Order for 35 Dreamliners after Delays," *Bloomberg,* August 23, 2012, http://www.bloomberg.com/news/2012-08-22/qantas-airways-has-first-annual-loss-as-fuel-costs-rise.html; Paul Ausick, "Why a Boeing 787-9 Costs $250 Million,"*24/7 Wall Street,* June 25, 2014, http://247wallst.com/aerospace-defense/2014/06/25/why-a-boeing-787-9-costs-250-million/.

36. Tripp Mickle, "Lateness Bedevils Apple CEO Cook," *The Wall Street Journal,* January 6, 2018, pp. A1–A5.

37. Omera Khan, Martin Christopher, and Bernard Burnes, "The Impact of Product Design on Supply Chain Risk: A Case Study," *International Journal of Physical Distribution and Logistics Management*28, no. 5 (2008), pp. 412–432.

38. Mike Esterl and Tripp Mickle, "PepsiCo to Switch Diet Soda," *The Wall Street Journal,* April 25, 2015.

39. Jonathan Cheng and John D. McKinnon, "Samsung Recall's Fatal Flaw," *The Wall Street Journal,* October 24, 2016, pp. A1, A12.

40. Timpthy W. Martin, "Samsung Plays It Safe with New Note Smartphone," *The Wall Street Journal,* August 10, 2018, p. B4.

41. Bill Ford, Executive Chairman of Ford Motor Company.

42. Christina Rogers and Joann S. Lublin, "Bill Ford Thinks Ford Needs a Vision—His," *The Wall Street Journal,* August 9, 2018, pp. A1, A8.

43. Mike Esterl and Annie Gasparro, "Coming Soon: The Coca-Cola K-Cup," *The Wall Street Journal,* February 6, 2014.

44. Blake Morgan, "10 Recent Product Design Failures and What We Can Learn from Them," *Forbes,* September 9, 2019, https://www.forbes.com/sites/blakemorgan/2019/09/09/10-recent-product-design-failures-and-what-we-can-learn-from-them/?sh=59a5ace046f1.

45. Rachel Hosie, "Singapore Airlines Has Cancelled Its Proposed 'Flights to Nowhere' after Criticism from Environmental Campaigners," *Insider,* October 1, 2020. https://www.insider.com/singapore-airlines-drops-flights-to-nowhere-after-environmental-concerns-2020-10.

46. Sara Germano, "Under Armour Turns Ambitions to Electronic Apparel, Monitoring Apps," *The Wall Street Journal,* February 17, 2015.

47. Kalyan Parbat, "Nokia to Lower Lumia Prices in India," *The Times of India,* February 18, 2013, http://articles.timesofindia.indiatimes.com/2013-02-18/strategy/37159401_1_lumia-range-nokia-plan-stephen-elop.

48. Jim Blythe, *Consumer Behaviour*(London: Thomson Learning, 2008), p. 284.

49. Wayne D. Hoyer and Debra MacInnis, *Consumer Behavior* (Mason, OH: South-Western Cengage Learning, 2008), p. 424.

50. Newley Purnell, "BlackBerry Turns to Indonesia," *The Wall Street Journal,* May 13, 2014.

51. Lars Perner, "Product Issues in International Marketing," n.d., http://www.consumerpychologist.com/intl_Product.

52. Bob Tita, "3-D Printer Firms Fall Flat as Buyers Wait for New Models," *The Wall Street Journal,* August 7, 2015.

53. Tripp Mickle, "Apple Seeks Home Advantage," *The Wall Street Journal,* June 6, 2017, pp. A1–A2.

54. Farhad Manjoo, "The Future of TVs? There Is No Future," *The Wall Street Journal,* September 12, 2013.

55. Ellen Byron, "Going, Going, Gone," *The Wall Street Journal,* January 11, 2017, p. A11.

56. Sebastian Herrera, "Amazon Augments Streaming with Plans for Fire TV Sets," *Wall Street Journal,* September 10, 2021, B4.

57. Peter Evans, "Growth at Unilever Slows," *The Wall Street Journal,* January 22, 2014.

Chapter 7

Segmentation, Targeting, and Positioning

Steve Schaack

Learning Objectives

After reading this chapter, you should be able to

LO 7-1 Explain the importance of and criteria for effective market segmentation.

LO 7-2 Describe the bases for segmenting both B2C and B2B markets.

LO 7-3 Discuss international segmentation bases and the effect of international market segments on the marketing mix.

LO 7-4 Describe the factors and analytics involved in selecting target markets.

LO 7-5 Compare the most common target marketing strategies.

LO 7-6 Summarize the ethical issues in target marketing.

LO 7-7 Explain the three steps of effective market positioning and why firms may choose to use repositioning strategies.

Executive **Perspective** ... because everyone is a marketer

Pauline Thiros
Athletics Director
Idaho State University

Pauline Thiros

Although Pauline Thiros majored in health-care administration, she soon followed her passion for sports and making a difference by accepting a position as an assistant volleyball coach for a college program. After a very successful tenure in coaching, Thiros was recruited into fundraising and university development where she led a very successful capital campaign.

Today, Thiros serves as the athletics director at Idaho State University. She is one of less than 30 women to serve in that role out of nearly 400 Division I university athletic programs in the country. She works to create an excellent experience for athletes and all students, the greater community, and alumni. Beyond her work at ISU, Thiros currently serves on the prestigious NCAA Division I Women's Volleyball Committee and as the Chair of the Big Sky Conference Joint Athletics Committee.

What has been the most important thing in making you successful at your job?

Leadership skills are the key. Unlike technical and functional skills, which can be acquired, leadership is most critical to success in large organizations. High performance of a department including hundreds of staff and students all working together demands a leader who can maximize their many and varied strengths for the benefit of the entire unit. Determination, wisdom, compassion, vision, initiative, excellent communication . . . all are necessary to inspire a large workforce to commit themselves to a common goal. Without good leadership compelling the team to share values and move the organization forward with passion, other tactical skills cannot make an impact.

What advice would you give soon-to-be graduates?

Take every opportunity to learn about your strengths and lean into them. At the same time, proactively seek feedback about things you need to improve. Do not make the mistake of thinking you will ever "arrive" at success and no longer need to evolve and get better. Take on additional opportunities and duties with the goal of building your skill set and making yourself one who can be depended upon by your organization. People who excel go above and beyond what they are asked to do, always improving themselves and doing more to serve their team and organization. Be that person—the person who always shows up and performs at her best and with passion.

How is marketing relevant to your role at Idaho State University?

The department of athletics is often the most visible unit at a University, therefore must represent and promote an impeccable brand to help drive enrollment and private funding for the University as a whole. Recruiting the best coaches and student athletes, raising money, selling tickets and advertising, all center around building a brand that packs a punch with the public. Dynamic marketing built to attract active participation must be followed by creating a great experience for the marketplace—in other words, delivering on your brand. It has to be intentional and quality from start to finish in order to sustain success. To stay employed in athletics you must be great at marketing yourself to constituents, marketing your teams, and constantly demonstrating your value to the University and community.

What do you consider your personal brand to be?

I am strong willed, goal oriented, and focused relentlessly on making an impact. I tackle obstacles and opportunities alike with enthusiasm so BRING IT. A true competitor can always find a way to get better, and once I see a pathway to move my organization or program forward it is absolutely irresistible to me. If you want to languish in negative inward or outward facing talk or thought, keep your distance because a day breathing should be a great day.

LO 7-1

MARKET SEGMENTATION

Explain the importance of and criteria for effective market segmentation.

market segmentation

The process of dividing a larger market into smaller groups, or market segments, based on meaningfully shared characteristics.

market segments

The groups of consumers who have shared characteristics and similar product needs.

The days of one-size-fits-all mass marketing are largely over. Marketers who try to be all things to all people typically end up serving no one well. **Market segmentation** is the process of dividing a larger market into smaller groups, or market segments, based on meaningfully shared characteristics. **Market segments** are the relatively homogeneous groups of consumers that result from the segmentation process. There are 7.8 billion people in the world with different needs and wants that are impossible to attract with a single marketing mix. Market segmentation plays an important role in the success of almost every organization in the United States and throughout the world.

The Importance of Market Segmentation

Imagine going into a restaurant that has 85 items on the menu, featuring everything from hamburgers to pasta to sushi. You might suspect that a restaurant offering such a wide range of diverse choices does not prepare any of them very well. Compare this strategy with that of restaurant chain Five Guys Burgers and Fries, which has consistently offered a very limited menu. Potential customers have a wide variety of tastes and preferences, but Five Guys focuses on serving what works best for its specific business, which is the "better-burger segment" of the market.

When Five Guys first opened, people asked for coffee, so the company's restaurants began to serve it. Unfortunately, the people working at the restaurants knew little about coffee. The coffee they made tasted terrible, and Five Guys became concerned that negative word-of-mouth communication would hurt its core business. Five Guys stopped serving coffee. The company tried a chicken sandwich once, too, but took that off the menu as well when sales failed to materialize. The menu does include hot dogs, which have been profitable, but other than that, all you can get at Five Guys Burgers and Fries is . . . burgers and fries. It became the fastest-growing restaurant chain in North America serving a limited menu of quality food.[1]

Market segmentation helps organizations like Five Guys navigate the various needs and wants in three major ways:

Thoughtful market segmentation allows Five Guys Burgers and Fries to enjoy success serving only a limited number of menu choices that it knows will satisfy its target market. *Thomas Cordy/The Palm Beach Post/ZUMA Press Inc/Alamy Stock Photo*

1. *Market segmentation helps firms define the needs and wants of the customers who are most interested in buying the firm's products.* Five Guys customers typically pay more and wait longer than they would at other fast-food hamburger restaurants.[2] The better-burger market segment values taste, freshness, and quality. Customers in that segment are willing to pay a premium for a more "gourmet" hamburger experience.

2. *Market segmentation helps firms design specific marketing strategies for the characteristics of specific segments.* Using specific marketing strategies for specific segments, firms are able to gain a much larger share of the market segments they target. For example, because

the marketing department at Five Guys understands its customers' needs and wants, it is able to develop promotional campaigns and advertisements that focus on high-quality, fresh products. It does not spend resources promoting lower prices or quicker service, which are not high priorities for the targeted segment. Five Guys has capitalized on this knowledge, even using signs that urge people to seek their burgers elsewhere if they're in a hurry.[3] Such tactics reinforce that Five Guys focuses on preparing the best possible burger for customers rather than simply trying to get everyone through the line.

3. *Market segmentation helps firms decide how to allocate their marketing resources in a way that maximizes profit.* By understanding the needs and wants of its market segment, Five Guys has been able to funnel resources toward more profitable markets. It has identified markets in which hamburgers and fries are purchased more often and those with higher family income levels, like northern Virginia and Dallas, Texas.

Criteria for Effective Market Segmentation

While there are multiple ways to segment markets, none of them are *guaranteed* to prove helpful to marketers. Simply dividing a larger group of consumers or businesses into smaller ones serves no purpose, unless doing so improves how the firm markets its goods and services. To be effective, segmentation should create market segments that rate favorably on the following five criteria:

1. *Substantial.* The segments must be large enough for the firm to make a profit by serving them. For example, designing a cereal for people who are over 100 years of age or athletic shoes for people who wear larger than a size 24 shoe are not viable options; the market for each product is not substantial enough for the firm to make sustainable profits.

2. *Measurable.* The size and purchasing power of the segment should be measurable and clearly identified. There's a popular saying in business that if you cannot measure something, you cannot manage it. Managers today demand high levels of accountability from marketers, who must show measurable results of the success of specific marketing strategies. For example, Nissan marketers researched the size and purchasing power of the market segment that desired an all-electric vehicle. A critical factor in the long-term success of Nissan's Leaf vehicle will be tied to how well the company estimated the number of consumers who want this type of car and how much those consumers are willing to pay for it.

3. *Differentiable.* Dividing the market into segments does no good if all the segments respond the same to different marketing strategies. Effective segmentation requires that the segments must be able to be differentiated. Many marketers make this mistake. For example, segmenting students for a specific marketing class by gender or age would not provide a textbook firm any value since everyone in the class would be required to buy the book.

4. *Accessible.* Marketers must be able to reach and serve the segment. If the firm lacks the size, financial capital, expertise, or government permits to serve a certain market segment, all of the other criteria are irrelevant. For example, think about a small construction business: If it did not have the financial capital to buy land and pay for expenses or the local permits necessary to legally build houses, it could not access the homebuilding market.

5. *Actionable.* Marketers should be able to develop strategies that can attract certain market segments to their firms' goods and services. A firm should be reasonably certain that its marketing mix can inform consumers about the product, how it adds value to the consumer, and ultimately how to purchase it. Subway has marketed its products to a wider market segment with campaigns

featuring Tennis great Serena Williams and NBA star Steph Curry. Those campaigns appealed to consumers interested in how the restaurant chain could help them stay in shape.

A potential market segment must meet these five criteria. Keep them in mind as we examine the main characteristics marketers use to segment markets: demographic, geographic, psychographic, and behavioral.

LO 7-2

Describe the bases for segmenting both B2C and B2B markets.

SEGMENTATION BASES

Marketers divide markets into segments using *segmentation bases,* which are characteristics of consumers that influence their buying behavior. These bases help firms develop customer profiles that highlight the similarities within segments and the dissimilarities across segments. There are different segmentation bases for B2C and B2B markets. The majority of this section addresses the bases used in B2C markets. At the end of the section, we take a separate look at B2B segmentation bases.

Figure 7.1 shows the four broad bases of segmentation and the specific variables within each that can be used to segment the B2C market. We describe each of the four bases—demographic, geographic, psychographic, and behavioral—in more detail in the sections that follow.

Demographic Segmentation

demographic segmentation

Segmentation that divides markets by characteristics such as age, gender, income, education, and family size.

Companies divide markets using characteristics such as age, gender, income, education, and family size to achieve **demographic segmentation**. Age and gender are the most commonly used demographic variables because they are often given freely through short surveys.

If less accessible information is required, firms can find demographic information that may be useful for market segmentation in a number of places. One of the most important is the U.S. Census Bureau. The website www.census.gov provides marketers with information such as the net worth and asset ownership of households segmented by race, education, age, and occupation. Small businesses and other organizations that have a very limited marketing research budget find such free information a valuable tool.

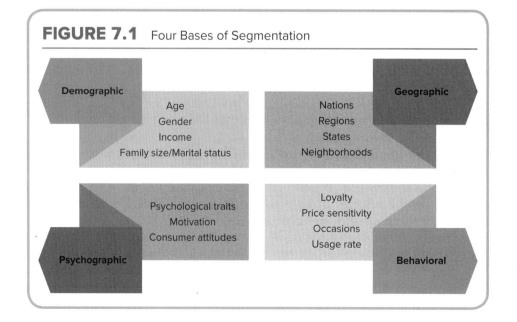

FIGURE 7.1   Four Bases of Segmentation

Demographic	Geographic
Age	Nations
Gender	Regions
Income	States
Family size/Marital status	Neighborhoods

Psychographic	Behavioral
Psychological traits	Loyalty
Motivation	Price sensitivity
Consumer attitudes	Occasions
	Usage rate

Age   Age is an especially valuable segmentation tool in areas such as food, housing, and health care. Older Americans spend significantly more in these areas than younger consumers. The median age for residents of the United States is the highest in the history of the country. Older consumers typically have two things that most of their younger counterparts do not: time and money. This large demographic group provides marketers with expanding market segments, representing billions of dollars in potential sales.[4]

Today's older consumers are not the same as older consumers from previous generations. Older consumers today want to stay active in retirement and seek out ways to look and feel younger.[5] Firms that develop marketing strategies for things like anti-aging products and natural and organic foods have found success appealing to older market segments. Products ranging from Viagra to Botox to Whole Foods have generated profits for their organizations by marketing the idea of youth to an older population.

Millennials represent a different set of challenges for marketers. Research has found that Millennials perceive themselves as particularly in tune with what they consider to be authentic and real. One of the most common mistakes made by organizations is marketing campaigns that come across as fake, overly forced, or condescending to Millennials. Marketers should select language, brands, and endorsers that are viewed as credible by Millennials, and develop marketing campaigns that are based on the actions the organization has taken.

McDonald's segments its market in part by age and develops products that effectively target each age group it identifies, from Happy Meals for children, Mighty Kids Meals for older kids, and the Dollar Menu that appeals to high school and college students with limited cash flow. *Eric Risberg/AP Images*

Marketers also have for many years targeted young consumers. McDonald's has sold Happy Meals to multiple generations of children. More recently, pay television service HBO signed an exclusive agreement to premier five seasons' worth of the popular children's television show *Sesame Street.* Netflix also started segmenting children's programming in 2011 and has produced thousands of hours of new content over the past decade, aimed at winning over this younger market segment.[6]

Segmenting by age also enables companies to target multiple age segments with the same product. For example, Disney Cruise Line has developed strategies to appeal to consumers of varying ages. Young children are attracted to the cruise as a magical adventure where they get to meet their favorite characters; teenagers like the unique interactive entertainment options designed just for them. Older consumers enjoy the opportunity to vacation with their grandchildren without the hassle of walking long distances through a large amusement park. Disney marketers have successfully offered a single cruise vacation that members of multiple age segments feel is designed just for them.

Gender   Gender is a valuable segmentation variable, for products ranging from clothing to soft drinks to medications. Marketers are expanding beyond traditional gender segmentation as new trends shift marketing dollars away from male- or female-oriented marketing, to try to appeal to multiple genders. For example, marketers for home improvement store Lowe's recognized that women were becoming an increasingly large part of their customer base but were largely being ignored by their promotional strategies. In an effort to target female consumers, Lowe's introduced a new line of Martha Stewart products and other home decor items.[7]

Gender segmentation is evolving for younger consumers as well. After targeting boys almost exclusively for more than 20 years, LEGO introduced the LEGO Friends line for girls when marketing research showed that girls enjoyed playing with LEGO toys in a distinctly different way than boys. That segmentation strategy has worked well: The LEGO Friends line, which features pastel colors and sets that involve building cafes rather than battleships, has sold twice as much as the company originally anticipated.[8]

Income   Income provides marketers with a valuable segmentation tool because it affects consumers' ability to buy goods and services. Of course, marketers can successfully define the needs and wants of customers at *all* income levels and design appropriate marketing strategies.

For example, the demand for wealth management and financial planning services in the United States has increased dramatically in recent decades. Firms like Merrill Lynch target American households that are considered *mass affluent,* that is, those who have between $100,000 and $250,000 in investible assets.[9] Mass affluents, one of the fastest-growing income segments in the country, need the type of financial planning that Merrill Lynch offers. They are also typically adopters of high-end technology, such as smartphones, tablets, and personalized web portals. Financial marketers therefore provide customers in this segment with products that track investments and pay bills without live input from a financial advisor. By segmenting the market in this way, Merrill Lynch can tailor its global investment advice and professional money management services to best meet the needs of these targeted consumers.[10]

Marital Status and Family Size   Marital status can be a helpful demographic segmentation tool. A company might discover that married individuals will pay higher prices than single individuals and promote certain products to that market. It might find that single customers purchase a certain product more frequently than married customers do and market that product to singles. A jewelry store, for example, might target married customers with promotions for anniversary bands and target unmarried customers with promotions for necklaces or bracelets.

Family size is also a useful demographic segmentation tool. In recent years, the size of families living under one roof has increased: More young adults and students are moving back home, and more adults are taking care of their older parents. Marketers at

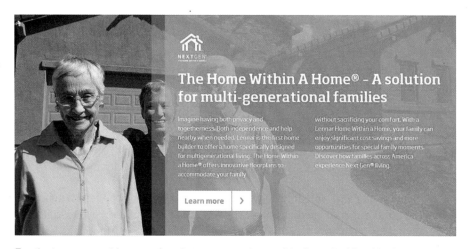

Family size can provide a good market segmentation tool for homebuilders like Lennar, which has developed a new type of home called Next Gen—The Home Within A Home that includes additional space for long-term guests, extended family, or adult children. *Lennar*

major U.S. homebuilders like Lennar hope to appeal to these larger family units by building and promoting houses that come with additional rooms or garage apartments with a separate entrance.[11] Some even have a second, small kitchen to allow for separate meal preparation.

Geographic Segmentation

The value consumers place on a product can vary greatly by region. For this reason, marketers often find it helpful to segment on the basis of geography. **Geographic segmentation** divides markets into groups such as nations, regions, states, and neighborhoods. Marketers pay special attention to local variations in the types of goods and services offered in different geographic regions. A Walmart located near the beach in Southern California might sell surfboards to meet demand for a popular local sport. It is doubtful that a similarly sized Walmart store in Denver, Colorado, will offer surfboards, due to the geographic difference. Walmart marketers empower local managers to stock products that are most appropriate for their local community.

geographic segmentation
Segmentation that divides markets into groups such as nations, regions, states, and neighborhoods.

Market Size The size of a market is an important geographic segmentation tool. IKEA marketers prefer to locate new stores in areas where at least 2 million people live within a 60-mile range.[12] This type of geographic segmentation requires information about the entire market, beyond just a city or county.

The U.S. Census Bureau divides cities and urbanized areas into Metropolitan Statistical Areas (MSAs), which are freestanding areas with a core urban population of at least 50,000. Table 7.1 shows the 10 largest MSAs in the United States and the cities and areas that are included in each.

Customer Convenience Segmenting by geography also allows marketers to capitalize on convenience to the customer. Cracker Barrel Old Country Store, for example, has developed a successful restaurant and retail business across the United States by locating its stores in convenient geographic locations. A major component of

TABLE 7.1 Ten Largest Metropolitan Statistical Areas in the United States

Rank	Core City	Metro Area Population	Metropolitan Statistical Area	Region
1	New York City	20,320,876	New York-Newark-Jersey City, NY-NJ-PA	Northeast
2	Los Angeles	13,353,907	Los Angeles-Long Beach-Anaheim, CA	West
3	Chicago	9,533,040	Chicago-Naperville-Elgin, IL-IN-WI	Midwest
4	Dallas	7,399,662	Dallas-Fort Worth-Arlington, TX	South
5	Houston	6,892,427	Houston-The Woodlands-Sugar Land, TX	South
8	Philadelphia	6,096,120	Philadelphia-Camden-Wilmington, PA-NJ-DE-MD	Northeast
6	Washington, D.C.	6,216,589	Washington-Arlington-Alexandria, DC-VA-MD-WV	South
7	Miami	6,158,824	Miami-Fort Lauderdale-West Palm Beach, FL	South
9	Atlanta	5,884,736	Atlanta-Sandy Springs-Roswell, GA	South
10	Boston	4,836,531	Boston-Cambridge-Newton, MA-NH	Northeast

Source: https://www.census.gov/newsroom/press-releases/2018/popest-metro-county.html#popest-tab9

Gas stations, banks, and retailers like Cracker Barrel Old Country Store make customer convenience based on geographic segmentation a central part of their marketing strategy.
Mark Dierker/McGraw Hill

Cracker Barrel's marketing strategy has been to place locations along interstate highways. Travelers make up approximately one-third of Cracker Barrel's guest base, so the percentage of people who travel mostly by automobile affects Cracker Barrel's revenue. The price of gasoline also plays a part. Cracker Barrel marketers have built on the need for traveler convenience by implementing an operating platform that focuses on getting customers through the door and eating in 14 minutes.[13] Dunkin' Donuts sought to increase customer convenience by opening dozens of new stores at nontraditional locations, including airport terminals, college campuses, and military installations throughout the country.[14]

Population Shifts   Finally, geographic segmentation can be a valuable tool for understanding population changes across different regions. In the United States, the population is calculated by census every 10 years. (The number of members each state has in the U.S. House of Representatives is determined by population, following the census.) The 2020 census illustrated a shifting U.S. population: Southern states like Texas and Florida grew substantially. Many northern states, including Ohio, Michigan, and New York, grew at a slower rate, or not at all.[15] Figure 7.2 shows the number of representatives each state has in the U.S. House of Representatives. (For example, Idaho has two.) More importantly, the figure highlights population shifts between 2010 and 2020: It shows, in green, which states have grown the most (and gained seats in the House of Representatives) and, in orange, which states have seen the smallest growth or biggest population declines (and lost seats in the House).

Population shifts occur for various reasons: Economic conditions, retirement, and even natural disasters can cause people to move. For example, in the 2010 census, the only southern state that lost seats in the House of Representatives was Louisiana. That loss occurred because Louisiana's largest city, New Orleans, lost 29 percent of its residents in the years following Hurricane Katrina.[16]

It is important for marketers to research patterns of consumer movement, to understand where and why consumers are moving. For example, real estate marketers can use this information when selecting locations in which to build new housing developments. The growth in states like Texas provides marketers an opportunity to deliver products that meet the growing demand for houses that comes with a rapidly increasing population.

FIGURE 7.2   Number of U.S. House Representatives in Each State, Showing States That Gained or Lost Seats Due to Population Shifts in the 2020 Census

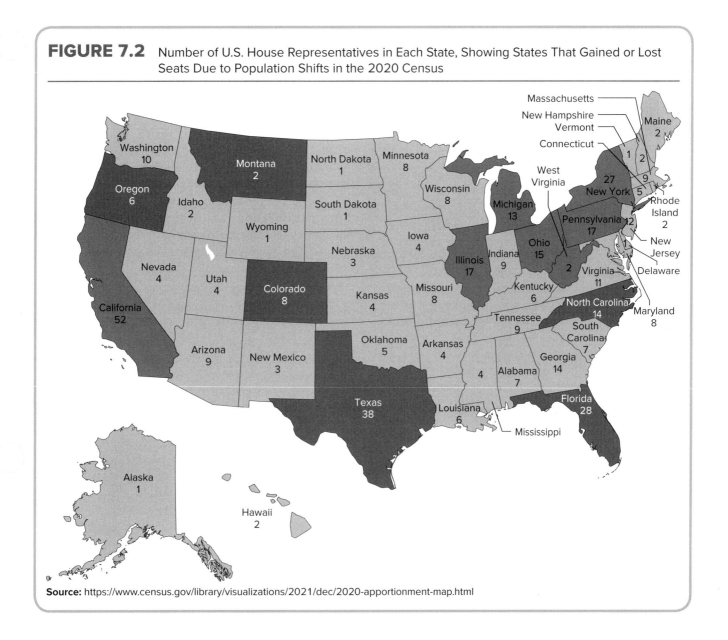

Source: https://www.census.gov/library/visualizations/2021/dec/2020-apportionment-map.html

Psychographic Segmentation

Segmentation that divides markets using demographics, psychology, and personality traits is called **psychographic segmentation**. Demographic characteristics such as age, gender, income, marital status, and family size give us multiple ways to segment markets. Within each of those demographic profiles, consumers can have very different psychological or personality traits that influence their purchasing behavior. Psychographic segmentation allows marketing professionals to create a more meaningful profile of market segments by focusing on psychological and personality traits.

When marketers segment based on psychographics, they divide a market into groups according to the reason the consumer made the purchase. For example, consumers purchase a new Mercedes automobile for a variety of reasons. One segment of consumers may buy a Mercedes for the status that a luxury car will provide them. A different segment may buy the car because of its superior safety features. When the Mercedes salesperson highlights the specific customer's needs and wants, they increase the likelihood of a sale.

psychographic segmentation

Segmentation that divides markets using demographics, psychology, and personality traits.

Executive Perspective. . .
because everyone is a marketer

Pauline Thiros
Athletics Director
Idaho State University

Pauline Thiros

What is something you would want students to know about working in college athletics?

Athletics must generate revenue and philanthropic support to sustain operations independently, while functioning in a highly competitive and constantly changing business and regulatory environment. It is extremely rewarding and dynamic work. Every day is different, whether working to hire coaches and staff, traveling for competition, advocating for legislation that will enrich collegiate sports, selling and fundraising, public speaking, strategically scheduling opponents for all sports, working on competition logistics, negotiating contracts, or diving into a crisis—athletics is always challenging and hugely rewarding.

lifestyle segmentation

Segmentation that divides people into groups based on their opinions and the interests and activities they pursue.

Lifestyle   Many firms have successfully segmented by lifestyle in recent years. **Lifestyle segmentation** divides people into groups based on their opinions and the interests and activities they pursue. For example, Kraft implemented a strategy to reach targeted tech-savvy consumers. Instead of just pushing out a mobile message as other companies were doing, Kraft created an iPhone app called "iFood Assistant." That app actually made mealtime easier for consumers by putting 7,000 recipes at their fingertips. By effectively segmenting the market into tech-savvy, professionals that frequently cooked for their family, Kraft was able to design a product that met the needs of its targeted consumers better than its competitors, thus increasing sales and customer loyalty.

VALS Network
Perhaps the most commonly used psychographic segmentation tool is the VALS framework. It classifies U.S. and Canadian adults (aged 18 years and older) into eight psychographic groups, on the basis of responses to 34 attitudinal and four demographic questions. The groups are Innovators, Thinkers, Believers, Achievers, Strivers, Experiencers, Makers, and Survivors. VALS measures two dimensions: primary motivation and resources. The ways in which motivation and resources combine explain different behaviors among consumer groups.

VALS identifies three primary motivations: *ideals, achievement,* and *self-expression.* The availability of resources affects each group's ability to act on its primary motivation. (Resources include emotional and psychological resources, such as self-confidence, as well as key demographics, such as income and education.) As an example, consumers who are motivated by achievement look to others for approval and acceptance. Resources determine how the motivation manifests itself:

- High-resource, achievement-motivated Achievers emulate the groups to which they aspire to belong.
- Low-resource, achievement-motivated Strivers seek identification with others like them.

Marketers use VALS to determine whether, for example, Achievers or Strivers are more likely to buy their product. They then tailor the marketing mix accordingly. Psychographic segmentation can be more difficult and expensive than demographic or geographic segmentation. For example, in order to place consumers into VALS segments, firms need to conduct product surveys that incorporate the VALS survey. In addition, if a firm is planning to market its products globally, it will need to evaluate its psychographic segmentation to be sure to capture cultural differences. Different countries require different frameworks because of language and cultural differences. In addition to the United States, VALS frameworks are available for the United Kingdom, Japan, Venezuela, the Dominican Republic, Nigeria, and China. We will discuss international market segmentation in more depth later in the chapter.

Hunting, fishing, and outdoor gear retailer Cabela's used lifestyle segmentation to develop a marketing campaign called "It's in Your Nature" that consisted of multiple videos promoting the various activities the retailer's customers pursue, including boating and camping. *Cabela's*

McGraw Hill connect Exercise **7-1**

Please complete the *Connect* exercise for Chapter 7 that focuses on the eight VALS segments. By identifying which goods and services are most attractive to specific segments, you will better understand how segmentation provides useful insights that can impact marketing strategy.

Behavioral Segmentation

Behavioral segmentation categorizes consumers according to how they behave with or act toward products. Behavioral segmentation variables include occasions (e.g., a wedding or business trip), loyalty, and usage rate. For example, marketers at Netflix might start with usage rate, by segmenting the market into groups of users and nonusers. Next, they may further segment current Netflix users into groups such as heavy, moderate, or light users. Heavy users form the firm's profit core and should be treated accordingly, such as receiving special offers or personalized attention from the company.

Many firms subscribe to the **80/20 rule**, which suggests that 20 percent of heavy users account for 80 percent of the total demand for a product. If firms can identify its heavy users, it is in a better position to create an effective marketing strategy to reach those consumers who contribute most to the firm's success.

When done well, behavioral segmentation helps marketers clearly understand the benefits sought by different consumer segments. For example, consider a customer who has been using the same brand of toothpaste for 12 years and has had no cavities in that time period. For this person, the benefit of no cavities will most likely outweigh a small price increase and will not be a problem. However, that same price increase might cause a less-committed user, for whom price is more important, to change brands. Understanding how changes to marketing-mix strategies affect different types of users enables the firm to evaluate the impact of such changes on sales and revenue.

behavioral segmentation
Segmentation that categorizes consumers according to how they behave with or act toward products.

80/20 rule
A theory that suggests that 20 percent of heavy users account for 80 percent of the total demand.

Marketing efforts toward heavy users are the goal of loyalty programs such as the IHG Priority Club, which rewards frequent guests by giving them points to use toward future stays at Holiday Inn hotels. *Ceri Breeze/Alamy Stock Photo*

Behavioral segmentation is often the most difficult of the four bases to use. The marketing research required to track and understand how consumers behave with a certain product is very expensive and time-consuming. Firms must weigh the benefits of such segmentation against the costs associated with obtaining the necessary information.

Business-to-Business Segmentation Bases

B2B firms generally segment their markets using different bases from those used in B2C markets. The three types of B2B segmentation bases are demographic, geographic, and behavioral. Although the names of these bases match those of the B2C bases discussed up to this point, they apply differently.

B2B Demographic Segmentation
The main B2B demographic variables include industry, size of the organization, and ownership structure. Segmenting by industry is an important first step that helps marketers determine which sectors of the economy might be most valuable to their business.

The size of the organization is a critical variable because organizations of different sizes often have different needs and wants. In addition, large organizations like Cisco or the U.S. Armed Forces might have more complex buying processes that might require more salespeople compared to a small business.

Finally, ownership structure can influence marketing decisions. For example, marketing a time-consuming product, such as a new smartphone made in a factory with significant logistical hurdles, to a publicly traded company like Verizon may prove challenging because the organization may fear upsetting its shareholders. In contrast, a privately held firm might have fewer layers of management and be able to make decisions more quickly.

B2B Geographic Segmentation
B2B geographic variables are similar to consumer variables. They include things like country, region, state, and climate. Geographic segmentation allows marketers to group B2B customers by geography-related needs or headquarters location. Such segmentation can help B2B marketers allocate resources to the parts of the country or the world with the highest concentration of economic- or climate-driven need.

B2B Behavioral Segmentation
Behavioral segmentation might be the most beneficial variable to B2B marketers: It enables them to segment based on purchasing patterns, supplier requirements, and technological orientation. Purchasing patterns, such as the time of year contracts come up for bid, can be helpful in the segmentation process. Supplier requirements, which include things like whether the supplier has e-commerce functionality, can help marketers determine which segments' capabilities and technological orientation make them attractive.

In both B2B and B2C markets, social media present marketing professionals with additional options for segmenting the market and then reaching targeted segments.

The Role of Social Media in Market Segmentation

Social media can be especially effective in market segmentation strategies. If they can segment the market by those who are active on social media, companies can, at minimal expense, expand their outreach. Individualized social media platforms such as Facebook, Instagram, and TikTok enable companies to engage and interact personally with a larger and more diverse consumer base.

Social media are, by their very nature, all about sharing personal behaviors, tastes, activities, desires, and connections. Nevertheless, questions remain as to exactly how to engage consumers on social networking sites and, more importantly, whom to engage. Airlines are an example of one industry that has sought to answer such questions. Airlines increasingly use social media channels to address and target key market segments, with significant success. Delta has sought to engage a younger audience using Instagram. Delta's page features images ranging from places all over the world to the inside of Delta's hangars and even aesthetically pleasing photos taken from the aisle of an aircraft. Delta also highlights photos submitted by users with fun tales of what travel has meant to them. By engaging younger age segments now, the airlines hope to develop a relationship with students who are likely to purchase significantly more airline tickets over the next decade of their lives as they begin their careers and travel with their young families.

Southwest, AirTran, Lufthansa, and Virgin Atlantic have launched their own social networking sites, allowing customers to interact and participate in contests and drawings. *Jaap Arriens/NurPhoto/Getty Images*

LinkedIn allows firms to segment by industry, company size, and function. For example, a telecommunications provider such as Lumen headquartered in Monroe, Louisiana, can use social media to segment potential small business customers by the size of their firm and the telecommunications functions of that organization. As social media develop and new platforms emerge, both B2C and B2B marketers will have increasing opportunities to use these powerful tools in market segmentation.

Mc Graw Hill connect Exercise 7-2

Social Media in Action

Marketers today interact with an empowered audience that is engaged in real-time social media conversations across many digital platforms. Customers are more than just a gender, age, and geographic location recorded in a database. By understanding customers' behaviors and preferences, marketers can segment customers in order to customize messages that will appeal to them.

Advocate Health Care, based in the midwestern United States, launched a GoPro giveaway and integrated marketing campaign to promote local health and wellness. Grounded in a hashtag to display user-generated content, #HealthiestLife aggregated more than 3,000 pieces of user-generated content. Advocate Health Care was able to collect opt-in permissions and segment potential consumers based on their social media activity. The improved segmentation strategy worked: Advocate saw a 26 percent increase in physician appointments, and a 126 percent jump in traffic to the user-generated content gallery on its website.

The Social Media in Action Connect exercise in Chapter 7 will let you develop social media strategies to segment markets based on readily available social media information. Segmentation and targeting are at the heart of successful marketing, and social media provide marketers from organizations of all sizes powerful tools to better understand consumers.

Source: See Rob Manning, "3 Strategies to Segment Audiences and Personalize Digital Marketing," *Adweek*, March 19, 2015, http://www.adweek.com/socialtimes/3-strategies-to-segment-audiences-and-personalize-digital-marketing/617284.

LO 7-3

Discuss international segmentation bases and the effect of international market segments on the marketing mix.

INTERNATIONAL MARKET SEGMENTATION

Even with the help social media platforms provide in reaching international markets, international market segmentation is a costly exercise, and often a very difficult one. For one thing, accessing demographic, geographic, psychographic, and behavioral information for international markets can be challenging. Even demographic information, which is typically the easiest to acquire, may be slow in coming or completely unavailable. Canada conducts a census, which provides important demographic information to marketers, about every five years. France conducts a census about every seven years. However, many emerging nations might not conduct an accurate census for decades at a time.

Another issue is that not all countries collect or classify their data in the same way. Data differences make it all but impossible to compare characteristics across nations. Then, even if marketing professionals obtain the information they seek, each nation and region has its own unique features that make establishing quality market segments problematic.

When possible, companies may try to identify several markets that exhibit behavior similar enough to form a segment. By identifying such segments, marketers can apply marketing research findings from one market to the rest of the segment. Let's look at the typical bases used to segment international markets.

International Segmentation Bases

global segmentation

Segmentation that identifies a group of consumers with common needs and wants that spans the entire globe.

Firms typically segment international markets using three general bases: global, regional, and unique.

1. **Global segmentation** identifies a group of consumers with common needs and wants that spans the entire globe. Firms use global segmentation when they believe they can identify such groups. Global segmentation usually results in

In Macau, China, McDonald's restaurants offer specialty food choices based on unique segmentation. *Rob Crandall/Alamy Stock Photo*

market segments made up of young people, those who have more money to spend, or those with access to the Internet.

2. **Regional segmentation** divides consumers into groups whose needs and wants extend across the region or several countries. Firms will often use this when they want to capitalize on the financial savings of global segmentation but still adjust for local customs and culture.

3. **Unique segmentation** identifies a group of consumers with similar needs and wants only within one country. If a firm wants to completely localize, it may choose to target a particular segment within one country. For example, the National Football League chose a unique segmentation strategy to market American football to British fans. The league's tactics included an exuberant street party with a marching band. It also posted on its UK website new digital content such as a "Rookie's Guide" to football and animated videos explaining the rules.[17]

regional segmentation

Segmentation that divides consumers into groups whose needs and wants extend across the region or several countries.

unique segmentation

Segmentation that targets the preferences of a group of consumers with similar needs and wants only within one country.

All three types of segments offer potential profits depending on how consumers within the segment respond to the marketing mix.

International Market Segments and the Marketing Mix

Companies can use international market segments to group together countries with market conditions that are materially the same in relation to the company's product. This means that a marketing-mix strategy that works well in one market may be successful for other markets in the same segment. When that's the case, the firm is able to standardize the marketing mix across segments.

However, marketers must also be mindful of the limits of international segmentation. In some instances, segmentation allows marketers to standardize elements of the market mix globally or regionally. There also will often be instances in which they need to localize the marketing-mix strategy within a segment. For example, some countries place a higher tariff on goods sold by foreign companies. Those tariffs may make product pricing in those markets less competitive than in other markets. In response, the firm may need to revise its marketing strategy and marketing mix in those countries.

Other aspects of the marketing mix can also fluctuate among markets in a segment. For example, advertising regulations and preferences vary substantially. Asian countries vary in their preference for which gender their promotional materials depict: In Malaysia, males are more likely to be seen in advertisements for food and soft drinks; in Japan, females are more likely to appear in ads for the same products.[18]

Marketers in the United States and throughout the world can use a single segmentation base to divide the marketplace, such as Mercedes appealing to affluent car buyers. Or they can use multiple segmentation bases to provide a more complete picture of the consumers within each segment, such as General Motors offering different models and price ranges for consumers in different parts of the world. Each strategy has its own advantages and disadvantages, depending on the firm, its products, and its budget.

Marketers today use an increasingly large number of consumer characteristics to divide markets, both domestic and international, into useful segments. Remember that segmentation should meet the five important effectiveness criteria discussed earlier to produce market segments that are: substantial (large enough for the firm to make a profit), measurable, differentiable (responsive to different marketing strategies), accessible, and actionable (able to be clearly accomplished).

SELECTING TARGET MARKETS

Market segmentation provides a good first step toward reaching potential consumers. The firm then must review the segments to determine which to target. **Targeting** occurs when marketers evaluate each market segment and determine which segments present the most attractive opportunity to maximize sales. The segments selected are the firm's target markets. A **target market** is the group of customers toward which an organization has decided to direct its marketing efforts.

targeting

Evaluating each market segment to determine which segments present the most attractive opportunity to maximize sales.

Factors in Selecting Target Markets

Firms should consider three important factors during the targeting process: growth potential, level of competition, and strategic fit.

target market

The group of customers toward which an organization has decided to direct its marketing efforts.

Growth Potential
Typically, the higher the future growth rate, the more attractive the segment is. For example, consumer spending on their pets has grown dramatically in recent decades. The COVID-19 pandemic accelerated this trend and led to a boom in the pet business.[19] Americans spent a record-high $99 billion in 2020 on their pets ranging from food to veterinary care. As more consumers increase spending on their pets, marketers have increasing opportunities in this market for growth.

Level of Competition
The more intense the competition within a segment, the less attractive it is to marketers. Competitors will fight extremely hard to prevent market share loss, and the potential for price wars can negatively impact success. Generally, more competitors means a firm has to work harder and invest more in promotion to earn business and increase market share.

When considering two market segments in which other factors, such as size and growth potential, are constant, the one with a less-competitive environment is more attractive. For example, marketers of a Chinese fast-food restaurant like Panda Express might want to reconsider entering a market where there are a high number of Chinese food restaurants offering all-you-can-eat buffets and delivery service. The high level of competition will make it more expensive to reach consumers in that community and maintain high profits.

Strategic Fit
Marketers should work to ensure that the target markets selected fit with what the organization is and wants to be, as defined in its mission statement. The SWOT analysis provides an excellent framework to determine if a firm will be successful targeting a specific segment.

Consumers are spending more money than ever on their pets providing marketers numerous growth opportunities from new flavors of cat treats to pet hotels in the years ahead. *Photo provided by Shane Hunt. Photograph by Jenifer Hunt*

Selecting an appropriate target market is crucial to a successful marketing strategy. Regardless of how clever and innovative a firm's marketing mix may be, if the strategic fit is wrong, the product will fail. McDonald's introduced an Angus burger to its menu in 2009 as a premium choice at its restaurants. The Angus burger was one of the priciest menu items; it did not fit well with the company's typical dollar-menu consumers. McDonald's target market did not want to pay four or five times more for a hamburger, even for a superior product. McDonald's eventually removed the Angus burger from its menu in 2013.[20]

Target Marketing Analytics

Marketers have a variety of decisions to make, such as the kinds of products to develop, the type of advertising to do, and what consumers to target. The more marketers understand the targeted market segment, the better able they will be to make those decisions. Marketing analytics can provide detailed data, such as gender, age, and lifestyle interests, of target markets.

Tools such as Google Analytics help marketers identify the demographics of valuable and potentially valuable customers. For an e-commerce site such as Etsy, Google Analytics can help identify segments with the highest e-commerce revenue. For a content-focused site such as ESPN.com or Unitedway.org, analytics tools help identify market segments with the highest engagement. (Engagement is measured by session duration or pageviews/screenviews per session for people who donate online.)

The age, gender, and lifestyle interest reports in Google Analytics all include engagement and conversion metrics. Marketers can start from any of these reports to build a picture of high-value customers to target in B2C, B2B, or nonprofit organizations. If you are running a B2B firm, for example, you can segment by a number of dimensions like *Product, Product Category,* or *Product Brand* to see the demographic composition of your potential target markets.

TARGET MARKETING STRATEGIES

LO 7-5

Compare the most common target marketing strategies.

The marketing department spends a great deal of time deciding which market segments are best to target. Once it has made that decision, the firm must develop a strategy for reaching those segments. The three basic strategies for targeting markets include undifferentiated targeting, differentiated targeting, and niche marketing.

Undifferentiated Targeting

An **undifferentiated targeting** strategy approaches the marketplace as one large segment. The major advantage of this type of mass-marketing strategy is the potential savings in developing and marketing the product. Because the firm doesn't segment the market further, it can approach all consumers with the same product offering and marketing mix.

undifferentiated targeting
A targeting strategy that approaches the marketplace as one large segment.

Undifferentiated targeting works best with uniform products, such as salt or bananas, for which the firm can develop a single marketing mix that satisfies the needs and wants of all customers. Only a limited number of products fall into this category, though. The majority of products satisfy very different needs and wants for different consumers.

Firms that offer only a general good or service are vulnerable to competitors that offer more specialized products that better meet consumer needs. The likelihood of success for a generic car or a restaurant that offers nothing unique or special is very small. Therefore, in most situations, marketers should use a more focused strategy.

Differentiated Targeting

Typically, firms can provide increased levels of satisfaction and generate more sales using a differentiated targeting strategy rather than a mass-marketing strategy. **Differentiated targeting** occurs when an organization simultaneously pursues several different market segments, usually with a different customized strategy for each.

differentiated targeting
A targeting strategy that simultaneously pursues several different market segments, usually with a different strategy for each.

General Motors (GM) provides a classic example of successful differentiated targeting. Nearly a century ago, GM segmented consumers by the price they could afford and the quality they desired. It then customized its products, messages, and promotions to the unique needs of each group. This practice was the beginning of the GM family—from Chevrolet to Buick to Cadillac.

Frito-Lay has made use of differentiated targeting by developing various flavors of potato chips to appeal to different regions of the country. *Pranay Chandra Singh/Shutterstock*

Firms that market a core product to multiple regions with different preferences often use differentiated target marketing. In such cases, the firm may adjust the product to ensure that it meets a need unique to each segment. For instance, some regions prefer food flavors that don't sell well in other areas. Frito-Lay offers more than 10 regional flavors. These include Fried Pickles with Ranch in the Midwest and a Thai sweet chili in the Pacific Northwest.[21] While the core product, potato chips, remains the same, differentiated targeting distributes select flavors to certain regions based on local preferences.

A firm marketing to a region outside the United States may also need to use differentiated targeting. It might modify products according to local government regulations or cultural preferences. For example, Walmart initially offended consumers in China by selling fish and meat in Styrofoam and cellophane, the way it sells these items in the United States. In China, consumers value fresh food, and they viewed the prewrapped products as old merchandise.[22] Walmart marketers responded quickly to this problem; they differentiated their offerings in Chinese locations by installing fish tanks and selling meat products uncovered. These moves, in combination with other differentiating strategies like elaborate cosmetics counters just inside the front door, have helped Walmart resonate with its target market in China.

Niche Marketing

niche marketing

A targeting strategy that involves pursuing a large share of a small market segment.

Niche marketing involves targeting a large share of a small market segment. Firms that do niche marketing offer a unique product or specialization that is desirable to their targeted customers. Consumers of niche marketing products typically have very specialized needs and will pay higher prices to meet those needs.

Ties.com is a successful Internet-based niche retail company. The business, which shares its name with its website, has been in operation since 1998.[23] It focuses exclusively on men's neckties and related products. Fashion retailer Kathy Marrou founded the company, replacing her general clothing retail operation with one focused only on ties. The company has now added scarves to its lineup, to target a niche market of female consumers who are passionate about neckwear.

Remember that one of the criteria for effective market segmentation is size. Whatever market niche a firm targets must be a segment that is substantial enough to be successful. If Ties.com sold neckwear to only 10 people who liked exotic ties, it would be virtually impossible for the company to turn a profit and sustain itself as a business. The market segment for neckwear is substantial enough that Ties.com was able to generate over $20 million in annual revenue, and revenue growth of over 30 percent annually.[24]

There can be multiple niche markets within the same product category. Pizza sales in the United States reached $37 billion annually in recent years, led by firms such as Pizza Hut, Domino's, and Papa John's. However, a number of pizza providers have found success targeting specific niche segments of the pizza market. Pizza Fusion targets consumers looking for a healthier and environmentally friendly alternative to the large pizza chains. Papa Murphy's leads the take-and-bake pizza niche. Little Caesars's $5 Hot-N-Ready Pizza targets customers looking for value and time savings.

Pizza Patrón has gained a following by implementing a niche marketing strategy specifically targeted toward the Hispanic population as a subset of the larger pizza-eating population.
Dave Einsel/Getty Images

ETHICAL ISSUES IN TARGET MARKETING

LO 7-6

Summarize the ethical issues in target marketing.

Regardless of what target marketing strategy firms use, they must keep in mind ethical concerns about targeting certain market segments. Segments of particular concern are children and older adults.

Beginning in the late 1990s, marketers at Abercrombie & Fitch, Juicy Couture, and similar firms began targeting "tween" consumers, children between the ages of 8 and 12. The tween segment accounts for over $51 billion in direct consumer purchases; it significantly influences another $170 billion spent by parents and family members.[25] With those sales dollars as the incentive, firms began to adjust the target age for their products downward. Before too long, they were marketing to tweens products like makeup and trendy clothing that had always been considered more appropriate for teenagers. In addition, embedded marketing programs in schools and product placements in popular television and movies by some of these companies made it difficult for tweens to differentiate between entertainment and a product promotion. An analysis of popular online children's retailers showed that almost 30 percent of children's clothes have sexualized characteristics; the highest proportion of sexualized clothing came from stores aimed at tweens.[26] Several grassroots organizations have been formed to promote ethical marketing to children.

A product called a *reverse mortgage* allows older homeowners to tap into the equity of their home and receive payments against its value. As traditional real estate sales have struggled since the collapse of the housing market in 2007, reverse-mortgage loans have become more widely used. Marketing of reverse mortgages has helped older adults access the equity in their home and "age in place" and avoid retirement housing. But it also has raised ethical questions from legislators and other stakeholders; they worry that this type of target marketing is potentially taking advantage of desperate older adults who may not fully understand what a reverse mortgage is or the associated upfront fees and costs.

Darrious Duffin

Sales Operations Analyst
Ritter Communications

Describe your job. I'm a sales operations analyst. My main responsibility is to provide our executive team with information to help them make data-driven decisions that increase sales and improve efficiency. I partner with our sales leadership to create and implement strategies that generate new sales leads, close more deals, shorten the sales cycle, and grow the overall enterprise sales chan-

Darrious Duffin

nel. I inform and advise management on current business trends, risks, and opportunities.

How did you get your job? During my senior year in college, I secured an internship with Ritter Communications. Through my internship, I was part of a sales strategy team that bid on two multimillion-dollar opportunities to provide data service to facilities across the region. Although I wasn't the one who closed the deal, the team recognized a young, eager, and driven student whose talents and personality aligned with the needs of the company. Five years later, I have been afforded the opportunity to learn and grow my skill set in a variety of ways.

What has been the most important thing in making you successful at your job? I've benefited from several opportunities to grow my business acumen and put my education to work, but my people skills have also been vital to my success. We are an extremely team-oriented company. I try to be open-minded and learn from others. I work very closely with people who identify the same goals and finish line but have different ideologies on how to get there. I have

the ability to adapt to every situation and find common ground with people to achieve an objective.

What advice would you give soon-to-be graduates? Start the job search early. Don't focus on finding the perfect first job. Pay, location, and job responsibilities are unlikely to be glamorous. Focus on landing a job with a company that will allow you to test your abilities, expose you to all parts of the business, and most important, make mistakes. With humility, realize you must start at the bottom. Your first opportunity will springboard you into many other ones. Also, know that it's going to be much harder to find a job than you think. It takes a lot of patience and persistence. Don't get discouraged!

What do you consider your personal brand to be? My brand is rooted in executive consulting. I help business leaders understand problems and possible routes to take for recovery. I'm a great assimilator of information and I have a strong command of material. While I'm invested in my own career, the success of those I work with is even more important than that of my own. I was trained to be servant-minded. I've worked to develop winning strategies that benefit employees and customers, and I was raised to be humble and never forget where I came from. I'm very team-oriented, and I want those around me to enjoy working with me. My mission is not to be respected for career highlights or personal advancement, but to be respected for using my experiences and the lessons I have learned to make a difference in the lives of others.

Marketers should consider the ethical implications of *any* target marketing strategies they implement and give particular consideration to whether certain segments might need extra protection.

MARKET POSITIONING

LO 7-7

Explain the three steps of effective market positioning and why firms may choose to use repositioning strategies.

Success within the target market depends, to some degree, on how the firm positions its product. **Positioning** consists of the activities a firm undertakes to create a certain perception of its product in the eyes of the target market. It assumes that consumers compare goods and services on the basis of their benefits. Positioning often takes into account the identity of the organization and where it fits relative to the competition. Successful positioning involves all of the marketing mix elements (price, product, place, and promotion).

positioning

The activities a firm undertakes to create a certain perception of its product in the eyes of the target market.

Steps in Market Positioning

Marketers should follow three major steps to decide how to best position their product:

1. Analyze competitors' positions.
2. Clearly define your competitive advantage.
3. Evaluate feedback.

Step 1: Analyze Competitors' Positions
First, firms must understand the position competitors have taken in the marketplace. Positioning does not occur in isolation, and it is important for marketers to have a realistic view of how customers perceive competitive offerings.

Competitive analysis becomes even more important when competitors appear to offer a similar good or service. Financial institutions like banks and credit unions face this challenge: Services like free checking and online banking are pretty much the same, regardless of the type of bank. Bank of America has tried to overcome this obstacle by using advertising; it emphasizes its ability to allow customers to pay bills online and deposit checks using their smartphone from anywhere in the world. Credit unions, on the other hand, promote other features. By explaining to potential members that a credit union is not designed to extract profit from them, credit unions may be able to position themselves as more customer-focused and convince individuals to switch from for-profit banks.

A perceptual map provides a valuable tool for understanding competitors' positions in the marketplace. A **perceptual map** creates a visual picture of product locations in consumers' minds. Figure 7.3 shows a sample perceptual map illustrating the domestic cell phone carrier market. It uses horizontal and vertical axes that reflect key elements of competitors' offerings, in this case, the size of the coverage area and the length of the contract required. Marketers can develop a perceptual map based on marketing research or from their knowledge about a specific market.

perceptual map

A competitive analysis tool that creates a visual picture of product locations in consumers' minds.

Perceptual maps provide guidance on potential market positions that might be underserved. For example, Figure 7.3 illustrates one of the reasons wireless provider T-Mobile decided in 2013 to promote new service plans that did not require an annual contract.[27] In doing so, T-Mobile became the only major wireless provider occupying the position of offering nationwide coverage to consumers purchasing an iPhone or Android device with no contract required. Contrast this to the number of major providers offering nationwide coverage but requiring a contract of at least one year. AT&T, Verizon Wireless, and Sprint already competed in that market position, making it difficult for T-Mobile to succeed using the same positioning strategy. By finding a unique

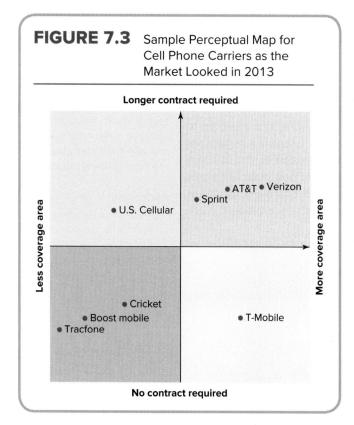

FIGURE 7.3 Sample Perceptual Map for Cell Phone Carriers as the Market Looked in 2013

position in the market, T-Mobile has been able to experience significant growth in the years since including record high customer results in 2021.[28]

Step 2: Clearly Define Your Competitive Advantage
Great marketers understand competitive advantage and why consumers buy their firm's goods and services. They know that consumers must have a clear answer to the question, "Why should I buy this product?" If a marketer cannot clearly establish an answer to this question in the mind of the consumer, the product may not realize its full potential.

A number of positioning strategies are available to highlight a firm's competitive advantage:

1. ***Price–quality relationship.*** Customers are often attracted to firms that offer them the same product quality as other stores, but at a more affordable price. Walmart is a great example of a low-cost retailer that has successfully positioned itself using a price–quality relationship strategy. Because of its thousands of stores globally, it can negotiate bulk discounts from wholesalers and keep its distribution costs low. These cost savings translate into low selling prices for goods with which rivals cannot compete. Shoppers know that Walmart offers the lowest prices, so they choose to shop there. This in turn enhances Walmart's brand, which only improves its competitive advantage.

2. ***Attributes.*** Often a product will have multiple attributes that create a unique position in the market. Marketers should evaluate those attributes that put its product in a special category of value to the customer. Successful attributes might include leadership, heritage, product manufacturing process, or the coolness factor. For example, Nike continued to have sales success marketing the Air Jordan line of shoes years after Michael Jordan retired from sports. The coolness factor of the shoes is an attribute that creates a unique position in the marketplace and resonates with consumers across generations.

3. ***Application.*** Apple has had success with its iPad product, in part, because of the competitive advantage it has when it comes to the application and use of the product. As new versions of the iPad have been introduced, Apple has had success emphasizing exclusive services like FaceTime and iCloud to further differentiate the iPad from competitors. In addition, Apple reminds customers that its app store is still the largest store of its type with the highest security standards.

Firms can choose to promote one or multiple competitive advantages, as long as they can clearly articulate those advantages to their target market.

Step 3: Evaluate Feedback
The third step in market positioning is constantly evaluating consumer feedback. Just as fashion styles change, consumer tastes for almost everything, including cars, food, and even educational learning formats, change. For example, as more students began to work while attending college, universities began offering a larger number of night classes than they had before. In recent years, to accommodate fluctuating student work schedules, high gas prices, and a the COVID-19

pandemic, universities began offering more online courses. Universities continue to position themselves as providers of quality higher education programs even as they have shifted their product to accommodate the additional features and conveniences their target market requires.

Disney provides another example. Disney used feedback from consumers who were concerned about childhood health to further position itself. The company required food and beverage products advertised on its networks to meet its specific nutritional standards by 2015. In the past decade, Disney began using a "Mickey Check" seal of approval to indicate that foods sold in its stores, theme parks, and resorts meet its nutritional standards.[29] The stated objective of these programs is combating childhood obesity. Listening to customer feedback on this sensitive issue has allowed Disney to position itself as a partner for parents in ensuring healthy lives for children.

Evaluating feedback is essential for universities and other organizations as they seek to position themselves with a target market increasingly focused on digital products through online classes and digital learning formats. *Rido/Shutterstock*

Mc Graw Hill connect Exercise 7-3

Please complete the *Connect* exercise for Chapter 7 that focuses on the steps in the market-positioning process. By understanding the decisions at each step of the process, you will better understand how to develop an effective market position.

Positioning Statement

Once a firm has completed the steps to decide how best to position its product, the hard part begins: The firm must determine how to succinctly communicate the market position it has chosen, first to its own organization and then to the world.

A **positioning statement** consists of a succinct description of the core target market to which a product is directed and a compelling picture of how the firm wants that core market to view the product. A successful positioning statement should clearly reflect the steps of the positioning process, including the competitive advantages of the product. However, positioning statements should also be short.

A succinct statement enhances the likelihood that stakeholders and consumers will understand the desired message. Zipcar is a membership-based car-sharing company that provides automobile reservations to its members, billable by the hour or day. Zipcar seeks to emphasize the superiority of its service in relation to the competitive alternative of owning one's own car. This approach is captured in its positioning statement. In fewer than 30 words, the statement outlines the target market, how Zipcar wants consumers to view its service, and how its service bests other options:

> To urban-dwelling, educated techno-savvy consumers [target market], when you use Zipcar car-sharing service instead of owning a car [picture of how they want consumers to view the service], you save money while reducing your carbon footprint [how they are better].[30]

A firm's positioning statement can be used as part of an external marketing strategy. First, though, it should serve as an internal guiding statement, keeping employees and other stakeholders aligned to the firm's guiding principles. The better all departments

positioning statement
A succinct description of the core target market to which a product is directed and a compelling picture of how the firm wants that core market to view the product.

understand an organization's market positioning, the more likely it is to be communicated and executed throughout the organization.

Firms that maintain the same position year after year, even if it has been successful, can lose touch with changing customer preferences. Smart marketers realize that positioning doesn't occur just when launching new products. Rather, it is an ongoing process. Consumer feedback, declining sales, or reduced market share can all suggest that the firm needs to undertake a major change in strategy.

Repositioning

repositioning

The act of reestablishing a product's position in response to changes in the marketplace.

In this digital age, marketers have to change and adapt their strategies if they want to continue to reach their target market. **Repositioning** involves reestablishing a product's position in response to changes in the marketplace. Dr Pepper Snapple Group, the Sunkist brand's licensee for soda in the United States, initiated a repositioning strategy aimed at trend-savvy teens and young adults. The soda brand now utilizes YouTube and Facebook platforms to promote its products.

Repositioning and the Marketing Mix
Repositioning typically involves changing one or more marketing-mix elements, often product or promotion. Elmer's changed promotion strategies when it launched the first-ever Ooey Gluey Slime Games to occur in 2018 to reposition its glue products as central ingredients for slime. The contest invited anyone over the age of six to express their creativity utilizing Elmer's glue and show off their unique slime-creating abilities. By guiding participants through a series of six different slime-making competitions, including Brightest, Coolest Texture, and Biggest Slime Bubble, Elmer's is creating more reasons for kids to continue making slime and purchasing glue. As the popularity of slime making has increased in recent years, sales of Elmer's glue more than doubled.[31]

Elmer's glue has successfully repositioned its traditional products as a key ingredient for making slime, which has increased in popularity and is helping product sales. *Shane Hunt*

Repositioning the Competition Sometimes marketers choose to reposition the competition rather than change their own position. For example, Apple had success repositioning its PC competitors like Dell and Hewlett-Packard using the popular "I'm a Mac, I'm a PC" advertisements that compared the capabilities and attributes of Macs and PCs. The promotion succeeded in characterizing the PC as formal and stuffy, while portraying Apple's Mac as the relaxed, easy-to-use alternative.

This type of repositioning strategy is also common in political marketing: Strategists look to define their opponent negatively without changing their own candidate's positions. Check out any major election cycle in your state or region, and you are likely to find plenty of examples of this type of repositioning strategy.

SUMMARY

Thomas Cordy/The Palm Beach Post/ ZUMA Press Inc/ Alamy Stock Photo

LO 7-1 Explain the importance of and criteria for effective market segmentation.

Market segmentation is the process of dividing a larger market into smaller groups, or market segments, based on meaningfully shared characteristics. *Market segments* are the relatively homogeneous groups of consumers that result from the market segmentation process.

Market segmentation plays an important role in the success of almost every organization in the United States and throughout the world. The process helps firms define the needs and wants of the customers the firm wants to target. Market segmentation also helps firms design specific marketing strategies for the characteristics of specific market segments.

Simply dividing a larger group of consumers into smaller ones serves no purpose unless it helps marketers sell their firm's goods and services. To be effective tools, market segments should rate favorably on five criteria; they should be substantial, measurable, differentiable, accessible, and actionable. Analytics also play an increasingly important role in properly segmenting markets.

Eric Risberg/ AP Images

LO 7-2 Describe the bases for segmenting both B2C and B2B markets.

Marketers use segmentation bases, which are characteristics of consumers that influence their buying behavior, to divide the market into segments. There are four broad bases of segmentation—demographic, geographic, psychographic, and behavioral.

Demographic characteristics include age, gender, income, education, and family size, among other things. Age and gender are the two most commonly used demographic variables. *Geographic segmentation* divides markets into nations,

regions, states, and neighborhoods, and other physical areas. Marketers pay special attention to local variations in the types of goods and services offered in different geographic regions. *Psychographic segmentation* divides markets using demographics, psychology, and personality traits. *Behavioral segmentation* divides consumers according to what they actually do with their goods and services.

Rob Crandall/Alamy Stock Photo

LO 7-3 Discuss international segmentation bases and the effect of international market segments on the marketing mix

International market segmentation is a costly exercise, and often a very difficult task. Firms typically segment international markets using three general bases: global, regional, and unique. *Global segmentation* is used when the firm can identify a group of consumers with common needs and wants that spans the entire globe. *Regional segmentation* may be used when the similarity in needs and wants extends across only the region or several countries. If a firm wants to completely localize, it may choose *unique segmentation,* which targets the preferences of a segment within one country. All three types of segments offer potential profits depending on how consumers within the segment respond to the marketing mix.

Photo provided by Shane Hunt. Photograph by Jenifer Hunt

LO 7-4 Describe the factors and analytics involved in selecting target markets

Targeting occurs when marketers evaluate each market segment and determine which segment presents the most attractive opportunities. The segments they select are called their *target markets.* When determining which market segments to pursue, marketers should consider the following important factors: growth potential, level of competition, and strategic fit.

Pranay Chandra Singh/Shutterstock

LO 7-5 Compare the most common target marketing strategies.

There are three general strategies for targeting markets. An *undifferentiated targeting strategy* approaches the marketplace as one large segment. *Differentiated targeting* occurs when an organization simultaneously pursues several different market segments, usually with a different strategy for each. A *niche marketing strategy* involves targeting a large share of a small market segment.

LO 7-6 Summarize the ethical issues in target marketing.

Regardless of what target marketing strategy firms use, they must keep in mind ethical concerns around targeting some market segments, in particular children and older adults. Several grass-roots organizations have been formed to promote ethical marketing to children. Marketers should consider the ethical implications of *any* target marketing decisions they make.

Rido/Shutterstock

LO 7-7 Explain the three steps of effective market positioning and why firms may choose to use repositioning strategies.

Positioning is the act of designing the firm's offering and image to occupy a distinctive place in the minds of the target market and involves three major steps: (1) understand the position other competitors have taken in the marketplace, (2) clearly define a competitive advantage, and (3) constantly evaluate consumer feedback.

Consumer feedback, declining sales, or reduced market share can all suggest that the firm needs to undertake a change in strategy. *Repositioning* involves reestablishing a product's position to respond to changes in the marketplace. It typically involves changing one or more marketing-mix elements. Marketers can also choose to reposition the competition in consumers' minds, rather than change their own position.

KEY TERMS

behavioral segmentation (p. 233)
demographic segmentation (p. 226)
differentiated targeting (p. 239)
80/20 rule (p. 233)
geographic segmentation (p. 229)
global segmentation (p. 236)
lifestyle segmentation (p. 232)

market segmentation (p. 224)
market segments (p. 224)
niche marketing (p. 240)
perceptual map (p. 243)
positioning (p. 243)
positioning statement (p. 245)
psychographic segmentation (p. 231)

regional segmentation (p. 237)
repositioning (p. 246)
target market (p. 238)
targeting (p. 238)
undifferentiated targeting (p. 239)
unique segmentation (p. 237)

MARKETING PLAN EXERCISE • Marketing Yourself

In this chapter, you read about the importance of targeting specific segments and developing a positioning strategy that appeals to those segments. Your assignment for this chapter is to apply these critical concepts to your marketing plan.

First, refer back to the career objectives (what company you want to work for or what graduate school you want to attend) that you have already developed. Next, think about and clearly articulate how you will position yourself for your target market. There are a limited number of openings for good jobs and quality graduate schools. To maximize your chances of success, you must plan ahead and use the

marketing strategies you have learned to position yourself properly in a very competitive environment. You should ask yourself questions such as:

- How can I best position myself for a job with one of these organizations?
- What classes have I taken or what experiences have I had that position me for the graduate school I want to attend?

Your Task: Write a one-paragraph personal positioning statement that includes succinct answers to these questions.

DISCUSSION QUESTIONS

1. Choose a company you have worked for or would like to work for and discuss how it could benefit from market segmentation. Does that company do a good job segmenting today? Why or why not?
2. Select a market segment for fast food. First, describe the segment. Then explain how the segment meets all five of the criteria to be considered an effective market segment.
3. Select a product that you use almost every day and explain how each of the major segmentation bases can be applied to you as a consumer of that product. What insights can each segmentation base provide to firms to help them develop a marketing mix that would win your business? (For example, you might say that geographic segmentation would help a firm market heavy coats to you because you live in a cold climate.)

4. Assume that your university is looking to increase enrollment. Choose the best targeting strategy (undifferentiated, differentiated, or niche) for achieving this goal. Describe how that strategy will be effective in bringing more students to your campus.
5. Select a company that you think has successfully positioned its products, and describe why it has been successful. Next, select a company that you think has done a poor job positioning its products, and explain why it hasn't been successful.
6. Select one firm that you think needs to reposition itself. Describe what you think isn't working about its current position. Then provide three specific recommendations for how it could reposition itself for a successful future.

 # SOCIAL MEDIA APPLICATION

Select a product that you like and that you would enjoy marketing. This could be a type of car, smartphone, restaurant, or other product. Segment the market for this product using the following questions and activities as a guide:

1. Select 20 friends, followers, or connections that you have on any social media platform and segment them as if they are potential customers of the product you have chosen to market. You need to identify at least three different segments.

2. What variables did you use to segment the potential customers?
3. How were social media helpful to you in assigning each person to a specific segment?
4. Decide which segment of the three you are going to target your marketing efforts to. Why did you make that decision?
5. How can social media help you reach the targeted consumers with your marketing message?

 # MARKETING ANALYTICS EXERCISE

Please complete the *Connect* exercise for Chapter 7 that focuses on using demographic data to select target markets.

ETHICAL CHALLENGE

Currently, users under the age of 13 are not permitted to create profiles on Facebook. Although many tweens lie about their age and create profiles, because Facebook can't identify users under 13, advertisers can't use Facebook to reach this demographic.

Allowing tweens to create profiles could reinvigorate Facebook's slowing growth. But Facebook has already come under fire for privacy issues, and it may want to avoid exposing itself to potential allegations about exploiting or

failing to protect children. In addition, the Children's Online Privacy Protection Act (COPPA) would require Facebook to allow parents to elect not to have their children's online activities tracked. If parents took advantage of this option, Facebook would have limited data and access to offer advertisers, compromising its ability to profit from the preteen demographic.

Facebook must weigh many risks and potential benefits in deciding whether to open up to tweens. Please use the ethical decision-making framework to answer the following questions:

1. Why do some people feel that Facebook shouldn't target children under 13? Do you agree?
2. Despite the current policy, surveys suggest that millions of children under the age of 13 lie about their age and use Facebook. How should Facebook, parents, and children share the responsibility for any adverse consequences the children might experience? Would the risk of such consequences be lessened if Facebook allowed children to have profiles?
3. What risks, costs, and benefits should Facebook consider in deciding whether to allow preteen users? To what extent should Internet companies be held accountable for children's online safety?

Source: See Jordan Roberston, "Will Facebook Friend Pre-Teens?" *Bloomberg Businessweek*, June 14, 2012, http://www.businessweek.com/articles/2012-06-14/will-facebook-friend-preteens.

VIDEO CASE

Please go to *Connect* to access the video case featuring Marriott that accompanies this chapter.

 # PODCAST

Please go to Connect to access the podcast that accompanies this chapter.

CAREER **TIPS**

Positioning Yourself at Various Stages of Life

You have read in this chapter about the critical marketing concept of positioning. In a personal context, positioning involves how you are perceived by those people who can affect your career success, such as employers, coworkers, customers, and classmates.

Coauthor Shane Hunt shares with you his thoughts about three major stages of your life at which successfully positioning yourself will help you have the career you desire.

1. **Position yourself during college.** You should give careful consideration to how you position yourself in college. Part of this process involves asking yourself, What am I doing that will give me a competitive advantage over my classmates? Ask yourself how the classes you are taking are helping you achieve your goals. Be selective in picking courses. In addition to the time and money you spend completing them, through them you have the opportunity to acquire differentiating knowledge. A course in the marketing program or a foreign language class might be time-consuming, but these kinds of classes are far more likely to help you carve a unique position for yourself as you complete your degree. Be thoughtful in considering how specific course knowledge, leadership activities, and work experiences make your position unique.

2. **Position yourself as a problem solver.** Once you start your career, you should work to position yourself in the mind of your manager as someone who can be relied on and, most importantly, can solve problems. Your ability to get paid more in your career is directly related to your ability to solve problems for your organization. Take on difficult assignments and volunteer for committees. These added activities might be stressful but they will raise your profile and advance your learning about the organization. If your manager perceives you as

someone whose problem-solving ability and attitude are superior to your peers, your likelihood for promotion and raises increases substantially.

3. **Don't be afraid to reposition yourself.** There might come a time when the job or career you have chosen ceases to be as personally or financially fulfilling as you had hoped. If this is the case, you need to consider how you can reposition yourself. You might consider going to

graduate school or learning a new skill at your current job. Sometimes repositioning is necessary because of technology or industry changes. Learn how to create an app for your small business or acquire new certifications relevant to your field. You must continue to learn when you finish college and develop new skills for the rest of your career so that you can reposition yourself to compete against future graduates.

CHAPTER NOTES

1. Monte Burk, "Five Guys Burgers: America's Fastest Growing Restaurant Chain," *Forbes*, July 18, 2012, http://www.forbes.com/forbes/2012/0806/restaurant-chefs-12-five-guys-jerry-murrell-all-in-the-family.html.
2. Rob Sachs, "High-End Burger Joints Raise the Stakes," *NPR*, April 21, 2011, http://www.npr.org/2011/04/21/135569985/high-end-burger-joints-raise-the-stakes.
3. Rob Sachs, "High-End Burger Joints Raise the Stakes," *NPR*, April 21, 2011, http://www.npr.org/2011/04/21/135569985/high-end-burger-joints-raise-the-stakes.
4. Lindsay M. Howden and Julie A. Meyer, "Age and Sex Composition: 2010," U.S. Census Bureau, May 2011, http://www.census.gov/prod/cen2010/briefs/c2010br-03.pdf.
5. Kaylene C. Williams and Robert A. Page, "Marketing to the Generations," *Journal of Behavioral Studies in Business* 3 (April 2011): 1–17.
6. Joshua Brustein, "Why HBO, Netflix, and Amazon Want Your Kids," *Bloomberg*, August 14, 2015, http://www.bloomberg.com/news/articles/2015-08-14/why-hbo-netflix-and-amazon-want-your-kids.
7. Stephanie Clifford, "Revamping, Home Depot Woos Women," *The New York Times*, January 28, 2011, http://www.nytimes.com/2011/01/29/business/29home.html.
8. Elizabeth Sweet, "Guys and Dolls No More?," *The New York Times*, December 21, 2012, http://www.nytimes.com/2012/12/23/opinion/sunday/gender-based-toy-marketing-returns.html?_r=0.
9. Colin Barr, "'Mass Affluent' Are Strapped Too, BofA Finds," *CNNMoney*, January 24, 2011, http://finance.fortune.cnn.com/2011/01/24/mass-affluent-are-strapped-too-bofa-finds/.
10. Colin Barr, "'Mass Affluent' Are Strapped Too, BofA Finds," *CNNMoney*, January 24, 2011, http://finance.fortune.cnn.com/2011/01/24/mass-affluent-are-strapped-too-bofa-finds/.
11. Penelope Green, "Under One Roof, Building for Extended Families," *The New York Times*, November 29, 2012, http://www.nytimes.com/2012/11/30/us/building-homes-for-modern-multigenerational-families.html?pagewanted=1.
12. Ryan Poe, "IKEA in Birmingham? Metro Falls Short of Retailer's Population Target," *Birmingham Business Journal*, October 29, 2012, http://www.bizjournals.com/birmingham/blog/2012/10/ikea-in-birmingham-dont-hold-your.html.
13. Joshua Caucutt, "Cracker Barrel Is Cracklin,'" *InvestorGuide*, May 25, 2010, http://www.investorguide.com/article/6467/cracker-barrel-is-cracklin-cbrl/.
14. "Dunkin Donuts Targets Small Markets in North Texas Growth," *Dallas Business Journal*, April 1, 2016, https://www.bizjournals.com/dallas/news/2016/04/01/dunkin-donuts-targets-small-markets-in-north-texas.html.
15. U.S. Census, "2020 Census: Apportionment of the U.S. House of Representatives," Census.gov, April 26, 2021, https://www.census.gov/library/visualizations/2021/dec/2020-apportionment-map.html.
16. David Mildenburg, "Census Finds Hurricane Katrina Left New Orleans Richer, Whiter, Emptier," *Bloomberg*, February 3, 2011, http://www.bloomberg.com/news/2011-02-04/census-finds-post-katrina-new-orleans-richer-whiter-emptier.html.
17. Alexandra Jardine, "NFL Ramps Up U.K. Marketing as It Seeks Mainstream Audience beyond U.S.," *Ad Age*, November 11, 2015, http://adage.com/article/news/nfl-ramps-u-k-marketing-seeks-mainstream-audience/301302/.
18. Mary Jiang Bresnahan, Yasuhiro Inoue, Wen Ying Liu, and Tsukasa Nishida, "Changing Gender Roles in Prime Time Commercials in Malaysia, Japan, Taiwan, and the United States," *Sex Roles* 45, nos. 1–2 (July 2001): 117–131.
19. Emily DeCiccio, "The Pet Business Is Booming as Americans Spend More on Their Animals While They Work from Home," *CNBC*, December 5, 2020, https://www.cnbc.com/2020/12/05/americans-are-spending-more-money-on-their-pets-during-the-pandemic.html.
20. NBC News Staff, "Where's the Beef? McDonald's Dropping Angus Burgers from U.S. Menu," *NBC News*, May 9, 2013, http://www.nbcnews.com/business/wheres-beef-mcdonalds-dropping-angus-burgers-us-menu-1C9864163.
21. Frito-Lay North America, "Lay's Releases the Most new Flavors Ever, Bringing Fans a Regionally Inspired 'Summer of Flavor,'" *PR Newswire*, July 18, 2018, https://www.prnewswire.com/news-releases/lays-releases-the-most-new-flavors-ever-bringing-fans-a-regionally-inspired-summer-of-flavor-300682744.html.
22. Keith Naughton, "The Great Wal-Mart of China," *Newsweek*, October 29, 2006, http://www.thedailybeast.com/newsweek/2006/10/29/the-great-wal-mart-of-china.html.

23. Sebastian Weiss, "Husband and Wife Team Ties into Rising Tide of E-Business," *San Antonio Business Journal*, December 12, 1999, http://www.bizjournals.com/sanantonio/stories/1999/12/13/story5.html?page=all.

24. Ryan Erskine, "How This Tie Shop Accidentally Became a Content Marketing Master," *Forbes*, March 17, 2018, https://www.forbes.com/sites/ryanerskine/2018/03/17/how-this-tie-shop-accidentally-became-a-content-marketing-master/#341962a61a71.

25. Leslie Jane Seymour, "Tween 'R' Shoppers," *The New York Times*, April 22, 2007, http://www.nytimes.com/2007/04/22/nyregion/nyregionspecial2/22RSHOP.html?pagewanted=all&_r=0.

26. Samantha M. Goodin, Alyssa Van Denburg, Sarah K. Murnen, and Linda Smolak, "Putting on Sexiness: A Content Analysis of the Presence of Sexualizing Characteristics in Girls' Clothing," *Sex Roles* 65 (2011): 1–12.

27. David Pogue, "Breaking Free of the Cellphone Carrier Conspiracy," *The New York Times*, April 3, 2013, http://www.nytimes.com/2013/04/04/technology/personaltech/t-mobile-breaks-free-of-cellphone-contracts-and-penalties.html?pagewanted=all&_r=0.

28. "T-Mobile Posts Record-High Customer Results, Adding 1.2 Million Postpaid Accounts and 5.5 Million Postpaid Customers in 2021," *T-Mobile.com,* January 6, 2022, https://www.t-mobile.com/news/business/t-mobile-preliminary-results-2021.

29. Brooks Barnes, "Promoting Nutrition, Disney to Restrict Junk-Food Ads," *The New York Times*, June 5, 2012, http://www.nytimes.com/2012/06/05/business/media/in-nutrition-initiative-disney-to-restrict-advertising.html?pagewanted=all&_r=0.

30. Alice M. Tybout and Bobby J. Calder, eds., *Kellogg on Marketing*, 2nd ed. (Hoboken, NJ: John Wiley & Sons, 2010), p. 89.

31. Matt Kates, "How Evoking Creativity from Children Can Lead to the Next Big Idea," *Adweek*, September 24, 2018, https://www.adweek.com/creativity/how-evoking-creativity-from-children-can-lead-to-the-next-big-idea/.

Part **THREE**

Reaching Your Customer

Erik Isakson/Blend Images

ER Productions/Blend Images/Getty Images

Wesley Hitt/Photolibrary/Getty Images

supparsorn/Shutterstock

TY Lim/Shutterstock

Anatolii Babii/Alamy Stock Photo

Chapter **8**

Promotional Strategies

Erik Isakson/Blend Images

Learning Objectives

After reading this chapter, you should be able to

LO 8-1 Describe the elements of the promotion mix and how they relate to an integrated marketing communications strategy.

LO 8-2 Compare the advantages and disadvantages of different types of advertising.

LO 8-3 Summarize the various types of sales promotion.

LO 8-4 Explain the importance of personal selling.

LO 8-5 Describe the role of public relations within the promotion mix.

LO 8-6 Describe metrics that measure the effectiveness of an organization's promotional strategy.

LO 8-7 Summarize the promotion-mix budgeting strategies.

Executive **Perspective** . . . because everyone is a marketer

Anderson Childress was a finance major in college who was passionate about marketing himself to help build a great career. Childress started his career working for a regional bank where he took advantage of his opportunity to learn as much as he could about all aspects of the business. Through hard work and personal branding, he had the opportunity to work in global cash management at eBay.

Today, Childress is a treasury manager at PayPal whose open digital payments platform gives PayPal's 254 million active account holders the confidence to connect and transact in new and powerful ways, whether they are online, on a mobile device, in an app, or in person.

What has been the most important thing in making you successful at your job?

Identifying what is most important to my company and its senior leaders, and then aligning my goals and objectives with theirs. This is a sure way to be called to the front. When your opportunity presents itself, own it! I have spent many hours rehearsing scenarios with myself to help develop business acumen for key moments.

What advice would you give soon-to-be graduates?

Anyone can tell you where he or she wants to end up in his or her career; the challenge is figuring out how to get there. My advice to up-and-coming graduates is to analyze each career decision thoroughly. Identify what intangibles each particular role can offer. An opportunity that pays more may not give you the tools you need to be successful in your path to your dream job. Think of this as chess, not checkers.

Anderson Childress
Treasury Manager
PayPal

Anderson Childress

How is marketing relevant to your role at PayPal?

Marketing is relevant to everything I do as we work with consumers and clients each day. We have established a culture that embraces integrity, ethics, and values not just on the face of the company but throughout all organizations within PayPal. Within my current role, I hold my colleagues to these standards and I am accountable to them as well.

What do you consider your personal brand to be?

I have always viewed my personal brand to be closely associated to my professional reputation within the company where I work. I place a strong emphasis on collaboration, transparency, and execution in every task or project that I am delegated or assigned. I remember to be respectful and patient to individuals that I encounter because good relationships are key to one's growth in this industry. I want the people that I encounter and work with to be assured that I am bringing my best to the table every day. This is my brand.

Describe the elements of the promotion mix and how they relate to an integrated marketing communications strategy.

PROMOTION MIX

Red Bull marketers were seeking a creative way to promote their brand and products that would communicate the firm's slogan, "Red Bull Gives You Wings." They developed a strategy that involved hiring extreme athlete Felix Baumgartner to break the world record for the longest free-fall jump. Baumgartner jumped from 120,000 feet above Earth, reaching a speed of 690 miles per hour during his descent.[1] The event promoted the Red Bull lifestyle and has been watched by over 50 million people on YouTube.[2] Images from the jump also became part of Red Bull's television advertising campaign. Red Bull marketers were able to integrate the success of the event to enhance the impact of their promotional strategy in everything from television to social media.

Promotion, one of the four marketing-mix elements, is where most of an organization's communications with the marketplace occur. **Promotion** consists of all the activities that communicate the value of a product and persuade customers to choose it over other options. The tools marketing professionals use to promote their products are referred to as the promotion mix. The **promotion mix** consists of four main elements of marketing communication: advertising, sales promotion, personal selling, and public relations.

promotion

All the activities that communicate the value of a product and persuade customers to buy it.

promotion mix

A subset of the marketing mix that includes four main elements of marketing communication: advertising, sales promotion, personal selling, and public relations.

Elements of the Promotion Mix

Figure 8.1 shows each element of the promotion mix. Each element represents a different way for the organization to communicate with its customers.

1. *Advertising.* Nonpersonal communication about goods, services, or ideas that is paid for by the firm identified in the message.
2. *Sales promotion.* A set of nonpersonal communication tools designed to stimulate quicker and more frequent purchases of a product.
3. *Personal selling.* The two-way flow of personal communication between a salesperson and a customer that is paid for by the firm and seeks to influence the customer's purchase decision.
4. *Public relations.* Communication focused on promoting positive relations between a firm and its stakeholders.

Athlete Felix Baumgartner's free-fall jump from 23 miles above Earth generated significant publicity and free media for Red Bull, the company that sponsored the event, as it appeared on dozens of news programs and websites. *Abaca Press/Alamy Stock Photo*

Historically, the elements of the promotion mix were handled by self-contained areas within an organization. Very little attention was paid to how the elements fit together. The advertising department would plan and implement advertising messages without coordinating with the sales force, which might be focusing on a different message during customer visits. Today, firms work to integrate the elements, so that the contribution from the whole promotion mix exceeds the sum of the individual elements.

Integrated Marketing Communications

An integrated communications solution involving multiple elements of the promotion mix allows a firm to effectively create and develop relationships with customers. An **integrated marketing communications (IMC)** strategy involves coordinating the various promotion-mix elements to provide consumers with a clear and consistent message about a firm's products.

For example, Taco Bell's IMC campaign encourages consumers to "Live Más" (live more). That brand essence reflects customers' evolving mindset from "food as fuel" to "food as an experience." Taco Bell's advertising, public relations, sales promotion, and in-store employees all focus on the "Live Más" theme.[3] Taco Bell used a sales promotion sweepstakes in which the winner received a trip to the MTV Video Music Awards to promote its "Big Box Rewind" product. Consumers could enter the sweepstakes by liking the Taco Bell Facebook page. Marketers also tied this sales promotion to their "Feed the Beat" music program that helps feed and support up-and-coming bands on tour.

A major part of the "Live Más" strategy involved the launch of Locos Tacos, which leveraged IMC elements to become the most successful product launch in the history of the company.[4] Television advertising for the launch included the popular commercial titled "Road Trip." The commercial was inspired by the true story of a group of friends from New York who traveled to Ohio to try Taco Bell's Doritos Locos Tacos. The IMC strategy enjoyed almost immediate success; the company sold over 100 million Doritos Locos Tacos in the first 10 weeks.

Each of the promotion-mix elements can influence different segments of the target market, and marketers should try to understand the impact of each element within the IMC strategy. For the Locos Tacos launch, Taco Bell relied heavily on its television advertising. Firms should use marketing research techniques to assess which promotion-mix elements have the most influence on different market segments at different points in the product life cycle. Using this research, the marketing

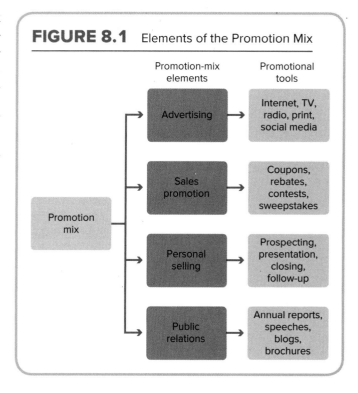

FIGURE 8.1 Elements of the Promotion Mix

integrated marketing communications (IMC)

A promotional strategy that involves coordinating the various promotion-mix elements to provide consumers with a clear and consistent message about a firm's products.

Taco Bell used an integrated marketing communications campaign to coordinate the promotion-mix elements to provide its target market with a clear and consistent message. *Jim R. Bounds/AP Images*

department can allocate more of its promotion budget to the elements that are most effective. Effective elements are those that increase sales, build brand equity, and improve customer relationships.

Finding the Optimal Promotion Mix

Finding the optimal promotion mix presents a great challenge to marketers. The optimal mix might include additional advertising for new products or high levels of sales promotion for mature products. Other firms might decide the best way to leverage their promotion mix is by adding additional salespeople. Regardless of where a product is in its life cycle, public relations often requires significantly more marketing resources in the months following a crisis.

The mix of promotional tools and how marketers integrate them can also change from year to year, or even from week to week, as environmental factors and consumer demands change. For example, in recent years marketers for everything from Adidas to political campaigns switched some of their advertising investment away from traditional television and radio commercials to Snapchat because of the social media platform's high popularity with young consumers. From sponsored geo-filters and video content, to shoppable augmented reality posts, there are numerous ways for marketers to reach Snapchat's 191 million daily active users, who each spend an average of between 25 and 30 minutes sending photos and consuming content on the platform every day.[5] Marketers should thoughtfully consider what mix of promotional elements will be most effective for their target market. They also should utilize marketing research to measure how successful each element of the promotion mix is, making adjustments as necessary to maximize the value of each promotional dollar spent.

In order to choose the optimal promotion mix, marketers need to understand the unique advantages and disadvantages of each promotion-mix element. These are described in detail in the sections that follow.

LO 8-2   ADVERTISING

Compare the advantages and disadvantages of different types of advertising.

advertising
Nonpersonal communication about goods, services, or ideas that is paid for by an identified sponsor.

advertising campaign
A collection of coordinated advertisements that share a single theme.

informative advertising
A type of advertising that attempts to develop initial demand for a product.

persuasive advertising
A type of advertising that attempts to increase demand for an existing product.

Advertising is the element of the promotion mix most consumers think of first. **Advertising** is nonpersonal communication about goods, services, or ideas that is paid for by an identified sponsor. Two words in the definition, *nonpersonal* and *paid,* are key to understanding how advertising fits into the promotion mix. The *nonpersonal* component refers to the fact that advertising uses media (e.g., Internet, television, radio, or print) to transmit a message to large numbers of individuals, rather than marketing to consumers face-to-face. The *paid* aspect of the definition indicates that the time or space for an advertising message is purchased. Because it is paid for, advertising has the advantage of control: The purchaser decides how to present the message to the public.

Firms spend hundreds of billions of dollars on **advertising campaigns**. An advertising campaign is a collection of coordinated advertisements that share a single theme. Marketers use advertising campaigns to achieve three primary objectives: to inform, to persuade, and to remind.

1. **Informative advertising** attempts to develop initial demand for a product. It's especially important in the introductory stage of the product life cycle. A flyer for a new bank that opened a branch in your neighborhood classifies as informative advertising.
2. **Persuasive advertising** attempts to increase demand for an existing product. Persuasive advertising is common during the growth stage of the product life cycle. At this stage, firms compete directly and attempt to take market share from one another. Persuasive advertising would include a television commercial

highlighting the benefits of becoming a member of a local gym that is trying to grow. The ad might highlight new equipment or flexible payment options in an effort to persuade consumers to join.

3. **Reminder advertising** seeks to keep the product before the public in an effort to reinforce previous promotional activity. Reminder advertising is most common in the maturity and decline stages of the product life cycle. A Facebook ad from the athletic department of your college, encouraging you to renew your season tickets to support one of your college's sports teams, is an example of reminder advertising.

reminder advertising

A type of advertising that seeks to keep the product before the public in an effort to reinforce previous promotional activity.

Marketers must also decide on the media to use to convey their message. Choice of media depends on the firm's objective—whether it seeks to inform, persuade, or remind—and where the audience it wants to reach is. Different advertising media reach different audiences.

Figure 8.2 illustrates the percentage of global advertising delivered via each major medium: television, the Internet (both desktop and mobile), print such as magazines and newspapers, radio, outdoor (billboards, signs in sports arenas, skywriting, and ads on the side of buildings, buses, and cars), and cinema. Notice the changes between 2016 and 2019: Newspaper and television advertising declined while mobile Internet advertising almost doubled.

You will learn more about digital and mobile marketing in a later chapter in this book. Each type of media has its own unique advantages and disadvantages that firms must understand if they want to determine the best fit for their specific product and budget.

Television Advertising

When they hear the term *marketing,* people often think first of television advertising because it is a form of advertising they experience a lot. Television advertising is very

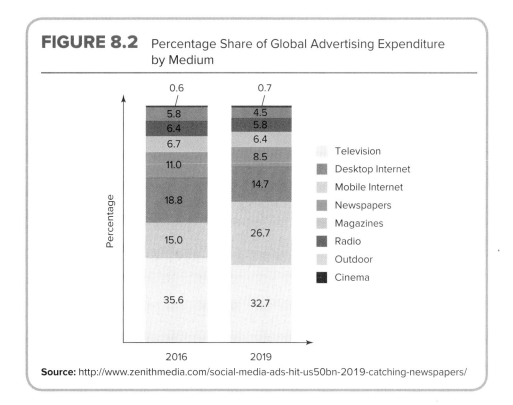

FIGURE 8.2 Percentage Share of Global Advertising Expenditure by Medium

Source: http://www.zenithmedia.com/social-media-ads-hit-us50bn-2019-catching-newspapers/

The Paramount show *Yellowstone* was one of the most watched shows of the 2021 television season, yet averaged a far smaller audience than the number of viewers for a highly rated show a generation ago.[7]

TCD/Prod.DB/Alamy Stock Photo

different today from what it was a generation ago. In the mid-1980s, the most popular television show was *Dallas:* More than 30 million people tuned in every week to watch J. R. Ewing and the drama that surrounded his family.[6] Today, the most popular shows on television often average fewer than 12 million viewers per week. Running ads during such shows comes at an increasingly high cost to firms as the price of television commercials has gone up dramatically in recent years.

One reason for the decreased viewership of top-rated TV programs is the greater number of channels available to consumers. In the early 1980s, the average American home had access to fewer than 20 channels. Today the average American household can choose from over 189 channels, plus a variety of streaming and on-demand options.[8]

Marketing professionals must understand the changing landscape of television advertising and consider the various advantages and disadvantages of trying to reach consumers in this way.

Advantages of TV Advertising

A major advantage of television advertising is the ability to combine sight, sound, and motion to appeal to consumer senses. Television ads can develop messages that entertain or emotionally appeal to consumers in ways that radio and print media cannot. In addition, television ads can demonstrate a product in use, for example, a new Toyota product with a rear camera that allows drivers to see the child's bike sitting behind it, or the absorption power of the ShamWow. Such demonstrations give consumers a better understanding of what owning the product would mean to their daily lives.

A more recent advantage of TV advertising comes from the increased number of television channels, which provides marketers an opportunity to target specific markets through narrowcasting. **Narrowcasting** is the dissemination of information to a fairly small, select audience that is defined by its shared values, preferences, or demographic attributes. For example, firms that marketed products to tennis fans a generation ago might have advertised heavily on ESPN, which at the time was the only all-sports channel on many basic cable subscriptions. Now these same firms can promote their tennis equipment and apparel on The Tennis Channel.[9] While the average viewership of The Tennis Channel is far lower than ESPN's, the audience is almost exclusively tennis enthusiasts, who are the most affluent viewing audience.[10] Focusing on this audience enables marketers of tennis products to target affluent customers efficiently. Because ads on The Tennis Channel are far less expensive than those on ESPN, marketers reach their target market at a lower cost and without wasting a significant amount of advertising on people who prefer other sports.

narrowcasting

The dissemination of information to a fairly small, select audience that is defined by its shared values, preferences, or demographic attributes.

Disadvantages of TV Advertising

Perhaps the biggest disadvantage of television advertising is cost. The cost to air a single 30-second ad on a major broadcast network (NBC, ABC, CBS, or Fox) during prime time averages well over $100,000 and can be much higher for popular shows. A 30-second ad on the popular NBC series *This Is Us* cost over $400,000 in 2018.[11] Ads for special events, such as the Super Bowl or the Academy Awards, can cost significantly more. In recent years, a 30-second television ad during the Super Bowl cost between $3 and $5 million.[12] Creating television ads is also expensive relative to other types of advertising. Television commercials can cost tens or even hundreds of thousands of dollars to make, depending on the length, complexity, and method used.

Complicating the use of television advertising is the widespread use of digital video recorders (DVRs). A majority of all American households that subscribe to cable or satellite television services now have some type of DVR for recording and watching their favorite programs.[13] Consumers love the ability to skip or fast-forward through ads to reduce the time it takes to watch shows or events. That ad-skipping ability leaves marketers paying for television ads that viewers aren't watching. In response, firms are exploring new technologies to ensure that viewers see their ad content. It has become common practice to hold the camera on a product for an extended period of time so that a viewer who is fast-forwarding through the commercial still has enough time to register the product. Firms are also implementing new strategies to put their ads directly into the program content using *product placement.*

Another concern is the growing number of customers who are abandoning traditional television service. In 2021, millions of cord-cutters in the United States—consumers who have ever canceled traditional pay-TV service and do not resubscribe—had reduced the percentage of consumers with cable or satellite subscriptions to 60 percent.[14] Consumers are increasingly using streaming services such as Netflix and Peacock to watch programs on demand across any device they choose. This change will reduce the impact of traditional television advertising in the years ahead. It also will provide marketers new opportunities to reach consumers by placing advertising in the new streaming services.

Product Placement

Product Placement The use of product placement has expanded in the past decade, as marketers look for ways to get their products in front of their target audience despite the prevalence of DVRs. **Product placement** is an advertising technique in which a company promotes its products through appearances in movies or on television shows or other media. For example in 2022, Lexus used the movie *Moonfall* to promote the new Lexus NX, positioning it as the luxury crossover best-suited to take on apocalyptic challenges. In the movie, actor Michael Peña plays a Lexus dealer, and there is an entire scene shot at a Lexus dealership. Plus, the Lexus GX 460 SUV also makes an appearance in the flick as a government vehicle.[15] In *Spectre,* James Bond wears an Omega Seamaster 300 watch and drives an Aston Martin DB10 coupe that was designed specifically for the movie.

product placement
An advertising technique in which a company promotes its products through appearances in movies or on television shows or other media.

Product placement has expanded beyond television and movies in recent years. In 2013, the National Football League (NFL) signed an agreement with Microsoft to make the Microsoft Surface the official tablet computer of the NFL. Microsoft now powers 269 NFL events each year with more than 2,000 Surface devices and 170 Windows servers installed at 30 stadiums.[16] Each week, millions of football fans of all ages see players, coaches, and announcers using Microsoft Surface tablets throughout the game. This use of product placement has generated over $400 million in new revenue for the NFL since the agreement was signed and helped Microsoft Surface revenue increase significantly in recent years.

The Microsoft Surface tablet computer has been a successful product placement seen by millions of NFL fans each week. *Robin Alam/Icon Sportswire/ Getty Images*

Internet Advertising

As Figure 8.2 shows, Internet advertising—combining desktop and mobile advertising—is now the second-largest global advertising medium and is growing every year. Internet advertising takes many forms. Paid *search advertising* typically involves offering consumers advertising links to brand content based on what they're searching for. Paid *display advertising* typically consists of banner advertising—a graphic display that appears on a website in an effort to get you to click on the content.

Social media platforms like Facebook offer new strategies for online advertising, and so are an ever-more-popular choice for Internet advertisers. Facebook's sponsored stories feature posts from friends about a product, which firms pay to highlight to make them more visible to other potential consumers.[17] Coca-Cola, Levi's, UNICEF, and other organizations increasingly spend part of their ad budgets on these new strategies.

The Internet has also made it easier for organizations to advertise directly to consumers. **Direct marketing** is advertising that communicates directly with consumers and organizations in an effort to provoke a response. You have likely received an e-mail advertisement directed to you based on information that marketers have about you from your previous purchases or marketing research. The e-mail might contain information about a new product that might interest you or might promote a special offer at a restaurant you frequent. By individually customizing their advertising using direct marketing strategies, firms seek to increase interest and awareness and, ultimately, generate additional revenue.

Internet streaming service Hulu is increasingly popular. Viewers use it to catch up with missed episodes of their favorite program or binge watch full seasons of shows in one sitting. Hulu leverages customer information to marketers who want to target a specific segment within the Hulu audience; viewers see the advertisement in order to continue watching the content. Hulu also uses a proprietary ad-serving technology that provides digital feedback about viewer habits and interests. That software enables marketers to maximize the benefit of their Internet advertising efforts.

Internet advertising does have some disadvantages as well. For example, banner ads have become so common that many consumers simply ignore them as they find their desired content. Banner or pop-up ads can also be potentially intrusive for consumers. Online ads that prevent or delay a customer from finding desired content can lead to a negative impression from the very consumers marketers are trying to reach.

We will discuss Internet advertising in greater detail in Chapter 13.

direct marketing

Advertising that communicates directly with consumers and organizations in an effort to provoke a response.

---

connect Exercise 8-1

Social Media in Action

Instagram used to be a simple photo-sharing app where users could show off their latest cool pics. Today, with over 1 billion active users, the social media giant has sellers excited over its potential as a place to market everything from dresses to furniture. Of those users, 150 million interact with over 25 million businesses that have a presence on the app. Instagram has counted several retailers as partners, including Macy's and J.Crew.

Instagram has become a carefree shopping experience that is desirable to many consumers. Amazon Fashion sells clothing through the store's Internet presence and offers a try-before-you-buy wardrobe service. Virtually all major department stores have their own Instagram accounts, driving people to their websites either by highlighting individual products or promoting clearance events. Instagram is looking to capitalize on this gap by being much more social and relevant to consumers.

On Instagram, the process of buying something can start on the app, but it doesn't end on the app. Marketers on platforms such as Shopify can tag products in their Instagram posts, and boxes designate what's available for purchase. Users can click to find the product description, which appears with more information. Then, users can click through to the retailer's own website, where the item is listed, and complete the purchase there.

The Social Media in Action Connect *exercise in Chapter 8 will let you develop potential advertisements utilizing Instagram to reach targeted consumers. By understanding strategies that can integrate social media tools and terminology, you will be prepared to develop effective advertising for consumers of various demographic groups and interests.*

Source: See Kim Bhasin, "How to Make Piles of Money Using Instagram," *Bloomberg,* July 2, 2018, https://www.bloomberg.com/news/features/2018-07-02/ inside-instagram-s-master-class-for-future-social-media-tycoons

Print Advertising

Print advertising media typically consist of newspapers and magazines. Advertising in print media requires a greater degree of involvement on the part of the consumer than in broadcast media. Readers choose what they want to read and then can spend as much time as they want reading it. This makes print advertising especially appealing for high-involvement (significant) consumer products, such as a house or a car.

Newspapers have been a valuable tool for marketers, especially retailers, for well over a century. Marketers spent over $8 billion in 2021 on newspaper advertising, although that number is less than a quarter of what it was in 2005.[18] As people increasingly move to resources other than newspapers for the daily news, though, marketers are likely to spend less on newspaper advertising.

In addition to newspapers, there are thousands of special-interest magazines in the United States and throughout the world, covering almost every possible subject or interest. Approximately half of all U.S. adults look through at least one magazine on a regular basis.[19] Marketers divide magazines into two categories: business magazines (e.g., *Bloomberg Businessweek, Fortune,* and *Money*) and consumer magazines (e.g., *People, Better Homes and Gardens,* and *Sports Illustrated*). Consumer magazines take a more general approach to subject matter than do business magazines, and thus have a wider audience.

Advantages of Print Advertising
Newspaper advertising has two major advantages. First, it is an effective way for small businesses to advertise their goods or services to the local community. Small-town newspapers or local community inserts in larger city (or even national) newspapers help marketers attract the local population that is most likely to buy their products. Grocery stores often run ads in local newspapers, highlighting current discounts or specials for that week in an effort to increase store traffic.

Second, firms can run their ads in a particular section of the newspaper if their business or product is specific to that section. For example, if you run a sporting-goods store, you might specify that your ad should appear in the paper's sports section; if you are a financial advisor, you can run your ad in the business section.

Magazine advertising enables marketers to target very specific audiences. Both business and consumer magazines allow firms to segment based on a variety of demographic, geographic, and behavioral variables. For example, *AARP Bulletin, Cosmopolitan,* and *Parenting* offer marketers the ability to reach very precise target markets with their ads. Fashion mags aimed at various income and age segments offer places to market clothes and makeup, as do magazines such as *Better Homes and Gardens* and *Martha Stuart Living,* aimed at lifestyle interests.

Magazine advertisements also have a longer shelf life than daily newspapers. Imagine that a consumer is traveling for the weekend and gets home to find three editions of the daily newspaper waiting; it's unlikely that he or she will read any of them. Compare that to readers of *Bloomberg Businessweek* who have a full week to read the content before a new issue arrives. Or think about the magazines you may have read while waiting at the dentist's office, which sometimes are months past their issue date.

Disadvantages of Print Advertising   The major disadvantage of print advertising is that fewer and fewer Americans use print as their primary information source. Younger consumers often receive news, entertainment, and employment information via computers and portable electronic devices. Even if they still rely on newspapers and magazines for information, they may choose to access the content online rather than buying the hard copy.

An additional disadvantage for newspaper advertising is that newspaper ads compete with other ads and editorial content for the consumer's attention. Firms with small or unimaginative ads risk the possibility that readers will pass over them completely while they engage with larger or more interesting graphics. Readers viewing multiple ads may also subconsciously spend less time on each individual ad.

Magazine advertising has several disadvantages as well, beginning with the lead time necessary to place an ad. The timeframe for designing a magazine forces marketers to plan and prepare advertisements months in advance of publication. As a result, the target audience might not see the ad until after the firm has committed the time and resources to the advertisement. If you own a small start-up business, the amount of time you spend waiting for your ad to bring in revenue could determine whether the business succeeds or fails. Beyond this, events may occur between when the ad is placed and when it is seen that limit the impact of the ad or affect the way readers perceive it.

In addition, marketers typically do not control where their advertisements are placed in relation to the features and stories contained in the publication. Effective placement of an ad is essential to its success or failure. An advertisement placed in the back of the magazine may not receive the same attention as those at the front.

Radio Advertising

There are thousands of radio stations in the United States, ranging from satellite radio stations that reach consumers across the country to local terrestrial stations that reach only small, rural communities. Radio advertising remains a powerful promotional tool because consumers can listen to the radio in their cars, online, and virtually anywhere else through their smartphones. Marketers spend approximately $27 billion per year on radio advertising.[20]

Advantages of Radio Advertising   Radio advertising has two major advantages. First, radio advertising is often the most cost-effective medium available. Buying radio ad time is far cheaper than buying television ad time. Also, the production costs of radio advertising are comparatively low, or even nonexistent if the ad is read live during a broadcast.

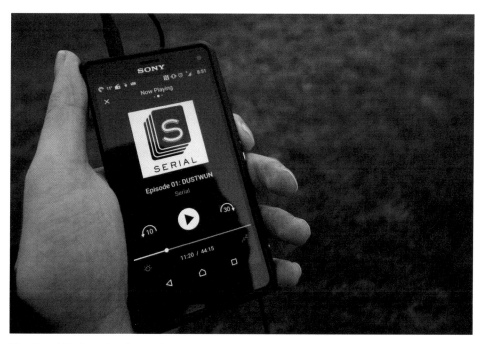

The Serial Podcast has been downloaded more than 250 million times and provides an example of the widespread use of podcasts which some consumers choose over traditional radio content.[21] *Hennell/Alamy Stock Photo*

A second advantage of radio advertising is that it allows marketers to segment effectively based on the geographic location and format of a radio station. The narrow transmission of terrestrial radio stations provides a great way to market to small geographic regions. Most regions of the country have radio stations that serve very small or rural communities. The local nature of radio makes it a perfect advertising medium for small merchants in the listening area. Marketers can also segment consumers by what they listen to: country, pop, gospel, hip-hop, heavy metal, sports talk, politics, and numerous other formats. Advertising on stations that cater to these different audiences is a form of narrowcasting that allows firms to target more effectively.

Disadvantages of Radio Advertising Traditionally, the biggest disadvantage of radio advertising has been that radio ads are audio-only. Being able to appeal to only one sense makes it difficult for companies to illustrate the uses and benefits of their products.

In recent years, technology advances have created several additional disadvantages for radio advertising. Most cars today have digital presets that allow listeners to switch stations when a commercial comes on simply by touching a button. For traditional music-based radio stations, the popularity of satellite radio represents an emerging challenge. Though satellite channels devoted to sports and news typically air ads, music stations on satellite radio are commercial-free. Finally, most new cars today come with the ability to plug in an MP3 player or smartphone. Over 50 percent of Americans listen to content on digital devices in their car; that number is expected to increase in the years ahead, making it harder for traditional radio advertising to reach these customers.[22]

In response to these challenges, firms like Subway are exploring creative ways to reach consumers listening to podcasts and other digital content. As another example, ticket search-engine SeatGeek partnered with Bill Simmons to sponsor his popular podcast, "The Bill Simmons Podcast." The podcast is free and averages millions of downloads per month.[23] Each podcast includes several mentions of SeatGeek products, allowing the firm to reach listeners of the show in a new way.

Outdoor Advertising

Outdoor advertising includes billboards, signs in sports arenas, skywriting, and ads on the sides of buildings, buses, and cars.

Advantages of Outdoor Advertising

Outdoor advertising has several advantages, including its flexibility and reduced costs, that are very appealing to marketers. Outdoor ads can be located where they will most likely be seen. For example, a company selling organic foods might advertise on a billboard near a farmer's market. A new college night club might advertise outside of a popular restaurant to target diners looking for a place to go later in the evening. These same ads, if placed in a newspaper or on the radio, may be missed altogether by the target market.

Tech companies like Facebook and Google generate billions of dollars in online advertising, but both companies spend part of their own marketing dollars on billboards and other forms of outdoor signage. In 2018, Facebook ran an outdoor campaign to promote its new approach to user safety and privacy. Music-streaming pioneer Spotify teamed up with the Brooklyn Museum to honor music legend David Bowie in subway advertising, and semiconductor maker Intel Corp. promoted its artificial-intelligence technology that's used to help find criminals in a crowd.[24]

Outdoor advertisements are also one of the most cost-efficient ways to reach potential customers and clients and are generally cheaper than television, print, or radio advertisements.[25]

Disadvantages of Outdoor Advertising

Outdoor advertising also has several disadvantages. First, because of the speed people travel in cars, the exposure time for outdoor ads is generally very short. This limits the number of words or images that firms can use effectively. Too much information on an outdoor ad can make it difficult to see, read, and understand in the limited amount of time consumers have as they walk or drive by.

The other major disadvantage is wasted coverage. While outdoor advertising allows companies to target specific areas, it is unlikely that everyone driving past an outdoor ad is part of the target market. An outdoor advertisement for a new local restaurant might look great, but its effect is wasted on those audiences who do not like the type of food or price range promoted.

Nontraditional Advertising

Business spending on traditional advertising like television, newspapers, and radio has been declining over the past decade. In that time, spending on nontraditional advertising has increased, as firms place messages on everything from valet tickets to hubcaps. For example, KFC used nontraditional advertising to help an Indiana town in need of new fire hydrants. The firm paid the town to place Fiery Grilled Wing ads on three hydrants, helping to offset the cost of the new hydrants. Nontraditional advertising encompasses some of the newest forms of advertising.

mobile advertising
Advertising that is communicated to the consumer via a handheld device.

A growing type of nontraditional advertising is **mobile advertising**, advertising that is communicated to the consumer via a handheld device. Over 75 percent of U.S. adults use smartphones, and most keep their devices within arm's reach for the majority of the day. Tech-savvy marketers can easily reach consumers at virtually any time.[26] Marketers spend over $70 billion each year on mobile advertising and new methods are emerging constantly as technology evolves.[27] We will discuss mobile advertising, including its advantages, disadvantages, and strategy, in greater detail in Chapter 13.

Another fast-growing area for advertisers is video games. More than half of Americans play video games, and marketers across industries are increasingly looking to reach

A tea and biscuit food truck in New York City is used to promote a new season of the popular series *Downton Abbey.* *Ben Hider/Getty Images*

these consumers.[28] The market for ads in video games globally is expected to grow from $4.0 billion in 2020 to almost $5.0 billion in 2024.[29] For example, the popular video game *FIFA International Soccer* prominently displays an Adidas ad on an onscreen billboard as users play. Video game advertising benefits from widespread Internet connectivity and larger bandwidth; both enable manufacturers to deliver advertisements remotely and update advertisements after the game is launched. In 2018, Google offered "rewarded ads" where a video game player's character dies on the game followed by the game asking the user to watch a short video ad in return for an extra life. That's actually a feature of Google's AdMob advertising service, and today it's extending this with playable ads, a new type of ad that fits far better into a game.[30] By giving players the choice to see the ad, advertisers can maximize brand recall and brand affinity throughout the game. For example, a fashion brand like J.Crew could implement an opt-in video showcasing its summer collection and reward the interested viewer with in-game currency or bespoke perks for watching the ad, creating a positive brand association.[31]

As consumer behavior continues to evolve, firms will turn more and more to nontraditional advertising at the expense of traditional advertising. Marketers must be on the lookout for new and better ways to get their message in front of their target consumers.

Mc Graw Hill connect Exercise **8-2**

Please complete the *Connect* exercise for Chapter 8 that focuses on the advantages and disadvantages of different advertising media. By understanding the benefits and challenges of each form of advertising, you will be able to choose the appropriate advertising media to successfully execute your organization's marketing strategy.

LO 8-3

Summarize the various types of sales promotion.

sales promotion

A set of nonpersonal communication tools designed to stimulate quicker and more frequent purchases of a product.

SALES PROMOTION

Sales promotion activities account for the bulk of most firms' promotion budgets. **Sales promotion** is a set of nonpersonal communication tools designed to stimulate quicker and more frequent purchases of a product. Firms often use sales promotion to support the other elements of their promotion mix. For example, McDonald's implemented a sales promotion in which young customers received plastic figures of the characters from the *Ralph Breaks the Internet* movie in their Happy Meals. The promotion prompted more consumers to buy Happy Meals in an effort to add cars with Vanellope, Felix, and other characters from the movie to their collections.

Successful sales promotions have the potential to build short-term excitement and long-term customer relationships simultaneously. We'll discuss some common sales promotions in the sections that follow.

coupons

Documents that entitle the customers who carry them to a discount on a product.

Coupons

Coupons remain the most common type of sales promotion. **Coupons** are documents that entitle the customers who carry them to a discount on a product or service. Traditionally, coupons have come in the form of printed vouchers that customers present to claim their discount.

However, the expansion of mobile advertising is changing the form and use of coupons: Websites like RetailMeNot have enabled companies to distribute coupons digitally to a smartphone device; the targeted consumer can then redeem the coupon directly from that device at a specific business. During the 2018 holiday season, Burger King offered a coupon for customers to purchase a 1 cent Whopper through its BK app. The BK app unlocked the coupon once customers got within 600 feet of a McDonald's. Orders had to be picked up from the nearest Burger King within one hour as part of its "Whopper Detour" sales promotion.[32]

Coupons provide firms with an effective method for stimulating sales and encouraging customers to make additional or repeat purchases. In addition, a firm can control the timing and distribution of coupons in a way that does not dilute potential revenue from a customer who is happy paying full price.

Coupons, whether in traditional or electronic form, for products such as cosmetics, hair care, and diapers continue to be in demand. *iPhone/Alamy Stock Photo*

However, coupons also have several disadvantages. Coupon fraud is a serious problem in the form of *misredemption* practices. Misredemptions can range from illegal copying of coupons by the consumer to innocent mistakes by an employee who gives too large a discount or forgets to take the coupon from the customer after the purchase. All misredemptions have the effect of reducing the firm's profitability. Care must be taken to anticipate and discourage such practices.

Rebates

rebates

Sales promotions that allow consumers to recoup a specified amount of money after making a single purchase; most rebates require consumers to mail their receipt and proof of purchase to manufacturers.

Many promotional strategies make use of rebates. **Rebates** allow consumers to recoup a specified amount of money after making a single purchase. Most rebates require customers to mail their receipt and proof of purchase to manufacturers. Marketing professionals offer over 400 million rebates each year.[33] Statistics show, though, that between 40 and 60 percent of all rebates are not redeemed.[34]

Most customers prefer coupons because they're easier to use, but most marketers prefer rebates. Rebates provide the incentive of a price decrease, but because customers often fail to redeem them, the firm typically earns greater profits than it would by issuing coupons. Rebates work most effectively when offered in conjunction with a high-involvement purchase in which the perceived value of the rebate is magnified. A $200 rebate for a flat-screen television or a $2,000 rebate for a new car typically generates more purchases than small rebates for everyday items that consumers tend to forget about.

Samples

Samples offer potential consumers the chance to actually try the product. They have been an effective sales promotion tool for decades. Sampling includes everything from trying a new type of sausage at your local grocery store or Costco to getting a free weekend of HBO's TV programming.

Samples can be expensive because marketers are giving away products in many cases. However, they can also be a powerful tool for getting customers to actually buy the product. Marketers of baby formula, for example, often send samples to new parents in the hope that the family will like it and start using that brand of formula during the child's first years of life.

Contests and Sweepstakes

Firms spend approximately $2 billion per year on contests and sweepstakes. The terms *contest* and *sweepstakes* are often used interchangeably, but there is a distinct difference between the two:

- **Contests** are sales promotions in which consumers compete against one another and must demonstrate skill to win. Contests provide marketers with a way to engage consumers and empower them to promote an organization's products and brand. For example, Oreo sponsored an "Oreo and Milk Jingle" video contest that offered cash prizes and trips to the group who did the best job designing and singing the "Oreo and Milk" jingle.[35]

- **Sweepstakes** are sales promotions based on chance. The only requirement to win is that you enter. Every entry has an equal chance of being drawn as the winner. An example of sweepstakes includes the HGTV Dream Home Giveaway, in which HGTV randomly selected a viewer to win $500,000 and a cottage in Hawaii.[36] Sweepstakes have the advantage of creating interest and excitement from a broad group of consumers. The HGTV sweepstakes also helped bring the network to a wider audience.

contests
Sales promotions in which consumers compete against one another and must demonstrate skill to win.

sweepstakes
Sales promotions based on chance such that entry is the only requirement to win.

Contests and sweepstakes do have some disadvantages. Contests can be expensive to administer. Because each entry must be judged, firms can't rely on random selection. A potential disadvantage of sweepstakes is the legal and regulatory issues that can arise. Publishers Clearing House was fined millions of dollars to resolve allegations that it misled the public in its advertising campaign portraying average Americans winning millions of dollars by participating in the company's well-known sweepstakes. Multiple federal and state government agencies monitor contests and sweepstakes to make sure they are fair and properly represented to the public.

Premiums

A **premium** is a promotional item that is given as an incentive for performing a particular act, typically buying a product. Premiums can come in a variety of forms including toys, collectibles, and souvenirs. Examples of premiums include receiving a prize in a

premium
A promotional item that is given as an incentive for performing a particular act, typically buying a product.

IHG Rewards Club and other loyalty programs help companies retain customers even in the face of fierce competition and a decrease in the natural loyalty customers feel toward firms and products. *Stephen Barnes/Travel/Alamy Stock Photo*

loyalty programs

Sales promotions that allow consumers to accumulate points or other benefits for doing business with the same company.

trade sales promotions

Sales promotions directed to B2B firms, including wholesalers, retailers, and distributors, rather than individual consumers.

allowances

Trade promotions that typically involve paying retailers for financial losses associated with consumer sales promotions or reimbursing a retailer for an in-store or local expense to promote a specific product.

children's meal or a free garden tool for visiting the grand opening of a hardware store. In 2018, Kellogg's used premiums when it offered special edition cereal boxes from the movie *Jurassic World: Fallen Kingdom* that featured branded content including art and images from the film, an embedded screen that plays more than five minutes of behind-the-scenes content, free movie tickets, and *Jurassic World*–themed ice pop molds. The premiums encouraged fans of the popular movie to eat Frosted Flakes more frequently so they could collect the entire set.[37]

Loyalty Programs

Designed to strengthen customer relationships, **loyalty programs** allow consumers to accumulate points or other benefits for doing business with the same company. Loyalty programs are especially popular in the airline and hotel businesses. Holiday Inn, for example, has had success with its Priority Club loyalty-rewards program. Global membership in this loyalty club has reached over 65 million, and members are rewarded with points that increase more rapidly the more often they stay at a Holiday Inn hotel.[38] The points can then be turned into free hotel stays, gift cards, and even charitable contributions.

Loyalty programs have grown in importance as natural loyalty to products has decreased in many industries. Increasingly, consumers view things like flights to Boston or hotel rooms in Chicago as commodities, and they make the decision about which company to buy from based solely on price. Loyalty programs offer incentives that encourage satisfied consumers to go out of their way to fly Delta Air Lines or stay at a Holiday Inn in an effort to receive additional rewards.

Trade Sales Promotions

The sales promotion tools discussed up to this point are often directed to individual consumers. **Trade sales promotions** are promotion tools directed to B2B firms, including wholesalers and retailers, rather than to individual consumers. Trade sales promotions often include the same tools discussed earlier (coupons, rebates, contests and sweepstakes, and loyalty programs), plus three other major approaches:

1. *Trade shows.* A *trade show* is an event at which organizations in a specific industry promote their offerings to firms they hope will buy them. Marketers use trade shows to identify potential customers, inform current customers about new and existing products, and demonstrate products and materials. For example, the International Pizza Expo in Las Vegas allows firms a single place to promote equipment and supplies to owners and managers of pizza restaurants across the globe.

2. *Allowances.* **Allowances** typically involve paying retailers for financial losses associated with consumer sales promotions or reimbursing a retailer for an in-store or local expense to promote a specific product. For example, a local grocery store might be reimbursed for a radio ad that mentions that Diet Dr Pepper is on sale over the next few days. Typically, the firm will pay the retailer only after it has proof of the financial loss or local promotion costs.

3. *Training.* The other major trade sale promotion is training the reseller's sales force. Training activities such as brochures or on-site demonstrations help retail

and wholesale personnel understand the product's benefits. This in turn makes the resellers better equipped to speak with consumers and sell the firm's products. Training also helps ensure that employees at every level understand the features, advantages, and benefits of the products they are trying to sell.

PERSONAL SELLING

Personal selling takes many forms. It can include someone trying to sell you insurance as an individual. It can include someone selling business software that will be used in each of your firm's stores. It can even take the form of the person behind the fast-food counter trying to get you to upsize your order. **Personal selling** is the *two-way* flow of communication between a buyer and a seller that is paid for by the seller and seeks to influence the buyer's purchase decision.

Personal selling differs from the other tools of the promotion mix because messages flow directly from the salesperson to the customer, often face-to-face. Despite economic and technological changes, the role of personal selling is more important today than ever before. Salespeople often serve as the critical link between the firm and the customer. They are the eyes and ears of the organization and help marketers understand what customers like and dislike and what changes are happening within an industry.

A major challenge of personal selling is the cost involved. The average cost of a sales call varies across industries, but almost always averages several hundred dollars per visit.[39] The costs are even higher when you consider that, for most products, one sales call will not result directly in an order.

Historically, the other challenge for personal selling has been ensuring that each salesperson communicates a message that is consistent with other salespeople as well as the full integrated marketing communications strategy. Inconsistent messaging is the equivalent of a firm having as many marketing strategies as it does salespeople. Firms can overcome this challenge by offering information and training to the sales force.

While personal selling is one of the most expensive elements of the promotion mix, it offers two unique advantages over the other promotional elements:

1. Personal selling results in immediate feedback from the customer. Perhaps most importantly, the salesperson can see the nonverbal communication that might give insight into the customer's mindset and the likelihood that he or she will buy. In addition, the salesperson can listen directly to the customer's feedback, objections, and concerns. This allows the salesperson to adjust the sales presentation accordingly and provide detailed and customized solutions that can generate more sales.
2. Personal selling allows the firm to develop a personal relationship with the customer. **Relationship selling** is a sales approach that involves building and maintaining customer trust over a long period of time. Relationship selling is increasingly important; very few firms can survive on the profits generated from one-time transactional sales.

Because of the importance of personal selling in both B2C and B2B settings, we have devoted an entire separate chapter to the topic (Chapter 12). There, you will find detailed discussion of the personal selling process and strategies for sales success.

LO 8-4

Explain the importance of personal selling.

personal selling

The two-way flow of communication between a salesperson and a customer that is paid for by the firm and seeks to influence the customer's purchase decision.

relationship selling

A sales approach that involves building and maintaining customer trust over a long period of time.

Anderson Childress

Executive Perspective...
because everyone is a marketer

Anderson Childress
Treasury Manager
PayPal

From a sales perspective, what do you think is most important to communicate to your customers?

PayPal is a payments company that has a significant global presence. Understanding the importance of this, we as a company have communicated our commitment to our customers that they are our upmost priority. When the public hears the name PayPal, we want them to associate us with security, reliability, and trust.

LO 8-5

PUBLIC RELATIONS

Describe the role of public relations within the promotion mix.

Public relations strategies provide information and build a firm's image with the public, including customers, employees, stockholders, and communities. **Public relations** is nonpersonal communication focused on promoting positive relations between a firm and its stakeholders.

public relations

Nonpersonal communication focused on promoting positive relations between a firm and its stakeholders.

Public Relations Tools

Organizations use a variety of tools for public relations, including the following:

- *Annual reports* provide a forum for the organization to share with its stakeholders what it has achieved over the past year. They present the firm with an opportunity to highlight financial successes as well as charitable and philanthropic work that portray the organization in a positive light.
- *Speeches* provide an avenue for members of an organization to market their message directly to a group in a longer form speech. These speeches, usually given by key members of the organization, can generate positive press and help to develop relationships with stakeholders and the public at large.
- *Blogs* are an emerging social media tool through which individuals can share their thoughts and knowledge with the public. Blogs can be a mix of insights, humor, or other personal interests. They have become increasingly popular with marketers focused on public relations. Established industry executives such as Bill Gates and Reid Hoffman also make use of blogs. An executive at an organization of any size who blogs consistently and well can build goodwill for the company they lead.
- *Brochures* typically are intended to inform and/or engage the public. A modern public relations brochure can be on paper or online. It provides a forum for educating the public about a firm, its mission, or a specific cause. Brochures often present information similar to that found in an annual report, but in a shorter, more accessible way. Marketers should ensure that the brochure contains useful information, is visually engaging, and is consistent with the rest of the company's promotion-mix elements.
- *Media kits* are typically a package of information provided to reporters and the general press. They often promote a new product or promotion. They can contain product samples, press releases, answers to frequently asked questions, and contact information for reporters who want to interview someone within the organization. Media kits can reduce or eliminate the need for employees of an organization to continually answer the same questions over and over.
- *Sponsorships* involve an organization paying to have its name associated with projects, programs, or facilities. Examples include M&M's sponsorship of the Special Olympics or Oracle's sponsorship of the arena where the Golden State Warriors play their home games. In 2018, Elk Grove Village paid $300,000 to attach its marketing slogan "Makers Wanted" as the sponsor of a college football bowl game. The goal would be to utilize the Makers Wanted Bahamas Bowl sponsorship to raise awareness nationally and attract manufacturers to its industrial park next to O'Hare International Airport.[40] Even though sponsorships are expensive,

Elk Grove Village sponsored the Bahamas Bowl College Football game with the goal of raising awareness for its industrial park near Chicago. *Bahamas Bowl*

The sports-entertainment company WWE has received positive publicity for its charitable work, including its partnership with the Make-A-Wish foundation. During the foundation's World Wish Day initiative, WWE superstar John Cena agreed to personally match every frequent-flier mile donated to help reduce travel expenses for the organization so that it can grant more wishes. *John Carucci/AP Images*

they are growing in popularity as organizations seek ways to strengthen their corporate image and reach their target markets.

- *Event marketing* involves developing a themed exhibit, display, or presentation to promote an organization to its target market. Macy's Thanksgiving Day parade has become an annual tradition to many consumers and an effective way to introduce the brand to new consumers.

Each of these public relations tools promotes a positive image and serves as a way to educate stakeholders about company developments.

Another public relations tool is publicity. **Publicity** involves disseminating unpaid news items through some form of media (e.g., a television story or on Instagram) to gain attention or support. The major advantage of publicity is that, when done well, it allows marketers to communicate with consumers at an extremely low cost. During the most recent economic recession, firms often used publicity as a way to lower the cost of their public relations efforts.

The major disadvantage of publicity is that organizations have less control over how the information is presented because they don't pay for it. Bad publicity and negative news can harm an organization's reputation and image.

publicity
Disseminating unpaid news items through some form of media (e.g., television story, newspaper article, etc.) to gain attention or support.

The Impact of Social Media on Public Relations

Social media have revolutionized the way companies present themselves to the public. Social media have increased the speed at which marketers, politicians, athletes, and virtually anyone can get direct contact with their target audience very quickly. Social media platforms ranging from Facebook to Twitter to Instagram allow marketers and organizations to tell their story and promote positive relationships with their stakeholders.

Case studies are a powerful PR tool that marketers can maximize using social media. Organizations can quickly and cost-efficiently provide engaging content about the impact of their goods and services on customers to the people who are most engaged in the brand. For example, Microsoft used social media to share a video telling the story about how its technology helped Sarah Churman hear for the first time. This powerful case study resonated with Microsoft's Facebook and Twitter followers who then shared the story with thousands of their friends. The case study ultimately led to over 25 million views on social media, extending the positive message to potentially new and previously unreached customers.[41]

Since marketers face the challenge of dealing with positive as well as negative publicity, monitoring social media is essential. Organizations in various industries sometimes have failed to respond to negative feedback they were receiving from customers via social media sites. That failure allowed the negative buzz to spread and be shared with friends and followers, potentially harming the company's reputation.

Crisis Management

Public relations can be especially important when an organization faces a crisis. BP's response after the 2010 oil spill in the Gulf of Mexico is an example: The company filled its website with the typical press releases and financial statements you would expect to see on a corporate site. It posted technical briefings with BP officials and maps and charts detailing the company's efforts to contain the leak. BP also produced and posted short films featuring BP officials, representatives of government agencies, and area residents helping in the Gulf cleanup effort. In addition, the company publicized other positive actions it was taking, such as donating $1 million to help a food bank feed people whose incomes were negatively impacted by the spill[42] and actively hiring laid-off workers to clean beaches and animals contaminated with oil. Finally, BP gave the Gulf States money to promote the region's seafood industry in an effort to improve economic conditions in the area.

It is essential that marketers communicate to their stakeholders via social media as quickly as possible when a crisis occurs. Organizations that try to cover up or delay informing stakeholders about the crisis are generally criticized afterward on social media more for their delay than for the incident itself. When Sony lost 77 million credit card details, it was the delay in informing the public that caused the most public relations damage.

It's safe to say that no company *wants* to use public relations for crisis management, but it needs to have access to marketers who know how to do so if the occasion arises.

As part of its crisis management strategy following the oil spill in the Gulf of Mexico, BP posted to its website videos and briefings about cleanup and response efforts to help mitigate the effects of the negative publicity it received. *Maurice Savage/Alamy Stock Photo*

The Changing Face of Public Relations

Public relations today is a 24-hours-a-day, 7-days-a-week job for marketers across for-profit industries, government entities, and nonprofit organizations. Advances in technology cause information to spread faster than ever before and amplify the influence of that information on potential customers.

Marketers should use all of the tools discussed, including social media, to make sure the public perceives the company in the most positive way possible. A simple truth in marketing is that people want to do business with organizations they like and respect. Effective marketers will share the organization's actions with the public in a way that entices customers to buy a product, give money to a charitable organization, or support a specific person or idea.

PROMOTIONAL METRICS

Because promotion is such a big part of an organization's budget, it is essential that marketers measure the effectiveness of the promotional strategy. Almost every organization, ranging from large for-profit businesses to small, local nonprofits, uses some form of advertising and social media. In this section, we'll examine metrics that measure the success of those two forms of promotion.

Measuring Advertising Effectiveness

Companies typically measure the effectiveness of advertising before and after an advertising campaign to understand its impact. To do so:

- Marketers typically conduct a **pretest** in which a sample of targeted consumers evaluates advertisements before an ad campaign begins. Pretests help set a baseline measure for marketers, against which to evaluate the subsequent campaign.
- After the ad campaign, marketers conduct a **posttest**, an evaluation after the campaign of the ads by the same targeted segment of consumers.

Together, these two measures help the firm gauge the ad campaign's success.

What gets measured in the pretests and posttests? Companies often measure print and digital advertising based on whether consumers see the ads and how well they *recognize and remember* them. A **recognition test** involves showing consumers the print advertisement and asking if they recognize the ad. While recognition tests can help the firm determine whether its ad has caught the attention of the target market, recognition alone may not prompt consumers to buy a product.

Marketing professionals often go a step further and assess what consumers recall about an advertisement, using either unaided or aided recall tests. **Unaided recall tests** require consumers to recall ads from memory, without any clues. In **aided recall tests**, respondents receive clues to help stimulate their memory. If consumers don't recognize or recall the firm's print advertisements, marketers may change the size or message of the ad or deliver it through an alternative medium.

Marketers also measure *how many* consumers have been exposed to their various promotional efforts. **Reach** is the percentage of the target market that has been exposed to a promotional message at least once during a specific time period. A prime example is the Super Bowl, which serves as a powerful tool to increase reach. The game typically garners the highest ratings of any television program of the year. It is one of the few televised events during which viewers *actively* watch the commercials. In an attempt to reach as many people as possible, marketers in 2022 paid $7 million per 30-second commercial to advertise during the Super Bowl.[43]

Unfortunately, no matter how effective a single advertisement might be, it generally takes multiple exposures to move a consumer to make a purchase or change their buying habits in some way. Therefore, marketers seek to increase both the reach and the frequency of their promotional exposure to their target market. **Frequency** measures how often the audience is exposed to a promotional message during a specific time period.

An old adage remains true in marketing today: A person has to hear something multiple times to remember it. Imagine that you sell golf equipment and have a $100,000

pretest

An evaluation of advertisements by a sample of targeted consumers before an ad campaign begins.

LO 8-6

Describe metrics that measure the effectiveness of an organization's promotional strategy.

marketing analytics

posttest

An evaluation of advertisements after the ad campaign is launched by a sample of targeted consumers.

recognition test

A performance metric that involves showing consumers an advertisement and asking if they recognize it.

unaided recall test

A performance metric that requires consumers to recall advertisements from memory, without any clues.

aided recall test

A performance metric in which respondents are asked to recall advertisements based on clues they receive to help stimulate their memory.

reach

A measure of the percentage of the target market that has been exposed to a promotional message at least once during a specific time period.

frequency

A measure of how often the target market has been exposed to a promotional message during a specific time period.

television advertising budget. If you choose to advertise on ESPN (the largest sports cable network in the United States), you might be able to run approximately five commercials for that investment. Or, you could choose to take those same dollars and advertise on the Golf Channel, where you could run dozens of commercials for less than the price of five ads on ESPN. While the Golf Channel has lower average viewership ratings than ESPN, the frequency of your target market's exposure to the ad may outweigh its limited reach.

revenue per ad dollar

A performance metric that is calculated by comparing total revenue to the amount of money spent on advertising.

This strategy of cultivating high-frequency advertising at a low cost can improve **revenue per ad dollar**. That metric is calculated by comparing total revenue to the amount of money spent on advertising. If your strategy of running ads on the Golf Channel increases revenue for your golf products without your having to increase your advertising budget, you have increased your revenue per ad dollar.

Companies should also explore the use of *qualitative research tools* as a way of understanding the effectiveness of their advertising, public relations, and other promotional programs. Techniques like focus groups and consumer interviews often generate in-depth responses. These responses give marketers insight into consumers' subtle likes and dislikes and can be valuable as the firm refines its promotion message.

Measuring Social Media Effectiveness

Companies also want to measure the effectiveness of their investments in social media. Marketers use a variety of tools to evaluate the success of their social media marketing strategies and guide their decisions going forward. Key tools for measuring the effectiveness of social media are the following:

1. *Google Analytics.* Google has a comprehensive analytics service that helps track user activity on an organization's website in real time. A company can set up Google Analytics quickly and easily. The service then provides a variety of useful data, including the number of daily visits to the company's site, the demographics of its users, how users got to the site, how long they stayed, and the relative popularity of each piece of content on the site.
2. *Kred.* Kred measures both social influence and outreach, providing a score for each on a user's profile. For influence, it works primarily by measuring retweets, replies, mentions, and follows on Twitter. Outreach is a cumulative score based on how often users retweet, reply, share, and mention other people. Each social action by users or their followers results in a certain number of points, and there is an activity page where they can see exactly what has contributed to their Kred score, making it very transparent for marketers.
3. *Buzzsumo.* Buzzsumo is an excellent way to analyze and monitor Facebook pages. Along with metrics around each individual post, users have the ability to see what content performs best. Buzzsumo can tell marketers what day is the best to post, how long their posts should be, what types of content works best, and monthly metrics over time.

LO 8-7

Summarize the promotion-mix budgeting strategies.

PROMOTION-MIX BUDGETING STRATEGIES

Determining the appropriate promotion budget is an important decision within any marketing strategy. Firms that set the budget too low risk blending into the competition and are often ineffective in communicating value to potential customers. Firms that set the budget too high open themselves up to waste and lower profits.

Promotion-budget decisions should consider a variety of factors, such as the types of products sold by the firm, the geographic location of the firm's customers, and the level of competition in the industry. Firms typically determine their promotion budget using one of three methods: the affordable method, the percentage-of-sales method, or the objective-and-task method.

Affordable Method

Firms that use the **affordable method** set their promotion budget based on what they believe they can afford. The affordable method is a top-down approach that is particularly common in small businesses. It also can occur in firms of any size when a firm does not view promotional strategies as an investment. The affordable method is simple and fiscally conservative, but offers no other benefits for the organization.

A major disadvantage of the affordable method is that it is not tied to specific organizational objectives. Firms that allocate a random dollar amount to the promotion mix guarantee virtually nothing except that the money will be spent. There are countless stories of marketing departments spending money on promotion at the end of the fiscal year simply because it was there to spend. Since the promotion budget is not tied to specific organizational objectives in this approach, it tends to be allocated haphazardly with no real focus on what the promotional strategies should achieve.

affordable method
A promotion-mix budgeting strategy in which firms set their promotion budget based on what they believe they can afford.

Percentage-of-Sales Method

One of the most widely used budgeting approaches is the percentage-of-sales method. Companies that use the **percentage-of-sales method** allocate a specific percentage of a previous period's sales or an upcoming period's forecasted sales to the promotion budget for that period. The method has the advantage of being simple because the promotion budget increases at the same rate that firm sales increase.

The primary disadvantage of the percentage-of-sales method arises when a firm's sales decline. Imagine that you own a car dealership and that your sales have declined 30 percent over the past year. You attribute that sales decrease to increased competition and economic concerns. It's not necessarily the case that your best promotional strategy for the following year is to reduce promotional expenditures by 30 percent. Quiznos, for example, saw its total sales decline by more than 50 percent between 2007 and 2011 as the company lost market share to competitors like Subway; it ultimately filed for bankruptcy protection in 2014.[44] Quiznos marketers realized that reducing the promotion budget by more than half to match sales would not help turn around their revenue or market-share numbers. After being purchased in 2018, Quiznos embarked on a new promotional campaign, allocating significant resources to advertising and sales promotion including offering participants in its Toasty Points program a 20 percent discount on Black Friday for orders placed remotely through the sandwich chain's app.[45]

percentage-of-sales method
A promotion-mix budgeting strategy in which firms allocate a specific percentage of a period's sales to the promotion budget for that period.

Objective-and-Task Method

The objective-and-task approach is typically considered the best of the budgeting methods. It incorporates many of the strengths of the other budgeting methods without having their weaknesses. The **objective-and-task method** takes a bottom-up approach to promotional budgeting: It defines specific objectives, determines the tasks required to achieve those objectives, and then estimates how much each task will cost. By focusing on what the organization wants to achieve, the marketing department invests each dollar in the specific promotion-mix elements that best deliver on those objectives.

objective-and-task method
A promotion-mix budgeting strategy in which a firm defines specific objectives, determines the tasks required to achieve those objectives, and then estimates how much each task will cost.

Hope Sparks

VIP Owner Concierge
Vistana Signature Experiences

Describe your job. I work for Marriott Vacations Worldwide at a resort in the vacation ownership segment. I am a VIP Owner Concierge, and I work directly with owners during pre-arrival and their stay at the resort. Every two weeks, I am assigned a list of leads who will be arriving to the property. I contact them pre-arrival, retrieve all of their villa requests, estimated arrival time, number of room keys, need for tickets and attractions—all to ensure they have a smooth check-in at the resort. The selected owner arrivals are considered VIP and receive a separate check-in area on the property, with complimentary refreshments while they wait for their unit to be ready. Upon check-in, I go over their requests and, if we are able to accommodate them, go over property details and surrounding attraction information and make them feel at "home." Although this seems easy, my job is very challenging, and customer service is key to building trust with the owners and setting up a presentation for them.

Photo provided by Hope Sparks

How did you get your job? A guest speaker came to visit with my marketing class about her career and how college had set her up for success. She helped me get a few interviews with the company, and I was hired for an entry-level guest service position. Shortly after, I moved into the sales and marketing role at one of the resorts. After a few years, I decided it was time for me to grow in my career, and my manager told me about this amazing company and position that was about to open. I interviewed with my current company, and management loved my personality and experience and thought I would be a great fit for this role. In return, I was excited to have a role where I go above and beyond for the guests and, in return, help drive the vacation ownership industry from the frontline.

What has been the most important thing in making you successful at your job? The most important thing that has made me successful at my job is keeping a positive mindset.

In any customer service role, you have a lot of different personalities to deal with and very challenging situations to handle. Also, my position is performance-based, meaning if you do not perform and meet monthly standards and capture rates, you will not keep your job long. You need to provide the best customer service but also be strong and persuasive, like in any sales role. After every "no" you will finally hear that "yes," and finding the stamina to keep a positive mind is critical. I was raised being taught to always look for the best in everything. I think that is the best way to keep yourself focused on your end goal, and knowing you win some and you lose some.

What advice would you give soon-to-be graduates? My advice to soon-to-be graduates is work hard, love what you do, and do it well. Nine times out of 10, if you are passionate about what you do, then it's not a "job." Do not rush into to a position because it is expected of you. Your parents, grandparents, teachers, or anyone else are not the ones that have to show up every day—it's your life and your happiness. Through hard work and desire, you will achieve success. And please . . . VACATION! Not just because I work for a company that sells the dream; you have to take time off to give your mind, body, and spirit a break. This is one of the driving factors of health and stability in any industry.

What do you consider your personal brand to be? I think I was asked this during college and it has really stuck with me over the past few years. I am a people person—people are my passion. I think this is what has drawn me to this industry. My whole life I have spent time being a friend to those in need, volunteering and helping others, calming people when things do not go the way they want, and being a positive light to others. I am outgoing and personable and people trust me. If I can rub off a little "spark" onto someone else and turn around their perspective, I feel like I have made some kind of impact on the world.

The only major disadvantage of this method is the time and judgment required to decide on the required tasks. However, firms should consider this time an investment: It leads marketers to allocate resources in the best possible way to achieve the desired results.

McGraw Hill connect Exercise 8-3

Please complete the *Connect* exercise for Chapter 8 that focuses on the different promotion-mix budgeting strategies. By identifying the rationale and benefit of each, you will understand which one is an appropriate budgeting strategy for your organization and how each will affect the success of your promotional strategy.

SUMMARY

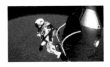

Abaca Press/Alamy Stock Photo

LO 8-1 Describe the elements of the promotion mix and how they relate to an integrated marketing communications strategy.

Promotion is all the activities that communicate the value of a product and persuade customers to buy it. The promotion mix is a subset of the marketing mix. It includes four main types of marketing communication: advertising, sales promotion, personal selling, and public relations. An integrated marketing communications (IMC) strategy involves coordinating the various promotion-mix elements. Many firms have adopted the IMC perspective in an effort to provide consumers with a clear and consistent message about their products.

TCD/Prod.DB/Alamy Stock Photo

LO 8-2 Compare the advantages and disadvantages of different types of advertising.

Advertising is nonpersonal communication about goods, services, or ideas that is paid for by an identified sponsor. Advertising comes in various forms, each of which has its own advantages and disadvantages: *Television advertising* provides marketers with an opportunity to target specific markets as well as to combine sight, sound, and motion to appeal to consumer senses. *Internet advertising* is the fastest-growing type and holds the most promise for future innovation. Although it's losing ground to other forms, *print advertising* continues to offer marketers the ability to reach local and narrowly segmented audiences. *Radio advertising* is often the most cost-effective medium available to an advertiser. *Outdoor advertising* is flexible and relatively inexpensive but doesn't always reach the target market effectively. *Nontraditional advertising*, which includes ads on everything from valet tickets to hubcaps, can attract consumer attention in a way traditional advertising no longer does.

iPhone/Alamy Stock Photo

LO 8-3 Summarize the various types of sales promotion.

Sales promotion is a set of nonpersonal communication tools, including coupons, rebates, contests, sweepstakes, and loyalty programs, designed to stimulate quicker and more frequent purchases of a product. Trade sales promotions are promotion tools directed to B2B firms—wholesalers, retailers, and distributors—rather than individual consumers. Unique trade sales promotions include allowances and training. Most firms use sales promotion tools to support their advertising, public relations, and personal selling activities.

LO 8-4 Explain the importance of personal selling.

Personal selling is the two-way flow of communication between a salesperson and a customer that is paid for by the firm and seeks to influence the customer's purchase decision. Salespeople often serve as the link between the firm and the consumer. A major challenge of personal selling is the cost involved. However, it provides the firm with immediate feedback from the market and allows the firm to develop a personal relationship with the customer. Relationship selling is increasingly important as very few firms can survive on the profits generated from one-time transactional sales.

John Carucci/AP Images

LO 8-5 Describe the role of public relations within the promotion mix.

Public relations is nonpersonal communication focused on promoting positive relations between a firm and its stakeholders.

Organizations use a variety of tools for public relations, including annual reports, speeches, blogs, brochures, and media kits. Publicity involves disseminating unpaid news items through some form of media (e.g., television story or Instagram story). When done well, public relations allows marketers to communicate with consumers at an extremely low cost.

LO 8-6 Describe metrics that measure the effectiveness of an organization's promotional strategy.

It is essential that marketers measure the effectiveness of their promotional strategy. Metrics that measure the success of advertising and social media are particularly relevant because almost every organization uses those two forms of promotion. Marketers measure *how many* consumers have been exposed to their various promotional efforts. *Reach* measures the percentage of the target market that has been exposed to a promotional message at least once during a specific time period. *Frequency* measures how often the audience is exposed to a promotional message during a specific time period. *Revenue per ad dollar*, calculated by comparing total revenue to the amount of money spent on advertising, measures the cost-effectiveness of the promotional strategy. Three key tools with which to evaluate the effectiveness of social media marketing strategies are Google Analytics, Kred, and Buzzsumo.

LO 8-7 Summarize the promotion-mix budgeting strategies.

Promotion budget decisions should consider a variety of factors, including the types of products sold by the firm, the geographic location of the firm's customers, and the level of competition in the industry. Firms typically determine their promotion budget using one of three methods: Firms using the *affordable method* set their promotion budget based on what they believe they can afford. The *percentage-of-sales method* allocates a specific percentage of a period's total sales for the promotion budget for that period. It is the most widely used approach. The *objective-and-task method* defines specific objectives, determines the tasks required to achieve those objectives, and then estimates how much each task will cost.

KEY TERMS

advertising (p. 258)
advertising campaign (p. 258)
affordable method (p. 277)
aided recall test (p. 275)
allowances (p. 270)
contests (p. 269)
coupons (p. 268)
direct marketing (p. 262)
frequency (p. 275)
informative advertising (p. 258)
integrated marketing communications
    (IMC) (p. 257)
loyalty programs (p. 270)

mobile advertising (p. 266)
narrowcasting (p. 260)
objective-and-task method (p. 277)
percentage-of-sales method (p. 277)
personal selling (p. 271)
persuasive advertising (p. 258)
posttest (p. 275)
premium (p. 269)
pretest (p. 275)
product placement (p. 261)
promotion (p. 256)
promotion mix (p. 256)
public relations (p. 272)

publicity (p. 273)
reach (p. 275)
rebates (p. 268)
recognition test (p. 275)
relationship selling (p. 271)
reminder advertising (p. 259)
revenue per ad dollar (p. 276)
sales promotion (p. 268)
sweepstakes (p. 269)
trade sales promotions (p. 270)
unaided recall test (p. 275)

MARKETING PLAN EXERCISE • Marketing Yourself

The marketing plan exercise for this chapter focuses on developing your own promotional strategy. You can think about this using the same four promotion-mix elements discussed in this chapter: advertising, sales promotion, personal selling, and public relations.

First, how are you advertising yourself? For example, what does your resume look like? What does it say about

you? If your resume is the same basic template that looks just like everyone else's, how will you stand out from others competing for the same job? Please read the *Career Tips* at the end of this chapter for suggestions.

Also consider what your social media profile says about you. If prospective employers were to look at your Facebook, LinkedIn, or Twitter profile, would they like what they saw? Would it reflect the image of a thoughtful, driven professional?

Next, consider using a sales promotion tool such as sampling. Unpaid internships give firms an opportunity to sample your work, increasing the likelihood that you could be hired there on a permanent and paid basis. Do the companies you want to work for offer unpaid internships? If so, how do you go about applying for them? How can you adjust your personal financial situation to take an unpaid internship if it helps advance your career?

Next, consider your ability to personally sell yourself. What will you say in an interview that will convince a prospective employer that he or she is better off with you than without you? The same strategies salespeople use to make a good first impression, such as appearance,

grooming, professional dress, and a firm handshake, are all things you want to fine-tune as you get ready for the job market.

Finally, public relations are essential as you start to develop your career. What do your colleagues think about you? Would your professors or classmates recommend you? Think about what you can do to improve or enhance others' perceptions of you.

Your Task: Create an outline of the specific advertising, sales promotion, personal selling, and public relations strategies you plan to use as you begin your career. For each type of promotion, answer the questions posed in the Marketing Plan Exercise and summarize how each can help you market yourself.

DISCUSSION QUESTIONS

1. What advertising medium is most effective for reaching *you* as a consumer? Has that changed in the past five years? What do you think the most effective medium for advertising to you will be five years from now?

2. If you had to advertise a new product to your marketing classmates, what media would you choose and why?

3. Describe a company that you think does a poor job of advertising. Why is its advertising ineffective? Anyone can criticize something that is not working, but those who offer creative solutions to fix advertising strategies that are broken have a bright future ahead. With this in mind, make two specific suggestions about how the company could improve its advertising.

4. Imagine you are in charge of getting students at your school to attend a lecture on campus. Would you choose a contest or a sweepstakes as a tool for promoting the event and increasing attendance? Explain your answer.

5. List two organizations that you think do a good job handling public relations and explain why you think so. List two organizations that you think do a poor job handling public relations and make specific suggestions as to how they might improve.

6. Based on your understanding of reach and frequency, would you recommend a company advertise during the Super Bowl? Why or why not? Would your answer vary depending on the type of business running the ad?

 # SOCIAL MEDIA APPLICATION

Select two firms that offer sales promotions through social media. These could include any of the strategies discussed in this chapter—coupons, rebates, contests, or sweepstakes. Describe which sales promotions each firm offers through which social media platforms. Then analyze those promotions using the following questions and activities as a guide:

1. In your opinion, which firm is doing a better job using social media to enhance its sales promotions? Explain your answer.

2. Who are the target markets for these social media sales promotions? Are the sales promotions an effective way to generate additional sales and profits from these target markets? Explain your answer.

3. Provide at least two specific recommendations for sales promotion strategies that each of these firms can implement through social media. Be sure to discuss why you think your recommendations would succeed in generating additional sales and profits from the firm's target markets.

MARKETING ANALYTICS EXERCISE

Please complete the *Connect* exercise for Chapter 8 that focuses on using metrics to measure advertising effectiveness (reach and frequency) and to calculate revenue per ad dollar.

ETHICAL CHALLENGE

There is an increasing public backlash over marketers who make false or misleading statements about their products. In recent years, numerous consumer lawsuits have resulted in multimillion-dollar settlements for several major companies. Dannon made claims that its yogurt products prevent sickness. Kellogg claimed that Rice Krispies help immunity. Ferrero USA made false claims about the healthiness and sugar content of Nutella. These claims have led to financial losses for the firms involved and also have the potential of eroding consumer trust. The U.S. Food and Drug Administration (FDA) is responsible for enforcing truthful labeling for food products, and some believe that these lawsuits are an effective way to improve the truth and transparency of food labeling and advertising.

However, some marketers have fought back, suggesting that many of these cases are "silly." They contend that consumers don't care that Quaker Oats calls its granola products "wholesome" even though they contain some trans fats. This debate leaves food marketers with an ethical dilemma: On the one hand, they want to promote their product in the best, most persuasive way possible. On the other hand, they must weigh the risks of saying something on the label that might potentially open up the firm to a consumer lawsuit.

Please use the ethical decision-making framework to complete the following:

1. Consider the various claims being made in consumer lawsuits against food companies. Do you consider the claims legitimate or "silly"?
2. What might be motivating the growing number of consumer lawsuits against food companies?
3. Many of the lawsuits against food companies involve foods consumed by children. Do food companies have more responsibility for the truth and transparency of their advertising and labeling when their products are consumed by children?

Source: See Katherine Campbell, Education Resource Center, "Mom and Dad vs. Snap, Crackle, and Pop," *Bloomberg Businessweek,* June 25, 2012, http://resourcecenter.businessweek.com/reviews/mom-and-dad-vs-snap-crackle-and-pop.

VIDEO CASE

Please go to *Connect* to access the video case featuring the Minor League Baseball team, the Cleburne Railroaders, that accompanies this chapter.

PODCAST

Please go to Connect to access the podcast that accompanies this chapter.

CAREER **TIPS**

How to Craft Your Resume as a Promotion Tool

You have read in this chapter about the importance of promoting products to communicate value to current and prospective customers. Similarly, as you embark on your career, you will need to be comfortable promoting yourself to prospective employers.

Debbie Pilgrim is the executive vice president of PeopleSource, a staffing and recruiting service with offices located throughout the central United States. She has spent nearly a quarter century helping people find jobs and careers. She offers the following advice for ensuring your resume is an effective promotional tool:

"In today's job market, it sometimes takes a little extra personal marketing to get noticed. Stacks of resumes make it difficult for a plain, basic resume to stand out, regardless of what the candidate's accomplishments are. Soon-to-be college graduates should view their resume as a marketing tool to creatively communicate why they bring value to a potential employer.

"The question I get from most job seekers is, How do I get organizations to notice my resume? A resume not only reflects your personality, it also speaks to your capability and creativity. Your resume is usually the first thing any employer sees, and if it is not good, it is the *only* thing they will see. Putting more effort and thought into creating an impressive resume is definitely worthwhile. I have heard of people printing their resume on fluorescent paper, sending baked goods along with a cover letter, or buying online ads to promote themselves.

"You can search online to find examples and ideas of possible resume templates. I encourage you to search sites like Mashable or Business Insider to get ideas for creative resumes that can help you stand out and communicate your value. I strongly encourage you to choose one that reflects your personality. Don't try to be something you are not. The worst possible career path in my opinion is to market yourself as something you are not and then, if you get that job, have to be that other person every day."

CHAPTER NOTES

1. Red Bull, "Red Bull Stratos," October 14, 2012, http://www.redbull.ca/cs/Satellite/en_CA/Article/Red-Bull-Stratos-Watch-the-mission-LIVE-NOW-021243270035378.
2. Mallory Russell, "Fearless Felix Baumgartner Is Second Fastest to 50 Million Views," *Advertising Age*, October 19, 2012, http://adage.com/article/the-viral-video-chart/fearless-felix-baumgartner-fastest-50-million-views/237870/.
3. Shirley Brady, "Taco Bell Promotes New 'Live Más' Tagline in New Campaign," February 24, 2012, http://www.brandchannel.com/home/post/2012/02/24/Taco-Bell-Live-Mas-Doritos-Locos-Tacos-Spots-022412.aspx.
4. Taco Bell Press Release, "It's About Time: Taco Bell's Cool Ranch Doritos Tacos Available Nationwide Today, March 7," March 7, 2013, http://www.tacobell.com/Company/newsreleases/cool_ranch_doritos_locos_tacos.
5. Ellen Hammett, "Advertising on Snapchat: Fleeting Fad or Marketing Goldmine?," *Marketing Week*, June 5, 2018, https://www.marketingweek.com/2018/06/05/snapchat-fad-goldmine/.
6. Michael O'Connell, "TNT's *Dallas* Premiere Scores just South (Fork) of 7 Million Viewers," *Hollywood Reporter*, June 14, 2012, http://www.hollywoodreporter.com/live-feed/dallas-premiere-ratings-tnt-337831.
7. Victor Luckerson, "Pay TV: You're Not Watching More Channels, but You're Definitely Paying for Them," *Time*, May 6, 2014, http://time.com/89813/nielsen-data-shows-people-watch-same-number-of-tv-channels/.
8. Rick Kissell, "Ratings: Fox's 'Empire' Dips, Still Dominates Wednesday; CW's 'Arrow' Returns Up," *Variety*, October 8, 2015, http://variety.com/2015/tv/news/ratings-empire-down-still-dominates-arrow-premiere-up-1201613460/.
9. Matt Cronin, "Tennis Channel's Complaint against Comcast in Jeopardy," *Tennis*, February 26, 2013, http://www.tennis.com/pro-game/2013/02/tennis-channels-complaint-against-comcast-jeopardy/46604/.
10. Staff writer, "Tennis Channel Is No. 1 Affluent Ad-Supported Network on Television," *BusinessWire*, May 26, 2015, http://www.businesswire.com/news/home/20150526005839/en/Tennis-Channel-No.-1-Affluent-Ad-Supported-Network.
11. Jeanine Poggi, "Here's How Much It Costs to Advertise in TV's Biggest Shows," *Ad Age*, October 2, 2018,

https://adage.com/article/media/tv-pricing-chart/315120/.

12. Suzanne Vranica, "Costly Super Bowl Ads Pay Publicity Dividend," *The Wall Street Journal*, February 3, 2013, http://online.wsj.com/article/SB100014241278873249002045782823600080857 52.html.

13. Associated Press, "Study: DVRs Now in Half of US Pay-TV Homes," *USA Today*, November 30, 2012, http://www.usatoday.com/story/tech/2012/11/30/study-dvrs-now-in-half-of-us-pay-tv-homes/1737637/.

14. Stephen Silver, "The Cord-Cutting Trend Continues to Rise," *The National Interest,* February 10, 2022, https://nationalinterest.org/blog/buzz/cord-cutting-trend-continues-rise-200482.

15. Kendra Clark, "Lexus and Lionsgate Co-promote New SUV and Halle Berry–Patrick Wilson Flick *Moonfall*," *The Drum,* January 14, 2022, https://www.thedrum.com/news/2022/01/14/lexus-and-lionsgate-co-promote-new-suv-and-halle-berry-patrick-wilson-flick-moonfall.

16. Talyor Soper, "Surface Saver: How Microsoft's Deal with the NFL Turned into a Marketing Boon for Its Tablet," *GeekWire,* December 5, 2021, https://www.geekwire.com/2021/surface-saver-how-microsofts-deal-with-the-nfl-turned-into-a-marketing-boon-for-its-tablet/.

17. Geoffrey Fowler, "Facebook Friends Used in Ads," *The Wall Street Journal*, January 26, 2011, http://online.wsj.com/article/SB1000142405274870401360457610453 2107484922.html.

18. A. Guttmann, "Newspaper Advertising Spending in North America 2000–2024," *Statista,* December 10, 2021, https://www.statista.com/statistics/882001/newspaper-advertising-expenditure-in-north-america/#:~:text=In%202021%2C%20newspaper%20advertising%20spending,billion%20U.S.%20dollars%20by%202024.

19. Carolyn Miller, Kristen Purcell, and Lee Rainee, "Reading Habits in Different Communities," *Pew Internet*, December 20, 2012, http://libraries.pewinternet.org/2012/12/20/reading-habits-in-different-communities/.

20. A. Guttmann, "Global Radio Advertising Expenditure 2000–2024," *Statista,* February 17, 2022, https://www.statista.com/statistics/272947/global-radio-advertising-expenditure/#:~:text=In%202021%2C%20radio%20advertising%20spending,30%20billion%20dollars%20in%202024.

21. https://variety.com/2017/digital/news/s-town-podcast-10-million-downloads-serial-productions-1202020302/.

22. Pew Research Center, "Audio Fact Sheet," April 29, 2015, http://www.journalism.org/2015/04/29/audio-fact-sheet/.

23. Ricardo Bilton, "A Solo Bill Simmons Nets 4 Million Podcast Downloads in Less Than a Month," *Digiday*, October 22, 2015, http://digiday.com/publishers/solo-bill-simmons-netted-4-million-podcast-downloads-less-month/.

24. David Caleb Mutua, "Facebook Pushes Online Ads, Then Spends Its Cash on Billboards," *Bloomberg*, August 6, 2018, https://www.bloomberg.com/news/articles/2018-08-06/big-tech-is-spending-big-in-a-decidedly-old-school-way.

25. Paul R. Lamonica, "Look Up: Big Bucks in Billboards," *CNNMoney*, April 5, 2006, http://money.cnn.com/2006/04/05/news/companies/billboards/.

26. Pew Research Center, "Mobile Fact Sheet," February 5, 2018, http://www.pewinternet.org/fact-sheet/mobile/.

27. Greg Sterling, "Report: Digital Now Makes Up 51% of US Ad Spending," *Marketing Land,* September 20, 2018, https://marketingland.com/report-digital-now-makes-up-51-of-us-ad-spending-248617.

28. Ashley Rodriguez, "How to Reach Gamers—An Affluent, Young and Fast-Growing Consumer Base," *Ad Age,* August 4, 2015, http://adage.com/article/cmo-strategy/reach-gamers-affluent-young-fast-growing-consumer-base/299764/.

29. Statista Research Department, "Value of Video Games Advertising Market Worldwide 2015–2024," *Statista,* January 12, 2022, https://www.statista.com/statistics/558502/value-video-games-advertising-market-global/#:~:text=In%202020%2C%20the%20global%20video,reach%204.8%20billion%20by%202024.

30. Frederic Lardinois, "Google Is Launching Playable In-Game Ads," *TechCrunch*, March 15, 2018, https://techcrunch.com/2018/03/15/google-is-launching-playable-in-game-ads/.

31. Welby Chen, "It's Time for Brands to Stop Ignoring the Mobile Gaming Market," *Adweek*, August 8, 2018, https://www.adweek.com/digital/its-time-for-brands-to-stop-ignoring-the-mobile-gaming-market/.

32. Geoff Herbert, "Burger King Selling Whopper for 1 Cent: How to Get Yours," *Syracuse.com,* December 5, 2018, https://www.syracuse.com/restaurants/index.ssf/2018/12/burger_king_whopper_cent_mcdonalds.html.

33. Brian Grow, "The Great Rebate Runaround," *Bloomberg Businessweek*, November 22, 2005, http://www.businessweek.com/stories/2005-11-22/the-great-rebate-runaround.

34. Patrick M. Dunne, Robert F. Lusch, and James R. Carver, *Retailing*, 7th ed. (Mason, OH: South-Western Cengage, 2011), p. 295.

35. Oreo Press Release, "Oreo Announces Casting Call for National 'Milk's Favorite Jingle' Contest," June 7, 2005, http://www.prnewswire.com/news-releases/oreor-announces-casting-call-for-national-milks-favorite-jingle-contest-54538802.html.

36. HGTV, "Congrats to the HGTV Dream Home 2013 Winner!" n.d., http://www.hgtv.com/hgtv-dream-home-2013-giveaway/package/index.html.

37. Tom Higgins, "*Jurassic World*'s Huge Promo Push Now Includes Limited Edition Cereal Boxes with Built-In Video Screens," *Promo Marketing*, June 18, 2018, https://magazine.promomarketing.com/article/jurassic-worlds-promo-budget-kelloggs-packaging/.

38. Barbara De Lollis, "IHG's Loyalty Club to Raise Point Rates for 25% of Hotels," *USA Today*, January 6, 2012, http://travel.usatoday.com/hotels/post/2012/01/ihg-priority-club-to-raise-point-rates-but-phase-in-change/591898/1.

39. Mark W. Johnston and Greg W. Marshall, *Relationship Selling*, 3rd ed. (New York: McGraw Hill, 2010).

40. Brent Schrotenboer, "Why College Football Bowl Game Industry, with ESPN's Help, Is Poised to Get Even Bigger," *USA Today,* December 13, 2018, https://www.usatoday.com/story/sports/2018/12/13/college-football-bowl-game-industry-espn/2286401002/.

41. Tom Warren, "Microsoft's Super Bowl ad Reminds the World Why Its Software Matters," *The Verge,* February 1, 2014, https://www.theverge.com/2014/2/1/5368820/microsoft-super-bowl-2014-ad.

42. Betsy Rate, "Spinning the Spill: BP's PR Ballet," *Need to Know on PBS*, June 14, 2010, http://www.pbs.org/wnet/need-to-know/environment/spinning-the-spill-bps-pr-ballet/1460/.

43. Frank Pallotta, "Super Bowl Commercials Cost $7 Million. It's Still a Good Deal," *CNN Business,* February 11, 2022, https://www.cnn.com/2022/02/11/media/super-bowl-commercials-nbc/index.html.

44. Steve Raabe, "Denver-Based Quiznos Seeks Recovery with New Marketing Strategy," *Denver Post*, July 8, 2012, http://www.denverpost.com/business/ci_21025259/quiznos-recovery-new-marketing-strategy.

45. Peter Romeo, "Restaurants Try New Lures for Black Friday Shoppers," *Restaurant Business,* November 21, 2018, https://www.restaurantbusinessonline.com/marketing/restaurants-try-new-lures-black-friday-shoppers.

Chapter **9**

Personal Selling

ER Productions/Blend Images/Getty Images

Learning Objectives

After reading this chapter, you should be able to

LO 9-1 Describe the strategic role of the sales force and the factors that influence use of personal selling.

LO 9-2 Understand the different types of sales positions.

LO 9-3 Explain the steps in the personal selling process.

LO 9-4 Describe the foundational elements necessary for sales success.

LO 9-5 Describe the use of sales technologies and social network platforms in professional selling.

LO 9-6 Discuss ethical issues in personal selling and sales management.

Executive **Perspective** . . . because everyone is a marketer

During his time in college, Tyler Cornwell interned and eventually became a graduate assistant for a Division 1 Athletics program. He left that position to work in the private sector before returning to serve as director of development for a University in the Southeastern United States. Over the next decade, his success led to promotions and opportunities at some of the best universities in the United States.

Today, Tyler has taken a new role where his talent and experience can help organizations raise funds to help others. He serves currently as the assistant vice president of Palmetto Philanthropy where he helps lead fundraising strategy for schools in higher education and build regional remote fundraising teams for a variety of nonprofits across the country.

Tyler Cornwell
Assistant Vice President
Palmetto Philanthropy

Joe and Robin Harbison

What has been the most important thing in making you successful at your job?

I believe we're all in the business of people—and people do business with those they like and trust. I would like to think I have had some measure of success because I've committed to connecting with and serving others, while always being true to myself.

What advice would you give to soon-to-be graduates?

Just get started. Each of us have personal and professional goals that we hope to one day achieve, but we often fall victim to seeking permission or approval from others. We tell ourselves that we need to be at a certain position or title before attempting to make progress on our goals. What I've learned in my career is that you will never feel ready to chase after your goals and dreams, but don't let it stop you from starting. This is especially important for young people. No matter what position you are in today or how far you are

away from that goal, just get started. Focus on making small improvements every day—you will be amazed by your progress and the journey that unfolds.

How is marketing relevant to your role at Palmetto Philanthropy?

In the traditional sense, most wouldn't look at my work as a fundraising consultant and recognize its relevance to marketing. Of course, at its core, marketing is about people. As a fundraiser and consultant, I've spent the better part of a decade learning about human behavior. What motivates us, inspires us, worries us, and ultimately why we choose to impact the lives of others through philanthropy. In my work with Palmetto Philanthropy, I spend much of my time equipping and training fundraising professionals and nonprofit organizations to better understand, communicate, and inspire the next generation of philanthropists.

What do you consider your personal brand to be?

My father taught me two important lessons at a very young age—integrity and determination define your reputation. I strive daily to ensure those qualities continue to guide my steps. Ultimately, I hope my reputation is more defined by how I serve others and less about what I've accomplished.

IMPORTANCE OF PERSONAL SELLING

LO 9-1

Describe the strategic role of the sales force and the factors that influence use of personal selling.

personal selling

The two-way flow of communication between a salesperson and a customer that is paid for by the firm and seeks to influence the customer's purchase decision.

In Chapter 8, we learned that advertising is typically one-directional—it communicates the seller's message to the buyer. **Personal selling**, in contrast, consists of the *two-way* flow of communication between a buyer and a seller, one that is paid for by the seller and seeks to influence the buyer's purchase decision. The salesperson and customer share information and feedback, often in a face-to-face setting. The interpersonal aspect of personal selling helps companies create and maintain strong customer relationships. In contrast to advertising and sales promotion, personal selling is a much more effective tool in complex purchase situations.

Personal selling activities play a crucial role in driving firms' competitive advantage and superior financial performance. Salespeople are a critical link that connects the business with its customer. In fact, for many buyers, their assigned salesperson is more than simply the face of the company; *they are* the company. As such, salespeople represent the firm to customers. As the eyes and ears of an organization, salespeople gather information about customer likes and dislikes and share it with marketers and product designers. They also provide market feedback on competitors and trends in the macro-environment.

Virtually everything we do in the course of the day—from the trivial to the truly miraculous—is a direct result of someone selling something to someone else. The range of personal selling activity is wide:

- A medical device representative advocating the benefits of a new heart pacemaker to a group of physicians at a hospital.
- A jeweler showing a heart-shaped pendant to a customer seeking to buy a Valentine's gift for their spouse.
- A sales team from Lockheed Martin working diligently over several years to secure a $200 billion bid for a new fleet of fighter jets.
- A single inside sales representative at a Southwest Airlines call center in San Antonio spending 15 minutes to help a grandmother in Orlando schedule a round-trip flight to visit grandchildren in Pittsburgh.

Personal selling activities, including examples like Lockheed Martin selling a new fighter jet or a jeweler selling an engagement ring, are an important element of marketing for organizations of any size. *B Christopher/Alamy Stock Photo*

While these situations are distinct, there are a number of common factors that combine to highlight the importance of personal selling as a marketing activity. We'll explore those commonalities in this chapter.

The Strategic Role of the Sales Force

Just as the nature of marketing has evolved considerably over the years, so too has the practice of personal selling. For one thing, today's buyer has much greater access to information about products and services. Traditionally, it was the salesperson who controlled the sales process, educating and guiding the prospect along the way until a purchasing decision was finally made. This is no longer the case. Customers' use of the Internet and social networking technologies has brought greater transparency with respect to price, product quality, and customer service. As a result, buyers are initiating contact with sellers much later in the sales process. In some cases, depending on the product type and whether it's B2B or B2C, prospects could be as much as 90 percent through the buying process before contacting a salesperson.[1]

The selling environment has also grown increasingly complex. Globalization has brought greater competition to many markets. As sellers leapfrog each other with innovations, the number and complexity of features can overwhelm customers. This is especially true when multiple features require the customer to make trade-off decisions.

Over time, the changing selling environment has led to a fundamental rethinking of the *strategic nature* of the sales force. For years, the dominant view of sales involved some or all of the following:

- The mission of the sales force was to enhance firm cash flow by communicating value to customers about basic goods and services.
- Value creation was largely the domain of marketing and R&D, the result of branding and product innovation efforts.
- The primary emphasis for the sales force was on increasing the volume of sales transactions.
- Attainment of sales objectives as a "numbers game," whereby increased revenue targets were achieved resulted mostly from the amount of effort made by sales personnel in identifying opportunities and closing deals.

Today, many leading firms are reorganizing critical business processes, including selling efforts, around the lifetime value represented by their most important accounts. **Customer lifetime value (CLV)** focuses on the net present value of a customer's business over the span of their relationship with an organization. Salespeople often play a strategic role in helping firms identify ways to grow CLV by selling additional products and providing high levels of service to improve customer retention rates.

As a result of this shift, **relationship selling** is at the core of all modern selling strategies. This sales approach involves building and maintaining customer trust over a long period of time—not just doing whatever it takes to meet periodic sales quotas. Since it is widely thought that it costs several times more to acquire new customers than it does to retain them, firms put greater emphasis on developing long-term, consulting-type relationships with downstream partners and critical customers. In fact, in some organizations there may be sales representatives dedicated to serving the needs of a single large customer!

customer lifetime value (CLV)
The total amount a customer will spend from acquisition through the end of a relationship with a brand.

relationship selling
A sales approach that involves building and maintaining customer trust over a long period of time.

Factors That Influence Use of Personal Selling

In general, sales investments are highly profitable for businesses. According to the Marketing Science Institute, firms on average gain a $31 increase in sales revenue for every $100 in increased sales expenditures.[2] In practice, it turns out that personal selling is more effective in promoting some products more than others. For instance, new goods and services tend to enjoy higher elasticity levels than do existing goods and services. This suggests

Marketers across the globe increasingly focus on developing relationships with large partners and critical customers to better serve the needs of their customers. *Westend61 GmbH/Alamy Stock Photo*

that when launching and establishing new products, companies may be better off investing more in their direct sales forces. As the product matures, they can then afford to start shifting resources toward other means of marketing communications.[3]

Figure 9.1 shows additional factors that influence the degree to which a firm should invest in personal selling. Personal selling is more effective when a good or service is:

- New-to-the-world (e.g., a self-driving vehicle).
- Infrequently purchased (e.g., a young couple buying a new home).
- Highly technical or complex. Such products often require the services of a salesperson to educate customers on product benefits and proper use (e.g., purchase of a communications satellite by the U.S. Navy).
- Viewed as risky. Purchases of high-priced or high-involvement items typically elevate buyers' risk perceptions. In such cases, salespeople play a critical role in helping build customers' trust in the firm and its products (e.g., investing in an emerging markets mutual fund).
- Customizable. Such products may require the assistance of sales personnel to properly configure the offering to match customer needs (e.g., a university medical center buying and implementing a new information system).

FIGURE 9.1   Factors That Influence Emphasis on Personal Selling

If the product is higher priced or involving

If the purchase is a new task for customer

If the product can be customized

Factors That Influence Level of Firm Emphasis on Personal Selling

If the product is not purchased frequently

If the purchase is considered "risky"

If the product is highly complex or technical

B2B versus B2C Sales   There are many parallels between selling products to consumers and to businesses. Both center on helping customers resolve problems, and both follow a similar sequence of steps. However, B2B sales are often much larger financially and take longer to complete. There are often multiple decision makers. In many cases, B2B buyers possess extensive information about the product and are experienced, professional negotiators. In part due to these differences, personal selling has emerged as arguably the most important decision factor in the large, complex sales that are common to B2B settings.[4]

Whether the context is B2B or B2C, effective sales professionals are able to guide these buyers through complex decision processes. They are able to bring together resources from across their extended organization, to craft a solution aimed at meeting customer needs. Their overall aim is to establish mutually beneficial long-term relationships with customers.

Personal Selling in the Digital Age It seems like every few years, some self-proclaimed "business guru" boldly pronounces the approaching decline, or even death, of personal selling as a cost-effective tool for communicating business value. After all, they say, in a world in which anybody can find anything nearly instantly with just a few keystrokes, who needs salespeople?

Yet sales remains the second-largest occupational category (behind office and administrative workers) in the U.S. workforce—as it has been for decades. According to the U.S. Bureau of Labor Statistics (BLS), each day more than 15 million people earn their living trying to convince someone else to make a purchase.[5] That's one out of every nine American workers. The chances are that if you are not a sales professional yourself, you are related to one or you know one quite well.

The digital transformation of advanced economies has not erased the need for salespeople. However, the scope and nature of personal selling activities are changing. In his book *To Sell Is Human: The Surprising Truth about Moving Others,* Daniel Pink observes that the very technologies that were supposed to make salespeople obsolete have in fact transformed more people into sellers.[6] According to his research, people spend roughly 40 percent of their work time—24 minutes out of every hour—persuading, influencing, and convincing others in ways that don't involve making a purchase. Pink calls these activities "non-sales selling." What's more, people consider this aspect of their work most crucial to their professional success.[7]

Television shows and movies like *Mad Men* and *The Wolf of Wall Street* tend to depict images of fast-talking, do-anything-for-the-buck salespeople. In general, that era is long past. Today's trained sales professional is much more likely to adopt an approach that fosters a long-term, consultative relationship with customers. In fact, in many B2B and services contexts, world-class salespeople are among the most highly regarded and well-trained professionals within their industries.

Career Opportunities in Sales

Professional selling offers attractive career choices. First, job listings for entry-level sales representatives are among the most plentiful. Many firms, of all sizes and across a multitude of industries, actively recruit on university campuses in search of new sales talent. In response, more universities are introducing bachelor and master's degree programs in sales. Because knowledge of personal selling offers added career options, minoring in sales has become a popular option for students majoring in other business disciplines, engineering, and even hard sciences, like chemistry and biology. Sales courses are designed to give students a head start in developing the basic skills, knowledge, and experience for entry-level sales positions. According to research from the Baylor University Center for Professional Selling, students in sales programs, nationally, average 2.8 job offers before graduation.[8] Many new graduates find that this career path provides a tremendous amount of flexibility and freedom.

TABLE 9.1   Sales Salaries by Job Title

Sales Job Title	National	Chicago	Atlanta	Austin	L.A.	Boston
Inside Sales	$ 39,584	$ 36,500	$38,000	$41,625	$ 37,120	$46,736
Sales Representative	39,300	39,300	40,010	28,273	42,672	48,575
Account Executive	56,000	45,000	47,409	45,720	49,679	52,000
Sales Manager	59,715	64,725	58,877	54,206	66,139	67,583
District Sales Manager	74,509	82,467	91,357	79,248	74,765	81,280
Key Account Manager	74,960	71,120	70,059	71,115	81,494	91,962
Regional Sales Manager	105,290	92,655	88,729	85,000	88,381	88,318
Vice President of Sales	149,854	158,811	n/a	n/a	134,961	n/a
Sales Engineer	87,633	79,571	85,601	91,834	72,720	95,505
Sales Analyst	60,000	61,575	57,270	58,183	58,781	60,128
All "Sales"	52,000	57,658	50,200	60,720	57,750	62,000

Source: Data from Glassdoor, "Entry-Level Sales Salaries," n.d., https://www.glassdoor.com/Salaries/entry-level-sales-salary-SRCH_KO0,17.htm.

Second, professional selling and sales management can be among the most financially rewarding careers. This is true for new hires and experienced reps alike, particularly in B2B settings. According to Glassdoor.com, the national average salary for an entry-level sales position in 2016 was $46,000 per year.[9] Table 9.1 provides details of national average sales salaries by job title. High-performing salespeople earn incomes far above these national averages. They also enjoy great visibility within the organization. Within many firms, excellent salespeople tend to move quickly into higher-level sales and marketing management roles. Third, sales positions offer qualities that appeal to Millennials: autonomy, rewards linked to personal effort, and the opportunity to interact with a variety of people.[10] Many people find the selling process requires a high level of innovativeness and creativity. Many field sales personnel are self-directed with little day-to-day supervision. Even though sales roles often require a fair amount of travel, many field-based sales representatives work out of their homes or virtual offices. Such arrangements offer flexibility and contribute to a work–family life balance and high job satisfaction.

Great Sales People Are Made, Not Born

As attractive as a sales career may appear on paper, some people respond, "That's fine, but I don't think I'm cut out for sales." Such feelings lead to the question, *Are great salespeople born or made?* That is, to what extent is sales success influenced by deeply ingrained traits, like personality? To what extent can qualities that lead to sales success be taught or gained through experience?

Sales managers and researchers have long debated such questions. It is true that individuals with certain personality characteristics, such as extroversion, seem more drawn to selling careers. Yet a comprehensive analysis of research has shown the relationship between personality and sales performance is negligible.[11] At the same time, differences in other individual characteristics—like a positive self-concept, high motivation, and an optimistic outlook—can have a tremendous impact on long-term sales success. Fortunately, these are attributes that can be strengthened through proper training, experience, and personal discipline.[12]

Whether or not you currently intend to work in sales, it is important to understand professional sales career opportunities and personal selling processes. Regardless of your major, in a few short years you will be "selling" employers on how your unique talents and experiences will contribute to the success of their organization. Once you start your career, your professional achievement and advancement hinge on your ability to introduce new ideas to customers, peers, and managers in a persuasive and convincing manner.

So far, we've talked in general terms about the role of the sales force and the importance of personal selling. Let's now get more specific, by looking at different types of sales positions.

TYPES OF SALES POSITIONS

LO 9-2
Understand the different types of sales positions.

Not all sales positions are the same. Field sales representatives often work out of their homes and often travel substantial distances to meet with customers at their places of business. In contrast, many new salespeople today start out with "inside-sales" positions. In these jobs, multiple reps at a centralized call-center location interact with customers by phone or via web-based communications.

As you might guess, the duties and compensation associated with different types of sales jobs can widely differ. Here, we'll look more closely at some of the most common types of sales positions.[13]

New-Business Salespeople

New-business salespeople are responsible primarily for finding new customers and securing their business. Typically, the sales prospect is likely to be a client of a competing firm. (Exceptions would be when the customer is a new business entity or when the good or service being sold is new-to-the-world.) New-business sales typically involve convincing the prospective customer to drop one or more competitors. Given the highly competitive nature of this type of selling, new-business salespeople must exhibit high levels of credibility, creativity, and professionalism. As a result, they are often very highly paid for their efforts.

Instead of finding new customers, some new-business salespeople focus on securing new distribution channel outlets. **Channel sales representatives** look to win, maintain, and expand relationships with channel partners. These partner relationships may be assigned to the rep based on geography, channel type, or market sector. Whether they sell directly to customers or seek to secure new distribution intermediaries, all new-business salespeople may be accurately described as *order-getters*.

Order-Takers

In contrast to new-business salespeople, **order-taker salespeople** are sales representatives who primarily process orders that a customer initiates. They are most commonly found within retail and inbound call-center settings. Examples are the salesperson helping you find a new interview suit at the department store and the Lands' End call-center employee assisting you with the purchase of a new winter coat.

Another typical order-taker sales role is **delivery salespeople**, also sometimes known as a *route salespeople*. As the name implies, the chief role of the delivery salesperson is product delivery. Responsibilities such as checking inventories, stocking shelves, and writing up new orders also may be part of the job. Manufacturers and wholesalers, such as Frito-Lay, Coca-Cola, and Mars Inc., are typical employers of delivery salespeople. Because their principal duties relate to order-taking, not order-getting, delivery salespeople often make upward of 20 sales calls per week; they may manage 100 or more accounts within their assigned territories. Compared with the other categories, delivery salesperson positions tend to attract younger, less-well-educated candidates and offer lower pay.

new-business salespeople
Sales representatives who are responsible primarily for finding new customers and securing their business.

channel sales representatives
New-business sales representatives who focus on securing new distribution channel outlets.

order-taker salespeople
Sales representatives who primarily process orders that a customer initiates.

delivery salespeople
Sales representatives whose chief role is product delivery; sometimes called *route salespeople*.

Delivery salespeople for firms like Frito-Lay are responsible for a range of tasks, including checking inventories, stocking shelves, and confirming new orders for their products.
David Goldman/AP Images

Consultative Sellers

consultative sellers

Sales representatives who focus on developing long-term relationships by developing a deep knowledge of the customer's industry, business issues, and needs.

Many new-business and delivery salespeople focus on short-term outcomes; as a result, they often use transactional-sales approaches. **Consultative sellers**, instead, focus on developing long-term relationships. This type of sales job is found across many sectors. It is particularly concentrated within traditional industrial settings, such as machinery, electronic, and metal products. Much like a management consultant hired to solve a problem, consultative sellers strive to become trusted advisors to customers. In order to effectively create customized solutions, a consultative seller must develop a deep knowledge of the customer's industry, business issues, and needs.

Missionary Salespeople

missionary salespeople

Sales representatives who generate sales by promoting the firm and encouraging demand for its products.

Missionary salespeople generate sales by promoting the firm and encouraging demand for its goods and services. Unlike other types of sellers, missionary salespeople do not actually get or take orders from customers. For example, Pfizer's pharmaceutical representatives do missionary sales work; they call on physicians to influence them to prescribe the latest-and-greatest Pfizer medications. However, no sales actually get made until the doctor calls in patient prescriptions to pharmacies, which then order the drug through wholesalers.

Key-Account Sellers

key-account sellers

Sales representatives who focus on establishing and maintaining partnership relationships with a small set of three to five named accounts.

The cost of acquiring a new customer is up to five times more than retaining an existing one; for the largest, most-strategic customer accounts, this ratio may be even higher. As a result, many B2B organizations have sought a more systematic approach to growing and protecting the business of their most strategically important customers. They have augmented their traditional sales force structure with **key-account sellers**. These sales reps typically focus on establishing and maintaining partnership relationships with a small set of three to five named accounts.

By developing a deeper understanding of their customer's business, key-account sellers are able to add value to the relationship. They engage in joint planning and guiding investments that help ensure mutual long-term success. In many instances, achieving these objectives requires key-account salespeople to lead cross-functional—and even interorganizational—teams dedicated to helping a customer achieve its goals. This highly specialized role tends to require higher levels of education and prior sales experience.

Sales Management and Support

The final category of sales positions is sales force management and support. **Sales force management** involves the planning, direction, and control of personal selling activities. Sales managers have oversight of selling efforts at varying levels of the organizational hierarchy:

- They establish sales objectives, and forecast and develop annual sales quotas for their assigned territories.
- They work with human resource personnel to recruit, select, train, supervise, and evaluate sales employees.
- They often work directly in the field with their assigned reps to help uncover or close sales opportunities.
- They serve as a conduit for information received from the front lines to senior management about ongoing market trends and competitive actions.

sales force management
The planning, direction, and control of personal selling activities, including recruitment, selection, training, motivating, compensation, and evaluation as they apply to the sales force.

Great sales managers are more than just supervisors—they are leaders who inspire their employees and help them achieve *their* personal and career goals. Like all good coaches, top sales managers strive to place people in positions where they can succeed. In the past, this type of mentoring took place on a face-to-face basis; now, much of it is digitally mediated. In fact, some sales playbook systems enable sales managers to provide deal-specific coaching to help their reps in real time. However, technology can never replace one-to-one interpersonal bonds. In fact, research shows that a salesperson's interpersonal identification with their sales manager contributes to superior customer satisfaction ratings for the representative *and* stronger sales performance.[14]

Sales Support Roles
There are also several common nonmanagerial sales support roles. For instance, in many complex sales settings, **sales engineers** interact with counterparts within the customer's buying center to address technical questions and issues that arise over the course of the entire sales process. In high-tech sectors like aerospace and enterprise software, these technical specialists typically have educational backgrounds in fields like engineering, computer science, and physics. They contribute expertise in the form of product demonstrations and trials, offer recommendations for complex equipment and the setup of machinery, and provide systems integration support.

sales engineers
Technical specialists who work in high-tech sectors and typically have educational backgrounds in fields like engineering, computer science, and physics.

More companies are shifting responsibility for onboarding new customers, identifying account growth opportunities, and long-term client retention to a **customer success manager**. Customer success management differs from traditional customer service in several important ways. Rather than reacting to customer problems to ensure the product meets expectations, customer success managers proactively look out for their customers' business, suggesting new and innovative ways to keep them succeeding with the company's products and services. This approach entails adopting a long-term perspective on the customer relationship (as opposed to a transactional view). In addition, individuals in these roles must be strong communicators and be comfortable in coordinating efforts across multiple functional areas within the organization.

customer success manager
A sales support position that is typically charged with successful onboarding of new customers, identifying account growth opportunities, and ensuring long-term client retention.

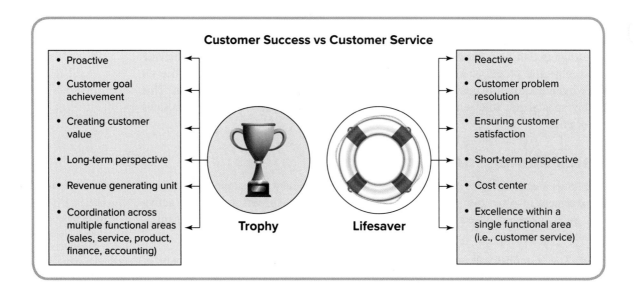

Customer Success vs Customer Service

- Proactive
- Customer goal achievement
- Creating customer value
- Long-term perspective
- Revenue generating unit
- Coordination across multiple functional areas (sales, service, product, finance, accounting)

Trophy   **Lifesaver**

- Reactive
- Customer problem resolution
- Ensuring customer satisfaction
- Short-term perspective
- Cost center
- Excellence within a single functional area (i.e., customer service)

Sales operations refers to the unit, role, activities, and processes within a sales organization that support, enable, and drive frontline sales teams to sell better, faster, and more efficiently.[15] Sales operations personnel apply data-analytics tools to improve sales forecasting, develop training programs, help to inform customer and territory allocation decisions, guide implementation of new sales technology, conduct performance metrics analysis, and more. Because of its broad scope and deep impact on sales force performance, a sales ops department has become a strategic component of many large sales organizations.

> **Mc Graw Hill connect** Exercise **9-1**
>
> Please complete the *Connect* exercise for Chapter 9 that focuses on the types of sales positions. By understanding what is involved in each, you will better understand the strategy in hiring different types of salespeople as well as which roles might fit you best in your career.

LO 9-3   THE PERSONAL SELLING PROCESS

Explain the steps in the personal selling process.

The **personal selling process** consists of a sequence of seven steps that salespeople follow to acquire new customers and obtain orders: prospecting and qualifying, pre-approach, approach, presentation, handling objections, gaining commitment, and follow-up. The steps numbered as 1 and 2 take place in advance of the sales call. The steps numbered 4 through 6 occur during the sales call itself. Step 7 happens after the sales call. We present a graphical depiction of the personal selling process in Figure 9.2.

The personal selling process is similar across nearly all sales contexts. However, changes in the selling environment have in many cases altered the manner in which sales organizations accomplish each task. For instance:

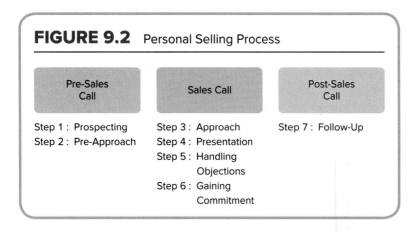

FIGURE 9.2 Personal Selling Process

Pre-Sales Call	Sales Call	Post-Sales Call
Step 1 : Prospecting	Step 3 : Approach	Step 7 : Follow-Up
Step 2 : Pre-Approach	Step 4 : Presentation	
	Step 5 : Handling Objections	
	Step 6 : Gaining Commitment	

- In order to allow salespeople more face-to-face time with customers, some organizations hire specialists to do activities such as prospecting and lead qualification.
- Customers may circumvent earlier stages of the personal selling process by finding company information on the Internet or social networking platforms.
- Not every sale goes through all of the stages: If you've worked with the same buyer for many years, there may be no reason to go through the first couple of stages.

Note that the amount of time allocated to each activity varies from one sales representative to the next.

Prospecting and Qualifying

A sales **prospect** is an individual (or group) capable of making the decision on a good or service a salesperson is selling. Identifying and qualifying such individuals and organizations in search of new business opportunities is the lifeblood of most businesses.

Prospecting involves the search for potential customers—those who need or want a product and fit into a firm's target market. Potential customers can be found in a variety of ways: customer referrals, trade shows, industry directories, websites, and networking.

The main goal of this step is to find *qualified* prospects. The activity of **qualifying** prospects involves identifying potential customers within the firm's target market who have a desire for the product, the authority to purchase it, the resources to pay for it, and timeframe for purchase. Salespeople qualify prospects using a number of techniques. The most obvious approach is simply talking with the target customer. Qualifying also involves doing market research to better understand the target customer's needs, wants, and ability to pay.

BANT approach to qualifying sales prospects

Budget — How much does the customer have to spend?

Authority — Who makes the final decision on what and when to buy?

Need — Is the purchase an urgent need or merely a want?

Timing — How quickly will the customer need to make a decision?

Once a prospect has been qualified, the salesperson can adjust the amount of effort directed toward securing a sale. That effort will be based on the probability of obtaining the sale and on the amount of expected revenue. Firms will approach higher-rated prospects with greater effort than lower-rated prospects.

Pre-approach

In the **pre-approach** stage of the personal selling process, the salesperson does research and preparation before contacting the customer. They should identify key decision makers, review account histories, ascertain customer needs, and prepare sales presentations.

personal selling process

A sequence of seven steps that salespeople follow to acquire new customers and obtain orders: prospecting and qualifying, pre-approach, approach, presentation, handling objections, gaining commitment, and follow-up.

prospect

An individual (or group) capable of making the decision on a good or service a salesperson is selling.

prospecting

The search for potential customers.

qualifying

Identifying potential customers within the firm's target market who have a desire for the product, the authority to purchase it, and the resources to pay for it.

pre-approach

The stage in the personal selling process in which the salesperson does research and preparation before contacting the customer.

Quality pre-approach research focuses on the environmental forces at work in the customer's life or in the organization's industry. Well-trained sales representatives do their homework before making their first contact. The entire personal selling process can result in failure if the salesperson doesn't know as much as possible about the prospect before approaching them about the sale. Every question you ask, every sentence you utter, can either enhance or detract from your credibility.

How does a salesperson find out all he or she needs to know about a prospect and the prospect's business? Asking customers directly can make the salesperson appear unprepared. In today's world, plenty of information about companies, industries, and individuals is available online with just a few clicks. There is zero excuse for not tailoring your approach and need assessment questions. Detailed information on many individuals is available through their public social media accounts, online press releases and news articles, bio pages, and the like. Do you know anyone in common? Perhaps useful information or even an introduction may be possible by reaching out to a shared friend or acquaintance. Additional information on businesses and industries can be found through keyword targeted web searches, annual reports, white papers, customer testimonials, representatives from other supplier organizations, and company brochures and other sales materials. As sales author Jeffrey Gitomer writes, salespeople must "prepare to win or lose to someone who is!"[16]

Approach

approach

A part of the personal selling process that involves meeting the prospect and learning more about his or her needs and wants.

In the **approach** stage, the sales rep meets the customer for the first time. A key element of the approach is gaining a sufficient level of customer interest in order to schedule an appointment. Setting the first appointment is arguably the most important, and most difficult, step in the sales process. In effect, it involves engaging the attention of a busy decision maker long enough to obtain a commitment that he or she will give you—who are, in most instances, a complete stranger—their undivided attention for a specified period of time.

For many years, salespeople were advised to always be ready with their "elevator pitch." The idea was that if you found yourself in an elevator with a key decision maker, you would be able to explain who you are and what your business has to offer between the time the elevator doors closed shut and opened back up again.

The ability to succinctly summarize your company's value proposition remains a worthwhile goal. In today's business world, though, we have far more opportunities to get our message to decision makers than simply through a chance elevator ride. Decision makers today are faced with a flood of information. The McKinsey Global Institute estimates that the typical American hears or reads more than 100,000 words every day—e-mails, texts, tweets, meetings, webcasts, commercials, blog posts, videos, and more.[17] Cutting through the clutter to get through to message receivers presents a great challenge to salespeople and marketers.

Experts offer several tips on increasing effectiveness in appointment setting:

- Carefully plan your approach to ensure that you present a strong value proposition that speaks to a valid buyer need. This is important whether you are reaching out to the prospect for the first time by phone, e-mail, or in person.
- Whenever possible, use the name of a trusted resource and reference him or her in the introductory e-mail or phone call. Or even better, get the referral partner to reach out and let the prospect know that the salesperson will be making contact.
- Most important, be persistent, patient, and professional. If the first few attempts are unanswered, continue to politely follow up with relevant information and ideas. The follow-up should help establish credibility and position the rep as a useful resource. If e-mails and voicemails are not working, try sending a handwritten note or connecting via a social network, such as LinkedIn.

Once the salesperson has succeeded in obtaining a meeting, the next goal is to build *rapport*—a friendly relationship—with the decision maker or key influencers. Personal affinity between the decision maker and the salesperson forms the basis of a positive customer relations. When rapport is strong, each new sale deepens the quality of the relationship, making successive sales easier. When rapport is weak, selling becomes difficult and awkward. When that bond is missing altogether, selling can become an exercise in futility. Therefore, learning how to build and maintain rapport should be at the top of every salesperson's list of critical skills to master.[18]

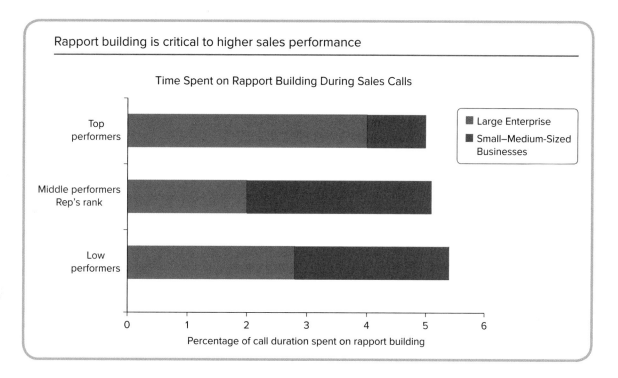

Rapport building is critical to higher sales performance

Time Spent on Rapport Building During Sales Calls

Rapport building comes naturally to some. For others, it's an ability that can be learned and taught. The most fundamental way to begin making a connection with a prospect is simply to try to see things from the customer's perspective. This in turn will influence how you look, what you say, and how you say it. Showing genuine interest conveys the level of concern you will show in attending to the needs of the customer.

The Dale Carnegie Institute offers a few additional tips on building rapport:

- *Keep smiling.* Studies show that we tend to overestimate the number of times we smile. A cheerful, friendly expression is the greatest predictor of a person's likability. Get in the habit of offering a sincere smile each time you meet your prospect or are introduced to someone new.
- *Be helpful.* Show your interest in others by asking questions about them, researching their social media profiles, and in general, finding out what you can do to help them. We can all use help from others in our quest for success. People you help may in turn be more than happy to help you.
- *Be positive.* People always want to hear when they're doing a great job. Find reasons to compliment your customers and give positive feedback on what they do well. The better you make people feel about themselves, the more likely they are to appreciate your presence.[19]

Finally, remember that creating rapport is an ongoing process. Rapport building takes place during every customer interaction, not simply in a first meeting or a formal sales call. This advice extends to virtual interactions as well as to publicly viewable social media posts or tweets. Taking the time to craft well-reasoned, grammatically correct e-mails and cover letters establishes your professionalism. Such communications send a strong statement about your personal brand. Likewise, it pays to review your public presence on all social media networks—even those on which you are no longer active. Make sure that the hard work you have put into building up your credentials is not undone by embarrassing pictures or inflammatory online comments.

The Presentation

After the approach, the salesperson prepares the *sales presentation*. Ideally, the sales presentation will do the following:

- Accurately convey the product's major *features*.
- Describe its *advantages* in comparison with alternatives.
- Detail how it will provide *benefits* for the potential customer.

feature-advantage-benefit (FAB) approach

Sales approach that conveys the product's major features, describes its advantages compared with alternatives, and details the benefits it will provide the customer.

Most successful salespeople use some variation of this **feature-advantage-benefit (FAB) approach** as a natural way of communicating the value of their product to their prospects and clients.

In the FAB approach, **features** are attributes or facts relating to the product being sold or demonstrated. For example, when showing outdoor sporting equipment to a customer at REI, a retail salesperson might point out, "An important feature of this sleeping bag is that it has a 2-inch layer of insulation." Features tend to be integral characteristics of the good or service being offered.

features

In the FAB sales approach, attributes or facts relating to the product being sold or demonstrated.

But simply providing customers with a litany of product features alone generally will not advance the sale. "Feature dumping"—listing features without tying them to benefits— is one of the worst mistakes a salesperson can make. Features alone don't explain how a solution will solve the buyer's specific problem. Failure to highlight a solution leaves it up to the buyer to draw his or her own conclusions about benefits of the features. Some buyers will come up with the right answers; others won't bother.

advantages

In the FAB sales approach, general statements about what the features do; they may or may not be connected to an expressed or actual customer need.

Skilled salespeople help their customers connect features with benefits, by incorporating advantage statements. **Advantages** are general statements about what the features do; they may or may not be connected to an expressed or actual customer need. For example, the REI salesperson may note, "The 2-inch insulation layer helps retain body heat during cold nights." The advantage a product has may be stated in comparison with the good or service the customer is currently using. If the customer talks about a competitor's product, the salesperson can show the advantages that their product has over a competing product (and perhaps how they are more important for your customer).

Sometimes the sales rep can talk about *disadvantages* of a customer's current approach or of a competing product. However, this approach should be used with caution. If not done carefully, it can seem as if the salesperson is criticizing a customer's past decisions, ultimately provoking objections and counterarguments.

benefits

In the FAB sales approach, individual values attached to the advantages offered by various product features.

Benefits are the individual values attached to the advantages offered by various features of the product. They are the bridges that connect the advantages of the various features to the specific needs of a customer.[20] For instance, the REI salesperson might conclude by telling the customer, "If you are able to sleep more comfortably at night, you will be more rested for the day ahead and will find your overall camping experiences even more enjoyable."

Effective sales presentations are thoughtfully created with a few key points in mind:

- First, prepare presentations with an understanding of the value of the customer's time. Presentations should quickly and efficiently link the firm's goods, services, and ideas to solutions that help the customer.

Salespeople share the benefits of a product, which connects the advantages of various features to the specific needs of the consumer. *Morsa Images/DigitalVision/Getty Images*

- Second, spend time thinking about what you want the customer to remember about the presentation. Customers will use these memories as they make purchase decisions. Focusing on key words, phrases, or images during the presentation can be critical.
- Third, customers want to do business with organizations they like and trust. The sales presentation should reinforce why the organization will be a good partner to the customer.
- Finally, do not underestimate the value of asking questions and listening during the presentation. Talking too much can signal a lack of real interest in the prospect's needs and wants. The more a salesperson knows about the prospect's needs, the better position he or she is in to meet those needs. Remember: Talking is sharing, listening is caring!

Handling Objections

Objections are the concerns or reasons customers offer for not buying a product. Objections actually are useful: When a customer raises an objection, the salesperson has an opportunity to clarify and reassure the customer about pricing, features, and other potential issues.

objections
The concerns or reasons customers offer for not buying a product.

Handling objections requires professionalism, strong communication skills, and a sincere respect for the prospect's concerns. Common techniques of overcoming objections include:

- *Acknowledging the objection: "Yes, our prices are higher because our product is better."* The objection allows the salesperson an additional opportunity to stress the benefits of the product. For example, consumers are willing to pay higher prices provided they've been given a clear reason (higher quality, better safety, more efficient) for spending more.
- *Postponing: "We'll discuss the delivery option in a few minutes, but first let me ask about your needs in this area. . . ."* Salespeople should postpone addressing

objections if the full context of an appropriate answer has not been developed. This strategy works best if the salesperson plans to address an objection shortly. Postponing for too long will frustrate customers and reduce their level of trust.

- **Denial:** *"That is not accurate. Here's what the situation actually is. . . ."* If a customer mentions something that is completely false, the salesperson should strongly deny the point, but only in a way that is not offensive or insulting to the customer.

In B2B contexts, the most common sales objections fall into four buckets: budget, authority, need, and time (known as *BANT*). While the sales rep may not need to have a detailed response to all four within a single sales call, he or she should be prepared to discuss each objection. The key is to offer up a reply that shows value to your buyer.

New salespeople often try to go through an entire presentation without any objections from the prospective customer. That's often a mistake: After all, the ability to draw out specific objections and remove obstacles to purchase is one of the major advantages of personal selling. Salespeople should make sure to validate the customer's objection, no matter how trivial it might seem, because the customer finds it important. Successfully dealing with objections, large and small, can strengthen the customer relationship and encourage sales both now and in the future.

Gaining Commitment

There is a famous, and instructive, story about the industrialist Henry Ford: Detroit newspapers reported that Ford had purchased a sizable life insurance policy. A close friend of Ford's, who was in the insurance business, was considerably upset and asked why Ford had not bought the policy from him. Ford's answer is a lesson to anybody who sells anything to anybody at any time or circumstance—and that's all of us: He said simply, "You didn't ask me."[21]

gaining commitment

Asking a sales prospect to move forward with the sales process, ultimately leading to a purchase.

Gaining commitment occurs at the point when the salesperson asks the prospect for agreement to move forward with the sales process, ultimately leading to a purchase. This is often the most difficult part of the personal selling process; it requires the salesperson to overcome the basic human fear of being rejected. Nonetheless, it is an essential step, because most customers will not take initiative to close the sale on their own. The act of asking for a customer's business is very important to securing it.

In order to reduce the uncertainty and tension associated with a final close, many sales training programs emphasize the use of *trial closes*. In this approach, sales reps ask questions throughout the sales presentation that test the buyer's readiness to commit. These questions enable the salesperson to ascertain (1) where the buyer is in the process and (2) the right time to ask for the sale. Examples of a few basic trial-closing questions include:

- *How do you feel about what we have discussed so far?*
- *Based on what you've heard so far, what questions do you have about the solution I've shared with you?*
- *If you had your way, what changes would you make to the proposal?*

After having tested the waters and gained agreement on key points using trial-close questions, asking for the buyer's business becomes a natural conclusion to the sales meeting. Several common closing approaches are:

- **Summary close.** The summary close works by repeating what has already been agreed to in the course of the presentation, typically via earlier trial closes. *"Let's summarize: In addition to getting the basic service, you will be receiving free installation, our 30-day free return policy, and a full 2-year manufacturer's warranty. How does that sound?"* In this type of close, the salesperson summarizes key benefits and how they meet the customer's stated needs before asking for the sale.

- *Alternative close.* The alternative close works by offering more than one clearly defined alternative to the customer. *"Would you prefer the red model or the yellow one?"* This technique works well in many different situations when you are seeking agreement, not just selling products.
- *Assumptive close.* In the assumptive close, the salesperson acts as if the buyer has already decided to purchase. The salesperson asks something like, *"What date would you like the product delivered?"* If the customer responds with a specific date, the salesperson knows the customer has decided to make the purchase.

No salesperson can rely on just one closing strategy. The most effective close depends on the customer and the specific situation. Salespeople who listen and watch closely for clues given by the customer during the earlier steps of the selling process will be best prepared to select the appropriate closing strategy.

Also, it is important to remember that closing can be different in more-complex sales. These situations typically have longer buying cycles, involve multiple decision makers, and often entail a sequence of sales meetings. In these sales settings, closing may mean simply obtaining a commitment from the prospect to agree to a subsequent meeting or some other clearly defined objective that moves the sale forward.

Follow-Up

Salespeople must not overlook the huge potential for revenue and profits of existing customers. Most businesses today depend on repeat sales of products and add-on services to existing clients. Also, as noted earlier, it's much more expensive to acquire a new customer than to keep an existing one. Thus, it is essential for the salesperson to do everything possible to retain existing customers as long as possible. The *follow-up stage* is a critical step in creating customer satisfaction and building long-term relationships with customers.

A sound follow-up strategy includes, at a minimum, checking in after the sale to ensure that the customer is satisfied. The customer should feel that he or she is actually receiving the sought-after benefits of the product. If the customer experienced any problems, the salesperson can intervene and become a customer advocate to ensure satisfaction.

Important by-products of the follow-up stage are positive word of mouth, customer testimonials, and direct referrals. Experienced sales reps know that customers share their good *and* bad experiences with others. They may talk with a few friends, family, and business colleagues. Or they may share their thoughts with hundreds, thousands, or even millions of others through social media.

Diligent follow-up can also lead to uncovering new customer needs and wants, securing additional purchases, or obtaining customer testimonials and referrals that can be used to open the door for new accounts. In fact, in B2B settings, some of the most valuable referrals may be to someone else within the buyer's organization. According to Salesforce.com, 84 percent of prospects respond to a salesperson referred by someone else within their organization.[22]

Follow-up after the close nurtures the ensuing relationship over the long term. From that perspective, follow-up should never end. The pace may slow and the type of follow-up may change, but making good on earlier commitments and constantly looking for new ways to be of service to the customer is vital to sustaining the customer relationship.

Applying the Personal Selling Process to Your Future Job Search

Many of these same guidelines apply when you begin the process of interviewing for an internship or new job. It is important for graduates to do their homework and research what is likely to be happening in the prospective employer's business right now. Develop several questions in advance of an interview. Asking great questions will help you demonstrate your knowledge and preparation; the answers will enable you to learn about the business and whether it is a proper fit for you. Make sure the question is open-ended (e.g., *How is this particular trend impacting your business these days?*) not closed-ended questions that can be answered as yes/no or multiple choice. Obtaining commitment with respect to next steps in the hiring process as well as a strategy of respectful follow-ups reflect professionalism and a sincere interest in the position.

Mc Graw Hill connect Exercise **9-2**

Please complete the *Connect* exercise for Chapter 9 that focuses on the personal selling process. By identifying the necessary actions and decisions at each step, you will understand how to navigate the process successfully and increase sales for your organization.

LO 9-4

Describe the foundational elements necessary for sales success.

FOUNDATIONS OF SALES SUCCESS

Legendary sales trainer and author Zig Ziglar had a personal credo that he shared at every opportunity: "You can have anything you want in life if you help enough other people get what they want."[23] Great opportunities await any new salesperson who truly keeps customers' long-term best interests at heart.

It follows then, that first and foremost, the achievement of long-term success in professional sales must be centered on serving the interests of the customer. **Customer-oriented selling** can be viewed as the adoption of the marketing concept at the level of the individual salesperson and customer.[24] Highly customer-oriented salespeople do the following:

customer-oriented selling

The adoption of the marketing concept at the level of the individual salesperson and customer.

- Engage in behaviors likely to lead to long-term customer satisfaction.
- Avoid actions that sacrifice customer interest for the sake of short-term benefit to the salesperson or their company.
- See things from the buyer's perspective.
- Recognize the social landscape under which large, complex sales are typically made.
- Understand that the impact on a customer of a bad buying decision is usually greater than the impact on a salesperson of a lost deal.

In doing all these things, customer-oriented salespeople are more likely to adopt a solution-centric approach to the sale—one that is better in the end for both the seller and the buyer.

Customer-oriented sales approaches are most effective when the salesperson has certain traits, knowledge, and abilities: a positive self-concept, market knowledge, and sales-related knowledge. In the next three sections, we explore in more detail these elements needed for sales success.

Maintaining a Positive Self-Concept

In sales, marketing, and many other career fields, fear and self-doubt are often the greatest enemies of human potential. These issues can manifest themselves in various ways, but within the sales context, the most common warning sign is procrastination. In fact, research suggests nearly 85 percent of all salespeople, regardless of experience or age, regularly experience some degree of reluctance before they contact a potential customer.[25] This finding underlines the extreme importance of strong self-belief and positive attitude to the achievement of personal success in the field of sales.

What elevates the most highly successful sales professionals above others who are equally knowledgeable and skilled? Maintaining a positive self-concept in the face of uncertainty and periodic adversity underlies long-term success in sales careers. In rough times, successful salespeople are able to muster the necessary mental and emotional discipline to stay focused and constructive. This trait may best be described as *grit,* a personality trait defined as perseverance and passion for achieving long-term goals. Grit emphasizes having the strength of mind to maintain realistic optimism while not letting failures slow you down.

Steps to Strengthening Grit   Research suggests that in many fields, a person's grittiness may have a bigger impact on success than IQ or talent do. What can sales professionals (or students) do to strengthen their grit?

First, it is important for salespeople to monitor how they approach failure. Individuals with a growth mindset—that is, who accept failure as an opportunity to learn—do much better in sales over the long run. This can be tricky because strengthening grit requires challenging oneself by setting ambitious goals. When a sale falls through, gritty salespeople avoid labeling their efforts as wasted. Instead, they ponder over lessons learned or how the experience helped strengthen new skills.

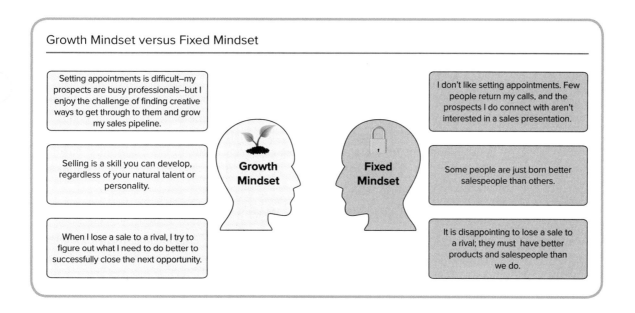

Growth Mindset versus Fixed Mindset

Setting appointments is difficult—my prospects are busy professionals—but I enjoy the challenge of finding creative ways to get through to them and grow my sales pipeline.

Selling is a skill you can develop, regardless of your natural talent or personality.

When I lose a sale to a rival, I try to figure out what I need to do better to successfully close the next opportunity.

Growth Mindset

Fixed Mindset

I don't like setting appointments. Few people return my calls, and the prospects I do connect with aren't interested in a sales presentation.

Some people are just born better salespeople than others.

It is disappointing to lose a sale to a rival; they must have better products and salespeople than we do.

Second, improving grit requires practice, practice, and more practice. Hard work sharpens skills; people are more likely to stick with things they are good at. But it is important to note that the type of practice matters. Simple repetition is not enough. Grit entails deliberate actions that push the salesperson beyond their comfort zone. They use the resulting feedback to identify weak areas, then focus on improving them.

Finally, it is difficult to understate the importance of passion. Passionate individuals are more likely to keep going, even when things get tough. Gritty salespeople don't merely have a job—they feel a life calling. By reflecting on how their work performance makes a positive contribution to customers, their company, fellow employees, their family, or even society at large, salespeople can find greater meaning in their work routines and a deeper passion for their careers.

Executive Perspective . . .

because everyone is a marketer

Tyler Cornwell
Assistant Vice President
Palmetto Philanthropy

Joe and Robin Harbison

How did you add to your market-related knowledge as a salesperson?

Market-related knowledge is essential to success in sales. Very few of you reading this book are being trained to work in a specific industry, so when you accept a new position it will be critical that you work hard to understand that industry and domain with as much depth as possible. For me, the biggest way I have always added to my market-related knowledge is seeking out and talking with smart professionals in my industry, asking them questions, and developing relationships where I can continue to grow while also sharing my insights with others and helping them expand their knowledge as well.

market-related knowledge

An understanding of the goods, services, and processes within one's firm and of key business issues that affect the customer's success.

selling-related knowledge

Sales abilities and an understanding of selling techniques.

adaptive selling

The altering of sales behavior during a customer interaction based on perceived information about the selling situation.

Market-Related Knowledge

In order to gain trust and effectively co-create value with customers, sales professionals must continuously improve their **market-related knowledge**. Sometimes this is referred to as *domain* knowledge. This includes strong understanding of (1) the goods, services, and processes within their own firm, and (2) the key business issues that affect their customer's success.

Being highly knowledgeable about the goods and services being offered by the firm is a prerequisite for any competent salesperson. But product knowledge is typically not enough to achieve high levels of sales performance. Sales prospects frequently feel rushed for time and starved for good information. They want to work with sellers who "know their stuff" and can bring them fresh ideas that can help their business. High-performing sales reps are able to use knowledge of how their prospects create value for their customers in order to win a greater share of new accounts. More significantly, high-performing reps attract profitable customers who are less price-conscious and exhibit greater loyalty.

What the salesperson says in conversation with customers demonstrates their market-related knowledge. Salespeople must be able to "speak" the technical language of the customer's field. This can be very challenging for salespeople who are generalists, selling into many different sectors. Salespeople who lack domain expertise must rely more on their own likability than on the benefits of their goods and services. Successful salespeople with high domain-area expertise can discuss in some detail how their products and services can bring value to the customers' business. Moreover, they are able to do so convincingly, in terms the buyer understands and can appreciate.

Selling-Related Knowledge

All successful salespeople commit themselves to their craft. **Selling-related knowledge** includes sales abilities and an understanding of selling techniques. Salespeople encounter different selling situations over a wide range of needs, buying motives, personalities, and social styles. Winning the sale often depends on the salesperson's ability to recognize buyer types and customize the sales message. **Adaptive selling** refers to the altering of sales behavior during a customer interaction or across customer interactions based on perceived information about the selling situation.[26]

Rather than relying on a canned presentation, adaptive sellers use information gathered about prospects before an interaction. They then use real-time feedback obtained during a presentation to customize the content, format, or delivery of their messages during the sales encounter. Not surprisingly, marketing studies have consistently shown that adaptive selling behavior has a strong positive effect on salesperson performance and job satisfaction.[27]

Chances are you already use a form of adaptive selling in your everyday life: For example, you probably speak to your professors in a different way than you talk with your roommates. Such intuitive tailoring of interpersonal communications does not mean that people know how to do so in the sales context, though. In order to successfully increase their repertoire of sales approaches, salespeople must be able to do two things:

Technology salespeople can provide value to their customers by offering them market-related knowledge about specific products they might consider purchasing. *Justin Sullivan/Getty Images News/Getty Images*

1. Quickly and accurately categorize prospective customers based on implicit buyer needs.
2. Use this information to craft a sales message that conveys an appropriate value proposition in a persuasive manner.

How do salespeople address these twin challenges? One way is to use a questions-based sales method—SPIN selling—that many top-flight sales organizations around the globe have adopted.

SPIN Selling In successful sales calls, who does most of the talking—the buyer or seller? To answer this question, one research team conducted a comprehensive analysis of more than 35,000 B2B sales calls. The study found that in successful meetings it is the *buyer,* typically prompted by a salesperson's questions, who does most of the talking.[28] As the complexity and size of the sales opportunity grew, salespeople who asked smart questions in a particular sequence were most likely to achieve sales success. This research ultimately led to the development of the *SPIN selling framework*. It has been widely adopted by many sales organizations, including over half the Fortune 500.

SPIN is an acronym that refers to the questions that feature most prominently in successful sales calls:

- *Situation questions* are designed to obtain background facts about the buyer's current circumstances. Answers to effective situation questions provide a starting point for deciding which potential problems and dissatisfactions to explore.
- *Problem questions* ask about buyers' problems, difficulties, or dissatisfactions with an existing situation. Problem questions clarify and make more explicit buyers' implied needs. They provide the raw material upon which to build the rest of the presentation.
- *Implication questions* ask about the consequences or effects of the buyer's situation. They show that the buyer's problem is significant enough to justify action.

TABLE 9.2 SPIN Questions

SPIN Question Type	Definition	Examples	Impact	Advice
Situation questions	Finding out facts about the buyer's existing situation.	*How many people do you employ at this location? Could you tell me how the system is configured?*	• Least powerful of SPIN questions. • Most salespeople ask too many.	Eliminate unnecessary situation questions by doing research in advance.
Problem questions	Asking about problems, difficulties, or dissatisfactions experiencing with the existing situation.	*What makes this operation difficult? Which parts of the system create errors?*	• More powerful than situation questions. • Salespeople ask more problem questions as they gain experience.	Think of your firm's offerings in terms of the *problems they solve* for buyers—not in terms of attributes and features.
Implication questions	Asking about the *consequences* of effects of a buyer's problems, difficulties, or dissatisfactions.	*What effects does that problem have on output? Could that lead to added costs?*	• The most powerful of all SPIN questions. • Top salespeople ask lots of implication questions.	These questions are the hardest to create.
Need-payoff questions	Asking about the value or usefulness of a proposed solution.	*How would a quieter printer help? If we did that, how much could your business save?*	• These versatile questions are used a great deal by top salespeople. • Positive impact on customers.	Use to get buyers to *tell you* the benefits that your solution can offer.

Implication questions help transform problems into explicit needs in the mind of the buyer and expand the perceived value of finding a solution.

• *Need-payoff questions* are designed to get the buyer thinking about the value of finding a solution to the problem. By focusing on the solution, need-payoff questions reduce objections, moving the discussion toward action and commitment.

Table 9.2 summarizes the SPIN approach, including impact of and advice about each type of question.

SPIN is but one of many sales techniques advanced in popular trade books or by sales training consultants. There is no one right method for every buyer or seller. What *is* certain, though, is that customers respond to sincere interest, intelligence, and authenticity, not tricks. Ultimately, sales success depends on building trust and creating value for customers. Salespeople who use gimmicky tactics or try to adopt methods that feel unnatural will come across as phony or worse.

LO 9-5

Describe the use of sales technologies and social network platforms in professional selling.

SALES TECHNOLOGY AND SOCIAL SELLING

Sales organizations today are using innovative technologies to dramatically reinvent selling processes, elevate productivity, and increase customer satisfaction. Next, we discuss three technology-driven innovations that are impacting the practice of personal selling: customer relationship management (CRM), virtual selling, and social selling.

Customer Relationship Management (CRM) Systems

Any discussion of sales technology should begin with an understanding of **customer relationship management (CRM)**, discussed more fully in Chapter 15. CRM is a strategy and set of processes used for better managing an organization's relationships and interactions with customers and potential customers.[29] A **CRM system**, a set of software tools used for contact management, sales management, productivity, and more, supports implementation of CRM-based strategies. CRM software is the biggest enterprise software category in the world by sales and its growth isn't slowing down. In fact, CRM spending is expected to reach more than $80 billion in revenues by 2025.[30]

CRM systems gather and store information about prospects and customers from various business touchpoints, including sales records, contact forms, e-mail and social media marketing, search engines, and more. Sophisticated systems can automatically pull in information from outside sources, such as recent news about a company's initiatives or changes in key personnel. A CRM system stores and organizes this information in a manner that provides sales and marketing personnel with an evolving 360-degree view of the customer. While CRM systems share many key features, some of the most important capabilities for sales and marketing include:

- **Contact management** that records key information about customers and organizes them into segments, making personalization possible.
- **Robust reporting and analytics** capabilities, helping sales and marketing managers to track outcomes and metrics corresponding to each customer interaction.
- **Powerful marketing and customer support automation** capabilities, allowing companies to automate routine tasks and create more consistent customer experiences.
- **Inventory tracking and forecast demand** based on information such as customer habits and seasonal variations.[31]

In addition, forward thinking companies are adopting sales-friendly enhancements to their CRM systems, which we discuss next.

Mobile CRM
One of the key factors behind the unrelenting growth of CRM has been the need for salespeople to have remote access to customer data, no matter where the user is located. Increasingly, this means being able to access customer information using an Internet-enabled mobile device or smartphone. In response, firms have increasingly adopted mobile CRM apps that allow their sales teams to manage customer relationships, contacts, deals, events, and tasks on the go. For instance, CRM software maker Pipedrive's mobile app syncs to its web app. Users are able to call and create e-mails with a single tap, add notes, log calls, update to-do lists, and access real-time CRM data from their smartphone.

Artificial Intelligence (AI) and CRM
Many believe artificial intelligence (AI) can help firms better leverage the investments they've made into CRM. Some have even gone so far as to suggest AI applications, like chatbots, may one day eliminate the need for human salespeople. However, this perspective understates the complexity of many buying situations and the role of buyer trust in driving the sales process.

While it is unlikely that a machine can replace the human aspect of sales, the use of AI can help take a lot of the guesswork out of the sales process and eliminate mundane administrative tasks. This allows sales professionals to devote more time, energy, and resources into educating prospects and nurturing relationships with their most profitable customers. There are several examples of ways in which AI-empowered CRM can help improve sales force performance:

customer relationship management (CRM)

The process by which companies get new customers, keep the customers they already have, and grow the business by increasing their share of customers' purchases.

CRM system

A set of information technology tools used to help companies stay connected to customers and prospects, streamline processes, and improve profitability.

- *Price optimization:* Knowing what discount, if any, to offer a client is always tricky. You want to win the deal, but at the same time you don't want to leave money on the table. AI algorithms can review specific features of past proposals that were won or lost and suggest an ideal pricing program.

lead scoring

Analytics-based sales approach in which a company numerically rates its best prospective customers.

- **Lead scoring:** Using historical data from past prospects and current customers, companies can apply AI tools to identify traits that predict purchase likelihood and CLV. Based on these statistical models, the company can prioritize incoming prospects based on purchase propensity and estimated long-term profitability.
- *Upselling and cross-selling:* The fastest, most economical way to grow revenue is to sell more to an existing client base. But the million-dollar question is, *who* is more likely to buy *what?* AI algorithms can help identify which existing clients are more likely to upgrade to a better version of what they currently own (upsell) and which are most likely to want a new product offering altogether (cross-sell).[32]

Virtual Selling

Over recent years, buyers have shown increasing reluctance to engage in face-to-face interaction with sellers until deeper in the sales process. However, the 2020 COVID-19 pandemic drove a radical shift to virtual selling for both B2B and B2C sellers. **Virtual selling** is the collection of processes and technologies by which salespeople engage with their customers remotely using a mix of synchronous and asynchronous communications. Multiple studies by firms like Bain and McKinsey indicate virtual selling is likely to remain even once opportunity for more face-to-face selling returns.

virtual selling

A collection of processes and technologies by which salespeople engage with their customers remotely, using both synchronous and asynchronous communications.

Virtual selling involves the strategic blending of communication channels (asynchronous and synchronous) in the sales process to increase the probability of engaging a prospect, scheduling an appointment, advancing the sale to the next phase, closing sales, and retaining customers.[33] Table 9.3 provides examples of synchronous and asynchronous communication channels. In determining the appropriate mix of sales communication channels and messaging, sales professionals must carefully consider questions such as: "Which communication channels are most cost-effective at each step in the sales process? When does communication need to be face-to-face? When should salespeople use video instead of e-mail or phone?"

Emphasis on Video-Based Communications   Even though virtual selling encompasses a variety of communication channels, it is most distinguishable from traditional face-to-face selling based on its heavy use of video technology. This includes conducting sales meetings and presentations through video calls, communicating with prospects through video messages, or making e-mails and follow-up text

TABLE 9.3   Examples of Synchronous and Asynchronous Communication Channels

Synchronous Channels (Talking with People)	Asynchronous Channels (Talking at People)
Face-to-face (not virtual)	E-mail
Video calls	Video messaging
Phone calls	Direct messaging
Live chat	Voice mail
Texting	Social media posting and commenting
	Snail mail

messages more engaging through use of video. In addition, virtual selling uses video throughout all phases of the selling process.

Virtual Selling as a Prospecting Tool Prospecting is a powerful application for virtual selling videos. Buyers are busy and their e-mail inboxes are flooded with messages from managers, employees, and other vendors. By creating a brief, personalized video and attaching it to an e-mail, sellers can stand apart from the noise. Such videos need not be something that is overly produced or rehearsed. In fact, it should appear natural and unplanned, a video that speaks specifically to the prospect, taking what is usually said in e-mail copy but providing deeper context and value.

Virtual Sales Meetings Virtual sales meetings and presentation have fast replaced in-person meetings and phone calls, especially during the earlier stages of the sales process. Typically, these conversations are held using video conferencing technologies. More advanced systems help salespeople facilitate collaboration during virtual sales meetings by incorporating special features, like live polls and interactive whiteboards.

While video is not as effective as face-to-face meetings in terms of developing rapport with buyers and reading nonverbal cues, it may be the next best thing. In preparation for the sales call, it is always a good idea for the salesperson to let the prospect(s) know that they plan to use their video camera during their presentation. This is an implicit signal that the prospect should do the same. Assuming the prospect's camera is on, a well-trained salesperson should then be able to detect when a prospect is confused, disinterested, or is responding positively, based on body language and expressions. Being able to detect those moments provides the seller with opportunity to ask probing follow-up questions and keep the prospect engaged in the conversation.

Video for Meeting Follow-Up and Closing Video is also useful for following up on virtual sales meetings, moving the sales process forward, and closing deals. Just like during the prospecting phase, inclusion of a professional video in a follow-up e-mail or proposal submission can help the seller stand out. These videos can also be used to help forestall common objections before they arise. In addition, in many complex B2B sales there may be influencers that the seller may never get to communicate with in-person. Including video as part of post-meeting e-mails and proposals enables the salesperson to communicate with these decision makers in a manner that would not be otherwise possible.

Video Production Guidelines
Given heavy use of video-based channels in virtual selling, companies and salespeople should take steps to apply best practices from photography and film in their home or office studio setups. Marketing students who will soon be entering the job market and participating in virtual job interviews can easily adopt many of these same tips.

- **Camera angle:** The camera should be directly in front, at eye level. The camera frame should include the torso above the waist. If possible, you should use a high-quality webcam mounted on a tripod, instead of an internal laptop webcam. And always make sure the camera lens is clean before starting the meeting.
- **Quality lighting:** Proper lighting makes it easier to see facial features and expressions, leading to increased engagement, attention, and trust. Never sit in front of windows. Ideally, lighting sources should be directly behind the camera.
- **Backdrop:** The backdrop is a direct reflection of your personal and professional brand. Avoid clutter, bland walls, and big open rooms. Experts suggest using bookshelves, professional artwork, or a logo as a background instead.

- **Color contrast:** Make sure your clothes contrast well against the background. Avoid black clothing if the background is dark. Otherwise, your head will appear to be floating.
- **Audio:** Proper audio is the most important element of an effective video call. Select a location that minimizes background noise. Avoid rooms with echo. If possible, use a high-quality external microphone.

What Is Social Selling?

social selling

The use of online, mobile, and social media to engage customers, build strong customer relationships, and increase sales.

Many leading sales organizations today have embraced the power of social networking tools to improve the ability of their sales representatives to initiate conversations and develop meaningful customer relationships. In a relatively short time, *social selling* has transformed selling practices for many companies and industries. **Social selling** is the practice of using social networking platforms to find, connect with, understand, and nurture relationships with sales prospects. To be sure, social selling is *not the same* as social media marketing. It does not entail broadcasting promotional material over social media platforms, nor does it involve the indiscriminate sharing of information online. It is a purposeful activity aimed specifically at bolstering seller credibility, facilitating insightful conversations with prospects, and establishing long-term customer relationships.

LinkedIn is recognized as a leading proponent of social selling. Mr. Koka Sexton, the company's global senior manager of social marketing describes it as "leveraging your professional brand to fill your pipeline with the right people, insights, and relationships."[34] LinkedIn provides users with an SSI (social selling index) score, which tells salespeople and marketers how effectively they are using the platform. SSI divides performance into four "pillars," so users can identify strengths as well as areas that need more attention. The four pillars of social selling on LinkedIn are:

1. Developing your brand.
2. Connecting with the right people.
3. Engaging with insights.
4. Establishing relationships.

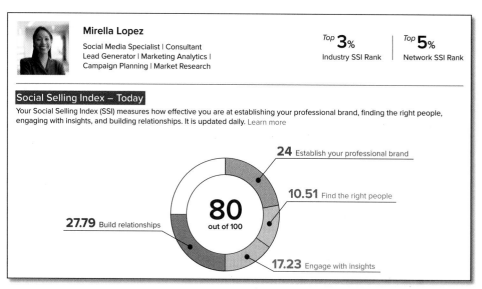

Example of a LinkedIn SSI score *(Businesswoman) Jose Luis Pelaez Inc/Blend Images LLC*

LinkedIn's reporting also provides salespeople and marketers with easy to read graphics that help them evaluate their social selling performance in context of other users in their field. With so many rivals actively prospecting and engaging customers using LinkedIn, it's important for salespeople to see how well they are doing in a competitive context.

Why Are Companies Adopting Social Selling? There are several factors driving adoption of social selling strategies. For one, prospective customers today routinely share information online about the most significant business or personal challenges they are facing. Adept social sellers leverage social networks to increase their understanding of industry trends as well as events impacting their prospect's lives or businesses. Internalizing this information enables them to provide customers with more timely insights and useful solutions.

Another reason sales organizations are turning to social media is because that is where their customers are spending their time. A recent study indicated that 83 percent of B2B executives use social media in their information searches; 92 percent of the executives report that the information found through their social media engagements had influenced buying decisions.[35] As a result, salespeople who are not actively engaged in social selling are less likely to show up in buyers' pre-purchase research, leading to missed sales opportunities. While the most appropriate platforms may vary by industry (e.g., Instagram for sellers in the fashion industry), Twitter and LinkedIn are primary outlets B2B buyers utilize to learn about potential products and vendors.

How Companies Are Using Social Selling What are some of the ways that company's are using social selling techniques? Figure 9.3 illustrates the ways in which B2B sales forces are using social selling techniques.[36]

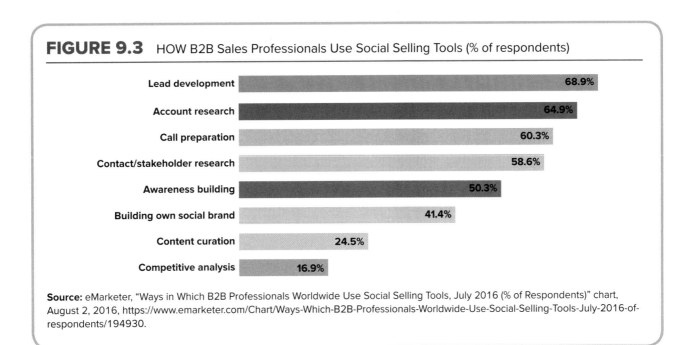

FIGURE 9.3 HOW B2B Sales Professionals Use Social Selling Tools (% of respondents)

Lead development	68.9%
Account research	64.9%
Call preparation	60.3%
Contact/stakeholder research	58.6%
Awareness building	50.3%
Building own social brand	41.4%
Content curation	24.5%
Competitive analysis	16.9%

Source: eMarketer, "Ways in Which B2B Professionals Worldwide Use Social Selling Tools, July 2016 (% of Respondents)" chart, August 2, 2016, https://www.emarketer.com/Chart/Ways-Which-B2B-Professionals-Worldwide-Use-Social-Selling-Tools-July-2016-of-respondents/194930.

connect   Exercise 9-3

Social Media in Action

The use of social technologies has also affected the degree to which buyers desire or require face-to-face relationships. Technologies are enabling prospective customers to develop deep knowledge of the firm's offerings before direct engagement with a salesperson. These technologies can effectively replace early stages of the personal selling process.

Social technologies are also changing customer expectations with respect to accessibility and responsiveness of salespeople and account managers. Salespeople are increasingly using social network platforms, e-mail, video, web conferencing, and text messaging to communicate with potential customers. As use of such Sales 2.0 tools increases, the volume of face-to-face interactions is decreasing. The new technologies provide sales and marketing an alternative means to build credibility and interpersonal trust. According to former IT sales executive and speaker Jill Rowley, "The modern sales professional doubles as an information concierge—providing the right information to the right person at the right time in the right channel."[37]

The Social Media in Action Connect exercise in Chapter 9 will let you choose social media tools to develop more profitable relationships with potential customers. By understanding the strategies associated with social selling, you will be prepared to use these tools to their maximum benefit in helping your organization succeed.

The success of online marketing software firm HubSpot has been fueled, in part, by its use of social selling techniques. *M4OS Photos/Alamy Stock Photo*

One example of a firm that has been successful in its use of social selling approaches is HubSpot, a provider of cloud-based CRM software and services. The company uses insights from social media to develop original content that triggers interest in its services. It has an active social listening campaign to identify questions of interest from small business owners and managers that match the profiles of its ideal buyers. Based on this information, whenever something changes in online marketing, HubSpot is always among the first to release guidebooks and white papers that contain precisely the information its customers are interested in.[38]

Social Selling Tactics for Sales Professionals
In order to strategically leverage social media platforms such as LinkedIn, Facebook, and Twitter, social sellers must be thoughtful and systematic in their efforts to: establish a professional brand; identify and focus their energies on the most valuable prospects; bolster credibility by engaging customers with timely and insightful information; and build and maintain trust-based relationships.

Crafting a Professional Brand on Social Platforms
Today's world of B2B buyers are very selective and will work only with vendors they trust. Social media tools can increase a salesperson's visibility within an industry and enable them to define a distinct professional brand. Through commenting, liking, or sharing content with prospects, salespeople can boost their own credibility by showing an active interest in what their buyers are posting and talking about. This can lead to more unsolicited inquiries from prospects as well as improved responsiveness to the salesperson's own outbound communications.

In creating their professional brand, salespeople should thoughtfully optimize their social media profiles to showcase the value they bring to customers. Experts suggest social sellers should always invest in a professional headshot. A descriptive headline works better than simply listing a job title; for example, "Customer-Centric B2B Software Sales Professional" is more compelling than "Sales Executive." Finally, summaries of professional experience and work histories should be buyer-centric, offering prospects a glimpse into how the salesperson is helping clients succeed. It should not read like a resume intended to attract interest from recruiters.[39]

Use Social Tools to Focus Attention on the Right Prospects
Social selling can enable salespeople to find and connect with prospects more effectively than traditional prospecting, pre-approach, and approach techniques. For instance, B2B sellers can utilize search features within LinkedIn to identify prospects that match the profiles of their best clients—such as role, function, education, industry, or firm size. Social media tools can also make it easier to determine whether the prospect has a personal connection with a friend or professional colleague. If so, the salesperson may feel comfortable to request a personal introduction. After all, a "warm" lead is always preferable to a "cold" call.

In addition, social sellers can set up alerts about customers, prospects, and target companies using Twitter, Google, or other social listening tools. This helps sales professionals stay on top of the latest industry news, insights, and customer conversations. Another approach is to set up a search that identifies buyers who have recently left a key account that has been successfully serviced by the seller's organization. These decision makers will likely want to work with the same people, processes, and technology that made them successful in their previous roles.

Engage Prospects and Customers with Relevant Insights
Sales is all about influence without authority. According to a recent study by LinkedIn, over 62 percent of B2B buyers respond to salespersons that connect with relevant insights and opportunities.[40] Engaging customers with meaningful information via social selling

entails a thoughtful approach to being the first to share industry news, surveys, reports, case studies, and ideas. By adding their own voice to carefully selected content, social sellers can further bolster prospects' perceptions of their thought leadership.

As a first step, social sellers must create or find quality content. *Content curation* is the process of continually finding, grouping, and sharing the most relevant content across social networks. Effective content curation requires an ongoing commitment to stay on top of emerging ideas in areas of concern for customers and share the most useful information with the right audiences. In addition to outside content, social sellers should selectively mix in company-created materials, such as white papers and customer success stories. Many sales organizations have augmented their CRM systems to include **sales enablement** tools, making it easier for salespeople to find and share internal content based on the prospect's needs and stage of the sales process.

Using Social Selling to Build Trust-Based Relationships
How do interpersonal relationships typically begin? What relationships in your personal life have stood the test of time? Your likely answers to these questions are not terribly unlike answers to these questions in a business context.

Buyers and sellers typically connect based on some shared interest or desire for positive change from the status quo. Buyers aim to establish long-term relationships with vendors who consistently provide economic value and demonstrate high levels of trustworthiness. Social selling simply offers salespeople new ways to initiate and maintain trust-based relationships with buyers. For instance, instead of reaching out to a prospect with a potentially intrusive telephone call or anonymous e-mail blast, social sellers can start with a tweet or retweet, a follow, a LinkedIn request, or comment. Participating in online groups that attract your target prospects is another great place to start. There are over 2 million groups on LinkedIn alone.

Once a social connection is made, sellers can provide value and build trust by providing insightful information in their online conversations, posts, and news feeds. Whether sharing original content or curated content, everything you put out must have credible, value-adding information. By providing relevant information and sharing their own unique perspectives—focusing on helping, not selling—salespeople gain a reputation for industry expertise and establish buyer trust. When a buyer is seeking out solutions to a future problem, it is only natural that they will first turn to the most knowledgeable individuals they know within their social sphere.

sales enablement

The process of providing the sales organization with the information, content, and tools that help salespeople sell more effectively.

LO 9-6

Discuss ethical issues in personal selling and sales management.

ETHICAL ISSUES IN PERSONAL SELLING AND SALES MANAGEMENT

The potential for ethical and legal issues pervades all areas of business decision making. There is no doubt, however, that such concerns are often spotlighted within personal selling contexts due to the one-to-one nature of salesperson–customer interactions. *Sales ethics* refers to a set of behaviors that ensure that every lead, prospect, and customer is treated with respect, fairness, honesty, and integrity.[41] To put it simply, it means salespeople should always place the customer first. Over the next section, we discuss factors that can lead to ethical dilemmas for sales personnel.

Causes and Implications of Unethical Sales Behaviors

If a salesperson's aim is to establish long-term, mutually beneficial relationships with their customers, it is logical for them to make sure that each step of the sales process is guided by ethical considerations. Conflicts can originate from social or financial demands in a salesperson's personal life. For instance, a sudden need to pay for unplanned medical expenses for a wife or child.

Sales employees can also suffer psychologically when they are caught in a struggle between their internal values and pressure from their company or manager to meet sales quotas. They may feel compelled to close sales "at any and all costs" under these circumstances. In a highly publicized case, Wells Fargo Bank was cited and fined by federal regulators in 2016 for the creation of millions of fraudulent savings and checking accounts on behalf of Wells Fargo clients without their consent. The scandal resulted from top-down pressure from top management on sales to open as many accounts as possible through cross-selling activities. Subsequent news coverage tarnished the bank's reputation, ultimately resulting in the resignation of the bank's CEO and payment of nearly $3 billion in civil and criminal penalties.

With rising use of social media networks among consumers and business buyers, sellers' ethical infractions can become highly visible to external stakeholders—including prospective customers, employers, investors, and competitors. If a salesperson takes a shortcut—if there is even the appearance of impropriety—it can sidetrack more than a single deal. These events have the potential to cause significant damage to corporate reputation and can cause irreversible damage to a sales career. Conversely, research has shown that maintaining high ethical standards on the part of sales personnel is a critical driver of sales force performance: It affects the firm's capacity to (1) build relationships with customers and (2) develop a positive work environment for employees.[42]

Standards of Sales Professional Conduct

Many firms seek to promote ethical behavior by emphasizing core organizational values and strictly enforcing codes of ethics. However, reports of damaging transgressions among sales, marketing, and other areas of the firm remain commonplace. One study of sales and marketing executives revealed that more than 50 percent of respondents believed that their salespeople have lied on a sales call. Nearly 75 percent agreed that the pressure to meet sales goals encourages salespeople to lose focus on customers' needs.[43]

What are some common examples of unethical conduct in sales context? In order to accelerate the sales process, a salesperson may be tempted to say exactly what they think the prospect wants to hear in order to close the sale. For example, they may overstate the performance capabilities of the company's product or exaggerate results other customers received after implementing the seller's solution. When discussing competitive offerings, it may be tempting to cast aspersion on a rival. Salespeople are well advised to *always* adopt the high road when discussing competitors. When pressed by a customer to address why they should choose their product over that of a rival, the salesperson should take it as an opportunity to demonstrate their professionalism and industry knowledge. They can use the competitor question as a chance to highlight illustrative customer success stories, offer feature comparisons, and discuss differentiating features that make their product offering unique.

Another common area of ethical concern involves salespeople's behaviors toward their own firm, such as improper use of expense accounts or misreporting account information. Illegal or unethical behavior may also be initiated by customers, such as buyer solicitation of bribes, favors, or gifts.

Many companies invest in training programs to better prepare employees to make good decisions when confronted with a potentially unethical situation. In addition, trade organizations such as Sales and Marketing Executives International (SMEI) and the Canadian Professional Sales Association (CPSA) have incorporated ethical codes of conduct into their sales and marketing certification programs. Salespeople must abide by these codes of conduct in order to maintain their certification. The SMEI code

Today's **Professional**... because everyone is a marketer

Tyler Garnett

State Farm Agent

Describe your job. I always say my job is to "Help life go right" for everyone I encounter in my office. I not only get to help people understand coverage better for cars and homes, but I also get to build a relationship by helping with their mortgage, vehicle loan, retirement saving, and life insurance.

How did you get your job? State Farm has a program for new employees who want to work in an agent's office and get "approved" to be in the agency pool. I got married and moved straight to Nashville, Tennessee. I worked at an office for almost two years until we decided to move back home, where I started working for an agent here. State Farm allows you to see EVERY opening across the nation and interview for it!

What has been the most important thing in making you successful at your job? Listening. This is a very underrated skill that many people don't understand. My job is not to tell people what to do; it is to listen, ask the right questions, and match the customers with the products that fit their specific needs. When done correctly you are always

Photo provided by Tyler Garnett

putting the customers' needs first, building strong relationships, and building trust with the community.

What advice would you give soon-to-be graduates? Work Hard!!! You will never get where you want to be if you don't work for it. No matter what the position is, you will always have someone competing with you. Working hard brings not only experience, but also a testament to what kind of person you will be when you finally get the job! When times get hard just remember, if it was easy, everyone would do it!

What do you consider your personal brand to be? When people think of Tyler Garnett State Farm, I want them to think of the most trustworthy, knowledgeable, and customer-serving agency in town. We want everyone to know they can trust us to do what is best for them, and that we care about the people in our community! Even though the slogan has changed, we still think of ourselves as the "Good Neighbor."

of conduct begins with three pledges that serve as excellent guides for all sales professionals.

1. **I hereby acknowledge** my accountability to the organization for which I work and to society as a whole to improve sales knowledge and practice and to adhere to the highest professional standards in my work and personal relationships.
2. **My concept of selling** includes as its basic principle the sovereignty of all consumers in the marketplace and the necessity for mutual benefit to both buyer and seller in all transactions.
3. **I shall personally maintain** the highest standards of ethical and professional conduct in all my business relationships with customers, suppliers, colleagues, competitors, governmental agencies, and the public.[44]

Today's business environment calls for transparency and customer-oriented behaviors. Deviating from these norms in pursuit of short-term gains will ultimately prove detrimental to an individual's—and an organization's—reputation for sales and marketing professionalism.

SUMMARY

B Christopher/ Alamy Stock Photo

LO 9-1 Describe the strategic role of the sales force and the factors that influence use of personal selling.

Personal selling consists of the *two-way* flow of communication between a buyer and a seller that is paid for by the seller and seeks to influence the buyer's purchase decision. It is a strategic activity closely linked to firm competitive advantage and financial performance. Personal selling is most effective as a promotional tool when a product is new-to-the-world, infrequently purchased, technical, viewed as risky, or customizable.

The changing selling environment has led to a fundamental rethinking of the *strategic nature* of the salesperson's role. The traditional emphasis for the sales force was on increasing the volume of sales transactions. However, *relationship selling* is now the core of modern selling strategies. Firms today place more emphasis on developing long-term, consulting-type partnerships with their most valuable downstream partners and customers.

Professional selling offers attractive career choices to new graduates. There are typically many opportunities for new hires with excellent starting salaries. To meet rising industry demand, many universities have launched sales centers and certificate programs.

David Goldman/AP Images

LO 9-2 Understand the different types of sales positions.

There are many different types of sales positions. *New-business* salespeople are responsible primarily for finding new customers and securing their business. *Channel* sales representatives look to win, maintain, and expand relationships with channel

partners. *Order-taker* salespeople primarily process orders that a customer initiates. They are most commonly found within retail and inbound call-center settings. *Consultative sellers* focus on developing long-term relationships. *Missionary* salespeople generate sales by promoting the firm and encouraging demand for its goods and services. They do not actually get or take orders from customers. *Key-account sellers* typically focus on establishing and maintaining partnership relationships with a small set of three to five named accounts.

Sales managers oversee selling efforts at varying levels of the organizational hierarchy. They establish sales objectives, and they forecast and develop annual sales quotas for their assigned territories. In addition, sales managers work with human resource personnel to recruit, select, train, supervise, and evaluate frontline sales employees. *Customer success managers* straddle the gap between service and sales, proactively seeking ways to improve customers' business performance through use of their firm's products.

Morsa Images/ DigitalVision/ Getty Images

LO 9-3 Explain the steps in the personal selling process.

The personal selling process consists of a sequence of seven steps that salespeople follow to acquire new customers and obtain orders: prospecting and qualifying, pre-approach, approach, presentation, handling objections, gaining commitment, and follow-up. This selling process is similar across nearly all sales contexts. Although finding new customers is crucial for sales growth, salespeople must not overlook the huge potential for revenue and profits of existing customers. Most businesses today depend on repeat sales of products and add-on services to existing clients

LO 9-4 Describe the foundational elements necessary for sales success.

Success in professional sales centers on serving the interests of the customer. *Customer-oriented selling* is the adoption of the marketing concept at the level of the individual salesperson and customer. Customer-oriented sales approaches are most effective when the salesperson has certain resources and abilities: a positive self-concept, market-related knowledge, and sales-related knowledge.

Keeping a positive self-concept in the face of uncertainty underlies high performance in sales careers. Successful salespeople are often characterized by their *grit,* a trait that emphasizes maintaining realistic optimism without letting failures slow you down. In order to be trusted advisers and effectively co-create value with customers, sales professionals must continuously improve their *market-related knowledge.* This includes understanding the goods, services, and processes within their own firm and key business issues affect their customers.

Successful salespeople commit themselves to their craft. *Sales-related knowledge* includes understanding of the sales process and selling techniques. Winning a sale can depend on a salesperson's ability to recognize buyer types and customize their message. *Adaptive selling* is a salesperson's ability to alter sales behavior during a customer interaction or across interactions based on perceived information about the sales situation.

LO 9-5 Describe the use of sales technologies and social network platforms in professional selling.

Sales technology plays an increasingly important role in driving sales performance. *Customer relationship management (CRM) systems* gather and store information about prospects and customers from various business touchpoints, including sales records, contact forms, e-mail and social media marketing, search engines, and more.

Virtual selling is the collection of processes and technologies by which salespeople engage with their customers remotely using both synchronous and asynchronous communications. Its most distinguishing feature involves its heavy use of video technology. This includes conducting sales presentations through video calls, communicating with prospects via video messages, and making e-mails and follow-up text messages more engaging by use of video.

Social selling involves the use of online, mobile, and social media to engage customers, build strong customer relationships, and increase sales. In order to strategically leverage social media platforms, social sellers must be thoughtful in efforts to: establish a professional brand; identify and focus energies on their most valuable prospects; bolster credibility by engaging customers with timely and insightful information; and build and maintain trust-based relationships.

LO 9-6 Discuss the ethical issues in personal selling and sales management.

The potential for ethical and legal issues pervades nearly all areas of business and marketing decision making. Such concerns are often spotlighted within personal selling contexts, due to the one-to-one nature of salesperson–customer interactions. Many firms seek to promote ethical behavior by emphasizing core organizational values and strictly enforcing codes of ethics. Companies also invest in training programs to better prepare employees to make good decisions when confronted with a potentially unethical situation.

KEY TERMS

adaptive selling (p. 306)
advantages (in FAB approach) (p. 300)
approach (p. 298)
benefits (in FAB approach) (p. 300)
channel sales representatives (p. 293)
consultative sellers (p. 294)
CRM system (p. 309)
customer lifetime value (CLV) (p. 289)
customer-oriented selling (p. 304)
customer relationship management (CRM) (p. 309)
customer success manager (p. 295)
delivery salespeople (p. 293)

feature-advantage-benefit (FAB) approach (p. 300)
features (in FAB approach) (p. 300)
gaining commitment (p. 302)
key-account sellers (p. 294)
lead scoring (p. 310)
market-related knowledge (p. 306)
missionary salespeople (p. 294)
new-business salespeople (p. 293)
objections (p. 301)
order-taker salespeople (p. 293)
personal selling (p. 288)
personal selling process (p. 297)

pre-approach (p. 297)
prospect (p. 297)
prospecting (p. 297)
qualifying (p. 297)
relationship selling (p. 289)
sales enablement (p. 316)
sales engineers (p. 295)
sales force management (p. 295)
selling-related knowledge (p. 306)
social selling (p. 312)
virtual selling (p. 310)

MARKETING PLAN EXERCISE • Marketing Yourself

In this chapter we discussed the importance of selling and also of asking good questions. Discovering the right information from decision makers and prospective future employees is a very important skill on your personal journey. In the next section of the marketing plan exercise, your assignment is to create specific questions to obtain the information you will need to decide whether a job in an organization or graduate school will be a good fit for your career goals.

New graduates consistently struggle at the part of interviewing or networking where prospective employers or graduate school admissions officers ask, "Do you have any questions for us?" The SPIN selling technique in this chapter provides a good framework as you work to develop the most relevant and efficient questions at this stage:

- *Situation* questions are designed to obtain background facts about the buyer's current circumstances.
- (In this example, the *buyer* is the potential employer or the committee making the decision to admit you to a graduate school program.)
- *Problem* questions ask about buyer's problems, difficulties, or dissatisfactions with an existing situation. Knowing this helps you understand how your skills

might help improve the organization or add value to a university's graduate school program.

- *Implication* questions help transform problems into explicit needs in the mind of the buyer and expand the perceived value of finding a solution. This type of question can help the decision makers think more closely about how hiring you or accepting you into their program will make their organization better.
- *Need-payoff* questions are designed to get the buyer thinking about your value, importance, or usefulness in finding a solution to the problem.

The SPIN framework questions will help you sell yourself to potential employers or schools. They also will help you better understand how the organizations you are interested in fit into your personal marketing plan.

Your Task: Write one question for each component of the SPIN selling framework. Your answer should include a situation question, problem question, implication question, and need-payoff question focused on either your targeted job or graduate school program. Please also include a sentence or two for each on what you hope to find out from each specific question and how that information might benefit you.

DISCUSSION QUESTIONS

1. Imagine that a company was looking to sell to you. How could social selling help that company sell its products to you? Please provide at least two specific recommendations.

2. Based on your personal strengths and weaknesses, which type of sales position do you think would be best for you? Explain your answer and also share which type of sales position you would least like to hold.

3. Think about a product you would like to sell. If you were going to sell that product to your class, what would you do to make sure that you included each of the four characteristics of a great sales presentation?

4. Remember a time when you had objections about buying a product from a salesperson. Based on those objections, what would you recommend the salesperson do in order to handle those objections and to increase the likelihood that you would buy that product? Explain your answer.

5. Based on what you have read about compensating salespeople, do you think salespeople should be compensated using only fixed salary, only commission, or a combination of the two? Please explain your answer. If you choose the combined approach, what would you consider the optimal ratio of fixed salary to commission?

 # SOCIAL MEDIA APPLICATION

Find a salesperson whom you know of and visit their LinkedIn profile. Analyze that profile using the following questions and activities as a guide:

1. What skills has the salesperson been "recommended" or "endorsed" for? Do you think these are the most valuable skills for a successful salesperson?

2. Has the salesperson you are analyzing joined any relevant groups on LinkedIn? Based on the

salesperson's job, are there any groups that you suggest they join?

3. Provide at least two recommendations as to how this salesperson could better highlight their market or sales-related knowledge to current and potential clients.

MARKETING ANALYTICS EXERCISE

Please complete the *Connect* exercise for Chapter 9 that focuses on using analytics to compare prospects in a lead scoring system.

ETHICAL CHALLENGE

How much investing terminology do you need to master while saving for your retirement? For example, do you know what the word *fiduciary* means? A Financial Engines survey found that only 18 percent of Americans are sure what the word means. U.S. financial advisers are divided between fiduciaries, who are required to put your interests first (like a doctor or lawyer), and nonfiduciaries, similar to salespeople, who push "suitable" products that may profit them more than you.

Nonfiduciary advisers, typically called *brokers,* are free to recommend only the products that earn them the highest commissions, which can come from both load fees and annual fees. These advisers typically get paid in a variety of complicated ways, so it can be hard to tell how much they're making off a client and what their incentives are. Fiduciary advisers tend to get paid in more transparent ways, often by charging an annual fee based on the assets they manage.

Despite years of resistance from Wall Street, the U.S. Department of Labor announced in 2016 the final version of a rule that may force financial advisers to abandon the way they've done business for decades. For the first time, all advisers may need to act as fiduciaries, putting their clients' interests first when handling retirement accounts.

Many on Wall Street counter that a strong fiduciary rule will make it less profitable to offer advice to lower- and middle-income Americans. They argue that the proposal will limit the ability of consumers to continue to receive personalized investment guidance for retirement plan accounts, which would result in a less secure retirement for many Americans.

Advocates of the new rule say it may generate new insurance and investment business models that cost less and aren't as likely to exploit less knowledgeable retail investors. It is not clear how the final rule would be enforced, though it might leave noncomplying firms open to penalties or lawsuits.

Please use the ethical decision-making framework to answer the following questions:

1. Do you think that all financial advisers should act as fiduciaries?
2. Identify the stakeholders that will be affected by this decision. Be sure to think through all of the potential internal and external stakeholders.
3. How will this decision affect each of the financial advisers stakeholders?

Source: Ben Steverman, "At Last, Brokers Must Put Your Retirement Needs First," *Bloomberg Businessweek,* March 31, 2016, http://www.bloomberg.com/news/articles/2016-03-31/new-law-may-force-brokers-to-put-your-retirement-investment-first.

VIDEO CASE

Please go to *Connect* to access the video case featuring the real estate brokerage Marcus & Millichap that accompanies this chapter.

PODCAST

Please go to Connect to access the podcast that accompanies this chapter.

CAREER **TIPS**

Breaking Out of a Sales Slump

Coauthor George Dietz offers the following advice if you ever find yourself in a sales slump. As you will see, you can apply it to other life challenges as well:

Most salespeople have at one time or another struggled to meet goals. There may be a variety of external causes for lower-than-desired performance. But before placing blame elsewhere, it's important for a salesperson to take a closer look at their own lifestyle, work habits, and belief systems.

Personal selling is a mentally demanding and highly competitive field. A sales rep who keeps late nights or is not conscious of healthy eating and drinking habits will soon feel insufficiently prepared, physically drained, and at a decided disadvantage to his or her competitors. Individuals in sales roles often work without regular direct supervision. Without the proper discipline, it is very easy for inexperienced and experienced salespeople alike to fall into poor work habits, such as getting to work late or not spending enough time qualifying prospects or preparing for sales calls.

Finally, slumping reps should reevaluate their belief system to make sure they are approaching their workday with the right attitude: *Do you believe your company or product is the best solution for the prospect? Do you think that you are the best?* If the answer to either question is "no," then you take action in one or more of the following ways:

- Proactively seek ways to improve the value proposition you are presenting.
- Reevaluate your prospecting and lead-qualification processes.
- Seek feedback on ways to improve your personal selling techniques.

Students often face similar challenges when they are seeking entry-level employment after graduation, or even later, as they pursue career advancement. If you are facing struggles in your school work or in finding the right internship or job, before placing blame elsewhere, you should ask yourself: *Am I getting enough sleep? Am I eating healthy and getting enough exercise? Am I really doing all that I can do to become the best in my field?* Whether you are seeking to sell a product, a service, or yourself, if you cannot comfortably answer "yes" to these types of questions, then it is critical that you proactively seek ways to correct the issue. Experts offer a few helpful tips:

- Hang around positive, successful people.
- Start your day an hour before everyone else.
- Talk to some of your best customers, friends, professors, or a mentor and ask them to evaluate your situation.
- Rearrange your work space.
- Set activity goals.
- List five things you could do to work harder *and* smarter to achieve your goals.

Ultimately, the best way to get out of a rut is to accept the fact that it is temporary and believe in your ability to change it. After all, if you don't believe that you are the best person to fulfill the opportunity you are applying for, then it will be exceedingly difficult to convince someone else that you are!

CHAPTER NOTES

1. D. M. Hanssens, ed., *Empirical Generalizations about Marketing Impact: What We Have Learned from Academic Research,* 2nd ed. (Cambridge, MA: Marketing Science Institute, 2015).
2. D. M. Hanssens, ed., *Empirical Generalizations about Marketing Impact: What We Have Learned from Academic Research,* 2nd ed. (Cambridge, MA: Marketing Science Institute, 2015).
3. S. Albers, M. K. Mantrala, and S. Sridhar, "Personal Selling," in *Empirical Generalizations about Marketing Impact,* 2nd ed., ed. D. M. Hanssens (Cambridge, MA: Marketing Science Institute, 2015), Chapter 12.
4. H. Stevens and T. Kinni, *Achieve Sales Excellence: The 7 Customer Rules for Becoming the New Sales Professional* (Avon, MA: Adams Media, 2006).

5. Bureau of Labor Statistics, "Sales Occupations," *Occupational Outlook Handbook,*n.d., http://www.bls.gov/ooh/sales/home.htm.

6. D. H. Pink,*To Sell Is Human: The Surprising Truth about Moving Others* (New York: Penguin, 2012).

7. https://knowledge.wharton.upenn.edu/article/daniel-pink-on-why-to-sell-is-human/.

8. Sales Education Foundation website, http://www.salesfoundation.org/.

9. Glassdoor, "Entry-Level Sales Salaries," n.d., https://www.glassdoor.com/Salaries/entry-level-sales-salary-SRCH_KO0, 17.htm.

10. Suzanne Fogel, Dave Hoffmeier, Rich Rocco, and Dan Strunk, "Teaching Sales," *Harvard Business Review,* July/August 2012.

11. Murray Barrick, Michael Mount, and Timothy Judge, "Personality and Performance at the Beginning of the New Millennium: Where Do We Go Next?"*Journal of Selection and Assessment* 9, no. 1 (2001): 9–30.

12. A. L. Dixon and S. M. Schertzer, "Bouncing Back: How Salesperson Optimism and Self-Efficacy Influence Attributions and Behaviors Following Failure," *Journal of Personal Selling & Sales Management* 25, no. 4 (2005): 361–369.

13. W. C. Moncrief III, "Selling Activity and Sales Position Taxonomies for Industrial Salesforces,"*Journal of Marketing Research* (1986): 261–270; W. C. Moncrief, G. W. Marshall, and F. G. Lassk, "A Contemporary Taxonomy of Sales Positions,"*Journal of Personal Selling & Sales Management* 26, no. 1 (2006): 55–65.

14. M. Ahearne, T. Haumann, F. Kraus, and J. Wieseke, "It's a Matter of Congruence: How Interpersonal Identification between Sales Managers and Salespersons Shapes Sales Success,"*Journal of the Academy of Marketing Science* 41, no. 6 (2013): 625–648.

15. Max Altschuler, "Sales Operations Demystified: What It Is, Why It Matters, and How to Do It Right,"*Sales Hacker,* June 3, 2021, https://www.saleshacker.com/what-is-sales-operations/.

16. J. Gitomer,*The Little Red Book of Selling* (Austin, TX: Bard Press Austin, 2005).

17. "Wordy Goods,"*The Economist,* August 22, 2012, http://www.economist.com/blogs/graphicdetail/2012/08/daily-chart-5.

18. Geoffrey James, "Train Your Sales Team, How to Build Rapport,"*SellingPower,* February 2, 2010, http://www.sellingpower.com/content/article/?a=6738/train-your-sales-team-how-to-build-rapport.

19. Lance Tyson, "The One Key Ability You Need for Building Rapport," Tyson Group, February 27, 2018, https://tysongroup.com/2018/02/key-ability-building-rapport/.

20. "Features Advantages Benefits Selling (FABS)," n.d., MBASkool.com, http://www.mbaskool.com/business-concepts/marketing-and-strategy-terms/12284-features-advantages-benefits-selling-fabs.html.

21. Z. Ziglar, *Selling 101: What Every Successful Sales Professional Needs to Know* (Nashville, TN: Thomas Nelson, 2003).

22. Stuart Leung, "How to Make a Good Sales Pitch in 7 Steps,"*Salesforce.com,* February 4, 2014, https://www.salesforce.com/blog/2014/02/how-to-make-good-sales-pitch.html.

23. Z. Ziglar, *Selling 101: What Every Successful Sales Professional Needs to Know* (Nashville, TN: Thomas Nelson, 2003).

24. Robert Saxe and Barton A. Weitz, "The SOCO Scale: A Measure of Customer Orientation on the Part of Salespeople,"*Journal of Marketing Research* 19, no. 3 (1982): 343–351.

25. G. W. Dudley and S. L. Goodson, *The Psychology of Sales Call Reluctance: Earning What You're Worth in Sales* (Dallas, TX: Behavioral Sciences Research Press, 1999).

26. Bart Weitz, Harish Sujan, and Mita Sujan, "Knowledge, Motivation, and Adaptive Behavior: A Framework for Improving Selling Effectiveness," *Journal of Marketing* 50, no. 3 (1986): 174–191.

27. G. R. Franke and J. E. Park, "Salesperson Adaptive Selling Behavior and Customer Orientation: A Meta-Analysis,"*Journal of Marketing Research* 43, no. 4 (2006): 693–702.

28. N. Rackham, R. Kalomeer, and D. Rapkin, *SPIN Selling* (New York: McGraw Hill, 1988).

29. Salesforce.com, "CRM 101: What Is CRM?," n.d., https://www.salesforce.com/crm/what-is-crm/.

30. Mark Taylor, "18 CRM Statistics You Need to Know for 2021 (and Beyond),"*SuperOffice,* May 4, 2021, https://www.superoffice.com/blog/crm-software-statistics/.

31. Amanda Sellers, "What Is CRM? 2021 Guide to CRM Software for Marketing and Sales Teams," *YokelLocal,* February 2, 2021, https://www.yokellocal.com/blog/what-is-crm.

32. Victor Antonio, "How AI Is Changing Sales," *Harvard Business Review,* July 30, 2018, https://hbr.org/2018/07/how-ai-is-changing-sales.

33. Jeb Blount, *Virtual Selling: A Quick Start to Leveraging Video, Technology, and Virtual Communication Channels to Engage Remote Buyers and Close Deals Fast* (Hoboken, NJ: Wiley, 2022).

34. "The How-To Guide to Social Selling," LinkedIn, (n.d.), https://business.linkedin.com/sales-solutions/social-selling/how-to-guide-to-social-selling-ebook.

35. Elliot Schimel, "Strategic Social Media Is Essential for Driving B2B Sales," *Forbes,* March 22, 2018, https://www.forbes.com/sites/forbesagencycouncil/2018/03/22/strategic-social-media-is-essential-for-driving-b2b-sales/?sh=6630661b1db0.

36. Staff writer, "The 8 Best Social Media Success Stories the World Has Ever Seen," *Cultbizztech,* January 15, 2018,https://cultbizztech.com/the-8-best-b2b-social-media-success-stories-the-world-has-ever-seen/.

37. Ken Krogue, "Sales Tips and Sales Quotes from 62 Top Sales Experts," *Forbes,* December 20, 2013, https://www.forbes.com/sites/kenkrogue/2013/12/20/sales-tips-and-sales-quotes-from-62-top-sales-experts/#2ffe1c8941be.

38. Staff writer, "The 8 Best Social Media Success Stories the World Has Ever Seen," *Cultbizztech,* January 15, 2018,https://cultbizztech.com/the-8-best-b2b-social-media-success-stories-the-world-has-ever-seen/.

39. "The How-To Guide to Social Selling," LinkedIn, (n.d.), https://business.linkedin.com/sales-solutions/social-selling/how-to-guide-to-social-selling-ebook.

40. "What Is Social Selling?" LinkedIn, (n.d.), https://business.linkedin.com/sales-solutions/social-selling/what-is-social-selling.

41. "Sales Ethics: Is There a Code of Ethics for Marketing and Sales?" PipeDrive, (n.d.), https://www.pipedrive.com/en/blog/sales-ethics.

42. J. P. Mulki, F. Jaramillo, and W. B. Locander, "Effects of Ethical Climate and Supervisory Trust on Salesperson's Job Attitudes and Intentions to Quit," *Journal of Personal Selling & Sales Management* 26, no. 1 (2006): 19–26.

43. E. Strout, "To Tell the Truth," *Sales and Marketing Management* 154 (July 2002): 40–47.

44. Sales & Marketing Executives, International, *Sales & Marketing Creed: The International Code of Ethics for Sales and Marketing,* https://www.smei.org/?16.

Chapter **10**

Supply Chain and Logistics Management

Wesley Hitt/Photolibrary/Getty Images

Learning Objectives

After reading this chapter, you should be able to

LO 10-1 Describe the various flows within a supply chain.

LO 10-2 Describe the push, pull, and hybrid supply chain strategies and their relationship to a company's competitive strategies.

LO 10-3 Summarize the importance of collaboration and resilience to effective supply chains.

LO 10-4 Describe how the primary logistics functions support a firm's supply chain strategy.

LO 10-5 Describe the various logistics functions and their importance to marketing.

Executive **Perspective** ... because everyone is a marketer

Sankha Basu
Senior Manager, Agile Transformation
CVS Health

Sankha Basu

Although Sankha Basu majored in civil engineering, he took a marketing class during his undergraduate studies out of curiosity; little did he know the impact it would have on his career. Following graduation, Sankha worked in various industries including travel and tourism, consulting, education, and most recently health care in a variety of sales, marketing, product development, digital strategy, and transformation roles.

Today, Sankha is with CVS Health, a Fortune 100 company, leading a team within the digital department responsible for the successful execution of digital programs and strategies across the organization.

What has been the most important thing in making you successful at your job?

I love the work I do. In my prior companies I have loved the roles I've had and the work I've done. I was happy to put in the effort needed because it never felt like a job for me. Whether I was selling a honeymoon package to newly-weds or launching education software that will help students learn better or going live with vaccination scheduling on an app, I have always loved the work I do and it drives me forward every day to do better.

What advice would you give soon-to-be graduates?

I am a civil engineer who went on to became a sales rep, consultant, marketer, editor, product manager, and am now a digital agilest. If you asked me 5 years ago if I knew the role I would be in today, I probably didn't know . . . and

that's OK. With the rapid advances in technology happening all over the world, the only constant in my career has been change. Regardless of industry or role—be ready for change and be prepared to adapt.

How is marketing relevant to your role at CVS?

I work at the intersection of technology and people, and I help build exceptional teams to deliver the value our customers seek. This relentless pursuit of innovation and value requires us to constantly think about what will resonate with customers and to evolve our marketing to benefit them.

What do you consider your personal - brand to be?

I consider myself to be a customer-centric, servant leader; someone who is invested in helping their team learn and grow, feel purposeful, motivated, and perform as highly as possible all the while keeping the customer at the core of everything I do.

SUPPLY CHAINS

If people learned one thing from the COVID-19 pandemic, it is that the world is an interconnected place in which the actions of people in one part can affect everyone. This is nowhere truer than in supply chains. The COVID-19 crisis forced people to stay in place, which in turn caused manufacturing companies to shut down. This was at the same time in which consumers switched to ordering goods online instead of spending money on dining out, travel, and other forms of services. Severe transportation delays occurred causing 61 percent of container ships to arrive late, the cost to ship a container to rise 333 percent, U.S. trucking rates to increase 15 percent from a year earlier, and customer service to plummet. These are just some of the problems faced by businesses as entire supply chains for many goods ground to a halt.[1]

A supply chain is the linked set of companies that perform or support the delivery of a company's products or services to customers. More formally, a supply chain is "a set of three or more companies directly linked by one or more of the upstream and downstream flows of products, services, finances, and information from a source to a customer."[2] Organizations make use of and are part of many supply chains, without which they cannot survive. When you work for an organization, it's likely you will take part in some way in its supply chain. This is true regardless of your job title and regardless of whether the organization sells products or services. Whatever functional area you end up working in, you will benefit from understanding what is involved in operating a successful supply chain strategy.

In Chapter 1, you learned that marketing consists of functions that create, communicate, and deliver value to customers. A supply chain *delivers value* to the end-user of products and services by leveraging the core competencies of its company members to cut costs, provide innovation, ensure quality, and deliver products and services to the right place at the right time at the right price. Without a well-run supply chain, all the efforts of marketers to design and promote products and services that will satisfy customers will not be as effective because they will cost too much, be less innovative, be of lower quality, and will not be delivered when and where the customer wants them.

Supply Chain Flows through Marketing Channels

A supply chain consists of flows of products and services, financial resources, and information among the companies in the chain. The image of a stream can help you visualize these flows. Imagine that you are standing in the middle of a stream (fly fishing, perhaps). The source of the water flowing toward you is *upstream* from you. The water flowing away from you is moving *downstream* toward its eventual destination in the ocean or lake.

In the case of a supply chain, instead of moving water we have products, which are primarily going from suppliers to customers. The terms *upstream* and *downstream* also apply to the flows in a supply chain:

- The flow of products and the services involved in getting the products to customers is said to move *downstream*.
- The flow of financial resources that move from the customer to the companies that were part of the supply chain is said to move *upstream*.

On their way downstream, products pass through distribution channels. *Distribution channels* or *marketing channels* are intermediaries, such as wholesalers, distributors, and retailers, through which the flow of products travels.[3] All along the supply chain, distribution channels add value to the product: They make it available to ship to the next step in the supply chain, take customer orders, and ship the product to the next step in the chain.

A *wholesaler* is a company that sells to other businesses, such as retailers and other industrial companies. Wholesalers buy products in large quantities, typically directly from producers of the products. United Natural Foods is an example of a wholesaler. It is a distributor of natural and organic foods, specialty foods, and related products in the United States and Canada. A *distributor* is similar to a wholesaler in that it sells products to other businesses. The main difference between a wholesaler and distributor is that a distributor will have exclusive rights to selling products from a producer to customers within a certain geographic territory. W. W. Granger is an example of a distributor that sells industrial supplies to other businesses. A *retailer* sells goods to consumers for their own use, rather than for resale to others. Individual sales are in much smaller quantities for retailers than for wholesalers and distributors. Target and Dollar General are examples of retailers.

IS098RK9I/Cultura Creative RF/Alamy Stock Photo

Containers have been a driving factor in the globalization of supply chains because they allow a large amount of goods to be shipped inexpensively and can be quickly and easily loaded onto and removed from ships.

In order to get a better idea of what a supply chain may look like, let's examine the journey of a pair of jeans from point of origin to point of consumption:

- First, a cotton grower harvests cotton and delivers it to a cloth manufacturer.
- The cloth manufacturer processes the cotton, spins it into yarn, dyes it, and ships it to a jeans manufacturer.
- The jeans manufacturer cuts the cloth, assembles it into jeans, embroiders, and labels them. Each of these steps require components such as thread, rivets, zippers, and labels that must be purchased from suppliers and delivered to the factory.
- When the jeans are finished they are typically moved by truck to a seaport, loaded onto a container ship, and sent to a port in the region where they are to be sold.
- From that port they are moved by train and/or truck to a distribution center owned by the jeans company. That distribution center stores the jeans until they are ordered by retailers.
- They are then sent to a retailer's distribution center. The retailer's distribution center sends the jeans by truck to individual stores, where people like you buy them.

All along this supply chain, we can see the different flows of products and services:

- Services such as ocean-freight companies assist the movement of the goods downstream.
- Information such as demand for the jeans moves upstream.
- Information about when the goods will arrive at the stores moves downstream.
- Finances in the form of payments to the suppliers move back upstream in the supply chain.[4]

Figure 10.1 illustrates these three types of supply chain flows.

The concept of a supply *chain* is actually a simplified version of what is actually a *network* of companies made up of many suppliers, selling to many intermediate customers. For example, a company producing cosmetics may buy from hundreds of suppliers. Some of those suppliers may be selling the same or similar raw and packaging materials to other cosmetics manufacturing companies. The cosmetics manufacturer may sell to a retailer that buys cosmetics from a number of other manufacturers. Thus, companies

FIGURE 10.1   Example of Supply Chain Flows for a T-Shirt

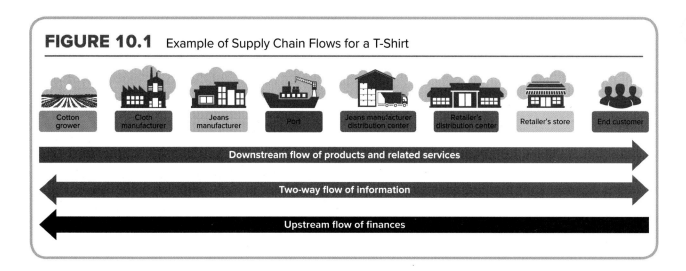

regularly are members of multiple supply chains or networks that can share many of the same suppliers, manufacturers, service providers, and customers. In the present global economy, supply chains incorporate members throughout the world. This presents many challenges to supply chain managers, who have to control the movement of goods and the performance of services throughout the globe.

Opportunities for college graduates to get high paying, interesting jobs in the supply chain field are plentiful. Careers in supply chain management and logistics include such positions as inventory specialists, customer service representatives, transportation sales, transportation management, transportation pricing, freight forwarding, production planning, purchasing, and warehouse management. Ample higher-level jobs such as global logistics manager, operations director, transportation director, international logistics manager, and chief supply chain officer are available to those who prove their abilities.

LO 10-2

Describe the push, pull, and hybrid supply chain strategies and their relationship to a company's competitive strategies.

SUPPLY CHAIN STRATEGY

Effective supply chain management requires a strategy that helps the firm establish a network of suppliers and customers to meet its supply chain objectives. This strategy will determine how the supply chain should be designed. This design will, in turn, determine how products are made and delivered to customers. Supply chain objectives should be based on the firm's marketing objectives. They can include things such as:

- Types and locations of markets to be served.
- Market share and customer service desired.
- Speed with which new products should be developed.
- Cost reduction and profitability goals.[5]

In the sections that follow, we will focus on three supply chain strategies: push, pull, and hybrid (push-pull). As you'll see in the sections that follow, the supply chain push and pull strategies essentially describe whether or not the company has orders in hand when it begins the supply chain activities.

push strategy

A supply chain strategy in which a company builds goods based on a sales forecast, puts those goods into storage, and waits for a customer to order the product.

Push Strategy

A **push strategy** is one in which a company builds goods based on a sales forecast, puts those goods into storage, and waits for a customer to order the product. A supply chain push strategy is also sometimes called a *speculation strategy* because the company speculates on the type and amount of products that the market will want.

There are two main advantages of a push supply chain strategy:

- Firms can achieve economies of scale. This means that purchasing can buy in larger lots which lowers purchase prices, transportation can move full vehicles which lowers the per-unit transportation costs, and manufacturing can make long production runs which are more efficient than short runs. The automotive industry, for example, relies on sales forecasts to plan production well in advance. A carmaker can drive down costs by placing large orders of raw materials, such as steel and glass. For that reason, a company whose marketing strategy includes objectives related to cost competitiveness and good customer service is a good candidate for this strategy.
- Push strategies often positively affect customer service because the goods are already in stock, awaiting the customer's order.

Automobile manufacturers often use a push supply chain strategy so that they can maximize their buying power when purchasing raw materials and making sure that dealers have cars available and in stock for customers to purchase and drive home. *Norman Wharton/Alamy Stock Photo*

However, there are disadvantages to using a supply chain push strategy:

- If sales forecasts are not accurate, the company will have too much of a product no one wants or not enough of a product consumers do want.
- Production facilities set up to manufacture one good over a period of time will respond slowly to changing demand patterns. For example, if gasoline prices suddenly increase and demand for SUVs slows, it is extremely expensive and time-consuming to retool an automotive plant to produce a small, fuel-efficient car instead of an SUV.
- Inventory carrying costs are expensive. They typically can be 25–30 percent of the cost to produce and deliver the goods. This expense can cut into the cost savings achieved through economies of scale in manufacturing, purchasing, and transportation. The ability to accurately forecast customer sales therefore becomes a priority for companies utilizing a push strategy.

pull strategy

A supply chain strategy in which customer orders drive manufacturing and distribution operations.

Pull Strategy

Firms whose marketing strategy requires agility and product customization may choose to pursue a supply chain pull strategy instead. A **pull strategy** is one in which customer orders drive manufacturing and distribution operations. It is also sometimes known as a *responsive supply chain.* The supply chain pull strategy and the promotion pull strategy both rely on customer orders. However, the supply chain version depends on an initial level of customer demand to even initiate manufacturing.

Boeing uses a pull strategy. It builds aircraft to customer specifications, and only when an order is received. Imagine the millions of dollars Boeing would tie up if it built aircraft to hold in inventory until an order came through.

Advantages of the supply chain pull strategy are:

- This method eliminates the risks associated with producing unwanted products because the good is not made until a customer order is received.

Manufacturers like Boeing often utilize a supply chain pull strategy to manage inventory costs and meet specific customer demands. *Stephen Brashear/Getty Images*

- Firms can customize products specifically to customer requirements.
- Inventory carrying costs are minimized.
- The firm can respond rapidly to changing market conditions.

The flexibility and customization of a pull strategy comes with a price. Its disadvantages are:

- A pull strategy doesn't often allow firms to take advantage of economies of scale. Because the company orders only what it needs to meet immediate production requirements, it typically orders small quantities. Such orders eliminate the possibility of quantity discounts.
- To effectively implement a supply chain pull strategy, a firm needs flexible production and distribution facilities. Production must be able to change rapidly to produce different products. Likewise, the distribution system must be able to deliver the product quickly once it's made. Such flexibility is hard to achieve, which explains why few companies practice a pure pull strategy.

Hybrid (Push-Pull) Strategy

hybrid (push-pull) strategy
A supply chain strategy in which the initial stages of the supply chain operate on a push system, but completion of the product is based on a pull system.

A third strategy is a hybrid of the other two: In a **hybrid (push-pull) strategy**, the initial stages of the supply chain operate on a push system, but completion of the product is based on a pull system. That is, as it would in a push strategy, a company might forecast sales, build an inventory of components based on the forecast, and hold those components in inventory until a customer order is received. Then, as in a pull strategy, the company would finalize the product based on the customer order. Lego, for example, builds its minifigures but delays their decoration, which can be in many different forms, until an order is received.[6]

The advantages of a hybrid strategy are:

- It combines the economies of scale of the push strategy with the flexibility of the pull strategy.
- It produces more accurate sales forecasts because firms tend to be more accurate at an aggregate level than at a specific product level. For example, Lego can more accurately forecast the number of minifigures it will sell in a given period much earlier than it can the number of each type of figure decoration it will sell.

A hybrid strategy also has disadvantages:

- It may not be as cost competitive as a push system because the firm cannot take advantage of manufacturing and transportation economies of scale.
- The firm will still incur costs to store components in inventory.
- As in a pure pull system, the company will need to develop a distribution system that can deliver products quickly to avoid customer service complaints.

Figure 10.2 compares the three different types of supply chain strategies.

Selecting the Appropriate Strategy

Which of the three supply chain strategies is appropriate for a company? The answer depends on one or more of the following factors:[7]

Push-pull supply chain strategies often work for firms like LEGO, which use sales forecasts to build up the expected inventory of base products such as minifigures and then wait for customer demand, such as popular characters at that moment, before customizing them. *Lewis Tse Pui Lung/Shutterstock*

FIGURE 10.2 Comparing Supply Chain Strategies

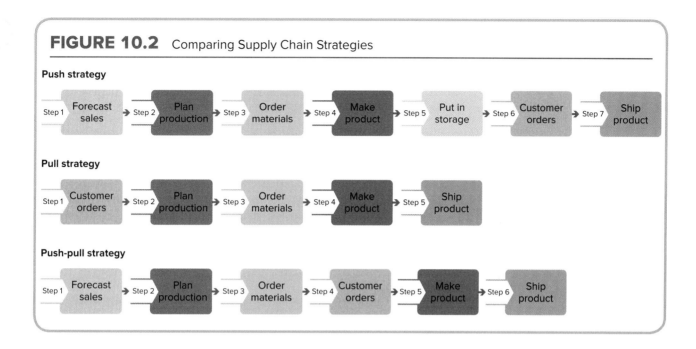

Push strategy

Step 1 Forecast sales → Step 2 Plan production → Step 3 Order materials → Step 4 Make product → Step 5 Put in storage → Step 6 Customer orders → Step 7 Ship product

Pull strategy

Step 1 Customer orders → Step 2 Plan production → Step 3 Order materials → Step 4 Make product → Step 5 Ship product

Push-pull strategy

Step 1 Forecast sales → Step 2 Plan production → Step 3 Order materials → Step 4 Customer orders → Step 5 Make product → Step 6 Ship product

1. *Stability of demand.* If a firm can't predict demand for its product, it can't create an accurate sales forecast that would allow it to enjoy the benefits of a pure push strategy. Demand uncertainty often occurs when products are in the introductory and growth stages of the product life cycle. During these stages, a firm may want to stick with the maximum flexibility a pull strategy allows. Or the firm may choose a hybrid strategy that commits to inventory of raw and packaging materials without committing to a large amount of finished goods inventory.

   Electric cars are an example of a product in its growth stage. Uncertainty about future sales due to the changing technology of these cars would suggest that car companies will want to utilize a pull strategy. By doing so, they will ensure a better fit of inventory to potential sales.

   Many products, though, are in their maturity phase. In that stage, they experience steady, predictable demand. Pepsi and Coke are examples of products in their maturity phase. The needed supply of products in the maturity phase can be accurately forecast, and therefore a push strategy makes sense for them.

2. *Degree of cost competitiveness.* A push strategy will allow a firm to achieve cost savings through economies of scale in purchasing, manufacturing, and transportation. If cost reduction is part of a firm's strategy, then a push strategy is the obvious choice. Consumer packaged goods, such as Crest toothpaste, have a lot of competition, and many of the brands are low cost. Therefore Procter & Gamble would want to use a push strategy to ensure that Crest is cost competitive.

3. *Degree of customization.* A pull or hybrid strategy would be a good choice for a company that competes on either (a) its ability to deliver customized products or (b) a high level of customer service built on manufacturing and distribution flexibility. Dell computers is an example of delivering customized products on a hybrid strategy.

Dell uses a hybrid push-pull strategy, so that it can concentrate on its core competency—building computers to customer specifications. Dell then partners with UPS, which ensures speedy product delivery and maintains Dell's high customer service levels. *Stew Milne/AP Images*

4. ***The speed at which customers need the product.*** *Lead time* is the time it takes from placement of an order to delivery of the goods. If customers want a short lead time, the company will need to have products already made and ready to deliver. A push strategy is best for this scenario. Big-box retailers such as Target and Kmart want their orders from manufacturers filled quickly. For the major types of products these retailers carry, manufacturers would use a push strategy.

Companies can use different strategies depending on the product or service. For example, General Electric makes light bulbs, home appliances, and jet engines. A push strategy would be appropriate for light bulbs and appliances, but definitely not for jet engines (because of their high cost to produce and unstable demand). Companies that are significantly affected by all of the factors listed may choose a hybrid strategy to achieve both the cost savings of a push system *and* the flexibility of a pull system. Whichever supply chain strategy a firm chooses, effective implementation is affected by logistics operations, which we will discuss in the next section.

Mc Graw Hill connect Exercise **10-1**

Please complete the *Connect* exercise in Chapter 10 that focuses on supply chain strategies. By identifying the appropriate strategy for various situations, you will be able to establish the right network of suppliers and customers necessary to meet your objectives.

LO 10-3

Summarize the importance of collaboration and resilience to effective supply chains.

supply chain management

The actions the firm takes to coordinate the various flows within a supply chain.

inventory carrying costs

The costs required to make or buy a product, including risk of obsolescence, taxes, insurance, and warehousing space used to store the goods.

SUPPLY CHAIN MANAGEMENT

What Is Supply Chain Management?

Supply chain management refers to the *actions* the firm takes to coordinate the various flows within a supply chain. For example, when a company sets up technology, such as Walmart's Retail Link program, to enable the sharing of demand information with suppliers so they can better plan their manufacturing activities, it is practicing supply chain *management.* By viewing the total system of interrelated companies that make up the supply chain as something they can manage, companies have greater control over the customer value they provide. This greater control, in turn, generates higher revenue for the company.

The key idea behind supply chain management is that no company is an island. All companies rely on related companies whose activities add value to the final product. This reliance could take the form of sharing sales forecasts and product-delivery information. Or it might involve enlisting another company to perform a function if the other company can do it more efficiently or effectively than the firm itself. Companies can collaborate with supply chain members in a variety of supply chain activities: new-product development, operations planning, sales forecasting, or logistics activity coordination. Through such collaboration, companies make the entire supply chain more efficient and effective.

Supply chain management decisions often involve trade-offs. Decisions made about one area of the supply chain will affect other areas, sometimes negatively. For example, a salesperson might offer a volume discount to a customer, without knowing whether that amount of product can be produced and delivered on time without incurring extra cost. That sale might actually end up costing the company money in overtime production and expensive transportation modes.

Another important trade-off exists between inventory and customer service. When there is not enough inventory to satisfy customer demand, the firm may lose sales. Or it may ramp up production to quickly increase inventory, incurring unplanned production costs. To combat such situations, companies sometimes store (carry) extra inventory. However, any money tied up in inventory is not available to the company to use for other things, such as capital investment, advertising, or bill paying. It is important to note that because of the COVID-19 pandemic many companies built extra inventory to buffer the constant disruptions in supply chains so their customers can be better serviced. It remains to be seen whether this trend continues long term.

Inventory costs money, both to produce or purchase and to store. **Inventory carrying costs** are the costs required to make or buy a product. These costs include risk of obsolescence, taxes, insurance, and warehousing space used to store the goods. It is important to compare the cost of carrying inventory to the potential cost of lost orders and possibly lost customers due to lack of inventory to fill orders.

These examples show the importance of understanding supply chain trade-offs and their implications for supply chain management decisions.

Supply chain management involves making decisions that involve trade-offs, for example, about how much inventory to keep in stock. Too much extra stock can end up costing the company a great deal of money over time; too little can leave the company unprepared to meet demand. *George Frey/Getty Images News/Getty Images*

Important Concepts in Supply Chain Management

Three concepts are important to understand concerning the management of supply chains: supply chain process integration, supply chain resiliency, and logistics operations.

Supply chain process integration: The ultimate objective of supply chains is to deliver goods and services in a timely manner to the place where they will be consumed by the final user. This requires that companies work *collaboratively* both internally (between functions) and externally (between companies) to provide value to the final consumer.

Resilience: Resilience is the ability to anticipate, prepare for, and effectively respond to supply chain disruptions.

Logistics operations: These are the functional areas of a supply chain that sources materials and finished goods, warehouses and manages inventories of those products, moves those products within stages of a supply chain, and handles the distribution of products to business customers or consumers. These operations have far reaching impact on the four Ps of marketing as we shall see.

Supply Chain Process Integration
A firm that recognizes and responds to the impact supply chain flows have on its business possesses a supply chain orientation.[8] A **supply chain orientation** is a management philosophy that guides the actions of a company toward actively managing the supply chain. With this philosophy, a company would consider upstream and downstream flows of goods, services, finances, and information across the supply chain as activities it would be involved in, even though they may be performed by other companies. A company with a supply chain orientation is willing to help coordinate supply chain activities that add value to the end-customer. A supply chain orientation is necessary to be successful at supply chain management, which is in part built on supply chain integration between companies.

supply chain process integration

When companies work *collaboratively* both internally (between functions) and externally (between companies) to provide value to the final consumer.

resilience

The ability of a company to anticipate, prepare for, and effectively respond to supply chain disruptions.

logistics operations

The functional areas of a supply chain that sources materials and finished goods, warehouses and manages inventories of those products, moves those products within stages of a supply chain, and handles the distribution of products to business customers or consumers.

supply chain orientation

A management philosophy that guides the actions of company members toward the goal of actively managing the upstream and downstream flows of goods, services, finances, and information across the supply chain.

Today's global business environment makes supply chain integration even more of an imperative for firms trying to overcome the time and distance obstacles that can stand in the way of efficient supply chain operations.
Julio Cortez/AP Images

The objective of a company practicing supply chain management is to coordinate processes across the supply chain, including within its own firm, with the goal being to improve the entire chain's performance in delivering goods and services to customers. This requires firms in the chain to take actions that are aligned with other firms' actions and consider the impact of its actions on other firms in the chain. In a high-performing supply chain, individual firms integrate their activities to such a degree that the supply chain functions as one extended enterprise.[9] This involves collaboration between functions within a company, and with other companies as well. Integrated supply chains typically realize multiple benefits: reduced costs, better customer service, efficient use of resources, and an increased ability to respond to changes in the marketplace.[10]

For an integrated supply chain to work, companies must be willing to embrace relationship-based strategies. Such strategies involve close, long-term collaboration for mutual benefit. One retail example was mentioned earlier in the section: Walmart's Retail Link program, which enables suppliers to see daily sales of their products and plan for replenishment of inventories of their products at Walmart. Another example is a program that a Unilever factory had with Weyerhaeuser, which produces boxes to hold Unilever products. Unilever shared with Weyerhaeuser data about its production schedules and inventories of boxes. Based on this information, Weyerhaeuser more efficiently scheduled its own manufacturing and delivery of boxes. In turn, Unilever planning personnel did not have to spend time determining when to order boxes or how many to order. Both members of this integrated supply chain gained from the strategy.

In the next section, we will investigate some of the strategies that firms can use to achieve effective supply chain process integration through internal and external collaboration.

Types of Supply Chain Collaboration

Internal Collaboration *Internal collaboration* involves departments or functions within a company working together to achieve a common goal. Surprisingly, interdepartmental/functional collaboration is not always the norm in companies due to conflicting goals, methods of operation, and behavioral norms. Often, trust between areas in a company is low, and this leads to a lack of communication and cooperation that is detrimental to achieving company objectives.

In the area of a manufacturing company's supply chain management function, a major objective is balancing supply and demand. This is accomplished by procuring the right number of materials and producing the right amount of product to meet market demand. When communication and cooperation between departments is low, it is extremely difficult to achieve a good supply/demand balance. The most common way that companies deal with this problem is to implement a *sales and operations planning process* (S&OP).

S&OP is a widely used process. It is based on a sales forecast developed by the demand side of the business (marketing and sales) and a capacity forecast developed by the supply side of the business (sourcing and production planning). S&OP has three basic purposes:

- Balancing the supply of product to meet demand.
- Planning volumes to guide detailed production plans.
- Integrating financial, new-product development, and operational plans.

The process includes monthly and sometimes weekly meetings during which demand and supply plans are reconciled and a plan is built to fulfill demand for a specified period of time, usually a month. Any areas where supply cannot meet demand are highlighted, and an executive-level meeting is held to make decisions concerning ways to meet demand, such as contact manufacturing or overtime production, or ways that demand can be adjusted.

At its best, S&OP not only results in higher customer service and lower overall inventories, it also can create spillover benefits that permeate the entire company. The collaboration needed in S&OP can lead to inter-functional collaboration in other processes as well: It can increase awareness of the problems faced by other parts of the organization and promote trust between departments. Moreover, the process can change the company's operational culture from one that is internally focused to one that better understands the potential benefits of working with other companies in the supply chain. The opportunities for integrating demand and supply are significant when companies are willing to work together to make it happen.[11]

External Collaboration The trust that develops from internally collaborative processes can become the foundation upon which external collaborative programs are built. These programs include vendor-managed inventory (VMI); collaborative forecasting, planning, and replenishment (CPFR); efficient consumer response (ECR); retail-event collaboration; and various stock-replenishment methods currently in use by major manufacturers and retailers. These processes require sharing information between companies, joint agreement on the responsibilities of the individual companies, and a good deal of trust among all parties, since the responsibility for integrating supply and demand is often delegated to the supplier.

These arrangements for external collaboration have been used primarily in the fast-moving consumer-goods industry, but vendor-managed inventory can also be used for components, raw materials, and work-in-process.

Vendor-Managed Inventory

In VMI, the supplier is given the responsibility of replenishing a customer's inventory, but the process is based upon rules agreed to by both parties. The supplier, not the customer, then decides how much inventory to produce and when to have it delivered. In the case of a manufacturer and its supplier, the supplier's responsibility is to replenish component, raw material, and/or work-in-process inventories in a factory. For retailers, the supplier's scope of responsibilities can include stock replenishment into a retailer's distribution center, or even all the way into the retailer's store shelves.

Underpinning the VMI process is a computer-guided system that determines at what point inventory should be replenished and how much inventory should be delivered. The customer establishes a replenishment point and inventory level, and when the customer's inventory hits that reorder point a set quantity is ordered. In addition, to assist the supplier in deciding the timing and quantities of shipments, retailers may provide data on distribution-center shipments to stores as well as its point-of-sale (POS) information. Benefits of VMI include the ability of the supplier to better plan manufacturing operations, manage shipment lot sizes, control the timing of deliveries, and more effectively react to changes in demand.

Collaborative Planning, Forecasting, and Replenishment (CPFR)

CPFR is a process through which suppliers and customers jointly plan demand fulfillment. The companies share information about promotions, sales forecasts, manufacturing plans, inventory levels, and planned orders; this information is then used to develop a plan of expected sales and inventory replenishment. (While this is typically how the CPFR process works, in some cases the retail POS data is used.)

The process is implemented via a joint calendar of events in which demand and supply plans are shared, discussed, and agreed upon. CPFR results in a consensus on sales forecasts, production schedules, and shipments.

Benefits of CPFR include improved intercompany relationships, higher levels of customer service, lower supply chain inventories, and lower costs for both parties. Additionally, through the CPFR process, potential issues around matching supply with demand can be amicably resolved before they become serious. Examples of companies using CPFR are Nabisco, Wegmans, Kimberly-Clark, Kmart, Walmart, Sarah Lee, Procter & Gamble, and Hewlett-Packard.[12]

Efficient Consumer Response (ECR)   ECR involves direct links, via a paperless flow of information, between members of the supply chain to accurately match production with consumer demands. ECR normally has four elements:

- Implementation of electronic data interchange (EDI) among all tiers of the supply chain to speed the flow of demand-and-supply data among exchange partners.
- Use of POS data to give suppliers more accurate and up-to-date demand information concerning their products.
- Fostering of cooperative rather than adversarial relationships between supply chain members, which is critical to creating the trust essential to processes where proprietary data is transmitted between companies.
- Continuous replenishment of inventory based on demand data.

Implemented and conducted properly, ECR can lead to both cost savings and service improvements because the right amount of inventory is flowing through the supply chain at all times. This technique has been used effectively in the grocery industry to manage product assortments, inventory, and replenishment of inventory.

Other External Collaboration Processes   Another set of processes designed to help match demand and supply revolve around *collaborative stock replenishment.* Retail-event collaboration is one such intercompany program; it is designed to help businesses match supply with demand following a promotional event. Too often, promotional events catch suppliers unawares, leading to stockouts, overproduction due to a misreading of demand signals from customer orders, and excess logistics costs such as premium shipments.

The retail-event collaboration process requires agreement between supplier and customer on which SKUs will be included in the collaboration, as well as the development of a sales forecast specific to the promotion and the formulation of manufacturing and shipment plans. During the promotional event, both parties monitor sales, identify any shortfalls or overages in inventory, and adjust replenishment plans as necessary. Procter & Gamble is one company that has used this technique with its retail customers.

Another technique commonly used in the drugstore, hardware, and grocery industries is *distribution center (DC) replenishment* collaboration. In DC replenishment, the supplier and customer collaborate on forecasting withdrawals from the customer's DC to replenish store inventories. These anticipated withdrawals are used to establish DC replenishment orders to the supplier (manufacturer), who commits to these future orders.

This stream of orders assists the manufacturer in planning its purchasing, production, and logistics activities in a proactive manner, leading in turn to reduced manufacturing and logistics costs, inventory carrying costs, and customer-service failures. In more advanced applications of this arrangement, the supplier may take over the planning and replenishment activities altogether. This relieves the customer of the burden of planning these activities, allowing them to focus on more value-added functions such as promotions and merchandizing. This type of collaboration does not require sophisticated processes such as POS data transfer. As such, it can be implemented fairly quickly and easily.

Store Replenishment Collaboration Used by so-called "big box" retailers such as Home Depot and club stores like Costco, *store replenishment collaboration (SRC)* involves direct store or retail DC-to-store deliveries based on collaborative store-level sales forecasts. These forecasts are used to create replenishment orders over a specified time. Similar to DC collaborative replenishment, manufacturers get better information concerning demand for their products, leading to more manufacturing control, better customer service, and reduced logistics and inventory costs. This type of collaboration can be very useful to manufacturers that are launching new products or are running product promotions at the retail level.

Summary All of the collaborative methods discussed here depend on the sharing of information between suppliers and customers. A combination of internal and external collaboration can become a competitive advantage for a company by reducing costs, improving customer service, and developing closer and more trusting relationships with important customers and suppliers.

Supply Chain Resilience Supply chain disruptions happen at both small and large scales. Examples of supply chain disruptions at a large scale include the eruption of the volcano Eyjafjallajökul in Iceland in 2010 affecting air traffic in Europe, the earthquake and tsunami that struck Japan in March of 2011 affecting manufacturing plants, the port strikes at Long Beach and Los Angeles California in 2015 affecting cargo movement to and from the ports, and the 1,100 foot cargo ship that got stuck in the Suez Canal in 2021 that prevented ships from traversing the canal. Some of these types of disruptions last a few days, or at most a few months. However, the COVID-19 pandemic is an example of what can go wrong throughout a supply chain that had serious effects for several years. The pandemic prevented supply chains from delivering goods and services throughout the world, and its effects pointed out to many companies that they were unprepared for a disruption of such magnitude. This is because supply chains intricately join together factories, distributors, retailers, and consumers, and a breakdown anywhere along the chain can mean a breakdown of the entire system.[13] An excellent example of such a breakdown is a shortage of microprocessors that has shut or slowed down many types of businesses, including major automobile companies like Ford. This in turn has affected car rental companies and automobile dealers who are unable to get enough cars to meet demand. It also drew attention from the U.S. government, which has been concerned about reliance on international sources such as Taiwan Semiconductor Manufacturing Co. for computer chips that are essential to both the civilian and military markets in the United States. For national security reasons, the U.S. government is working with chip manufacturers to build factories in domestic locations that can ensure supply of these vital components.[14]

If companies want to survive long term, they must be prepared for changes that can negatively affect their chance of remaining viable. A powerful approach that companies can use is to make their supply chains as resilient as possible to supply chain disruptions. Companies can try to solutions such as inventory management, sourcing strategies, manufacturing capacity flexibility, and transportation flexibility.

Holding inventories of components, raw materials, work-in-process, and finished goods can tide a company over a short-to-medium term supply disruption. *Safety stock,* which is used to buffer short-term variations in demand and order lead times, is used by most companies because demand and supply vary over time. However, safety stocks are inadequate to buffer longer-term disruptions. *Anticipatory stock* differs from safety stock in that it only needs to be held during times of potential supply risk or periods of possible extraordinary consumer demand. For example, a company may be able to anticipate a supply chain disruption if it is aware of labor unrest at a port or political upheaval in a supplier's country and build extra inventory before the supply chain shuts down. This can be an especially useful method if there are common components used across several different products and the company builds extra inventory of those materials.

Sourcing is the set of business processes required to purchase goods and services. Companies can use a sourcing strategy that takes advantage of multiple suppliers of components, raw materials, work-in-process, or finished goods in different parts of the world, so that if a disruptive event occurs in one region they can be obtained from a different region. The objective is to have multiple sources for all goods and services needed. This may require a combination of *in-shore* and *off-shore* suppliers to provide multiple ways to obtain what is needed to meet customer demand. For example, Branch Furniture in New York City recently chose to work with two U.S. manufacturers to launch a new line of products. While most of its manufacturing is done overseas, this collaboration allows the company to have some domestic capacity.[15] Another idea that is used is *regionalization*. This involves sourcing components or building manufacturing plants through the world and using each region to supply its own geographic customers. If a factory is incapacitated, the shortage will only be felt in nearby markets.[16] An example is Benetton, an Italian clothing company. Benetton has started to pivot from producing in Asian countries to producing clothing in countries closer to its markets, such as Serbia, Croatia, and Turkey.[17] This shift helps reduce the problems associated with long supply chains such as transportation disruptions and increasing costs to move products.

Manufacturing capacity flexibility involves such tactics as gaining time flexibility from employees, adding production shifts and/or lines, use of *subcontracting,* and the use of multiple facilities to produce the same product. These tactics allow a company to be more resilient to increases in demand, such as occurred for paper products during the COVID-19 pandemic. Time flexibility involves asking employees to work more hours in a shift or to work weekend hours. This tactic enables a company to use trained workers to make the products but can be detrimental to the health and safety of employees if used to excess. Another tactic is to add additional work shifts; for example, going from two to three shifts in a day. This requires hiring new employees and training them, which can be expensive. A third tactic is to go to a third party, called a subcontractor, to make the product(s) along with your own production facilities. This can be very effective because many subcontractors are quite capable of making quality products in high volumes. There are some potential issues such as intellectual property theft and underperformance by the third party, but it is a common and usually successful way of adding additional capacity quickly.

Transportation disruptions such as port strikes and slowdowns, ships getting stuck in the Suez Canal, and lack of truck drivers can have devastating effects on supply chains for many months. This issue is especially acute due to the high-level offshore sourcing in today's supply chains. Companies have several options to become more resilient to transportation problems. One way is to change the mode of transportation. For example, for critical products or components such as microprocessors, a company can change from ocean to air freight. This is an expensive tactic but can be effective in keeping a supply chain open. Another is to change a shipment's routing to go through

Heorshe/Alamy Stock Photo

another port of entry. Shipments from Asia to North America, for example, could be re-routed to a Canadian or Mexican port if the U.S. ports are shut down. An additional tactic is to use multiple carriers so that if one carrier goes out of business or has labor problems, the other carriers can take up the slack.

Vertical integration is when a company controls two or more stages of production or distribution normally operated by separate companies. Companies vertically integrate to gain more control over their supply chains, thus gaining more resiliency. Automobile companies are a good example of using this strategy. Ford is partnering and helping to fund new battery plants for South Korean battery maker SK Innovation in order to ensure a supply of batteries for EVs. GM and Ford are looking to get into semiconductor manufacturing due to the extreme shortage of chips. Ford is partnering with U.S.-based semiconductor manufacturer GlobalFoundaries Inc. to develop chips. GM is working on an agreement with Qualcomm and NXP Semiconductors NV to co-develop and make semiconductors. Such partnerships should help companies weather disruptions in their supply chains that prevent them from making as many automobiles as the market demands.[18]

Supply chain resiliency continues to grow in importance. Companies that anticipate problems and have alternative plans in place will likely fair much better than those that do not when a disruption in the supply chain occurs.

In the next section, we will investigate the logistics functions and their importance to supply chain management.

WHAT IS LOGISTICS?

Logistics functions are just part of the many activities that occur in a supply chain. For example, while manufacturing and finance are supply chain functions, they are not part of logistics operations. **Logistics** is that part of supply chain management that plans, implements, and controls the flow of goods, services, and information between the point of origin (such as the mine in which silicone is extracted for use in making computer chips) and the final customer (the user of a personal computer).[19] *Logisticians* are people who specialize in the area of logistics. They do such jobs as:

- Supervising trucking and warehousing personnel.
- Determining how much inventory should be stored in warehouses and distribution centers.
- Analyzing how much product to ship from distribution centers to stores and when.
- Arranging for materials and products to be bought and moved from suppliers to customers.

Logistics comprises some specific functions that enable a supply chain to operate smoothly and effectively. Broadly, these functions include managing inventories; purchasing; and materials management, warehousing, and distribution (including transportation). Through these various functions, logistics adds value to products moving through the supply chain.[20] The goal is to achieve "the seven Rs of logistics"—delivering the *right* product, to the *right* place, to the *right* customer, at the *right* time, in the *right* quantity, in the *right* condition, and at the *right* price. How well companies provide value by performing the seven Rs of logistics will determine how satisfied are their customers. This is of great importance to marketing because logistics influences the marketing mix (the four Ps) in many ways.

Executing logistics functions successfully can serve as a competitive advantage for some companies. We will discuss most of these functions later in this chapter. First, we will discuss how these functions affect the four Ps of marketing.

LO 10-4

Describe how the primary logistics functions support a firm's supply chain strategy.

logistics

That part of supply chain management that plans, implements, and controls the flow of goods, services, and information between the point of origin and the final customer.

The Food Bank of Northeast Arkansas delivers food to over 125 sites. It has partnered with Arkansas State University to develop delivery routes to more efficiently utilize its delivery trucks and save on fuel costs. *Food Bank of Northeast Arkansas*

The Impact of Logistics

Managers from all areas of business should be aware of the impact logistics operations and personnel have on their own functional areas. Arguably the biggest impact is on the four Ps of marketing.[21] Logistics activities relate to the marketing mix in many ways:

- *Place:* The most obvious relationship is with the *place* element: delivering goods and services to the correct location and in a timely manner. Satisfying customers through logistics activities is a prerequisite for maintaining and increasing market share. Having products at the right place and at the right time is critically important to marketers because, if the product is not available for purchase, all of the company's other marketing efforts will be wasted.
- *Price:* Logistics affects *price* through efficient purchasing, inventory warehousing, and transportation processes that help keep costs down for the consumer.
- *Product:* The *product* element is influenced by input from logistics managers about packaging needs for safe and efficient storage of goods and shipment of those goods to customers.
- *Promotion:* Marketing promotions are expected to result in increased sales volume. Logistics managers must be part of promotions planning, to ensure that sufficient materials, inventory, storage, and transportation are available to handle the increased sales volume.

Marketing is the most obvious, though not the only, area of an organization affected by logistics. Other areas include:[22]

- *Manufacturing operations:* Logistics personnel support manufacturing operations by receiving, storing, and retrieving materials needed in production. Coordination between the two operations is critical to ensure a smoothly running manufacturing facility.

UPS uses its established network of facilities and logistics technology to help customers reduce costs, improve customer service, and increase a firm's global reach. *PictoKraft/Alamy Stock Photo*

- *Finance:* The amount of inventory a company holds and the costs of warehousing and transportation affect return on investment (ROI).
- *Customer service:* How well the logistics managers perform affects customer service, which ultimately can affect revenue positively or negatively.

Logistics also applies to services and nonprofits. Dairy Queen, for example, must have the components of meals, such as frozen french fries, hamburger buns, and take-out containers, on hand in order to deliver customer orders. Similarly, the nonprofit food bank Feeding America must manage the inventory of more than 30 million pounds of food it delivers every year from its warehouses to people in need. It uses logistics software to keep track of the many food items it stocks.[23]

As you can see, logistics operations affect and are affected by all areas of a company. As a result, regardless of your major or what type of job you plan to pursue after you graduate, you will benefit from understanding what logistics is and what it does.

Aligning Logistics with Supply Chain Strategies

As we saw earlier, firms can employ push, pull, or hybrid (push-pull) supply chain strategies, depending on their objectives. As an important aspect of supply chain management, logistics operations have to be properly configured to meet the different challenges presented by each type of supply chain strategy.[24]

Companies pursuing the economies of scale that come with a *push strategy* will have to set up logistics operations that can handle large volumes of product. Specifically, they will benefit from:

- Modes of transportation, such as container ships and railroads, that can inexpensively handle large amounts of product.
- Large warehouses equipped to efficiently store, retrieve, and load goods onto vehicles at a fast pace. Companies looking for efficiency will have fewer, but larger, facilities to take advantage of economies of scale. For example, Williams-Sonoma has a distribution center in Mississippi that is over 2 million square feet in size. From there, Williams-Sonoma ships products to various UPS warehouses across the country for final delivery to customers.

Companies that employ a *pull* or *hybrid strategy* typically establish logistics operations based on service quality, innovation, and flexibility. Such companies benefit from:

- Suppliers that produce and deliver quickly. Purchasing managers try to find suppliers that can offer short lead times so that customers can get their products quickly.
- Transportation that ensures on-time delivery.
- Use of advanced technology to increase the responsiveness and flexibility of logistics operations. For example, *enterprise resource planning (ERP) systems* are data management systems that integrate information across all the departments of an organization. ERP systems can communicate with the IT systems of other companies through *electronic data interchange (EDI)*. EDI enables an almost-instantaneous transfer of information from one company's computer to another, enabling firms to react quickly to customer demand.

Next, we will investigate in detail the operational aspects of logistics functions.

LOGISTICS FUNCTIONS

LO 10-5

Describe the various logistics functions and their importance to marketing.

U.S. corporate spending on logistics and related business functions is approximately 8 percent of gross domestic product, which indicates the impact logistics has on the economy.[25] Logistics operations have a large impact on consumers as well as business. For example, when you go to a store to purchase a product, you expect it will be on the shelf. If you order an item from an online site, you expect it to be delivered to you quickly. Logistics is a big part of making that happen. A breakdown in any logistics function will result in back orders, empty shelves, and customer dissatisfaction.

As noted earlier, the main logistics functions are:

- Managing inventories
- Purchasing
- Materials management, warehousing, and distribution (including transportation)

Executive Perspective . . .
because everyone is a marketer

Sankha Basu
Senior Manager, Agile Transformation
CVS Health

Sankha Basu

How has technology changed your role with CVS?

My role is to help transform CVS Health's consumer experience across all digital touchpoints, accelerating the company's digital transformation so we can meet the customer by delivering convenience, personalization, and value.

We'll discuss each of these functions in more depth in the sections that follow. The purpose of this closer look is to get a fuller understanding of how logistics managers and personnel add value for customers and help achieve company goals.

Managing Inventories

Marketing relies on inventory management for several reasons. The primary reason is that unless the right amount of inventory is available at the right location, customer service will suffer. Yet if companies stock too much inventory, they pay more in inventory carrying costs than they need to. Those extra costs could, instead, have been used for things like new-product development or advertising. The challenge of inventory management is to manage inventories in a way that balances supply and demand in a cost-effective manner.

Aldi, the German grocery chain that is rapidly expanding in the United States, has an approach toward inventory that cuts cost. It limits the number of brand-name goods it sells, but buys large quantities of those goods. This gives it considerable bargaining power with producers, and this has allowed it to price its goods on average almost 17 percent lower than Walmart.[26]

Inventory Costs   To manage inventory effectively, firms try to balance product availability with the costs of carrying inventory. To determine the level of inventory to keep in stock, a firm must track three types of costs:

1. ***Purchasing costs.*** Purchasing costs include the costs to place and process orders of materials and finished goods. The more often a company places orders for an item, the higher the annual purchasing costs.
2. ***Inventory carrying costs.*** Inventory carrying costs are important to companies because they negatively impact profits. As discussed earlier in the chapter, these include storage and handling expenses, the cost of tying up capital in inventory, service costs such as property taxes and insurance, and costs associated with damage to or obsolescence of the good while it is in storage. Inventory carrying costs differ somewhat between companies, so companies calculate their carrying costs based on their own actual cost for each individual part of the overall costs of a product. Table 10.1 shows a sample calculation of inventory carrying costs for a smartphone. Any amount of carrying costs that the company could save would improve the profit margin the firm earns on the phone.
3. ***Out-of-stock costs.*** A **stockout** occurs when a company does not have enough inventory available to fill an order. In such cases, a customer can either place a back order or cancel the order. A canceled order, of course, means lost revenue. But if the customer places a back order, the company incurs *out-of-stock costs.* Such costs typically are those associated with processing the back order, overtime production, and expedited shipping to deliver the product as soon as it is available.

stockout

A situation in which a company does not have enough inventory available to fill an order.

While satisfying demand for customers in a domestic market is often difficult, satisfying customers in international markets is much more complex, requiring thoughtful and efficient inventory management. *ms_pics_and_more/Shutterstock*

TABLE 10.1 Calculating Inventory Carrying Cost Percentage for a Smartphone

Inventory Carrying Costs per Unit	Annual Cost per Unit
A. Manufacturing cost, including direct labor, materials, and overhead, per unit	$450.00
B. Transportation	5.00
C. Warehouse space	3.50
D. Insurance	10.00
E. Obsolescence	26.00
F. Damage and pilferage in storage and transit	29.00
G. Interest	25.00
H. Taxes	22.00
I. Total inventory carrying costs per unit (sum of lines B through H)	$120.50
Carrying cost (line I) divided by manufacturing cost (line A) = Annual inventory carrying cost %	26.78%

Purchasing

Purchasing involves the sourcing and procurement of raw materials, component parts, finished goods, and services. Purchasing is an important function for several reasons:

- Materials purchased for manufacturing typically account for 40 to 60 percent of product costs. Any savings a company can make in purchasing costs can add significantly to its profits.
- Purchasing is a major factor in the quality of both goods and services. Selecting suppliers that can provide high-quality goods and services enables companies to compete with, or even surpass, the quality of other companies.
- By involving appropriate suppliers early in the product design process, purchasing can help improve product design and time-to-market for new products.
- Sourcing materials and products from reliable suppliers ensures that the flow of goods in a firm's supply chain meets demand, leading to superior customer service.

Purchasing Activities To carry out the purchasing strategy of a company, purchasing managers perform a variety of activities:

- *Select and qualify appropriate suppliers.* A company selects suitable suppliers based on criteria established by the purchasing manager.[27] The criteria will be those that fit the company's particular needs, such as cost or service capability.

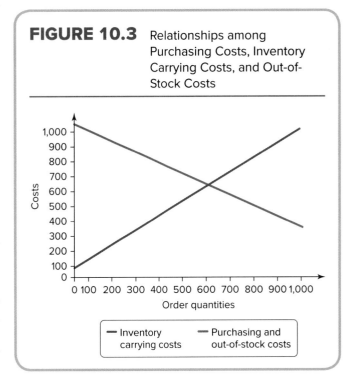

FIGURE 10.3 Relationships among Purchasing Costs, Inventory Carrying Costs, and Out-of-Stock Costs

Challenges are constant. For example, for decades companies have been out-sourcing production and sourcing products depending on labor costs. However, as trade barriers are rising, and backlashes against global sourcing increase, purchasing managers are being tasked with finding suitable local suppliers for their production or finished products needs.[28] An example of this is Inditex SA, which owns the fashion retailer Zara. It sources its material close to its Spanish home, which cuts delivery time and allows the company to ship new clothing around the world faster than its competitors.[29]

purchase order

A legal obligation to buy from a supplier a certain amount of product, at a certain price, to be delivered at a specified date.

- *Negotiate contracts and place purchase orders.* Purchasing managers negotiate with a supplier about contract terms and conditions. Based on the terms of the negotiations, the purchasing manager writes a **purchase order**, which is a legal obligation to buy from a supplier a certain amount of product, at a certain price, to be delivered at a specified date.

- *Monitor supplier performance.* Purchasing managers establish performance expectations for suppliers and develop ways to measure their performance. Expectations often relate to quality, on-time delivery, rapid response to problems, and accuracy of invoices. If performance does not meet expectations, purchasing managers may reduce the business awarded to the supplier, levy monetary fines, or refuse to do business with the supplier in the future.

- *Develop suppliers.* Sometimes suppliers need extra help in meeting the expectations of the buying company. Purchasing managers may visit the supplier's operations to better understand issues. They may organize supplier training by company experts or provide financial assistance to suppliers for needed equipment purchases.

Given the global nature of business and the desire of purchasing managers to create a world-class supply chain, many companies rely on *global sourcing.* That approach gives companies access to the highest-quality materials, goods, and services at the lowest-possible price. A number of additional costs are involved in sourcing goods and services from other countries—transportation costs, inventory

New trends like sustainability have affected how companies purchase equipment, materials, and components from suppliers. The military is only one of many organizations whose procurement personnel increasingly seek out environmentally friendly products. *Jason M. Graham/U.S. Navy*

carrying costs for goods in transit, and customs duties (tariffs), among other things. Inexpensive labor and materials and high-quality goods and services often offset these higher costs.

However, the cost of labor from international sources has begun to rise. For example, labor costs in China rose approximately 65 percent from 2000 to 2015.[30] As a result, some companies are looking at *reshoring,* that is, sourcing goods and services domestically that were once purchased internationally. It is up to the purchasing manager to find the best suppliers, wherever they are located, and to understand the trade-offs involved in global sourcing. One outcome of reshoring is that while supply chains may gain resiliency, customers who are used to having a great deal of choice and low costs may be disappointed in the lower varieties of products and higher costs that could result from domestic sourcing. [31]

Materials Management, Warehousing, and Distribution

The next logistics function we'll explore has a longish name: materials management, warehousing, and distribution. The basic meaning of each of those is pretty straightforward:

- *Materials management* involves managing materials for manufacturing.
- *Warehousing* involves holding inventories of both intermediate materials and finished goods.
- *Distribution* involves distributing (transporting) goods from a warehouse to stores or directly to customers. *Transportation management* is part of the distribution activities.

This section looks at each of those functions.

Materials Management

Materials management involves the inbound movement and storage of materials in preparation for those materials to enter and flow through the manufacturing process. Effective materials management benefits the company in the following four ways:[32]

1. Reduces procurement, transportation, and production costs through economies of scale.
2. Coordinates supply and demand for materials. Cyclical, safety, and anticipative stocks are held in warehouses until needed.
3. Supports manufacturing activities. Materials management ensures that stored or recently received materials get to the production floor when they are needed.
4. Supports marketing objectives by making sure that goods are available to ship to customers in an efficient and effective manner.

Materials management typically occurs in a warehouse. To maximize the benefits of materials management, logistics personnel must effectively coordinate various warehouse functions.

Warehousing Functions

Warehousing activities can be organized into three basic functions: storage, movement, and production.[33]

Storage *Storage* involves holding inventories until they are needed. Proper storage procedures are important to marketing: The product must be warehoused properly to ensure there is no damage. For example, fresh fruit must be refrigerated promptly after it has been received from a supplier. In addition, the goods must be easily found by stock pickers when a customer orders the product.

materials management
The inbound movement and storage of materials in preparation for those materials to enter and flow through the manufacturing process.

Activities like picking—retrieving and delivering materials or goods to fulfill production or shipment orders—make up one of the movement functions provided by warehouses. *Geoffrey Robinson/Alamy Stock Photo*

put-away

Moving goods to their temporary or semipermanent storage location and updating inventory records.

picking

Retrieving materials from storage and bringing them to manufacturing to fulfill a production order, or retrieving finished goods from storage and preparing them for shipment to fulfill a customer order.

Movement The movement functions of a warehouse include receiving, put-away, picking, and shipping:

- *Receiving* involves unloading goods from a carrier, updating inventory records, and quality inspection, if required.
- **Put-away** refers to moving goods to their temporary or semi-permanent storage location and updating inventory records.
- **Picking** involves retrieving packaging and raw materials from storage and moving them to manufacturing to fulfill needs for those materials in production. For finished goods, picking involves retrieving items from storage and preparing them for shipment to fulfill a customer order.
- *Shipping* involves loading picked items onto transportation vehicles, updating inventory records, and preparing the necessary documents to transport the items.

Movement is greatly affected by technology. Robots, for example, are being used by companies such as Amazon to pick orders. Specialized equipment such as carousels bring products to pickers rather than the pickers going to the products, saving travel time and making picking operations less fatiguing. And motorized conveyors move bar-coded boxes over hundreds of feet to the correct warehouse location, enabled by bar code readers and computers that know the location the box should be transported to.

All of these movement activities are important to marketing: They ensure that the right product is shipped, that it is shipped to the right place, in the right quantity, in the right condition, and in a timely manner.

Motorized conveyors in the process of moving small orders from picking to packing/shipping areas, enabled by bar codes, bar code readers, and IT systems. *Geoffrey Robinson/Alamy Stock Photo*

Production Some warehouses also perform a production function. This may include such activities as light assembly of products, like store displays. It might involve customizing products for customers, such as mixing different products into a shipment for customers that do not need large quantities of any one product. It also can include refurbishing returned goods.

Distribution

Distribution occurs when a company ships its goods from a warehouse to its stores or customers. There are multiple ways that companies can distribute products. The way a company establishes its distribution network should be aligned with its objectives for servicing its customers, and with the costs involved in meeting customer needs. We will discuss the main distribution methods next.

The first distribution method is for the manufacturer to produce goods and store them in a distribution center for shipment either to a retailer's distribution center or directly to a store. A **distribution center (DC)** is a type of warehouse used specifically to store and ship finished goods to customers. Thus, stores can be restocked by the retailer's own distribution centers, or by the manufacturer. Shipments from manufacturing DCs can take advantage of full vehicle load shipping rates, adding value to the customer by reducing costs. When the manufacturer ships to stores it is called *direct store delivery.* This method helps reduce inventory in the retailer's distribution centers. However, unless the shipments to the stores are in full vehicle load quantities, the shipping costs will be higher.

For retailers, another distribution option is to use an omnichannel. **Omnichannels** offer consumers the ability to purchase goods at a retail store (brick-and-mortar) or through a website (click-and-mortar). The latter method is becoming increasingly popular because it offers the consumer value through providing shopping convenience. Both the store and the Internet consumer can be serviced from the same DC, as Target is now piloting with its Perth Amboy, New Jersey, DC.[34] Or the retailer can dedicate specific DCs to service stores, and other DCs to service Internet shoppers. Dedicated fulfillment will be more costly in that there will be more facilities, which means higher overhead and inventory costs. However, dedicated fulfillment can provide higher levels of service to Internet buyers because the DC dedicated to servicing them will have equipment and trained personnel specifically for those orders, and there will be no confusion over what inventory to allocate to store and Internet orders.

Small companies can also get into Internet orders, either by servicing the consumer themselves, or through a third party. Suburban Sports in Berlin, Connecticut, for example, has been in business since 1974, but until recently it was strictly a brick-and-mortar retailer with one store. It has since branched out to Internet sales, setting up a website (suburbanskiandbike.com) where a customer can order its products. The products ship from a recently acquired building that was turned into a distribution center for Internet orders. Companies can also use third-party distribution companies to inventory their goods, take customer orders, and ship the goods to their customers. Examples of such third-party service providers are ShipBob and Red Stag Fulfillment.[35]

A rapidly growing way to better service consumers, especially in the grocery business, is to offer in-store pickup of orders placed on the company's website. For example, Kroger's and Walmart offer the ability for a consumer to place an order, and for a small fee the company will have its employees pick the order and make it available for the shopper to pick up in a dedicated location at the store. Employees will even load the groceries into the consumer's car.

distribution center (DC)

A type of warehouse used specifically to store and ship finished goods to customers.

omnichannel

A type of retail that offers different methods of shopping and delivery of products to consumers (e.g., online or in a physical store).

Suburban Sports is an example of a small company that has recently made the transition to an omnichannel capability by setting up a website to take orders and a dedicated warehouse from which to ship those orders to its online customers. *Suburban Sports*

Faster shipments from distribution centers to consumers are being driven by Amazon's Prime program. Amazon built 75 distribution centers and 25 sortation centers (which organize shipments by region) in order to be physically closer to its customers. While expensive, this has proven to be a competitive advantage in delivery times. Walmart, Target, and Overstock.com are examples of companies that followed Amazon's example and offer their customers two-day shipping. There are several ways this is being accomplished. Walmart uses dedicated fulfillment centers, Target ships most of its orders from its stores, and Overstock.com uses a combination of its own distribution centers and a network of vendors that ship direct from their locations to the consumer.

It is important that companies design their distribution network around adding value to the consumer. Such considerations as total cost to service the consumer, value added services that make the company more attractive to do business, and availability of products to consumers are among the issues that companies must consider in setting up or changing their methods of distribution. These factors can help a company achieve competitive advantage in the market.

Transportation Management
Transportation management is one of the most important logistics functions. Transportation creates place and time utilities that are essential to keeping customers satisfied. Cost-effective transportation can enable companies to market goods to greater distances while maintaining competitive pricing. Transportation management is particularly important for companies that compete globally—it enables them to build global supply chains and compete in new markets.

The availability and reliability of transportation also affect the number and location of suppliers, production facilities, and distribution centers. These, in turn, affect customer service capabilities, product and package design, and inventory management strategies. Decisions regarding choice of transportation modes, choice of carriers, and in-house versus private carriage all affect how well a company can carry out its competitive and supply chain strategies.

There are six transportation modes: rail, motor, air, water, pipeline, and cyberspace. Each has advantages and disadvantages for marketers. Knowledge of these modes, including their advantages and disadvantages, is essential to building a transportation network that can most efficiently and effectively add value for customers. Reducing costs or speeding up delivery of products can provide a competitive advantage over other companies.

intermodal transport

Using multiple types of transportation for the same shipment.

Rail   Railroads provide long-haul carriage of a wide variety of products. Historically, railroads have carried bulk products such as chemicals, coal, produce, and automobiles. Today, **intermodal transport** uses multiple types of transportation for the same shipment. Thus, companies can load products into containers that are carried part of the way by rail and part of the way by truck.

Rail transport provides the advantage of carrying a wide variety of goods in large quantities at a low cost. Its primary role in logistics is to move large shipments long distances. Disadvantages include damages, inconsistent service, and lack of accessibility. **Accessibility** in this context refers to a carrier's ability to provide service from the source of the shipment (a factory, for example) to its destination (a store or even an individual customer).

accessibility (of transportation)

A carrier's ability to provide service from the source of the shipment (a factory, for example) to its destination (a store or even an individual customer).

Motor   Motor carriers, primarily trucks, account for 64 percent of the value, 58 percent of the tonnage, and 32 percent of the ton-miles of the nation's total commercial freight.[36]

The primary role of this mode is to move small to midsize shipments. It also is used as a companion mode with railroads in intermodal transport, moving container and trailer shipments to the ultimate consumers of the cargo.

Advantages of motor freight are accessibility, reliability, and fast service. Disadvantages include a fairly high cost per ton-mile and limited vehicle capacity. Due to the universal accessibility of motor transport, most shipments will include some leg of the journey that will be completed by a truck. One major issue in the United States is a shortage of truck drivers. There is somewhere between 75,000 and 100,000 fewer drivers than are needed to move all shipments, causing delays and rising prices. The combination of older drivers retiring and fewer young people interested in the job has made this an acute problem. Companies such as Embark, Starsky Robotics, and Drive.ai are developing technology to enable self-driving trucks. While still a few years away, there is plenty of investment capital pouring into these type of companies, and it may not be that far in the future when we will see trucks driving themselves.[37]

Intermodal transport allows shipments to be easily transferred from mode to mode, such as from rail to a truck, which expedites delivery times. *Leo de Groot/Alamy Stock Photo*

Delivery of packages to consumers (known as the "last mile") is especially critical to online retailers. Online retailers typically use a package delivery service such as UPS to perform this service. However, some companies are starting to develop their own last-mile delivery capability. Walmart, which has its own fleet of trucks to deliver to stores, is testing its own network of independent delivery drivers to bring groceries to customers in approximately 100 metropolitan areas. The company is using Spark Delivery, a crowd-sourcing driver network, to recruit and pay drivers who will use their own cars to perform home grocery deliveries.[38] The company is also offering two-day shipping on thousands of household products. Walmart has doubled Spark's coverage to more than 500 cities nationwide, providing access to more than 20 million households.[39] Amazon is building its own fleet of delivery vehicles, and is for the first time inviting entrepreneurs to create delivery companies to work for the company.[40]

Air Air transportation accounts for less than 1 percent of the intercity ton-miles in the United States, yet it plays an important role in supply chains. The main advantage of airfreight is speed. For certain types of goods and shipments, air is the only viable option. For example, for flowers to arrive fresh in New York City from South America, they must be flown in; no other mode will do.

The main reason why airfreight is used sparingly is its cost: Air is far and away the most expensive way to move goods. Another issue is accessibility; with very few exceptions the last mile will need to be covered by truck. Airfreight makes sense only for goods that are so expensive that they can bear the high cost of transportation, or for those that "absolutely, positively have to be there overnight" (FedEx's former ad slogan).

Water Water transportation has taken on great significance due to offshoring of production to low-cost producers in Asia and other parts of the world. The use of containers to move goods has

Amazon utilizes air freight to move goods rapidly from one place to another. It then uses ground transportation to deliver to business customers and consumers (the "final mile"). *Fabrizio Gandolfo/SOPA Images/LightRocket/Getty Images*

significantly changed the way finished goods are shipped because containers can be loaded and unloaded from ships quickly and efficiently. Container ships cross oceans on regular schedules, carrying thousands of containers of goods across thousands of miles each trip.

Water transport's advantages are low cost and high capacity. However, it is slow: For international shipments, water transport is slower than air. For domestic shipments, water transport (by barges on rivers, for example) is slower than both air and surface modes. Water transport must be considered of prime importance for international shipments, but is of much less importance for domestic ones.

Pipeline   Pipeline is a very specialized mode of transportation that services only a few industries. Pipelines play an important role in providing fuel for industrial, personal, and utility use. Most businesses, however, will not be able to take advantage of pipelines due to the types of products that can be shipped through pipelines. Pipelines have a huge impact on national economies in North America, Europe, and the Middle East. This mode is very efficient and low cost, but it is slow and very limited in the products it can carry.

Cyberspace   The sixth mode of transportation, cyberspace, is one you likely use frequently but may not think of as a transportation mode. Anything that can be digitized can be sent through the Internet and delivered to businesses and homes. Software, documents, and media such as music, pictures, and film are examples of products that can be sent electronically. Businesses such as Amazon, with its wide selection of digitized books that can be downloaded to a Kindle, are a good example of a company that can make transportation in cyberspace part of its supply chain strategy. Once a firm sets up the technology to transmit data over the Internet, the shipment costs very little and arrives at its destination almost instantaneously.

In order to get the most advantage from their logistics operations, firms must match the modes of transportation they choose to use with (1) the types of products they are selling and (2) the competitive strategies they are basing their marketing efforts on. Global operations add complexity to transportation choices; the supply chain of a global company covers vast distances and will require several modes of transportation. Factors companies must consider in choosing transportation modes include:

- Transit times.
- Mode accessibility.
- Ability of the mode to handle necessary volumes (capacity).
- Ability of the mode to consistently meet lead time requirements (reliability).
- Cost, which is always a factor but is more important for certain products than for others.

Table 10.2 compares the six main modes of transportation.

TABLE 10.2   Comparing the Six Main Modes of Transportation

Mode	Accessibility	Speed	Capacity	Cost	Service	International Capabilities
Rail	Low	Moderate	High	Moderate	Moderate	Intermodal
Truck	High	Moderate	Low	Moderate	High	Intermodal
Water	Low	Slow	Very high	Low	Moderate	Intermodal
Air	Low	Fast	Low	High	High	Intermodal
Pipeline	Low	Very slow	Very high	Very low	High	Limited
Cyberspace	Very high	Very fast	Very limited	Very low	Very limited	Very high

C. Bryant Estes

Customer Logistics Specialist
Danone

Describe your job. My job as customer logistics specialist is to act as an advocate for our customers in relation to the supply chain. We want to benefit our stakeholders as much as possible without disrupting the supply chain network. It is a combination of cultivating customer relationships while balancing the capabilities and needs of our company. It is my duty to represent the customer within internal meetings and throughout my day-to-day processes.

How did you get your job? One of my former classmates who graduated the semester before me recommended the position to me. I was nearing graduation and was testing the waters of the job market so to speak. After talking with him, I learned the company he worked for had its headquarters in Denver, Colorado. I have always had an affinity for the outdoors and thought this would also be a great opportunity for me to push my boundaries and advance my professional career—the perfect combination. I asked him to send my resume to the hiring manager in the Denver office. About a week later, I drove out to Denver, interviewed, and accepted my current position.

What has been the most important thing in making you successful at your job? Perseverance. To me, there was so much to learn moving from a comfortable environment in the classroom which I had figured out to navigate long ago to getting plugged in at a large corporation where almost nothing seemed familiar. The interactions, the jargon, the expectations were all something that I had to adapt to. The main thing that has helped me thrive has been trying to

C. Bryant Estes

learn as much as possible. I continue to take this attitude into my job every day. Things may seem hard or impossible to learn or get through, but I have learned to take it day by day. Eventually, I start to piece it together a little bit at a time until I have succeeded or completed a project.

What advice would you give soon-to-be graduates? Continue to grow and utilize your network as well as your personal brand. College is an incredible place. Everyone around you is studying and working toward the next step in launching a career for themselves. My network was the number-one reason I received an interview for my job. That being said, once you're in an interview, a reference will take you only so far. From that point on it becomes about your work ethic, attitude, persona—your personal brand.

What do you consider your personal brand to be? My favorite hobby is distance running. The thing that is incredible about it to me is that you don't have to be the fastest or the strongest out on the course, you just can't quit. Perseverance is the most important quality. Other runners can be faster than you during a race, but if they quit at any point then it was all for nothing. All a runner must do is continue to persist and he or she will be successful in completing the course. I think that same lesson has been applicable to my career. I didn't start my job with the most knowledge in supply chain or the best ability to handle a customer, but what I did do was continue to grow and learn from those around me. I want people to see that resiliency and teachability in my work. I pride myself on that.

Social Media in Action

As consumers shift their shopping experience from brick-and-mortar to online stores, retailers must increasingly embrace social media sites as a tool for reaching their target market. Firms ranging from Starwood Hotels to nutrition store GNC have invited customers to spend money through company fan pages on social media platforms. *Forbes* found that two-thirds of shoppers did some shopping on social media, and that trends indicate that more of the shopping process is going to happen on social media and similar platforms.[41]

Retailers want to go where their customers are. Increasingly, those places are social media platforms. The average consumer now spends more time each month on social media than on the top 500 online shopping sites combined. The popularity of "social commerce" also provides the added benefit of generating marketing research that helps retailers and their entire supply chain track trends and manage inventories.

The Social Media in Action Connect exercise in Chapter 10 asks you to make decisions about social commerce strategies for retailers and use customer-generated marketing research to manage the supply chain. By doing this exercise, you will better understand how social media tools can help retailers sell more and also create a more efficient supply chain.

Source: See Dana Mattioli, "Retailers Embrace Social Commerce," *The Wall Street Journal,* May 19, 2011, http://online.wsj.com/article/SB10001424052748703367004576289461779663904.html.

SUMMARY

ISO98RK9I/Cultura Creative RF/Alamy Stock Photo

LO 10-1 Describe the various flows within a supply chain.

A *supply chain* is the linked set of companies that perform or support the delivery of a company's products to customers. More formally, it is "a set of three or more companies directly linked by one or more of the upstream and downstream flows of products, services, finances, and information from a source to a customer."

Products primarily move *downstream* from a supplier to a customer, adding value to the final customer along the way. On their way downstream, they pass through distribution channels. These channels are intermediaries such as wholesalers, distributors, and retailers. Finances flow *upstream* in a supply chain. Information flows both upstream and downstream. Real-world supply chains typically involve a complex network made up of many suppliers and customers. A company can be a member of a number of supply chains.

Norman Wharton/Alamy Stock Photo

LO 10-2 Describe the push, pull, and hybrid supply chain strategies and their relationship to a company's competitive strategies.

To effectively perform supply chain management, firms must first develop a supply chain strategy. Three variations are push, pull, and hybrid (push-pull) strategies. In a *push supply chain,* the company builds goods based on a sales forecast, puts the goods into storage, and waits for a customer to order them. In a *pull supply chain,* production and distribution operations are driven by customer orders. In a *hybrid (push-pull) supply chain,* the initial stages of the supply chain operate on a push system, but the finalization of the product is based on a pull system.

George Frey/Getty
Images News/Getty
Images

LO 10-3 Summarize the importance of collaboration and resilience to effective supply chains.

The ultimate objective of supply chains is to deliver goods and services in a timely manner to the place where they will be consumed by the final user. This requires companies to work collaboratively both internally and externally to provide value to the final consumer. For an integrated supply chain to work, companies must be willing to embrace relationship-based strategies. Such strategies involve close, long-term collaboration for mutual benefit.

Resilience is the ability to anticipate, prepare for, and effectively respond to supply chain disruptions. If companies are to survive long term, they must be prepared for changes that could negatively affect their chances of remaining viable. A powerful approach that companies can use is to make their supply chains as resilient as possible through methods that include inventory management, sourcing strategies, manufacturing capacity flexibility, and transportation options.

Food Bank of
Northeast
Arkansas

LO 10-4 Describe how the primary logistics functions support a firm's supply chain strategy.

Logistics is that part of supply chain management that plans, implements, and controls the flow of goods, services, and information between the point of origin and the point of consumption to meet customers' requirements. Logistics operations add value to products moving through the supply chain. Though logistics is often associated with the place aspect of the four Ps, it affects all aspects of the marketing mix. By aligning logistics activities with its supply chain strategies, a firm can ensure that it adds value to a customer at all stages.

Geoffrey Robinson/
Alamy Stock Photo

LO 10-5 Describe the various logistics functions and their importance to marketing.

The primary logistics functions include inventory management, purchasing, materials management, warehousing, and distribution. *Inventory management* allows companies to maintain as low an inventory carrying cost as possible while still maintaining good customer service. *Purchasing* provides materials and goods at the lowest cost and highest quality needed to meet a company's marketing strategy. *Materials management, warehousing, and distribution functions* store goods until needed by manufacturing or a customer, then pick those goods, and prepare them for delivery. *Transportation* delivers goods to customers at the right time, to the right place, and in the right condition.

KEY TERMS

accessibility (of transportation) (p. 350)
distribution center (DC) (p. 349)
hybrid (push-pull) strategy (p. 332)
intermodal transport (p. 350)
inventory carrying costs (p. 334)
logistics (p. 341)
logistics operations (p. 335)

materials management (p. 347)
omnichannel (p. 349)
picking (p. 348)
pull strategy (p. 331)
purchase order (p. 346)
push strategy (p. 330)
put-away (p. 348)

resilience (p. 335)
stockout (p. 344)
supply chain management (p. 334)
supply chain orientation (p. 335)
supply chain process
    integration (p. 335)

MARKETING PLAN EXERCISE • Marketing Yourself

In this chapter, we discussed the importance of distribution. Getting your name, skills, and profile in front of decision makers is critical for you to achieve career success. In this next section of the marketing plan exercise, your assignment is to create a specific plan for how you will distribute your information and qualifications to reach your career objectives.

Job seekers upload and share millions of resumes every day on the Internet, even though the success rate of finding a job online is less than 20 percent in the United States. What do you plan to do to increase your success rate using

this distribution channel? A growing number of professionals use online services like LinkedIn. If you are thinking about LinkedIn or other social media distribution methods, which sites are best for your specific career path? What strategies should you employ on each site to maximize your efforts? Are there specific keywords you should use? Are there resume formats that work better on specific job sites?

If your career goals focus on graduate school, this process is equally important. Many graduate school entrance exams allow you to send your scores to a limited number of schools. Which schools will you choose?

If you plan to seek a job or graduate school opportunity using e-mail, what is the best strategy for designing that e-mail? Hiring managers and admissions personnel will pay attention to the e-mail text, the subject line, and even the time of day that you sent the e-mail. (What would a manager think if your resume arrives at 2:30 a.m.?)

Spending time now planning a personal distribution strategy will help as you prepare for your job or graduate school search.

Your Task: Write a one- to two-paragraph explanation of how you will distribute your information and qualifications. Your answer should include the websites or companies to which you plan to distribute your resume or the five schools to which you will send your graduate entrance exam scores. Also include any social media platforms you plan to use as part of your distribution strategy and how you plan to use them.

DISCUSSION QUESTIONS

1. Acme Manufacturing buys raw materials from Apex Unlimited. Acme gives Apex a monthly forecast of what it thinks it will buy and pays for the goods within 30 days of receipt. Better Retailing Inc. is one of Acme's customers. It provides Acme with data that record the sales of Acme's products at Better Retailing's checkout counters. Better Retailing pays for the goods it receives from Acme within 30 days of when the products sell. Do Acme, Apex, and Better Retailing constitute a supply chain? Explain your answer.

2. Mumbai Grocery in India buys produce directly from farmers. It provides the farmers with information: It tells them the amount it would like the farmers to harvest each day to avoid having too little, thus losing sales, or too much, causing some of the produce to spoil and become unsellable. Does Mumbai Grocery have a supply chain orientation? Is it practicing supply chain management? Defend your answers.

3. Shanghai Computers uses a sales forecast to purchase components for desktop and laptop computers. The firm also uses the sales forecast to schedule the production of partially assembled computers that are missing random-access memory (RAM), hard drives, and other components. Shanghai Computers

waits until it receives a customer order, then finishes assembling the computers to the configuration ordered by the customer. What supply chain strategy is Shanghai Computers using? Explain why you chose that answer.

4. How do the various types of functions provided by logistics operations help companies achieve their marketing objectives?

5. Explain the various types of inventories and how each type is used by companies to meet their marketing objectives.

6. Just-a-Buck is a low-cost retailer that sources its goods from factories in Asia. Just-a-Buck built its competitive strategy around providing products for exactly one dollar. Just-a-Buck has a distribution center located in Los Angeles that services the western half of the United States. Another distribution center in Atlanta services the eastern half of the United States. What modes of transportation would Just-a-Buck logically want to use to transport the goods it purchases from Asia to the United States? What modes would it use to get the goods to its distribution centers? What modes would it use to get the goods to its stores? Explain your answers.

 SOCIAL MEDIA APPLICATION

Assume that you are hired by the purchasing department at your university and your first task is to decide what type of PCs, laptops, or tablet computers the university will buy for its students. Analyze the social media presence of potential suppliers, using the following questions and activities as a guide:

1. Decide on a list of three to five potential suppliers. What criteria, such as cost or service capability, did you use to determine the list?

2. Carefully read through the social media platforms used by each of the potential suppliers from which

the university might purchase. Based only on what you read across the social media platforms, how would you rank the potential suppliers as preferred vendors? Explain your answer.

3. Is there anything that you have found on your preferred suppliers' social media presence that can help you in negotiating with those firms? For example, do any of them appear to be having customer service issues that you might be able to use as leverage to negotiate a lower price?

MARKETING ANALYTICS EXERCISE

Please complete the *Connect* exercise in Chapter 10 that focuses on using marketing analytics in inventory management—specifically, calculating the cost of holding inventory.

ETHICAL CHALLENGE

Tony Dauginas is a purchasing agent for a consumer packaged-goods company based in the United States. His company manufactures various goods in the health and beauty industry, such as cosmetics, skin lotions, toothpaste, and shampoo. Tony's company has come under assault from another, much larger company. The larger company can use its large purchasing volume as leverage to buy components for its products much less expensively than Tony's company can. This has put a lot of pressure on Tony's purchasing group to get the best price possible on the components it buys for manufacturing.

One of the types of materials that Tony buys is corrugated boxes. The boxes are used as secondary packaging for all of the company's goods. The price of wood pulp used to make the boxes has been steadily rising, causing prices of corrugated boxes to rise along with it. Tony has been very concerned about this price trend because the company spends a large percentage of its product-related costs on boxes.

Tony just got back from a trade show, at which he received some interesting insider information about one of his suppliers. While talking to a fellow purchasing manager at a noncompeting company, he found out that the other purchasing manager's company was terminating its contract with one of Tony's corrugated-box suppliers, Amalgamated

Boxes Inc. The company Tony's friend works for is Amalgamated's biggest customer, constituting about 50 percent of its business. The loss of this business will likely be a damaging, if not fatal, blow to Amalgamated.

Tony is considering calling on Amalgamated's sales office to chat with the vice president of sales. He figures that Amalgamated will be desperate for business and will be willing to do just about anything to secure Tony's company as a customer. Tony is thinking that he might be able to negotiate a long-term contract that locks in prices over several years. While in effect, that contract would prevent Amalgamated from passing on rising wood pulp prices to his company. He is also thinking about making a deep reduction in Amalgamated's prices a condition of the contract.

Please use the ethical decision-making framework to answer the following questions related to this scenario:

1. What are the ethical implications of Tony's plan to negotiate a long-term contract under the conditions presented in the scenario? Explain your answer.
2. What other approaches could Tony take with Amalgamated?
3. If you were in Tony's shoes, what would you do, and why?

VIDEO CASE

Please go to *Connect* to access the video cases featuring (1) FedEx and (2) Mary Kay that accompany this chapter.

PODCAST

Please go to Connect to access the podcast that accompanies this chapter.

CAREER **TIPS**

How to Succeed in a Logistics Career

You have read in this chapter about supply chain management and logistics functions. This area of marketing is rapidly growing and can be a great career path. Coauthor John Mello spent over 25 years as an employee and manager in the field of logistics and supply chain management. Here are four important tips, based on his experience, to consider if you choose to pursue a career in this field.

1. **Be flexible.** Be willing to relocate to a new city or state when applying for a job. You will greatly limit your chances for getting a good job if you tell the employer you are not willing to move.

    In addition, be flexible about what type of job you are willing to do. An offer for an off-shift job or one that involves working in an area open to the weather may not seem appealing. However, such jobs usually lead to higher-paying and more prestigious positions because they give you invaluable operations experience.

2. **Be collaborative.** If you cultivate good relationships with the people you work with, they will cooperate with you when you need them to. You will also develop a reputation as someone with whom it is easy to work.

Beyond this, if you attempt to make someone else's job easier, you will gain their admiration and respect. This applies to your employees, your peers, your boss, and the people you are in contact with outside the company such as suppliers or customers. Do what you can to help others. You never know when you will need their help to get something done. Personal relationships are key to your success and ultimately your career.

3. **Be honest.** First, be honest with yourself. Ask yourself whether you are a person others would like to be around. If the answer is no, work on improving your interpersonal skills. Second, be honest with others. Don't tell people just what they want to hear. That may make them feel better, but it doesn't help them solve personal or company problems.

4. **Keep learning.** The more you know about your job and your industry, the more valuable you will be to the firm and to yourself. Learning includes asking questions on the job, shadowing experienced professionals, reading information about your field, and obtaining additional certifications and degrees. Find out what certifications are available in your field of interest.

    Once you're established in a company, look for opportunities to further your formal education with a master's degree. Often, your company will pay for all or part of your continuing education.

CHAPTER NOTES

1. Justin Lahart, "Time Is Money in Transport Snarl," *The Wall Street Journal,* July 15, 2021, B12.
2. John T. Mentzer, ed., *Supply Chain Management* (Thousand Oaks, CA: Sage, 2001), p. 14.
3. John J. Coyle, John C. Langley Jr., Robert Novack, and Brian J. Gibson, *Supply Chain Management: A Logistics Perspective,* 9th ed. (Mason, OH: South-Western Cengage Learning, 2013).
4. "The Journey of Jeans," http://www.gtnexus.com/infographics/journey-of-jeans-supply-chain-collaboration.
5. James R. Stock and Douglas M. Lambert, *Strategic Logistics Management,* 4th ed. (New York: McGraw Hill, 2001).
6. Saabira Chaudhuri, "Lego Races to Stack Enough Bricks for the Holiday," *The Wall Street Journal,* November 12, 2015, pp. B1–B2.
7. David Simchi-Levi, Philip Kaminsky, and Edith Simchi-Levi, *Designing and Managing the Supply Chain: Concepts, Strategies and Case Studies,* 3rd ed. (New York: McGraw Hill, 2008), pp. 191–193.
8. John T. Mentzer, ed., *Supply Chain Management* (Thousand Oaks, CA: Sage, 2001).
9. John J. Coyle, John C. Langley Jr., Robert Novack, and Brian J. Gibson, *Supply Chain Management: A Logistics Perspective,* 9th ed. (Mason, OH: South-Western Cengage Learning, 2013).
10. David Simchi-Levi, Philip Kaminsky, and Edith Simchi-Levi, *Designing and Managing the Supply Chain: Concepts, Strategies and Case Studies,* 3rd ed. (New York: McGraw Hill, 2008).
11. Mello, John and Stahl, Robert, "How S&OP Changes Corporate Culture: Results from Interviews with Seven Companies." No. pages: 11. *Foresight: The International Journal of Applied Forecasting,* (Winter 2011), issue 20.
12. J. VanDuersen and J. Mello, "A Roadmap to Implementing CPFR," *Foresight: The International Journal of Applied Forecasting* 33 (Spring 2014): 8–12.
13. Jacob M. Schlesinger, "Coronavirus Reshapes World Trade," *The Wall Street Journal,* June 20, 2020, pp. A1, A10.

14. Asa Fitch, Kate O'Keefe, and Bob Davis, "Chip Makers, Trump Pursue Plants in U.S.," *The Wall Street Journal,* May 11, 2021, p. A6.
15. Mike Cherney, "Supply-Chain Woes Lead to New Thinking," *The Wall Street Journal,* December 28, 2020, p. A2.
16. Mike Cherney, "Supply-Chain Woes Lead to New Thinking," *The Wall Street Journal,* December 28, 2020, p. A2.
17. Thomas Gryta and Chip Cutter, "CEOs Rethink Global-Production Playbook," *The Wall Street Journal,* November 2, 2021, p. A1.
18. Mike Colias and Ben Foldy, "Ford, GM Move to Expand Into Chip Making," *The Wall Street Journal,* November 19, 2021, pp. A1–A2.
19. Council of Supply Chain Management Professionals, "Supply Chain Management Terms and Glossary," February 2010, http://cscmp.org.
20. John J. Coyle, John C. Langley Jr., Robert Novack, and Brian J. Gibson, *Supply Chain Management: A Logistics Perspective,* 9th ed. (Mason, OH: South-Western Cengage Learning, 2013).
21. John J. Coyle, John C. Langley Jr., Robert Novack, and Brian J. Gibson, *Supply Chain Management: A Logistics Perspective,* 9th ed. (Mason, OH: South-Western Cengage Learning, 2013).
22. John J. Coyle, John C. Langley Jr., Robert Novack, and Brian J. Gibson, *Supply Chain Management: A Logistics Perspective,* 9th ed. (Mason, OH: South-Western Cengage Learning, 2013).
23. Erica Phillips, "Tech Helps Food Banks Track Donations," *The Wall Street Journal,* December 3, 2015, p. B4.
24. John J. Coyle, John C. Langley Jr., Robert Novack, and Brian J. Gibson, *Supply Chain Management: A Logistics Perspective,* 9th ed. (Mason, OH: South-Western Cengage Learning, 2013).
25. Jennifer Smith, "Post-Pandemic Supply Chains Seek 'Resilience,' Report Says," *The Wall Street Journal,* July 23, 2020, https://www.wsj.com/articles/post-pandemic-supply-chains-seek-resilience-report-says.
26. Zeke Turner, "Aldi Bets Limited Choice Will Lure U.S. Shoppers," *The Wall Street Journal,* June 22, 2018, pp. A1, A9.
27. W. C. Benton Jr., *Purchasing and Supply Management,* 2nd ed. (New York: McGraw Hill, 2010).
28. Greg Ip, "Globalization Is Starting to Go Into Reverse," *The Wall Street Journal,* June 28, 2018, p. A2.
29. Jeannete Neuman, "Zara's Owner Battles Pressure on Sales from Shift to Online," *The Wall Street Journal,* June 14, 2018, p. B3.
30. Kathy Chu and Bob Davis, "A Nation of 1.4 Billion Faces a Labor Shortage," *The Wall Street Journal,* November 24, 2015, pp. A1, A10.
31. Greg Ip, "Globalization Takes Hit from Supply Crunch," *The Wall Street Journal,* October 21, 2021, A2.
32. Ronald H. Ballou, *Business Logistics/Supply Chain Management,* 5th ed. (Upper Saddle River, NJ: Pearson, 2004), pp. 330–331, 470.
33. James R. Stock and Douglas M. Lambert, *Strategic Logistics Management,* 4th ed. (New York: McGraw Hill, 2001).
34. Jennifer Smith, "Target Tries Out New Strategy to Improve Its Supply Chain," *The Wall Street Journal,* May 15, 2018, p. B3.
35. Brian Basket, "Shippers Go Small in Strategy Shift," *The Wall Street Journal,* April 11, 2017, p. B6.
36. U.S. Department of Transportation, n.d., http://www.rita.dot.gov/bts/sites/rita.dot.gov.bts/files/publications/freight_shipments_in_america/html/entire.html.
37. Tim Higgins, "On the Road to Self-Driving Trucks," *The Wall Street Journal,* March 3, 2017, pp. B1, B4.
38. Kimberly Chin and Saraj Nassauer, "Walmart Tries Out Own Deliveries," *The Wall Street Journal,* September 6, 2018, p. B2.
39. Anne Innocenzio, "Walmart to Launch Delivery Service to Other Businesses," *AP News,* August 24, 2021, https://apnews.com/article/business-eaeadc42654212fa434799327c307c67.
40. Laura Stevens, "Amazon Beefs Up Its Fleet of Vans," *The Wall Street Journal,* September 6, 2018, p. B2.
41. Rebecca Brooks, "How Shoppers Are Using Social Media," *Forbes,* August 27, 2021, https://www.forbes.com/sites/forbesagencycouncil/2021/08/27/how-shoppers-are-using-social-media/?sh=748139bb72eb.

Chapter **11**

Pricing

supparsorn/Shutterstock

Learning Objectives

After reading this chapter, you should be able to

LO 11-1 Explain the importance of pricing strategy to every organization.

LO 11-2 Outline the objectives, steps, and decisions involved in setting a price.

LO 11-3 Compare the pricing tactics marketers can use.

LO 11-4 Explain the influence of technology on pricing.

LO 11-5 Summarize the major challenges of pricing for international markets.

LO 11-6 Explain the major legal and ethical issues associated with pricing.

Executive **Perspective** ... because everyone is a marketer

Tina Cassidy
Chief Marketing Officer
GBH

Gulnara Niaz

As a journalism major in college, Tina Cassidy began a career that would lead her from being a reporter to leading strategic communications for complex issues to being vice president for a marketing agency with clients across a wide variety of industries.

Today, Tina is the chief marketing officer at GBH, a Boston-based media company that creates most of the content for PBS with national series such as Masterpiece, NOVA, Antiques Roadshow, American Experience, FRONTLINE, *and kids programs such as* Arthur and Molly of Denali. *Tina is the first CMO to have this title in the company's 70-year history and considers herself the steward of a legacy brand at a time of massive change in how audiences consume media.*

What has been the most important thing in making you successful at your job?

Understanding audiences and what they want is key because you're never going to be successful marketing content they don't want or didn't ask for. That's why ensuring that market research and data insights are infused into the entire life cycle of content production is essential for growth and impact. Also, given that GBH is practically a house of brands (my team supports hundreds of unique content strands) having an internal culture of collaboration and innovation makes the work not just possible but excellent.

What advice would you give soon-to-be graduates?

I came to my role after being a journalist, author, and agency executive. When I was 18 (or even 22) I am not sure I knew what a CMO did so I could not have imagined being one. But there is a thread throughout my entire working life—and that is storytelling, which is foundational to who I am and what I love. So my advice is: figure out what you enjoy doing, not what job you want. There are many different paths that one can enjoy, and it's ok to try them all. I've loved all of my roles!

How is marketing relevant to your role at GBH?

Marketing is central to my role because it's central to GBH achieving our mission, which is to enrich people's lives through programs and services that educate, inspire, and entertain, fostering citizenship and culture, the joy of learning, and the power of diverse perspectives. In a fractured media landscape, marketing has become more and more important to keeping us connected to audiences and our community.

What do you consider your personal brand to be?

I will never forget the time when I was a young journalist finding my voice with a new column, and an editor told me I was doing a great job building my personal brand. It never had occurred to me that an individual could have such a thing but his comment opened my eyes. When you are intentional about how you spend your time—with a goal or a vision in mind—a brand emerges. So, what am I known for? I am excited by change: understanding why it's necessary and how to make it happen. I like creating new things, innovating, to make life—or work—better.

LO 11-1 # THE IMPORTANCE OF PRICING

Explain the importance of pricing strategy to every organization.

Pricing affects your life each day; it is part of almost every consumer decision that you make. Whether you are buying a new car or ordering lunch, the prices of the products you are considering typically factor into your decision about what to purchase. If the price for a lunch special is too high, you may buy something else to eat. But consider that, if the restaurant charges less than you would have been willing to pay, it has reduced its revenue.

Keep these factors in mind when, after you graduate, you negotiate the price an organization is willing to pay you as an employee. If the price to hire you is too high, the company you are interviewing with may hire someone else. However, if you ask for a lower salary than what the company is willing to pay, you have sacrificed initial earnings potential. This, in turn, could affect your earnings for years to come if your raises are based on percentage increases in your initial salary. Thus it is critical that you understand the strategy and tactics of pricing and how they impact your future and the future of the organizations you work for.

The other three elements of the marketing mix—product, promotion, and place—come together to determine how marketers capture value through pricing. **Price** is the amount of something—money, time, or effort—that a buyer exchanges with a seller to obtain a product. Pricing is one of the most important strategic decisions a firm faces: It reflects the *value the product delivers* to consumers as well as the *value the product captures* for the firm. When used correctly, pricing strategies can maximize profits and help the firm take a commanding market position. When used incorrectly, pricing strategies can limit revenue, profits, and brand perceptions.

Pricing is the essential element for capturing revenue and profits. **Revenue** is the result of the price charged to customers multiplied by the number of units sold. **Profits** are the firm's "bottom line": revenue minus total costs. These two calculations, represented in the following equations, underlie the firm's entire marketing strategy:

price

The amount of something—money, time, or effort—that a buyer exchanges with a seller to obtain a product.

revenue

The result of the price charged to customers multiplied by the number of units sold.

profits

Revenue minus total costs.

$$\text{Revenue} = \text{Units sold} \times \text{Price}$$
$$\text{Profits} = \text{Revenue} - \text{Costs}$$

The objective of strategic pricing is profitability. The majority of marketers and firms throughout the world seek to increase revenue, which can ultimately lead to increased profits. There are only two ways to increase revenue: sell more products or sell them at a higher price. As a result of this reality, in order to maximize profits, marketers must make strategic trade-offs between volume and price.

Ultimately, marketers want to charge as much as they possibly can, as long as the consumer still perceives value in the product at that price. Integrating the pricing strategy with other marketing-mix elements ensures that the firm's products include only those features that add value to customers. For example, consider customers who stop buying cable television or fast-food combo meals because the price included channels or menu items they didn't want to pay for. If the price is set too high, customers will simply choose another good or service. To avoid such pitfalls, marketers use a systematic process to evaluate relevant factors when setting a price.

Companies that charge a higher price than the value the customer places on a product run the risk that the customer will choose another good or service. In recent years, some cable customers have disconnected their service in favor of less-costly alternatives like streaming Netflix or Google TV. *Marvin Tolentino/Alamy Stock Photo*

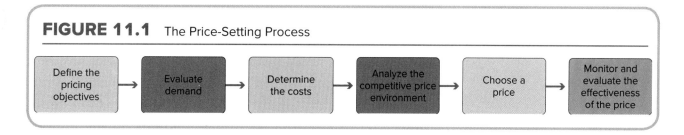

FIGURE 11.1   The Price-Setting Process

Define the pricing objectives → Evaluate demand → Determine the costs → Analyze the competitive price environment → Choose a price → Monitor and evaluate the effectiveness of the price

THE PRICE-SETTING PROCESS

LO 11-2

Outline the objectives, steps, and decisions involved in setting a price.

Many factors influence how a firm sets prices. A firm's various stakeholders may voice a preference for higher or lower prices, depending on their point of view: Marketing executives in search of substantial profits typically want high prices across the products they sell. Salespeople often want lower prices, to increase the perceived customer value and ultimately the number of units sold. Customers, too, want low prices, to maximize their purchasing power. Thoughtful consideration of the impact on all stakeholders at each step in the price-setting process, illustrated in Figure 11.1, increases the likelihood that the final price captures value for the firm and delivers value to the customer.

Step 1: Define the Pricing Objectives

The first step in setting a price is to clearly define the pricing objectives. Pricing objectives should be an extension of the firm's marketing objectives. They should describe what a firm hopes to achieve through pricing. Similar to the firm's marketing objectives, pricing objectives should be specific, measurable, and reflect the market realities the firm faces. Common pricing objectives include profit maximization, volume maximization, and survival.

profit maximization

A pricing objective that involves setting a relatively high price for a period of time after the product launches.

Profit Maximization   Profit maximization is designed to maximize profits on each unit sold. **Profit maximization** involves setting a relatively high price for a period of time after the product launches. Profit maximization assumes that customers value a product's differentiating attributes; as a result, they are willing to pay a higher price to take advantage of those attributes, especially early in a product's life cycle. Apple's pricing of a newly released watch series provides a good example of profit maximization.

volume maximization

A pricing objective that involves setting prices low to encourage a greater volume of purchases; also called *penetration pricing*.

For profit maximization to work, firms must use the other marketing-mix elements to ensure the product is produced, delivered, and promoted in a way that clearly differentiates it from competing alternatives. For example, a luxury brand like Mercedes-Benz does not sell inexpensive products or use promotional gimmicks to increase the volume of its sales. The firm wants customers to associate Mercedes-Benz with higher levels of quality and elegance than a regular car company. By consistently selling at a higher price, Mercedes-Benz maximizes profits and reinforces the added value and superior experience of buying its cars.

Luxury brands like Mercedes charge high prices as part of a profit maximization strategy that relies on a customer's willingness to pay more for a product they attach more value to. *1Roman Makedonsky/Shutterstock*

Volume Maximization   Volume maximization is designed to maximize volume and revenue for a firm. **Volume maximization** is the process of setting prices low to encourage a greater volume of purchases. Because the goal is to gain a large market share due to the low price, the strategy associated with volume maximization is often referred to as *penetration pricing*. DirecTV, for example, aggressively promotes a pricing strategy in which customers get access to over 150 channels for less than $40 per month during their first year of service. While the pricing package requires a two-year contract (and prices typically increase in the second year to a specified rate), consumers see immediate savings in their monthly bill and receive a home digital video recorder (DVR) and other added features. The penetration pricing strategy has increased the volume of DirecTV customers to more than 20 million subscribers.[1]

For a volume maximization strategy to work over the long term, the firm must have a significant cost or resource advantage over competitors. For example, Walmart leverages its bulk buying power and efficient supply chain to reduce costs. Volume maximization has helped make Walmart the largest retailer in the world.

survival pricing

A pricing objective that involves lowering prices to the point at which revenue just covers costs, allowing the firm to endure during a difficult time.

Survival Pricing   Survival pricing involves lowering prices to the point at which revenue just covers costs, allowing the firm to endure (survive) during a difficult time. The survival objective is designed to maximize cash flow over the short term and is typically implemented by a struggling firm. It should not be a permanent pricing objective, though it can be useful as a temporary means of staying in business: During the recession that began in late 2007, General Motors (as well as a number of other companies) reduced prices in an effort to avoid bankruptcy and sustain the firm.[2]

Step 2: Evaluate Demand

The second step in setting a price is evaluating demand for the product at various price levels. The concept of supply and demand sits at the heart of setting prices. According to traditional economic theory, setting prices is as simple as finding the point at which the quantity demanded of a good or service at a particular price equals the quantity supplied by producers at that price. Determining the quantity that producers are willing and able to supply involves looking at costs. No company can afford, for very long, to sell its goods or services at prices that do not cover costs. For producers, the optimal price is the point at which marginal revenue equals marginal cost. **Marginal revenue** is the change in total revenue that results from selling one additional unit of product. **Marginal cost** is the change in total cost that results from producing one additional unit of product.

marginal revenue

The change in total revenue that results from selling one additional unit of product.

marginal cost

The change in total cost that results from producing one additional unit of product.

Pricing in today's market isn't as easy as applying economic theory. To start, external environmental forces can significantly affect market demand. For example, during the recession, demand for houses declined significantly. The economic situation reduced demand to such a degree that house prices in many parts of the country declined by more than 15 percent from their previous values.[3] Those who wanted to sell homes—existing homeowners and banks holding foreclosed properties—often were not willing to reduce prices to the point where would-be buyers were willing and able to buy.

price sensitivity

The degree to which the price of a product affects consumers' purchasing behavior.

Marketers need to project not only the overall market demand but also the specific product demand at various price points. This requires an understanding of consumers' **price sensitivity**, which is the degree to which the price of a product affects consumers' purchasing behavior. Price sensitivity varies from product to product and from consumer to consumer. As Table 11.1 shows, a number of factors influence price sensitivity. For example:

- A consumer shopping for a new car who cannot afford to spend more than a certain amount on such a large purchase will be more price-sensitive than a consumer with more money to spend on a car or a consumer shopping for a smaller purchase like a new piece of clothing. So, the size of the expenditure affects price sensitivity.
- Consumers are also more price-sensitive if the price they see for a new car at the dealership is outside the range of what the consumer believes is fair. Regardless of the car's features, a consumer is less likely to pay the price if it's more than they consider reasonable.

TABLE 11.1 Factors Influencing Price Sensitivity

Factor	Description
Size of expenditure	Customers are less sensitive to the prices of small expenditures that, in the case of households, are defined relative to income.
Shared costs	Customers are less price-sensitive when some or all of the purchase price is paid by others.
Switching costs	Customers are less sensitive to the price of a product if there is added cost (both monetary and nonmonetary) associated with switching to a competitor.
Perceived risk	Customers are less price-sensitive when it is difficult to compare competing products and the cost of not getting the expected benefits of a purchase is high.
Importance of end benefit	Customers are less price-sensitive when the product is a small part of the cost of a benefit with high economic or psychological importance.
Price–quality perceptions	Customers are less sensitive to a product's price to the extent that price is a proxy for the likely quality of the purchase.
Reference prices	Customers are more price-sensitive the higher the product's price *relative to* the customers' price expectation.
Perceived fairness	Customers are more sensitive to a product's price when it is outside the range that they perceive as "fair" or "reasonable."
Price framing	Customers are more price-sensitive when they perceive the price as a "loss" rather than as a forgone "gain." They are more price-sensitive when the price is paid separately rather than as part of a bundle.

Source: Thomas Nagle, John Hogan, and Joseph Zale, *The Strategy and Tactics of Pricing*, 5th ed. (Upper Saddle River, NJ: Pearson, 2011), pp. 132–133.

- Consumers often become more price-sensitive as they become aware of potential substitute products. If a consumer can review and compare the prices and performance of available cars throughout the region, the perceived risk for the buyer declines, and the consumer becomes more price-sensitive.

Marketers consider each of the price-sensitivity factors during the price-setting process to understand their impact. Once marketers understand the price sensitivity exhibited by members of their target market, they can use this measure to calculate how changes in price will affect demand for a product and thus the amount of product the firm can sell at various price levels.

Price elasticity of demand is a measure of price sensitivity that gives the percentage change in quantity demanded in response to a percentage change in price (holding constant all the other determinants of demand, such as income). It is one of the most important concepts in marketing and should be considered when pricing any product.

Consider the following example: Suppose a car dealership reduces prices on its entire stock of new inventory by 10 percent. You would expect the quantity of cars demanded, and consequently sales, to increase. But by what percentage would sales increase? Would they increase enough to offset the decrease in price? If the dealership reduced prices by 10 percent but sold only 4 percent more cars in the following month, it would be worse off than it was initially, as the following equations illustrate:

price elasticity of demand

A measure of price sensitivity that gives the percentage change in quantity demanded in response to a percentage change in price (holding constant all the other determinants of demand, such as income).

Sales before price cut:
  1,000 cars sold × $20,000 (average price for new cars) = $20,000,000

Sales after price cut:
  1,040 cars sold (4% increase) × $18,000 (10% price decrease) = $18,720,000

inelastic demand

Demand for which a given percentage change in price results in a smaller percentage change in quantity demanded.

This scenario, which happens all too often, illustrates the concept of inelastic demand. **Inelastic demand** is demand for which a given percentage change in price results in a smaller percentage change in quantity demanded.[4] As a marketing professional, if salespeople or others in an organization approach you asking for a price reduction to sell more units, your first question should be: "How many more units do you expect to sell at the reduced price?" If the additional sales don't offset the price reduction, you would not want to approve the request.

Now consider a different scenario. Suppose the car dealership's 10 percent reduction in price leads to a 20 percent monthly increase in the number of cars sold. In that case, the firm would be better off than it was originally, as shown in the following equations:

Sales before price cut:
 1,000 cars sold × $20,000 (average price for new cars) = $20,000,000

Sales after price cut:
 1,200 cars sold (20% increase) × $18,000 (10% price decrease) = $21,600,000

elastic demand

Demand for which a given percentage change in price results in an even larger percentage change in quantity demanded.

In this scenario, the car sales demonstrated elastic demand. **Elastic demand** is demand for which a given percentage change in price results in an even larger percentage change in quantity demanded. Prices are generally more elastic in the early stages of the product life cycle and increasingly inelastic in the later stages of the product life cycle.

To see these concepts at work in the real world, consider how the principle applies to cost increases at Netflix. In 2011, Netflix raised prices on its DVD and online streaming services by over 50 percent.[5] The company received a significant amount of negative publicity, but fewer than 4 percent of paid subscribers stopped using the service. Thus, demand was inelastic.

If we plug these percentages into our fictional car example, look at what the equivalent results would be for the car dealership:

March: 1,000 cars sold × $20,000 (average price for new cars) = $20,000,000
April: 960 cars sold (4% decrease) × $30,000 (50% price increase) = $28,800,000

Because demand for Netflix's DVD and online streaming services is inelastic—not significantly affected by changes in price—the additional revenue it earned when it increased prices for each service more than outweighed the revenue it lost due to unhappy customers. *jvphoto/Alamy Stock Photo*

In the case of Netflix, because of inelastic demand, the firm could raise prices significantly and realize only a small reduction in units sold. In fact, because Netflix's remaining customers were paying a 50 percent higher rate, its quarterly revenue and profit after the change were both significantly higher. In light of this, the company's decision to raise prices to increase profitability was a good one.

Marketers should also be aware of how the external environment affects price elasticity. For example, research suggests that consumers tend to be more sensitive to prices during difficult economic times.[6] In addition, inflation has been shown to lead to substantially higher price elasticities over the past several decades.[7]

Step 3: Determine the Costs

A marketer should understand all of the costs associated with its product offering, whether the product is a good, service, idea, or some combination of these. Accurately determining the costs sets a lower price limit for marketers. It also ensures that the company will not lose money by pricing its products too low. Although a firm may temporarily sell products below cost to generate sales as part of a survival-pricing strategy, it cannot endure for very long employing this strategy. Setting a price begins by knowing the fixed and variable costs that go into producing a good or service.

Fixed Costs versus Variable Costs Calculating the total cost of a product begins with an understanding of the two major types of costs—fixed and variable:

- Costs that remain constant and do not vary based on the number of units produced or sold are called **fixed costs**. Examples of fixed costs include salaries, rent, insurance, and advertising costs. Because these costs will be incurred regardless of the level of production or sales activity, they must be recovered during the course of doing business. Marketers must set a final price that allows the firm to cover fixed costs over the long term.
- Costs that vary depending on the number of units produced or sold are called **variable costs**. Variable costs include things such as raw material, sales commissions, and delivery costs.

To illustrate the difference between the two types of costs, let's use our car dealership example again: Fixed costs for a car dealership include rent for the offices and showroom and employee salaries and benefits. These costs exist each month. They do not change even if, for example, an additional 10 cars are sold in one month. Variable costs for a car dealership would include things like commissions for the dealership's salespeople.

Organizations must ensure that the prices they set generate profit after accounting for *both* fixed and variable costs. A $20,000 car might generate an $800 per-car profit for the dealership after all of the fixed costs are accounted for. However, if the dealership offers its salespeople a 5 percent commission ($1,000) on each new car sold, the dealership would actually lose money on sales of the car. Marketing professionals must watch costs closely and set prices accordingly to avoid such scenarios.

Executive Perspective . . .
because everyone is a marketer

Tina Cassidy
Chief Marketing Officer
GBH

Gulnara Niaz

How has technology impacted some of the marketing decisions you make?

My role, big picture, is to grow audiences and support for public media, but of course doing that includes many functions: marketing, communications, media relations, government relations, station relations, community relations, research, and creative services, which includes branding. One of the first things I did upon arrival was to rebrand the organization from WGBH to GBH. Dropping the W is a reflection of the fact that we are not just a broadcaster, but a creator that distributes on many platforms and engages in many ways.

Break-Even Analysis

Break-Even Analysis Once a company estimates fixed and variable costs, it can incorporate them into a break-even analysis. **Break-even analysis** is the process of calculating the break-even point, which equals the sales volume needed to achieve a profit of zero. Specifically, the **break-even point** is the point at which the costs of producing a product equal the revenue made from selling the product. Once the firm has established the break-even point, it can determine how much it would need to sell to earn a profit on the product.

To calculate the break-even point, we divide total fixed costs by the unit contribution margin. The *unit contribution margin* is the amount of revenue a product contributes per unit; it is calculated as the selling price per unit minus the variable costs per unit. In equation form:

$$\frac{\text{Total fixed costs}}{\text{Unit contribution margin}} = \frac{\text{Total fixed costs}}{\left(\begin{array}{c}\text{Selling price} \\ \text{per unit}\end{array} - \begin{array}{c}\text{Variable cost} \\ \text{per unit}\end{array}\right)} = \begin{array}{c}\text{Break-even} \\ \text{point in units}\end{array}$$

Consider this simple example of break-even analysis: A firm wants to know the break-even point of a product at two prices: $100 and $250. If fixed costs are $1,000 and variable costs per unit are $50, we can calculate the break-even point as follows:

$$\frac{\$1,000 \text{ fixed costs}}{\$100 \text{ price per unit} - \$50 \text{ variable cost per unit}} = \frac{\$1,000}{\$50} = \begin{array}{c}\text{Break-even} \\ \text{point of 20 widgets}\end{array}$$

$$\frac{\$1,000 \text{ fixed costs}}{\$250 \text{ price per unit} - \$50 \text{ variable cost per unit}} = \frac{\$1,000}{\$200} = \begin{array}{c}\text{Break-even} \\ \text{point of 5 widgets}\end{array}$$

fixed costs

Costs that remain constant and do not vary based on the number of units produced or sold.

variable costs

Costs that vary depending on the number of units produced or sold.

break-even analysis

The process of calculating the break-even point, which equals the sales volume needed to achieve a profit of zero.

break-even point

The point at which the costs of producing a product equal the revenue made from selling the product.

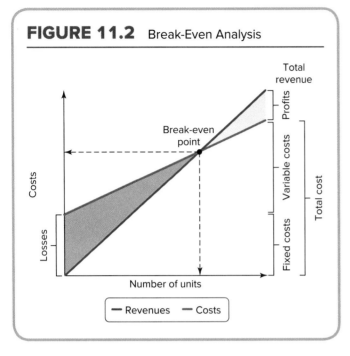

FIGURE 11.2 Break-Even Analysis

Thus, at a price of $100, the firm will need to sell 20 widgets to break even. At the break-even point, it will earn no profit and it will suffer no loss. At a price of $250, with the same fixed and variable costs, the firm will break even when it sells 5 widgets.

Another way to determine the break-even point is by using a graph (often called a *cost-volume-profit, CVP, graph*). Figure 11.2 illustrates break-even analysis by this method. It plots lines representing a product's estimated revenues and costs. The point at which the two lines intersect is the break-even point. Notice that the graph also shows the influence of fixed and variable costs. The fixed costs remain flat, while variable costs increase as the amount of sales increases. Once unit sales pass the break-even point, the firm begins to generate a profit. (Also, sales lower than the break-even point result in losses to the firm.)

Note an important point: Break-even analysis analyzes only the costs of the sales. It does not reflect how demand may be affected at different price levels; in other words, it doesn't measure price sensitivity. Just because the firm will break even selling 5 widgets at a price of $250 each doesn't mean customers are willing to buy widgets at that price.

While marketers must understand a firm's costs to set prices effectively, costs should never totally dictate price. Strategic pricing requires firms to integrate costs into other aspects of the marketing mix, including what value the customer places on the product and the price environment in the industry.

Step 4: Analyze the Competitive Price Environment

Pricing does not occur in a vacuum. Marketers must consider what competitors charge for their products. Setting prices to compete against other firms is challenging and complex, with various possible strategies:

- Match competitor prices.
- Price lower than competitors, thus offering customers greater value.
- Price higher because the firm offers a superior product.

This decision should be consistent with the overall marketing objectives of the firm and the other three marketing-mix elements.

Industry structure plays an important role in analyzing the competitive price environment. For example, in a market structure in which there are a large number of buyers and sellers, as is the case for our car dealership, the pricing impact of any single firm will be fairly small. If a car dealership in Dallas reduced or raised prices on certain types of cars, it is doubtful the change in price would significantly influence pricing at other car dealerships in the area. However, in an industry in which a small number of firms compete, firms will typically match the price of competitors. A common example is the multibillion-dollar wireless phone industry, in which only a few major competitors fight for market share. Marketers at AT&T, Verizon Wireless, and other firms compete on nonprice strategies, such as rollover minutes and better product features.

Marketers also should consider how competitors might respond to their pricing. Pricing can resemble a game of chess. You should always be thinking about what your

Marketers in industries with few competitors, like the domestic airline industry, increasingly look to avoid price wars by competing based on rewards programs, enhanced flight offerings, and other nonprice strategies. *David Paul Morris/Bloomberg/Getty Images*

opponents' future moves might be. How a firm reacts to a change in a competitor's prices depends on whether the competitor is a stronger or weaker rival and whether the price reduction is cost-justified. For example, if a weaker competitor initiates a price decrease that would leave your firm unable to cover its costs if you met the price, you are likely to ignore the competitor's price cut and maintain your current pricing. However, if the price cut is initiated by a stronger competitor and is cost-justified, your firm will likely reduce prices to defend its existing customer base and market share.

Marketers must also take online competitors into account. This applies to both in-store and online-only items. For example, retailer Brookstone separated its team of pricing employees into an in-store group and an online-commerce group. Every day the online team scours competitors' websites to check the prices of their online electronics and then adjusts the prices of thousands of Brookstone's online-only items accordingly.[8]

Step 5: Choose a Price

So far, we've seen that determining the costs provides a lower price limit, and analyzing the competition narrows the range of prices that can be charged. After completing these two steps, it is time for marketers to choose a price. Again, the pricing decision should be made with the goal of maximizing long-term, sustainable profits. Because choosing a price is a complicated process, firms rarely do it perfectly. The next major section of the chapter discusses the most common tactics for determining price. Before we get there, we'll discuss two often-overlooked factors that influence price: reference prices and underpricing.

Reference Prices Chances are you routinely compare the prices of almost everything you buy, from textbooks to coffee to gasoline. Marketers can capitalize on this tendency by identifying the reference prices of their targeted consumers when setting their own prices. **Reference prices** are the prices that consumers consider

reference prices
The prices that consumers consider reasonable and fair for a product.

Retailers like TJ Maxx and Marshall's use reference prices to illustrate the savings they offer customers by listing both the original price of the good and the retailer's discount price on the merchandise tags. *Paul Morigi/Getty Images*

reasonable and fair for a product. Reference prices matter to marketers because consumers are typically more price-sensitive the higher a product's price is relative to expectations.

Salespeople can be a valuable tool when identifying reference prices. In most cases, salespeople have the most direct contact with customers and thus a good sense of what customers are willing to pay. Salespeople who have developed relationships with customers often understand the most attractive price points; they can leverage the quality of that relationship to obtain higher profits. Marketers should work closely with the sales force to understand how high they can price a product before customers stop considering the product a good value. Customer surveys, focus groups, and other forms of marketing research also are helpful in understanding how consumers view a certain product and how much they are willing to pay for it.

Instead of just seeking to *identify* reference prices, marketers can also seek to *establish* reference prices for consumers. Apple, for example, launches a variety of products at various price points so that buyers can compare the products and begin to associate features with dollars. As a result of this strategy, customers don't mind paying a higher price for a product with more capacity or better features. They are willing to pay $239 for the iPod Touch with 16 gigabytes (GB) of storage because it has many sought-after features that earlier versions of the iPod, such as the 16GB Nano (priced at $149), don't have. If customers are willing to pay an even higher price for more storage capacity, they may choose the 64GB iPod Touch for $344.

Even if a firm doesn't seek to establish reference prices as Apple does, its marketers should always question what reference prices potential customers will compare the firm's prices with.

underpricing

Charging someone less than they are willing to pay.

Underpricing One of the most common mistakes in modern pricing is charging someone less than they are willing to pay, or **underpricing**. Customers place different values on the goods and services they buy. As Charlie Sheen's character Budd Foxx famously said in the movie *Wall Street,* "You should not charge a guy $30 for an airline ticket if he is willing to pay $300." Because revenue is simply the number of units sold multiplied by the price per item, marketers too often make the mistake of setting prices too low in an effort to increase the units-sold side of the equation. Instead, they need to consider all of the other factors that contribute to the value a customer places on a product.

Airlines have for years considered the ramifications of underpricing in their pricing strategies. If you purchase an airline ticket today for a flight from Dallas to Los Angeles three months from now, you might pay $500. However, if you wait until the day before that flight to buy the same ticket, you may pay something in the range of $1,500. The customer buying three months in advance, whether he or she is attending a conference or taking a family trip to Disneyland, has plenty of time to comparison shop. However, the person who needs to fly to Los Angeles tomorrow may have an urgent business meeting or a new baby in the family, either of which increases the value of the airline ticket. Could the airline charge the last-minute customer the same price as the recreational traveler? Yes, but why should it, if the value the customer places on the ticket differs? The airline would be, as the saying goes, "leaving money on the table."

Step 6: Monitor and Evaluate the Effectiveness of the Price

Choosing a price is not a one-time decision. Pricing strategy evolves throughout the product life cycle; it needs repeated monitoring and evaluation, to determine how effectively the strategy meets the pricing objectives. For example:

- Marketers in the introduction stage for a new type of smartphone might select a price-skimming strategy; its goal would be to achieve maximum profits from innovators and early adopters.
- As the product enters the growth stage, its customer base expands. The firm might gradually lower prices as it achieves economies of scale and more competitors enter the market.
- Once the product enters the decline stage of the product life cycle, the firm might decide to use survival pricing to clear out remaining inventories and sustain the product for as long as possible.

One of the most challenging aspects of pricing is initiating price increases. It is hard to imagine a customer being excited about paying more for the same product. However, in an effort to recover increasing costs or improve profits, firms often face situations that require price increases. For example, restaurants Wendy's and Arby's were both forced to raise prices after the cost of beef and other key ingredients increased by more than 5 percent.[9] This challenge was especially relevant as organizations across industries managed the highest inflation level in decades throughout 2021 and 2022. Three of the most common and effective strategies for raising prices are *unbundling, escalator clauses,* and *shrinkflation.*

Unbundling Unbundling involves separating out the individual goods, services, or ideas that make up a product and pricing each one individually. Such a strategy allows marketers to maintain a similar price on the core product but recover costs in other ways on related goods and services. For example, a restaurant might unbundle a meal so that the hamburger sells for the same price, but the customer now must pay extra for the french fries. Airlines have pursued an unbundling strategy over the course of the last decade. They now charge separate fees for baggage rather than bundling luggage fees into the cost of the ticket. Netflix used an unbundling strategy when it separated its streaming service from its DVD-by-mail service. Customers could still get one service or the other for less than $15 per month, but not both; that change amounted to a price increase for those customers who wanted to continue utilizing both services. In general, unbundling provides value for customers who are focused on a specific price point rather than the complete product offering.

unbundling

Separating out the individual goods, services, or ideas that make up a product and pricing each one individually.

Escalator Clauses An **escalator clause** in an agreement provides for price increases if certain, specified conditions occur. The escalator clause ensures that providers of goods and services do not encounter unreasonable financial hardship as a result of uncontrollable factors relating to the product. Those factors could involve either increases in the costs of materials or decreases in the availability of something required to deliver products to customers. For example, an escalator clause in a logistics contract can take the form of a fuel surcharge that allows trucking companies to adjust prices based on the current price of fuel.

Many rental agreements provide a good example of how an escalator clause can be enacted. Landlords often include an escalator clause in a rental contract, allowing them to increase the monthly rent if taxes on the property go up. Firms that decide to use escalator clauses should make them as transparent as possible. They should specify whether price adjustments will be made at fixed intervals (e.g., quarterly, semiannually, or annually) or only at the expiration of the contract.

escalator clause

A section in a contract that provides for price increases if certain, specified conditions occur.

Construction contracts often have built-in escalator clauses to protect construction firms in the event of increases in the price of materials like copper, asphalt, lumber, and concrete. *Jat306/Shutterstock*

shrinkflation

The process of items shrinking in size or quantity while their prices remain the same or increase.

Shrinkflation Shrinkflation is the process of items shrinking in size or quantity while their prices remain the same or increase. In recent years, numerous companies have shrunk the size of products to keep prices stable and to retain customers. For example, Nestlé SA's Häagen-Dazs brand reduced the size of its "pint" containers from 16 ounces to 14, keeping prices stable. Sometimes the tactic is even considered a product innovation. Coca-Cola introduced 8.5-ounce bottles that can cost up to six times more per ounce than sodas sold in traditional 12-packs of 12-ounce cans.[10]

When undertaking any of these strategies, the firm must take the time to clearly explain the price change to customers. Even if customers are not happy with the change, at least they will understand why it's being done. If the firm doesn't communicate the purpose of the increase effectively, customers who are unwilling to accept the increase may use social media platforms or other word-of-mouth strategies to protest against the new policies. In 2016, after Mondelēz International Inc. changed its bars to reduce the grams of chocolate to cut costs, angry fans complained on the company's Facebook page. In 2018, Mondelēz reverted to the original size.

Mc Graw Hill **connect** Exercise **11-1**

Please complete the *Connect* exercise for Chapter 11 that focuses on the price-setting process. By understanding the dynamics of each step of the process, you will gain insight into how marketers set prices that maximize both profits and customer value.

LO 11-3

Compare the pricing tactics marketers can use.

PRICING TACTICS

Once marketers have completed their analysis of demand, costs, and the competitive environment, they can use a number of different tactics to choose a final price. In this section, we will discuss several of the most common methods and discuss the advantages and disadvantages of each. Pricing tactics are short- or long-term attempts to adjust the pricing of a product to achieve a particular pricing objective. Which tactic to use depends on the value customers perceive the product to have, their ability to pay, and how they intend to use the product.

Markup Pricing

Markup pricing (also known as *cost-plus pricing*) is one of the most commonly used pricing tactics, largely because it is easy. In **markup pricing**, marketers add a certain amount, usually a percentage, to the cost of the product, to set the final price. The general formula for calculating markup price is:

markup pricing
A pricing method in which a certain amount is added to the cost of the product, to set the final price; also called *cost-plus pricing.*

$$\text{Markup price} = \text{Unit cost of product} + (\text{Desired \% return} \times \text{Unit cost})$$

For example, a pricing analyst can easily implement markup pricing by reviewing a spreadsheet and adding 20 percent to the cost of each item, such as a lawn chair, as illustrated in the following equation:

$$\text{Markup price} = \$10 \text{ unit cost of lawn chair} + (0.2 \times \$10) = \$12$$

Though markup pricing has the advantage of being easy, it's not very effective at maximizing profits, which is the ultimate objective of a good pricing strategy. Let's look at an example of how markup pricing does *not* capture value for our lawn chair. As we have discussed, different customers place different values on the products they purchase. Imagine we have four target customers who personally value the lawn chair at $10, $14, $15, and $20, respectively. The information about the value that each customer places on the lawn chair comes from the firm's marketing research and salespeople.

Table 11.2 shows how much profit margin the firm would earn on each lawn chair if it uses a 20 percent markup. **Profit margin** is the amount a product sells for above the total cost of the product itself. Notice that if the firm uses the 20 percent markup, the profit margin for *each customer* who purchases a lawn chair will always be $2 ($12 selling price − $10 unit cost) due to the 20 percent markup. Customer #1 would not purchase the chair because its perceived value is less than the $12 price. Customers #2, #3, and #4 would purchase the chair, giving the firm a total profit of $6 ($2 profit margin × 3). But if the firm were to use markup pricing, it would lose the difference between the amount of each customer's perceived value and the $12 price.

profit margin
The amount a product sells for above the total cost of the product itself.

Now compare the markup pricing scenario to a research-based approach that considers the competitive price environment. The cost of producing the product is still $10 per lawn chair. Marketing research has told the company that competitors charge $16 or more per chair and that many customers value their lawn chairs at $15 or more.

TABLE 11.2 The Profit Implications of Using a Markup Pricing Strategy

	Perceived Value of the Lawn Chair to the Customer	Does the Customer Purchase at the 20% Markup Price ($12)?	Profit Margin for Firm
Customer #1	$10	No	$0
Customer #2	$14	Yes	$2
Customer #3	$15	Yes	$2
Customer #4	$20	Yes	$2

TABLE 11.3   The Profit Implications of Using a Research-Based Pricing Strategy

	Perceived Value of the Lawn Chair to the Customer	Does the Customer Purchase at the Research-Based Price ($15)?	Profit Margin for Firm
Customer #1	$10	No	$0
Customer #2	$14	No	$0
Customer #3	$15	Yes	$5
Customer #4	$20	Yes	$5

As a result, the firm sets its price at $15. Table 11.3 shows the firm's improved profit margin outcomes using this alternate pricing strategy. The firm ends up with one fewer sale because customer #2 perceives the price to be too high. But the firm has a total profit of $10, which is close to 50 percent higher than the $6 total profit the firm earned using a simple markup strategy.

Odd/Even Pricing

odd pricing

A pricing tactic in which a firm prices products a few cents below the next dollar amount.

Have you ever seen a product sitting on a shelf at Target with a price of $19.95 and wondered why the price wasn't set at an even $20.00? Chances are it's because Target is pursuing an odd-pricing strategy, as do many other retailers. **Odd pricing** is a tactic in which a firm prices products a few cents below the next dollar amount. For the strategy to succeed, customers must perceive a product priced at $19.95 as offering more value than a product priced at $20.00. Though the price difference seems immaterial, if customers feel they received a deal, they are more likely to share that feeling with others, which can lead to additional sales.

Firms that use odd pricing still need to consider the impact of price elasticity of demand at odd-pricing points. For example, would a fast-food restaurant that offers a value meal for $4.95 see any decrease in sales if it raised the price to $4.99? Probably not, and the resulting $0.04 increase could result in significant profits over millions of customer transactions throughout the year.

even pricing

Pricing tactic that sets prices at even dollar amounts.

There are also potential benefits for firms using even pricing. **Even pricing** sets prices at even dollar amounts. Prices that end with zero are often easier for customers to process and retrieve from memory. In addition, luxury product marketers often use even pricing; odd pricing, often ending in 9, can sometimes convey a message of discount or sale that is not consistent with a luxury pricing objective. Research has even suggested that prices ending in 00 increased the likelihood of consumers rating the quality of the items advertised as "above average."[11]

Prestige Pricing

prestige pricing

A pricing tactic that involves pricing a product higher than competitors to signal that it is of higher quality.

In addition to even pricing, firms that want to promote an image of superior quality and exclusivity to customers may also pursue a strategy of prestige pricing. **Prestige pricing** is a pricing tactic that involves pricing a product *higher than competitors* to signal that it is of higher quality. Luxury brands such as Louis Vuitton, Cartier, Rolex, and Mercedes-Benz are perfect examples of this strategy. Such companies use high prices to suggest their products are high quality and stylish. Simply improving the look, packaging, delivery, or promise of a product can justify a higher price and support prestige pricing.

Starbucks pursues prestige pricing by setting its prices high to convey increased value compared to other coffee purveyors like Dunkin' Donuts. *(left): Xiang yang/AP Images; (right): Joe Raedle/Getty Images*

Loss-Leader Pricing

Loss-leader pricing involves selling a product at a price that causes the firm a financial loss. Although the firm may lose money selling the product at that price, it might attract customers who will also buy other, more profitable products in the future. For example, department stores often drop the price of well-known products to increase overall store traffic. This worked better at a time when consumers would do most of their shopping on-site; their additional purchases at the store would make up for the loss-leader item. However, consumers today have more pricing information at their fingertips and more options for purchasing online. The result can be that firms sell only the loss-leader product and never make up the profits, as customers go elsewhere to buy the more profitable products.

loss-leader pricing
A pricing tactic that involves selling a product at a price that causes the firm a financial loss.

Seasonal Discounts

Price reductions given to customers purchasing goods or services out of season are called **seasonal discounts**. Disney World pursues this strategy by offering its best rates when demand is at its lowest due to cold weather (e.g., January and February) and the fact that children are in school.[12] Seasonal discounts enable Disney World to maintain a steady stream of visitors to its parks year-round. The strategy also exposes new customers to the brand. Young families (those with children younger than school age) can try Disney World during its value season; many go on to become loyal customers, purchasing Disney vacations during the peak summer seasons once their children start school. Marketers for a variety of firms and industries, such as ski lodges in the summer and cruises during nonpeak times, utilize seasonal discounts to keep attendance high throughout the year.

seasonal discounts
Price reductions given to customers purchasing goods or services out of season.

Price Bundling

There are usually two ways to purchase products: à la carte (individually) or as a bundle. **Price bundling** is a pricing tactic in which two or more products are packaged together and sold at a single price. Marketers often use bundling as a tool because they can charge higher prices for the bundle than they could for the elements individually.

Assume you are buying a new Ford Escape SUV. Would you prefer to purchase the base model and then handpick options, such as a moon roof or satellite radio? Or are you better off buying the vehicle as one all-inclusive bundle? Conventional wisdom says that à la carte pricing benefits the customer, and bundled pricing benefits the firm. Undoubtedly, price bundling simplifies things for marketers. The company can sell the same bundle to

price bundling
A pricing tactic in which two or more products are packaged together and sold at a single price.

everyone, which results in reduced advertising and selling costs. Think of the success that bundled software packages such as Microsoft Office enjoy, despite the fact that many of the software's users need only a fraction of the available functionality.

Companies across sectors are going from a product-based to a subscription-based business model, from Microsoft, Google, and Nike to auto manufacturers, industrial manufacturers, and brick-and-mortar retailers, making the price-bundling strategy critical to many marketers' success. Amazon is known for making very deliberate choices about what to bundle in with a standard Prime membership, when, and for how long. For example, if you want to watch Eddie Murphy in 2021's *Coming 2 America* then that is free with your Prime membership, but if you want to check out the Murphy classic *Beverly Hills Cop* from 1984, that'll cost you an additional $2.99. Marketers have to determine what to offer as standalone versus adding to the basic Prime bundle. Because the value of shows and movies tends to depreciate, some titles will lose their value after a certain period. At that point, the standalone charge can no longer be justified, so Amazon moves these titles under the standard Prime membership. A strategy often used by marketers is called biphasic subscription monetization, in which businesses roll out novel services as standalone offerings and quickly monetize them by targeting enthusiastic consumers. For example, Disney+ charged $30 to watch the live action movie *Mulan* when it debuted, before adding *Mulan* to its pre-existing bundle in 2021.[13]

Mc Graw Hill connect Exercise **11-2**

Please complete the *Connect* exercise for Chapter 11 that focuses on pricing tactics. By understanding the dynamics of different tactics and being able to perform the necessary pricing calculations, you should gain insight into how marketers choose specific prices and when those tactics will be most effective.

LO 11-4

Explain the influence of technology on pricing.

TECHNOLOGY AND PRICING

Technology influences pricing strategy in a significant and growing way. Technology has helped shift the balance of power from companies to customers, who are better informed about prices than ever before. The Internet has made it possible for customers to comparison shop for products literally around the world. If you had taken this course a generation ago, your pricing options for buying this product would have been whatever the campus bookstore charged. Today, you can comparison shop at bookstores throughout the United States and online marketplaces such as Amazon or buy digital copies directly from the publisher. In addition to the power of the Internet, mobile applications and dynamic pricing are rapidly changing the nature of pricing.

Mobile Applications

Smartphone and tablet technology have unleashed a new era of pricing transparency. Consumers now use wireless apps and search engines on their mobile devices in stores to compare prices. In response, marketers at traditional brick-and-mortar stores more aggressively review the prices of online stores when setting the initial price of an item as part of their analysis of the competitive price environment.

With more people using their mobile devices to order products, apps are becoming increasingly important in directing users to online purchasing sites. Popular price-comparison apps like ShopSavvy have been downloaded more than 16 million times and provide consumers the chance to compare prices throughout much of the world.[14] ShopSavvy and other popular apps like BuyVia allow users to scan bar codes, take a photo, or search a product while in a store. The app then displays how much online competitors charge for that product and allows customers to immediately purchase the product through their mobile device. Recent research suggests that over 40 percent of consumers search for and purchase a low-priced product using an in-store shopping app or online search engine.[15]

Dynamic Pricing

Dynamic pricing is a pricing tactic that involves constantly updating prices to reflect changes in supply, demand, or market conditions. While dynamic pricing is not new, its popularity has grown explosively due to improving and readily available technological tools that facilitate its use. Digital sales environments can provide marketers with an abundance of sales data. These data may contain important insights on consumer behavior, in particular, on how consumers respond to different selling prices. Marketers can apply these insights to their own dynamic pricing policies.[16]

Dynamic pricing helps marketers emphasize **yield management**, which is a strategy for maximizing revenue even when a firm has a fixed amount of something (goods, services, or capacity). A sports teams, for example, has only a finite number of seats in its stadium. A team might want to charge the maximum possible price for a ticket, but if the price is too high, actual attendance at the game might suffer. In contrast, if prices are set too low, the team's marketers have missed an opportunity to improve their revenue.

To solve this problem, some sports leagues have implemented yield management systems, offered by firms like SAP and Oracle. Such systems enable marketers to estimate price elasticity of tickets and then use dynamic pricing to maximize revenue. As a result, teams are able to sell tickets for a specific event at the price that reflects the true value to fans. A majority of NFL teams were using dynamic ticket pricing by 2022, and increasing numbers of teams have used it since then. Dynamic pricing allows teams to reset individual-game tickets periodically as demand changes based on the quality of the opponent or the excitement surrounding a single player. More attractive games, such as when teams are playing superstars like Aaron Rodgers or Patrick Mahomes, carry higher face values and generate additional revenue for the team for those games. Dynamic pricing also allows teams to set lower season-ticket prices for less-attractive games, so the difference for the prices on secondary-market sites like StubHub does not appear as drastic for those particular games. As a result of the use of yield management systems and dynamic pricing, several NFL franchises enjoyed significant, double-digit percentage increases on single-game ticket revenue.[17]

Dynamic pricing websites like StubHub constantly update prices to reflect changes in supply and demand and provide valuable information to marketers. *Kalki/Alamy Stock Photo*

dynamic pricing

A pricing tactic that involves constantly updating prices to reflect changes in supply, demand, or market conditions.

yield management

A strategy for maximizing revenue even when a firm has a fixed amount of something (goods, services, or capacity).

name-your-own-price (NYOP) auction

A pricing tactic in which the consumer submits a bid at the price he or she is willing to pay for a product or service, and the auction site conducts a search to find matches with prices set by participating suppliers.

Name-Your-Own-Price

The power of technology is allowing companies to experiment with the name-your-own-price auction, a pricing tactic popularized by firms like Priceline.com. In a **name-your-own-price (NYOP) auction**, the consumer submits a bid at the price he or she is willing to pay for a product or service, and the auction site conducts a search to find matches with prices set by participating suppliers. Specifically, the auction site looks to see whether the bid price matches or exceeds any unrevealed threshold prices set by participating suppliers. If it does find a match, the bid is accepted. The auction site retains as its revenue any difference between the bid price and the supplier's threshold price. If no match is found, the bid is rejected. Use of NYOP auctions is common among companies that consolidate and offer hotel and airline tickets.

The NYOP model is attractive to marketers for various reasons: It has the potential to help suppliers reduce inventory (fewer unsold airline tickets and hotel rooms), while generating additional revenue (for the airline or hotel). It also potentially provides savings to consumers.[18]

Websites including Priceline .com allow consumers to participate in name-your-own-price auctions for a variety of products such as hotel rooms, potentially providing savings to consumers who participate. *pictoKraft/Alamy Stock Photo*

LO 11-5

Summarize the major
challenges of pricing for
international markets.

GLOBAL PRICING

Pricing is a critical component of a successful global marketing strategy. Historically, companies have set prices for products sold internationally higher than the same products sold domestically. However, technological advancements and Internet access throughout the world have made global pricing more transparent and, in many cases, more competitive.

In addition, challenging economic conditions over the past decade have affected pricing in a global context. China experienced an economic slowdown beginning in 2011 that affected pricing strategy, both for Chinese companies selling to other nations and for firms selling to Chinese consumers. The slowdown forced U.S. marketers to modify their prices to reach increasingly price-sensitive shoppers from China.[19] For example, McDonald's introduced a value dinner starting at 15 yuan (approximately $2.40, at the time) to combat declining sales.

In addition to technological and economic factors, firms seeking additional revenue and profits by marketing their products globally encounter unique challenges related to global pricing, including the gray market, tariffs, and dumping.

Gray Market

gray market

The sale of branded products through legal but unauthorized distribution channels.

The **gray market** involves the sale of branded products through legal but unauthorized distribution channels. This form of buying and selling often occurs when the price of an item is significantly higher in one country than another. Individuals or groups buy new or used products for a lower price in a foreign country and import them legally back into the domestic market, where they sell them for less than the normal market price.

Gray-market goods can be a boon for consumers, allowing them to obtain legally produced items for less than they could normally. However, gray-market goods cut into a firm's revenue and profits, leaving marketers looking for ways to control and repress such activity. The increasingly interconnected nature of world economies makes gray-market exchanges easier than ever. Firms find it difficult, if not impossible, to track exactly how much of their products sell in this manner.

tariffs

Taxes on imports and exports between countries.

As they set international prices, U.S. marketers must be cognizant of the potential for gray-market exchanges. If they price their products significantly lower in foreign countries than in the domestic market, they may open the door to gray-market buyers. Using modern technology, those buyers will buy the products internationally and then sell them in the United States at a price that undercuts the standard rate paid by U.S. consumers.

Tariffs levied on products can affect the overall price of a product in other countries and thus how companies set their baseline prices. An American-made surfboard that carries a 20 percent tariff in another country may need to be priced lower to be competitive in that market. *Joe Raedle/Getty Images*

Tariffs

Many nations place tariffs on a variety of products. **Tariffs** are taxes on imports and exports between countries. Fruits and vegetables are popular goods on which to place tariffs, in some countries reaching to over 25 percent.[20] The goal of tariffs is usually to protect domestic industries from lower-priced foreign competition. In 2018, for example, the United States levied tariffs of 10 percent on a variety of Chinese-made products, to make American-produced products more price-competitive.[21] Similarly,

Today's **Professional**... because everyone is a marketer

Amber Rahman

Pricing Manager
J.B. Hunt Transport Services Inc.

Describe your job. As an intermodal pricing manager, my job is to provide rates for moving freight from one location to another via truck and railroad. The process begins when customers request a rate because they are in need of transportation service and they decide they want to move their freight via Intermodal. My job consists of providing rates to customers on lane level freight. Typically, a lane is a city and state combination. An example of a lane is Chicago, Illinois, to Los Angeles, California.

How did you get your job? I joined J.B. Hunt Intermodal operations after graduating from college and worked several years honing my skills and learning as much as I could about how the JBI network operates. This created the stepping stone I needed to approach customers from a pricing perspective. Knowing operations helps pricing determine how freight will operate within the network. Having operations experience was the main factor in how I got the job I currently have.

Amber Rahman

What has been the most important thing in making you successful at your job? Two things that go hand in hand: personal drive and company drive. As a company we set operational goals in providing premier service to our customers. This motivates me to be the best at what I do so that as a company we can be the best at what we do, which is being an industry leader in intermodal transportation.

What advice would you give soon-to-be graduates? Work hard and enjoy what you do, but also be prepared for when things don't work out the way you want them to. There are days when nothing goes right in the transportation world—delays, traffic congestion, turnover, weather surges, and so on. Anything and everything can happen in one day.

What do you consider your personal brand to be? Dependability. My management recognizes this about me and knows that I will always get the job done.

tariffs put on U.S. products sold abroad raise the price that foreign customers must pay for goods produced in the United States. Such tariffs negatively impact a U.S. firm's ability to be price-competitive in those markets.

The international pricing strategy of any U.S. firm must take into account the potential tariffs foreign countries will place on its goods. Marketers typically prefer targeting international markets that have low (or no) tariffs. Countries with which the U.S. has international trading agreements also offer lower-tariff markets. For example, the North American Free Trade Agreement (NAFTA) enabled companies and consumers in those countries to trade without tariffs.

Dumping

dumping

A protectionist strategy in which a company sells its exports to another country at a lower price than it sells the same product in its domestic market.

In recent years, the removal of tariffs due to international agreements has caused some countries to switch to nontariff barriers, such as anti-dumping laws, to protect their local industries. **Dumping** occurs when a company sells its exports to another country at a lower price than it sells the same product in its domestic market.[22] For example, Indian silk producers once claimed that the price of Chinese-produced silk sold in India was so cheap that Indian firms could not compete. The Indian silk producers declared that Chinese producers must be dumping the products. Indian companies complained that the unreasonably low price of Chinese silk left them only two options: lose customers to the Chinese producers or sell their own silk at a loss.[23]

As indicated in an earlier chapter, the World Trade Organization (WTO) is the forum that regulates trade among participating companies. The WTO hasn't classified dumping as illegal. Therefore, many countries enact their own laws to curb the strategy. As they develop an international pricing strategy, companies must monitor how anti-dumping laws affect similar companies in the industry and calculate the potential impact of anti-dumping regulations on sales.

LO 11-6 LEGAL AND ETHICAL ISSUES IN PRICING

Explain the major legal and ethical issues associated with pricing.

Many legal and ethical issues affect pricing decisions. Pricing is one of the most watched and regulated marketing activities because it directly affects the financial viability of both organizations and individuals. In this section, we'll discuss some of the ethical issues marketers may face as they seek to set prices for their products. These issues include price discrimination, price fixing, predatory pricing, and deceptive pricing. We'll then look into some of the regulations the U.S. government has put into place to combat such practices.

Price Discrimination

You may be surprised to hear that you have likely benefited from discriminatory pricing in various ways. If you've paid student prices at a movie theater, or have been given an introductory price to switch cell phone or cable providers, you've taken advantage of price discrimination.

Price discrimination is the practice of charging different customers different prices for the same product. Price discrimination sounds negative, but it is illegal *only if it injures competition*. It is perfectly legal for organizations to charge customers different amounts for legitimate

A variety of companies, including many restaurants, engage in legitimate price discrimination by offering meals to students for a lower price than other customers. *Ian Francis/Alamy Stock Photo*

reasons. This is especially common in B2B settings, in which different customers might be charged different rates due to the quantities they buy, the strategic value of the company, or simply because one firm did a better job negotiating the contract. Later in this section, we'll discuss the Robinson–Patman Act, which has helped clarify when price discrimination can and cannot be used.

price discrimination

The practice of charging different customers different prices for the same product.

---

connect Exercise 11-3

Social Media in Action

Social media are influencing the prices consumers see when buying products online. Rosetta Stone, which sells language-learning products, varies the prices for some of its products and the product bundles offered depending on whether a consumer comes to its site through a social media link.

Some organizations also offer different online prices based on what type of mobile device consumers use to access the site or where consumers are located. Office supply company Staples discounted the price of its online products for consumers who lived within a 20-mile range of major competitors. Some firms, such as travel website Orbitz, modified the prices consumers saw depending on whether the customer was using a specific type of mobile device. Consumers using an iPhone or Android phone saw discounts of up to 50 percent compared with what a person searching the site on a traditional computer saw.

Such pricing differences are legal, as long as they do not stifle competition. However, marketers should be careful about pricing differences: Studies suggest that over 75 percent of consumers say they would be bothered if they knew that someone paid a lower price for the same product.

The Social Media in Action Connect exercise in Chapter 11 will let you make decisions about setting consumer prices based on the social media profiles of consumers. By understanding the insights that social media can provide, you will be able to develop pricing strategies that maximize profits from each individual consumer.

Source: See Jennifer Valentino-Devries, Jeremy Singer-Vine, and Ashkan Soltani, "Websites Vary Prices, Deals Based on Users' Information," *The Wall Street Journal*, December 24, 2012, http://online.wsj.com/article/SB100014241278873237772045781 89391813881534.html.

Price Fixing

When two or more companies collude to set a product's price, they are engaging in **price fixing**. Price fixing is illegal under the Sherman Antitrust Act of 1890 and the Federal Trade Commission Act (both of which we discuss later in the chapter).

An example of price fixing occurred when British Airways and its rival Virgin Atlantic agreed to simultaneously increase their fuel surcharges.[24] Over the next two years, fuel surcharges increased from an average of 5 British pounds a ticket to over 60 pounds. When the price-fixing scheme was reported by Virgin, British Airways was

price fixing

When two or more companies collude to set a product's price.

punished with record fines: The British Office of Fair Trading fined the airline £121.5 million, and the U.S. Department of Justice levied an additional $300 million fine. Virgin was given immunity for reporting the collusion and was not fined.

Predatory Pricing

predatory pricing

The practice of first setting prices low with the intention of pushing competitors out of the market or keeping new competitors from entering the market, and then raising prices to normal levels.

Consider a situation in which a chain supermarket opens across the street from a locally owned grocery store. Theoretically, the prices at both stores should be similar because the costs and customer demand will be similar. However, because the chain supermarket can rely on corporate backing for support, it decides to radically lower prices, attracting more customers to its facility and eventually driving the competition out of business. It then can raise its prices to normal levels. This example illustrates a strategy called predatory pricing. **Predatory pricing** is the practice of first setting prices low with the intention of pushing competitors out of the market or keeping new competitors from entering the market, and then raising prices to normal levels.

This type of long-term aggressive pricing strategy could be considered an attempt to create a monopoly. It is therefore illegal under U.S. law. However, predatory pricing is difficult to prove. The Supreme Court has ruled that the victim must prove that the company being accused of predatory pricing (the chain supermarket, in our example) would be able to recoup its initial losses by charging higher prices later on, once it has driven others out of business.[25]

Deceptive Pricing

deceptive pricing

An illegal practice that involves intentionally misleading customers with price promotions.

Deceptive pricing is an illegal practice that involves intentionally misleading customers with price promotions. Deceptive pricing practices can lead to price confusion, with consumers finding it difficult to discern what they are actually paying. The most common examples of deceptive pricing involve firms that falsely advertise wholesale pricing or promise a significant price reduction on an artificially high retail price. Deceptive-pricing practices have come under fire in recent years in industries ranging from credit cards to home loans. In these cases, important information was often buried deep within little-noticed and hard-to-read disclaimers and information.

In 2011, China accused Walmart and its French competitor Carrefour of deceptive pricing.[26] Chinese officials cited instances in which Carrefour and Walmart overcharged their consumers or quoted a higher original price to make the discounts they offered on products seem more substantial. For example, a Walmart store in the city of Nanning priced Nescafé coffee at $5.44, discounted from an advertised price of $6.67; in fact, the original price was $5.66. Similarly, a Carrefour store in Changchun, the capital of Jilin province, allegedly discounted men's cotton undershirts to around $7.00 from an advertised original price of just over $25.00. The original price was verified by regulators to be $18.07.

In the United States, deceptive pricing is regulated by the Federal Trade Commission (FTC). Cases may be prosecuted by a state attorney general or by a district attorney at the state or local level.

U.S. Laws Affecting Pricing

The U.S. government and other major economies, such as Japan and the European Union, are committed to stopping and punishing anticompetitive and harmful pricing behavior through a variety of laws and regulations, as discussed below.

Robinson–Patman Act

A law passed in 1936 that requires sellers to charge everyone the same price for a product; also called the *Anti-Price Discrimination Act.*

Robinson–Patman Act
To combat price discrimination that injures competition, in 1936 the U.S. government passed the Robinson–Patman Act as an amendment to the Clayton Antitrust Act of 1914. The **Robinson–Patman Act** (also called the *Anti-Price Discrimination Act*) requires sellers to charge everyone the same

price.[27] It grew out of concerns that large companies would leverage their buying power to purchase goods at lower prices than smaller companies could. Though the purpose of the act was to reduce injurious price discrimination, it did provide for three scenarios in which price discrimination may be allowed:

- A firm can charge different prices if it is part of a quantity or manufacturing discount program. For example, a company selling 5,000 laptops to a multibillion-dollar company can charge less per unit than if it sells the same laptop to an individual consumer buying just one.
- A firm can lower prices for certain customers if a competitor undercuts the originally quoted price. This rule affects Walmart and several large retailers that promise to match any competitor's price if the consumer produces proof of the lower price. These retailers are not legally required to extend this same discount to customers who do not present proof of the lower price, effectively resulting in different prices for different customers.
- Finally, market conditions such as going-out-of-business sales or situations in which the quality of products has changed give firms the opportunity to charge different prices for the same product. For example, a bakery may sell loaves of French bread for $3 each on the day it bakes them. However, it would be allowed to sell the same loaves the next day at a steep discount because the quality and freshness of the bread has deteriorated.

Lowe's price match guarantee provides an example of price discrimination allowed by the Robinson–Patman Act. It allows Lowe's to offer a different price to those customers who can prove that a local or online retailer is offering the same product for a lower price. *Kevork Djansezian/Getty Images*

Federal Trade Commission Act

The **Federal Trade Commission Act (FTCA)** was passed in 1914. It established the Federal Trade Commission (FTC), which had the authority to enforce laws aimed at prohibiting unfair methods of competition.[28] The FTCA was later broadened to prevent practices such as price fixing and deceptive pricing that:

- May cause injury to customers.
- Cannot be reasonably avoided by customers.
- Cannot be justified by other outcomes that may benefit the consumer or the idea of free competition.

Wheeler–Lea Act

The **Wheeler–Lea Act** of 1938 (also called the *Advertising Act*) is an amendment to the FTCA.[29] Its passage removed the burden of proving that unfair and deceptive practices had to injure competition as well as customers. It also broadened the FTC's powers to include protecting consumers from false advertising practices.

Sherman Antitrust Act

As described in an earlier chapter (but worth repeating here), the **Sherman Antitrust Act** was passed in 1890 to eliminate monopolies and guarantee competition. It combats anticompetitive practices, reduces market domination by individual corporations, and preserves unfettered competition as the rule of trade. As described above, the Sherman Antitrust Act makes price fixing illegal.

These four U.S. laws provide much of the regulatory framework for the most common legal challenges associated with price discrimination, price fixing, predatory pricing, and deceptive pricing.

Federal Trade Commission Act (FTCA)
A law passed in 1914 that established the Federal Trade Commission and sought to prevent practices that may cause injury to customers, that cannot be reasonably avoided by customers, and that cannot be justified by other outcomes that may benefit the consumer or the idea of free competition.

Wheeler–Lea Act
An amendment to the Federal Trade Commission Act passed in 1938 that removed the burden of proving that unfair and deceptive practices had to injure competition; also called the *Advertising Act*.

Sherman Antitrust Act
A law passed in 1890 to eliminate monopolies and guarantee competition.

McGraw Hill connect Exercise **11-4**

Please complete the *Connect* exercise for Chapter 11 that focuses on important laws that affect pricing. By recognizing the specific requirements of each law, you will understand the legal requirements of pricing decisions and be able to help your firm avoid violating pricing rules and regulations.

SUMMARY

Marvin Tolentino/ Alamy Stock Photo

LO 11-1 Explain the importance of pricing strategy to every organization.

Price is the amount of something—money, time, or effort—that a buyer exchanges with a seller to obtain a product. It is the essential element for capturing revenue and profits. Revenue is the result of the price charged to customers multiplied by the number of units sold. Profits equal revenue minus total costs. The objective of strategic pricing is to maximize profits. If the price is set too high, customers will simply buy another product. If the price is set too low, the firm loses revenue it can never recover.

1Roman Makedonsky/ Shutterstock

LO 11-2 Outline the objectives, steps, and decisions involved in setting a price.

Common pricing objectives include profit maximization, volume maximization, and survival.

Marketers use a systematic six-step process to evaluate relevant factors when setting a price and should thoughtfully consider the decisions at each step in the price-setting process to increase the likelihood that the final price captures value for the firm and delivers value to the customer. The six steps include the following: (1) Select the pricing objective, (2) evaluate demand, (3) determine the costs, (4) analyze the competitive price environment, (5) choose a price, and (6) monitor and evaluate the effectiveness of the price.

Marketers need to project not only the overall market demand but also the specific product demand at various price points. This requires an understanding of consumers' *price sensitivity.* One of the most important concepts in marketing, which should be considered when pricing any product, is *price elasticity of demand;* it is a measure of price sensitivity that gives the percentage change in quantity demanded in response to a percentage change in price. Demand may be *elastic* or *inelastic.*

Setting a price begins by knowing the *fixed* and *variable costs* that go into producing a good or service. A company then can use these estimated costs in a break-even analysis,

to find the *break-even point,* the point at which the costs of producing a product equal the revenue made from selling the product.

Xiang yang/AP Images

LO 11-3 Compare the pricing tactics marketers can use.

Markup pricing is a pricing method in which a certain amount, usually a percentage, is added to the cost of the product to set the final price. It is one of the most common pricing tactics used, largely because it is easy, but it's not very effective at maximizing profits.

Odd pricing is a tactic in which a firm prices products a few cents below the next dollar amount. This strategy is effective with customers who perceive they are getting a good value for their money when a product is priced slightly below a whole number value. *Even pricing* sets prices at even dollar amounts. Prices that end with zero are often easier for customers to process and retrieve from memory. *Prestige pricing* involves pricing a product high to signal that it is of high quality.

Seasonal discounts involve price reductions given to customers purchasing goods or services out of season. *Price bundling* involves packaging two or more products together to be sold at a single price, allowing marketers to earn greater profits than if they priced the elements individually.

Kalki/Alamy Stock Photo

LO 11-4 Explain the influence of technology on pricing.

Technology has helped shift the balance of power from companies to customers, who are better informed about prices than ever before. The Internet has made it possible for buyers to comparison shop for products literally around the world. Smartphone technology allows consumers to use wireless apps and search engines in stores to compare prices. In response, marketers at traditional brick-and-mortar stores review prices at online stores when setting the initial price of an item. Technology has also increased the role of *dynamic pricing,* a strategy that involves constantly updating prices to reflect changes in supply, demand, or market conditions. In a *name-your-own-price (NYOP) auction,* the consumer submits a bid at the price he or she is willing to pay for a product or service, and the auction site conducts a search to find matches with prices set by participating suppliers.

Joe Raedle/Getty Images

LO 11-5 Summarize the major challenges of pricing for international markets.

Firms that price their products to be sold internationally face several unique challenges. The *gray market,* which involves the sale of branded products through legal but unauthorized distribution channels, continues to expand. *Tariffs,* taxes on imports and exports between countries, raise the prices that customers must pay for goods, thus negatively impacting a company's ability to be price-competitive in countries that impose tariffs. *Dumping* occurs when a company sells its exports to another country at a lower price than it sells the same product in its domestic market. Dumping and the laws imposed to prevent it

are increasingly important to multinational corporations as they determine their global pricing policy.

Ian Francis/ Alamy Stock Photo

LO 11-6 Explain the major legal and ethical issues associated with pricing.

Many laws, regulations, and ethical issues affect pricing decisions. *Price discrimination* is the practice of charging different customers different prices for the same product. It is illegal only if it injures competition. *Price fixing* occurs when two or more companies collude to set a product's price. Price fixing is illegal under the Sherman Antitrust Act and the Federal Trade Commission Act. *Predatory pricing* is the practice of first setting prices low with the intention of pushing competitors out of the market or keeping new competitors from entering the market, and then raising prices to normal levels. *Deceptive pricing* involves intentionally misleading customers with price promotions and is illegal under the Wheeler–Lea Act and the Federal Trade Commission Act.

KEY TERMS

break-even analysis (p. 367)
break-even point (p. 367)
deceptive pricing (p. 382)
dumping (p. 380)
dynamic pricing (p. 377)
elastic demand (p. 366)
escalator clause (p. 371)
even pricing (p. 374)
Federal Trade Commission
    Act (FTCA) (p. 383)
fixed costs (p. 367)
gray market (p. 378)
inelastic demand (p. 366)
loss-leader pricing (p. 375)
marginal cost (p. 364)
marginal revenue (p. 364)

markup pricing (p. 373)
name-your-own-price (NYOP) auction
    (p. 377)
odd pricing (p. 374)
predatory pricing (p. 382)
prestige pricing (p. 374)
price (p. 362)
price bundling (p. 375)
price discrimination (p. 381)
price elasticity of demand (p. 365)
price fixing (p. 381)
price sensitivity (p. 364)
profit margin (p. 373)
profit maximization (p. 363)
profits (p. 362)
reference prices (p. 369)

revenue (p. 362)
Robinson–Patman Act (p. 382)
seasonal discounts (p. 375)
Sherman Antitrust Act (p. 383)
shrinkflation (p. 372)
survival pricing (p. 364)
tariffs (p. 378)
unbundling (p. 371)
underpricing (p. 370)
variable costs (p. 367)
volume maximization (penetration
    pricing) (p. 363)
Wheeler–Lea Act (p. 383)
yield management (p. 377)

MARKETING PLAN EXERCISE • Marketing Yourself

In this chapter you learned about setting prices based on costs and market conditions. For the next part of your marketing plan exercise, you will conduct a pricing analysis of your own future career plans.

First, you should consider the costs you expect to have in the next decade, including things like repaying your student loans, paying your rent, saving for a house, or starting a family. Take time to consider the potential costs of these things on a monthly and annual basis. Then compare these

costs with the career information you put together in an earlier chapter. How do they match up?

Next, consider your market value within your company or industry, either now or after graduate school. The price elasticity you inspire in future employers will be an important consideration as you develop in your career. For example, if you possess a unique combination of experience, education, personality, and work ethic, demand for your services might well be inelastic. In this scenario, you might be able to negotiate a higher salary because the demand for your services is high.

Conversely, if demand for your brand is elastic, you should understand your lessened bargaining power and work to develop unique skills or take on difficult assignments within your company to increase the value others place on your brand.

Knowing whether demand for your personal brand is inelastic or elastic is essential. Too many employees undervalue their brand and work for less than what market prices would dictate, leaving money on the table over a significant period of their career.

Your Task: Develop a detailed list of the costs necessary to have the career you desire 10 years from now (e.g., student loans, training seminars, graduate school costs, or any fixed or variable costs). Next, compare these costs with the prices that organizations are paying for people with your skill set. Finally, determine your own personal break-even point for your salary level. Also, identify when you expect to reach the salary that you desire.

DISCUSSION QUESTIONS

1. Why is it difficult to determine reference prices? Consider a new pizza restaurant opening near your campus. What challenges would the restaurant's marketers encounter as they attempt to determine their customers' reference prices? How could they find this information?

2. What is the problem with standard markup pricing? How do buyers and sellers lose from this type of pricing strategy?

3. Name a product that you think is underpriced. What price do you think should be charged, and what would be the benefits of that higher price for the company that produces the product?

4. Name one product for which your demand is elastic and one product for which your demand is inelastic. For example, if Subway raised its prices by 10 percent, would you reduce the number of times you eat there by 10 percent, by more than 10 percent, or would the price increase not change your purchases at Subway at all? Do you think most other consumers of these two products feel the same way? How should this information affect the pricing of those products?

5. Go to the StubHub website (www.stubhub.com) and find an event for which you might be interested in buying tickets. Are prices higher or lower than you could buy directly from the venue? Why do you think that is? Why is StubHub not violating price discrimination laws?

6. Think of your favorite brand of potato chip and then discuss what considerations would affect how you would price that product in a neighboring country such as Mexico or Canada.

 ## SOCIAL MEDIA APPLICATION

Pick two companies whose products you currently buy, and look at all of the social media platforms the company employs (for example, Instagram, TikTok, YouTube, etc.). Analyze what is being said about pricing either by the company or customers on these platforms, using the following questions and activities as a guide:

1. How much is pricing discussed? Provide specific examples.

2. Is pricing mentioned by the company, social media users, or both?

3. Is pricing discussed on social media by one company more than the other? If so, why do you think this is?

4. If you worked in marketing for either firm, is there anything you have read on social media that would make you consider changing the price of that company's products? Explain your answer.

 ## MARKETING ANALYTICS EXERCISE

Please complete the *Connect* exercise for Chapter 11 that focuses on using analytics in break-even analysis.

ETHICAL CHALLENGE

National Basketball Association (NBA) teams play an exhausting 82-game regular season before they reach the playoffs, if they're lucky enough to do so. The playoffs are a reward not just for the organization but also for its fans.

Playoff tickets are generally in far more demand than regular season tickets, and marketers for a number of teams attempt to use pricing strategies to improve their yield management. For example, many teams require that fans make a deposit to secure season tickets for the following year before they can buy playoff tickets at face value. Or teams might offer single-game playoff tickets to those who don't hold season tickets, but at a price that runs from between 200 and 400 percent more than what season ticket holders would pay.

While such tactics can generate additional revenue and increase a team's season ticket holder base, the team also risks alienating nonseason ticket holders who may be able to attend only a few games a year but who follow the team faithfully on television and the Internet.

Please use the ethical decision-making framework to answer the following questions:

1. Is an NBA team's charging nonseason ticket holders more than season ticket holders an example of price discrimination? Explain your answer.
2. Do you agree with the idea of NBA teams requiring fans to place deposits for season tickets for the following year? What about the NBA charging higher single-game prices to nonseason ticket holders? Explain your answers.
3. Since season ticket holders probably represent a team's most devoted fans, would it make sense to charge them the higher playoff ticket prices on the assumption that, because their demand is inelastic, they will pay almost any price?

VIDEO CASE

Please go to *Connect* to access the video case featuring Amy's Candy Bar that accompanies this chapter.

PODCAST

Please go to Connect to access the podcast that accompanies this chapter.

CAREER **TIPS**

Consider a Job in Pricing

You have read in this chapter about the importance of developing an effective pricing strategy. Coauthor Shane Hunt began his career as a pricing analyst for The Williams Companies, a Fortune 500 company specializing in energy and telecommunications based in Tulsa, Oklahoma; he considers that job one of the best things that ever happened to him. Based on his experience, he has provided three things to remember if you are considering a job in pricing.

1. Supply and demand works in your favor. Some jobs in marketing are highly sought after because

they are glamorous or sound cool to new graduates. Everyone wants to be the salesperson who accompanies clients to the Super Bowl or the event planner who throws elaborate parties for important people. Product manager and brand manager jobs have impressive sounding titles. In my years as a professor, I have taught thousands of students with all kinds of career goals, and not one has come to me on the first day of class and said, "Dr. Hunt, I want to be a pricing analyst." This is a good thing. Here's why: This chapter talks about the fact that pricing is an essential element for virtually every organization on the planet, yet most new graduates don't consider working in pricing. When demand for a job is high, and the supply is low, the wages for that job increase. I encourage you to consider pricing as a career in this challenging economic environment.

2. **Pricing is a great way to combine marketing with other disciplines.** Perhaps you are pursuing a major other than marketing but think marketing might make for a great career. I want to especially encourage you to consider pricing, which requires a combination of skills in addition to marketing, such as a knowledge of finance and psychology. Pricing jobs also can lead to career paths in marketing or finance, which will give you increased flexibility as your career develops.

3. **Develop your skills using Excel.** One important piece of career advice I would give you, regardless of your major, is to become proficient at using Excel. While PowerPoint, Word, and other products may be most common in your college courses, Excel is by far the most frequently used tool in day-to-day pricing jobs (and many other jobs as well). I would encourage you to take courses that utilize Excel and develop skills that will help your career in pricing and many other areas.

CHAPTER NOTES

1. Meg James, "Streaming Gains Make Up for DirecTV's 188,000 Lost Satellite Customers," *LA Times,* April 26, 2018, https://www.latimes.com/business/hollywood/la-fi-ct-directv-now-subscribers-20180425-story.html.

2. Nick Bunkley, "Sales Decline 20%, but GM Sees a Bright Spot," *The New York Times,* September 3, 2008, http://www.nytimes.com/2008/09/04/business/04auto.html.

3. Nick Timiraos and Kelly Evans, "Home Prices Rise Across the U.S.," *The Wall Street Journal,* July 29, 2009, http://online.wsj.com/article/SB124878477560186517.html.

4. Campbell R. McConnell, Stanley L. Brue, and Sean M. Flynn, *Economics* (New York: McGraw Hill, 2012), p. 76.

5. Cliff Edwards, "Netflix Seen Cracking Down on Sharing to Bolster Profit," *Bloomberg,* April 22, 2013, http://www.bloomberg.com/news/2013-04-22/netflix-seen-cracking-down-on-sharing-to-bolster-profit.html.

6. Brett R. Gordon, Avi Goldfarb, and Yang Li, "Does Price Elasticity Vary with Economic Growth? A Cross-Category Analysis," *Journal of Marketing Research* 50, no. 1 (February 2013): 4–23.

7. Tammo H. A. Bijmolt, Harald J. Van Heerde, and Rik G. M. Pieters, "New Empirical Generalizations on the Determinants of Price Elasticity," *Journal of Marketing Research* 42 (May 2005): 141–156.

8. Dana Mattioli, "Retailers Try to Thwart Price Apps," *The Wall Street Journal,* December 23, 2011, http://online.wsj.com/article/SB10001424052970203686204577114901480554444.html.

9. Lisa Baertlein, "Wendy's/Arby's Mulls Price Increases," *Reuters,* May 10, 2011, http://www.reuters.com/article/2011/05/10/us-wendysarbys-idUSTRE74935120110510.

10. Robert Williams, Justin Bachman, Gabrielle Coppola, Keith Naughton, and Craig Trudell, "How Companies Get You to Pay More for the Same Product," *Bloomberg Businessweek,* November 16, 2018, https://www.bloomberg.com/news/articles/2018-11-16/how-companies-get-you-to-pay-more-for-the-same-product.

11. Robert M. Schindler, "Symbolic Meanings of a Price Ending," in *Advances in Consumer Research* 18, ed. Rebecca H. Holman and Michael R. Solomon (Provo, UT: Association for Consumer Research, 1991), pp. 794–801.

12. Isaiah David, "Tips to Save Money on a Disney Vacation," *USA Today,* http://traveltips.usatoday.com/tips-save-money-disney-vacation-14495.html.

13. Stamos Kanellakis, "What Belongs in Your Basic Bundle?" *Harvard Business Review,* July 20, 2021 https://hbr.org/2021/07/what-belongs-in-your-basic-bundle.

14. Dan Butcher, "ShopSavvy Mobile Shopping Assistant App Exceeds 16M Installs," *Retail Dive,* n.d., https://www.retaildive.com/ex/mobilecommercedaily/shopsavvy-mobile-shopping-assistant-app-exceeds-16m-installs.

15. James K. Willcox, "Free Shopping Apps for Black Friday Deals," *Consumer Reports,* November 22, 2017, http://www.consumerreports.org/cro/news/2015/11/7-free-shopping-apps-that-grab-holiday-discounts-and-deals/index.htm.

16. Arnoud V. Den Boer, "Dynamic Pricing and Learning: Historical Origins, Current Research, and New Directions," *Surveys in Operations Research and Management Science* 20, no. 1 (2015): 1–18.

17. Daniel Kaplan, "Dynamic Ticket Pricing Makes Successful Debut in NFL," *Sports Business Journal,* October 26, 2015, http://www.sportsbusinessdaily.com/Journal/Issues/2015/10/26/Leagues-and-Governing-Bodies/NFL-dynamic.aspx.

18. K. L. Gwebu, J. Wang, H. Wei, and M. Hu, "Effects of Price Recommendations in Name-Your-Own-Price Auctions," *Journal of Electronic Commerce Research* 12, no. 1 (2011): 61–77.

19. Justina Lee, "China Slowdown Forcing Discounting at McDonald's," *Bloomberg,* August 1, 2012, http://www.bloomberg.com/news/2012-08-01/china-slowdown-forcing-discounting-at-gome-to-mcdonald-s.html.

20. Renee Johnson, "The U.S. Trade Situation for Fruits and Vegetable Products," *Congressional Research Service,* December 17, 2012, http://www.nationalaglawcenter .org/assets/crs/RL34468.pdf.

21. Angus Whitley, Blruce Einhort, and Daniela Wei, "The Winners and Losers from Trump's Tariffs," *Bloomberg,* September 18, 2018, https://www.bloomberg.com/ news/articles/2018-09-18/winners-and-losers-from-trump-tariffs-apple-bikes-americans.

22. World Trade Organization, "Anti-Dumping," n.d., http://www.wto.org/english/tratop_e/adp_e/adp_e.htm.

23. Charlotte Windle, "China Faces Indian Dumping Allegations," *BBC News,* July 31, 2006, http://news.bbc .co.uk/2/hi/business/5224370.stm.

24. "BA's Price-Fix Fine Reaches £270m," *BBC News,* August 1, 2007, http://news.bbc.co.uk/2/hi/business/ 6925397.stm.

25. Thomas T. Nagle, John E. Hogan, and Joseph Zale, *The Strategy and Tactics of Pricing,* 5th ed. (Upper Saddle River, NJ: Pearson, 2011).

26. Parija Kavilanz, "China Accuses Wal-Mart of Deceptive Prices," *CNNMoney,* January 26, 2011, http://money.cnn. com/2011/01/26/news/international/walmart_china_ fines/index.htm.

27. Robert J. Toth, "A Powerful Law Has Been Losing a Lot of Its Punch," *The Wall Street Journal,* May 21, 2012, http:// online.wsj.com/article/SB10001424052702304746604 577380172754953842.html.

28. Federal Trade Commission, "FTC Fact Sheet: Antitrust Laws: A Brief History," n.d., http://www.ftc.gov/bcp/edu/ microsites/youarehere/pages/pdf/FTC-Competition_ Antitrust-Laws.pdf.

29. Federal Trade Commission, "Appendix 1—Laws Enforced by the FTC," n.d., http://www.ftc.gov/opp/gpra/ append1.shtm.

Chapter **12**

Retailing

TY Lim/Shutterstock

Learning Objectives

After reading this chapter, you should be able to

LO 12-1 Discuss the importance of retailing, differences in retail organizations, and career opportunities in retail.

LO 12-2 Describe the major types of physical-store retailers.

LO 12-3 Describe the major types of nonstore retailing, including online retailing.

LO 12-4 Discuss key strategic issues in retailing.

LO 12-5 Discuss emerging practices, trends, and technologies that are reshaping the face of retailing.

Executive **Perspective** ... because everyone is a marketer

What has been the most important thing in making you successful at your job?

In order to make sure we have a clear path to success for any objective or even a simple marketing campaign, everyone must be clear on what the success metrics should be. I always seek to collaborate as much as possible cross-functionally so everyone has a unified vision of what we are trying to achieve and why.

What advice would you give soon-to-be graduates?

If you are unsure of what your career path looks like, explore several roles and projects within your chosen field. It helps tremendously to rotate through several functional areas to better prepare you for strategic and leadership positions. Always ask a lot of intentional questions, if you want something don't be afraid to ask for it—have a clear vision, figure out what it will take to get there, then do it. It took me nearly 10 years to find out the area of marketing I was passionate about pursuing.

How is marketing relevant to your role at AutoZone?

Despite going to college for Advertising, I was never the "creative" one—but I was always the resourceful one. Ever since the beginning of my career, I was always pretty strong at making data-driven marketing decisions. In corporate, we are held to numbers and it is important that you are not only able to read and manage KPIs, but make decisions that will ultimately drive those numbers. My current role allows me to explore customer segmentation and run

Julie Acosta
Web Analytics Manager
AutoZone

Julie Acosta/Antwoine J. McClellan/AJM Images

in-depth behavioral and transactional analysis that is used in planning marketing campaigns, product offerings, messaging approaches, and benchmarking against competitors. Everyday there is something new that we learn about our customers allowing us to be much more effective marketers and merchandisers. A greater understanding of this information allows us to calculate the customer's lifetime value (CLTV) and determine how much benefit we can gain from each customer we are able to engage and convert into a loyalty member.

What do you consider your personal brand to be?

I help organizations evolve their mindset by creating a transformative and adaptable omnichannel vision that marries traditional business logic with digitally native ideas typically instigated by industry disrupters. I'm a teacher at heart and am passionate about mentoring and onboarding new team members, helping them uncover their strengths and better understand the vital roles they play in their organizations.

LO 12-1

Discuss the importance of retailing, differences in retail organizations, and career opportunities in retail.

retailing

All of the business activities involved in the sales of goods and services to an end consumer for their personal, family, or household use.

retailer

A company that sells goods to consumers for their use, rather than for resale to others.

WHAT IS RETAILING?

Do you know that special feeling you get when you have given someone the perfect gift? Retailers get to be part of the path customers take to get there each and every day.

The practice of **retailing** encompasses all business activities involved in the sales of goods and services to the ultimate consumer for their personal, family, or household use.[1] A **retailer** is any organization that sells directly to end-user consumers. The scope of retail includes the sale of items ranging from luxury automobiles to apparel to the movie tickets and popcorn you bought at the theater last weekend. Some retailers, such as Home Depot and Staples, are also wholesalers: They provide goods and services to other businesses as well as to consumers. While retailing often takes place in physical stores or service locations, the concept also includes nonstore-based retailers, such as online shopping sites, as well as services retailers.

Importance of Retailing to the Global Economy

Given the close link between consumer spending and economic growth, retailing is an important economic activity that affects nearly everyone, either directly or indirectly. From the part-time sales associate at a local store on Main Street to an app-developer for a major retailer, the retail industry directly employs 32 million Americans, making it the largest private sector employer in the economy.[2] Total retail sales in the United States amounted to 5.57 trillion U.S. dollars in 2020.[3] (See Figure 12.1.)

Where do U.S. consumers spend their money? Figure 12.2 breaks down annual sales by retail category.

People tend to think of retailing in terms of very large organizations. But retail is a tremendous outlet for entrepreneurially minded small business owners and investors. Nearly 9 out of 10 retail companies employ fewer than 20 employees; over 95 percent of retailers operate just one store.

With that said, a few giant companies, such as Walmart and Amazon, do play an outsized role in the retail sector. Consider the following facts about Walmart:

- Walmart employs over 2.3 million associates, making it the third-biggest employer in the world, behind the U.S. Department of Defense and the Chinese army.

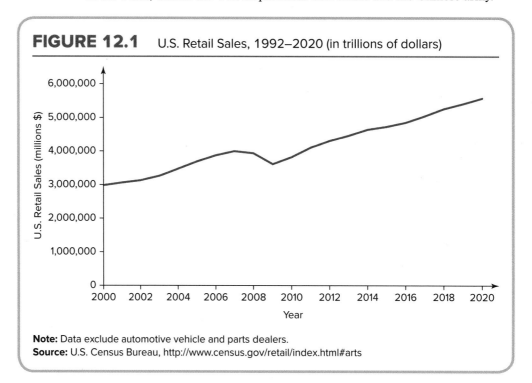

FIGURE 12.1 U.S. Retail Sales, 1992–2020 (in trillions of dollars)

Note: Data exclude automotive vehicle and parts dealers.
Source: U.S. Census Bureau, http://www.census.gov/retail/index.html#arts

- Walmart's fiscal year 2021 global sales of $560 billion exceeded the combined sales of the next four-largest retailers.
- In addition, a staggering 37 million people shop at Walmart every day, more than the entire population of Canada.[4]
- If Walmart were a country, it would be the 25th-largest economy in the world, slightly behind Belgium and ahead of Iran.[5]

Impact of the Pandemic on the Retail Industry

Despite the continuing success of Walmart and Amazon, many large retailers were already struggling when COVID-19 hit. Debt from store overexpansion and the residual effects of the Great Recession on consumer spending habits had led several iconic retailers to fall into bankruptcy. Industry experts even coined this phenomenon as a *retail apocalypse*. In 2020 alone, major retailers closed a record 12,000 stores amid pandemic-induced stay-at-home orders, social distancing measures, and increased online shopping.

Just one year later, however, physical store retailers seemed poised for a comeback, registering more openings than closings in 2021. Are brighter days ahead for the sector? Retail analyst Jay Sole suggests that the pandemic forced out weak retailers and bolstered heavyweights, largely based on how well companies adjusted to the new digital world *before* the virus struck the country.[6] Consumer spending on groceries actually grew during the pandemic, even as restaurant spending declined. Major retailers like Walmart and Home Depot weathered the pandemic and were back to beating profit expectations by the fourth quarter of 2021.

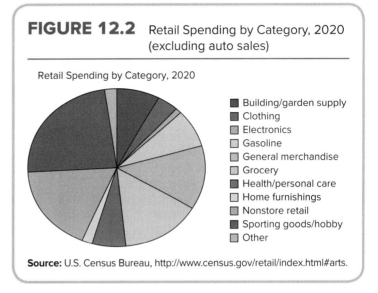

FIGURE 12.2 Retail Spending by Category, 2020 (excluding auto sales)

Retail Spending by Category, 2020

- Building/garden supply
- Clothing
- Electronics
- Gasoline
- General merchandise
- Grocery
- Health/personal care
- Home furnishings
- Nonstore retail
- Sporting goods/hobby
- Other

Source: U.S. Census Bureau, http://www.census.gov/retail/index.html#arts.

Walmart is the world's largest retailer and resells products to millions of consumers across the world each day. As retailing evolves, Walmart will have to continue to adapt to meet the needs of its customers. *Susana Gonzalez/Bloomberg/Getty Images*

Self-service ordering kiosks like this one at Panera are becoming increasingly popular. They offer convenience for customers and improved efficiency for retailers. *Raymond Deleon/Alamy Stock Photo*

How Do Retailers Differ?

Retailing includes many different types of organizations and store formats. Marketers commonly classify retailers along four key dimensions: level of service, ownership and organization, breadth and depth of merchandise assortment, and merchandise pricing. We will briefly discuss each of these areas.

Level of Service

Level of service refers to the amount of individual attention the retailer provides the consumer. Service levels can vary considerably depending on customer segments or the complexity of the products sold. In order to meet varying service-level needs, retailers may provide some combination of self-service, full service, or limited service. *Self-service* requires customers to perform certain tasks on their own in order to save time or money. Common self-service activities are locating items and checking out without the help of a store employee. Typically, self-service makes the most sense for retailers that sell a high percentage of low-margin products. By enabling customers to perform actions on their own, retailers are able to become more efficient while better meeting customer price and convenience preferences.

In contrast, *full-service retailers* assist customers through every step of the shopping process. High-end specialty (e.g., Tiffany's) and department stores (e.g., Nordstrom) are examples of full-service retailers. In most instances, products sold by full-service retailers are of high quality or possess more complex features than those in the standard offering in its class. Consumers who seek out full-service retailers often have greater disposable income. They favor premium brands and expect customized service from highly skilled and knowledgeable employees. These customers also expect to find engaging, and even elegant, store environments. As a result, prices and margins for products sold in full-service retail settings tend to be much higher.

Limited service falls between the two extremes. This category would include most retailers. For instance, department stores like JCPenney or big-box stores like Best Buy would be considered limited-service providers. In limited-service outlets, one would expect to find a higher percentage of shopping goods in the store's merchandise assortment. Customers may still need additional information and reassurance in order to feel comfortable purchasing items like larger appliances and flat-screen TVs. However, it is rare to find the same level of highly skilled, personalized attention in limited-service settings as one might find in a full-service retailer.

Ownership and Organization

The majority of retail operations are *independent retailers,* owned and operated by a single person or group. Other retailers are bound together under some form of corporate or contractual organization. Most of these retail organizations are either corporate chains, retailer cooperatives, or franchise organizations. **Corporate chains** are two or more retail outlets that are commonly owned and controlled. By virtue of their size, chains are often able to buy merchandise and supplies in greater quantities at much lower prices. As corporate chains grow in size, these scale-related advantages also enable them to hire more specialized managers in areas such as e-commerce, merchandising, promotions, inventory control, pricing, and predictive analytics.

corporate chains

Two or more retail outlets that are commonly owned and controlled.

The dominance of corporate chain stores has led many independents to find ways to collaborate to increase their competitiveness. A **retailer cooperative** is a group of independent retailers that band together to create a mutually owned, central wholesale operation that also conducts joint merchandising and promotion. By facilitating cooperation, retailers like Ace Hardware and NAPA provide their independent members with the economies of scale needed to combat lower-priced chains.

Another common form of retail organization is franchising, which is an arrangement in which a supplier (or franchisor) grants a dealer (or franchisee) the right to sell products in exchange for financial considerations. In a typical franchise system, the franchisee agrees to pay a lump sum plus a royalty on future sales in return for the right to operate a business in a specific location. Franchising has been particularly prominent in areas such as the quick-service restaurant industry (for instance, Taco Bell, Chick-fil-A), automotive services (Firestone), real estate (Century 21), and tax preparation services (H&R Block). But would it surprise you to learn that about 40 percent of retail sales in the United States are accounted for by franchise operations?

There are two types of franchising relationships: business format franchising and product distribution franchising. In a **business format franchise**, the franchisor provides not just its trade name, products, and services but an entire system for operating the business. Franchisee support often includes financing, site selection and development, operating manuals, training, quality control, marketing, and business advisory services. Examples include McDonald's, Subway, and UPS Stores. Product distribution franchising, while less common, actually accounts for a larger percentage of franchise-based sales. In a **product distribution franchise** arrangement, the focus is not on a system of doing business, but is instead based on the franchisee gaining preferred or exclusive access to products supplied by the franchisor. Examples include Coca-Cola bottlers, Exxon gas stations, and John Deere distributorships.

NAPA (which stands for National Automotive Parts Association) Auto Parts is a well-known retailer cooperative, with more than 6,000 stores nationwide. *Allen Eyestone/The Palm Beach Post/ZUMA Press/Alamy Stock Photo*

retailer cooperative

A group of independent retailers that band together to set up a jointly owned, central wholesale operation that also conducts joint merchandising and promotion.

business format franchise

Business organization in which the franchisor provides to the franchisee not just its trade name, products, and services but an entire system for operating the business.

product distribution franchise

Business organization in which the franchisee gains preferred or exclusive access to the products manufactured or supplied by the franchisor, but not the franchisor's system of doing business.

Breadth and Depth of Assortment

Retailers may also be classified by merchandise assortment (or mix). An **assortment** is the selection of merchandise a retailer carries. **Breadth of assortment** refers to the number of distinct goods or service product lines that a retailer carries. **Depth of assortment** refers to the number of individual items offered within any single product category. For instance, specialty retailers offer a deep assortment of goods or services within just a few select, interrelated categories. Wilsons Leather is a specialty store that sells an assortment composed primarily of leather-based outerwear as well as accessories, like handbags and briefcases. Alternatively, department stores and general merchandise discounters may offer only a limited number of better-selling or higher-margin items across a broad range of product categories.

assortment

The selection of merchandise a retailer carries.

breadth of assortment

The number of distinct goods or service product lines that a retailer carries.

depth of assortment

The number of individual items offered within any single product line.

Scrambled Merchandising

If you were pressed for time and needed to buy a greeting card or flowers, where would you shop? For most shoppers, the answer is not a card shop, like Hallmark, or a local florist. Instead, many people would think of going to a drugstore or supermarket.

scrambled merchandising

Selling goods and services that may be unrelated to each other and to the firm's original business.

Retailers seek to increase their breadth of assortment via **scrambled merchandising**, adding goods and services that may be unrelated to each other or the firm's original business. Scrambled merchandising is popular for several reasons. Consumers like one-stop shopping. Adding fast-selling, highly profitable goods and services leads to more impulse purchases by consumers. On the down side, offering broader assortment increases costs.

One implication of the spread of scrambled merchandising is increased competition across different types of retailers. For instance, drugstores, florists, and bookstores are deeply affected by supermarkets selling items such as prescription drugs, flowers, and books. In response, drugstores have responded by practicing scrambled merchandising themselves, offering food and drink items, toys, greeting cards, and the like.

Mc Graw Hill connect Exercise **12-1**

Please complete the *Connect* exercise for Chapter 12 that focuses on the forms of retail organizations. By understanding what is involved with different forms of retailers, you will better understand the potential marketing strategies to be successful in each.

Merchandise Pricing A final way to classify retailers is by the relative prices they charge for goods and services. The distribution of retailers along a price continuum follows a bell curve: Most retailers offer standard pricing, accompanied by moderate levels of service. On the low-price end, extreme-value retailers and discount retailers tend to offer extremely limited service in exchange for a broader selection of low-to-moderate-quality merchandise. On the high-price end are specialty store boutiques and upscale department stores. They offer a limited selection of high-margin, premium merchandise along with knowledgeable, individualized customer services.

Careers in Retailing

When students first think about retail, many may reflect back on a part-time, seasonal job they held as a senior in high school. However, retail involves much more than stocking shelves or working a cash register! No matter your major, new grads would be shortsighted to overlook career opportunities in retail.

As the retail industry is the largest private-sector employer, there are always positions to be filled. Moreover, it is a diverse industry with plenty of room for career development and growth. In fact, only about half of all retail jobs involve working on the retail sales floor. Also, because many retailers tend to hire internally, there is greater opportunity for rapid advancement and responsibility. In addition, experience gained in dynamic retail environments is highly valued by employers in other industries.

The retail industry offers graduates flexible, collaborative careers in supply chain, data science, marketing, human resources, technology, finance, engineering and design—to name just a few. Let's review a few of the key roles within retail organizations. Retail *store managers* and *assistant store managers* oversee the day-to-day operations of a retail store location. In larger store settings, they work with *department managers* to ensure floor sales staff, service representatives, cashiers, and other frontline employees perform their duties to a high standard and that customers are satisfied with their shopping experiences. Some common store management tasks include hiring, scheduling, and motivating employees; developing and executing sales promotions; monitoring sales figures and forecasting future sales volume; and addressing questions and complaints from customers.

Supply chain managers at Nike Inc. make the impossible happen every day, ensuring that almost a billion units of footwear, apparel, and equipment arrive on time at the doorsteps of retailers and customers. *Roman Tiraspolsky/Alamy Stock Photo*

Many other workers contribute to the success of retail organizations behind the scenes, without regular customer interaction. For example, supply chain and logistics managers play a vital role in the retail industry, ensuring the effective storage, distribution, and tracking of store merchandise. At Nike Inc., supply chain experts must ensure almost a billion units of footwear, apparel, and equipment each year arrive at the right place, at the right time. To make sure this complex job goes off without a hitch, team members work with a network of more than 50 distribution centers, thousands of accountants, and more than 100,000 retail stores worldwide. With the growth of online retail, supply chain knowledge and experience have never been in higher demand.

What are some of the specific positions within retail supply chain teams? *Sourcing managers* develop global and domestic sourcing strategies for their assigned product categories. This role requires understanding of global market conditions that impact the supply chains for their assigned categories, such as raw material costs, tariffs, social compliance issues, and freight challenges. *Distribution center managers* oversee all inbound and outbound activities involving the retailer's warehouses and distribution facilities. *Inventory specialists* are responsible for executing, monitoring, and benchmarking inventory best practices and standard operating procedures for the entire store chain, including both front end and distribution warehousing.

Merchandise management is also an important functional area within retail operations. **Merchandise planners** are responsible for planning, controlling, and monitoring the purchase, intake, and distribution of merchandise to stores. Planners must work across seasons and countries to maximize sales and profit margin within the assigned departments or categories. Merchandise planners work closely with retail **buyers**, who are responsible for purchasing wholesale merchandise to sell in store and online. In the course of their duties, buyers will typically evaluate vendors, negotiate prices, order merchandise, and arrange delivery schedules. These professionals must also track inventories and sales trends in order to adjust purchase levels and stay on top of consumer demand for new products. **Visual merchandisers** often work closely with buyers to

merchandise planner
Retail management position responsible for planning, controlling, and monitoring the purchase, intake, and distribution of merchandise to stores.

buyer
A retail professional responsible for purchasing wholesale merchandise for retailers to sell in store or online.

visual merchandiser
A retail professional that develops layout plans and displays aimed at improving store sales by highlighting select items using visually appealing displays.

develop layout plans and displays that improve sales by highlighting select items in a way that grabs shoppers' attention and boosts purchase interest.

Over the next sections, we introduce the various types of retail store and nonstore formats and review ongoing trends affecting these organizations and sectors.

LO 12-2 IDENTIFY RETAIL STORE FORMATS

Describe the major types of physical-store retailers.

Now that you understand the ways in which retailers can differ, let's take a closer look at the various types of retail formats. In the sections that follow, we'll highlight some of the unique opportunities and challenges currently facing these retail organizations. Table 12.1 summarizes information about the different aspects of retail strategy by selected store type.

TABLE 12.1   Aspects of Retail Strategy by Selected Store Type

Type of Retailer	Examples	Merchandise Mix	Service Level	Pricing
Full-line discount store	Walmart, Target	Extensive breadth and depth of assortment; average to good quality	Slightly below average to average	Competitive
Specialty discount store	Best Buy, Dick's Sporting Goods	Narrow to average breadth, extensive depth of assortment; good to excellent quality	Average	Competitive
Conventional supermarket	Kroger, Albertson's	Extensive breadth and depth of assortment; average quality	Average to above average	Competitive
Warehouse club	Costco, Sam's Club	Moderate breadth and low depth of assortment; average to excellent quality; low continuity of merchandise array	Very low to average	Very low
Convenience store	7-Eleven, Sheetz	Medium breadth, low depth of assortment; average quality	Average	Average to above average
Specialty store	Kay Jewelers, Barnes & Noble	Narrow but deep, in a specific market segment	Average to excellent	Competitive to above average
Off-price retailer	TJ Maxx	Moderate breadth but poor depth of assortment; average to good quality; changing merchandise array	Low	Low
Upscale department store	Nordstrom	Extensive breadth and depth of assortment; good to excellent quality	High to very high	High to very high
Low- and mid-tier department store	Kohl's, Sears	Extensive breadth and depth of assortment; average to good quality	Above average	Average to above average
Extreme-value retailer	Dollar General	Good breadth and depth of assortment; below average to average quality	Average	Low

Source: Adapted from Barry Berman and Joel Evans, *Retail Management: A Strategic Approach*, 12th ed. (Upper Saddle River, NJ: Prentice-Hall, 2012).

Discount Stores

Discount stores are general merchandise outlets that offer brand-name and private-label products at low prices. Discount retailers accept lower margins on their merchandise in exchange for high customer traffic and transaction volume. In order to maintain high inventory turnover, discount stores choose merchandise breadth over depth: They carefully select fast-moving items across select categories. Poor-selling products are quickly discontinued. Discount retailers are broadly grouped into two groups: full-line discount stores and specialty discount stores.

discount stores
General merchandise outlets that offer brand-name and private-label products at low prices.

Full-Line Discount Stores
Full-line discount stores carry a wide assortment of merchandise across popular categories. Full-line discount stores like Walmart and Target sell apparel, cosmetics, sporting goods, toys, electronics, kitchenware, home furnishings, garden accessories, and automotive items. Over the past 30 years, full-line discount stores have created massive economies of scale by opening thousands of stores around the globe. Did you know that 90 percent of the entire U.S. population lives within a 15-minute drive to Walmart?[7] The company's massive size has given full-line discounters considerable leverage over suppliers in negotiating lower costs and process improvements.

full-line discount stores
General merchandise outlets that carry a wide assortment of merchandise across popular categories.

Some full-line discount stores have expanded facilities to a **supercenter format**, adding grocery, pharmacy, and other services. For companies like Target and Walmart, supercenters represent avenues for stable revenue growth. Although groceries offer lower margins, food as a purchase category is resistant to macroeconomic downturns. With aging populations in many Western countries, demand for prescription drugs and health care–related items will remain high. In addition, consumers drawn in to pick up grocery items or prescriptions at a supercenter often end up making additional unplanned purchases.

supercenter format
Full-line discount store format that includes grocery, pharmacy, and services.

Specialty Discount Stores
Specialty discount stores offer a wide selection of merchandise within a single category. Examples include Dick's Sporting Goods for athletic apparel and sporting equipment and Bed Bath and Beyond for home decor. Specialty discount stores compete on the basis of low prices, wide selection, and product availability. These stores are sometimes referred to as **category killers** because they are able to gain high market share within their chosen category. Higher-margin rivals and discounters find it difficult to compete effectively within that space. Other examples of category killers include Best Buy (consumer electronics), Home Depot and Lowe's (home improvement), and Office Depot (office supplies).

specialty discount stores
General merchandise outlets that offer a wide selection of merchandise within a single category.

category killers
Specialty discount stores that are able to gain high market share within their chosen category.

Supermarkets and Grocery Stores

Supermarkets are large, departmentalized retailers that carry a wide and complex line of groceries, meat, dairy, produce, and baked goods plus a limited array of nonfood products like beauty aids, personal care, and general merchandise. Large supermarkets often carry additional goods and services, such as pharmacists, florists, dine-in options, and salad bars.

supermarkets
Merchandise outlets that carry a wide and complex line of groceries, meat, dairy, produce, and baked goods plus a limited array of nonfood products.

U.S. consumers make 1.5 grocery trips per week, making supermarkets and other types of grocery stores the most frequently visited retail category. Not surprisingly, supermarkets and grocery stores represent a large portion of overall retail in the United States, accounting for annual sales of nearly $760 billion. In fact, the average supermarket generates more than $585,000 in sales each week![8]

Growth in Asian, Latin American, and Indian immigrant populations in various parts of the United States has led to a rising number of ethnic grocery stores. One such grocery chain is Fiesta Mart, which operates 60-plus stores located mainly in large metro areas in Texas. Fiesta Mart caters to its Latino customers through a large selection of foods and

Fiesta grocery stores cater to a growing population of Latino customers in large Texas cities, offering a large selection of food items and ingredients that are not widely available through most U.S. grocers. *Suzanne Cordeiro/AFP/Getty Images*

ingredients generally not available at most U.S. grocers. Fiesta stores often include stores owned by independent operators, such as discount jewelry and bank vending.

Impact of COVID-19 on Food Retailers
Grocery was one of just a few retail sectors that grew in 2020. With remote working, social distancing, and restrictions on restaurant dining, grocery store's share of food spending increased by around 10 percent. While this pace of growth is not sustainable, new consumer habits underlying the trend—like working from home and cooking more often—seem likely to stick. For instance, as consumers sought out safe food shopping alternatives, many individuals tried online grocery shopping for the first time. Having experienced the convenience of buying groceries online, experts predict many consumers will continue to use online channels for some portion of their food purchasing even after the pandemic abates.

The pandemic also resulted in consumers showing greater interest in nutrition and healthy lifestyles. As a result, spending on organic, sustainable, and local food products increased. More people than ever are mindful of the food they put into their bodies. Many are even willing to pay a premium for healthy, sustainable foods, which can be a source of new revenue in this low-margin industry.[9]

Warehouse Clubs

warehouse clubs

Merchandise outlets that operate in warehouse-like facilities that offer merchandise in bulk quantities, at ultra-low prices, to shoppers who pay an annual fee to join; also known as *wholesale clubs* or *membership warehouses.*

Warehouse clubs (also known as *wholesale clubs* or *membership warehouses*) operate in warehouse-like facilities that offer merchandise in bulk quantities, at ultra-low prices, to shoppers who pay an annual fee to join. While these stores offer few frills, members enjoy surprise deals on select branded and private-label merchandise. Examples of warehouse clubs are Costco, Sam's Club, and BJ's.

Costco is the number-two U.S. retailer after Walmart (which owns Sam's Club). Costco keeps prices low by buying in bulk and religiously limiting its markups to a maximum of 15 percent (supermarkets average 25 percent markup by comparison). "All we're trying to do is sell stuff cheaper than anybody else," says cofounder and former

Costco continues to grow as a retailer for several reasons, such as exposing customers to more products by changing the location for certain staples throughout the store and offering a simplified selection of items to reduce choice overload. *A katz/Shutterstock*

CEO Jim Sinegal, "but there's a lot more work that goes into it." The recipe underlying Costco's success is based on two key ingredients:

1. *A culture that emphasizes simplicity, sustainability, and frugality:* Costco's floors are bare concrete slabs, which are more durable and easier to maintain than linoleum or carpet. Merchandise is stacked on the same industrial pallets upon which it is shipped, saving millions in labor costs. Each warehouse uses around 150 skylights, providing most of the store's illumination. These efforts to maximize efficiency help Costco scale worldwide while still offering great benefits to customers and employees.
2. *An impressive understanding of consumer psychology:* Costco constantly rotates the location of selected staples such as light bulbs, detergents, and paper towels, which the store refers to as "triggers." Shoppers must search storewide for trigger items, which exposes them to a greater number of products. With this "treasure hunt" strategy, Costco creates a sense of urgency among consumers, leading to more impulse purchasing. Also, despite its cavernous size, a typical Costco warehouse stocks only around 4,000 SKUs (**stock-keeping units**)—many fewer than the 100,000 typically found at a Walmart supercenter. By limiting the number of items in its assortment, Costco reduces shopper anxiety associated with choice overload.

stock-keeping unit (SKU)
A distinct item available for sale within a retail store or e-commerce website.

Convenience Stores

Convenience stores are small, self-service stores that are open long hours and carry a limited number of frequently purchased items. Usually located along highly trafficked roads, they aim to capture sales from those who are willing to pay premium prices in exchange for an easy, in-and-out shopping experience. Convenience stores account for more than one-third of all retail outlets in the United States.[10] While around 80 percent of convenience stores sell gasoline, margins for fuel are thin. To increases profits, convenience stores also sell food products, snacks, beverages, and newspapers.

In recent years, some convenience store operators have sought to shed their gritty, gas station image in order to attract more females and business travelers. Few convenience stores have attracted as many avid fans as Sheetz, a family-owned, 640-store chain based in Altoona, Pennsylvania. "Everything they do is focused on food and

convenience stores
Small, self-service stores that are open long hours and carry a limited number of frequently purchased items.

Convenience stores like Sheetz have tried hard to shed their gas station image by offering new amenities such as premium coffee and better-tasting, made-to-order food. *Wirestock, Inc./Alamy Stock Photo*

delighting customers inside the store," says Jeff Lenard, a spokesperson for the National Association of Convenience Stores, an Alexandria, Virginia, trade group.[11] Sheetz customers rave about store amenities, including premium coffee drinks served by trained baristas (at half the price of Starbucks); a lengthy made-to-order menu including pizza, wings, sub sandwiches, pretzel melts, salads, and wraps; touch-screen ordering; and great customer service. The company is even expanding its footprint in urban areas and college campuses by pushing a new store model—one without the gas pumps—that focuses on higher-margin sales of food and beverages.[12]

Drugstores

Drugstores are specialty retailers that concentrate on selling over-the-counter (OTC) and prescription pharmaceuticals as well as health products, personal grooming items, and general merchandise. As insurers and government agencies seek to streamline health-care costs, some drugstore chains have started offering additional health-maintenance services, such as blood pressure tests, diabetes monitoring, and immunizations. However, prescription pharmaceuticals still represent almost 70 percent of drugstore sales.

Over the years, the prescription drugs space has attracted competition from full-line discounters, grocery stores, and new e-commerce providers. However, drugstores are not standing still. In 2015, CVS Health paid $1.9 billion to acquire all 1,700 of Target's in-store pharmacies and clinics.[13] The deal helped CVS incrementally increase market share and provided the retailer with a growth platform for its MinuteClinic primary-care offering. In 2018, CVS followed up with a $69 billion merger with health insurer Aetna. The deal has enabled CVS to leverage its pharmacy and clinic assets by directing more insured patients to its stores.[14]

Pharmacy providers played a key role on the frontlines of the fight against the COVID-19 virus. Working in conjunction with public health officials, drugstore chains launched a string of diagnostic products and services, including at-home test kits, at-home antibody tests, and COVID-19 tests for people with no symptoms or exposure. Once the vaccines became available in 2021, Walgreens distributed shots to more than 29 million people. In 2022, the company added a free public health tracking app, its branded "Walgreens COVID-19 Index." The tool reflects testing results from 5,000 Walgreens locations across the United States, providing national and state-by-state updates of the spread of omicron and other variants.

Department Stores

department stores

Merchandise outlets that carry a wide variety of product lines, with each line operated as a separate department and managed by specialist merchandisers and buyers.

Department stores carry a wide variety of product lines, with each line operated as a separate department and managed by specialist merchandisers and buyers. Common departments include: clothing, shoes, home furnishings, household goods, tools, and hardware. Industry experts generally cluster department stores into three tiers:

- The upper tier includes upscale stores like Nordstrom and Neiman Marcus.
- The mid-tier includes chains such as Macy's and Dillard's.
- The lower tier includes chains like Sears, Kohl's, and JCPenney.

The golden age of the department store began in the 1920s. Iconic retail palaces known for their ornate design and bewildering array of merchandise were built in busy downtown business districts. During the 1950s and 1960s, department store chains

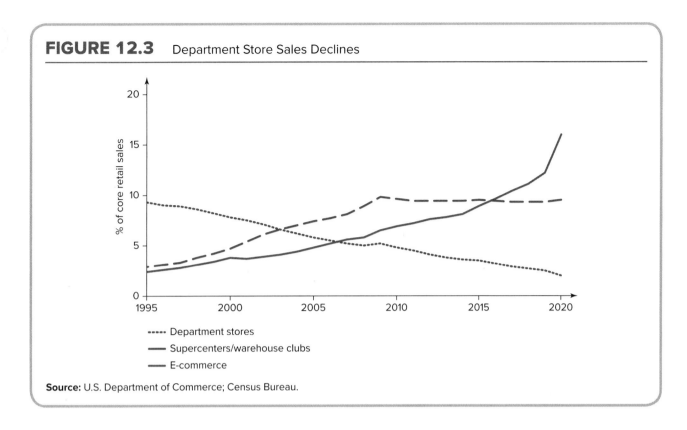

FIGURE 12.3   Department Store Sales Declines

----- Department stores
——— Supercenters/warehouse clubs
——— E-commerce

Source: U.S. Department of Commerce; Census Bureau.

boomed as they followed population growth into the suburbs, where they anchored new shopping malls. In recent years, however, mall traffic has declined. Department stores' share of retail sales has shrunk from 5.54 percent in 1998 to 2.01 percent in 2020 (see Figure 12.3). "In the old days, department stores offered convenience," said Greg Portell, a partner with consulting firm Kearney. "But now that we can get that without leaving the couch, it's no longer enough. Department stores have to offer more: They need smart curation, high-touch service and personalization."[15]

The emergence of the pandemic set off a chain reaction that rippled through the country's department store chains, sending many into a deeper tailspin. Overall sales at department stores plunged more than 40 percent at the beginning of the pandemic as Americans conducted more of their shopping online and gravitated toward off-price and discount chains. As a result of the downturn, Neiman Marcus, JCPenney, Lord & Taylor, and Belk all filed for bankruptcy re-organizations during 2020–2021. Even companies on relatively stable footing, like Macy's, shuttered dozens of stores permanently to save on expensive mall leases. Figure 12.4 illustrates the number of department store locations that have closed over the past several years.

"The COVID pandemic forced the department store sector to innovate, invest in digital, and diversify product offerings to reach new customers," said Erin Schmidt, a senior analyst at Coresight Research.[16] To that point, Saks Fifth Avenue has doubled down on e-commerce, spinning off its website into a stand-alone company. Nordstrom is offering virtual styling appointments and recently launched an online channel where shoppers can buy merchandise during live-streamed events. Neiman Marcus has also invested heavily in digital technology, hosting "shoppable" virtual events and making store employees available by text, e-mail, and video chat.

Mid- and lower-tier department stores like Macy's, Kohl's, and JCPenney are seeking to bounce back by tightening inventories, closing unprofitable locations, and leveraging vendor partnerships. Macy's has established **leased department** partnerships with brands like Lids, Sunglass Hut, Sketchers, Best Buy, and Toy-R-Us, which have given customers better selection. In addition, trained sales associates with in-depth knowledge

leased department

A section within a retail store that is rented to an outside party.

FIGURE 12.4   Decline in Department Store Locations (2016–2021)

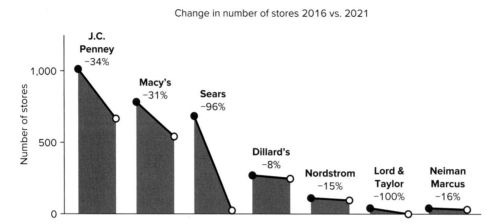

Change in number of stores 2016 vs. 2021

https://www.washingtonpost.com/business/2021/04/16/half-countrys-remaining-mall-based-department-stores-are-expected-shutter-by-2025/

JCPenney has partnered with cosmetics firm Sephora in adding Sephora Inside JCPenney counters at most of its U.S. locations. These leased departments have helped JCPenney increase foot traffic to its stores and drive added sales in beauty as well as other products. *Taylor Jones/The Palm Beach Post/ZUMA Press/ Alamy Stock Photo*

specialty store

A store that concentrates on selling one line of goods or services and carries a narrow but deep merchandise assortment.

fast fashion

The rapid translation of high-fashion design trends by lower-cost manufacturer-retailers.

of their respective product lines helps to make customers more comfortable in their purchases.[17]

Judging by the 2021 holiday traffic and sales figures, it would appear these strategies might be paying off, at least for now. But to be certain, the structural challenges facing the department store sector—which existed before the pandemic—have not disappeared. Will this department store revival persist? Only time will tell.

Specialty Stores

A **specialty store** competes by concentrating on one line of goods or services, such as jewelry, tea, batteries, tools, young women's apparel, or hair salons. It usually carries a narrow but deep merchandise assortment and tailors its strategy to a specific market segment. Examples of specialty retailers include Tiffany & Co. (jewelry), Jos. A. Bank (men's apparel), Pearle Vision (eye wear), Anne Klein (apparel), lululemon (yoga/athletic wear), Sunglass Hut (sunglasses), and Northern Tool.

Due to their specialized nature, specialty stores often offer greater selection and more knowledgeable, personalized service. Because they do not have aisles of unrelated products, specialty stores can also offer a more intimate and intuitive shopping experience. Among the most popular categories of specialty stores are apparel, jewelry, home furnishings, electronics, books, pet supplies, and athletic wear.

Fast-Fashion Retail   As many consumers have reduced their spending, specialty retailers like H&M, Forever 21, and Zara have turned apparel retail on its head with their "fast-fashion" approach. **Fast fashion** refers to the rapid translation of high-fashion design trends by lower-cost manufacturer-retailers. The Spanish retailer Zara is a pioneer in this field. Leveraging its production and supply chain expertise, Zara is able to restock its stores twice each week with on-trend, knock-off fashion apparel at

Fast-fashion retailers such as H&M, Zara, and Uniqlo have upended traditional apparel retail. These stores feature low-priced knock-offs of emerging fashion trends using quick manufacturing techniques and nimble supply chain systems. *Ymgerman/Shutterstock*

bargain prices. Shopping for inexpensive clothing provides customers with a source of cheap, endlessly available entertainment. Consumers also appreciate the ability to frequently update their wardrobe with fresh, new, affordable clothing items.

Fast fashion encourages customers to make frequent visits to stores and encourages impulse shopping. Despite its popularity with customers, fast fashion has been criticized for encouraging a "throw-away" attitude that is ultimately harmful to the environment. The trend has also been critiqued on intellectual property grounds: Some designers allege their designs have been illegally mass-produced by fast-fashion retailers.

Off-Price and Extreme-Value Retailers

The global economic downturn in the late 2000s helped create a generation of price-conscious shoppers. As a result, two retail formats that have experienced great success in recent years are off-price and extreme-value retailers.

Off-Price Retail Stores

Off-price retail stores feature brand-name (sometimes designer) merchandise bought at less-than-regular wholesale prices and sold at less-than-retail prices. They offer a broad and inconsistent array of merchandise—everything from shoes to shirts to picture frames—at major discounts from department store prices. Off-price retail chains, such as TJ Maxx and Ross, negotiate especially low prices for certain categories of merchandise. These include end-of-season goods, products returned by consumers to the manufacturer or other retailers, and closeouts. The popularity of this retail format has grown rapidly in recent years. In fact, off-price retail pioneer TJ Maxx recently surpassed Macy's in annual sales.[18]

Because it is not buying full lines, TJ Maxx's merchandise flow is similar to those of fast-fashion giants Zara and H&M. Since the stores maintain little inventory, TJ Maxx is able to introduce new merchandise, brands, styles, and fashion each week. Shoppers realize many items are likely to be gone within a day or two. This sense of scarcity compels consumers to visit the store more often to hunt for what's new.

off-price retail stores

Stores that feature brand-name (sometimes designer) merchandise bought at less-than-regular wholesale prices and sold at less-than-retail prices.

Like all retailers, the off-price chains took a hit during the darker lockdown period of the pandemic. But once stores reopened, off-price shoppers returned to seek out shopping entertainment and inexpensive new "treasures." Financial uncertainty resulting from the pandemic also helped off-price retailers attract new value-conscious buyers away from department and specialty stores. "It's a true testament to the off-price model given how quickly customers returned once stores began to reopen," said retail analyst Chuck Grom.[19]

extreme-value retailers

Stores that carry an assortment of inexpensive and popularly priced merchandise; heirs to the traditional Main Street "five-and-dime" variety stores from decades past.

Extreme-Value Retailers   Extreme-value retailers are heirs to the traditional "five-and-dime" variety stores from decades past. These stores carry an assortment of inexpensive merchandise, such as apparel, costume jewelry, toys, small wares, candy, and party supplies. Broadly speaking, there are two types of extreme-value retailers:

- *Dollar discount stores,* such as Dollar General and Family Dollar, offer a wide range of merchandise, both off-brand goods and closeouts of name-brand items, at very low prices.
- *Closeout chains,* such as Big Lots, sell similar types of merchandise as dollar stores, but feature closeouts and production overruns.

The dollar-discount sector has been ratcheting up growth in both sales and square footage over the past decade or more. According to retail research firm Nielsen, about 11,000 more of these stores have opened across the United States between 2007 and 2017.[20] Dollar stores have proven to be formidable competitors for discount stores like Target and Walmart.[21] Figure 12.5 shows that dollar store retailers have demonstrated the strongest growth in terms of new stores opening over the past decade or so.

Services Retailers

In contrast to the retailer types previously discussed, the primary products sold by services retailers are intangible, typically involving the sale of mechanical or human knowledge and effort rather than merchandise. There are a wide variety of services retailers. Some, such as movie theaters and quick-service restaurants, solely target end consumers. Other providers, such as airlines and premium hotel chains, offer the same mix of goods and services to both consumers and business customers.

FIGURE 12.5   Changes in U.S. Retail Open Store Counts by Category, 2007–2017

Source: https://www.marketingcharts.com/industries/retail-and-e-commerce-83023.

Due to the inherent characteristics of services (i.e., their intangibility, perishability, inseparability, and variability), services retailers also differ in terms of distribution and service delivery strategies. Does the nature of the service or the firm's positioning strategy require customers to be in direct physical contact with its personnel, equipment, and facilities? If so, do customers have to visit the facilities of the service organization, or will the service provider send personnel and equipment to the customer's site? Answers to these questions have strong implications in terms of store location and design, equipment, and human resource practices. Alternatively, there are some services retailers, such as the Google Play Store, that deliver value to customers virtually through using electronic channels of distribution.

Service retailers were especially hard-hit during the COVID-19 pandemic. Owing to the close interpersonal nature of service delivery, many restaurants and hair salons were shut down or reduced staffing due to health ordinances and low customer traffic. Many of those that remained open found innovative ways to offer limited services and maintain a revenue stream. For instance, some spas set up "smart salons," with each client in a "pod" separated from the person next to them. Many restaurants began offering new services, including curbside delivery, outdoor dining, and prepared meals that patrons could reheat at home.

Services retailers include providers such as hair salons, restaurants, and movie theaters. Rather than selling primarily physical products, these businesses create value for consumers through the provision of knowledge and expert skills of their employees. *Nancy Honey/Getty Images*

Mc Graw Hill connect Exercise **12-2**

Please complete the *Connect* exercise for Chapter 12 that focuses on the types of physical-store retailers. By identifying different characteristics of each, you will better understand which might offer you the best opportunities in your future career.

ONLINE RETAILING AND OTHER NONSTORE RETAIL FORMATS

The retail formats we've looked at up to this point have been in physical-store environments. Retailing now also includes various forms of nonstore retailing. In these, customers shop for products without visiting a retail store. Nonstore retailing includes online retailing as well as automated vending and direct selling.

Online Retailing

Online retailing, also known as *e-commerce,* is B2C electronic commerce in which individual consumers directly buy goods or services over the Internet. Online retailing may be conducted via a desktop computer, laptop, smartphone, or tablet. **Mobile commerce (or m-commerce)** refers more narrowly to online business or purchases conducted over mobile devices like smartphones or tablets. The rapid growth of mobile commerce has been driven by several factors, including increased wireless handheld device computing power, a proliferation of mobile shopping apps, and the broad resolution of security issues.

LO 12-3

Describe the major types of nonstore retailing, including online retailing.

online retailing

B2C electronic commerce in which individual consumers directly buy goods or services over the Internet; also known as *e-retailing.*

mobile commerce

Refers to consumers use of Internet-enabled mobile devices to conduct business or shop online.

As lockdowns became the new normal during COVID-19, businesses and consumers increasingly "went digital," providing and purchasing more goods and services online, raising e-commerce's share of global retail trade from 14 percent in 2019 to about 17 percent in 2020.[22] This upsurge in e-commerce was not limited to the U.S. and European economies. In fact, consumers from emerging economies made the greatest shifts toward online shopping. Latin America's online marketplace Mercado Libre, for example, sold twice as many items per day in the second quarter of 2020 compared with the same period the previous year. African e-commerce platform Jumia reported a 50 percent jump in transactions during the first six months of 2020.

While online retailing provides many benefits for consumers and marketers, e-commerce retail sites do still have certain limitations:

- For many consumers, shopping in a physical store is an inexpensive and pleasurable form of entertainment. While online shopping can be enjoyable, it does not provide that same customer experience.
- Online shopping does not provide the sensory elements of shopping that many customers enjoy, such as the hustle and bustle of a mall or the feel and smell of a new garment.
- Many retail goods and services actually require the physical presence of a consumer, such as fitting a wedding dress, getting a haircut, or having car tires rotated.

While such factors place some constraints on the growth of e-retail, there is little question that the rise of the commercial Internet and development of business-to-consumer (B2C) commerce have changed the face of modern retailing. This is exemplified by the growth of online retail giants like Amazon.com. These same technologies also fueled the rise of C2C (consumer-to-consumer) commerce, in which millions of individuals around the globe sell items through platforms such as Amazon Marketplace, eBay, and Alibaba. Online sales comprise around 10 percent of global consumer spending. However, as seen in Table 12.2, this percentage is much higher for certain product categories, like apparel, computers, and consumer electronics.

TABLE 12.2   U.S. Retail E-commerce Sales Share by Product Category, 2015–2020

	2015	2016	2017	2018	2019	2020
Apparel and accessories	18.6%	18.7%	18.7%	18.7%	18.7%	18.7%
Computer and consumer electronics	15.7	16.3	16.7	16.6	16.5	16.5
Auto and parts	10.6	10.6	10.7	10.7	10.7	10.7
Books/music/video	8.4	8.4	8.4	8.4	8.4	8.4
Furniture and home furnishings	7.9	7.9	7.9	8.0	8.0	8.0
Health and personal care	7.2	7.2	7.2	7.3	7.3	7.3
Toys and hobby	4.3	4.3	4.4	4.4	4.5	4.5
Office equipment and supplies	2.7	2.6	2.6	2.6	2.5	2.5
Food and beverage	2.4	2.5	2.5	2.5	2.5	2.5
Other	22.3	21.5	21.0	21.0	21.0	21.0

Note: Includes products or services ordered using the Internet, regardless of the method of payment or fulfillment; excludes travel and event tickets.
Source: eMarketer, December 2020.

TABLE 12.3 Amazon Share of U.S. E-commerce Sales, by Product Category, 2020 millions and % of total

	Total E-commerce Spending	Amazon GMV	Amazon Share of E-commerce
Books and magazines	$ 14,829	$ 11,864	80%
Consumer electronics	188,808	94,404	50
Consumer packaged goods	121,017	57,483	48
Toys and hobbies	19,373	8,718	45
Apparel and accessories	107,934	42,094	39
Office supplies	26,204	10,219	39
Sports and fitness	16,913	6,596	39
Furniture, appliances, and equipment	47,491	15,435	33
Home and garden	26,249	7,875	30
Flowers, greetings, and miscellaneous gifts	11,353	2,838	25
Jewelry and watches	14,366	3,591	25
Other	98,619	38,168	39
TOTAL (billions)	—	**$299,285**	**39%**

Note: Includes products ordered using Amazon.com (browser or app), regardless of the method of payment or fulfillment; excludes travel and event tickets, Amazon Web Services (AWS) sales, advertising services, and credit card agreements.
Source: https://www.emarketer.com/chart/248093/amavzon-share-of-us-ecommerce-sales-by-product-category-2020-millions-of-total.

Rise of Amazon Amazon.com (www.amazon.com) is probably the most famous online retailer in the world today. Founded by former Wall Street investment banker Jeff Bezos as an online bookseller in 1995, Amazon started out quite modestly: Every time someone made a purchase, a bell would ring on Amazon's computers, and everyone in the office would gather around to see if anyone knew the customer.[23] Over the years, Amazon has implemented its own complex distribution network, and the company has expanded into selling just about everything. It is now the Internet's top retailer and a leading platform for third-party sellers. In 2015, its 20th year of operation, Amazon achieved $107 billion in sales, becoming the fastest retailer in history to surpass $100 billion in sales.[24] Table 12.3 details Amazon's e-commerce sales share for several major consumer product categories.

Two of Bezos's guiding principles for the firm are (1) thinking for the long term and (2) always putting the customer first. Thinking for the long term has meant forgoing short-term financial gains and continuously reinvesting profits into its technology. Putting customers first, the company has successfully introduced a long string of retail innovations that have reduced obstacles to purchase and build incredible loyalty among Amazon's customer base. Examples include:

- *1-Click ordering.* This e-commerce feature eliminated the need to fill out multiple forms and visit multiple pages to place an order. Amazon 1-Click ordering streamlined the order and payment process, making it quick and painless.
- *Kindle.* Kindle is the e-reader that revolutionized bookselling. Amazon gave people a quick, convenient, and affordable way to get books and the medium surged. By working to put a Kindle in the hands of as many people as possible with a low price tag, Amazon took control of the e-book market—becoming *the* destination for purchasing content.

Amazon continues to develop new products and technologies to make the customer experience better. *NYCStock/Shutterstock*

- *Amazon Echo.* The voice-controlled, hands-free speaker lets customers use AI assistant Alexa and specially created "Skills" to play music, shop, order food, turn on lights, check the weather, and much more.
- *Amazon Prime.* Not only did Amazon Prime give people fast and free (aside from the yearly subscription fee) shipping on thousands of items, it also made people come to expect fast and free shipping from every other company. Now it's a letdown for Amazon users when they buy something online from anyone and don't get it in two days.[25] Its Prime Now service has upped the delivery ante in certain urban markets by guaranteeing products arrive within two hours. Inclusion of streaming video services also helps the company retain customers and increase its share of online purchases.

Continuing to think for the long term and put customers first, Amazon is working on new ideas, still in the development phase, such as same-day delivery and home delivery by drones. Amazon also has positioned itself as a cutting-edge technology business, selling basic computer infrastructure like storage, databases, and raw computing power. Customers of Amazon Web Services include start-ups such as Pinterest and Instagram, larger companies such as Netflix, and divisions of the U.S. government, including NASA and the Central Intelligence Agency (CIA).[26]

Catalog Marketing and Video Commerce

Catalog Marketing
Catalogs have been one of America's favorite ways to shop for over 200 years. In fact, garden and seed catalogs were in circulation in the United States before the Revolutionary War. **Catalog marketing** is a retail sales technique used to group many items together in a printed piece or an online store. Consumers use information in the catalog to buy directly from the catalog sender by phone, mail, or online.

catalog marketing

A retail sales technique used to group many items together in a printed piece or an online store.

This form of retailing has experienced a recent resurgence. This uptick includes upgrades by traditional catalogers, such as Lands' End and J.Crew. However, even digital retailers such as Bonobos, the menswear retailer, and Birchbox, the beauty subscription service, have started mailing catalogs. Why the sudden renewed interest in catalog marketing?

Marketers are increasingly challenged to produce a specific return on investment for their efforts. The sales effect of a commercial or print campaign can be difficult to determine. But catalogs—with their definitive mail dates and customer identifiers—are easier to track. In addition, new digital media and print production capabilities have made it cost-efficient to personalize catalogs to appeal to different customer segments. Steve Fuller, chief marketing officer for outdoor apparel manufacturer L.L.Bean, explains that instead of sending every customer his brand's largest book (catalog), he looks for frequent website visitors and asks, "Can I only send them 50 pages, or 20, as a reminder of, 'Oh, I've got to go to the website'?"[27]

shop-at-home television networks

A type of specialty television channel in which on-air presenters provide live demonstration and sales pitches for merchandise that viewers can buy online or by phone.

Shop-at-Home Video Commerce
Lights. Camera. Action! With lineups of trusted celebrities and a changing array of new merchandise, **shop-at-home television networks** have become a very popular form of nonstore-based retailing. Regardless of the day or hour you tune in, these networks are always selling *something.* Qurate Retail Group—owner of retail channels QVC and Home Shopping Network (HSN)—is the

leader in video commerce, reaching approximately 370 million homes worldwide via 16 television networks and an array of e-commerce and social media sites. The company is the third-largest e-commerce provider in North America, with 2020 revenues just over $14 billion.[28]

QVC and HSN have adapted to changes in the marketing environment remarkably well. For instance, HSN has a sophisticated social media plan in place to deepen relationships with its loyal base of avid shoppers—existing customers order 25 items per year, on average! QVC has centered its strategy on the "second screen," the tendency to watch TV while also swiping and tapping on a smartphone or tablet. Over half of its sales come from customers using mobile devices to order from its website, making it one of the largest mobile commerce retailers in the United States.[29]

Automated Vending

Many consumers think of *automated vending* primarily in terms of cash-operated machines used to distribute inexpensive food items, such as snacks and soft drinks. However, most people use automated vending systems regularly to acquire valuable services as well. For instance, automated vending includes kiosks at the airport that enable travelers to purchase or upgrade tickets, pay baggage-check fees, and print their boarding passes. Automated teller machines (ATMs) are another common form of service vending machines; they provide bank customers with time-saving capabilities, such as account balance information, check deposits, and cash withdrawals.

Automated vending is the most impersonal form of retailing. Yet the small space requirements and 24/7 availability make automated vending a cost-efficient alternative for certain products, particularly in high-traffic areas. For instance, Best Buy Express kiosks at airports and train stations dispense items like Beats headphones, iPads, and

Automated vending machines like Best Buy Express provide customers in airports, train stations, and other locations quick access to products while providing the operators of the machines the chance for high profit margins. *Robert Alexander/Archive Photos/Getty Images*

even video game consoles with the swipe of a credit card. ZoomSystems, a San Francisco-based company, designed these kiosks; it earns a fee from every transaction on the 200 kiosks in the United States. According to a source close to Zoom, Best Buy Express generates anywhere from $10,000 to $50,000 a month per kiosk. When you consider that Best Buy Express machines don't require human employees, advertising, or price discounts, you can assume that the profit margins from those blue kiosks are sky high.[30]

Direct Selling

direct selling

Retailing in which an independent representative of a company conducts retail and sales-related activities away from a fixed retail location, most often at consumers' homes or place of business. Also known as *direct retailing.*

Some companies distribute their products and services through **direct selling** (or *direct retailing*). In this form of retailing, an independent representative of a company conducts retail and sales-related activities away from a fixed retail location, most often at consumers' homes or place of business. Companies like Mary Kay Cosmetics, Amway, Avon, and The Pampered Chef are well-known direct retail organizations. Direct retail sales representatives often introduce their products via some sort of party or event at the home of a customer. The customer invites relatives, friends, and neighbors to watch or participate in product demonstrations, and typically receives a small discount on the order. Although the industry has its detractors, many consumers enjoy the direct retailing experience, include personal demonstration of products, home delivery, and generous satisfaction guarantees.

According to the World Federation of Direct Selling Associations (WFDSA), direct selling organizations accounted for 2017 global sales of $189.6 billion through the activities of more than 117 million independent sales representatives. For independent representatives, the cost to start a direct retailing business is typically very low compared to franchising opportunities. Due to these low start-up costs, however, turnover rates can be fairly high. Nonetheless, direct selling remains an attractive option for individuals looking for a secondary source of income. Nearly 90 percent of direct sellers elect to work part time, offering busy parents, caregivers, military spouses, veterans, and others

Mary Kay has provided direct selling opportunities to hundreds of thousands of people each year who are looking to start their own business and have increased flexibility in their professional lives. *Eddie Seal/Bloomberg/Getty Images*

flexible schedules and work–life balance.[31] Direct selling attracts large numbers of Millennial, female, and minority entrepreneurs. For instance, cosmetics retailer Mary Kay Inc. highlights the following facts:

- 47 percent of the more than 325,000 people who started a Mary Kay business in the United States in 2015 were between ages 18 and 34.
- 51 percent of the women who started a Mary Kay business were Latina, Asian, or African American.
- 35 percent of new Mary Kay beauty consultants are Latinas, who comprise 22 percent of the company's total sales force.[32]

McGraw Hill connect Exercise **12-3**

Social Media in Action

Facebook is making it easier for you to shop directly in Facebook. The company has partnered with e-commerce service Shopify to enable merchants who use Shopify's services to sell their products directly in a new Shop section on Facebook Pages. Facebook is pushing this new feature as a better mobile alternative for businesses than the web.

At a 2015 event at its Silicon Valley headquarters, Facebook highlighted its success at helping 45 million businesses launch digital storefronts with Pages on Facebook's app and site. With over 175,000 merchants, Shopify helps Facebook make it easier for some of those businesses to make those Pages true online stores. If a user clicks on a product, stores can either push shoppers from Facebook to their websites, or let them check out directly on Facebook.

Shopify will handle payment processing and transaction tracking, and Facebook will not be taking a cut for items sold on the site. Shopify is not the only e-commerce site trying to make it easier for people to buy on their phones. Nor is Facebook the only social network hoping to make it easier for people to buy without bothering with the web. Recent innovations from Twitter, Pinterest, and other social media platforms let users make purchases on the site.[33]

The Social Media in Action Connect exercise for Chapter 12 will let you use different social media platforms and products to allow different organizations to sell directly to their target markets. By understanding how different social media platforms can best allow your customers to shop directly, you will be prepared to develop and utilize these strategies to benefit your future organization.

RETAIL MARKETING STRATEGY

LO 12-4

Discuss key strategic issues in retailing.

The development of retail marketing strategy generally follows the approach outlined in Chapter 2. However, retail strategy development is distinctly characterized by hard-to-predict shifts in consumer preferences and changes in the external factors that make up the competitive landscape. The dynamic pace of retail industry change was further accelerated during the 2020 pandemic, which turned several widely held assumptions about retailing on their heads:

- Direct interaction with shoppers, once the foundation of retail customer service, was replaced by virtual or contactless touchpoints.
- Returns processing took on increasing importance as online sales increased.
- Physical stores turned into mini-fulfillment centers and pickup points.
- Retailers were required to constantly modify safety standards in order to safely meet employee and customer expectations.
- Supply chains were restructured to fulfill specific orders to households rather than shipments to large-format stores.

Even as the effects of the pandemic on public health diminish, industry experts do not expect customer behaviors or their expectations of retailers and service providers to return to their pre-COVID-19 norms. Forward-looking retail executives today recognize the need to continuously re-structure store operations, integrate emerging technologies, and modify their marketing strategies in response to shopper preference shifts and market conditions.

In the next few sections, we examine managerial decision making in three key areas that are highly pertinent to retail strategy makers: omnichannel retailing, improving operational efficiency, store location decisions, and crafting a distinctive store image.

Omnichannel Retailing

Bricks or clicks? This distinction is no longer so clear-cut for retail businesses. Most traditional brick-and-mortar (physical-store) retailers have introduced online and mobile e-commerce websites. This "bricks-and-clicks" strategy allows shoppers to purchase the same merchandise available in their stores from the comfort of their couch. Similarly, nonstore retailers, such as catalogers Lands' End and Eddie Bauer, have incorporated online retail into their distribution networks. Likewise, online retailers like Warby Parker, lingerie brand Adore Me, and custom men's suit seller Indochino have all added physical retail outlets.[34]

omnichannel retailing

The retailing practice of integrating customer experiences across the physical and online channels.

Recognizing the macro-environmental trends that have reshaped consumer preferences and expectations, retailers have sought to more closely integrate customer experiences across physical and online channels, a practice known as **omnichannel retailing**. The aim of omnichannel retailing is to deliver a seamless, cohesive, and personalized shopping experience, no matter whether the customer is shopping using a smartphone, a laptop, a voice-activated digital assistant, a wearable device, or are actually present within a brick-and-mortar store. By embracing an omnichannel strategy, retailers are able to effectively differentiate themselves from rivals, better enabling them to sustain or even build market share during market downturns.

Gen Z and Millennial shoppers expect much more from the products they buy and the brands they support. These 80 million consumers have been raised online, have had smartphones since childhood, and have low tolerance for obsolete processes getting in the way of their shopping pleasure. The business case for omnichannel, however, extends far beyond simply making a targeted segment of younger customers more satisfied. Evidence suggests that shoppers who use more channels are actually more attractive to retailers. An industry study found that omnichannel customers spent on average 4 percent more in brick-and-mortar stores and 10 percent more online compared to their single channel customers.[35] Furthermore, customer profitability increased in line with the number of channels used. Another study found that omnichannel customers who research online and buy offline spend 13 percent more in-store.[36]

Based on these results, it seems clear that digitally integrating physical stores with added customer touchpoints can provide omnichannel retailers with a distinct competitive edge. Starbucks is an example of a retailer that excels at providing seamless omnichannel user experiences. Every time a Starbucks customer pays with a Starbucks card, via a physical card or mobile, that user accumulates reward points. The linked app also allows coffee aficionados to locate stores nearest to them, send gifts to friends, order drinks ahead of time for a quicker experience, and view new additions to the menu. Its Spotify integration even enables consumers to view what songs are playing in a specific store and add them to their personal music playlists.

Buy Online, Pickup In-Store In terms of creating a seamless shopping experience for omnichannel consumers, in-store pickup technology has arguably made one of the most transformational impacts within retail in recent years. Home delivery options may be preferable if there is no urgency to an order. But consumers can get orders faster by reserving a product online and picking it up the same day at their closest store. In addition, they can avoid the costly shipping and delivery charges that often cause hesitation at checkout.

The Kroger supermarket chain has introduced its Pickup (formerly ClickList) service. Kroger Pickup enables shoppers to purchase grocery items online and pick them curbside at a convenient time. The introduction of the service has helped the grocery chain secure online-curious shoppers while building loyalty with longtime customers who value the added convenience. The retailer has also introduced home delivery services to help it address new challenges from other online grocery rivals. In similar fashion, online retailer Amazon is using extra space in its Whole Foods supermarkets to accommodate delivery and pickup of online orders. In fact, the online retail giant is building larger Whole Foods stores across the United States, enabling it to expand its Prime Now 2-hour delivery service and 30-minute online grocery pickup in more cities.[37]

During the pandemic, many retailers augmented their traditional in-store pickup service with new technology that facilitated curbside delivery. In many cases, the technology was integrated within the retail mobile app; once arriving to the store, the consumer simply needs to indicate a parking space number within the designated curbside delivery area and their order is brought out. Retail lockers also witnessed increased use in supplementing touchless in-store pickup options for online purchases. Even when the pandemic subsides, 75 percent of consumers who subscribe to multiple delivery services say they will likely continue opting for curbside delivery.

Retailer Operational Efficiency

The average amount of a single sales transaction is much less in retail than other types of businesses, typically under $100 per visit. Because of the smaller per-transaction revenue, retailers must emphasize being cost-conscious, driving traffic to their stores and e-commerce sites, and converting visitors into satisfied, long-term customers. Although the majority of retailers consider operational efficiencies to be of the utmost importance, most struggle to figure out how to achieve them. To meet the demands of today's consumer, for example, a retailer likely has to allow the customers the ability to shop online and pick up in the store. Even the best in-store pickup functionality will fail, however, if a retailer's underlying supply chain, inventory, and sales systems are not able to "talk" to each other.

Not surprising, optimizing supply chain management and other back-end processes is typically a major focus of process improvement efforts. Best in practice retailers constantly evaluate warehouse layout, making sure to place bestselling items near the packing station to ensure rapid and accurate order fulfillment. Items frequently sold together should be located close together in the warehouse. Stores should closely monitor product inventories and set rules for automated merchandise allocation and replenishment. Point-of-sale systems should capture customer and product data needed to market to customers better.

Brick-and-mortar grocery retailers, like Kroger and Walmart, now provide curbside pickup tactics aimed at improved convenience for time-strapped customers. *Duncan Selby/Alamy Stock Photo*

While it is good to know which items are best sellers, understanding which items *aren't* flying off the shelves is also valuable information. Reducing or eliminating these products from your inventory will lower carrying costs and allow retailers to dedicate that shelf space to better-selling products. It can also provide managers with the insight needed to move inventory without having to mark down—such as which items to bundle so you can move lower-selling items along with best sellers.

Store Location and Site Selection

Even with the rise of online channels, it is still hard to understate the importance of the store location decision for physical retailers. Opening a store involves high costs and commitment of company resources over a substantial period of time, even when leasing property. Regulatory factors, changing demographics, and economic factors can make it hard to identify and secure good locations. As a result, competition for premium retail locations is high.

Think about a new retail outlet that recently opened in your community. Prior to breaking ground on the space, retail managers had to take into account a variety of factors:

1. The distance to major housing communities, employers, and business districts and parking availability.
2. Traffic congestion and other transportation infrastructure issues.
3. Whether to lease and remodel existing retail space or build a new store.
4. How compatible are other nearby retailers in terms of store image and clientele.
5. Whether to build a freestanding structure or acquire space in a business district, strip mall, or shopping center.

After a retailer evaluates alternative trading areas and identifies a trading area, it must next decide on the preferred type of location. There are three different location types:

isolated store

A freestanding retail outlet located on either a highway or major road.

unplanned business district

A type of retail location where two or more stores are situated together or in close proximity.

planned shopping center

A group of architecturally unique business establishments on a site that is centrally owned or managed.

- An **isolated store** is a freestanding retail outlet located on either a highway or major road. There are no adjacent retailers with which a freestanding store shares traffic.
- An **unplanned business district** is a type of retail location where two or more stores are situated together or in close proximity. In this location, the overall mix of stores is not the result of prior long-range planning. For instance, a downtown business district may consist of a department store, a gastropub, a fashion boutique, and a pharmacy.
- A **planned shopping center** is a group of architecturally unique business establishments on a site that is centrally owned or managed. Dedicated parking is another typical feature. Even as large regional malls have declined, *lifestyle shopping centers* have gained in popularity. These retail centers are often located in affluent neighborhoods, featuring upscale retailer, fine dining, and entertainment options.

Because different retailers need different kinds of locations, the merits of any given site will depend on the nature of a given retailer's business. For instance, a convenience store would rather be in an area with heavy vehicular traffic; it does not need to be close to other stores. On the other hand, a shoe store would likely benefit from heavy pedestrian traffic and proximity to department stores and other specialty stores.

Store Image and Retailer Positioning

Store image refers to how consumers perceive a retailer. To succeed, a retailer must communicate a clear, distinctive, and consistent image. Numerous factors combine to shape a retailer's image. These include:

- Quality of a store's customer service.
- Merchandise attributes.
- Brand communications (including social media).
- Characteristics of the retailer's physical facilities or website.

A lifestyle center is a shopping center or mixed-used commercial development that combines the traditional retail functions of a shopping mall with leisure amenities oriented toward upscale consumers. *Jamie Pham/Alamy Stock Photo*

Crafting and maintain a distinct, favorably received store image does not happen by accident. It involves a thoughtfully managed, ongoing process. This task is even more complex for marketing managers working for chain retailers, franchisees, and global retailers. They must find ways to maintain image consistency across far-flung branch locations. Here, we discuss the importance of store atmospherics, store layout, and merchandise management as tools for managing retailer image.

Store Atmospherics
Consumer views of a retailer's image are heavily grounded in the store's "atmosphere"—the psychological feeling a person gets when visiting the retail store, catalog, vending machine, or website. These feelings can arise even before a shopper sets foot in the store, based on storefront and location. After entering the store, consumer feelings are influenced by lighting, music, width of aisles, and displays. **Atmospherics** refers to sensory-based stimuli within the retailer's environment—the sights, sounds, smells, and other attributes—that project an image and draw customers to the store. Retail atmospherics have been shown to contribute greatly to people's shopping enjoyment. They also influence consumer behaviors such as time spent in the store, willingness to engage with store personnel, likelihood of purchase, purchase size, and future patronage.

atmospherics

Sensory-based stimuli within a retailer's environment—the sights, sounds, smells, and other attributes—that project an image and draw customers to the store.

Store Layout and Product Display
Store layout also has an impact on retailer image. Stores must consider the following in their layouts:

- Total amount of floor space allocated to selling (e.g., display areas, counters, checkout areas).
- Merchandise storage.
- Customer space (e.g., aisle width, fitting rooms, lounge area, public restrooms).
- Personnel space (e.g., break rooms, employee restrooms).

Store layout also encompasses traffic flow patterns within the store. For instance, many supermarkets, drugstores, and convenience stores employ a *gridiron* traffic flow pattern, in which display and aisles are laid out in a rectangular grid. Department stores often encourage more of a curving traffic flow, placing aisles and display in more of a free-flowing pattern. Some retailers utilize a combination of these approaches in their

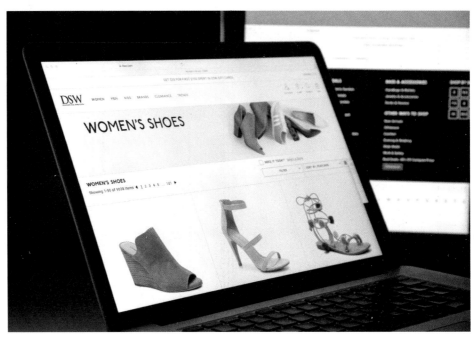

Retailers like DSW focus on the layout of product pages on their website in an effort to improve customers' online shopping experiences. *Casimiro PT/Shutterstock*

slotting allowances

Payments made by manufacturers to retailers to ensure that products are preferentially displayed by the retailer.

merchandising

The activities involved in acquiring particular goods and services and making them available at the places, times, prices, and quantities that enable a retailer to achieve its goals.

category management

A merchandising technique that focuses on the performance of a product category rather than individual brands.

micro-merchandising

A category-management technique in which a retailer adjusts its shelf-space allocations in response to overall consumer demand as well as differences in local markets.

cross-merchandising

A category-management technique in which a retailer carries complementary goods and services to encourage shoppers to buy more.

designs. Whichever approach is used, the goal is to optimize shopper convenience while creating an enjoyable environment and encouraging browsing behavior.

After allocating space and establishing traffic flows, the last step in store layout planning involves arranging individual merchandise and placing in-store signage and displays. Ideally, the most profitable products appear in the best locations: End-of-aisle, eye-level, and checkout counter positions are the most likely to increase sales for individual products. Similarly, for online retailers, the layout of product pages and links that enable the user to move intuitively from page to page are critical to customer conversion and a positive online store experience.

Product arrangement is so critical in some retail environments that manufacturers are often willing to pay **slotting allowances** to the retailer. These are payments that manufacturers make to retailers, to ensure products are preferentially displayed by the retailer. All changes in store location for higher demand and more profitable items should be carefully thought through to avoid consumer confusion.

Merchandise Management Merchandising consists of the activities involved in acquiring particular goods and services and making them available at the places, times, prices, and quantities that enable a retailer to achieve its goals. A retailer should align its merchandising approach with the needs of its target-market consumers, its marketplace positioning, its internal capabilities, and the strengths of its supplier network.

Category management is a merchandising technique that focuses on the performance of a product category rather than individual brands. Essentially, each category is run like a "mini-business." Retailer managers make merchandising decisions based on maximizing the total return on all assets assigned to their category. Frequent users of category management are supermarkets, drugstores, hardware stores, and discount retailers.

Many retailers today are incorporating analytics into their category-management decisions, practicing techniques such as micro-merchandising and cross-merchandising. With **micro-merchandising**, a retailer adjusts its shelf-space allocations in response to overall consumer demand as well as differences in local markets. In **cross-merchandising**, a retailer carries complementary goods and services to encourage shoppers to buy more.

Robert Morris

Associate Director of Donor Experience
UAMS

Describe your job. I am an Associate Director of Donor Experience for University of Arkansas for Medical Sciences in Little Rock, AR. In this position, I help to raise funds to both enable the UAMS system to perform needed services for its patients and help to empower the next generation of health-care professionals to complete their education through scholarship opportunities. I work with administration to match greatest needs for fundraising with donors and foundations with personal affinities for those specific needs.

How did you get your job? After receiving my Bachelor's degree, I realized my passion for marketing matched my passion for service through philanthropy. As such, I completed a Masters of Public Service and a Masters of Public Health as I wanted to approach philanthropy through a health-care lens. This position matched my ability to market health-care organizations with my passion for enabling change through philanthropic efforts.

What has been the most important thing in making you successful at your job? By far, building relationships is the most important thing in my position. With philanthropy, there is always going to be an amount of trust between donor and organization. We are lucky to have donors that are

Photo by Evan Lewis

passionate about the work that we do at UAMS, and we are glad to be able to match that passion to funds and donations that are meaningful to them. With that, we are able to peer into their lives and get to know the "why" more so than the "what" of their philanthropic giving, which makes for an incredibly enriching experience for myself, the donor, and the institution.

What advice would you give soon-to-be graduates? I would say to not close yourself into a box based on your major or interest area. Many of the things that I have been able to experience came as a result of doing something that was out of my comfort zone, which I feel has helped to make me more of a well-rounded professional and person in general. My background has undoubtedly brought me to where I am today, but opening yourself up to new and unfamiliar opportunities can help to take your professional life to the next level.

What do you consider your personal brand to be? I strive to promote change through radical authenticity. Throughout both my life and work, I hope that the things I accomplish will help to bring a positive influence to people in their daily lives.

LO 12-5

Discuss emerging practices, trends, and technologies that are reshaping the face of retailing.

TWENTY-FIRST-CENTURY RETAILING

The face of retail is changing. In the past few years, major retailers like Bon-Ton department stores have gone out of business, while JCPenney, Sears, and Macy's have experienced re-organizations and announced store closures. With e-commerce garnering more and more business, many traditional brick-and-mortar retailers are struggling to stay relevant. Retailer debt from store overexpansion and the residual effects of the Great Recession on consumer spending habits have contributed to the decline of some retailers.

But the truth is, brick-and-mortar retail is far from dead—U.S. shoppers still prefer to make most purchases in-store. What *has* changed is consumer expectations of retail businesses. They expect stores to provide a convenient, safe, personalized, and engaging shopping experience, whether they are online or in-store. Otherwise, consumers reason they can simply stay at home and buy the lowest-priced item online.

Retail companies that are thriving today have several things in common:

- Utilization of Big Data and analytics in managerial decision making.
- Focus on creating engaging customer experiences.
- Effective integration of emerging retail technologies.

Big Data and Retail Analytics

Data science and analysis allow retailers to collect and fuse data from multiple customer touch points such as web, store, social media, and call centers. Studying analytics is vital to understanding your customer. Information, like demographics and customer traffic, allows businesses to make smarter decisions based on customer details, as well as to personalize the customer experience. Retailers are constantly finding innovative ways to draw insights from the ever-increasing amount of structured and unstructured information available about their customers' behavior. Big Data analytics is now being applied at every stage of the retail process:

- Working out what the popular products will be by predicting trends.
- Forecasting where the demand will be for those products.
- Optimizing pricing for a competitive edge.
- Identifying the customers likely to be interested in the products and working out the best way to approach them.
- Figuring out what to sell next.[38]

The opportunity to achieve competitive advantage from retail analytics is enormous. A few leading retailers have already achieved dramatic benefits. Kroger, for example, reports a 40 percent redemption rate from its analytically targeted coupons, compared with an industry average of 2 percent. The supermarket chain believes the promotions have increased overall sales by 5 percent. Overstock.com used an analytics-based gift recommendation system on its website, and customers who used it bought 2.5 times more than those who didn't.

Another leading application for Big Data and retail analytics is sales forecasting. Perhaps one of the more interesting data points for forecasting demand is the weather. Brands like Walgreens and Pantene worked with the Weather Channel to account for weather patterns in order to customize product recommendations for consumers. Walgreens and Pantene anticipated increases in humidity—a time when people would be seeking anti-frizz hair products—and served up ads and in-store promotions to drive sales. The purchase of Pantene products at Walgreens increased by 10 percent over two months and Walgreens saw a 4 percent sales lift across the hair care category during that same period.[39]

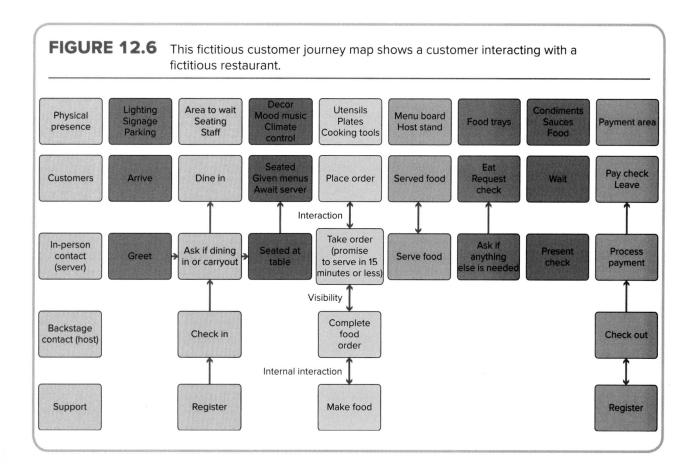

FIGURE 12.6 This fictitious customer journey map shows a customer interacting with a fictitious restaurant.

Competing on Customer Experience

Consumer expectations with respect to their retail experiences are changing quickly. A thoughtful and proactive approach to understanding customer experiences, whether online or store-based, is essential in this day and age. Leading retailers often use "journey mapping" to trace the end-to-end experiences of their consumers. A customer journey map is a visual representation of the process a customer or prospect goes through to achieve a goal with a company (see Figure 12.6). This technique helps retail managers identify points in their customers' journey where that process breaks down. Using this information, retailers are better able to design customer experiences that move the consumer from awareness and discovery to purchase, use, and advocacy of a good or service.

Experiential Retail Today's consumers crave experiences. Customers no longer want to simply walk into a shop, buy a product, and leave. Why would they, when they could do this less expensively from the comfort of their own home? By creating immersive retail experiences, retailers can drive consumers back to their stores, ensuring they not only leave with their products, but also with memories and an emotional connection to the brand.

Consumers are increasingly seeking unique and exciting experiences both offline and in brick-and-mortar store environments. Some interesting examples include:

- **Lululemon,** the yoga-inspired apparel chain that debuted in 1998, offers yoga classes in its stores, serving as a sort of one-stop community for both seasoned practitioners and novices.

- **Adidas's** 5th Avenue location in New York City has a miniature track set up on one floor, where customers can take a run or get their stride analyzed. Another floor includes a turf field with soccer balls, kettle bells, and other workout equipment.
- **REI,** the employee-owned outdoor retailer, is also an outdoor educator. The company offers in-house and in-the-field classes in kayaking, hiking, rock climbing, and more.
- **Whole Foods** and **Williams-Sonoma** aren't just places to buy cookware, they're also places where you can take cooking classes.
- **Pirch** is shaking up the home space with stores that offer guided, interactive tours of working kitchens and bathrooms, letting consumers experience high-end equipment from manufacturers around the globe.

Located inside a transformed sports arena on the banks of the Mississippi River, store guests at the Bass Pro Shop at the Pyramid in Memphis, Tennessee, can explore an immersive cypress swamp with nearly 600,000 gallons of water features and soaring 100-foot-tall trees. In addition to a vast assortment of outdoor gear, the Pyramid includes a wilderness hotel, an underwater-themed bowling alley, the Ducks Unlimited National Waterfowling Heritage Center, and the Lookout restaurant featuring a glass-floored observation deck at the top of the 32-story steel Pyramid.

Retail Technology

If brick-and-mortar stores want to stay open and stay competitive with digital natives, they must revolutionize the way they reach customers. However, implementing technology for the sake of doing so isn't productive. Instead, retailers must turn their attention to the customers, and how they have changed in recent years. "So many retailers are failing (with technology) because there's still a disconnect with who the consumer is, and what they shop, and why they shop, and how they shop," states Brian Solis, a principal analyst at Altimeter Group.[40]

Bass Pro Shop at the Pyramid in Memphis, TN is one of the most dynamic, immersive retail experiences in the world. *Bass Pro Shops*

So, what are a few of the ways that retailers are effectively implementing new technology to enhance their customers' experiences? Next, we explore a few of the most exciting emerging retail technologies and discuss ways in which organizations are using them to help create added value for their customers.

Geofencing enables brands to target mobile customers within a specified geographic area. *Plot Projects*

Geofencing Sensor data are revolutionizing brick-and-mortar retailers. **Geofencing** refers to the use of GPS or RFID (radio-frequency identification) technology to create a virtual boundary around a particular location, which can trigger a response when a mobile device enters or leaves a certain area. The most popular vessel of sensor data is RFID beacons. Major retailers strategically place small beacon sensors throughout their stores, which connect to customers' phones if Bluetooth is enabled and the retail app is installed. For example, using the Home Depot app, shoppers are able to walk into a store, switch the app to "in-store" mode, and gain access to helpful features. The Product Locator, for example, is a mapping function that helps customers navigate the exact store they're in to find their desired product. Other features include bar code scanning, price comparison, and an image search, allowing shoppers to save time and find similar products.[41]

Geofencing is also commonly used to offer consumers rewards to encourage purchases. American Eagle's app gives customers rewards to incentivize try-ons, an example of a practice known as retail **gamification**. Shoppers become more likely to try on additional items in order to see what they might receive in return. This behavior leads customers to seriously consider items they might have otherwise left on the rack, increasing purchase likelihood. Even if the customer does not make an immediate purchase, American Eagle can use these data to send a related e-mail or product offer at a later point in time.[42] A few additional things to keep in mind with respect to geofencing marketing campaigns are:

- A geofence does not have to be in close proximity to your store. Smart marketers build geofences around key physical sites; arenas, airports, schools, and even competitor outlets may be great target locations for a geofencing campaign.
- A geofence is not just a place on a map, it is also a place in time. *When* you take action on a trigger and *when* you notify a customer to do something is just as important as where.
- Geofencing also offers great opportunities to gather data on customers' shopping habits, such as when they are in proximity to your store, and whether they always come in or pass by. This information can be used to create more detailed customer profiles and tailored promotions.

Augmented Reality (AR) and Virtual Reality (VR) Did you or someone you know get caught up in the Pokémon Go trend of a few years ago? If so, this may have been your first exposure to augmented reality technology.

Augmented reality (AR) is an interactive experience of a real-world environment where the objects that reside in the real world are "augmented" by computer-generated perceptual information. Today, AR is rapidly becoming a core retail technology that

geofencing

A location-based technology that uses small sensors to send messages to smartphone users who enter a nearby, defined geographic area.

gamification

The application of typical elements of game playing (e.g., point scoring, competition with others, rules of play) to other areas of activity, typically as an online marketing technique to encourage engagement with a product or service.

augmented reality (AR)

An interactive experience of a real-world environment where the objects that reside in the real world are "augmented" by computer-generated perceptual information.

The IKEA Place app uses AR technology to help customers more easily visualize how its furniture and homeware products would look in their own homes. *IKEA*

is changing customers' shopping experiences. For instance, rather than requiring customers to visit a physical-store location, AR-enabled apps allow customers to experience certain products and services right from their homes. In one case, the IKEA Place app enables customers to tap one of over 2,000 products in its catalog— nearly the company's full collection of umlauted sofas, armchairs, coffee tables, and storage unit—then hold up your phone and use the camera to place the digital

TOMS Virtual Giving Trip VR experience takes you on a ride in the back of a jeep, where you end up at a giving destination with a team of TOMS employees, carefully measuring kids' feet for shoes. *Joe Scarnici/Getty Images*

furniture anywhere in a room. Want to see how the Strandmon winged chair looks by the window? Done. Can you really squeeze in that 7-foot-long area rug? Open the app, point your camera at the floor, and watch it appear at scale. You can even place a futon where it would go in the guest room, then see what it looks like when it unfolds into a bed.[43]

Brick-and-mortar retailers and manufacturers are also using AR to enhance customers' in-store experiences. Cosmetics brand Charlotte Tilbury took AR out of customers' hands and embedded it within a "magic mirror" place within one of its store counters. Customers sit in front of the mirror, which uses AR technology to scan an image of their face. In less than one minute, shoppers are able see their face with up to 10 of the brand's iconic looks—all without physically wearing any makeup.

Retailers are also incorporating virtual reality into their store operations and marketing. **Virtual reality (VR)** is an interactive, computer-generated experience that takes place within an immersive simulated environment, typically incorporating multisensory feedback. Shoe retailer TOMS, known for its buy-one, give-one business strategy, has introduced a VR-based campaign to help spread and reinforce its socially oriented message with customers. Now, fans of the brand are able to travel around the globe on a Virtual Giving Trip at its retail stores and department store trunk shows. Recorded with 360-degree HD cameras and advanced audio technology, the VR experience immerses the brand's fans in the scenes. Customers are able to see and feel firsthand the ways that TOMS is helping improve children's education and health around the world.

virtual reality (VR)
An interactive, computer-generated experience that takes place within an immersive simulated environment, typically incorporating multisensory feedback.

artificial intelligence (AI)
An area of computer science that emphasizes the creation of intelligent machines that work and react like humans.

Artificial Intelligence and Voice-Activation Technology
Artificial intelligence (AI) is an area of computer science that emphasizes the creation of intelligent machines that work and react like humans. The application of AI in retail contexts promises to improve internal operations and enhance customer experiences. One interesting application of AI in retail is toward the improvement of shelf intelligence. Computer vision platform Trax Retail analyzes what happens on physical shelves using images from in-store cameras, robots, or mobile phones to create a digital version of the physical store. Meanwhile, Walmart is using robots to monitor price tags and missing items on its shelves.

In 2016, online retailer 1-800-Flowers.com launched a service called Gifts When You Need (GWYN), which the company labeled as an AI gift concierge. The software took information about a gift recipient, then tailored gift recommendations by comparing the specifics provided by the customer to previous gifts purchased for similar recipients. The company reported that within two months of its introduction, GWYN was completing 70 percent of online orders.[44]

Another major AI movement is the development of cashier-less stores. Amazon introduced its first Amazon Go store, a fully automated grocery store in Seattle, that employs AI along with advanced imaging technology to eliminate checkout lines and cashiers. The company is set to open two more Amazon Go stores in San Francisco and Chicago in 2019.

Voice-activation-based AI is also emerging as an important application within retail. Whether it's

Julie Acosta/
Antwoine J.
McClellan/AJM
Images

Executive Perspective . . .
because everyone is a marketer

Julie Acosta
Web Analytics Manager
AutoZone

What are some issues that you believe will be important to the future of retailing?

I look at this from a digital perspective, so absolutely the use of artificial intelligence (AI) and machine learning (ML) to provide unique customer experiences in their brick-and-mortar or digital shopping journey. Many marketers tend to think about the utilization of AI and ML for things like customer-facing augmented reality—such as shopping for furniture by laying out the piece in their room using their phones; however, we actually use ML early on in the planning process for things like data modeling to create dynamic segments based on customer engagement, seasonality and trends (think "recommended for you" or "top selling items" sections on some retailer sites) and optimization of media mix. The latter helps us make our media spend most effective by automating the shifting of budgets toward the channels that provide the highest ROAS (return over ad spend).

Japanese telecom provider has introduced an AI-enabled humanoid robot known as Pepper in its retail stores. The robot is able to interact with customers and even perceive human emotions. *Yoshikazu Tsuno/AFP/Getty Images*

instructing your Google Home to buy you things or asking Siri to search for an item online, voice control has gained popularity in the retail space. Voice activation is also helpful for improving the performance of retail employees: For example, using the Theatro app, employees can communicate with each other throughout a store via voice-controlled wearables.

SUMMARY

Susana Gonzalez/ Bloomberg/Getty Images

LO 12-1 Discuss the importance of retailing, differences in retail organizations, and career opportunities in retail.

A retailer is any organization that purchases products for the purpose of reselling them to the ultimate consumer. The practice of retailing encompasses all of the business activities involved in the sales of goods and services to the ultimate consumer for their personal, family, or household use. Marketers commonly classify retailers along four key dimensions: level of service, breadth and depth of merchandise assortment, merchandise pricing, and ownership/organization. The modern retail environment is one that is increasingly global and dynamic. Industry consolidation and flattening sales growth in established markets have led more retailers to seek out global and online growth opportunities. Today, dozens of large, multinational retailers do business across multiple countries. Retail offers a wide range of interesting career opportunities for new graduates to consider.

A katz/Shutterstock

LO 12-2 Describe the major types of physical-store retailers.

Retailing includes many different types of organizations and store formats. The majority of retail operations are *independent retailers,* owned and operated by a single person or group; they are not operated as part of a larger network. The major forms of *retail organizations* are corporate chains, retailer cooperatives, voluntary chains, and franchise organizations. There are a variety of retail formats. *Full-line discount stores* carry a wide assortment of merchandise across popular categories. Full-line discount stores like Walmart and Target sell apparel, cosmetics, sporting goods, toys, electronics, kitchenware, home furnishings, garden accessories, and automotive items. *Warehouse clubs* operate in warehouse-like facilities that offer merchandise in bulk quantities, at ultra-low prices, to shoppers who pay an annual fee to join. *Convenience stores* are small, self-service stores that are open long hours and carry a limited number of frequently purchased items. *Off-price retail stores* feature brand-name (sometimes designer) merchandise bought at less-than-regular wholesale prices and sold at less-than-retail prices. In contrast to the retailer types previously discussed, *services retailers* primarily offer mechanical or human efforts (services), rather than merchandise, to consumers.

NYCStock/ Shutterstock

LO 12-3 Describe the major types of nonstore retailing, including online retailing.

Nonstore retailing includes online retailing as well as automated vending and direct selling. *Online retailing,* also known as *e-retailing,* is B2C electronic commerce in which individual consumers directly buy goods or services over the Internet. *Automated vending* is the most impersonal form of retailing. Yet the small space requirements and 24/7 availability make automated vending a cost-efficient alternative for certain products, particularly in high-traffic areas. Some companies distribute their products and services through *direct selling* (or *direct retailing*). In this form of retailing, an independent representative of a company conducts retail and sales-related activities away from a fixed retail location, most often at consumers' homes or place of business.

Duncan Selby/Alamy Stock Photo

LO 12-4 Discuss key strategic issues in retailing.

The complex, fast-moving nature of retail means that decision makers must continuously adjust strategies to match shifts in shopper preferences. The section focuses on four key areas retail strategists must continuously evaluate: omnichannel retailing, maintaining and improving operational efficiency, store location and site selection, and store image and positioning. Omnichannel retailing involves firm efforts to ensure a consistent customer experience across retail touchpoints. Retail operational efficiency is a source of constant scrutiny. Much performance gains come from integrating back-end and front-end systems and processes. Opening a retail store involves high costs and commitment of company resources. Because different retailers need different kinds of locations, the merits of any given site will depend on the nature of a given retailer's business. Finally, retail managers seek to establish a distinctive brand image through careful attention to store design, atmospherics, and merchandising tactics.

IKEA

LO 12-5 Discuss emerging practices, trends, and technologies that are reshaping the face of retailing.

With e-commerce stealing more and more business, brick-and-mortar locations are struggling to stay relevant. Since 2010, more than 12,000 physical-store locations have closed, what industry experts have termed a *retail apocalypse.* Retailers who have thrived during this period share several key characteristics. These include reliance on Big Data and advanced analytics in decision making, focus on creating engaging and memorable customer experiences, and effective integration of emerging retail technologies.

KEY TERMS

MARKETING PLAN EXERCISE • Marketing Yourself

In this chapter we discussed the rapidly changing retail environment. Emerging issues that range from technology to operational efficiency to organizations competing on the basis of customer experience will likely be a major part of your career, regardless of industry. In the next section of the marketing plan exercise, your assignment is to consider how the changing retail landscape in your targeted profession will potentially be affected by emerging strategic issues.

For example:

- If you are targeting a B2C company for employment after graduation, how will retailing changes affect that organization? You need to consider things like

the shift to online buying, increased usage of factory outlets, and automated vending changing your organization.

- If you are planning to be an attorney or an accountant, how is your targeted firm positioned to compete on customer experience or in a virtual world where customers can get legal or financial advice online, often for a very small investment?

Your Task: Write one paragraph on how the changing retail landscape might potentially affect your career plans. Your answer should include at least two specific retail changes that could alter the way your targeted employer or industry functions in the future.

DISCUSSION QUESTIONS

1. Discuss whether you think the average amount of a retail transaction will be higher or lower a decade from now and explain why you think so. Based on your answer, identify at least two companies that you think will benefit from this shift and explain your answer.

2. Describe your preference for retailer's level of service. What do you think the majority of your class would answer to this question? Identify two retailers that do a great job at providing you the level of service you prefer.

3. Which type of physical-store retailer do you think has the brightest future? Which type do you think faces the most challenging future? Explain your answer to both.

4. For the community where you live, provide an example of a quality retail store location and an example of a less-effective retail store location. Describe why you categorize each location as you do.

5. Assume you are in charge of a retail bookstore on your campus. What would you recommend the bookstore do in terms of store atmospherics, product display, and retail positioning?

 # SOCIAL MEDIA APPLICATION

Select two firms that allow you to purchase their products directly through social media. These could include any products that you can "buy" on Facebook, in-tweet purchases, or any organization from which you can purchase something directly through a social media platform without having to visit the physical store or company website. Discuss this type of retailing experience using the following questions as a guide:

1. How easy is it to make the purchase? What could the company do to make it easier and more likely that you would make purchases directly from social media platforms?

2. Who do you think are the main target markets for the two firms you identified? How does allowing their customers to buy directly from social media help them reach their targeted customers?

3. Provide two specific recommendations to a company in your community that should introduce or increase their ability to allow customers to buy directly from a social media platform. How will this benefit the local company?

 # MARKETING ANALYTICS EXERCISE

Please complete the *Connect* exercise for Chapter 12 that focuses on using analytics in retail store site selection.

ETHICAL CHALLENGE

As traditional retailing struggles, online merchants are reaping the rewards. People like the convenience of e-commerce and the feeling that they are getting a deal. The perception of a bargain is fostered by online retailers' use of something variously labeled *list price, suggested price, reference price,* or *manufacturer's suggested retail price.* Whatever its name, the implication is that people are paying more somewhere else.

But with many products online, you could not pay the list price even if you wanted to. That is because hardly anyone actually charges it. Citing a list price for selling at a lower price is a sales tactic that is drawing legal scrutiny, as well as prompting ethical questions about the integrity of e-commerce. The use of list prices online was at the heart of a case in a California Court of Appeal. Overstock.com, a popular online merchant, was found liable in a lower court for using misleading reference prices to exaggerate potential customer savings. The company was fined $6.8 million for false advertising in California. In its appeal, Overstock said it followed "standard industry practices" to come up with its reference prices. Internet retailers including Walmart, Crate & Barrel, and Williams-Sonoma employ list prices to varying degrees. Amazon, the biggest e-commerce player, uses them extensively and prominently.

Amazon has a section on its website where it says the list price can have many origins: It can be the price on the product itself; it can be the price suggested by the manufacturer or supplier; or it can be Amazon's guess as to what the list price should be. The retailer also said its list prices "may or may not" represent the prevailing price "in every area on any particular day." Retailers, as Amazon indicates, often are supplied with list prices by the manufacturer or the brand. The Overstock case went to trial in

late 2013. In one example cited by the district attorneys, a man bought a patio set from the retailer. It cost him $450, a discount of 55 percent from the list price of $999. The buyer was somewhat alarmed to find a Walmart price tag on his purchase for $247, a price he confirmed was the going retail price.

In an earlier era, list prices were intended to prevent retailers from gouging customers. If $40 was printed on the box, a customer might flee if charged $60. Manufacturers also wanted to signal quality by discouraging deep discounting. They hoped retailers would stick to the printed price. List or reference prices are still used as selling tactics in the physical world, and companies routinely are sued for abusing them. JCPenney, for example, set aside millions of dollars in 2015 to settle a class-action suit in which it was accused of tricking customers into thinking they were getting big discounts.

Use the ethical decision-making framework to answer the following questions:

1. What is the major ethical issue at hand in the Overstock example?
2. Who are the stakeholders affected when a company uses misleading reference prices to exaggerate potential customer savings?
3. If you are an executive for a retail store, what would be your policy on this topic? Explain why your decision will be best for the long-term success of the retailer you are working for.

Source: David Streitfeld, "It's Discounted, But Is It a Deal? How List Prices Lost Their Meaning," *The New York Times,* March 6, 2016, http://www.nytimes.com/2016/03/06/technology/its-discounted-but-is-it-a-deal-how-list-prices-lost-their-meaning.html.

VIDEO CASE

Please go to *Connect* to access the video case featuring Gearhead Outfitters that accompanies this chapter.

PODCAST

Please go to Connect to access the podcast that accompanies this chapter.

CAREER **TIPS**

Adjusting to Life after College

And now, a word from your coauthors: "Be quick. Don't hurry." This quote from legendary UCLA college basketball coach John Wooden is important for you to think about as you go through your career journey in a digital and social world. Similar to the retailers discussed in this chapter dealing with unprecedented change, you need to be quick as a new graduate. You need to quickly learn that if you don't think, solve problems, and work hard, your career will show it. We have seen countless new graduates waste their first year or two after graduation, ruin their personal brand, and incur lots of debt. You must be quick in adjusting from the protective structure of school to the self-accountability of professional life. You are responsible for your actions, and as long as you embrace that, you can have a fulfilling career and life.

But don't try to hurry through life, taking the shortest route you can find. Despite what anyone may have told you, your college degree doesn't entitle you to anything. It doesn't guarantee you a job, a career, or the life you want. Your ability to succeed in your career is directly tied to your ability to solve problems for organizations and customers. There are no scantron tests or study guides as you begin your career. You will not be judged by whether you make a 91 percent or a 78 percent, but rather by how much better your organization is because you are there. Be quick to engage in the incredible experience of building a career and a life, but don't hurry, because you may miss out on the skills, relationships, and experiences that will give you the best memories and the highest-quality career going forward.

Be quick to find something you are passionate about. We love being marketing professors, and we have loved creating the materials you have read and engaged with this semester. Our lives are better in every way because we love what we do. Your career will consume over half of your life; if you are doing something you hate, we doubt that the money you make from it will ever be enough. Once you find the career you are passionate about, don't hurry, because the best, most meaningful parts of your career are ahead. Good luck to you!

CHAPTER NOTES

1. Joseph Barry Mason, Morris Lehman Mayer, and Judy Bonner Wilkinson, *Modern Retailing: Theory and Practice* (Homewood, IL: Irwin, 1993).
2. National Retail Federation, "About Retail Jobs," (n.d.), https://nrf.com/insights/economy/about-retail-jobs.
3. "U.S. Retail Sales Top $5,570 Billion," U.S. Census Bureau, January 13, 2022, https://www.census.gov/newsroom/press-releases/2022/annual-retail-trade-survey.html.
4. Ashley Lutz and Mike Nudelman, "13 Mind-Blowing Facts about Wal-Mart," *Business Insider,* June 5, 2015, http://www.businessinsider.com/facts-about-wal-mart-2015-6.
5. Fernando Belinchon and Qayyah Moynihan, "25 Giant Companies That Are Bigger Than Entire Countries," *Business Insider,* July 25, 2018, https://www.businessinsider.com/25-giant-companies-that-earn-more-than-entire-countries-2018-7.
6. Leticia Miranda, "2021 Was a Turning Point for Retailers, with Store Openings Outpacing Store Closures," *NBC News,* December 29, 2021, https://www.nbcnews.com/business/business-news/2021-was-turning-point-retailers-store-openings-outpacing-store-closur-rcna10051.
7. Statistic Brain Research Institute, "Walmart Company Statistics," n.d., http://www.statisticbrain.com/wal-mart-company-statistics/.
8. FMI, "Supermarket Facts," n.d., https://www.fmi.org/our-research/supermarket-facts.
9. McKinsey & Company, "Disruption & Uncertainty—The State of Grocery Retail 2021, Europe," March 2021, https://www.mckinsey.com/~/media/mckinsey/industries/retail/our%20insights/the%20path%20forward%20for%20european%20grocery%20retailers/disruption-and-uncertainty-the-state-of-grocery-retail-2021-europe-final.pdf.
10. "US Convenience Stores Continue Retail Channel Growth," *Retail Customer Experience,* January 29, 2015, http://www.retailcustomerexperience.com/news/us-convenience-stores-continue-retail-channel-growth/.
11. Hayley Peterson, "9 Reasons People Are Obsessed with Sheetz," *Business Insider,* February 5, 2015, http://www.businessinsider.com/why-people-love-sheetz-2015-2.
12. Jason Black, "Sheetz to Add Food-Only Stores to Promote Growth in Urban Areas, Exec Woodley Says," *Trib Live,* March 17, 2015, http://triblive.com/business/headlines/7934196-74/woodley-trib-stores.
13. Paul Ziobro, "CVS to Buy Target's Pharmacy Business for $1.9 Billion," *The Wall Street Journal,* June 15, 2015, http://www.wsj.com/articles/cvs-to-buy-targets-pharmacy-business-for-1-9-billion-1434367874.
14. Brittany De Lea, "CVS, Aetna Merger: What It Means for You," *Fox Business,* November 28, 2018, https://www.foxbusiness.com/markets/cvs-aetna-merger-what-it-means-for-you.
15. Abha Bhattarai, "Mall Department Stores Were Struggling: The Pandemic Has Pushed Them to the Edge of

Extinction," *The Washington Post,* April 16, 2021, https://www.washingtonpost.com/business/2021/04/16/half-countrys-remaining-mall-based-department-stores-are-expected-shutter-by-2025/.

16. https://www.retaildive.com/news/can-this-years-department-store-recovery-last/611622/.

17. Walter Loeb, "Macy's and Kohl's Define Post-Pandemic Department Stores' Look," *Forbes,* August 23, 2021, https://www.forbes.com/sites/walterloeb/2021/08/23/macys-and-kohls-define-post-pandemic-department-store-look/?sh=4bab806923fb.

18. Sapna Maheshwari, "The Owner of T.J. Maxx and Home Goods Keeps Beating Macy's," *BuzzFeed,* February 24, 2016, http://www.buzzfeed.com/sapna/the-owner-of-tj-maxx-and-home-goods-keeps-beating-macys#.miQVXzDyP.

19. Rob Walker, "Why TJ Maxx Doesn't Need E-Commerce to Survive the Pandemic," *Marker,* August 5, 2020, https://marker.medium.com/why-tj-maxx-doesnt-need-e-commerce-to-survive-the-pandemic-2b9cb766cedc.

20. "The Retail Apocalypse: Which Store Categories Have Been Hit the Hardest?," Marketing Charts, April 13, 2018, https://www.marketingcharts.com/industries/retail-and-e-commerce-83023.

21. Daphne Howland, "What's Next after Wal-Mart's Store Closings?," *Retail Dive,* February 16, 2016, http://www.retaildive.com/news/whats-next-after-wal-marts-store-closings/413703/.

22. United Nations Conference on Trade and Development, "How COVID-19 Triggered the Digital and E-Commerce Turning Point," March 15, 2021, https://unctad.org/news/how-covid-19-triggered-digital-and-e-commerce-turning-point.

23. Brad Stone, *The Everything Store: Jeff Bezos and the Age of Amazon* (New York: Random House, 2013).

24. MarketWatch, "Amazon.com Inc.," n.d., http://www.market-watch.com/investing/stock/amzn/financials.

25. "8 Ways Amazon Changed the World," *Speaking Human,* n.d., https://thinkmonsters.com/speakinghuman/media/amazon-game-changing-innovations/.

26. Brad Stone, *The Everything Store: Jeff Bezos and the Age of Amazon* (New York: Random House, 2013).

27. Denise Lee Yohn, "Why the Print Catalog Is Back in Style," *Harvard Business Review,* February 25, 2015, https://hbr.org/2015/02/why-the-print-catalog-is-back-in-style.

28. https://www.qurateretailgroup.com/lp/investors/.

29. https://www.pymnts.com/news/retail/2017/mobile-trumps-e-commerce-sales-for-qvc/.

30. Thomas Lee, "Best Buy Express Kiosks Dispense Electronics—and Lots of Profits," *SFGATE,* November 6, 2014, http://blog.sfgate.com/mindyourbusiness/2014/11/06/best-buy-express-kiosks-dispense-electronics-and-lots-of-profits/.

31. Direct Selling Association, "What Is Direct Selling?" n.d., http://www.dsa.org/about/channel.

32. Georgina Caldwell, "Millennials Sign Up in Droves to Become Mary Kay Consultants," *Global Cosmetics News,* January 20, 2016, https://globalcosmeticsnews.com/millennials-sign-up-in-droves-to-become-mary-kay-consultants/.

33. See Julia Greenberg, "Now That You Can Buy Stuff in Facebook, You'll Never Leave," *Wired,* September 16, 2015, http://www.wired.com/2015/09/facebook-now-lets-buy-stuff-never-leave/.

34. Alexander Neely, "Clicks to Bricks: Why Online Retailers Are Opening Physical Stores," *DMN News,* January 5, 2017, https://www.dmnews.com/clicks-to-bricks-why-online-retailers-are-opening-physical-stores/.

35. Mario Toneguzzi, "Study: Retailers in Canada Struggle to Implement Omnichannel Experience Due to Customer Data Conundrum," *Retail Insider,* April 27, 2021, https://retail-insider.com/retail-insider/2021/04/study-retailers-in-canada-struggle-to-implement-omnichannel-experience-due-to-customer-data-conundrum/.

36. Emma Sopadjieva, Utpal M. Dholakia, and Beth Benjamin, "A Study of 46,000 Shoppers Shows That Omnichannel Retailing Works," *Harvard Business Review,* January 3, 2017. https:// hbr. org/2017/01/a-study-of-46000-shoppers-shows-that-omnichannel-retailing-works.

37. Heather Haddon and Laura Stevens, "Amazon Plans to Add Whole Foods Stores," *The Wall Street Journal,* December 31, 2018, https://www.wsj.com/articles/amazon-plans-to-add-whole-foods-stores-11546178520.

38. Bernard Marr, "Big Data: A Game Changer in the Retail Sector," *Forbes,* November 10, 2015, http://www.forbes.com/sites/bernardmarr/2015/11/10/big-data-a-game-changer-in-the-retail-sector/#fa69f8d678aa.

39. Ron Barasch, "The Power of Big Data in Retail," *Envestnet,* January 14, 2019, https://www.yodlee.com/blog/the-power-of-big-data-in-retail/.

40. Macy Bayern, "10 Technologies Leading Digital Transformation in Retail," *ZDNet,* July 3, 2018, https://www.zdnet.com/article/10-technologies-leading-digital-transformation-in-retail/.

41. Molly St. Louis, "Here's How Geofencing Helps Brick-and-Mortar Stores Compete in an Increasingly Digital World," *Adweek,* December 11, 2017, https://www.adweek.com/digital/heres-how-geofencing-helps-brick-and-mortar-stores-compete-against-online-retailers/.

42. Nikki Gilliland, "How Retailers Are Using Geofencing to Improve In-store CX," *Econsultancy,* January 15, 2018, https://econsultancy.com/how-retailers-are-using-geofencing-to-improve-in-store-cx/.

43. Arielle Pardes, "IKEA's New App Flaunts What You'll Love Most about AR," *Wired,* September 20, 2017, https://www.wired.com/story/ikea-place-ar-kit-augmented-reality/.

44. Grace Caffyn, "Two Months In: How the 1-800 Flowers Facebook Bot Is Working Out," *Digiday,* June 24, 2016, https://digiday.com/marketing/two-months-1-800-flowers-facebook-bot-working/.

Chapter 13

Digital and Social Media Marketing

Anatolii Babii/Alamy Stock Photo

Learning Objectives

After reading this chapter, you should be able to

LO 13-1 Understand the impact of mobile and social digital technologies on consumers and marketing practices.

LO 13-2 Explain how search marketing contributes to digital marketing strategy.

LO 13-3 Discuss how companies are employing social media marketing to strengthen customer relationships and achieve business objectives.

LO 13-4 Explain the importance of content marketing in driving digital marketing strategies.

LO 13-5 Discuss key performance indicators commonly utilized in managing digital and social media marketing campaigns.

LO 13-6 Identify potential moral hazards arising from digital and social media marketing and offer best practices for ethical application of these tools.

Executive **Perspective** . . . because everyone is a marketer

A passion for research made a marketer of Donielle Xu, but it didn't happen overnight. During college, her interests led her to study math and economics. Following graduation, she spent five years working in the nonprofit sector leading recruitment efforts and managing volunteers. Donielle then took a position in sales for a publishing company, which led to new opportunities to utilize her research skills as a senior marketing manager.

Today, Donielle is a data center solution principal for Dell EMC and provides scoping and solutioning support for deployment services for Dell EMC, which is part of a unique family of businesses that provides the essential infrastructure for organizations to build their digital future, transform IT, and protect their most important asset: information.

Donielle Xu
*Data Center
Solution Principal*
Dell EMC

Donielle Xu

What has been the most important thing in making you successful at your job?

I believe my career success is primarily attributed to three things—One, a strong work ethic. I show up every day with enthusiasm and dedication to perform a job well done, and a day that I can be proud of. Two, I approach my job from the viewpoint of management. I try to think every day what would make my manager's life easier. Rather than wait for direction, I try to anticipate what would my manager want from me that day, and not only do that, but more. And finally, I recognize that every relationship, whether personal or business, is a possible networking opportunity. I wouldn't have my current job if not for a volunteer opportunity I signed up for in my community—which led to a great job!

What advice would you give soon-to-be graduates?

For all those soon-to-be graduates, I would say to do your best to follow your passion. Find a role that suits your lifestyle and goals, and know that you have so much more to learn. Be open to the wisdom of the people who cross your path.

How is marketing relevant to your role at Dell?

As a sales professional, marketing is so important. Our marketing teams make my job easier. They are creating collateral, promoting products and solutions, and working to establish a brand image that ensures that customers have a positive idea about the product and solution I am selling before I show up at their door.

What do you consider your personal brand to be?

My personal brand is summed up in my LinkedIn headliner—with an expertise and background in sales, marketing, and sales support, I bring energy and enthusiasm into every role I've had. I enjoy a challenge, embrace opportunity, and build relationships to create value for the organizations I work for.

433

LO 13-1

THE DIGITAL MARKETING REVOLUTION

LO 13-1

Understand the impact of mobile and social digital technologies on consumers and marketing practices.

"Markets are conversations." This simple statement was the first of 95 theses outlined in a visionary 2001 business book titled *The Cluetrain Manifesto.* It challenged business-as-usual views of the then-emerging digital economy and predicted the Internet would upend the nature of consumer–brand interactions.[1]

The authors note that until the rise of mass media in the early 20th century, markets were a bazaar where people came to buy what others had to sell—and to talk. Buyers and sellers spoke directly without the filter of media or shade of advertising. With the introduction of broadcast media, the traditional one-to-one communications model was replaced by a one-to-many model. Markets were soon dominated by large corporations pumping out brand messaging via mass advertising campaigns.

Fast-forward to today. The diffusion of digital and social technology has fundamentally returned modern commerce to its pre-industrial roots. The ability to make one-to-one connections, be responsive to consumers, and inspire positive word-of-mouth have reemerged as the most important business considerations.[2] These changes have led to the rapid emergence of digital and social media marketing. **Digital marketing** is an umbrella term that refers to the marketing of goods or services using digital media, such as search engines, websites, e-mail, and social media. **Social media marketing** involves a company's use of social media and social networking platforms to establish relationships with customers and market their products and services.

In this section, we discuss the implications of digital and social technologies—first, on society and consumers generally, and second, on the practice of marketing.

digital marketing

The marketing of goods or services using digital media, such as e-mail, websites, search engines, and social media platforms.

social media marketing

Use of social media and social networking platforms by companies in order build relationships with customers and promote their products and services.

Marketing to the "Always-Connected" Consumer

Smartphones, tablets, and other mobile devices provide powerful and unprecedented access to information, commerce, and entertainment opportunities any time of the day or night, with only the tap, pinch, or swipe of a fingertip. In 2022, it is estimated the average American will spend nearly a month and a half on their phones. In one survey, over one-third of American users indicated in a recent survey that they would rather give up their pets than do without their smartphones![3]

It is hard for many to imagine life without digital and social technology. As a result, the historic significance of these innovations often goes unrecognized by even its most avid users. For instance, it took Facebook just 9 months to achieve 100 million users—by comparison it took 13 years for TV to reach half that total.[4] As of early 2022, there are 2.91 billion monthly active Facebook users (MAUs) worldwide. Approximately 1.84 billion users visit Facebook on a daily basis (DAUs).[5] While these numbers indicate the massive reach and scale of Facebook, they stop short of showing the pervasiveness of digital and social technologies in modern life. Consider the following stats:

- The average American spends just over two hours per day on social media.
- There are 500 hours of video uploaded to YouTube every minute.[6]
- Roughly 500 million tweets are sent per day on Twitter.[7]
- There are more than 200 million business accounts on Instagram.[8]

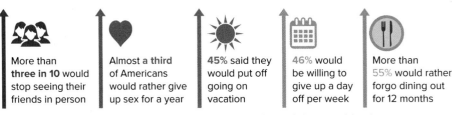

| More than **three in 10** would stop seeing their friends in person | Almost **a third** of Americans would rather give up sex for a year | **45%** said they would put off going on vacation | **46%** would be willing to give up a day off per week | More than **55%** would rather forgo dining out for 12 months |

According to a recent study, one-third of Americans claimed they would rather give up sex for a year than live without their smartphones! Source: *Blue Corona, https://www.bluecorona.com/blog/mobile-marketing-statistics.*

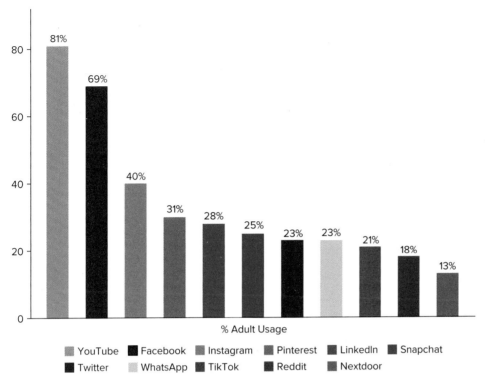

Social media platform usage as a percentage of total U.S. adult population. Source: *Hootsuite,* *https://blog.hootsuite.com/facebook-statistics/.*

Digital and social technologies link individuals with each other as well as with the brands and causes that matter most to them. As such, they have emerged as powerful information distribution ecosystems whose influence rivals that of the most powerful broadcast networks. In order to reach today's always-on consumers, marketers must understand and engage in this digital revolution.

To be certain, despite their prevalence, some observers see a darker side of the impact of digital and social technologies on individuals and society. Next, we consider the societal implications of the digital revolution.

Impact of Social Media on Individuals and Society Can you think of an acquaintance who can't ever seem to put down her phone, constantly text messaging or checking her Instagram account in the middle of a conversation? Or a friend who uses Google to look up trivial facts over an intimate meal or spends time tweeting during a movie or a live concert? Most of us can.

Sociologists and organizational scientists have expressed growing concern that use of smartphones and social media to verify information and virtual connections makes people *less social* in face-to-face settings. The effect of this phenomena can be very damaging to real-world personal and business relationships. One widely cited report suggests that the mere presence of a nearby mobile device (not even in use) can divert individuals from face-to-face exchanges and weaken interpersonal connections.[9] According to Julian Kabab, cofounder of FlashGap, a popular photo-sharing app, too much focus on looking at social media when people are out at events may be costing them in social interaction: "People miss out on parties because they want to see what's going on social networks, take beautiful selfies, and add filters to their pictures."[10]

As mentioned in the discussion of Maslow's hierarchy of needs in Chapter 4, humans are strongly motivated—even biologically driven—to seek out social connections and establish a sense of belonging. Given these instinctual drives, it would be

Smartphones, tablets, and other mobile computing devices are changing the world in a variety of ways, including how people access information, consume content, and interact with each other. *Ridofranz/iStock/Getty Images Plus/Getty Images*

fear of missing out (FOMO)

A feeling of isolation and concern about missing out on what is occurring in the world around us.

naïve to minimize the impact of digital and social technologies on interpersonal behaviors, relationships, and norms. But an always-on digital lifestyle can take a mental toll. Research has shown that when people shut off their attention to social networks, many begin to feel isolated and grow concerned over missing out on what is occurring in the world around them. People have termed this feeling **fear of missing out (FOMO)**. As more members of society increase social media usage, observers caution individuals' perceptions of reality can become skewed and affect their life satisfaction.[11]

Impact of the Digital Revolution on Marketing Practice In order to create value and strengthen brand relationships, brands must meet and interact with consumers where they spend time. Increasingly, that interaction occurs via a mobile device, involving a social networking platform, a mobile app, or website. It is important for students to understand—both as consumers and future managers—the many ways organizations employ these tools to enhance their value propositions and deepen customer relationships. Digital technologies have also changed customers' expectations of the brands they interact with, whether they are businesses, nonprofit organizations, or governmental institutions.

One way to discuss these changes would be to look *solely* at the creative ways in which companies are integrating social network platforms such as Facebook, Twitter, Instagram, Pinterest, YouTube, and TikTok into their marketing mix. However, to shoehorn these broad shifts into a discussion of new channels and platforms grossly understates the magnitude of this tectonic shift. Authors Charlene Li and Josh Bernioff describe these changes as a groundswell, "a social trend in which people use technologies to get things they need from each other, rather than from traditional institutions like corporations."[12] This ongoing wave of change continues to transform our society as well as the nature of marketing practice. Digital and social technologies are forcing all marketers to reassess, alter, and even, in some cases, forgo many tried-and-true ways of *thinking about* and *doing* marketing.

We next discuss some of the ways in which these ongoing trends are affecting how professional marketers think about and ply their craft.

Greater Emphasis on Owned and Earned Media Today, integrated marketing communications experts broadly categorize their media investments across three categories:

- *Paid media*—publicity gained through advertising, such as buying a 30-second Super Bowl commercial, taking out a billboard along a busy stretch of road, or sponsoring a local golf tournament.
- *Owned media*—publicity gained via a brand-controlled source, such as a website, blog, or Facebook page.
- *Earned media*—publicity gained through editorial influence or by grassroots actions, such as product reviews on *Consumer Reports,* online reviews via an online social source such as Yelp, unsolicited brand conversations on Twitter, or a viral YouTube video featuring a company's product or service.

In a two-way communication era, brands that do not seek to align and integrate elements of their paid, owned, and earned media are increasingly at a disadvantage.[13]

Brand Democratization During the mass-media era, a brand was—first and foremost—a way for companies to specify a set of differentiating attributes. For example, when Anheuser-Busch wanted Budweiser to be seen as a premium product, it started calling it the "King of Beers." After billions of dollars spent on advertising campaigns, the perception stuck.

Today, many experts see this type of company-controlled brand management as rapidly fading. Dan Lewis, chief public affairs officer at Molson Coors, suggests, "Brands don't belong to companies any more—they belong to the people who choose to buy them."[14] The process of defining, building, and maintaining a brand is now a collaborative one. Whether through Facebook, Twitter, Yelp, blogs,

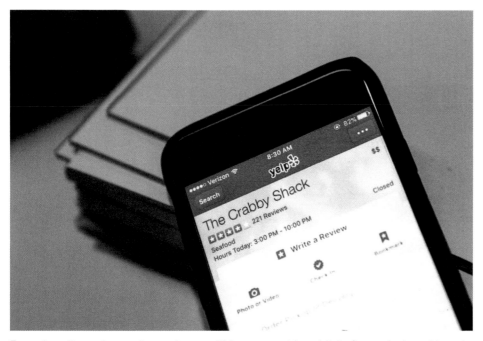

Earned media, such as online reviews on Yelp, can provide publicity for products and brands from ratings and comments supplied by consumers. Publicity from earned media can help future customers in their decision-making process. *Chris Goodney/Bloomberg/Getty Images*

The pace of cord-cutting of cable and satellite TV services is accelerating. In 2018, more than 33 million U.S. households have moved to streaming video-based TV services. *Ivan Marc/ Shutterstock*

product forums, or Pinterest, customers are sharing their experiences on platforms where audiences can readily find what others are saying about the brand—both positive and negative.

Relevant Messaging—Breaking through the Noise   The power of digital communications has lowered barriers to market entry in many market sectors. This shift has enabled many smaller, more nimble competitors to compete head-to-head with established brands. Thanks to digital distribution and promotions, a company can start in someone's bedroom and soon begin to eat into the market share of rivals listed on the New York Stock Exchange.

At the same time, the media landscape is changing. More and more households have "cut the cord," dropping pay cable and satellite TV in favor of Internet-based options like Hulu and Netflix. Popular new social media platforms seem to rise up every other year or so. In this fragmented media landscape, customer attention has become an increasingly scarce commodity. How do marketers break through the clutter to reach their audience?

Mc Graw Hill connect   Exercise **13-1**

Please complete the *Connect* exercise for Chapter 13 that focuses on digital marketing media investment categories. By exploring these categories, you should gain insight into the impact of digital technologies on consumers and marketing practices.

The answer is relevance. Simply having the most visible or creative branding is no longer enough. Consumers hold the power to tune in or tune out what messages they receive and where and when they want to receive them. To become the signal that consumers hear through the noise, marketers must thoughtfully produce messaging that is relevant to each individual consumer. In order to do so, marketers must:

1. Understand customers and provide them with content that is valuable—that is useful, informative, engaging, and entertaining.
2. Make content visible in places where customers spend their time.
3. Make sure that the message is delivered or accessible to the customer at the point in time when the consumer needs it most to make a purchase decision.

SEARCH MARKETING

In late 2005, news broke about Procter & Gamble's controversial strategy to increase the sophistication of its in-store marketing. These efforts included everything from more distinctive packaging to special in-store promotions and displays. Chairman and CEO A.G. Lafley suggested the companies efforts were based around P&G's brands winning "two moments of truth."[15]

- The *first moment of truth (FMOT)* is the short three-to-five second window after a shopper first encounters a product on a store shelf. In these few moments, marketers must appeal to shoppers' senses, values, and emotions.
- The *second moment of truth (SMOT)* is the actual experience a customer has with a product once he or she buys it and returns home.

In 2012, Google's Jim Lecinksi published an e-book titled *ZMOT: Winning the Zero Moment of Truth.* He describes the **zero moment of truth (ZMOT)** as "that moment when you grab your laptop, mobile phone, or some other wired device and start learning about a product or service (or potential boyfriend) you're thinking about trying or buying."[16] Figure 13.1 graphically illustrates the ZMOT concept.

LO 13-2

Explain how search marketing contributes to digital marketing strategy.

zero moment of truth (ZMOT)

The moment when a customer uses a digital device to begin learning about a potential purchase.

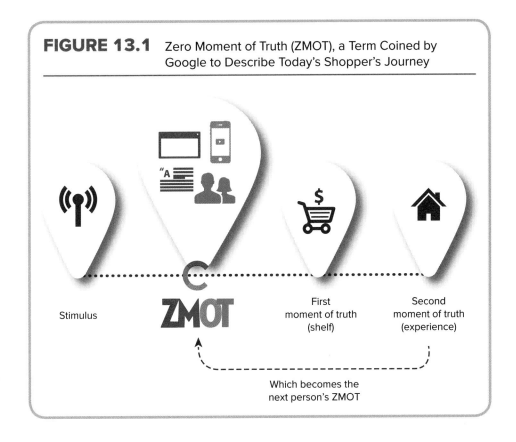

FIGURE 13.1 Zero Moment of Truth (ZMOT), a Term Coined by Google to Describe Today's Shopper's Journey

Stimulus

ZMOT

First moment of truth (shelf)

Second moment of truth (experience)

Which becomes the next person's ZMOT

While there is no denying the importance of the first and second moments of truth, consumers' newfound abilities to search for virtually anything at any time via the Internet has created new moments of decision before the consumer even gets to a store display case. What makes a zero moment of truth?

- It happens online—typically starting with a search on Google, Bing, Yahoo!, YouTube, or any other search engine.
- It happens in real time, any time of the day. More and more often, it happens on the go—even in the store itself—as consumers search from their smartphones.
- The consumer is in charge, pulling information they want rather than having it pushed at them by others.
- It is emotional. The consumer has a need they want to satisfy and an emotional investment in finding the best solution.

How do companies make sure their websites and other online content are part of that ZMOT experience? A big part of that answer is through search marketing techniques.

Search Marketing Techniques

search marketing

A form of Internet marketing that promotes websites by increasing their visibility in search engine results pages.

Search marketing involves techniques for generating greater online customer traffic from online search engines using both unpaid and paid efforts. It encompasses two closely related practices: *search engine optimization* and *search engine marketing*.

Search Engine Optimization

search engine optimization (SEO)

Adjusting or rewriting website content and site architecture to achieve a higher ranking in search engine results pages to enhance pay per click (PPC) listings.

Search engine optimization (SEO) is the process of getting more traffic based on higher rankings of free or "organic" search results on search engines. SEO targets various kinds of search, including image search, local search, video search, academic search, news search, and industry-specific search engines.[17] SEO tactics influence organic page rankings by influencing the relevance and popularity of web content. There are many aspects to SEO, from the words used on a web page to the way other sites link to a site from the web. SEO also takes into account whether a company's website is structured in a way that search engines understand. In addition, it is critical that online marketers continuously update their sites with new and interesting content. Websites and pages that remain stagnant signal to search engines that the content is likely to be less relevant to user searches.

Search Engine Marketing

search engine marketing (SEM)

The process of generating website traffic by purchasing advertisements on search engines.

In contrast, search engine marketing (SEM) is the process of generating website traffic by purchasing advertisements on search engines.[18] SEM uses **paid listings**—these are the purchased links that typically appear either at the very top or upper right of a search results page. Paid search spending in the United States is set to exceed $95 billion in 2022, accounting for roughly for 35 percent of spending for online advertisements.[19] Google AdWords is, by many measures, the most popular paid search platform used by search marketers. It is followed by Bing Ads, which also serves a significant portion of ads that appear on Yahoo!. After preparing a small ad to appear on either of these platforms, marketers choose search terms that will make an ad show up in the search results. With Google AdWords, the price-per-click for these search terms will vary based on demand. The marketer specifies a daily budget for the paid ad, and the ad is then ready to go live.

paid listings

Purchased links that typically appear either at the very top or upper right of a search results page.

Search Marketing Performance Is Key to Online Success

How important is search marketing to the success of companies' online initiatives? Consider the following facts:

- Ninety-three percent of online customer experiences begin with a search engine.[20]
- Click-through rates depend heavily on the link's position on the first page. Links from the first page of a Google results page obtain over 90 percent of clicks.[21]

- Studies have consistently shown that the first organic search result receives at least 30 percent of clicks. The first three organic search results get between 50 and 60 percent of clicks. That is, the difference between being the first and the second listing is much greater than that between the second and third listing, and so on.[22]

Google dominates the search market. Competing search engines include sites like Yahoo!, Bing, and DuckDuckGo. However, in 2018 Amazon surpassed Google in terms of total product searches. Nearly 90 percent of Amazon's product views came from the online retailer's own product search feature. "Amazon's dominance has really set it apart as the default place for product search, encroaching on Google's territory," said Deren Baker, CEO of digital market research firm Jumpshot, "They have started to leverage that strength with more sponsored placements, making billions on their product search even while their market share plateaus."[23]

Search marketing is an attractive area for marketing students and is a highly in-demand position. Successful search marketing specialists possess a rare blend of abilities. First, the position requires strong technical and analytical skills. Search professionals should be knowledgeable about current search algorithms and must routinely run tests to assess website ranking and keyword performance. Being able to interpret the statistics underlying search is crucial to making practical

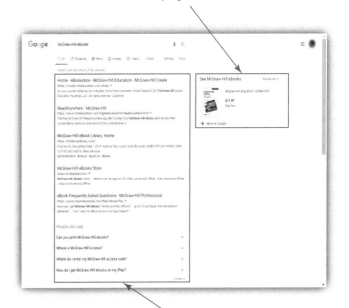

28% of the clicks   **Pay per click areas:** These results have been paid for by advertisers through Google's AdWords program.

72% of the clicks   These results are not paid for; they're the product of Google crawling the Web and processing what it finds.

Where People Click on Google Search Results Pages. Source: *Data from Fredrick Marckini's Search Engine Strategies 2008 Toronto keynote.*

design changes that enhance website and mobile app user experiences. Second, success in the position also requires "soft" people skills as well as strong communication ability. Being able to empathize with customers' needs and motives helps search managers to make real-world sense of the data. Strong oral presentation and writing skills are often useful to translate these findings into actionable managerial recommendations.[24]

Successful search marketing management requires, at minimum, a rudimentary understanding of (1) how search engines work and (2) why search engine performance is closely related to digital marketing success.

How Does Online Search Work?   Search engines have two major functions. The first is to build an index of all content on the web. The second is to provide users with a ranked list of websites that are most relevant to their search query.[25]

In order to create an index, search engines must first know what online content is available. Search engine companies use automated software programs, called *web crawlers,* to visit each page on the Internet—just as you or I would do, only very quickly. Sites and links that contain a larger amount of updated content are crawled more frequently than others and to a greater depth.[26] All of the data are stored in vast data centers with thousands of petabytes' worth of drives.

The second step is the part that you see as a user. When you perform an online search, your chosen search engine scours billions of pages, using specialized algorithms to determine the results most relevant websites and pages in relation to the entered search terms. In general, search engine algorithms assumes that the more popular a site or page is, the more valuable information it contains. So, regularly

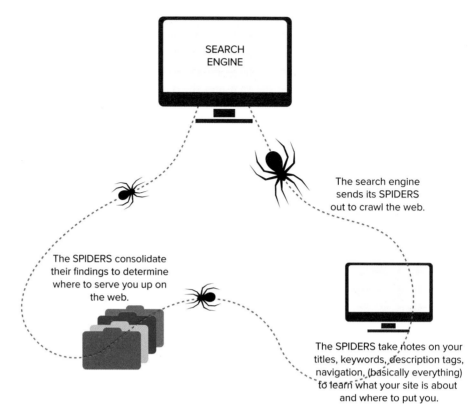

The search engine sends its SPIDERS out to crawl the web.

The SPIDERS consolidate their findings to determine where to serve you up on the web.

The SPIDERS take notes on your titles, keywords, description tags, navigation, (basically everything) to learn what your site is about and where to put you.

Search engines uses programs called *web crawlers* to continuously crawl the Internet and categorize website information. Source: *https://searchengineland.com/guide/what-is-seo*

FIGURE 13.2   Heat Map of a Google Search Results Page, Graphically Representing Data as Colors

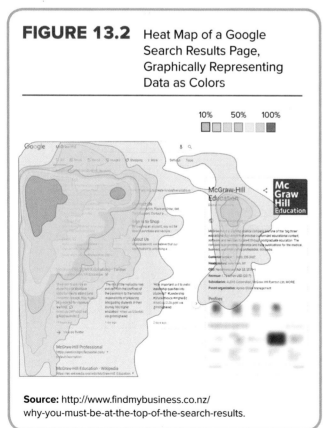

Source: http://www.findmybusiness.co.nz/why-you-must-be-at-the-top-of-the-search-results.

updating websites with new, engaging content is critical to search engine marketing success.

The Golden Triangle of a Search Results Page

Why do search results determine click-through success? It's due in large part to people's habits of visual attention. Figure 13.2 displays a heat map that shows the relative amount of visual attention devoted to search listings aggregated across dozens of study participants. The areas looked at most are shown in "hot" colors (red, orange, yellow), and the areas looked at the least are shown in "cold" colors (blue and gray). Experts refer to the top left part of the page as "the golden triangle." It is the area of the page where users read the title and the description of each search result, which eventually results in higher click-through rates. Getting a website listed within the golden triangle of any search result page is critical to increasing traffic to a site.

Using search marketing techniques, brands can increase the likelihood of appearing in the golden triangle. In general, the higher and more frequently a site appears in the results list, the more clicks it will receive.

Search Marketing Trends

Roughly two-thirds of organic online search activity is derived from a mobile device. Mobile search is a search engine querying technique that uses a wireless/mobile platform or handheld device with an Internet connection, such as a smartphone or tablet. Mobile search is typically location-specific with simplified data results, such as sports scores, versus a standard web search. Further, mobile search algorithms are evolving such that aspects like location have become more important.

A growing proportion of mobile search—roughly 40 percent—is voice-based search. Google has launched a mobile-friendly version of its search engine that accounts for voice clarity, lower bandwidth, and form factor limitations of mobile platforms. Google Voice Search is a function that allows users to search the Internet using Google through spoken voice commands rather than typing. Google Voice Search can be used on both desktop and mobile searches. In some instances, users must say a "wake" phrase (e.g., "OK, Google") or tapping the microphone icon to tell Google to begin analyzing what the user says next.

▇ connect Exercise **13-2**

Please complete the *Connect* exercise for Chapter 13 that focuses on search engine optimization and search engine marketing. By understanding the dynamics of both, you should gain insight into how to generate traffic to your organization's website and content.

SOCIAL MEDIA MARKETING

LO 13-3
Discuss how companies are employing social media marketing to strengthen customer relationships and achieve business objectives.

Social networks plays an increasingly important role in how consumers discover, research, and share information about brands. As a result, marketing organizations are devoting greater percentages of their resources to their social media marketing efforts. In the next section, we discuss some of the very creative ways marketers engage with customers across social networking channels.

Social Media Marketing Channels

What social media platforms are marketers using? Figure 13.3 displays data from a 2021 industry study that identified key social media marketing trends.[27] Some 96 percent of B2C marketing executives said their business uses Facebook as a marketing tool; about 89 percent of B2B respondents say the same. YouTube, Instagram, and Pinterest are more popular with B2C marketers. LinkedIn, Twitter, Google+, and SlideShare are more popular with B2B marketers.

Rising Use of Niche Social Platforms

Social media evolves rapidly. A handful of social media channels—Facebook, Twitter, Instagram, Pinterest, and LinkedIn—have consistently dominated advertising and marketing spending. However, the explosive growth of TikTok in 2019 and 2020 has ignited greater interest in how to use niche social platforms to strategically reach new audiences. Emerging channels such as TikTok, Twitch, and Houseparty provide brands with opportunities to tap into fresh segments in creative new ways.

Donielle Xu

Executive Perspective . . .
because everyone is a marketer

Donielle Xu
Data Center Solution Principal
Dell EMC

What is a way that social media is impacting marketing that people might not think of?

Beyond all of the consumer and branding strategy we typically think about, social media is a powerful tool for gathering information about what competitors are doing. It provides real-time feedback and what is working for competitors across different social media channels. Today, marketers for even very small businesses can find out a great deal about their competitors and why customers like or dislike them from social media.

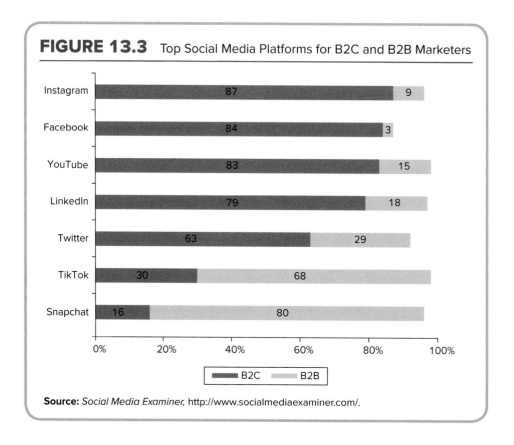

FIGURE 13.3 Top Social Media Platforms for B2C and B2B Marketers

Platform	B2C	B2B
Instagram	87	9
Facebook	84	3
YouTube	83	15
LinkedIn	79	18
Twitter	63	29
TikTok	30	68
Snapchat	16	80

Source: *Social Media Examiner,* http://www.socialmediaexaminer.com/.

Successfully diversifying across these "SoMe" channels requires brands to take the time to understand differences between the platforms and their respective audiences, then tailoring brand tone and tactics to match. While this extra time and effort may not seem worthwhile, getting on the ground floor of a new platform makes it easier to break through to an audience. There is typically less noise from messaging by other brands and little to no direct competition from rivals. Advertising on these emerging platforms is typically much less expensive than the more established social media sites. Early research on TikTok indicates that its users have more positive attitudes toward ads compared to other platforms.

Social Media Marketing Strategy

How can marketers use social media to achieve business-related goals? Generally speaking, nearly all social media marketing strategies and tactics can be grouped according to one of three main purposes:

1. Increase brand visibility.
2. Grow customer engagement and brand advocacy.
3. Improve customer responsiveness and retention.

Next, we briefly discuss each social media marketing strategy component, providing relevant examples of brands that are succeeding in using these tools to reach new customers, strengthen customer relationships, and grow brand loyalty.

Using Social Media to Increase Brand Visibility   More than half the people in the world today are using social media.[28] It follows that the need for companies to create a social presence for their brands has become essential. Social media is a great medium for distributing content and connecting with a wide

Firms like Starbucks are increasingly rewarding customers who connect and interact with the brand on social media as part of its loyalty program. *BestStockFoto/Shutterstock*

potential audience. In addition, all social media platforms come with features that enable brands and users to create engaging content and build strong brand communities. Traditional methods for building brand awareness, like advertising, come with comparatively much higher costs and lower ROI. Moreover, sharing information about products and services on social media presents a great opportunity for brands to reach purchase-ready customers.

In recent years, savvy brands have started to invest in influencer marketing to drive awareness. A **social media influencer** is someone who has built a loyal following through their online content creation. Influencer marketing involves collaborating (typically on a paid basis) with the content creator to promote the brand. Ideally, the influencer has a base of followers that is representative of one of the brand's key target markets. Because influencers already have a built-in audience that considers them experts within their niche area, influencer campaigns create awareness and lend credibility to the sponsor brand.

social media influencer
Someone who has built a loyal following through their online content creation.

Blenders Eyewear—Using Social Media to Build a Brand "from the Sand Up" Social media marketing has been instrumental in helping Blenders Eyewear transform from being just a couple of guys selling sunglasses out of their backpacks to a seven-figure business with hundreds of thousands of followers. A huge part of Blenders growth is due to Instagram. From its early days, Blenders focused on building relationships with professional photographers. It frequented InstaMeets, which are events where photographers and creators from Instagram meet up and take photos and network. According to Blenders cofounder Chase Fisher:

> I would show up in Ocean Beach and I would bounce around San Diego and just meet new photographers and bring a box of sunglasses. Just say, "Hey guys, I'm Chase. I've got a sunglass company. I follow all you guys already. Your photos are amazing. I would love to give you guys awesome pairs to photograph. If you guys would be so kind, send them to my email and I would love to share them and post about them on Instagram too."[29]

Blenders Eyewear blends reviews and star ratings into its ads using Facebook's Dynamic Product Ads format. *Blenders Eyewear*

So instead of strictly trying to get high-priced influencers to work with the company, Blenders builds relationships with photographers by sponsoring InstaMeets and offering free products. In addition to the photographers, Blenders also has plenty of satisfied customers who post photos on Instagram with the branded #blenderseyewear hashtag included in their bio. The hashtag has been used in over 60,000 posts, so it's clear the brand has built up a very engaged audience.

Growing Customer Engagement via Social Media Marketing

Thanks to social media, personalized interactions between brands and consumers are fast becoming the new normal in the online world. Social interaction begins with establishing and maintaining a strong social presence. Inbound marketing firm HubSpot asked nearly 600 consumers what kind of social media presence they expect of any brand. Consumers reported that they expect brands to be active on at least three to four social channels. Figure 13.4 details results from the study with respect to preferred social channels. There was some generational variation in social media usage and preferences. While use of Facebook by younger users is declining, the research almost universally suggests that a Facebook presence remains a must. Consumer expectations for Twitter presence were about 10 points lower. They were lower still for Instagram, LinkedIn, Pinterest, YouTube, and Google+.[30]

If consumers expect a brand to be active on Facebook and possibly two or three other social channels, the next question is, "What do they want from companies there?" A good way to determine this is to examine which companies have the most loyal social media following. One study examined posts by some of the brands with the most loyal followings on Facebook.[31] Typical posts from these brands included:

- Costco (1.2 million fans): Deals on items consumers need.
- Ziploc (1.5 million fans): Holiday cake recipes like cakes encrusted with peppermint stick crushed in Ziploc bags.
- St. Jude Children's Research Hospital (1.7 million fans): Photos of children recovering from cancer.
- Reese's Candy (12 million fans): Information about peanuts and dessert ideas incorporating Reese's Cups and Reese's Pieces.

Marketing professionals from these organizations understand the impact of social media in establishing a unique brand identity and building social connections with consumers. Customers don't go to social media to buy. In fact, they tend to respond negatively to blatant sales attempts. By interacting with consumers in a fun, helpful, and interesting manner, social media can help build a successful brand by:

- Allowing the firm or brand to develop deeper relationships with customers.
- Generating positive word-of-mouth communication about the brand.

Let's take a deeper look at a few brands that are succeeding in their use of social media marketing.

LEGO Ideas—Using Social Media to Strengthen Fan Engagement

LEGO is a brand that is synonymous with play. In fact, its name is derived from the Danish words for "play well"—*leg godt.* But did you know that LEGO has been recognized as one of the world's most powerful brands?[32]

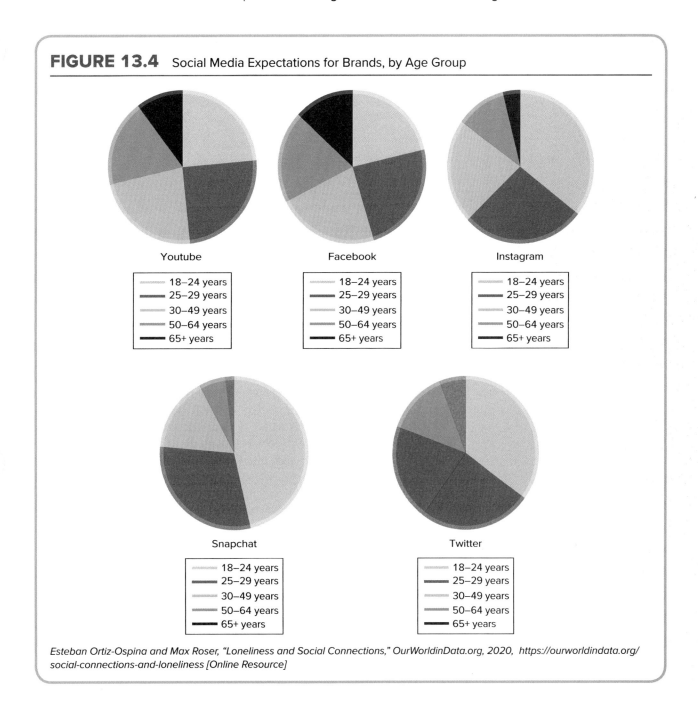

FIGURE 13.4   Social Media Expectations for Brands, by Age Group

Youtube
- 18–24 years
- 25–29 years
- 30–49 years
- 50–64 years
- 65+ years

Facebook
- 18–24 years
- 25–29 years
- 30–49 years
- 50–64 years
- 65+ years

Instagram
- 18–24 years
- 25–29 years
- 30–49 years
- 50–64 years
- 65+ years

Snapchat
- 18–24 years
- 25–29 years
- 30–49 years
- 50–64 years
- 65+ years

Twitter
- 18–24 years
- 25–29 years
- 30–49 years
- 50–64 years
- 65+ years

Esteban Ortiz-Ospina and Max Roser, "Loneliness and Social Connections," OurWorldinData.org, 2020, https://ourworldindata.org/social-connections-and-loneliness [Online Resource]

Social media marketing is a key element to the brand's success. According to Lar Silberbauer, senior global director of marketing at LEGO Group, "Connecting with fans on social platforms isn't about the 'hard sell.' It's very important to understand that even though we often refer to them as 'channels,' they are still platforms for engagement and creation. Any company that fails to understand this, will struggle to leverage the full potential of digital media."[33] Perhaps the greatest testament to the brand's social commitment is its embrace of *user-generated content*. For instance, at its LEGO Ideas website, makers can submit ideas for LEGO products to be turned into potential sets available commercially, with the original designer receiving 1 percent of the royalties. This involvement in product development is just one part of brand activity that gives ownership of LEGO to its fans.

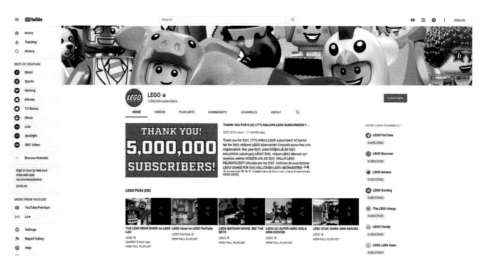

LEGO *is represented across most social media channels, reaching 50 million consumers in total each month.* LEGO

The key social media channel for LEGO is YouTube, where it reaches more than 30 million unique users monthly. Silberbauer highlights videos made by LEGO designers as a key example of its success on this channel. One designer video for its *Star Wars Millennium Falcon* model gathered more than 250,000 views; another for its Downtown Diner model clocked more than half a million. According to Silberbauer, "The LEGO designers are the rock stars of the company, and for us it was important to show how they work and the thought that goes into the creation of a LEGO set. We might have great ideas and great designers, but when we look to the millions of LEGO fans, there are always amazing ideas that we would never have thought of that we can then hopefully bring to the market and help showcase."[34]

Social Listening and Customer Care

It is not uncommon for some organizations and marketers to express fear over losing the ability to control brand conversations in the online environment. However, these conversations are already happening without the brand anyway—over breakfast tables and office water coolers, if not online.

With the social web, brands have the opportunity to "listen in" and even participate in those discussions. **Social media monitoring**, also known as *social listening,* is the process of identifying and assessing what is being said about a company, individual, product, or brand on the Internet. Many firms today are investing customer-support resources into programs that monitor social media. They seek to respond *before* complaints damage online reputations. Digital business guru Brian Solis suggests that the cost of reacting to experiences is far greater than the cost of proactively creating and defining those experiences from the onset:

> [Customer] experience is everything. . . . Businesses must invest in defining not only a positive experience, but also a wonderfully shareable experience. Doing so influences others to join the fray while offsetting negative inquiries and the damaging viral effects of shared negative experiences.[35]

For many customers, social media has become the *preferred* channel to engage with brands on customer service issues. Questions and complaints posted from customers on social media sites allow companies to make personal connections and potentially resolve problems faster than otherwise possible. However, social media has also raised customer expectations about how quickly their problems should be resolved. Some

social media monitoring (social listening)

The process of identifying and assessing what is being said about a company, individual, product, or brand on the Internet.

well-known brands have met the challenge of rising customer expectations and truly excel in their use of social
platform for their customer service efforts.

Netflix—Growing Customer Retention through Social Listening
Netflix's social customer service is
known for exhibiting the same charisma and wit that
characterizes the brand. As an entertainment company,
its social customer care team is trained to deliver great
service while maintaining the company's friendly, casual
tone.[36]

Businesses who invest resources into providing more
responsive social customer care can reap higher brand loyalty, reduced customer churn, stronger word of mouth,
and greater profits. For instance, one recent study found
customers who received a satisfactory brand response on
Twitter were willing to spend up to 20 percent more and were 30 percent more likely to
recommend the brand.[37]

Netflix

Mc Graw Hill connect Exercise **13-3**

Social Media in Action

In 2015 Lancôme introduced Lancôme Elite Rewards, one of the first
loyalty programs in the discount-averse luxury cosmetics category.
Customers can join Elite Rewards at no charge. They can begin to
rack up points not only by buying products but also by connecting
and interacting with Lancôme USA through social media.

In fact, consumers get more points for social media than for
shopping. For example:

- Lancôme Elite Rewards members earn 10 points per dollar spent.
- They earn up to 25 points for sharing products on Facebook,
  Instagram, and Twitter.
- They can earn up to 50 points when they connect with the
  brand on Facebook, Instagram, Twitter, and Foursquare.

Program members also accrue points when they watch makeup
tutorials on Lancome.com or check in at events via Foursquare. Each
member gets an online dashboard on Lancôme's U.S. website to track
and manage points. Members can redeem their points for full or trial
sizes of 100 selected Lancôme products, for beauty consultations
and treatments, and for access to events like New York Fashion Week.

In designing the program, the L'Oréal-owned brand carefully analyzed seven years of customer data to determine the long-term financial value of interactions at every customer touch point. According to
Alessio Rossi, vice president of Lancôme digital marketing, the program's aims are to increase new customer acquisition and improve
retention: "We didn't want to just throw another promotion or discount.
Instead, it's a bi-directional communications channel with consumers
to understand them better, collect information about how they go
through the decision-making journey, providing more insights so
ultimately we can provide an even more personalized experience."[38]

The Social Media in Action Connect *Exercise in Chapter 13 will let you develop a social media strategy to improve the effectiveness and engagement of an organization's loyalty program. By understanding how social media marketing can increase acquisition and improve retention, you will be able to use these tools to maximize the benefits of loyalty programs.*

LO 13-4

Explain the importance of content marketing in driving digital marketing strategies.

content marketing

A marketing approach focused on creating and distributing valuable, relevant, and consistent content to attract and retain a clearly defined and profitable audience.

CONTENT MARKETING

Content is the life blood of the social web. The success of any website, search marketing, or social media marketing campaign depends on the creation and management of useful and interesting digital content. **Content marketing** is a marketing approach focused on creating and distributing valuable, relevant, and consistent content to attract and retain a clearly defined and profitable audience.[39]

The essence of content marketing is the belief that if businesses deliver valuable information to buyers, customers will reward them with their business and loyalty. It focuses on delivering useful and relevant information that makes an interested buyer more intelligent, rather than wasting resources pitching goods or services to prospects with limited interest in the offering. Today, companies large and small, including many of the most highly regarded marketing organizations in the world, such as P&G, Microsoft, Cisco Systems, and John Deere, use content marketing. Content marketing can deliver powerful benefits:

- Search engines reward businesses that consistently publish quality content; search results pages are typically more relevant and popular with search users. Better search results should generate greater website traffic and interest in an organization's market offerings.
- By coupling useful content with a social media strategy, organizations and individuals are able to establish a reputation of expertise within their industries. Ultimately, the added credibility drives inbound traffic and sales leads.

Content Marketing Source and Techniques

Successful content marketing is not simply about how much content a business can produce and distribute by itself. Companies can and should use other existing sources of content. Examples are the press coverage a brand receives from public relations efforts or the user-generated content voluntarily contributed by satisfied customers. Content marketing categories can generally be broken into three types:

user-generated content

Content created by a brand's fans and followers.

- **User-generated content**: Content created by a brand's fans and followers; it is earned content. It communicates a brand's value in users' words rather than the company's or those of a neutral party (like a journalist). User-generated content can include reviews from users (like product reviews on Amazon.com) and other customer-contributed content (like posts on social media).
- **Branded content:** Any content developed and owned by the brand. This can include blog posts, white papers, research reports, infographics, or any other content that a brand produces for itself.
- **Expert content:** Credible, third-party articles and reviews from unbiased journalists. This is the earned media that is often the result of PR efforts.

Research conducted by the Content Marketing Institute recently investigated the impact of different content types at various stages of the consumer decision-making process.[40] Product categories included automotive, home appliances, insurance, video games, electronic toothbrushes, and more. Overall, the impact of expert content was most consistent across stages and categories. But study findings also suggest that each of the three types of content plays a role in the consumer's decision-making process. Moreover, the data show there is an optimal order to follow in content marketing:

1. A baseline of trust is critical to your brand's success with consumers. The quickest route to building a solid foundation of trust is to *lead with credible expert content.*
2. Once trust is established, you need to maintain that trust while also empowering consumers with additional information. That information comes via user-generated and branded content. Both content types help educate customers, enabling them to make better informed decisions.

Types of Branded Content
Next, we briefly introduce several of the most common forms of branded content used by B2C and B2B marketers.

Blog A **blog** (short for *web log*) is an online journal in which people or companies post their thoughts and other content. Blogs are usually related to narrowly defined topics. There are more than 31 million blogs in the United States today. Many bloggers use social networks like Twitter and Facebook to promote their content.

blog
An online journal in which people or companies post their thoughts and other content.

White Paper A **white paper** is a concise yet authoritative report or guide that seeks to inform readers about a complex issue. It is meant to help readers understand an issue, solve a problem, or make a decision.

white paper
A concise yet authoritative report or guide that seeks to inform readers about a complex issue and presents the issuing body's philosophy on the matter.

E-Mail Marketing **E-mail marketing** lets marketers send highly targeted, personalized, relationship-building e-mail messages. To address concerns relating to unsolicited *spam* e-mail messages, most legitimate marketers now practice permission-based e-mail marketing. They send product information only to customers who "opt-in," and they make it easy to "unsubscribe" if the recipient tires of the e-mail relationship.

e-mail marketing
Highly targeted, personalized, relationship-building e-mail messages.

Webinars Webinars are especially effective for B2B companies because 66 percent of B2B buyers prefer to watch a webinar *before* buying a product.[41] Great content is the backbone of webinar success. In order to create and deliver compelling webinar content, marketers must begin with a strong understanding of the target audience and how their brand addresses their identified needs. Increasingly, marketers are using outside vendors and tools to automate much of the administrative tasks involved with scheduling and promoting webinars. As long as the content remains relevant, companies can continue to attract prospects by offering the recorded content on an on-demand basis.

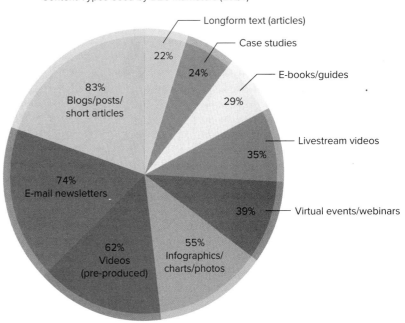

Content Types Used by B2C Marketers (2021)

Content types most frequently used by B2C marketers
Source: B2C Content Marketing Benchmarks, Insights for 2021.

Virtual Trade Shows Trade shows have long been an important way for companies to connect with customers.

However, during the course of the pandemic, most live trade shows and industry events were postponed or cancelled. Even in the post-pandemic world, most exhibit managers believe there will be lower trade show attendance and fewer events.[42]

Undeterred, many B2B organizations today have started hosting and participating in virtual trade shows and conferences. Virtual trade shows offer several unique advantages over traditional, in-person events, including:

- Access to larger audiences.
- Less expensive for vendors and customers.
- Improved ability to educate your prospective customers.
- Software tools that help vendors monitor contacts and content engagement.

video marketing

The posting of digital video content on brand websites or social media sites such as YouTube, Facebook, and others.

Video Marketing For years, video has been steadily rising as the dominant form of online content. As a result, video has become an integral piece to content marketing strategies at many B2B and B2C organizations. **Video marketing** involves posting digital video content on brand websites or social media sites such as YouTube, Facebook, Rumble, and others. Shoppers find visual content particularly helpful for informing decisions. To wit, research has found videos are up to 50 times more likely to receive an organic first-page ranking than traditional text pages.[43]

Video content used by marketers comes in many shapes and sizes. For instance, many marketers utilize both pre-recorded video as well as live streaming video content. Innovative realtors are now utilizing drone footage and 360-degree video formats when showcasing homes online. Recent neuromarketing research shows that animated videos are particularly effective in "hijacking" consumers' attention systems and help make content more memorable.[44]

Another trend is the use of "story" videos. Rather than post dry content about their products and services in their newsfeeds, many brands have popularized the use of stories as a more authentic way to resonate with audiences. While the stories do not necessarily require high production value, they do place a premium on creativity and innovation in storytelling. Often, story videos are short-form, an acknowledgment of the drop-off in video engagement beyond the two-minute mark.

Although a product may be highly technical, you can still write and create content that connects with your audience on a popular level. *Maxsattana/Getty Images*

Trends in Content Marketing

Marketers strive to differentiate themselves if possible through the quality and creativeness of their branded content. With the growing use of content marketing, a simple 500-word blog post with stock photos and a call to action is unlikely to stand out from the crowd.

Over the past few years, infographics have become a trendy way to share information about goods and services. *Infographics* are highly sharable, catchy to the eye, and more fun to read than a generic blog post. With more companies using infographics, the competition to stand out continues to increase.

Live Streaming   One new branded content approach that is catching on with content creators and audiences is *live streaming*—broadcasting real-time, live video footage or video feed to an audience accessing the video stream over the Internet. Live streaming does not require a huge investment in video production capabilities. In fact, many companies offer live streaming audio and video applications that can be launched from a smartphone.

Live streaming offers several unique advantages. As opposed to podcasting, it is real time, giving content the urgency of watching or listening now. A live video strategy engages viewers in an authentic way that is difficult to match using other social media formats. Another benefit is that it allows viewers to be involved, enabling users to participate and share with the tap of a tweet.[45]

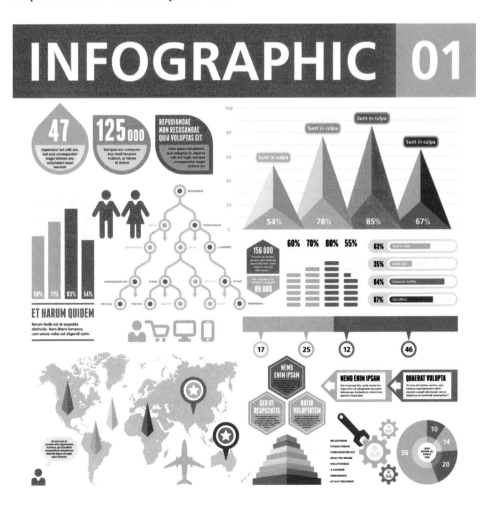

This infographic details the use of infographics as a way of distributing information. *Sergey Korkin/Shutterstock*

Smithsonian ✓
@smithsonian

☼ Louis Armstrong's trumpet at @NMAAHC. He was one of the 1st to record improvised jazz solos s.si.edu/1fb4Ypc

RETWEETS   LIKES
127   190

10:35 AM - 17 Jul 2015

Smithsonian

location-based marketing (LBM)

The use of GPS data transmitted from a mobile device to adapt content, messaging, or service delivery to a target's location.

Mobile applications by popular ride-sharing services, such as Uber and Lyft, have created great customer experiences by successfully integrating location-based technology with an intuitive user interface. *Thomas Hatherway/Alamy Stock Photo*

Ephemeral Content

The ephemeral (or disappearing) content format, which went mainstream with the Snapchat app, has become a fixture across multiple platforms. By design, ephemeral content is fast-paced and fleeting, offering more opportunities to interact with followers. Regardless of form, the content often tends to be scrappier and more down-to-earth, which enhances perceptions of brand authenticity. Another component that contributes to the success of ephemeral content is the previously discussed FOMO (fear of missing out). Since the content will eventually disappear, users are more likely to tune in and take action.

Emoji Marketing

In some instances, creating effective brand content and communications may not even require the use of words. According to data gathered by marketing agency Deep Focus, 4 out of every 10 Millennials would rather engage with pictures than read.[46] Most prominent among this shift to pictorial communication is the *emoji,* a small digital image or icon used to express an idea or emotion in digital communication.

Because Millennials are such an important demographic to reach, brands have been trying to capitalize on the emoji craze. For instance, on World Emoji Day, the Smithsonian Institute tweeted an emoji that corresponded to a particular piece in its museum along with a link to more information. An emoji trumpet, for instance, brought visitors to facts about Louis Armstrong's trumpet. Pizza maker Domino's Pizza co-opted the pizza emoji, turning it into a food-ordering mechanism for registered customers. Domino's attracted new customers with this novel campaign and reduced the time it takes to order a pizza to five seconds.

Location-Based Marketing: Adding Relevance to Content

Factoring location into marketing campaigns is an established practice. For example, marketers have for many years targeted people at the community level using media like a local newspaper. Mobile technologies are now making such information more precise and readily available in real time. Today, marketers can create targeted ads that are accurate to within a few feet in places such as the aisle of a grocery store or the shoe section of a department store.[47]

Brands, retailers, and advertising agencies use **location-based marketing (LBM)** to adapt content, messaging, or service delivery to a target's location, using GPS data transmitted from an individual's mobile device. Advances in technology have made this method accessible to organizations and marketers with budgets of all sizes. For instance, the owner of your favorite Indian buffet down the street may register for free with Google Maps, a GPS application used on smartphones. The restaurant then comes up on the Google Maps application when you look for directions or search for a restaurant in the area.[48]

Many location-based marketing campaigns incorporate the use of location-based services. A *location-based service* is a social, entertainment, or information service that allows a company to reach and engage with its audience using tools and platforms that capture the geographic location of the audience. The delivery mechanisms used for location-based services include mobile applications, short message service (SMS) text messaging, and even in-store digital signage. There are several really interesting examples of marketers using this technology to enhance their customers' experiences.

DIGITAL AND SOCIAL MEDIA MARKETING METRICS

Within top corporate strategy circles, the marketing function has historically suffered from a crisis of credibility. Many traditional marketing objectives and the corresponding key performance indicators (KPIs) used to track marketing performance, such as customer satisfaction and brand attitudes, are considered "soft." That is, they are either not directly observable and easily measured or aren't clearly linked to financial performance outcomes. As a result, chief marketing officers have often struggled to demonstrate the return on marketing investments.

The emergence of digital and social media marketing is changing this perspective. Marketing managers today are able to use web and social media analytics tools to create marketing **dashboards** that track consumer response to their campaigns. By integrating these tools with data from advanced CRM systems, marketers are better positioned to quantify the financial impact of their strategies. Next we briefly review some of the most commonly tracked digital and social media marketing metrics.

Digital Marketing Metrics

Digital marketing metrics are measurable values that marketing managers can use to track the performance of their digital marketing efforts. In reviewing these metrics, we break these KPIs into three groups: search performance, website analytics, and content performance.

Search Performance Consistently tracking SEO and SEM performance over time enables digital marketing managers to adapt their keyword strategies and make meaningful modifications to website design. Business that do not track their search performance over time are also vulnerable to updates in search engine algorithms or changes in competitors' strategies. Here are several important search performance metrics.[49]

- **Search engine rankings.** It makes sense that the higher your site ranks on search engines, the better. This crucial KPI ties in directly with the digital marketing team's SEO efforts. The higher your website or content appear in the search rankings, the more traffic, leads, and conversions your brand is likely to get. Search engine providers modify their algorithms on a regular basis. Of course, rival brands are likewise seeking to improve their ranking performance. By continuously monitoring search rankings, digital marketers can quickly identify and address issues with their digital strategies.
- **Organic traffic.** This is the number of visits to your website by someone who has found your site using a search engine. This reflects the effectiveness of the company's content and SEO efforts. It's irrelevant how good your content is if no one sees it. Looking at organic traffic is a great place to start to measure the performance of digital marketing campaigns.
- **Cost-per-click (CPC).** For paid search campaigns, it is important to track how much it costs for each click. This cost will depend on how much your competitors are bidding for a particular keyword or audience.

LO 13-5

Discuss key performance indicators commonly utilized in managing digital and social media marketing campaigns.

dashboard

A digital tool that provides data visualizations that enable marketing managers to assess performance over time across a range of relevant KPIs.

- **Traffic sources.** First visit metrics track how people are finding your website (e.g., via organic search, paid ad, or social media). In addition to search and social media traffic, many e-commerce brands also engage in *affiliate marketing,* whereby partners receive a portion of revenue that is generated from redirected traffic referred from their site. Identifying which sources attract the most traffic can help the digital marketing team improve overall performance and optimize digital marketing budgets.

Website Analytics

Website analytics is the analysis, collection, measurement, and reporting of Internet-generated user data for the purpose of understanding and optimizing web content and usage.[50] This includes simple statistics, such as the number of visitors to a website in a given week. But this category also includes more nuanced details that can help to clarify underlying trends in online customer behaviors.

- **Site speed.** How annoying is it when you land on a website or open a mobile app and it takes forever for it to load? If you are like most people, chances are you will close the app or try and find what you are looking for on a different site. Slow performance in the digital world places the brand at risk of losing customers. Test the website speed of your favorite (or least favorite) sites yourself for free using webpagetest.org. Mobile app performance can likewise be tested using resources like speedtest.net.
- **Bounce rate.** Bounce rate is the percentage of website visitors that exit a site after viewing just a single page. This helps digital marketers determine if the website design makes it easy for users to find the information they are looking for. A low bounce rate often correlates with a higher average time on site and a higher number of pages viewed per session.
- **Engagement.** Engagement is typically assessed based on average time on site or pages per visit. Once a threshold value has been defined (e.g., visited more than three pages), new visitors can be categorized as engaged or not engaged. By assessing engagement levels and other behaviors (including purchases) across traffic sources, marketers can understand which traffic sources are driving the most valuable traffic.
- **Lead conversion rate.** This metrics tells you how many of your website visitors convert to sales leads. This indicator is useful because it tells you the quality of your website traffic. It is possible to be fooled by the growing popularity of your website, even when it is having no financial impact. By tracking how many visitors turn into actual sales leads, digital marketers can more meaningfully quantify the impact of their efforts.

    The following is an example of how to calculate a website's lead conversion rate:

    100,000 Website Visitors ÷ 5,000 leads = 5% conversion

- **Returning Visitors.** By using web cookies, marketers can track return visitors. This allows digital marketers to determine the effectiveness of the website design and content with respect to establishing and growing an online audience.

Content Performance

Successful content marketing campaigns quite often depend on an iterative A/B testing approach, comparing various strategies against each other across a variety of performance indicators. While not an exhaustive list, here are a few of the metrics that are most commonly referenced.[51]

- **Open rate.** One of the simplest and most universally used metrics by e-mail marketers, open rate calculates the percentage of individual recipients who will open an e-mail message. For a opt-in e-mail list, this can offer insight into how engaged and interested subscribers are as well as how effective different e-mail subject lines can be. This can be particularly useful when testing different subject lines and running A/B tests.

- **Click-through rate (CTR).** CTR is another common metric to determine how well an e-mail marketing campaign is performing. This measures how many recipients have clicked on the links within your email. CTRs are typically lower than open rates, with an average CTR just above 2 percent.
- **Unsubscribe rate.** Most e-mail marketing platforms will tell you how many list members have unsubscribed (i.e., opted out) from your list upon receiving your e-mail. Users should be given the option to opt out of e-mails completely or update their e-mail preferences in relation to frequency and the content they are happy to receive.
- **Content downloads.** Keeping track of the number of times a piece of content is downloaded from a website or social media platform offers insights into the topics your audiences find most relevant. This information can help shape content strategy moving forward. Downloads are also a great tool to collect prospect's information, which can be used for subsequent outbound marketing efforts.

Social Media Marketing Metrics

Marketers track social media activity to help improve their marketing efforts. There are literally hundreds of different metrics that can be derived from social media–related sources. Some are more widely used than others. Table 13.1 provides a list of metrics commonly found on the dashboards of digital marketing analysts and managers. We'll discuss several of the most important social media metrics in greater detail next.

- **Brand reach.** Tracking the brand reach (i.e., the number of social media followers) across each channel can help digital marketers better understand the number and types of people who are viewing and interacting with social content. By tracking follower growth across time, marketers can also get a sense of the brand's momentum as well as assess how well brand messaging is resonating with users.
- **Brand mentions.** Are people talking about your brand? Another common metric—and one of the easiest to measure—is the volume of brand mentions. People tend to talk about things they either love or hate, but rarely do they talk about things they simply don't care about at all. So, volume of mentions is a great initial indicator of interest. Moreover, tracking the number of people talking about your brand over time and matching that to marketing actions can provide useful insights to managers.

    Google Alerts allows managers to set up notifications for instances in which a brand is mentioned online. On many social platforms, branded hashtags are commonly used, which allow marketers to easily determine how often a campaign is mentioned in online conversations. Facebook Insights offers a useful KPI called "People Talking about This." This metric assesses how many unique people have posted something to their walls about a given brand page.
- **Share of voice.** Determining share of voice helps marketers evaluate how conversations about their brand compare with conversations about its competitors. This might include determining what percentage of the overall conversation about brands within an industry is focused on one brand compared with its main competitors. Since so many social media conversations (and data) are public, you can measure your competitors' impact just as easily as you can measure your own.
- **Brand engagement.** Engagement is one of the most important areas to measure in social media. In most social media settings, content can be both shared and replied to. Engagement metrics aim to provide answers to questions such as:

TABLE 13.1   Key Social Media Marketing Metrics

Metric Type	Description
Reach Metrics	
Audience (or impressions)	Total number of people (e.g., fans, followers, etc.) within a brand's various networks.
Audience growth rate	Rate at which a brand adds (or loses) audience members across its social media networks.
Influence	Influence scores (offered by providers like Klout) measure a person's or brand's influence on a particular channel.
Volume	Overall number of online brand mentions per period.
Share of voice	Percentage of a brand's portion of the conversation on social media compared with others in its space.
Sentiment	Percentage of overall brand mentions that are positive, negative, or neutral in sentiment.
Engagement Metrics	
Average engagement rate	Percentage of audience that has engaged with a brand's content on a given social channel per reporting period.
Conversation rate	Number of conversations (e.g., comments, replies) going on about the brand per social media post.
Amplification rate	Number of shares, retweets, re-pins, etc. on average for each post.
Applause rate	Number of approval actions (e.g., likes, thumbs-ups, favorites) per post.
Virality	Rate at which a piece of content spreads across the social web—for instance, by measuring total shares per piece of content per day.
Acquisition Metrics	
Traffic ratio(s)	Percentage of visitors who reach your site based on various measures: • Directly typing a URL into their browser (direct visitors). • Creating a search query (search visitors). • Using a link from another blog or site (referral visitors). • Using social media (social media visitors).
Click-through (CT) rate	Percentage of audience members who click on a post.
Bounce rate	Percentage of visitors who went only to a single page of your site, bouncing back to the place they came from rather than clicking further into the site.
Conversion Metrics	
Conversion rate	Percentage of audience members or website visitors who take a desired action.
Social media conversion rate	Percentage of total conversions attributable to social media, found by dividing social media conversions by total conversions.
Cost per conversion	Dollar amount of how much a brand pays in order to obtain a single conversion.
Retention Metrics	
Churn rate	A measure of the number of audience members who leave over a specific period of time divided by the average number of audience members over that same time span.
Brand advocacy	Number (or percentage) of visitors (or social media mentions) who reflect brand advocacy.

Ross Hornish

SEO Manager
ServiceMaster

Describe your job. I am the SEO manager for all ServiceMaster brands including Terminix, American Home Shield, ServiceMaster Clean & Restore, Merry Maids, AmeriSpec, Furniture Medic, and the all-encompassing parent brand of ServiceMaster. To save some of you from a trip to a Google search bar, *SEO* stands for *search engine optimization*—but believe me, usually I want you to go to Google. My job is to position my brands as close as possible to the top of any searches you do in a digital environment. Search has evolved to be much more than just Google, so my job has evolved to include social search, voice search, and personal assistants, to name a few.

Ross Hornish

but to get to the position where you make the decisions, you have to know how the whole ecosystem works. That's where cross-training comes in. Throughout my career, I supported teams in a variety of areas: IT, Quality Assurance, Design, Development, User Experience, Project Management, Sales, Marketing, Merchandising, Finance, and Analytics. Learning these processes and how they fit into the whole corporate picture allowed me to build on my own job functions. I was able to better understand the capacity and limitations that other teams bring to the table. Knowing how everything operates allows you to prioritize and support initiatives that promote high-performing teams.

How did you get your job? I got my current position through a mix of doing things that interested me and doing things that no one else wanted to do. I would handle my normal job functions and do what I needed to do, while coupling those activities with what I wanted to do. In my last semester of my MBA, I started making my own websites. Fairly early in this process, I found that building a website is much like the old adage of the tree: "If a tree falls in the forest and no one is around to hear it, does it make a sound?" In the digital sphere, it's more like, "If you build a beautiful website and no one can find it, is it a website?"

I did a deep dive for 15 hours over a weekend taking online courses and studying multiple white papers on SEO. From there I held a number of positions in digital that weren't anything special—but they got me in the door to where I wanted to be. I kept immersing myself in all things digital to understand what makes a successful website. Eventually I was able to apply the things I learned during nonwork time to enterprise-wide projects. This experience mixed with the things that genuinely interested me allowed me to position myself in a very coveted position.

What has been the most important thing in making you successful at your job? Everyone wants a specialist,

What advice would you give soon-to-be graduates? Travel. Get out of your comfort zone. Take risks. You'll have so much time to make up those things that entry-level jobs teach, and you'll start to gain more of an understanding that in a global economy not everyone thinks, works, acts, or uses online platforms as someone with your upbringing. Don't be afraid to "fail young." You'd be surprised how much real-world experience you'll gain by running your own business or start-up. Past the risk taking, look into creative classes to understand how to think outside your norms or those of your company; you'll constantly have to find innovative ways to solve complex problems.

What do you consider your personal brand to be? This question is funny because I took a lot of time to brand myself. I'm in digital so my brand has to be digital. I have a logo. I have a website that's being built out as we speak. You have to pay attention to your social profiles and be true to what you're interested in to become a thought leader in those interests, even if they're not quite related. More than just a personal branding statement, you have to live what you speak.

To give you a background on my personal branding statement, in between undergrad and getting my MBA, I went to art school to earn a degree in digital design. I quickly found out that I am not a pure designer, but genuinely appreciate what I know now as User Experience or UX, so I ended up dropping out. It's important to know what you are—but almost more important to know what you are not. That leads to my personal statement now which is, "Art School Drop-out. Digital Marketing Pundit."

How is marketing changing and what would help a student's success in an increasingly digital environment? Ten years ago, leaders in education and business kept saying, "Take IT classes. Marketing and IT will become ever more fused than you will ever believe." This statement is so obvious today but is still overlooked time and time again. Learn how systems work and how they will be integrated with marketing functions.

Learn a different language. I'm not talking about Spanish (although that will go a long way). I'm talking about Hypertext Markup Language (HTML), Cascading Style Sheets (CSS), JavaScript, or any other programming language. Everyone who works in digital should learn how to code (or at least how to read code) to understand the framework of everything you will be working on. You'd be surprised to know how far even the basics in reading these languages can take you.

Services like SproutSocial help marketers track digital and social media marketing performance by crafting customizable performance dashboards. *Wordstream*

- How are people participating in the conversation about your brand?
- Do they engage in conversation by commenting?
- Do they share or retweet your posts or tweets?
- How many demonstrate their approval or agreement with a retweet, a like, or +1?

Engagement data can be contextualized and compared against internal benchmarks by taking into account the brand's social reach. Taking raw engagement metrics and dividing by the number of Facebook friends, Twitter followers, or another platform audience measure, digital marketers can add meaning to the raw engagement metrics by producing ratios reflecting *conversation rate, amplification rate,* and *applause rate.*

- **Brand sentiment.** If you were measuring mentions for your company's new product, you might assume a surge in mentions meant it was being well received. But what if most of those mentions were negative? Digital and social marketing managers often seek to assess the underlying *sentiment* toward a brand by examining the language customers use when speaking about it. **Sentiment analysis,** also known as *opinion mining,* examines the positivity or negativity of the feelings (attitudes, emotions, and opinions) behind the words, using natural language processing tools.[52]

sentiment analysis or opinion mining

The analysis of the feelings (attitudes, emotions, and opinions) behind the words, using natural language processing tools.

ETHICAL ISSUES IN DIGITAL AND SOCIAL MEDIA MARKETING

LO 13-6

Identify potential moral hazards arising from digital and social media marketing and offer best practices for ethical application of these tools.

With the advent of digital marketing, brands have felt increasing pressure to blur lines between what they consider ethical and unethical marketing strategies. At the same time, social media have given consumers a much bigger stage on which to stand and voice their displeasure at brands they find wanting.[53] In a digital world, organizations must not only be aware of ethical values such as trust, honesty, fairness, and confidentiality, they must actively use them to make sure they are doing the "right" thing by their customers.[54]

The rise of digital and social media marketing has raised the level of attention placed on three distinct areas: (1) online privacy and information security, (2) unethical targeting of digital customers, and (3) ethical best practices in use of social media for marketing purposes.

Online Privacy and Information Security

What reasonable expectations of privacy do social media users have with respect to information they post online? This is a complex issue. Certainly, the full moral, legal, and public policy implications of this question are continuing to take shape in society.

From a marketing perspective, however, the imperative for firms to act with transparency and integrity in using all forms of customer data must be clear. Being transparent and honest means that organizations must state their intentions regarding data usage and allow their customers to provide their consent. The concept of **informed consent** is a key principle within marketing ethics, referring to permission granted in the full knowledge of the likely consequences. However, obtaining informed consent for data use can represent a challenge to some organizations harvesting data; all potential uses of the data may not even be known at the time data are collected.

informed consent
Permission granted in the knowledge of the possible consequences.

What should be evident to marketers, though, is that breaches of trust resulting from improper use of data can be very damaging to brands. This is a lesson that Facebook found out the hard way. In 2017, reporters found that analytics firm Cambridge Analytica paid to acquire Facebook users' personal information through an outside researcher, Aleksandr Kogan. Kogan had created a data-harvesting personality quiz app that told users (in fine print) that it was collecting the information for academic purposes—a claim Facebook did not verify and was not true. Although only 305,000 people participated in the quiz and consented to having their data harvested, their friends also had their profiles scraped, bringing the estimated number of those affected to 87 million.[55] News of this ethical failure result in a next-day drop of 18 percent of Facebook's stock price, amounting to more than $109 billion in lost shareholder value.

Privacy Data Breaches and Information Security
Information security is another growing concern for many companies and brands. Over the past several years, there have been several well-publicized information security events involving the loss of tens and even hundreds of millions of consumer records. These events have become so commonplace that many individuals have become desensitized by their occurrence. For others, particularly those who have been personally victimized, these cybercrimes have led to greater caution in sharing personal data. In addition, the occurrence of large-scale privacy breaches has been shown to negatively impact brand trust, customer retention, and purchasing behaviors.

Firms that fail to invest sufficiently in safeguarding their customer data and establishing policies to deal with cybercrimes may also run into problems with consumer protection agencies. In 2018, Uber was forced to pay $148 million to settle a nationwide investigation of a data breach event. The massive data breach, which Uber covered up

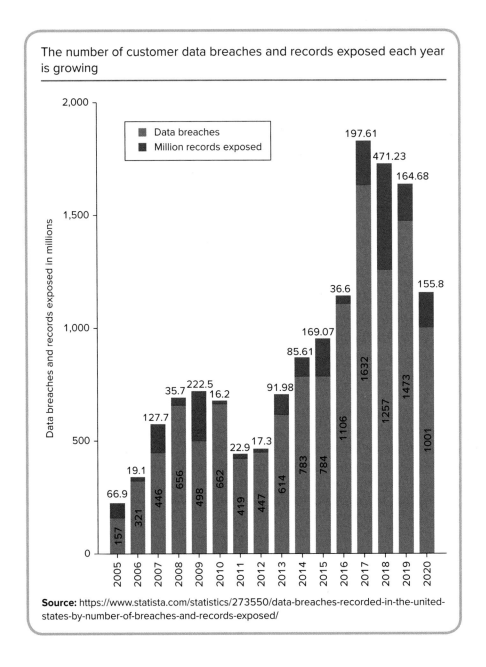

The number of customer data breaches and records exposed each year is growing

Source: https://www.statista.com/statistics/273550/data-breaches-recorded-in-the-united-states-by-number-of-breaches-and-records-exposed/

for more than a year, gave hackers unauthorized access to the personal information of 50 million riders as well as 7 million of its drivers. Of those drivers, 600,000 had their driver's license numbers compromised. Uber then failed to inform users of the breach, choosing instead to reward the attackers with a $100,000 payment, in effect paying ransom to the thieves in return for deleting the data and staying silent.[56]

Unethical Targeting of Digital Customers

Our every action in the digital world leaves a data trail. Use of digital technologies enables marketers to gather information from social media networks, e-mail accounts, purchase histories, ad tracking data, online reviews, and other sources to build sophisticated consumer profiles. This is a huge benefit to marketers—it allows firms to target customers with more personalized and attractive offers and messaging. In fact, the ability to target customers with advertising is largely why social media platforms are able to offer their services for free to their users. It is also why digital advertising has rapidly grown as a percentage of overall ad expenditures. However, as these profiles become more detailed, it raises the temptation for marketers to target customers in ethically questionable ways.

Vulnerable Consumer Populations Marketers should be cautious when targeting populations that may be considered vulnerable. For instance, marketing of any sort toward children is bound to attract scrutiny from public interest groups and regulators. While children and teens are often heavy Internet users, they may lack the sophistication to understand that they are being targeted with marketing messaging. For example, they may not realize that their every mouse click may be monitored, and they may be unable to evaluate the accuracy of information they view or be unable to understand the nature of the information they provide to advertisers. To ensure the safety of children and ultimately avoid consumer backlash from children's parents, companies should not attempt to hard sell online to these children, should do their best to involve the parents (e.g., ensure that information from children comes with express knowledge of the parents), and should think of their website as a service rather than an advertisement.[57]

Unethical targeting practices can also be exclusionary in nature. For instance, in 2016 ad agency ProPublica bought a Facebook ad for real estate that blocked users with an "affinity" for African Americans, Asian Americans, or Hispanics.[58] This violated the federal Fair Housing Act, which prohibits discriminatory marketing tactics in the sales or rental of real estate. In February 2017, Facebook was forced to bow to mounting pressure from activist groups who demanded that the company disable all ad targeting on the basis of race, gender, and sexual orientation.[59]

Ethical Best Practices in Social Media Marketing

Like all marketing efforts, social media marketing *should be* ethical. But the temptation for some companies and individuals to bend the rules to make a quick buck are always there. Over time, regular use of unethical social media tactics may cause enduring harm to the reputation of an individual or brand. Author Jacob Maslow offers guidance that will keep marketers from falling prey to unethical practices:[60]

1. **Remain transparent at all times.** Social media are very personal. When there is full transparency in a brand's social media communication, its motivations are perceived as more sincere. This can engender a greater sense of trust and connection to that brand. For instance, McDonald's took great strides to be more transparent with its "Our Food. Your Questions." social campaign. In one segment, viewers were taken behind the scenes at a Big Mac photo shoot to answer this consumer question: "Why does your food look different in the advertising than what is in the store?" It was a refreshing attempt to connect with viewers and be more transparent. The video received over 9 million views on YouTube.[61]

2. **Never give cause for privacy concerns.** Even though social media use in many cases entails voluntary sharing of personal information, privacy remains an important concern. Unfortunately, incidents of account hacking, identify theft, stalking, harassment, and worse on social media are not uncommon. The rise of location-based mobile apps gives cause to a whole new set of potential privacy concerns. If a company intentionally, or even accidentally, reveals sensitive personal information, this can lead to a tarnished reputation and backlash against the brand.

3. **Always credit when re-sharing someone else's content.** Crediting, and asking permission, is the least you can do when using someone else's content. Many content creators are actually happy to share their content, images, links, ideas, and even data. However, the social media marketing world is not without individuals

who attempt to take someone else's content and try to pass it off as their own. Whether this type of behavior results from a lack of scruples or lack of understanding of Internet etiquette, the negative reputational impact when uncovered is likely to be the same. When in doubt, the easiest way to give credit to another source is to just simply retweet or share the post from Twitter or Facebook. On Twitter, if you would like to manually retweet content, be sure to include *RT* before the original or add *MT* if you are modifying the content. Facebook makes sharing a post very easy—just click "share." You also have the ability to add your own thoughts to the post with the share option.[62]

4. **Always divulge your affiliation.** Whether working with social influencers on Instagram or participating yourself on a B2B topic board discussion on LinkedIn, it is unethical (and possibly illegal) for individuals to promote products or brands while being paid by that company without disclosing that information.[63] To preserve the trustworthiness and integrity of the brand or a person as an information source, it is critical to clarify potential conflicts of interest resulting from a paid relationship to a brand or company.

SUMMARY

Ridofranz/iStock/ Getty Images Plus/ Getty Images

LO 13-1 Understand the impact of mobile and social digital technologies on consumers and marketing practices.

We are in the midst of a revolution in which the business world is being reshaped via the convergence of social and mobile technologies. *Social media* refers to Internet-based platforms that enable users to create their own content and share it with others who access these sites. Empowered by the massive diffusion of wireless Internet access and mobile computing, social media play an increasingly important role in how consumers discover, research, and share information about brands and products.

The process of defining, building, and maintaining a brand is now a collaborative one. The use of social and mobile technologies provides marketers with new tools that can simultaneously serve to (1) deepen customers' brand engagement and (2) provide marketers with real-time feedback about what tactics are effective.

Source: https://search engineland .com/guide/ what-is-seo

LO 13-2 Explain how search marketing contributes to digital marketing strategy.

Search engine results are a key driver of online consumer click-through behaviors. As a result, ensuring websites appear near the top of relevant search results is a critical component to the success of digital marketing strategies. *Search marketing* involves a set of techniques and procedures designed to improve search engine results rankings. Search marketing encompasses two closely related practices: search engine optimization and search engine marketing. *Search engine optimization (SEO)* is the process of obtaining more traffic based on higher rankings of free or

"organic" search results on search engines. *Search engine marketing (SEM)* is the process of generating website traffic by purchasing advertisements on search engines. These paid listings are those links that typically appear either at the very top or upper right of a search results page.

LEGO

LO 13-3 Discuss how companies are employing social media marketing to strengthen customer relationships and achieve business objectives.

Consumers and business decision makers increasingly utilize social media for entertainment, communication, and information purposes. As a result, marketers are investing greater resources into social media marketing activities. Social media marketing uses combinations of digital tools such as websites, online videos, e-mail, blogs, social media, mobile ads, mobile apps, and other digital platforms. It seeks to engage consumers anywhere, anytime via their computers, smartphones, tablets, Internet-enabled TVs, and other digital devices. By interacting with consumers in a fun, helpful, and interesting manner, social media can help build a successful brand by enabling the firm to develop deeper relationships with customers, and by generating positive word-of-mouth communication about the brand across social networks.

Maxsattana/Getty Images

LO 13-4 Explain the importance of content marketing in driving digital marketing strategies.

The success of any digital marketing strategy begins and ends with a sound, organized approach to developing and managing interesting, relevant content.

While branded content created by the organization is often a central focus, marketers can strengthen interactions by integrating content created by experts and consumers. Content can take the form of e-mails, blogs, white papers, videos, infographics, tweets, and more.

Due to the rise of the global pandemic in 2020, many B2B organizations today have started hosting and participating in virtual trade shows and conferences. Virtual trade shows offer several unique advantages over traditional, in-person events, including: access to larger audiences, lower costs, and greater ability to educate and engage with prospects on a one-to-one basis. Additional content marketing trends include: live streaming, use of ephemeral content, and emoji marketing.

Wordstream

LO 13-5 Discuss key performance indicators commonly utilized in managing digital and social media marketing campaigns.

Marketing managers today are able to use web and social media analytics tools to create marketing *dashboards* that track consumer response to their digital and social campaigns. By integrating these tools with data from advanced CRM systems, marketers are better positioned than ever to quantify the direct financial impact of their strategies.

Digital marketing key performance indicators (KPIs) can be broken into three sets: search performance, website analytics, and content performance. Tracked search marketing metrics include search engine ranking, organic traffic, and cost-per-click. *Website analytics* is the measurement, analysis, and reporting of Internet-generated user data to optimize web content and usage. Marketers commonly track a variety of website statistics, including number of site visitors, site

speed, and visitor bounce rate. Content performance metrics include open rate and content downloads.

Marketers monitor response to their social media marketing activity across all platforms to help improve online response to their social messaging and branding efforts. Commonly observed social media marketing metric categories tracked by brands include reach, the number of brand mentions, the level of follower engagement, and brand sentiment.

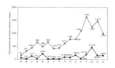

Source: *https://www .statista.com/statistics/ 273550/data-breaches- recorded-in-the-united- states-by-number-of- breachers-and-records- exposed/*

LO 13-6 Identify potential moral hazards arising from digital and social media marketing and provide best practices for ethical application of these tools.

In a digital world, marketers must not only be aware of ethical values such as trust, honesty, fairness, and confidentiality, they must actively use them to ensure they are doing the "right" thing by their customers. Digital marketers must guard against intrusive tactics that violate privacy norms and must remain steadfast in protecting their customers' personal information from misuse. Informed consent should be a driving principle in guiding how customer information is used. Using customer data as a means of targeting vulnerable consumer populations is a hot-button issue and is drawing increased scrutiny from industry watchdogs and policy makers. Finally, several best practices are presented for ethical use of social media as a marketing communications channel: transparency, respect for privacy, proper attribution of credit for shared content, and full disclosure of brand affiliations by marketers and spokespersons.

KEY TERMS

MARKETING PLAN EXERCISE • Marketing Yourself

While many college students use social media applications like Twitter and Instagram on a daily basis, they find the prospect of creating a professional profile in LinkedIn to be intimidating. But remember, it is perfectly normal to feel discomfort when writing about yourself. Don't be discouraged

by the polished profiles of other students or industry executives.

Millions of people in the workforce use LinkedIn to make professional connections and advance their career. Why wait to join them?

Here are 10 tips for creating an attention-grabbing LinkedIn profile.

1. **Include a profile photo.** Visuals are very important. Having a photo makes your profile 21 times more likely to be viewed, according to Ada Yu, director of product management at LinkedIn. For maximum impact, obtain a professional headshot. *Do not* use a photo of you with your friends during your recent spring break trip to the beach.

2. **Highlight soft skills.** Skills like time management and communication are increasingly important to employers. You can overcome limited work experience in a relevant field by emphasizing soft skills and your passion for learning.

3. **Use keywords.** Words that appear below your name and elsewhere in your profile are indexed in the platform's search as well as external search engines such as Google if your profile is public. Ms. Yu suggests students read job descriptions and mention sought-after skills they see listed—provided they actually have them.

4. **Write an elevator pitch.** Think for a minute about what you'd want someone you'd never met to know about you. Next, thoughtfully craft five to seven sentences that inform potential employers about you as a person. Avoid jargon. Alan Katzman, CEO of personal digital portfolio consulting firm Social Assurity, suggests, "Rather than using résumé talk, I want them [students] to talk about what they've learned about themselves," he said. "It could be volunteering, sports or family care."

5. **Turn on "Open to Work."** LinkedIn created a feature during the pandemic that allows people actively seeking jobs to indicate that by turning on a profile-photo frame with the label Open to Work. People who use it are 40 percent more likely to receive messages from recruiters, Ms. Yu said.

6. **Make meaningful connections.** Quality is better than quantity. There are numerous LinkedIn Groups organized around interest areas like independent filmmaking, economics, and marketing. Students can join them to network with people who share similar interests. Students can also make use of LinkedIn's university alumni network to find potentially helpful professionals.

7. **Be personal.** When sending messages to alumni or to people who work at companies you're interested in, take the time to write a personal note. Be specific about your reason for writing. The same goes for commenting on a post. If you don't know what to say, ask a question.

8. **Include your contact information.** Teens and 20-somethings are used to communicating via direct message, but not all employers are. Rather than relying solely on LinkedIn's internal messaging system, add alternate ways to contact you, such as an e-mail address.

9. **Don't try to be funny.** What's acceptable on other social media platforms with friends may not fly on LinkedIn. Without context or direct interaction, it can be hard to convey humor in text.

10. **Get a second opinion.** Before your LinkedIn profile goes live, ask a parent, professor, or trusted professional to proofread and provide other feedback. The same goes for comments on posts.

Task #1: Search through several entry-level job listings in your field using a free online job board like Indeed or Glassdoor.com. Which skills and attributes *that you possess* seem to be commonly sought-after by employers? Make a list of five potential keywords.

Task #2: Go to LinkedIn.com and search for Groups that correspond to personal or professional interest areas, companies that you might like to work for, or your university. Read through a few articles and posts. From a networking perspective, which three groups do you think would be most beneficial for you to join? Why?

DISCUSSION QUESTIONS

1. What organization provides you with the most consistently relevant content? How does this affect your purchasing habits? Name an organization that does not provide consistently relevant marketing content through social media. What would you recommend it do differently?

2. What are the two main reasons you go online? If a company were trying to reach you through digital and social marketing, what recommendations would you give it?

3. Do you think the abundance of social media platforms used by organizations makes it easier or harder to reach customers in a meaningful way? Explain your answer.

4. What is a call to action (CTA) that led you to some action? What made that specific CTA effective in influencing your behavior?

5. Think of a company in the town where you live and develop a strategy of how it could use geofencing to effectively promote products to its target market.

SOCIAL MEDIA APPLICATION

The use of social and mobile technologies provides marketers with new tools that can simultaneously serve to (1) deepen customers' brand engagement and (2) provide marketers with real-time feedback about what tactics are resonating. Pick a company that is located in the state where you live. Analyze that organization's social media platforms using the following questions as a guide.

1. What is the company doing to deepen brand engagement with customers using social media?

2. Looking at the last month, what feedback have customers provided on the firm's marketing efforts?

3. Based on the social media feedback customers have provided, what marketing recommendations would you make to this company?

 MARKETING ANALYTICS EXERCISE

Please complete the *Connect* exercise for Chapter 13 that focuses on analyzing the success of social media campaigns using different platforms.

ETHICAL CHALLENGE

The National Football League (NFL) generates the most television revenue of any major North American professional sport. Network deals with broadcast partners Fox, NBC, CBS, and ESPN generate $6 billion annually in rights fees for the NFL. In addition, the League decided to run 13 Thursday night games on its own NFL Network cable channel. *Thursday Night Football* on the NFL Network, which is available in over 70 million U.S. homes, averaged millions of viewers a night during the fall of 2015.

While some of the Thursday night games are simulcast on CBS and NBC, there are multiple games each year that can be seen only by watching the NFL network. Its success negatively affected the ratings of the prime-time comedy and drama shows that air on NBC, CBS, and the NFL's other broadcast partners on Thursday evenings. While *Thursday Night Football* is bringing more viewers to the NFL's cable channel, marketers at the League's broadcast partners might be wondering why they are paying $6 billion a year to an organization that is stealing television viewers on what had been traditionally one of the broadcast networks' best nights.

Please use the ethical decision-making framework to complete the following related to this scenario:

1. Analyze the NFL's decision to play more Thursday night games on the NFL Network. What about the proposal to broadcast all Thursday night games on the Amazon streaming service possibly encouraging more television customers to cut the cord? What are the ethical implications of this decision?

2. If you were a marketer at a broadcast network partner of the NFL, what action might you take in response to the fact that Thursday night games have hurt the television ratings and advertising revenue of your Thursday night programming?

3. If you were a marketer for the NFL, why would you not put televised games on every night of the week? Are there any advertising or marketing concerns about showing football games on Tuesday, Wednesday, or Friday nights?

Source: See Andy Fixmer, "Thursday Night Football Scores Big for the NFL," *Bloomberg Businessweek,* November 29, 2012, http://www.businessweek .com/articles/2012-11-29/thursday-night-football-scores-big-for-the-nfl.

VIDEO CASE

Please go to *Connect* to access the video case featuring Dell that accompanies this chapter.

PODCAST

Please go to Connect to access the podcast that accompanies this chapter.

CAREER **TIPS**

Tips for Students Looking to Break into Search Engine Marketing

Search marketing is an in-demand job area. While more and more universities are beginning to offer digital marketing classes that cover search topics, motivated students have plenty of opportunity to impress hiring managers with more than just a formal education. Clay Cazier, VP of search strategy for the marketing agency PM Digital, offers a few tips on how students can get a leg up on the competition for SEO positions:

> Those who succeed in SEO are self-starters by nature. A good signal that you, as a job candidate, have those skills is by showing that you've developed a website or a blog on your own with *some* specific focus. Maybe it's a Tumblr site with crafting how-tos; perhaps it's a fully developed travel blog; maybe it's even a website for a favorite local charity or church. . . . [Also] the ability to keep up with changes in the discipline is important. Your curiosity and willingness to learn are signaled by your self-directed research. I will ask candidates what things they read and what they think is "next" in SEO.[64]

Cazier suggests that students augment coursework with Google certifications, especially the Google Analytics individual qualification, to differentiate their resumes (visit https://analytics.google.com/analytics/academy/ for more information). Also, SEO industry leader Moz offers a highly recommended free course (https://www.udemy.com/whiteboard-seo/) as well as a variety of learning resources to the SEO community on its website (www.moz.com).

CHAPTER NOTES

1. R. Levine, C. Locke, and D. Searls, *The Cluetrain Manifesto* (New York: Basic Books, 2009).
2. M. W. Schaefer, *Social Media Explained: Untangling the World's Most Misunderstood Business Trend* (Schaefer Marketing Solutions, 2014).
3. Trevor Wheelwright, "2022 Cell Phone Usage Statistics: How Obsessed Are We?" *Reviews.org,* January 24, 2022, https://www.reviews.org/mobile/cell-phone-addiction/.
4. E. Qualman, *Socialnomics: How Social Media Transforms the Way We Live and Do Business* (Hoboken, NJ: Wiley, 2010).
5. Zephoria, "The Top Valuable Facebook Statistics," updated June 2019, https://zephoria.com/top-15-valuable-facebook-statistics/.
6. Maryam Mohsin, "10 YouTube Stats Every Marketer Should Know in 2022," *Oberlo,* May 17, 2022, https://www.oberlo.com/blog/youtube-statistics.
7. Claire Beveridge, "150+ Social Media Statistics That Matter to Marketers in 2022," *Hootsuite,* March 1, 2022, https://blog.hootsuite.com/social-media-statistics-for-social-media-managers/#instagram.

8. Shelley Walsh, "52 Instagram Statistics and Facts for 2021," *Search Engine Journal,* April 12, 2021, https://www.searchenginejournal.com/instagram-facts/314439/#close.
9. Tom Jacobs, "Even Just the Presence of a Smartphone Lowers the Quality of In-Person Conversations," *Pacific Standard,* updated June 14, 2017, https://psmag.com/even-just-the-presence-of-a-smartphone-lowers-the-quality-of-in-person-conversations-4b518f657b32#.jha7zbfoq.
10. Uptin Saiidi, "Social Media Making Millennials Less Social: Study," *CNBC,* October 19, 2015, http://www.cnbc.com/2015/10/15/social-media-making-millennials-less-social-study.html.
11. Ben Schreckinger, "The Home of FOMO," *Boston,* July 29, 2014, http://www.bostonmagazine.com/news/article/2014/07/29/fomo-history/.
12. C. Li and J. Bernoff, *Groundswell: Winning in a World Transformed by Social Technologies* (Cambridge, MA: Harvard Business Press, 2011).

13. Dave Chaffey, "The Difference between Paid, Owned, and Earned Media," Smart Insights, June 19, 2022, http://www.smartinsights.com/digital-marketing-strategy/customer-acquisition-strategy/new-media-options/.

14. Personal conversation with author, as detailed in Nick Johnson, *The Future of Marketing* (Old Tappan, NJ: Pearson Education, 2015).

15. Emily Nelson and Sarah Ellison, "In a Shift, Marketers Beef Up Ad Spending Inside Stores," *The Wall Street Journal,* September 21, 2005, http://www.wsj.com/articles/SB112725891535046751.

16. Jim Lecinksi, *Winning the Zero Moment of Truth* (New York: Vook, 2011).

17. B. Geddes, V. Anderson, H. Cannon, C. Tanner, T. Khachaturyan, and V. Golovanyov, *Introduction to Online Marketing* (St. George, UT: eLight Marketing, 2015).

18. Search Engine Land, https://searchengineland.com/guide/what-is-seo.

19. "Search Ad Spend in the U.S. 2109–2022," Statista Research Department, February 7, 2022, https://www.statista.com/statistics/190275/us-online-display-and-search-advertising-forecast-2010-to-2015/.

20. Danny Goodwin, "60 + Mind-Blowing Stats about Search Engine Optimization," *Search Engine Journal,* December 29, 2017, https://www.searchenginejournal.com/10-stats-to-justify-seo/36762/.

21. Pat Ahern, "25 Mind-Bottling SEO Stats for 2019 (and Beyond)," *Junto,* updated June 5, 2019, https://junto.digital/blog/seo-stats-2017/.

22. Philip Petrescu, "Google Organic Click-Through Rates in 2014," *Moz,* October 1, 2014, https://moz.com/blog/google-organic-click-through-rates-in-2014.

23. Dan Alaimo, "Amazon Now Dominates Google in Product Search," *Retail Dive,* September 7, 2018, https://www.retaildive.com/news/amazon-now-dominates-google-in-product-search/531822/.

24. "How to Become a Search Marketing Manager," Zippia, (n.d.), https://www.zippia.com/search-marketing-manager-jobs/.

25. Moz, "How Search Engines Work: Crawling, Indexing, and Ranking," n.d., https://moz.com/beginners-guide-to-seo/how-search-engines-operate.

26. James Bruce, "How Do Search Engines Work?" MUO, November 2, 2017, http://www.makeuseof.com/tag/how-do-search-engines-work-makeuseof-explains/.

27. "Social Media Platforms Used by Marketers Worldwide 2021, by Target Group," *Statista,* August 3, 2021, https://www.statista.com/statistics/259382/social-media-platforms-used-by-b2b-and-b2c-marketers-worldwide/.

28. Simon Kemp, "TikTok Gains 8 New Users Every Second (And Other Mind-Blowing Stats)," *Hootsuite,* January 28, 2022, https://blog.hootsuite.com/simon-kemp-social-media/.

29. Jose Angelo Gallegos, "The 7 Best User Generated Content: Examples from Brands on Facebook," Falcon.io, November 13, 2018, https://www.falcon.io/insights-hub/topics/social-media-strategy/the-7-best-examples-of-brands-leveraging-ugc-in-facebook/.

30. HubSpot, "The Social Lifecycle: Consumer Insights to Improve Your Business," October 29, 2014, http://www.slideshare.net/HubSpot/the-social-lifecycle-consumer-insights-to-improve-your-business.

31. LoudDoor, "Top 20 Brands with the Most Loyal Followers on Facebook," August 11, 2014, http://blog.louddoor.com/2014/08/top-20-brands-with-the-most-loyal-followers-on-facebook/.

32. Jeff Kauflin, "The Most Powerful Brands in 2017," *Forbes,* February 14, 2017, https://www.forbes.com/sites/jeffkauflin/2017/02/14/the-most-powerful-brands-in-2017/#525a6240f1f8.

33. Lars Silberbauer, "5 Secrets behind the LEGO Social Media Success," April 5, 2018, http://www.larssilberbauer.com/single-post/2018/04/05/5-Secrets-Behind-the-LEGO-Social-Media-Success.

34. Brad Howarth, "How Lego Infuses Social Media Marketing with Play," *CMO,* May 23, 2018, https://www.cmo.com.au/article/641387/how-lego-infuses-social-media-marketing-play/.

35. Brian Solis, *What's the Future of Business? Changing the Way Businesses Create Experiences* (Hoboken, NJ: Wiley, 2013), p. 8.

36. Joei Chan, "Social Customer Service: Lessons from 5 of Our Favorite Brands," Mention.com, n.d., https://mention.com/blog/social-customer-service/.

37. Wayne Huang, "Study: Twitter Customer Care Increases Willingness to Pay," Twitter.com, October 5, 2016, https://blog.twitter.com/marketing/en_us/topics/research/2016/study-twitter-customer-care-increases-willingness-to-pay-across-industries.html.

38. Susan Kuchinskas, "Lancôme Gives Points for Social Media in New Loyalty Program," *ClickZ,* April 21, 2014, https://www.clickz.com/clickz/news/2340735/lanc-me-gives-points-for-social-media-in-new-loyalty-program.

39. Content Marketing Institute, "What Is Content Marketing?," n.d., http://contentmarketinginstitute.com/what-is-content-marketing/.

40. Peyman Nilforoush, "New Data: Mix Types of Content for Successful Content Marketing," Content Marketing Institute, June 17, 2014, http://contentmarketinginstitute.com/2014/06/mix-content-types-for-successful-content-marketing/.

41. "Webinar Glossary Close-up: What Is Content Marketing," *ClickMeeting,* July 16, 2019, https://blog.clickmeeting.com/what-is-content-marketing.

42. "The Key to a Successful Virtual Exhibit Booth: Content Marketing," Cramer, (n.d.), https://www.cramer.com/insights/key-to-successful-virtual-exhibit-booth-content-marketing/.

43. https://www.impactplus.com/blog/seo-statistics.

44. https://www.neurosciencemarketing.com/blog/articles/neuromarketing-animation.htm.

45. Chelsea Harrigan, "Five Types of Content That Are Changing the Digital Marketing Game," *CopyPress,* May 22, 2015, http://www.copypress.com/blog/five-types-of-content-that-are-changing-the-digital-marketing-game/.

46. Matthew Kane, "Is Your Brand Fluent in Emoji? The 7 Best Examples of Emoji Marketing," *HubSpot,* updated July 28, 2017, http://blog.hubspot.com/agency/emoji-marketing.

47. The LBMA, http://www.thelbma.com/files/647-Turnstyle_LBM_WhitePaper_Final.pdf.

48. Andrew Latham, "What Is Location-Based Marketing?," Chron, n.d., http://smallbusiness.chron.com/locationbased-marketing-25650.html.

49. "The 40 Most Important KPIs for Marketers," Hurree, (n.d.), https://www.hurree.co/the-40-most-important-kpis-for-marketers-guide?

50. Zilvinas Alekna, "Importance of Website Analytics for Your Business," *Webnus,* June 22, 2022, https://webnus.net/importance-of-website-analytics/.

51. "The 40 Most Important KPIs for Marketers," Hurree, (n.d.), https://www.hurree.co/the-40-most-important-kpis-for-marketers-guide?

52. iProspect, "10 Sentiment Analysis Tools to Track Social Marketing Success," November 6, 2013, http://www.iprospect.com/en/ca/blog/10-sentiment-analysis-tools-track-social-marketing-success/#.

53. David Trounce, "Ethics in Online Marketing: Does Brand Morality Matter?" *Search Engine Journal,* January 4, 2017, https://www.searchenginejournal.com/ethics-online-marketing-brand-morality-matter/181863/.

54. David Yardley, "Are You Making Ethical Decisions during the Digital Transformation Process?" Kogan Page, March 29, 2018, https://www.koganpage.com/article/essential-ethics-for-digital-transformation.

55. Sarah Steimer, "The Murky Ethics of Data Gathering in a Post-Cambridge Analytica World," American Marketing Association, May 1, 2018, https://www.ama.org/publications/MarketingNews/Pages/marketers-are-wading-through-an-online-data-swampland.aspx.

56. Shannon Wu, "Uber and the Ongoing Battle over Consumer Data Privacy," *Bloom Blog,* September 28, 2018, https://blog.hellobloom.io/uber-and-the-ongoing-battle-over-consumer-data-privacy-a29d3f858f53.

57. "4 Ethical Issues in Digital Marketing," *StephenClarke49* blog, March 23, 2014, https://stephenclarke49.wordpress.com/2014/03/23/4-ethical-issues-in-digital-marketing/.

58. Laura Cox, "The Dark Side of Targeted Advertising," *Disruption,* December 5, 2017, https://disruptionhub.com/targeted-advertising-discriminatory/.

59. Ross Briggs, "The Ethics of Online Ad Targeting," *Red Door,* March 30, 2017, https://www.reddoor.biz/blog/the-ethics-of-online-ad-targeting/.

60. Jacob Maslow, "4 Layers of Ethics in Social Media Marketing," *Social Media Explorer,* November 12, 2018, https://socialmediaexplorer.com/social-media-marketing/4-layers-of-ethics-in-social-media-marketing/.

61. Canadian Marketing Association, "Why Transparency Is Important on Social Media," November 21, 2013, https://www.the-cma.org/about/blog/why-transparency-is-important-on-social-media.

62. Slava Vidomanets, "Citing the Site: A Guide to Giving Credit on Social Media," StrataBlue, September 8, 2014, https://stratablue.com/citing-site-guide-giving-credit-social-media/.

63. Jacob Maslow, "4 Layers of Ethics in Social Media Marketing," *Social Media Explorer,* November 12, 2018, https://socialmediaexplorer.com/social-media-marketing/4-layers-of-ethics-in-social-media-marketing/.

64. Clay Cazier, "Advice to Those Considering SEO as a Career," *Search Engine Land,* June 1, 2016, http://searchengineland.com/advice-considering-seo-career-250493.

Part FOUR

Responding to Your Customer

Kostic Dusan/fotokostic/123RF

Chapter **14**

Branding

Rob Wilson/Shutterstock

Chapter **15**

Customer Relationship Management

Rawpixel.com/Shutterstock

Chapter **16**

Social Responsibility and Sustainability

Chapter **14**

Branding

Kostic Dusan/fotokostic/123RF

Learning Objectives

After reading this chapter, you should be able to

LO 14-1 Explain the importance of building a successful brand.

LO 14-2 Describe the relevance of brand equity for marketers.

LO 14-3 Compare some common strategies for developing brands.

LO 14-4 Summarize the impact of packaging on brand building.

LO 14-5 Summarize the impact of social media on brand management.

LO 14-6 Discuss the major branding challenges facing global marketers.

LO 14-7 Explain the role of branding in nonprofit organizations.

Executive **Perspective** ... because everyone is a marketer

T.J. Thompson
Brand Manager
Valley View Agri-Systems

Photo provided by T.J. Thompson

T.J. Thompson majored in mechanical engineering in school and went to work in that field following graduation. As T.J.'s professional responsibilities expanded, he found himself focused much more on the business and marketing aspects of the organization he worked for. He took a position as a marketing and advertising manager where he got to learn and use his new skills to promote the business and win new customers. Thompson soon realized that building a brand for his organization would be critical to its success.

Thompson has helped develop a brand that is recognized and respected in the agriculture industry. He has a passion for marketing and a strong belief in the impact and importance branding has on organizations of all sizes and across industries. Today, Thompson serves as the brand manager for Valley View Agri-Systems and takes the lead role in continuing to build and manage the organization's brand.

What has been the most important thing in making you successful at your job?

I strive to be true to my values. That's not to say my values always support the popular position, but in the end, my values define who I am. This has allowed me to earn respect and build relationships along the way, though not without some setbacks and sacrifices. In the long-run, I believe being true to who I am and adhering to my values wins over selling out for personal or financial gain.

What advice would you give soon-to-be graduates?

Focus on people. Though technology is an ever-advancing and powerful tool, people still matter the most. It's easy to get caught up in the metrics and algorithms at the expense of people and doing the right thing. While we should leverage technology and data to provide insights that help guide our decisions, we should never lose sight of the value of people.

How is marketing relevant to your role at Valley View Agri-Systems?

Marketing is everything. As brand manager I am tasked with building and promoting our brand in the marketplace. Marketing methods inform those decisions daily. What is fascinating to me is the correlation that exists between internal and external branding. I believe when companies are not true to their internal brand, their culture, the marketplace sniffs them out and "feels" their inconsistencies. In today's world authenticity reigns. I believe the biggest winners in business are those who build a culture people want to be a part of and then find ways to effectively share that culture in the marketplace.

What do you consider your personal brand to be?

I am different, and I like it. I see the world through a unique lens, shaped by my experiences and values. Some of my brand elements are my desire to be an outstanding husband, father, son, family member, and friend—and my desire to connect with and serve people. I strive to be authentic, but I don't believe I have the authority to label myself "authentic." I believe such a labeling is reserved for someone else, only to be given if I've truly earned it.

LO 14-1

Explain the importance of building a successful brand.

brand

The name, term, symbol, design, or any combination of these that identifies and differentiates a firm's products.

brand loyalty

A consumer's steadfast allegiance to a brand, as evidenced by repeated purchases.

brand recognition

The degree to which customers can identify the brand under a variety of circumstances.

brand marks

The elements of a brand, not expressed in words, that a consumer instantly recognizes, such as a symbol, color, or design.

brand image

The unique set of associations target customers or stakeholders make with a brand.

BRANDING

For former, current, and potential customers, a brand represents everything that a good, service, or idea means to them. Think about brands, such as Apple, Disney, and Ford, and consider what they mean to you. The differentiating characteristics of the brands that matter to you might be tangible and related to the product (such as the towing capacity of a Ford F-150 truck). Or they might be emotional and focused on a special memory (such as your memories of Disney World). Specifically, a **brand** is the name, term, symbol, design, or any combination of these that identifies and differentiates a firm's products.

A successful brand adds value to organizations in numerous ways, including through brand loyalty and brand recognition:

- **Brand loyalty** is a consumer's steadfast allegiance to a brand, evidenced by repeated purchases. Brand loyalty typically develops because of a customer's satisfaction with an organization's products.[1] Brand-loyal customers typically exhibit less sensitivity to price. They therefore are an important contributor to a firm's long-term success and profitability. For example, Coca-Cola enjoys millions of brand-loyal customers who actively seek Coca-Cola products and will purchase them even if they are priced higher than the Pepsi products on sale down the aisle. Such brand loyalty adds to Coca-Cola's pricing power and its ability to maintain higher profits.
- **Brand recognition** is the degree to which customers can identify the brand under a variety of circumstances. Firms like Nike and McDonald's employ **brand marks**, which are the elements of a brand, not expressed in words, that a consumer instantly recognizes, such as a symbol, color, or design. The Nike swoosh and McDonald's golden arches are brand marks that have become powerful marketing tools for those companies.

The importance of brand recognition can perhaps best be seen when a company changes or updates its symbol or logo. Consumers often grow attached to certain brand logos or symbols and changes can cause a backlash. For example, Gap was forced to abandon a new logo only a week after it was launched, due to thousands of complaints online and throughout social media from unhappy consumers.[2]

Brand loyalty and brand recognition lead to more revenue for for-profit firms and more donations and support for nonprofit organizations.

The Nike swoosh is consistently one of the most recognized brands in the world. *2p2play/Shutterstock*

Developing Your Personal Brand

The benefits of branding also can apply to individuals, not just organizations. Regardless of what you do after graduation, you will engage in branding. The most important brand you will ever manage is *your* personal brand. Responsibility for building and managing the brand image that bears your name is a 24-hours-a-day, 7-days-a-week, 365-days-a-year job.

Brand image is the unique set of associations that target customers or stakeholders make with a brand. It signifies what the brand presently stands for in the minds of others. For example, Mountain Dew marketers built a brand image of a youthful, fun product that represents energy and excitement. Today, Mountain Dew products are associated with extreme sports, video gaming, and other youth activities. As you develop in your career, you should identify and monitor your brand image. Ask yourself questions such as:

- What do managers and coworkers think when they hear my name?
- What associations do they make with my brand?
- Do they consider me a hard worker, a team leader, and a thoughtful employee, or do they think of me as smart, but lazy and difficult to work with?

Throughout this book, you have had the opportunity to read the personal brand statements of executives across a variety of industries. For example, small business owner Erin Brewer, who provided the career tips in Chapter 3, described her personal brand this way:

> I strive to enjoy the moment, make decisions that leave me without regret, treat others with courtesy and respect, learn something every day, and be comfortable in my own skin. I love asking and trying to answer tough questions! I'm getting more and more comfortable not knowing all the answers.
>
> Also, I believe people—me included—can change if they choose. I have a running list of things to improve within myself. I proudly own my own history with all the failures, successes, decisions, friends, and experiences that have shaped me. In short, I'm trying to be the best me I can be.

Establishing a brand image in the minds of peers, colleagues, or customers begins with understanding the components of a successful brand.

Components of a Successful Brand

Whether you are building the brand for your firm's product or your personal brand, the process involves the following four essential components:

1. ***Deliver a product that provides value.*** The product should attract a positive reaction from consumers, whether that's achieved through packaging, delivery, or the value it offers to users. If a consumer does not perceive value in using a particular product, he or she will not remain a customer for very long. A strong brand provides continued value and quality to customers over time. Southwest Airlines has accomplished this by consistently offering low fares and refusing to charge baggage fees, even as other airlines are doing so.

2. ***Create a consistent brand image.*** All of the firm's marketing decisions, promotions, and employees should reinforce the brand by providing a consistent experience in the minds of consumers. Mountain Dew's efforts to be seen as a youthful, energetic, and extreme brand would be compromised if it began promoting its image by sponsoring senior golf tournaments and advertising in business trade magazines.

   For your personal brand, creating a consistent brand image is equally important. How you dress for work, how you treat others at your office, and the quality of the work you produce combine to create a narrative that becomes your brand. An inconsistent brand image, such as doing a great job on a presentation but then showing up 10 minutes late to the office or

Photo provided by T.J. Thompson

Executive Perspective . . .
because everyone is a marketer

T.J. Thompson
Brand Manager
Valley View Agri-Systems

What is the most important component of building your personal brand?

I think for me it is creating a consistent brand image by always striving to connect deeply with people. Compassion is sometimes a rare gem in the workplace. I believe true compassion requires vulnerability, and vulnerability can sometimes lead to disappointment and pain. But when we're willing to put ourselves out there consistently in an effort to connect with people on a deeper level, more often than not, the benefits outweigh the risks.

Southwest Airlines works to create a consistent brand image of a comfortable, casual company who is focused on providing a great experience for their customers. *David Paul Morris/Bloomberg/Getty Images*

dressing unprofessionally, will reduce the likelihood that your organization views you as someone on the fast track toward advancement and promotion.

3. ***Create consistent brand messaging.*** As with brand image, brand messaging should be consistent and concise. It should be easy to remember and remind consumers about the product attributes they care about most. Marketers commonly make the mistake of trying to share all of the individual good things about their organization's product. Multiple different messages can potentially confuse customers as to why they should purchase a specific brand. Auto insurance company GEICO has succeeded in providing one consistent brand message through a variety of ad concepts: a promise to save consumers money on their car insurance.

4. ***Capture feedback.*** Since the real power of a brand exists in the minds of consumers, marketers must always capture and analyze customer feedback. Companies with strong brands are typically great listeners and use a variety of marketing research to better understand the thoughts, feelings, and concerns of their customers. For example, Chick-fil-A offers random customers the opportunity to receive a free chicken sandwich if they go online and fill out a survey about their experience with the restaurant within 48 hours of their visit. The survey captures feedback on the quality of the food, the portion size of the order, the cleanliness of the restaurant, and the friendliness of the employees, all of which affect the company's brand image. Chick-fil-A then uses these data, which are tied to a specific restaurant and time of day, to identify potential problems and improve every part of the dining experience. Capturing and responding to feedback contributed to Chick-fil-A being recognized as a top restaurant brand in customer satisfaction by research firm J.D. Power.[3] Firms can also use social media tools to gather data about their brand. Later in the chapter we'll discuss the social media tools firms can use.

   You will receive feedback on the success of your personal brand from various stakeholders in your life, including your friends, family, classmates, managers, coworkers, and professors. Consistently monitoring your personal brand will allow you to see what changes need to be made. For example, if your firm continues to pass you over for a promotion, you should ask what it is about your brand that might be keeping you from a higher position. Is it the way you approach your job? Or perhaps how you dress (think of this as personal packaging) might be sending the wrong message? In the same way that a firm analyzes both the positive and negative feedback it receives for a product, so should you reflect on the feedback you are getting throughout your academic and professional career.

Understanding the components of a successful brand is important for a firm both internally and externally. Internally, a strong brand drives cohesion and helps an organization build the capacity and skills to implement its mission. Externally, a strong brand results in trust among the firm's many constituents, be they customers, donors to a nonprofit organization, suppliers, or communities. If a firm successfully executes on these four components and develops a successful brand, it can begin to benefit from the *brand equity* it creates. We'll discuss brand equity and the benefits it provides in the next section.

McGraw Hill connect Exercise **14-1**

Please complete the *Connect* exercise for Chapter 14 that focuses on the steps to building a successful brand. By understanding different strategies and the importance of each step, you will gain insight into how to effectively build a brand, whether it is a firm's, a nonprofit's, or your personal brand.

BRAND EQUITY

Large U.S. firms typically spend millions of dollars each year developing and promoting their brand in an effort to increase brand equity. **Brand equity** is the value the firm derives from consumers' positive perception of its products. Brand equity increases the likelihood that the consumer will purchase the firm's brand rather than a competing brand.

Young and Rubicam, a global advertising agency, developed the BrandAsset Valuator, which suggests that brand equity is based on four dimensions, as illustrated in Figure 14.1: differentiation, relevance, esteem, and knowledge.[4] Firms with high brand equity, like Apple and Disney, rate highly in these dimensions: They clearly stand apart from competitors (*differentiation*); are relevant to a large segment of consumers (*relevance*); are well known (*knowledge*); and are positively thought of by the majority of their target markets (*esteem*). Organizations with high brand equity enjoy significant advantages over other firms.

LO 14-2

Describe the relevance of brand equity for marketers.

brand equity

The value the firm derives from consumers' positive perception of its products.

Benefits of Brand Equity

High brand equity is an asset to an organization; it provides three major benefits to marketers:

1. *Brand equity increases a firm's ability to succeed in a difficult competitive environment.* Competitors of all sizes try to tempt consumers with new features, catchy slogans, and reduced prices. A consumer who has tried and likes a product has brand loyalty and is more likely to continue to buy it, regardless of outside influences.
2. *Brand equity facilitates a brand's expansion into new markets.* For example, Microsoft's brand equity helped facilitate its move into the video game industry when it introduced its Xbox gaming system. Microsoft's relevance and knowledge as a technology leader helped the Xbox gain popularity and in a relatively short time vault ahead of established gaming-focused companies like Nintendo.[5]
3. *Brand equity can contribute to positive perceptions of product quality.* Mercedes-Benz, another company that is near the top of brand equity rankings, benefits from the fact that most consumers consider a new automobile introduced by the company to be of the highest quality, even before they have had any interaction with it.[6]

Each of the benefits of brand equity discussed also applies to your personal brand. If the work you produce for your employer is of significant value and builds your personal brand equity, the firm will be much more likely to view your future work as high quality; as a result, you are more likely to be promoted to a new position. High personal brand equity translates into a larger salary and more career opportunities than you might have received otherwise.

FIGURE 14.1 The Four Dimensions of the BrandAsset Valuator

Differentiation	Relevance
The brand's point of difference	How appropriate the brand is to you
Esteem	**Knowledge**
How well regarded the brand is	An intimate understanding of the brand

Source:  Y&R, "Y&R BrandAsset Valuator," n.d., http://young-rubicam.de/tools-wissen/tools/brandasset-valuator/?lang=en.

Microsoft has been ranked near the top of a list of firms with the highest brand equity and sees many benefits as a result, including the ability for its products like Xbox to succeed in a very competitive industry. *1000 Words/Shutterstock*

As you seek to establish personal brand equity, you must have a way to identify it and measure it. You may do so through formal performance reviews with your supervisor as well as casual conversations with colleagues. Similarly, firms looking to create brand equity use various techniques to define and quantify it. In the next section, we'll discuss some of the common qualitative and quantitative techniques firms use.

Measuring Brand Equity

Measuring brand equity is fundamental to understanding how to build and manage a brand over time. Companies use several qualitative and quantitative research methods to measure brand equity.

Qualitative Methods to Measure Brand Equity Qualitative research is particularly helpful in identifying the sources of brand equity and its role in consumer decisions.[7] Two important qualitative research methods are free association and projective techniques.

Free association involves asking consumers what comes to mind when they think about the brand.[8] For example, consumers participating in a focus group might be asked to list what comes to mind when they hear the word *Lexus.* They may respond with words and phrases such as *luxury, high quality,* or *very stylish.* These responses give marketers insight into what consumers think of the firm's brand and whether those associations are consistent with the firm's marketing-mix strategies.

Projective techniques are tools used to uncover the true opinions and feelings of consumers when they are unwilling or otherwise unable to express themselves.[9] A common projective strategy involves asking a consumer to compare a brand to a person, animal, car, or country. For example, a consumer may be asked, "If Microsoft was a car, what kind of car would it be?" If the consumer likens Microsoft to a sports car, it might suggest that the consumer considers Microsoft a fast-moving, exciting brand. However, if the consumer compares Microsoft to a minivan, the consumer may believe Microsoft is a conservative, reliable brand that's less exciting than other tech firms like Apple or Google.

Quantitative Methods to Measure Brand Equity
Qualitative techniques can provide interesting, in-depth consumer insights. But they typically involve very small samples of consumers, whose perceptions may not be generalizable to those of the larger population. In an effort to get a more complete understanding of brand equity, marketers also use several quantitative research techniques. Two common quantitative research techniques focus on measuring consumers' recognition and recall of specific brands.

Brand recognition research helps marketers understand two things: (1) which brands stand out in a consumer's memory and (2) the strength of his or her association with the brand. One basic type of brand recognition measure presents a list of single product names, images, or slogans

Companies like Taco Bell can measure their brand equity using free association or projective techniques. Consider for a moment what comes to your mind when you hear the name *Taco Bell. Stan Rohrer/Alamy Stock Photo*

in a survey and asks consumers to identify which items they've previously seen or heard of. Marketers typically include decoys in the list, items that consumers could not possibly have seen. The decoys allow marketers to tell if consumers are truly able to identify the brands they've seen and to distinguish between those and brands they have not been exposed to.

Brand recall refers to consumers' ability to identify the brand under a variety of circumstances.[10] Researchers often use cues to understand brand recall, such as, "When you think of great pizza, what brands come to mind?" Brand recall measures can be used to determine whether consumers consider the firm's brand when they are planning to make a purchase, and if so, whether they think of the firm's brand before they think of competing brands.

It is important to understand the link between brand equity and other important outcomes such as *customer lifetime value.* **Customer lifetime value (CLV)** is the total amount a customer will spend from acquisition through the end of a relationship with a brand. CLV can be calculated using the following formula:

customer lifetime value (CLV)
The total amount a customer will spend from acquisition through the end of a relationship with a brand.

$$Customer\ lifetime\ value\ (CLV) = Average\ value\ of\ a\ sale$$
$$\times\ Number\ of\ repeat\ transactions$$
$$\times\ Number\ of\ repeat\ transactions\ or\ years$$
$$for\ a\ typical\ customer$$

For example, a local gym may offer special pricing to attract new residents in the community to become members. The marketers for the gym are willing to offer the first two months free because they know the average gym member will pay $20 per month every month for five years on average. As such, each new member whom the gym signs up can expect to generate $1,200 in revenue for the brand during their lifetime as a customer:

$$\$20\ (average\ value\ of\ a\ sale) \times 12\ months\ (repeat\ transactions\ per\ year)$$
$$\times\ 5\ years\ (average\ retention\ time)$$
$$= \$1,200\ customer\ lifetime\ value$$

Research has shown that brand equity has a predictable and meaningful impact on customer lifetime value and that marketing activities that built brand equity exerted both direct and indirect impacts on CLV. Marketers can use analytics to measure how effective different marketing tools, such as promotional strategies or pricing changes, are in building brand equity.[11]

As with any kind of marketing research, the tools for measuring brand equity have both advantages and disadvantages. Which method a company chooses depends on the costs of pursuing the research relative to the benefits from any insights uncovered. Firms use these insights to gauge the current strength of the brand. The insights also may reveal how firms may need to modify their brand strategy to be more successful in the future.

LO 14-3

Compare some common strategies for developing brands.

BRAND STRATEGIES

When choosing a brand strategy, marketers seek to maximize their brand equity without diluting profits or damaging the attractiveness of the brand. As always, the brand strategy should align with the overall marketing strategy the firm established in its marketing plan. It should be implemented with the goal of helping the firm accomplish its marketing objectives. Companies have a number of choices as they decide which brand strategies are best for their organization. We'll discuss some common strategies—brand extensions, brand revitalization, co-branding, and private-label brands—in the sections that follow.

Brand Extension

brand extension

The process of broadening the use of an organization's current brand to include new products.

Companies that already possess a strong brand and high brand equity may pursue a brand-extension strategy. **Brand extension** is the process of broadening the use of an organization's current brand to include new products. In an earlier chapter we discussed product extensions, in which a firm expands within the *same product category* (e.g., Coke and Coke Zero Sugar are both soft drinks). Brand extensions, in contrast, typically involve taking a brand name into a *different product category.* A brand-extension strategy enables new products to profit from the recognition and acceptance the brand already enjoys. For example:

- McDonald's extended its brand beyond convenience and Happy Meals to include healthier items such as salads, yogurt parfaits, and premium coffee.
- Crest extended its brand beyond toothpaste to include dental floss, mouthwash, and toothbrushes.
- Dove extended its brand from traditional soap products into hair care products. Because Dove customers already associate the Dove brand with quality, they were able to extend that association to shampoo and other hair care products. The company employed this same strategy to enter into the lotion and deodorant markets as well.

Dove used a brand-extension strategy to leverage its reputation for quality into new product categories, including hair care, lotion, deodorant, and others.

Editorial Image, LLC / Alamy Stock Photo   *AlenKadr/Shutterstock*

As a company implements a brand-extension strategy, it must remain mindful of the following two potential concerns:

1. The extension must live up to the quality consumers expect from the brand. If the quality of the extension products does not meet customer expectations, the firm jeopardizes sales, consumer trust, and brand loyalty.

2. Brand extensions must be implemented with an eye toward avoiding cannibalization. **Cannibalization** is the erosion of sales that occurs when new products eat into sales of a firm's existing products, rather than generate additional revenues or profits. For example, KFC targeted new customers looking for great taste and healthier options when it introduced its new grilled chicken products. But rather than winning over new customers, KFC soon realized that the grilled chicken seemed to be purchased mostly by existing KFC customers, who were buying it instead of the fried version. Despite a major promotional push, sales fell by 4 percent at some KFC locations in the first year after the launch, in part due to the cannibalizing effect the new product had on the company's traditional products.[12]

cannibalization

A reduction in sales volume or market share of a company's existing product due to the introduction of a new product made by the same company.

Brand Revitalization

Brands do not typically die natural deaths; they *can* be killed through mismanagement. Some firms mismanage brands into a position from which they cannot recover. Some brands can be revitalized. **Brand revitalization**, or **rebranding**, is a strategy to recapture lost sources of brand equity and identify and establish new sources of brand equity.

Revitalization begins with a determination to rebuild trust with consumers. That desire is often accompanied by an investment that shows the company's resolve. Following the major scandals from the past decade related to the Deepwater Horizon oil spill in the Gulf of Mexico, marketers at BP responded to consumer demand for more openness, more social responsibility, and more integrity. BP instituted a long-term strategy to rebuild trust that included donating millions of dollars to help the environment and promote tourism in the Gulf region.[13]

Similarly, following the largest recall in the history of the company, Toyota marketers embarked on a brand revitalization campaign with the motto, "Moving Forward."[14] Their efforts included advertisements communicating the company's desire to start fresh with consumers. By fixing defective products and promoting a brighter future, Toyota was able to begin rebuilding its brand image. It increased positive perceptions of the brand in the year following the start of the revitalization campaign.[15]

brand revitalization (rebranding)

A strategy to recapture lost sources of brand equity and identify and establish new sources of brand equity.

Co-Branding

Another alternative is to leverage the equity of another firm's brand to increase one's own brand equity. **Co-branding** is a strategy in which two or more companies issue a single product in an effort to capitalize on the equity of each company's brand. For example:

- The menu at casual dining restaurant T.G.I. Friday's has an entire section dedicated to Jack Daniel's–flavored food. The partnership started in 1997 and continues to be a customer favorite.[16]

- Betty Crocker, a brand introduced in 1921 and owned by General Mills, has been involved in numerous successful co-branding campaigns. The company has issued new products with the likes of Hershey's and Sunkist to create easy-to-make food products that leverage the equity of multiple brands to attract customers.

- Cold Stone Creamery restaurants and the Canadian restaurant chain Tim Hortons have co-branded nearly 150 restaurant locations in the United States and

co-branding

A strategy in which two or more companies issue a single product in an effort to capitalize on the equity of each company's brand.

A co-branding strategy, such as that pursued by Tim Hortons and Cold Stone Creamery, aims to leverage the strengths of two complementary brands to generate new revenue and profit sources for both companies. *Vince Talotta/Toronto Star/Getty Images*

Canada.[17] The co-branding initiative leverages the complementary strengths of each partner to provide value for customers and generate profits for both companies: Tim Hortons is known for its coffee and baked goods; its products are popular in the morning and during the lunch hour. The Cold Stone Creamery desserts sell mostly during the evening hours. Their partnership has allowed Tim Hortons, which faced stiff competition from Starbucks, Dunkin' Donuts, and McDonald's, to expand into the U.S. market; it has given Cold Stone Creamery a new way to entice customers into its stores in the morning and afternoon hours.[18]

Co-branding has many benefits. But negative publicity for one of the brands could affect the co-branding partner in a negative way. For example, consider a rental car company that enters into a co-branding agreement with a hotel chain to provide additional value for business travelers. If the hotel chain receives negative publicity because of poor customer service, the rental car company may be negatively affected because of its association with the underperforming brand. To avoid such pitfalls, marketers should develop processes to select appropriate co-branding partners. Organizations like AT&T have developed a co-branding decision tool that helps guide the firm's marketers as they make decisions related to co-branding opportunities.[19]

Private-Label Brands

private-label brands

Products developed by a retailer and sold only by that specific retailer. Also referred to as *store brands*.

manufacturer brands

Brands that are managed and owned by the manufacturer.

In recent years, as a sluggish economy forced consumers to closely watch their spending, more and more retailers have pursued the strategy of private-label brands. **Private-label brands**, sometimes referred to as *store brands,* are products developed by a retailer and sold only by that specific retailer. For example, Walgreens has developed its own private-label aspirin that competes against the well-known Bayer brand.

Private-label goods and services are available in a wide range of industries, from food to cosmetics to web hosting. They are often positioned as lower-cost alternatives to well-known **manufacturer brands**, brands that are managed and owned by the manufacturer. Private-label brands like Walgreens' aspirin can cost up to 50 percent less than Bayer aspirin.[20] Table 14.1 provides examples of private-label brands across several different types of grocery products.

Over the past decade, annual sales of private-label products have increased by 40 percent in U.S. supermarkets. In addition, over 40 percent of U.S. shoppers now say that at least half of the groceries they buy are private-label brands.[21] Private-label brands are often more profitable to national stores like Walgreens and Target, leading more retailers to develop private-label offerings.[22] Walmart's Great Value brand, and others like it, are even more popular in Europe, where private-label brands account for 35 percent of retail sales, a significantly higher market penetration than in the United States.[23]

Millennials often are ideal candidates for private-label purchases. Their definition of a cool product often does not correlate with high-end, expensive purchases. For a Millennial, a great brand can be a $3 tube of Burt's Bees lip balm. Price is not the determining factor of a brand's value. Archer Farms, Target's private-label food brand, uses artisanal imagery that appeals to Millennials, who are increasingly demanding a premium feel without the higher prices. When marketers can help Millennials justify affordable luxuries, they will likely be satisfied, returning customers for many years.

One of the ways that Walmart promotes its private-label Great Value brand is through packaging. The simple designs feature the Great Value logo in blue and a picture of the

TABLE 14.1 Examples of Private-Label-Branded Products

Gourmet/Premium	Environmentally Conscious
• Sam's Choice (Walmart)	• Bright Green (Safeway)
• Marketside (Walmart)	• Earth Essentials (CVS)
• Gold Emblem (CVS)	• Greenwise (Publix)
• Archer Farms (Target)	
Organic/Healthy Eating	**Pet**
• O Organics (Safeway)	• Ol' Roy (Walmart)
• Eating Right (Safeway)	• Pet Pride (Kroger)
• Simple Truth (Kroger)	• Pet Central (CVS)
• Simply Balanced (Target)	
• Central Market (H-E-B)	
Value	**Exclusive/Licensed**
• P$$T (Kroger)	• Urbini (Walmart)
• Shoppers Value (SUPERVALU)	• Better Homes & Gardens (Walmart)
	• Persil (Walmart/Henkel)
	• Circa (Walgreens/Eva Mendes)
	• Nuance (CVS/Salma Hayek)
	• C9 (Target/Champion)

Source: https://markettrack.com.

product; that simplicity signals to customers that this is a no-frills product that delivers value for their dollar. Whatever brand image a firm is trying to establish, it should understand the powerful tool that packaging can be in building a successful brand.

PACKAGING

LO 14-4

Summarize the impact of packaging on brand building.

Consider how many advertisements you see every day. You may think that virtually every product you buy is heavily promoted. The truth is that we all buy many products for which we never see, hear, or read a promotional message. For such products, the only tool marketers have to catch our attention, provide information, and build their brand is packaging. **Packaging** is all of the activities of designing and producing the container for a product. It is one of the most underappreciated tools in marketing.

packaging

All of the activities of designing and producing the container for a product.

Virtually every good comes in a package. Yet, many marketers do not take advantage of the opportunity to use packaging to promote the brand and cut through the growing amount of clutter consumers face. Packaging gives the product a chance to stand out among the other 30,000 items that are stocked by an average American retailer.[24] Companies use words, symbols, colors, pictures, and other brand marks on their packages to help communicate the brand attributes to consumers. In addition, packaging promotes and reinforces brand image.

Promoting Brand Image

Many organizations consider packaging only in the basic terms of containing, protecting, and shipping packages. This is a shortsighted view. Packaging provides marketers with an opportunity to promote the image they want others to associate with the brand. For example, packaging allows premium products to communicate class and sophistication. A classic example is the Tiffany gift box, which has come to indicate quality, both to the person receiving the gift and to the rest of the world. The Tiffany box and shopping bag a

The simple elegance of Tiffany's packaging is reminiscent of the luxury of the brand's physical store and reminds consumers of their in-store experience. *Elise Amendola/AP Images*

consumer carries out of the store serve as a type of mobile billboard seen by other consumers, particularly in large metropolitan cities. The shopping bag may also remain in a consumer's home for some time after the purchase, offering a continuing reminder of the luxury experience, which can increase brand recall.

Packaging is one of the few points of customer contact that upscale firms can directly control. As a result, they cannot afford to miss the chance to extend the luxury experience and promote brand image beyond the store's walls.

Reinforcing Brand Image

Marketers also can utilize packaging to reinforce their brand image with consumers. For example, demand for environmentally friendly packaging has changed the marketing landscape for U.S. consumer goods in many categories. Research suggests that a growing number of consumers are *green motivated,* or driven to make decisions based on concern about the environment.[25] They make purchasing decisions based not only on environmentally friendly ingredients and manufacturing procedures but also on packaging materials. In response to this trend, in 2009 Coca-Cola launched PlantBottle packaging, a recyclable plastic bottle made partly from plant materials. PlantBottle packaging received an Edison Award, which recognizes innovative products. Coca-Cola has shared the technology and entered into a partnership with Heinz, to allow Heinz to put its ketchup in PlantBottle packaging.[26]

Regardless of the industry, packaging is considered an important indicator of brand quality. The quality of the brand has to be communicated by good packaging, and not just by *promises* of quality made in the text on the packaging. Effective packaging results in an engaging and persuasive marketing tool in which the product and its packaging form a coherent whole, and the consumer forms their image of the brand based on this consistency.

The same relationship between packaging and brand quality holds true when branding yourself. From a self-branding perspective, the way you package your ideas, thoughts, and accomplishments influences others to listen to what you have to say. Consider the way you package yourself for an interview: Your resume and clothing project your brand image. Ineffective packaging of your personal brand could include typographical errors on your resume, grammatical mistakes in your e-mails, or unprofessional attire for an interview. Your ideas and potential may be phenomenal, but no one will listen to you if you package yourself the wrong way. Therefore, invest time and resources into packaging your personal brand in a way that promotes and reinforces your brand image.

Mc Graw Hill connect Exercise **14-2**

Please complete the *Connect* exercise for Chapter 14 that focuses on packaging. By analyzing different packaging strategies, you should gain insights into which strategies work and don't work and how packaging can play an important role in building a strong brand.

LO 14-5

Summarize the impact of social media on brand management.

THE ROLE OF SOCIAL MEDIA IN BRANDING

The idea that firms can manage their brands by simply crafting messages into print and digital materials and then handing them down from the corporate office is becoming more outdated every day. Consumers spend more time than ever using social media, trading opinions and feedback on everything they come into contact with. On Instagram alone, over 80 percent of users follow at least one business.[27] Marketing professionals who understand the impact social media can have on building their brands and connecting directly with their audience will be positioned for success.

Customer Engagement through Social Media

Customers engage with brands via social media for various reasons. Figure 14.2 lists the things consumers most want from brands on social media. We discuss some of these reasons in the sections that follow.

Consumers Seeking Discounts Figure 14.2 indicates that consumers increasingly express their brand loyalty via social media in the hope of reaping benefits from firms. Among those who connect with brands through social media, 72 percent say they do so to receive discounts.[28] Starbucks was ranked as one of the most "loved" brands by Millennials on social media in 2018, in part because of the specials it offers to its most loyal customers.[29] Starbucks has developed a huge social media presence: Over 50 million people have joined Starbucks's communities on such sites as Facebook, YouTube, Twitter, and Instagram. Starbucks also engages with customers and builds its brand through competitions. For example, the company put up advertising posters in six major U.S. cities and asked people to take a picture of them and tweet it; winners received a store gift card worth $20.[30]

Offering special discounts can increase positive feedback, but marketers should be aware of the potential risks of such promotional activities. Continually offering discounts or specials has the potential to devalue the brand and the company's relationship with customers. It can also have the effect of

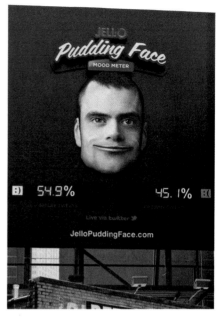

Jell-O engaged consumers with its brand by installing a billboard that analyzes the number of happy and sad emoticons used on Twitter at any given time. *Andrew Burton/Getty Images News/Getty Images*

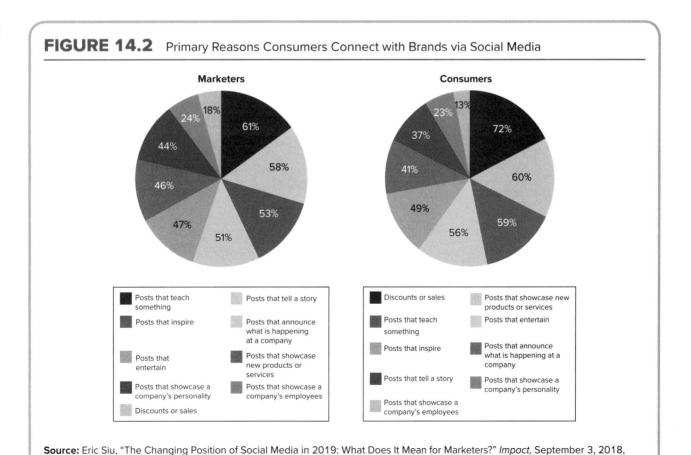

FIGURE 14.2 Primary Reasons Consumers Connect with Brands via Social Media

Marketers

- 61% — Posts that teach something
- 58% — Posts that tell a story
- 53%
- 51%
- 47%
- 46%
- 44%
- 24%
- 18%

Legend:
- Posts that teach something
- Posts that tell a story
- Posts that inspire
- Posts that announce what is happening at a company
- Posts that entertain
- Posts that showcase new products or services
- Posts that showcase a company's personality
- Posts that showcase a company's employees
- Discounts or sales

Consumers

- 72% — Discounts or sales
- 60%
- 59%
- 56%
- 49%
- 41%
- 37%
- 23%
- 13%

Legend:
- Discounts or sales
- Posts that showcase new products or services
- Posts that teach something
- Posts that entertain
- Posts that inspire
- Posts that announce what is happening at a company
- Posts that tell a story
- Posts that showcase a company's personality
- Posts that showcase a company's employees

Source: Eric Siu, "The Changing Position of Social Media in 2019: What Does It Mean for Marketers?" *Impact*, September 3, 2018, https://www.impactbnd.com/blog/changing-position-of-social-media-in-2018-marketers.

Companies like Delta offer special promotions to consumers on Facebook and other social media sites. While customers benefit from the deals, the companies benefit from the online endorsement they receive when customers engage with the brand. *Stephen Lovekin/Getty Images Entertainment/Getty Images*

underpricing the product, thereby reducing profits. Marketers must balance the desire to have a significantly positive social media presence with the brand equity measures discussed earlier in this chapter. If consumers' free association responses when asked to describe a brand include "constant discounts" or "wait for special promotions," such responses should be consistent with the firm's desired brand image. If they're not, the company may need to rethink how it's using social media (and other promotional) tools.

Posts That Showcase New Products and Services

With a large percentage of the world's population using social media platforms, they're a natural place to reach new and highly targeted potential customers. Sixty percent of Instagram users say they discover new products on the platform.[31] Social media also provides brands an opportunity to showcase different aspects of their product. The National Basketball Association (NBA) and its member teams are often recognized in the sports business community as innovators in showcasing their players and teams. The league and teams have embraced the use of social media channels to keep fans interested through behind-the-scenes access, game highlights, stats, and glimpses of players' lifestyles off the court. The NBA receives over one million logo exposures on official league and team profiles and its brands receive hundreds of millions of dollars worth of exposure via social media each season.[32]

Posts That Teach Something

Social media play an important role in how consumers discover, research, and learn information about brands and products. Data from the Nielsen research firm provide striking evidence of the growing role of social media in brand building: Sixty percent of consumers researching products through online sources learned about a specific brand or retailer through social networking sites.[33] Active social media users are more likely to read product reviews online, and three out of five create their own reviews of products. Female consumers are more likely than male consumers to tell others about products that they like (81 percent of females versus 72 percent of males).

Videos posted to social media sites demonstrating the ease with which Kryptonite bike locks could be opened with a pen prompted Kryptonite to redesign its product. *Elise Amendola/AP Images*

One of the earliest examples of social media's impact on a brand occurred with Kryptonite bike locks. Kryptonite has been a leading producer of bicycle locks for more than three decades. Several consumer-produced videos appeared on YouTube and other sites showing how to open a Kryptonite bike lock with a common Bic pen. The video spread rapidly, and negative consumer reviews began to appear as a result. To protect its brand equity, Kryptonite responded to these reviews by redesigning its product and offering free upgrades to those who purchased vulnerable locks.[34]

When researching products, social media users tend to trust the recommendations of their friends and family most. Firms like Starbucks are well aware of the influence these personal recommendations can have and make a concerted effort to reach *super influencers,* adults typically between 18 and 49 years old who reach a large number of potential consumers through social media.

Branding through Customer Service

Many customers use social media to engage with brands on a customer service level. Questions from customers on social media sites allow companies to provide direct feedback and potentially resolve a specific problem faster than they could have otherwise. While social media can spread complaints like wildfire, responding in a timely fashion can showcase the company's commitment to excellence. For example, Morton's Steakhouse was given this opportunity when a customer tweeted a request from aboard a flight that he would love it if the premium steak restaurant would have a porterhouse ready for him when he landed in Newark in two hours (Figure 14.3). The customer was Peter Shankman who had over 110,000 Twitter followers and is considered an influencer of social media. Morton's cleverly took advantage of this tweet by sending a representative to meet Shankman at the gate in Newark with a 24-ounce Porterhouse steak, an order of Colossal Shrimp, potatoes, bread, and silverware. Morton's was able to turn what most brands would have ignored as a throwaway request into a powerful example of its willingness to provide customer service by any means necessary.[35]

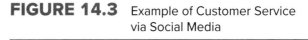

FIGURE 14.3   Example of Customer Service via Social Media

Peter Shankman ✔
@petershankman   ☼   ⚲ Follow

Hey @Mortons - can you meet me at newark airport with a porterhouse when I land in two hours? K, thanks. :)

RETWEETS   LIKES
16   28

4:08 PM - 17 Aug 2011

Source: Tabitha Jean Naylor, "How Brands Are Using Social Media to Boost Customer Engagement," *SocialMedia Today,* January 18, 2018, https://www.socialmediatoday.com/news/how-brands-are-using-social-media-to-boost-customer-engagement/514872/.

Though social media facilitate the speed and efficiency with which firms can respond to customer service issues, they also raise the expectations customers have for how quickly their problems should be resolved. According to Nielsen, 42 percent of 18- to 34-year-olds say they expect customer support within 12 hours of a question or complaint.[36] People expect brands to be available on social media and seek out their social accounts for customer service. Research shows that brands who don't meet those expectations damage their bottom line. For example, a recent study found that customers who receive a response to their tweet would be willing to spend more with the brand on a later purchase, especially if they get a response within five minutes. That holds true even when the initial tweet was a direct complaint.[37]

Social Media Branding Goals

Social media can support the goal of building a successful brand in two main ways:

1. By allowing the firm to develop deeper relationships with customers.
2. By generating positive word-of-mouth communication about the brand across social networks.

The marketers for Oreo cookies kept these two goals in mind as they implemented social media activities in their marketing strategy. Oreo has developed a robust online following and interacts regularly with those followers through a variety of social media platforms. The Oreo's team responds promptly to questions posed via the company's Facebook page. Oreo is consistently producing relevant content on its social media platforms. One of the brand's best campaigns called the #MyOreoCreation contest encouraged people to submit flavor ideas on social media with a $500,000 reward for the person whose idea is chosen. Oreo created a highly engaging contest for consumers, whereby they could send in their own Oreo cookie flavor ideas to Twitter or Instagram with the hashtags #MyOreoCreation. The over 800,000 Oreo followers suggested flavors from Kettle Corn to Marshmallow, generating lots of positive word of mouth across social networks.[38]

Marketers should consistently evaluate their social media presence to determine if these two key goals—deeper

Social Mention, which monitors multiple social media sites, is one of various tools firms can use to measure social media activity that affects their product, brand, or industry.
Source: *Oreo*

customer relationships and positive word-of-mouth communication—are being achieved. If they are not, marketers would be wise to consider what strategies they can take to use social media more effectively.

Monitoring a Social Brand

Regardless of what prompts consumers to follow and engage with a brand, marketers should closely monitor what is being said about their brands on social media. McDonald's learned this lesson firsthand when it launched #McDStories on Twitter as a way to encourage customers to share fun or heartwarming stories about their experiences at the restaurant. What McDonald's marketers did not expect, and thus were not prepared for, was people sharing negative stories about the McDonald's brand. Any consumer who searched for "McDStories" immediately saw thousands of tweets describing awful experiences users had with McDonald's.[39]

Whether a Fortune 500 firm, a small business, or a local nonprofit organization, all companies can use a number of tools to monitor their social media presence. Some of the most commonly used tools include the following:

- *Google Alerts.* Firms can set up alerts about their company, good, service, or brand and receive an e-mail whenever they appear online. Firms can also set up alerts to be notified when consumers search the Internet using keywords or industry terminology that is important to their business.
- *Social Mention.* Social Mention is a tool that captures mentions of brands across most social media sites. The Social Mention search engine monitors over 100 platforms, isolating relevant keywords and measuring a brand's impact online.
- *UTM Parameters.* UTM parameters are short text codes added to a URL to track important data about website visitors and traffic sources. UTM parameters work with analytics programs like Google Analytics to provide a detailed picture of a brands social media success, from which platforms are performing best down to which specific post drove the most traffic to a specific page.
- *Hootsuite Impact.* This tool helps marketers understand the revenue and marketing results generated by social media. Impact measures conversions by social channel and analyzes ROI between owned and paid media, which helps marketers improve performance by analyzing their content, spend, and conversions.

These and other tools are relatively inexpensive and easy to set up. Marketers who use these tools to monitor their brands are able to recognize potential threats to their brand equity quickly, and develop solutions if needed. They are also better prepared to facilitate an ongoing dialogue with customers to strengthen brand loyalty over time. Firms that monitor the social profiles they build and integrate the various ways they communicate with customers online can successfully leverage social media to help build a successful brand.

Since the beginning of the COVID-19 pandemic in 2020, 75 percent of U.S. consumers say they've tried new shopping behaviors for both economic reasons and shifts in personal priorities. Consumers are increasingly quick to adapt to changing circumstances making social media monitoring indispensable for marketers trying to keep their brands ahead of the curve.[40]

Mc Graw Hill connect Exercise **14-3**

Social Media in Action

By effectively expanding into social media, brands can foster closer relationships with their followers. They also can add extra credibility to marketing at a time when consumers are increasingly turned off by traditional advertising. In the past, a brand could use its marketing campaigns to present a consistent message. The meteoric rise of social media has forced companies, especially luxury brands, to reassess how they use, interact with, and respond to social media sites like Instagram and Snapchat.

That response includes finding new ways to engage with brand followers. Some companies engage with brand followers through regular digital interactions on popular social media sites. Others offer online extras, like behind-the-scene looks at fashion shows or photo shoots to reinforce their ties to a designer or fashion house. Brands also have turned to social media to extend their presence beyond the traditional customer base, partly to reach a new generation of consumers who have grown up online.

Some luxury brands have embraced social media and other digital activities with greater energy than others. Some digitally savvy brands have incorporated social media and other online platforms directly into their wider marketing campaigns. Burberry, for example, regularly posts on YouTube and Snapchat. Such social media activities give companies a greater reach in the online world, associating their brand with people's desire to be connected to the next online trend.

Marketing experts say that how a company is viewed online—not just by its primary customers, but also by the wider online population—can have a significant impact on a brand's overall reputation, particularly with digitally literate young shoppers. This change has been particularly acute for luxury brands such as Louis Vuitton and Chanel. These companies have traditionally fostered an image of exclusivity as part of their marketing strategies, portraying a lifestyle that is often out of reach for most people. In response to the digital free-for-all that characterizes the Internet, many companies have expanded their brands' online footprint, often teaming up with social media darlings and other celebrities to present a more populist image:

- Dior, for example, joined forces with music star Rihanna, whose social media following is four times as large as that of the Dior fashion label.
- Calvin Klein signed a deal with Justin Bieber, in part to tap into the Canadian singer's avid following on Instagram and Twitter, where his audience is up to 15 times as large as that of the brand.
- Instagram, the photo-friendly online platform, has become the social network of choice for luxury brands and their followers.

The ability to engage with a wider audience through sites like Instagram and Snapchat lies at the heart of how companies should use online platforms. The British label Karen Millen, for instance, has crowdsourced photos from social media as part of its online store, showing how its customers view the brand online. Coach turned to user-generated images in a recent advertising campaign to highlight its range of footwear; the campaign includes an interactive map showing where customers had taken their digital photos around the world.

These types of online interactions would happen irrespective of a brand's participation. But by engaging with both core consumers and the broader digital audience, luxury brands have an opportunity to use the marketing potential offered by social media.

The Social Media in Action Connect exercise in Chapter 14 will let you develop strategies by choosing which messages and platforms should be part of building your brand through social media. Brands can be built or destroyed faster than ever before due to the power of social media, and it will be important for you to consider how to use a variety of social media tools to best position your brand for success.

Source: Mark Scott, "Luxury Brands and the Social Campaign," *The New York Times,* December 1, 2015, http://www.nytimes.com/2015/12/02/fashion/luxury-brands-and-the-social-campaign.html?_r=0.

LO 14-6

Discuss the major branding challenges facing global marketers.

global brand

A brand that is marketed under the same name in multiple countries.

GLOBAL BRANDING

Building a strong brand is a complicated task, and the challenge is even greater when the branding becomes global. A **global brand** is a brand that is marketed under the same name in multiple countries. Table 14.2 lists the most valuable global brands in 2021 based on three criteria: (1) the financial performance of the branded product, (2) the role the brand plays in influencing consumers, and (3) the ability of the brand to draw a premium price or significantly affect the company's profits.

Coca-Cola is the only company to rank in the top six most valuable global brands every year since 2000. The Atlanta-based company has had marketing success throughout the world, including in Mexico, where the soft drink was introduced in 1898 and registered as a brand in 1903. To expedite its entry into the Mexican market, Coca-Cola provided free refrigerators to restaurants and taco restaurants to encourage distribution and trial. The strategy worked as increasing numbers of consumers in Mexico tried the product, and Coke became widely distributed even in the remotest parts of Mexico. Coca-Cola has used a similar strategy for success in many developed and emerging economies.

The Global Strength of U.S. Brands

The American economy rebounded from the financial crisis that began in December 2007 at a slightly faster pace than did the economies of many European countries. That rebound enhanced the marketing value of U.S. brands in the global marketplace. In addition, U.S. companies in general benefit from the collective success of U.S. tech companies like Apple, Facebook, and Google, due to the cachet of Silicon Valley in the global imagination. The Internet and the language associated with it are rooted in U.S. brands and U.S. imagery, increasing marketers' success building U.S. brands globally. Also, social networking sites such as Facebook and Twitter have been important tools in promoting U.S. brands internationally.

Research indicates that emerging middle-class consumers in developing countries desire American-sounding brand names. These socioeconomic groups in China, India, Brazil, Russia, and other developing countries associate status with U.S. brands. Consumers in China, for example, seek brands such as Budweiser, General Motors, Tiffany, Jack Daniels, Levi's, Harley-Davidson, KFC, and Pizza Hut.[41]

TABLE 14.2   The Top 10 Most Valuable Global Brands

1. Apple	6. Coca-Cola
2. Amazon	7. Toyota
3. Microsoft	8. Mercedes-Benz
4. Google	9. McDonald's
5. Samsung	10. Disney

Source: Interbrand, "Best Global Brands 2021 Rankings," https://www.rankingthebrands.com/The-Brand-Rankings.aspx?rankingID=37

Adapting Brands to the Global Market

Even with the strength of U.S. brands overseas, global branding is mainly about finding the right balance between being global and being local. With the abundance of digital platforms, many companies are deciding they will no longer follow different brand strategies in different countries. Instead, they are adopting a more unified branding approach. Although the brand image remains the same from country to country, the ways to communicate it and make it relevant to local consumers should adapt to each specific context. The biggest challenge in global branding is to remain easily recognizable at any location and, at the same time, be compatible with the local culture and traditions.

In 2018, a2 Milk Company more than doubled its Chinese market share by focusing its brand message on the fact that its product comes from New Zealand dairy herds that produce only a protein known as A2, which the company contends is easier to digest than the blend of A1 and A2 proteins found in most European and U.S. herds. Chinese parents, spooked by health and safety scares in recent years, are splurging on premium goods for their kids. a2 Milk's brand is positioned near the top of the market, with a week's supply generally selling online for over 200 yuan.[42]

Marketing professionals often appeal to local culture through packaging. Cultural differences can greatly affect product packaging:

- In Chile, the average consumer eats several pounds of mayonnaise each year, much more than the average U.S. consumer. As a result, mayonnaise in Chile is often sold in large two-pound bags.[43]
- When KFC first entered the Japanese market, its traditional "bucket" packaging did not meet the higher standards of Japanese consumers for food packaging and presentation. In response, KFC modified its packaging and presentation strategy, laying the chicken neatly in wide boxes.[44]

A common mistake marketers in the United States make is to group together nations, for example, Asian countries, and assume that consumers in those countries

Gucci, Chanel, and other luxury brands typically succeed in countries like Japan in which consumers accept, and sometimes prefer, foreign brands that project a particular self-image. *Wei yao/Imaginechina/AP Images*

Today's **Professional**... because everyone is a marketer

Justin Shaw

Marketing Manager
FedEx Services

Describe your job. I'm a marketing manager at FedEx Services and have responsibilities across three lines of marketing priorities: marketing alliances, our marketing relationship with a major credit card provider, and customer journey management. Within our marketing alliances, we manage relationships with member-based associations to drive acquisitions of new customers by providing the association with shipping benefits they pass on to their members. Our credit card relationship looks to utilize an exclusive agreement that enables our team to provide offers to cardholders to deepen their relationship with FedEx. Last, within journey management, we look to design and orchestrate customer experiences that combine digital and human touch points from FedEx to nurture, grow, and retain revenue from small and medium business customers.

How did you get your job? I started at FedEx as part of a Marketing Scholars program, in which I studied for my Master's full time

Photo provided by Justin Shaw

at the Fogelman College of Business and Economics at the University of Memphis and rotated through five different departments within the marketing organization. After completion, I spent the first portion of my FedEx career in a variety of digital roles from product managing an innovative refresh of a portion of our retail convenience network to leading the strategy of our Testing & Personalization practice on FedEx .com. I was recently promoted to manager and I attribute having this opportunity to the power of my internal professional network, valuable career experience, and a willingness to be a passionate champion for our customers and for FedEx.

What has been the most important thing in making you successful at your job? I believe the most important thing that has made me successful has been a willingness to continuously learn and my ability to cultivate and nurture relationships with coworkers. With the speed at which customer expectations are increasing, staying ahead of the learning curve is paramount to be able to answer to any macro-economic trends that affect your business. Also, working at a company the size and complexity of FedEx, there is next to nothing that can be accomplished without the help of stakeholders from a variety of functional areas.

What advice would you give soon-to-be graduates? I would say a couple of things: One, never stop learning. If you're not learning, you lose the opportunity to differentiate yourself. Two, never have regrets. You should always make decisions based off the information you have in front of you. If you make a bad decision, make a new one.

What do you consider your personal brand to be? I consider my personal brand to be one of loyalty, passion, and driven determination. I will always prioritize my family and friends because at the end of the day that's all we have. My passion can be seen on display during meetings and one-on-one sessions discussing our brand or our customers, and my determination can be witnessed on a daily basis. I enjoy being a self-starter and always look forward to the next challenge.

have similar tastes and brand preferences. Such a shortsighted view can cause problems as brands enter international markets. For example, Japanese consumers are the most brand-conscious and status-conscious of all developed countries and are generally accepting of foreign brands. Research suggests that Japanese consumers prefer global brands that contribute to their sense of identity and self-expression.[45] The most successful brands in Japan include Louis Vuitton, Gucci, Coach, Chanel, and other prestigious names. Korean consumers share a preference for premium brands, but in contrast to Japanese consumers, they hold relatively more negative attitudes toward foreign brands. For U.S. brands to be successful in Korea, marketers often look to rebrand their products or even pursue a co-branding strategy with a local brand.

The coming decade is likely to bring continued economic challenges to many parts of the world. It will become increasingly necessary for marketers to establish truly global brands that help them attract and retain customers. Marketers should be prepared to successfully manage their brand in whatever geographic location offers their firm the greatest chance for growth and success.

Mc Graw Hill connect Exercise **14-4**

Please complete the *Connect* exercise for Chapter 14 that focuses on strategies for localizing a global brand to maximize success in different international markets. By understanding the branding decisions required to best appeal to a particular country and culture, you should gain insights into how to market your brand in different regions of the world.

BRANDING FOR NONPROFIT ORGANIZATIONS

LO 14-7

Explain the role of branding in nonprofit organizations.

When it comes to building a strong brand, for-profit firms like Under Armour have a clear reason for doing so—they need to generate profits by satisfying customer needs and wants with products that customers perceive as better than competing products. In contrast, nonprofit organizations like United Way and Big Brothers Big Sisters have complex missions that are hard to achieve, difficult to measure directly, and typically require a number of partners. Nonprofits also have many customers, or stakeholder groups, that are critical to their success. The complexity of both the goals and the audiences that nonprofit marketers have to address makes branding even more critical for them. The organization's brand has to help motivate donors, staff, volunteers, beneficiaries, and partners.

An effective nonprofit brand should be unique, aesthetically pleasing, easy to remember, and, perhaps most importantly, reflective of the work the organization does. The World Wildlife Fund (WWF) provides an example of successful branding by a nonprofit organization. It has a portfolio of activities and partners, with programs spanning advocacy, market transformation, community-based conservation, and climate change. However, the brand image it established with its panda logo has been tied most closely to

The World Wildlife Fund has worked hard to ensure that its panda brand mark reflects the work the organization does in conservation, climate change, and species protection. *Evaristo Sa/AFP/Getty Images*

TABLE 14.3   The Most Valuable Nonprofit Brands

Category	Most Valuable Nonprofit Brand
Youth interest	Reading Is Fundamental (RIF)
Animal welfare	Best Friends Animal Society
Health	St. Jude Children's Research Hospital
Social service	Ronald McDonald House Charities
Disability	Autism Society of America
International aid	Food for the Poor
Environmental	National Wildlife Federation

Source: Harris Interactive, "2018 Harris Poll Non-Profit EquiTrend," April 25, 2018, https://theharrispoll.com/the-harris-poll-announces-this-years-brands-of-the-year-in-the-2018-equitrend-study/.

only its most well-known activity: species conservation. WWF marketers developed internal-story themes to help align the brand image with the brand mark. The recognizable panda logo conveys the breadth of the organization's work beyond species conservation without compromising either clarity or emotional pull.

In 2018, WWF marketers created a branding campaign called "Sack of Socks" to increase awareness and raise funds during the holiday season. For a $55 contribution, the organization sent three pairs of unique socks that supporters could wear or give as gifts. WWF created over 30 designs that feature some of the endangered animals it works with, from giraffes to honeybees to narwhals, and food patterns that represent its efforts to feed the world with environmentally friendly produce.

Nonprofit Brand Equity

Like a for-profit firm, once a nonprofit organization creates a brand image that matches its mission, it should seek to establish and increase its brand equity. A nonprofit with high brand equity can use the value stakeholders associate with the organization to raise the funds and support it needs to accomplish its mission.

The Autism Society of America and the National Wildlife Federation are examples of nonprofit organizations that command high brand equity. They were named the top nonprofit brands in their respective categories in 2018.[46] Table 14.3 lists the most valuable nonprofit brands in 2018 across several categories (youth interest, animal welfare, health, social service, disability, international aid, and environmental). The analysis, by the marketing firm Harris Interactive, used surveys to determine how well the public knows a brand, how positively they think of the brand, and whether they would do business with or donate to the brand.

Measuring Nonprofit Brand Equity

Similar to for-profit firms, nonprofit marketers should regularly measure their brand equity using the tools described earlier in this chapter. Social media tools are particularly important for nonprofit marketers because of their low cost relative to other traditional brand-building media, such as television advertising. Nonprofit organizations often do not have the resources to enhance their brand image through expensive ad campaigns or sponsorships. Social media help level the playing field by offering nonprofit marketers low-cost (and often free) tools to communicate with followers and potential donors about their work.

A nonprofit organization that can develop a strong brand image is far more likely to align supporters with the organization's mission and deepen their commitment as donors, volunteers, and advocates.

SUMMARY

2p2play/Shutterstock

LO 14-1 Explain the importance of building a successful brand.

A *brand* is the name, term, symbol, design, or any combination of these that identifies and differentiates a firm's products. For many current, former, and potential customers, a brand represents everything that a good, service, or idea means to a customer. A successful brand leads to increased brand loyalty and more recognizable products.

Brand-loyal customers exhibit less sensitivity to price, making them an important contributor to a firm's long-term success and profitability. *Brand recognition* based on symbols and logos can be a powerful marketing tool.

Developing a successful brand involves four essential components: (1) deliver a quality product, (2) create a consistent brand image, (3) create consistent brand messaging, and (4) capture feedback.

1000 Words/ Shutterstock

LO 14-2 Describe the relevance of brand equity for marketers.

Brand equity is the value the firm derives from consumers' positive perception of its products. Brand equity is based on four dimensions: differentiation, relevance, esteem, and knowledge.

High brand equity provides three major benefits to marketers: First, it increases a firm's ability to succeed in a difficult competitive environment. Second, it can facilitate a brand's expansion into new markets. Third, it can contribute to positive perceptions of product quality.

Measuring brand equity is fundamental to understanding how to build and manage equity over time. Two qualitative techniques that marketers use to measure brand equity are free association and projective techniques. Quantitative techniques that marketers use to measure brand equity include *brand recognition, brand recall,* and *customer lifetime value (CLV).*

Vince Talotta/Toronto Star/Getty Images

LO 14-3 Compare some common strategies for developing brands.

Marketers should choose a brand strategy that increases their brand equity without diluting profits or damaging the attractiveness of the brand. A *brand extension* is the process of broadening the use of an organization's current brand to include new products. Many new products are brand extensions, which provide the new good or service increased recognition and faster acceptance.

Brand revitalization is a strategy to recapture lost sources of brand equity and identify and establish new sources of brand equity. *Co-branding* is a strategy in which two or more companies issue a single product in an effort to capitalize on the equity of each company's brand. *Private-label brands* are products developed by retailers. They are often positioned as lower-cost alternatives to well-known manufacturer brands.

Elise Amendola/ AP Images

LO 14-4 Summarize the impact of packaging on brand building.

Packaging is all of the activities of designing and producing the container for a product. It is one of the most underappreciated tools in marketing. Packaging uses words, symbols, colors, pictures, and designs to help communicate the brand's attributes to consumers. Packaging promotes and reinforces brand image. The quality of the brand has to be communicated by good packaging and not just by promises of quality made in the text on the packaging.

Stephen Lovekin/ Getty Images Entertainment/Getty Images

LO 14-5 Summarize the impact of social media on brand management.

Social media play an important role in how consumers discover, research, and share information about brands and products. Consumers increasingly use social media to express their loyalty to their favorite brands; many seek to reap benefits from brands for helping promote their products. In addition, many customers use social media to engage with brands on a customer service level.

Two common ways social media support brand building across industries are by helping the company deepen its relationships with customers and generating positive word-of-mouth communication that can spread across social networks.

Wei yao/ Imaginechina/AP Images

LO 14-6 Discuss the major branding challenges facing global marketers.

Building a strong brand is a complicated task, and the challenge is even greater when the branding becomes global. A global brand is a brand that is marketed under the same name in multiple countries. Global branding is mainly about finding the right balance between being global and being local.

U.S. firms should understand and seek to capitalize on the strength of their brands in global markets. They should focus on the factors that drive consumers to pay a premium price for global brands, including the conviction that global brands represent better quality and the latest innovations.

Evaristo Sa/ AFP/Getty Images

LO 14-7 Explain the role of branding in nonprofit organizations.

The complexity of both the goals and the audiences that nonprofit organizations have to address makes branding perhaps even more critical in the nonprofit sector. An effective nonprofit brand should be unique, pleasing to the eye and ear, easy to remember, and reflective of the work the organization does. The nonprofit organization's brand has to further the mission at every step and motivate donors, staff, volunteers, beneficiaries, and partners to contribute funds and support.

KEY TERMS

brand (p. 474)
brand equity (p. 477)
brand extension (p. 480)
brand image (p. 474)
brand loyalty (p. 474)

brand marks (p. 474)
brand recognition (p. 474)
brand revitalization (rebranding) (p. 481)
cannibalization (p. 481)
co-branding (p. 481)

customer lifetime value (CLV) (p. 479)
global brand (p. 490)
manufacturer brands (p. 482)
packaging (p. 483)
private-label brands (p. 482)

MARKETING PLAN EXERCISE • Marketing Yourself

In this chapter we discussed the importance of building a strong personal brand. The next step in developing your personal marketing plan is to establish a strategy for building your personal brand that will help you achieve the objectives you identified in Chapter 1.

First, think about what your personal brand is now: What do people think of when they hear your name? Are you happy with the answer to that question? Remember that not having a brand at all can negatively influence your success, too. It prevents you from standing out from your classmates and others who will be applying for the same job or graduate school opening.

Next, develop specific brand-building action items for the next year that will help build, strengthen, or revitalize your personal brand. You might include things like running for office in a club or organization on campus or targeting a specific type of internship. You could also include things like going to your professors during their office hours to make yourself more than a face in the crowd, which can be very beneficial when it is time to list references or ask for letters of recommendation.

Give this exercise careful thought. Being aware of your current brand and planning specific actions to develop that brand will be one of the most important career steps you can take over the next year.

Your Task: Develop three to five specific brand-building action items for the next year. For each, clearly define the action you plan to take and set a deadline for taking that action. Finally, provide a description of what the expected outcomes will be for each brand-building action.

DISCUSSION QUESTIONS

1. Think of a brand to which you, as a consumer, are loyal. Why are you loyal to that brand? Does your brand loyalty extend to paying more if the price increases? Next, think of a type of product for which you feel no loyalty to any one brand. How does not being loyal to any brand change your buying patterns for that type of product?

2. Name a specific brand that you think needs to be revitalized. Why do you think this? What specific advice and suggestions would you give the company as it embarks on the brand revitalization process?

3. How high would you consider your personal brand equity to be? If you used the tools discussed in this chapter to measure brand equity, how might others in your life respond? For example, ask a friend, family member, or professor what they think of when they hear your name. Or ask, if you were a car, what kind of car would you be and why? Based on these responses, are you satisfied with your current level of brand equity? If not, what are you planning to do in the next 12 months to build more equity?

4. Look at your home or at a grocery store and identify two brands that you think use packaging in an effective way. Explain specifically why you think the packaging is effective. Then, reverse this and identify two brands that you think do not use packaging effectively. Again, explain specifically why you feel this way.

5. Consider a nonprofit organization in your life (this could be your church, a charity, an organization on campus, etc.) and analyze whether it does a good job of building its brand. Does it have high brand equity? If you chose to measure the organization's equity, how do you think people in your community would answer the qualitative and quantitative questions presented in this chapter? Give two recommendations to help the nonprofit build its brand (or further enhance it if you feel it already has a strong brand).

6. Think of a global brand, headquartered outside your home country, that you are loyal to (e.g., Honda if you live in the United States, or Coca-Cola if you live in South Africa). Why are you loyal to that brand? Why do you choose that brand over domestic brands?

 ## SOCIAL MEDIA APPLICATION

Select a public figure (celebrity, politician, professional athlete, etc.) who effectively leverages social media to build their personal brand. Analyze the person's efforts to build brand equity via social media, using the following questions and activities as a guide:

1. What specific activities does the person engage in via social media to build their brand?

2. Give two potential strategies for how you can use social media to build your personal brand.
3. Briefly summarize how social media can potentially harm the public figure discussed earlier or your own personal brand.

 ## MARKETING ANALYTICS EXERCISE

Please complete the *Connect* exercise for Chapter 14 that focuses on measuring customer lifetime value (CLV).

ETHICAL CHALLENGE

A university's brand is critical to how it is perceived by students, alumni, faculty, and staff. In 2013, marketers at Florida Atlantic University (FAU) were looking for new revenue to support its athletic teams and agreed to a deal with GEO Group. In this deal, the school would receive $6 million in exchange for allowing GEO to put its name on the FAU football stadium. The practice of putting a brand name on athletic facilities has become commonplace in recent years. However, the difference in this case is that GEO's business is running for-profit prisons.

Within months of the announcement, the deal was terminated. The termination quelled the negative backlash FAU had begun to receive on campus and from the community and media for agreeing to the deal. However, without the deal, FAU lost a substantial revenue source, making it more difficult for the school to compete on the field. The dilemma presented an ethical challenge to the FAU brand: Which is more damaging: a stadium named for a for-profit prison or a losing football team?

Please use the ethical decision-making framework to answer the following questions:

1. Do you think FAU made a mistake in agreeing to a naming-rights deal with a company that runs for-profit prisons? Explain your answer.
2. What value would putting its name on the stadium hold for GEO Group's brand?
3. What types of companies would you not want associated with your university, even if those companies were willing to give money to your school?

Source: See Ira Boudway, "Florida Atlantic University Backs Off on Naming Its Stadium after a Prison Company," *Bloomberg Businessweek,* April 2, 2013, http://www.businessweek.com/articles/2013-04-02/florida-atlantic-university-backs-off-on-naming-its-stadium-after-a-prison-company.

VIDEO CASE

Please go to *Connect* to access the video case featuring the Idaho Central Credit Union that accompanies this chapter.

 ## PODCAST

Please go to Connect to access the podcast that accompanies this chapter.

CAREER **TIPS**

Building Your Personal Brand

In this chapter and throughout this textbook, you learned that one of the most important contributors to a successful career is having a strong personal brand. As you build your personal brand, coauthor Shane Hunt urges you to focus on the following two key elements:

1. ***What do you want your brand to be?*** This is a personal question and focuses on who you are and what you want from your life. If you want your brand image to be that of a hardworking, responsible person, you have to make the decision not to be late for work, not to miss class, and not to forget to do things when others are counting on you. Just *wanting* your brand to be characterized by descriptors like *hardworking* and *responsible* is not enough if your day-to-day actions do not support them. Similarly, if you want to be considered a problem solver, find problems to solve. Simply sitting in your office doing the bare minimum will not convince anyone. I would encourage each of you to think about your own personal strengths and weaknesses, and decide while you are in college what you want your personal brand to be as you embark on your career.

2. ***How do you build your brand image?*** Your brand image involves how others see you. It is being shaped every second of every day. Your brand does not take a day off. If people from your office see you on the weekend acting markedly differently from the way you act in the office, they will see you in a different light and your brand will be forever changed in their eyes. How you treat a stranger at a grocery store can affect your brand image just as much as how you treat someone in a college class. Every assignment you turn in, every project you work on, every job you complete builds your brand. However, each also can be an opportunity to damage your brand if handled improperly. Remember to build and protect your brand image in everything you do.

CHAPTER NOTES

1. D. E. Schultz, "The Loyalty Paradox," *Marketing Management* 14, no. 5 (2005): 10–11.
2. Joseph Schumpeter, "Logoland: Why Consumers Balk at Companies' Efforts to Rebrand Themselves," *The Economist,* January 13, 2011, http://www.economist.com/node/17900472.
3. J.D. Power, "North America Restaurant Customer Satisfaction Study," September 17, 2010, http://www.jdpower.com/content/press-release/MQ4o1AS/north-america-restaurant-customer-satisfaction-study.htm.
4. Giep Franzen and Sandra Moriarty, *The Science and Art of Branding* (New York: M.E. Sharp, 2009), p. 427.
5. Don Reisinger, "Xbox 360 Again the Most Popular Gaming Console among U.S. Gamers," *CNET,* February 15, 2013, http://news.cnet.com/8301-10797_3-57569574-235/xbox-360-again-the-most-popular-console-among-u.s-gamers/.
6. Harris Interactive, "2012 Harris Poll EquiTrend Automotive Scorecard," June 25, 2012, http://www.harrisinteractive.com/NewsRoom/PressReleases/tabid/446/mid/1506/articleId/1035/ctl/ReadCustom%20Default/Default.aspx.
7. Kevin Lane Keller, "Measuring Brand Equity," in *Handbook of Marketing Research—Do's and Don'ts,* Rajiv Grover and Marco Vriens, eds. (Thousand Oaks, CA: Sage, 2006), pp. 546–568.
8. Kevin Lane Keller, "Measuring Brand Equity," in *Handbook of Marketing Research—Do's and Don'ts,* Rajiv Grover and Marco Vriens, eds. (Thousand Oaks, CA: Sage, 2006), pp. 546–568.
9. Kevin Lane Keller, "Measuring Brand Equity," in *Handbook of Marketing Research—Do's and Don'ts,* Rajiv Grover and Marco Vriens, eds. (Thousand Oaks, CA: Sage, 2006), pp. 546–568.
10. Kevin Lane Keller, "Measuring Brand Equity," in *Handbook of Marketing Research—Do's and Don'ts,* Rajiv Grover and Marco Vriens, eds. (Thousand Oaks, CA: Sage, 2006), pp. 546–568.
11. Florian Stahl, Mark Heitmann, Donald Lehmann, and Scott A. Neslin, "The Impact of Brand Equity on Customer Acquisition, Retention, and Profit Margin," *Journal of Marketing* 76, no. 4 (2012): 44–63.
12. Emily Bryson York, "KFC's Stunts Make Nightly News, but Don't Stop Sales Slide," *Advertising Age,* April 19, 2010, http://adage.com/article/news/fast-food-kfc-s-stunts-stop-sales-slide/143359/.
13. Kathy Finn, "Two Years after BP Oil Spill, Tourists Back in U.S. Gulf," *Reuters,* May 27, 2012, http://www.reuters.com/article/2012/05/27/usa-bpspill-tourism-idUSL1E8GP15X20120527.
14. Anne Marie Kelly, "Has Toyota's Image Recovered from the Brand's Recall Crisis?" *Forbes,* March 5, 2012, http://www.forbes.com/sites/annemariekelly/2012/03/05/has-toyotas-image-recovered-from-the-brands-recall-crisis/.
15. Anne Marie Kelly, "Has Toyota's Image Recovered from the Brand's Recall Crisis?" *Forbes,* March 5, 2012, http://www.forbes.com/sites/annemariekelly/2012/03/05/has-toyotas-image-recovered-from-the-brands-recall-crisis/.

16. *Bloomberg Businessweek,* "Twenty Co-Branding Examples," n.d., http://images.businessweek.com/ss/09/07/0710_cobranded/16.htm.

17. *Bloomberg Businessweek,* "Tim Hortons and Cold Stone: Co-Branding Strategies," July 10, 2009, http://www.businessweek.com/smallbiz/content/jul2009/sb20090710_574574.htm.

18. Courtney Dentch, "Tim Hortons, Cold Stone to Form 100 Co-Branded Stores," *Bloomberg,* February 6, 2009, http://www.bloomberg.com/apps/news?pid=newsarchive&sid=amENTv5wwAcU.

19. Steve McKee, "The Pros and Cons of Co-Branding," *Bloomberg Businessweek,* July 10, 2009, http://www.businessweek.com/smallbiz/content/jul2009/sb20090710_255169.htm.

20. Walgreens, http://www.walgreens.com/store/c/genuine-bayer-aspirin-325-mg-tablets/ID=prod5589359-product.

21. E. J. Schultz, "Grocery Shoppers Continue to Spend Less, Embrace Private Label," *Advertising Age,* June 10, 2011, http://adage.com/article/news/grocery-shoppers-spend-embrace-private-label/228107/.

22. Brad Tuttle, "Brand Names Just Don't Mean as Much Anymore," *Time,* November 1, 2012, http://business.time.com/2012/11/01/brand-names-just-dont-mean-as-much-anymore/.

23. Nielsen, "The Rise of the Value-Conscious Shopper," March 2011, http://hk.nielsen.com/documents/PrivateLabelGlobalReport.pdf.

24. *The Economist,* "The Tyranny of Choice: You Choose," December 16, 2010, http://www.economist.com/node/17723028.

25. Ernest Beck, "Do You Need to Be Green?" *Bloomberg Businessweek,* June 18, 2006, http://www.business-week.com/stories/2006-06-18/do-you-need-to-be-green.

26. Coca-Cola, "Annual Sustainability Reports," n.d., http://www.coca-colacompany.com/sustainabilityreport/world/sustainable-packaging.html#section-investing-in-recycling-programs.

27. Todd Clarke, "22+ Instagram Stats That Marketers Can't Ignore This Year," *Hootsuite,* March 5, 2019, https://blog.hootsuite.com/instagram-statistics/.

28. Eric Siu, "The Changing Position of Social Media in 2019: What Does It Mean for Marketers?" *Impact,* September 3, 2018, https://www.impactbnd.com/blog/changing-position-of-social-media-in-2018-marketers.

29. Tanya Dua, "Millennials Reveal the Top 100 Brands They Love," *Business Insider,* September 7, 2018, https://www.businessinsider.com/top-100-millennial-brands-2018-9#16-macys-91.

30. Tom McNamara and Asha Moore-Mangin, "Starbucks and Social Media: It's about More Than Just Coffee," *EContent,* August 3, 2015, http://www.econtentmag.com/Articles/Editorial/Commentary/Starbucks-and-Social-Media-Its-About-More-than-Just-Coffee-103823.htm.

31. Facebook Business, "Raise Awareness of Your Business with Facebook," n.d., https://www.facebook.com/business/goals/build-awareness.

32. Nielsen, "NBA Teams Score a Slam Dunk with Social Media," November 5, 2018, https://www.nielsen.com/us/en/insights/news/2018/nba-teams-score-a-slam-dunk-with-social-media.html.

33. Nielsen, "How Social Media Impacts Brand Marketing," October 14, 2011, http://www.nielsen.com/us/en/newswire/2011/how-social-media-impacts-brand-marketing.html.

34. Griff Witte, "Flaw Makes Bike Locks Easy to Crack," *The Washington Post,* September 18, 2004, http://www.washingtonpost.com/wp-dyn/articles/A30149-2004Sep17.html.

35. Tabitha Jean Naylor, "How Brands Are Using Social Media to Boost Customer Engagement," *SocialMedia Today,* January 18, 2018, https://www.socialmediatoday.com/news/how-brands-are-using-social-media-to-boost-customer-engagement/514872/.

36. Nielsen, "How Social Media Impacts Brand Marketing," October 14, 2011, http://www.nielsen.com/us/en/newswire/2011/how-social-media-impacts-brand-marketing.html.

37. Wayne Huang, John Mitchell, Carmel Dibner, Andrea Ruttenberg, and Audrey Tripp, "How Customer Service Can Turn Angry Customers into Loyal Ones," *Harvard Business Review,* January 16, 2018, https://hbr.org/2018/01/how-customer-service-can-turn-angry-customers-into-loyal-ones.

38. Tara Shah, "Oreo: A Smart Cookie," *Digital Society,* February 11, 2018, https://medium.com/digital-society/boasting-858k-followers-oreo-consistently-utilises-twitter-to-keep-up-to-date-with-current-social-b5d6348fe31b.

39. Kashmir Hill, "#McDStories: When a Hashtag Becomes a Bashtag," *Forbes,* January 24, 2012, http://www.forbes.com/sites/kashmirhill/2012/01/24/mcdstories-when-a-hashtag-becomes-a-bashtag/.

40. Tamara Charm, Becca Coggins, Kelsey Robinson, and Jamie Wilkie, "The Great Consumer Shift: Ten Charts That Show How U.S. Shopping Behavior Is Changing," McKinsey & Company, August 4, 2020, https://www.mckinsey.com/business-functions/marketing-and-sales/our-insights/the-great-consumer-shift-ten-charts-that-show-how-us-shopping-behavior-is-changing.

41. Felix Gillette, "Made in USA Still Sells," *Bloomberg Businessweek,* October 11, 2012, http://www.businessweek.com/articles/2012-10-11/made-in-usa-still-sells.

42. Carol Matlack, "The Australian Company Selling China on Easier-to-Digest Milk," *Bloomberg Businessweek,* December 5, 2018, https://www.bloomberg.com/news/articles/2018-12-05/the-australian-company-selling-china-on-easier-to-digest-milk.

43. Adam Wooten, "International Business: Cultural Tastes Affect International Food Packaging," *Deseret News,* June 17, 2011, http://www.deseretnews.com/article/705374644/Cultural-tastes-affect-international-food-packaging.html?pg=all.

44. Adam Wooten, "International Business: Cultural Tastes Affect International Food Packaging," *Deseret News,* June 17, 2011, http://www.deseretnews.com/article/705374644/Cultural-tastes-affect-international-food-packaging.html?pg=all.

45. Masaaki Kotabe and Crystal Jiang, "Three Dimensional," *Marketing Management* 15, no. 2 (March–April 2006): 39.

46. Harris Interactive, "2018 Harris Poll Non-Profit EquiTrend," April 25, 2018, https://theharrispoll.com/the-harris-poll-announces-this-years-brands-of-the-year-in-the-2018-equitrend-study/.

Chapter 15

Customer Relationship Management

Rob Wilson/Shutterstock

Learning Objectives

After reading this chapter, you should be able to

LO 15-1 Explain the importance of effective customer service and customer satisfaction to companies.

LO 15-2 Describe methods companies use to develop good customer relationships.

LO 15-3 Discuss how companies can improve relationships with B2B and B2C customers.

LO 15-4 Describe how customer relationship management uses customer information to improve relations between businesses and customers.

LO 15-5 Discuss the security and ethical issues involved in using customer relationship management systems.

LO 15-6 Describe how companies can judge the effectiveness of their customer relationship management efforts.

Executive **Perspective** ... because everyone is a marketer

Edward Craner
Vice President, Strategy and Marketing
Holt Cat Companies

Edward Craner

Edward Craner had a nontraditional, or perhaps more accurately, nonlinear career. As an undergraduate student pursuing a degree in radio and television production, he started his own plumbing business; he followed that up with a stint as a program director at a church, while obtaining an MBA. In such service-oriented roles, he learned the importance of customer satisfaction and effectively managing customer relationships.

After accepting a position in the procurement department with AT&T (SBC Communications, at the time), Craner held a variety of positions: in supply chain management, supplier quality, sales operations, strategic projects, and customer experience. All of these different roles provided him with invaluable experience and insights into the complexity of business operations and the importance of encouraging brand loyalty in all aspects of those operations.

With these insights in hand, he eventually joined Holt Cat Companies, one of the largest Caterpillar heavy equipment and engine dealers in the United States. It sells, services, and rents Caterpillar equipment, engines, and generators for construction, mining, industrial, petroleum, and agricultural applications. He was hired as the director of strategic marketing and was promoted four years later to vice president of strategy and marketing. In this role, Craner oversees all aspects of marketing for Holt's dealerships. In addition, he leads the strategic planning and execution process for Holt Cat Companies.

What has been the most important thing in making you successful at your job?

It's the unending quest to learn from the outstanding people I have had the privilege to work alongside. I have often worked with coworkers or managers who had a trait or skill that made them particularly effective at their job or appealing to others. I would challenge myself to emulate that trait or skill and adopt it as my own. These were things like building good presentations, communicating effectively across company levels, articulating ideas, analyzing data, actively listening, holding eye contact, showing authentic smiles (key to this: smile with your eyes!), and exhibiting consistent behavior (regardless of the circumstances). The key for me has been to make sure my learning and adopting of traits, skills, and behaviors is authentic and done with the proper motivation: to get better and be better.

What advice would you give soon-to-be graduates?

Regardless of what job you are in, make yourself invaluable through your individual contribution. Each one of us has something valuable and unique to bring to a job . . . something we do well that can set us apart. Identify your unique contribution, hone it to make it better, and then make it available to help your team, department, or company succeed. By doing so, you'll be the go-to person for that certain skill or contribution.

How is marketing relevant to your role at Holt?

Marketing is essential to almost everything I do at Holt. From targeting new markets to developing pricing strategies to making sure our team provides excellent customer service, marketing is very critical to our success as an organization.

What do you consider your personal brand to be?

I'm inquisitive. Everything has an optimum way to function. Whether it is a business, a relationship, a team, a product, or a process, I'm the guy who wonders what the secret sauce is to achieve optimum performance. This creates a continual learning environment and an ongoing state of "becoming." Trying to figure it all out can drive me batty at times. But hey, everyone needs a batty guy around occasionally!

LO 15-1

Explain the importance of effective customer service and customer satisfaction to companies.

WHAT IS CUSTOMER SERVICE?

In the course of your life you have probably experienced good and bad customer service. Perhaps you were in Best Buy trying to figure out what laptop to buy for school on a tight budget, and a friendly and knowledgeable customer service representative helped you select the right computer for your needs and budget. Or perhaps you went through the frustrating experience of trying to return a defective good to a store with a no-returns policy and were told to deal directly with the product's manufacturer.

Businesses, as well as consumers like you, experience both good and bad customer service. Trucking companies that can track goods in transit provide that extra bit of service that makes their customers happy. On the other hand, poor customer service from suppliers may force manufacturers to shut down production due to the late delivery of parts or may result in the delivery of the wrong product to retailers.

Companies need to know how well they are doing in keeping customers happy. Research studies have quantified reasons to be concerned about customer service:

- About 78 percent of consumers have changed their minds about buying a good or service because of a poor service experience.
- On average, over time, loyal customers bring in up to 10 times as much revenue as the value of their first purchase.
- It takes up to 12 positive experiences with a customer to make up for 1 unresolved negative experience a customer has.
- News of bad customer service reaches more than twice as many people as comments about a good service experience a person or business has.
- Perhaps most importantly, it is six to seven times more expensive to get a new customer than it is to keep an existing customer.[1]

Poor customer service is almost guaranteed to frustrate customers. But good customer service alone doesn't make customers happy. Even if a company offers good customer service, it still can lose customers if its service is not significantly better than that of a competitor. To maintain current customers, as well as gain new ones, firms must provide customer service that makes them stand out among competitors.

Firms like the Temkin Group and J.D. Power provide customer service rankings for a variety of companies. Table 15.1 lists the 10 top-rated organizations according *Forbes*. Most of these have global operations. Smart consumers use such ratings to select companies from whom to buy goods and services. Therefore, it is important for companies to maintain a good reputation for customer service.

Defining Customer Service

customer service

All of the activities a firm engages in to satisfy the needs and wants of its customers.

Anything a company does that directly touches the customer falls under the realm of customer service. **Customer service** involves all of the activities a firm engages in to satisfy the needs and wants of its customers. These activities consist of both *human* methods and *mechanical* methods for direct customer interaction. A human method would be ordering a catalogue item directly by talking with a customer service representative (CSR). A mechanical method would be placing an order for a product on a company's web page.

The company's philosophy toward dealing with its customers drives such activities. When companies commit to providing outstanding customer service, they elevate customer service to the highest priority level. A strategy for dealing with customers will follow from this philosophy. As General George S. Patton once said, "Always do more than is required of you." For example, Orvis and Territory Ahead provide liberal return policies and several convenient options for returning merchandise. These policies help customers feel confident that it will not be a hassle to return a product, if needed.

TABLE 15.1   Companies with the Best Customer Experience Ratings

Best Companies	Reasons for Rating
Chick-fil-A	Its employees were rated the most polite in their industry category.
Trader Joe's	From its private label staples to its organic produce, Trader Joe's has carved out a niche that has propelled its rapid growth.
Aldi	Aldi's no-frills approach seems to connect with consumers and has fueled rapid growth over the past decade.
Amazon	The world's largest internet retailer has mastered a combination of value, satisfaction, and delivery efficiency that consumers love.
Lexus	J.D. Power has repeatedly recognized Lexus for its outstanding customer service.
Costco Wholesale	Maybe it's the low prices, the liberal return policy, or the delicious free samples, but customers love Costco.
HEB Grocery	A regional supermarket serving Texas, HEB has quietly become one of the biggest and most popular private grocers in the United States.
Toyota	Despite a spate of recent large recalls, the world's second-largest automaker remains a favorite with owners.
Publix	The people that work there. They make shopping a pleasure!
Wegman's Food Markets	The brightness and decorations in the store. It is a very welcoming place.

Source: Christopher Elliott, "These Companies Have the Best Customer Service," *Forbes,* July 11, 2018, https://www.forbes.com/sites/christopherelliott/2018/07/11/these-companies-have-the-best-customer-service-heres-why/?sh=7a07e9e6b80a

A company's customer service strategy guides the establishment of customer service policies and procedures. Such policies might:

- Set rules for allowing customers to return unwanted goods.
- Dictate how often a salesperson should call on a customer in a given period of time.
- Determine the amount of discretion an employee has in handling a customer complaint.
- Establish the hours of a firm's customer service department.

For example, some companies provide directions and shipping labels for returning unwanted products up-front; customers do not have to contact the company before replacing or returning the product. High rates of returns for products ordered over the Internet make this an effective part of a customer service strategy for many companies. Beyond this, specific procedures for dealing with returns might define what information may be given to a customer, how customer returns are processed, or methods for dealing with complaints.

In addition, firms that want to improve their customer service strategy put measurements in place to track how well they are satisfying customers. Companies that understand the importance of customer service will develop such measures with input from customers. What might seem like good service to the company may seem like poor service to important customers. For example, does a 95 percent customer satisfaction rate seem like a good goal to you? A grade of 95 percent on an exam is an excellent

If you are not 100% satisfied with one of L.L. Bean's products purchased directly from L.L. Bean, you may return it within one year of purchase for a refund. *John Greim/LightRocket/Getty Images*

score. But what if a company failed to deliver 5 percent of the items a customer ordered? The customer might consider that an excessive amount of missed orders and stop doing business with the company.[2]

The ultimate goal of delivering superior customer service is to increase brand loyalty. Customers will usually remain loyal to a company or brand if they feel they receive more value from that company's goods and services than they do from its competitors. Offering superior customer service goes a long way toward ensuring that customers will stay loyal.

Establishing Customer Service Policies

A firm builds an effective customer service strategy around a set of common objectives for all company employees. These objectives dictate the firm's policies for interacting with and treating its customers. The following objectives apply, whether a company sells to other businesses (B2B) or directly to consumers (B2C):

- Deliver the good or service completely and in a *timely* manner.
- Ensure that the process for taking and fulfilling customer orders is *reliable.*
- Establish convenient customer *communication* channels.
- Encourage *ease of doing business,* so that the customer finds it convenient and pleasant to deal with the firm.

These four factors are critical to delivering customer service and, ultimately, maintaining brand loyalty.

Timeliness Consumers don't want to wait long for their products to arrive. Neither do retailers and manufacturers. Unfortunately, in B2B markets only about 75 percent of orders from large suppliers arrive on time and complete.[3] Timeliness concerns the ability of a company to deliver a good or service by the time a customer expects to have it available for sale or consumption. The process companies use to take a customer order and deliver goods to a customer is referred to as the order cycle. The **order cycle** is the total amount of time that elapses from the time a customer places an order until the time the product is delivered to the customer. It involves a number of activities, as shown in Figure 15.1.

timeliness

The ability of a company to deliver a good or service by the time a customer expects to have it available for sale or consumption.

order cycle

The total amount of time that elapses from the time a customer places an order until the time the product is delivered to the customer.

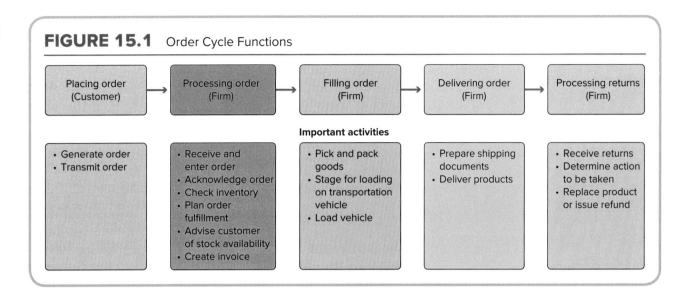

FIGURE 15.1 Order Cycle Functions

Placing order (Customer)	Processing order (Firm)	Filling order (Firm)	Delivering order (Firm)	Processing returns (Firm)
		Important activities		
• Generate order • Transmit order	• Receive and enter order • Acknowledge order • Check inventory • Plan order fulfillment • Advise customer of stock availability • Create invoice	• Pick and pack goods • Stage for loading on transportation vehicle • Load vehicle	• Prepare shipping documents • Deliver products	• Receive returns • Determine action to be taken • Replace product or issue refund

Two major trends drive the desire for shortened order cycles: inventory reduction due to lean manufacturing principles and good inventory management practices. Distribution systems that can quickly and efficiently get the product to a customer help firms satisfy this desire. In addition, firms must put in place efficient order-processing systems. These systems take in the order and check for stock availability; they then print pick tickets that help workers select products from warehouse locations and load orders onto transportation vehicles. Order processing plays an integral role in timely delivery. Thus, companies must maintain their order-processing system and ensure that it utilizes good data.

reliability

The company's ability to ensure that customers will receive a good or service within a stated lead time and that there will be no problems with the order.

Reliability A second customer service objective that guides the firm's policies and procedures is reliability. **Reliability** involves ensuring that customers can depend on receiving a good or service within a stated lead time and that there will be no problems with the order.

customer communication

The two-way information flow between the firm and its customer.

Reliability becomes a particularly important objective in B2B transactions. Business customers may accept a longer lead time from a reliable supplier because it involves less uncertainty. When business customers can depend on the delivery of products, they can hold less inventory; this reduces their inventory carrying costs.

Whether selling in B2B or B2C situations, firms develop a reputation for reliability by:

- Establishing effective inventory management policies.
- Performing accurate sales forecasts.
- Maintaining effective transportation and distribution operations (or hiring reliable third parties to perform those functions).

Customer Communication Customer

communication involves a two-way information flow between the firm and its customer. That is, firms communicate with customers, and they provide convenient ways for customers to communicate with them. Firms that fail at one, or both, likely will not perform well in the marketplace.

Edward Craner

Executive Perspective...
because everyone is a marketer

─────────────

Edward Craner
Vice President, Strategy and Marketing
Holt Cat Companies

What is the most important aspect of providing great customer service?

At Holt, we are passionate about all aspects of customer service, as I think you must be to be truly successful. If I had to pick just one aspect, I would say it is *reliability.* Our customers know that they can always count on us, and that when challenges arise, Holt will be there to help. Many of our customers are small business owners themselves, and our reliability helps them run their operations more efficiently and also builds brand loyalty with Holt.

A number of important types of information can flow between the firm and the customer. Order-status communication provides the customer with information about the completeness of the order, when it will ship, and when it will arrive. An example of order-status communication is the tracking number for a carrier (e.g., UPS) you receive from a firm like Amazon, enabling you to trace the delivery status of your order. Shipment-tracking capability is particularly important to business customers. They might need to know the status of materials required to keep a production line running, for example. Customer service departments can also provide information to the customer about inventory availability, back-order status, and pricing; they can answer questions from customers about their orders. Communication may be done by computer-to-computer links (e.g., via an EDI that automatically sends data about an order), by e-mail, or by telephone. All of these types of communications help a firm maintain customer satisfaction. All must be accurate and timely.

Ease of Doing Business   Convenience is a major part of ease of doing business. **Ease of doing business** is the amount of effort required on the part of a customer when dealing with a firm. For example, having a help line available to answer customer questions 24/7 provides convenience to customers who may need answers right away. At stores like Academy Sports + Outdoors, salespeople on the store floor armed with a smartphone can place an order for a customer and take a credit card payment; the merchandise is delivered at no additional charge, without the customer having to go through a checkout line. Websites also offer consumers convenience. They supply information about the product, the ability to compare products and prices quickly, and a simple checkout process.

In addition to convenience, ease of doing business extends to the financial aspect of a purchase. In B2B markets, offering favorable payment terms and discounts for quick payment can differentiate a firm from competitors that are less flexible. Also, simple things like training customer-facing employees, such as customer service representatives and salespeople, to treat customers professionally and in a friendly manner can make doing business with that firm easy for customers. Liberal return policies represent another way to enhance convenience. In short, anything a company can do to make a sales transaction go smoothly will help it gain loyal customers.

ease of doing business

The amount of effort required on the part of a customer when dealing with a firm.

Companies communicate important information to customers in many ways, including via shipment-tracking capability. *Brent Lewin/Bloomberg/Getty Images*

The Role of Social Media in Customer Service

Social media are used by people of all ages, around the world, to share information about themselves, including the kinds of goods and services they use. They also use social media to share their likes and dislikes with others. Marketers have learned how to use social media to send information about their company's goods and services. They also use social media to gather feedback from customers about those goods and services, and to provide assistance to customers when they have problems. The growing use of social media has shifted marketing communications from a traditional one-to-many format to one-to-one communications with individual customers.

In today's world of instant communication and social media, customers expect help immediately, at any hour of the day, on any day of the week. Customers also expect to be able to communicate using the method of their choice, which increasingly involves social media tools. Many of the world's companies use social media for activities that include some form of customer service:

- Responding to customer comments about a good or service.
- Resolving problems customers encounter with products.
- Answering requests for information.
- Addressing complaints.
- Gathering competitive information and new product ideas.
- Quantifying the number of people who like or show interest in the firm's products.

Companies build their social media strategy on **social media platforms**. These are web-based technologies that enable a company to build and manage social media solutions and services.[4] Top social media platforms with over 1 billion users include such websites as Facebook, YouTube, Instagram, Tumblr, Twitter, Snapchat, WhatsApp, and Pinterest.[5] These platforms enable companies to build relationships with customers in ways that were not available until fairly recently. Facebook and Twitter, for example, connect companies to their customers through direct interaction. This connection helps build brand loyalty through greater customer service. Many company websites allow customers to send questions, comments, or complaints. Other companies scan social media platforms to find out what their customers' needs and wants are. For example, e-Bags uses social media such as Facebook, Twitter, Google+, and Pinterest to get feedback on its products and ideas for product development.

social media platforms
Web-based technologies that enable a company to build and manage social media solutions and services.

Companies can also use certain websites set up specifically for consumer complaints. Sites such as complaints.com, my3cents.com, complaintsboard.com, measuredup.com, pissedconsumer.com, consumeraffairs.com, and ripoffreport.com monitor what consumers are saying about products that are making them unhappy.[6]

Many large companies have adopted social media as a way to enhance their customer service capabilities. FedEx, for example, offers its customers a number of ways to interact with the company, including through online chats, blogs, and Facebook and Twitter pages. The company has a dedicated team responsible for handling requests for customer care; the team follows up with customers to help solve problems or answer questions. Its goal is to respond to customers in a matter of minutes. The team also tracks online conversations to follow what customers say about the company and its products.[7]

Nonprofit organizations such as Special Olympics, UNICEF, and the Red Cross have also adopted social media to help them connect with people and improve customer service. Several resources are available, for example:

- Zoomerang enables nonprofits to set up accounts at a discount; through these accounts, an organization can conduct surveys about such things as program satisfaction and volunteer satisfaction.
- Facebook Causes also helps nonprofits conduct surveys, recruit donors, and provide information about volunteer opportunities.

Today, many companies use electronic technologies, including social media, to provide customer service at any hour of the day, any day of the week. Teams trained as customer-retention associates provide customer care within minutes. *ZUMA Press/Alamy Stock Photo*

- Twitter enables companies to launch online petitions and to connect with other nonprofit organizations.
- Google+ also has a community of nonprofit organizations working with it to connect with people.[8]

Nonprofit organizations typically have smaller budgets for marketing than for-profit corporations. Therefore, social media are a cost-effective way for a nonprofit to stay connected with donors and volunteers on whom they rely and want to keep satisfied. Though such activities are also supported by more traditional customer service activities, social media have become the front line for many organizations as they deal with customers.

Mc Graw Hill connect Exercise **15-1**

marketing analytics

Social Media in Action

Citibank, one of the five largest banks in the United States, has spent several years working to improve how it provides customer service using social media. The owner of a California-based small business who had been on hold for 40 minutes waiting for help from the bank decided to tweet her displeasure to the firm's @AskCiti Twitter account. She received a tweet back almost immediately asking for her phone number so a service representative could call her directly. Her problem was quickly resolved, and the small business owner now goes directly to Twitter when she has a problem. As a result of Citigroup's efforts, it has resolved the highest percentage of customer complaints through social media of any of the large U.S. banks.

Large banks have a history of scoring poorly on customer service. According to J.D. Power, nearly one out of five customers has had a problem with their bank. To combat this reality, other major banks, such as Wells Fargo, Chase, and Bank of America, have dedicated teams to quickly respond to both complaints and praise from customers on social media sites. While regulations and privacy issues restrict the ease with which banks can resolve customer issues via social media, marketers at large banks continue to search for ways to balance such concerns with the positive impact of social media on customer service.

The Social Media in Action Connect exercise in Chapter 15 will let you develop strategies for improving customer service through social media. Utilizing the unique characteristics of different social media platforms to improve customer responsiveness can be a powerful tool in the effort to provide excellent customer service and increase brand loyalty.

Source: See Suzanne Kapner, "Citi Won't Sleep on Customer Tweets," *The Wall Street Journal*, October 4, 2012, http://online.wsj.com/article.

Tracking Performance through Customer Service **Metrics**

How do companies know if they are doing a good job serving their customer? Primarily, they do so by establishing performance metrics, tied to the four objectives of customer service: timeliness, reliability, customer communication, and ease of doing business. Commonly used metrics for tracking B2B and B2C customer service performance include the following:

marketing analytics

- **Fill rate** is the percentage of an order shipped on time and complete. Companies can measure fill rate in various ways:
  - **Item fill rate** measures the percentage of the total number of items on the order that the firm shipped on time. Thus if there are a total of 501 items on the order, and the firm ships 489 on time, the item fill rate is 97.6 percent.
  - **Dollar fill rate** measures the value of goods shipped on time versus the total value of the order. If the items ordered are worth $12,290, and the items shipped are worth $12,098, then the dollar fill rate is 98.4 percent.
  - **Line fill rate** measures the percentage of item-stocking types, known as *stock-keeping units (SKUs)*, on the order shipped on time and complete. The SKU helps the company differentiate among similar items that may be stocked in various ways. For example, a promotional twin-pack of Pantene Lively Clean shampoo takes a different SKU than a single bottle of the same product. If there are 10 different SKUs on the order, and the firm fills 6 completely and puts 4 on back order, then the line fill rate is 60 percent.
- **Perfect order rate** judges the reliability of the order system. As the name implies, the metric measures how many orders have been filled perfectly. It leaves no room for error. A perfect order must be delivered to the right place, on the correct due date, with the right items in the right quantity, and with no damage. It also must be billed correctly. Any deviation from these requirements constitutes a failure and receives a zero. If the company fills 2 out of 10 orders perfectly, but the other 8 have errors, the perfect order fill rate is 0 percent. Note too that if the company fills 9 of 10 orders perfectly, the perfect order fill rate also is 0 percent. Perfect order fill rate is measured over a period of time, such as monthly or quarterly. The number of perfect orders divided by the number of orders shipped over the time period equals the perfect order fill rate. This metric has become important as customer expectations for exceptional service have increased over time.

fill rate

A metric that measures the percentage of an order shipped on time and complete.

item fill rate

A metric that measures the percentage of the total number of items on the order that the firm shipped on time.

dollar fill rate

A metric that measures the value of goods shipped on time versus the total value of the order.

line fill rate

A metric that measures the percentage of item types (SKUs) on the order shipped on time and complete.

perfect order rate

A metric that measures how many orders have been filled, delivered, and billed without error.

Warehouses and distribution centers often have thousands of different items that must be stored, picked, and shipped, making the perfect order metric difficult to achieve; however, companies that do achieve this level of excellence satisfy customers in a way that differentiates the company from competitors. *Mark Passmore/Alamy Stock Photo*

on-time delivery

A metric that measures how many shipments are delivered per the requested delivery date.

order cycle time

A metric that measures the length of the order cycle, or the ability of the order system to react to customer orders.

customer communication metrics

Measurements of a firm's effectiveness in communicating with customers at the pre-transaction, transaction, and post-transaction points.

responsiveness

A metric that measures the firm's ability and willingness to provide fast service, answer customer inquiries, and resolve problems.

- **On-time delivery** recognizes that it is not enough just to ship the goods on time; they must *arrive* on time as well. The only date that matters is the due date for the order to arrive at the customer's location. Firms base the on-time delivery measure on the actual delivery date versus the requested delivery date. In today's business world, in which firms watch inventories closely, delivering earlier than the requested date adds inventory that is not yet needed, increasing inventory carrying costs. Late deliveries are a problem because the goods will be unavailable for use or sale when needed. Both of these conditions, early *or* late delivery, constitute a failure for this metric.
- The **order cycle time** metric measures the length of the order cycle, or the ability of the order system to react to customer orders. Both B2B and B2C customers increasingly seek shortened order cycles.
- **Customer communication metrics** involve review of communication at three stages:
  - At the *pre-transaction point,* the firm measures the accuracy and timeliness of the information fed back to a customer concerning product availability and delivery dates. This aspect of the metric relates to being proactive with customers and keeping them informed.
  - The second communication point occurs *at the transaction.* It measures the ability of the firm to accurately provide shipment status and order tracking.
  - The third stage is *post-transaction.* It measures the ability of the firm to answer questions concerning the use of the product or to process returned goods in a timely manner.
- The **responsiveness** metric measures the firm's flexibility. Flexibility can involve the firm's ability and willingness to provide fast service, answer customer inquiries, and resolve problems.

Other methods for determining the effectiveness of customer service include the following:[9]

- **Post-incident surveys.** These surveys help measure the customer's service experience with the company. Included are questions about the customer service representative's customer service skills and technical knowledge, how long it took to respond and resolve the problem, and the customer's satisfaction with the solution.
- **Customer service website experience.** These surveys help companies determine whether customers found answers to their questions at the company's website. They also ask customers to suggest how to make the website more useful or user friendly.
- **Relationship surveys.** These surveys seek to gauge the strength of a customer's relationship with the company. These surveys ask customers about their overall customer service support experience, satisfaction with products or services, and the value the customer received from interacting with customer service. Often these surveys are offered immediately after a call or e-mail from a customer.
- **Customer loyalty.** This measure focuses on trends in repeat buying from current customers. It indicates whether the customer is satisfied with the product/service and with the overall customer service provided by the organization.
- **Hold time and abandonment rates.** These measures help a company gauge whether their customers are experiencing problems when they want to talk to a customer service representative. *Hold time* is the time a customer has to wait to talk to or receive a text back from a CSR. The longer the hold time, the less satisfied the customer is likely to be. The *abandonment rate* is the percentage of customers who hang up the phone or stop an e-mail conversation before reaching a customer service agent.

These metrics cannot be developed in a vacuum; customer input is critical. It does a company no good, for example, to establish a line-fill-rate goal of 95 percent if the company's customers expect perfect orders. Nor is it useful to have a goal of resolving a problem within 24 hours if the customer usually expects an immediate resolution. Some organizations use third parties to monitor their customer service. Client Heartbeat is one such third-party provider: It can provide customer service surveys or help a client develop its own surveys; identify unhappy customers; benchmark a company's customer service against the rest of its industry; measure and track customer satisfaction; get testimonials and share them with prospective customers; and link up with a company's customer relationship management system.[10]

Mc Graw Hill connect Exercise **15-2**

Please complete the *Connect* exercise for Chapter 15 that focuses on analyzing customer service metrics. By being able to calculate various fill and perfect order rates, you will be prepared to evaluate and manage customer service at your organization.

GAINING AND KEEPING LOYAL CUSTOMERS

LO 15-2

Describe methods companies use to develop good customer relationships.

In Chapter 1 we introduced the marketing concept, which is the idea that a firm's long-term success must include a companywide effort to satisfy customer needs. Ultimately, the goal of achieving customer satisfaction is to promote brand and company loyalty. If done in a cost-effective manner, achieving customer satisfaction will drive long-term

customer satisfaction

A state that is achieved when companies meet the needs and expectations customers have for their goods or services.

profitability. Companies achieve **customer satisfaction** when they meet the needs and expectations their customers have for their goods or services.

In today's business climate, customer satisfaction is merely a first step to ensuring that customers will remain loyal to the company or brand. Think of a good or service you regularly buy. How happy are you with it? If the product satisfies you, but you discover that another company's good or service can provide additional value, you probably would consider switching. In response to this reality, customer-driven companies strive to *delight,* rather than simply *satisfy,* their customers. Delighted customers obtain more value than they had expected from their purchase.

Companies delight customers in a variety of ways. They might:

- Make the customer's shopping experience easier.
- Offer a significantly superior product.
- Sell goods or services at a lower price.
- Provide follow-up customer service.
- Make an around-the-clock customer help line available.

Besides being loyal, delighted customers also may tell friends and family of their experience, post favorable reviews on social media, and rate the firm highly on websites such as Amazon and eBay. All of these positive actions help companies retain existing customers and gain new ones.

The Bases of Customer Satisfaction

A company's emphasis on customer satisfaction develops as a consequence of a *customer orientation.* Firms with a customer orientation set an expectation that all employees should seek to provide value to the customer in a way that meets, or exceeds, the customer's expectations. A customer orientation makes up a part of the **marketing concept**, the idea that a firm's long-term success must include a companywide effort to satisfy customer needs and wants.

marketing concept

The idea that a firm's long-term success must include a companywide effort to satisfy customer needs and wants.

The marketing concept is based on the following principles, actively applied by managers companywide:[11]

1. Awareness and appreciation of the consumer's role in the firm's existence, growth, and stability.
2. Awareness of and concern with the interdepartmental implication of decisions and actions of an individual department with regard to the customer.
3. Concern with innovation of goods and services designed to solve select customer problems.
4. Understanding of the effect of the introduction of new goods and services for the firm's profit position, both present and future.
5. Appreciation of the role of marketing intelligence in determining the needs and wants of customers.
6. Effort in determining corporate and departmental objectives based on customer satisfaction.

Companies that base their business on the marketing concept maintain a focus on *delivering value* to the customer in any profitable way they can. They put the customer in the center of the firm's thinking in terms of both strategy and operations. In such a company, *all areas of the firm,* not just sales and marketing, should be customer oriented: Purchasing, finance, engineering, manufacturing, and logistics focus on promoting customer satisfaction, not just on meeting their own individual department objectives.

Companies seek to delight customers so that, in addition to becoming loyal, they also will become advocates for the brand to family, friends, and their online community.
TomBham/Alamy Stock Photo

The GAP Model

It is important for companies to approach customer satisfaction in a systematic way. The GAP Model is an approach that helps companies identify major gaps facing organizations seeking to meet customer's expectations.[12] Using the GAP Model companies can identify and address gaps between what they provide customers and what customers actually want. The model identifies the following five gaps:

- Gap 1 is the distance between what customers expect and what a company thinks they expect. The best way to identify this gap is through direct feedback from customers, such as the use of customer satisfaction surveys.
- Gap 2 is between management perception of customer needs and the actual specification of how those needs are to be met. This can be achieved by defining the level of service that is to be delivered. For example, if a company believed that consumers want to be able to contact the company 24 hours a day, 365 days a week with questions or concerns, then it would define that level of customer service availability as what is required.
- Gap 3 is from the specification of customer service to how well it is actually delivered. An example would be the expectation of customer service availability of 24 hours a day, 365 days a year, and the actual availability of 16 hours a day, 5 days a week. This would indicate a substantial gap between expectations and delivery of customer service.
- Gap 4 is the gap between the delivery of the customer service and what is told it will be to customers. Companies should not promise one level of service, but deliver a lower level. This sets up expectations that are not met, which harms the relationships between companies and their customers. Thus, if a company can only provide 16 hours a day, 5 days a week of customer service availability, it should tell its customers that.
- Finally, Gap 5 is the gap between a customer's actual experience with customer service and the customer's expectations. Companies should follow up directly with customers to see how well the customers' experiences matched up with their expectations. Amazon, for example, routinely e-mails its customers and asks them to rate their recent transactions.

Limitations on Customer Satisfaction

Part of adopting a customer orientation also involves recognizing the things that limit satisfaction. As noted previously, merely meeting a customer's expectations does not always lead to loyalty.

Customer satisfaction ties into customer perceptions. If a gap exists between the company's capabilities and the customer's true needs or wants, other firms can exploit that gap. For example, a customer may want perfect orders but realize that the firm achieves a perfect order only occasionally. The customer isn't completely happy with the relationship, just satisfied that the firm is doing its best to provide good service. If the customer finds another firm that can provide a higher percentage of perfect orders for a similar product, the customer likely will buy from the other firm. Customer satisfaction doesn't always lead to brand loyalty.

Beyond this, one customer's needs and wants must be treated separately from those of other customers. What delights one customer does not necessarily satisfy or delight others. A one-size-fits-all customer service policy isn't likely to lead to a great many loyal customers if customer perceptions of value differ widely. *One-to-one marketing* individualizes the relationship between the firm and customer by gathering and using specific customer information to understand what will delight each customer.

Through personalized communication and customized product offerings, companies can improve customer satisfaction and loyalty. For example, Amazon uses an

Road Runner Sports offers the next best thing to being fitted in-store with live chats with fit experts. Customers are in full control of their camera, volume and microphone, and can choose whether they want to talk, type, or have a face-to-face video chat. Once customers start shopping, they will see a pop-up window inviting them to connect with a fit expert. Their fitters will then place their orders. *Kristoffer Tripplaar/Alamy Stock Photo*

collaborative filtering

A mechanism that filters large amounts of information about many consumers' previous purchases that may be related in some way in order to predict consumer preferences.

geofencing

A location-based technology that uses small sensors to send messages to smartphone users who enter a nearby, defined geographic area.

algorithm that performs a process called **collaborative filtering** to predict consumer preferences.[13] When a consumer searches the Amazon site for a sporty clip watch, the algorithm filters large amounts of information about many consumers' previous purchases that may be related in some way.[14] Amazon then sends out messages to buyers of a particular item, pointing out that others who purchased the same item also purchased other, similar products. This information offers individualized value to Amazon customers that can lead to high levels of satisfaction.

Another one-to-one marketing technique, discussed in detail in Chapter 12, is **geofencing**. This is a location-based technology that uses small sensors to send marketing messages to smartphone users who enter a nearby, defined geographic area, such as a store.[15] Macy's, American Eagle, Safeway, and other companies are using this technique.[16]

By understanding the typical buying patterns of its customers, a company can push product options and promotions directly to customers. A company called Turnstyle Solutions Inc., for example, has placed sensors in several hundred businesses in Toronto to track shoppers as they move about the city. These sensors track Wi-Fi-enabled cell phones; they enable the firm to build a database of people's habits from which the firm can direct promotional information to individuals.[17] This can be a very effective way of marketing. However, not all customers appreciate the intrusion or loss of privacy. Companies need to be careful in how they apply these marketing techniques so they do not alienate their customers.

LO 15-3

Discuss how companies can improve relationships with B2B and B2C customers.

IMPROVING CUSTOMER RELATIONSHIPS

We've seen that customer orientation should be a primary focus for businesses. But companies need to balance customer satisfaction with profitability. Providing *too much* value in terms of low prices, extra features, or custom services can lead to an unprofitable situation that actually costs the company money. Companies want to capture and retain customers that will be both loyal *and* profitable. Sometimes that means targeting fewer customers. After screening out potentially unprofitable customers (discussed later in the chapter), the firm can focus its efforts on the specific customers with which it most wants to develop good relationships.

Relationship Marketing

We've discussed the idea of relationship marketing at a number of other points in the book. Here, we look at it in a bit more detail. **Relationship marketing** is a strategy that focuses on attracting, maintaining, and enhancing customer relationships, thus building brand loyalty. Two basic keys to building good relationships with customers are (1) establishing customer value and (2) delivering value.

relationship marketing

A marketing strategy that focuses on attracting, maintaining, and enhancing customer relationships.

Establishing Customer Value First, the company must *establish customer value*. **Customer value** refers to the perceived benefits, both monetary and nonmonetary, that a customer receives from a product compared with the cost of obtaining it. Thus, the firm must establish the ways in which it will provide more value in its exchange with the customer than its competitors do. The customer can be either a business customer or an individual consumer. By making a special effort to understand the value the customer receives, the firm is able to build a relationship with the customer. Attention to customer value often leads to commitment between the two parties, which can result in a long-term mutually beneficial relationship. For example, suppliers that subscribe to Walmart's Retail Link software get daily updates on sales of their products. These updates enable suppliers to better anticipate the retailer's needs; in turn, suppliers offer better customer service, resulting in fewer stock shortages at Walmart stores.[18]

customer value

The perceived benefits, both monetary and nonmonetary, that a customer receives from a product compared with the cost of obtaining it.

Personal selling is another way to build relationships between companies. Salespeople are able to learn what their regular business customers want (and do not want) from their company; they can advise other departments of their company, such as marketing and R&D, about products and services tailored to important customers. By regularly visiting with their customers, salespeople can be aware of changes to the customer's needs and can also monitor what competitors are doing. Most important, an attentive salesperson can personally address any issues that the customer has with the company's products; they can suggest changes that can better address a customer's needs and desires. Going beyond the usual brick-and-mortar model, Men's Wearhouse salespersons tend to customers not only at their store but also on its website. Using their smartphones they can message, video chat, and send pictures of their clothing to consumers. This personal touch can make a big difference in ensuring the consumer gets helpful advice and suggestions.[19]

As part of relationship marketing, some companies adapt business processes specifically to the needs of their customers. For example, Dell created a special online store for certain important business customers, with an ordering process tailored to meet the customer's unique needs.[20] Companies can also set up special programs for customers. For example, a company might set up electronic data interchange (EDI) that allows computer-to-computer transactions with one of its customer companies for activities such as invoicing and bill payments, expedited shipping, and special pricing incentives.

A company also can differentiate its customer service by making a customer service representative (CSR) the first option on an automated service menu. Another customer service consideration is to make sure that the representative can be easily understood by the customer. This is especially important when the call is likely to involve a situation in which the customer needs empathy or a highly technical answer to a question.[21] Companies with a customer orientation train managers and CSRs how to properly talk to customers; they also seek to give CSRs adequate training to answer technical questions. These companies are better able to deliver phone or e-mail customer service that improves customer relationships.

transparency

Involves opening up the company to the outside world by making its practices, policies, and future plans available to customers.

Another way a company can differentiate its customer service is through transparency. **Transparency** involves opening up the company to the outside world by making its practices, policies, and future plans available to customers. Technology such as websites, chat rooms, and customer relationship modules allow a company to disseminate information about itself and receive feedback from current or potential customers about how it is currently doing business and its plans for the future. By increasing the level of participation of its customers, a company can learn a great deal about how well it is establishing customer value, and whether it is headed in the right direction.[22] Lyft, for example, provides its customers the opportunity to rate its drivers and shares those ratings with customers who are being paired up with a driver. That way the customer can make an informed decision about accepting the ride.

Delivering Value Second, the firm must *deliver* its goods or services in ways that meet or exceed the expectations of the customer. To do so, the firm must know what the customer wants and also know what it can consistently deliver in terms of value. It does the firm no good to make promises it cannot keep consistently. Sometimes companies want a customer's business so badly they offer prices, order cycles, or special features that they cannot reliably and profitably deliver. Such an agreement leads to dissatisfaction for both parties in the exchange. It is not enough to merely understand what the customer perceives as value; it is just as important to understand the capabilities of the company in delivering that value.

Exceeding customer expectations is a tricky thing. It begins by understanding what customers expect, then giving them more. One measure of customer satisfaction used by a number of companies is *Net Promoter Score.* Based on a single question: "On a scale of 0 to 10, how likely are you to recommend this company's product or service to a friend or a colleague?" Customers are placed in three categories: detractors, passives, and promoters. Detractors give a score lower or equal to 6, and through social media detract from the image of the product. Passives give a score of 7 or 8, and are satisfied but not thrilled. They are unlikely to spread the word, either good or bad, about the product. Promoters answer 9 or 10, and are likely to recommend the company's products. Higher Net Promoter Scores tend to indicate desirable levels of customer satisfaction, while lower Net Promoter Scores are a warning to investigate causes of poor customer satisfaction and brand loyalty issues.[23]

Companies find ways to deal with customer expectations in ways that make sense for their specific business:

- Managers at many restaurants, such as Olive Garden and Ruby Tuesday, roam through the dining area asking about the food and service. Managers can quickly resolve a customer complaint and can offer discounts or free appetizers or desserts, turning a potentially negative experience into a positive one.
- In order to help online shoppers choose correct sizes, Macy's and Nordstrom Inc. are working with True Fit Corp., which analyzes data to show customers how clothes would actually fit them.[24]
- Retailers such as Home Depot and Lowe's have highly knowledgeable employees who can quickly answer questions, give suggestions, and help customers who often are not familiar with tools, paint, appliances, and other aspects of home improvement.
- QVC Inc. e-mails customers when their products arrive, to give them instruction on assembly and use of the products they bought.[25]

Third-party logistics provider C.H. Robinson engages in relationship marketing by leveraging its expertise in the shipping business to offer customer value that differentiates it from competitors. *Robinson Worldwide.*

Being proactive about what customers expect can head off an issue that might lose a customer. Likewise, expert advice can often exceed what customers expect when they enter the store and can make them lifelong customers.

Personalizing service is another way to help exceed a customer's expectations. Some companies, for example, use a method called **clientelling**. This method tailors product information for individual customers, in order to provide an exceptional and personalized shopping experience. It involves:

- Identifying key information about a customer.
- Contacting the customer about a product or service that fits their individual profile.
- Having a service representative give personal service to the customer.
- Following up on the customer's experience with the purchase.

A key element of clientelling is empowering salespersons to provide an exceptional experience for the customer, our next topic.[26]

clientelling
A method of personalizing service by tailoring product information for individual customers, in order to provide an exceptional and personalized shopping experience.

Empowering Service Employees

Despite a company's best efforts to deliver value, customers may still have problems with a company's products. Negative experiences can damage the customer relationship and future business opportunities. Negative experiences carry more weight than positive ones when a customer is deciding whether to do business with a company again. Word-of-mouth criticisms to a customer's friends and relatives can also damage future sales. Effectively resolving a customer's problem is critical to repairing a customer relationship damaged by a negative experience.

Service employees are those like salespeople, retail employees, and others who have direct contact with customers and the public. Have you ever complained to a service employee who responded that they could resolve your problem without asking for permission from a supervisor? If so, you were lucky enough to be dealing with a company that believes in empowering its service employees. **Empowerment** means giving employees permission to make decisions and take action on their own to help customers. Empowerment usually involves training employees in what they should do to satisfy customers.

empowerment
Giving employees permission to make decisions and take action on their own to help customers.

Companies typically set boundaries beyond which the employee will need to ask permission from a supervisor to address a customer's issue. If the job is routine or the issue is minor, the company can develop a set of rules to guide the employee on the appropriate response. For example, a restaurant like Applebee's may put in place a policy that states that, if it takes longer than 20 minutes for food to reach a table in a restaurant, the server can automatically offer a free dessert or subtract a percentage off the bill. Similarly, retail employees at a store like Nordstrom may be empowered to offer damaged goods at a reduced price of 10 percent or extend the merchandise-hold policy for a profitable customer.

Empowerment programs have an added bonus: employee satisfaction. Empowered employees have a sense of ownership for how well they do their jobs. As a result, they have a strong affinity for their company and are happier in their jobs. Customers who deal with empowered employees experience high rates of satisfaction because their issues are resolved quickly and with little to no hassle. Happy employees and customers provide a good basis for company success in the marketplace.

Service Recovery

All companies make mistakes: The wrong products are shipped; products are damaged in transit; products or services are delivered late, or not at all. What a company does to resolve poor service can set it apart from its competition and help build customer loyalty. Customers who have had a service problem that is resolved quickly and to their satisfaction are significantly more loyal to a company than are customers who have never had a service failure.[27]

Maintaining and enhancing good customer relationships begins with a company culture that places customer service as a high priority. Such a culture puts in place procedures for recovering from service errors that can leave customers angry. Some commonsense steps can be used to recover from a service failure:[28]

1. **Apologize and ask the customer to forgive.** The apology must be real and perceived by the customer as sincere. If the customer believes that the company is truly sorry about an error, they will be much more likely to move on to the next recovery steps.
2. **Review the complaint with the customer.** The cause of the problem needs to be established at this point. This should be done diplomatically: The problem may have occurred because the customer made a mistake in ordering, and you do not want to insult them.
3. **Fix the problem, then check back with the customer to make sure that they are satisfied with your solution.** This can involve many techniques: free return shipping, discounts on future purchases, or free merchandise or services. The key is that the customer's sense of injustice is removed. For example, restaurants will often offer a free dessert or meal if a customer complains about the food or service.
4. **Document the problem and find its root cause.** Record service problems in order to identify and correct patterns or trends in service failures. Finding the root cause of the problem is critical. Often on the surface, a problem's cause may seem obvious, but under further investigation, there can be deeper causes. For example, UPS and FedEx were blamed for late delivery of products during several holiday seasons; looking deeper, part of the problem was retailers overpromising delivery dates to their customers. Once the company has determined the root cause, it can find ways to permanently fix it.

Not all customers will be satisfied with how a company handles their complaints. But a good process, backed up by a sincere effort to correct the problem, goes a long way to successful service recovery that maintains good customer relationships.

LO 15-4

Describe how customer relationship management uses customer information to improve relations between businesses and customers.

customer relationship management (CRM)

The process by which companies get new customers, keep the customers they already have, and grow the business by increasing their share of customers' purchases.

CUSTOMER RELATIONSHIP MANAGEMENT

Companies interested in improving customer relationships and empowering their employees to support that effort often formalize the process by making customer relationship management a large part of their marketing strategy. **Customer relationship management (CRM)** is the process by which companies get new customers, keep the customers they already have, and grow the business by increasing their share of customers' purchases. It is an overall strategy that unifies all of a company's activities under the overarching goal of achieving customer satisfaction through the right actions, attitudes, and systems. Companies that adopt CRM use data to understand customer needs and wants. Based on that understanding, they respond to and anticipate customer expectations in a way that delivers value to the customer. These activities, if done well, can foster favorable impressions of the company and its goods or services.

In modern times, companies use CRM software to capture, store, and analyze consumer data. With that information, they create and maintain customer profiles, including buying habits and purchasing patterns. The company can then leverage the information to help marketers design individualized fulfillment strategies for their customers. Company websites augment CRM software data. Through these sites, companies can track how customers navigate their websites, what customers look at, and what customers ultimately buy.

Companies with both a physical and an Internet presence (*click-and-mortar companies*) have the ability to track customers through various means: capturing point-of-sale data, cataloging direct interaction with salespeople, and monitoring traffic on the firm's website. Each of these opportunities represents a touch point. A **touch point** is any point at which a customer and the company come into contact. Best Buy, for example, has multiple touch points: when customers create an online account and order merchandise, when a customer goes to a store and talks to a salesperson, and when the customer purchases goods at a store.

touch point

Any point at which a customer and the company come into contact.

Objectives of Customer Relationship Management

CRM entails gathering data from all touch points (e.g., face-to-face, telephone, and Internet) and using those data to understand the customer's needs and wants. The firm can then develop tactics for building a long-term, mutually beneficial relationship with the customer. CRM technologies allow marketers to do the following:

1. Track consumer behavior over time.
2. Capture data that allow the firm to identify customers who are likely to be profitable.
3. Interact with customers to learn what they need and want.
4. Use the information gathered to tailor goods and services accordingly.

The Internet is an invaluable tool in CRM: It enables companies to collect individualized data and to send personalized marketing messages directly to individual consumers. For example, J.Crew offers its customers advice via e-mail from Jack O'Connor, a real stylist, in a friendly and conversational manner. Macy's tracks its customers' shopping patterns and sends them sales offers that complement previous purchases. Neiman Marcus sends an e-mail to its customers called a *gift dash* that offers big discounts for items not advertised through any other medium.[29]

CRM provides a structure for a company to establish and maintain valuable relationships with customers. Most products provide a searchable database to store customer information. Companies can use CRM tools to track performance based on activities entered into the CRM system, such as new customers, sales, and new orders placed. These tools can also be used for sales forecasting.[30]

Using CRM, companies can readily develop a customer orientation: They can gather data that help them understand the needs of individual customers, rather than an entire market segment as in a traditional marketing approach. This narrower focus enables companies to obtain maximum profits from customers they already have, rather than spending time and money prospecting for new customers.

There are a number of major software companies that provide firms with CRM systems. One such company is Salesforce. It provides CRM capabilities such as managing customer support, personalizing messages to customers, and enabling customer data analytics to companies. A company does not have to be very large to take advantage of what Salesforce offers, but midsize and large companies also use its services. Other CRM systems can be purchased from such companies as Oracle and SAP, which are typically modules within a larger system such as ERP (enterprise resource planning). Microsoft and Adobe also offer CRM applications, as well as a number of highly rated companies such as HubSpot CRM, FreeAgent CRM, Pipeliner CRM, and BoomTown.[31]

Companies use data collection and analysis technologies like HubSpot CRM to support their customer relationship management efforts. *Tada Images/Shutterstock*

The CRM Process

The CRM process revolves around a cycle of activities. As Figure 15.2 illustrates, CRM is an iterative rather than a linear process; the firm repeats the sequence of steps, as necessary, to reach the desired result.

Step 1: Identify Current Customers

The company initiates the CRM process by identifying its current customers. For example, a company like Dell that has both business customers and individual customers would identify its customers by:

- Finding out their locations.
- Breaking down computer purchases by customer type.
- Quantifying the frequency of both individual and business purchases.
- Determining how many computers each type of customer typically purchases.

Even within each type of customer, Dell would want to note distinctions. For example, though both Arkansas State University and the U.S. Department of Defense fall into the category of business customer, they might differ when it comes to the type and number of computers purchased.

Step 2: Understand How Customers Interact with the Firm

Next, the company seeks to understand how customers interact with the firm. The firm wants to know how customers purchase (what percentages purchase via the Internet, in brick-and-mortar stores, and through a salesperson). It also wants to know how customers, in general, communicate with the firm. Dell has several channels through which it sells computers to individuals. It would probably want to know which types of customers are more likely to order a computer on the company's website, and which would prefer to go to a retail store to buy one.

Interactions can take many forms: phone calls and e-mails to customer service, conversations with salespeople, purchases, questionnaire responses, coupon redemption, requests for information, and repair or product return requests. Understanding the interactions between the company and its customers is the backbone of a CRM system. Up to this point, the information gathered in the CRM system is general customer information.

Step 3: Gather Specific Customer Information

In step 3, the company gathers specific information on each individual customer's touch points with the company. These include any time the customer has had contact with the company in any way, such as website visits, purchase history, use of coupons or promotional codes, warranty card submissions, point-of-sale data, or customer inquiries.

A salesperson serves as an excellent source of information about in-person customer interactions. They can record information in the CRM system, including the customer's contact information and preferences for particular goods or services.

Kroger's use of free customer-loyalty cards is another example of gathering customer specific information that helps the company track information about customers. Purchase information is collected at the counter and tagged directly to the customer through the loyalty card. This information can then be used to target promotions to specific customers,

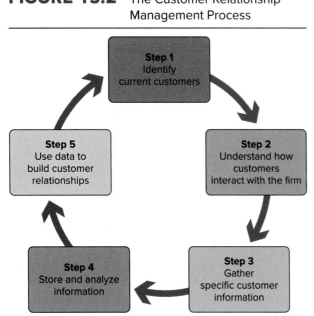

FIGURE 15.2   The Customer Relationship Management Process

Step 1
Identify
current customers

Step 2
Understand how
customers
interact with the firm

Step 3
Gather
specific customer
information

Step 4
Store and analyze
information

Step 5
Use data to
build customer
relationships

Red Lobster gathers specific customer service information at the customers' tables by asking diners to fill out a satisfaction survey after they use the pay-at-the-table touchscreen to pay for their meals. *Allen Creative/Steve Allen/Alamy Stock Photo*

such as offering a coupon for diapers to customers identified as parents with young children.

An increasingly popular way for companies to gather information is Internet interactions: a customer going to a company's website for information, purchasing goods or services, or providing feedback on a good or service. For example, Amazon tracks a customer's purchases and provides that information to its customers in case they want to reorder a product. It also has a recommendation engine that it has integrated into almost every purchase price to guide a consumer to one of their offerings. Up to 35 percent of Amazon's revenue is generated by its recommendation engine.[32] Additionally, Facebook, Twitter, and other social media sites offer avenues for companies to interact with individual customers.

Step 4: Store and Analyze Information

After the company has gathered the appropriate data, it must store the data so that CRM data analysis applications can access them. CRM databases store the information for individual or business customers. CRM data analysis applications can work only with the data stored. The information input into the CRM database must be accurate. If it is not, the company will not be able to use it effectively to create and maintain satisfied, profitable long-term customers.

To analyze the stored data, the CRM system uses data mining techniques. **Data mining** is a process that involves the computerized search for meaningful trends in a large amount of data. Using data mining software like ProClarity, Tableau, Pentaho, and Sisense, marketers can search for relevant data, organize the data based on select criteria, and create customer profiles that can be used to analyze customers.[33]

Data mining analysis can include one or more of the following techniques:

- **Customer segmentation analysis** involves creating customer profiles based on demographic characteristics, purchase patterns, and other criteria and placing them into various categories.
- **Recency-frequency-monetary analysis** involves categorizing customers by their buying patterns. Examples of patterns are how recently customers have purchased a good or service, how often they purchase from the company, and how much

data mining

A process that involves the computerized search for meaningful trends in a large amount of data.

customer segmentation analysis

A method of analyzing data that creates customer profiles and categorizes them.

recency-frequency-monetary analysis

A method of analyzing data that categorize customers by their buying patterns.

money they spend on the company's products. Based on this analysis, the system ranks customers according to how profitable they are (or their profitability potential). The firm can then target customers for appropriate further marketing efforts.

- **Lifetime value** is the total profit a customer brings to a company during the time the individual or firm is a customer. **Lifetime value (LTV) analysis** compares the costs of retaining customers with the costs of acquiring new customers, to determine how much money each type of customer requires. With this analysis in hand, a company can predict how valuable a customer will be over a period of time. Customers are assigned a *customer lifetime value (CLV),* and that number can affect the level of service a customer gets, including prices, the advertising the company directs to a customer, and the perks a customer might receive, such as upgraded airline seats and how quickly a wireless carrier customer service representative will pick up your service call.[34] The system can also help a company identify potential customers on whom it may be worth spending money to develop a long-term relationship. Lifetime value analysis helps ensure that a company is focusing on the most profitable customers.

- **Predictive modeling** uses sophisticated algorithms based on patterns of previous buying behavior to predict the future buying behavior of customers. For example, Norwegian Cruise Lines might use the timing and frequency of previous cruise purchases to predict which customers will purchase a cruise in the near future. Using the results of predictive modeling, marketers for the cruise company could focus promotional activities on those potential buyers.

Step 5: Use Data to Build Customer Relationships
The fifth step in the CRM process is to utilize the information gathered and analyzed in the previous steps to build customer relationships. The CRM system sends information to functional areas within the company, like sales and marketing. Those functional areas use the information to customize their activities to target specific customers. Norwegian Cruise Lines, for example, may offer a discount or cabin upgrade to frequent customers. We'll discuss these types of tailored examples, as well as additional ways a firm can increase the power of the information obtained through the CRM process, in the next section.

lifetime value

The net present value of a customer's business over the span of his or her relationship with an organization.

lifetime value (LTV) analysis

A comparison of the costs of retaining customers and the costs of acquiring new customers, to determine how much money each type of customer requires.

predictive modeling

Analysis that uses statistical techniques and algorithms based on patterns of past behavior to predict the future unknown events, such as future buying behavior.

Predictive modeling identifies patterns in past behavior to help firms, such as cruise lines, anticipate the future actions of customers and adapt their marketing activities accordingly.
Carl & Ann Purcell/Corbis/Getty Images

📊 connect Exercise **15-3**

Please complete the *Connect* exercise for Chapter 15 that focuses on the steps of the customer relationship management process. By understanding this process, you can improve customer relationships with your organization and increase the likelihood of maintaining long-term relationships with loyal and profitable customers.

Leveraging Customer Information

Firms can increase the power of customer information obtained from CRM systems in a number of ways beyond those already discussed.

Tailor Customer Promotions Perhaps the most obvious use of CRM data is to tailor promotions to match customer profiles. For example, Kroger offers discounts on gasoline purchases for members of its loyalty-card program. Based on past purchases and the customer's receipt, Kroger generates discount coupons to send to customers, creating an incentive for the customer to return to the store. Infrequent buyers could receive different incentives, such as a coupon good for their next purchase. Similarly, a Dell customer who mainly shops on the company's website might receive promotional materials through an e-mail; a customer who purchases a computer from a store might be targeted for mailed coupons or catalogs.

Firms can also leverage CRM data by targeting specific customers for direct-mail advertising. Mail-order companies that track customers' purchases and inquiries can use that information to predict how customers would react to a particular catalog sent to their home. Additionally, CRM systems can cross-reference promotions to specific categories of customers. With that information, companies can monitor the success of tailored promotional efforts and make adjustments as necessary. By gaining efficiencies in promotional efforts, companies maximize the ratio of promotional spending to profitability.

There are a number of Loyalty Systems software programs that can help companies in many ways. These include those sold by Qualtrics, Annex Cloud, and Salesforce Experience. Types of services offered by these companies include activity tracking, CRM, gift card management, loyalty cards, loyalty programs, and membership management.[35]

Combat Buyer's Remorse Firms also can use CRM information to combat cognitive dissonance (buyer's remorse) by congratulating the buyer on his or her choice and reinforcing the best aspects of the good or service. A car manufacturer, for example, could send an e-mail to a customer congratulating her for purchasing a car that was rated the highest in its class for initial customer satisfaction by J.D. Power.

Improve Business-to-Business Relationships B2B companies can use CRM systems to improve the profitability of their customer relationships in much the same way B2C companies do. They can:

- Cross-sell their products, promoting other products they sell that might be purchased by an existing business customer.
- Track customer service complaints and returned goods.
- Tailor promotional programs to specific business customers based on classification.

Beyond this, CRM systems offer several unique advantages to B2B firms: Suppliers can generate sales forecasts from information in CRM systems, such as past and current orders. The systems also can provide product availability information to manufacturers as they establish production runs or to retailers as they plan sales.

Companies can leverage data collected through customer relationship management to alleviate customers' post-purchase cognitive dissonance by reminding customers of the superiority of their purchase.
J.D. Power

LO 15-5

Discuss the security and
ethical issues involved in
using customer relationship
management systems.

SECURITY AND ETHICAL ISSUES IN CUSTOMER RELATIONSHIP MANAGEMENT

Not all customers feel comfortable having their information accumulated and stored in a company's computer system. The issue of privacy is becoming increasingly acute; customers now realize that any computer security system that stores birth dates, credit card numbers, addresses, and other personal information can be breached. Target Corp., Neiman Marcus, JCPenney, and Home Depot are among retailers suffering from high-profile cyberattacks. The attacks breached company security and stole personal information about their customers such as credit card numbers.[36]

Leaving aside cybertheft, a general discomfort with invasion of privacy has become widespread. Companies can capitalize on information about a customer's buying habits and product preferences, among other things. Such information could be sold to or traded between companies. Since good customer relationships are built in part on trust, any doubt about the security of personal data can lead the customer to take his or her business elsewhere.

Privacy is a concern of many people, especially when the collection of personal data is done without their knowledge or approval. The United States and other countries are considering limiting the type and amount of information that companies can collect about customers. Some companies already restrict their data-gathering activities: Some offer a "do-not-track" button at their websites; it enables customers to request that the company not collect information about their Internet activity. Others offer customers the ability to opt-out of using collected data for advertising or other purposes.[37]

To guard against security breaches, CRM systems must have robust firewalls to protect customers' privacy. In particular, companies using cloud-computing CRM applications should understand the increased risks involved in entrusting data to a third party. Their contract should require the third-party vendor to employ protective measures to discourage and prevent data hacking. Safeguarding the privacy and trust of a company's customers requires constant vigilance and regular upgrading of security systems. But establishing robust cybersecurity is not enough: Clever hackers can often breach firewalls,

Companies that collect and store customer information, such as Target, must be vigilant about identifying and addressing cyberattacks that compromise customer data. *Sam Hodgson/ Bloomberg/Getty Images*

and new methods for hacking are being developed every day. Marketers should be sensitive to the desires of customers for privacy and make accommodations for customers to opt-out of data collection when possible to avoid backlash on this sensitive topic.

The U.S. government has put in place laws for protecting the financial, health, telephone, and e-mail information of citizens. Still, companies should supplement these laws with company policies that govern various aspects of customer information:

- How the company can collect information.
- How it can use the information it collects.
- Whether it may share the information with other companies.
- How it will protect the information.

Though almost all companies have such policies, firms also must fully train employees in their application; they also must monitor and enforce the policies. Companies interested in protecting the privacy of customer information must make a concerted effort not only to develop such policies but also to make sure they are followed every day. Failure to do so could lead consumers to lose trust in the company and, as a result, switch to a competitor.

Another ethical issue involves a tactic some companies use to determine how far they can push their customers before they reach a "breakpoint" and stop doing business with them. For example, technology allows a company to determine how long a customer will wait for an actual person to answer a phone call or the number of advertisements a customer will put up with before closing a website. Used in a way that takes advantage of a customer is unethical, and probably not good business in the long run because customers are not afraid to get on a social media platform and complain. However, the same technology can be used to monitor the tone of voice and pace of speech of a customer. When it determines that the customer is upset or angry, the caller gets routed to a customer service representative who is trained in de-escalating situations. Additionally, transcriptions of call-center conversations can be used to train representatives to know when callers are becoming frustrated and how to handle such calls. Thus, such technology can be used in an ethical and productive manner to help firms better serve their customers.[38]

In the long run, customer service is not just about handling customer questions or product returns. More broadly, it is about gaining the trust of customers and building relationships with them, so that they will continue to do business with your company. This principle applies to both B2B and B2C customer relationships.

DETERMINING THE EFFECTIVENESS OF CUSTOMER RELATIONSHIP MANAGEMENT

How can a company determine whether its CRM strategy is working? Companies can use any of four basic metrics to judge the effectiveness of a CRM program:

1. **Share of customer. Share of customer** differs from market share in that it measures the quantity of purchase dollars each customer spends on the company's products, rather than the number of customers. If a company's CRM efforts lead to an increase in the number of goods or services purchased by a consumer, then it has been successful in increasing its share of customer. As share of customer increases, so do the company's profits.

   If the CRM efforts do not increase the company's share of customer, the company must evaluate them to determine why and apply corrective measures. For example, if a customer buys a Nissan Altima, the company contacts them when the warranty is about to run out with an offer for an extended warranty. If Nissan does not follow up, the company misses an opportunity to gain share of customer, which means its CRM program is not working to its highest potential.

LO 15-6

Describe how companies can judge the effectiveness of their customer relationship management efforts.

share of customer

A measure of the quantity of purchase dollars each customer spends on the company's products.

customer equity

A ratio that compares the financial investments a company puts into gaining and keeping customers to the financial return on those investments.

customer focus

A measure of the extent to which a company puts effort into servicing its customers' needs, based on an understanding of each customer's profitability.

2. **Customer equity.** **Customer equity** is a ratio that compares the financial investments a company puts into gaining and keeping customers to the financial return on those investments. A company can determine the value of its CRM program from this ratio. If a company determines that it is spending more on CRM than it is getting back in profit, it needs to evaluate the program and correct the problems. For example, if a salesperson neglects to follow up with B2B customers to offer post-sales service that other companies do not offer, the company has given up the chance to increase the financial return on investment in those customers. A well-designed CRM process would prompt the salesperson to offer such post-sales service; offering that additional service would show the customer there are services the company offers that competitors do not.

3. **Customer focus.** **Customer focus** measures the extent to which a company puts effort into servicing its customers' needs, based on an understanding of each customer's profitability. With that information, the company can direct its personal selling efforts, which are expensive, to those customers who are most profitable.

One way that a company can identify its most important customers is through ABC analysis. This technique is based on *Pareto's law,* also known as the *80/20 rule.* Applied to CRM, this principle would mean that 80 percent of profits come from 20 percent of the customers. ABC analysis can help identify which customers are most profitable. Customers that deliver 80 percent of the profits are placed in the "A" category; customers that deliver the next 15 percent of profits are placed in the "B" category; customers that deliver the final 5 percent of profits are placed in the "C" category (see Table 15.2). This is a better metric than

TABLE 15.2 ABC Analysis Example

Customer	Annual Profit $	Cumulative Profit $	% of Annual Profit	Cumulative Annual Profit %	Classification
Big-box retailer #1	$395,000	$395,000	27.17%	27.17%	A
Big-box retailer #2	335,000	730,000	23.04	50.21	A
Big-box retailer #3	245,000	975,000	16.85	67.06	A
Big-box retailer #4	189,000	1,164,000	13.00	80.06	A
Regional wholesaler #1	39,200	1,203,200	2.70	82.75	B
Regional wholesaler #2	36,200	1,239,400	2.49	85.24	B
Regional wholesaler #3	33,300	1,272,700	2.29	87.53	B
Regional wholesaler #4	31,700	1,304,400	2.18	89.71	B
Regional retailer #1	29,600	1,334,000	2.04	91.75	B
Regional retailer #2	25,500	1,359,500	1.75	93.50	B
Regional retailer #3	22,700	1,382,200	1.56	95.06	B
Regional retailer #4	21,800	1,404,000	1.50	96.56	C
Large-city supermarket #1	7,875	1,411,875	0.54	97.10	C
Large-city supermarket #2	7,450	1,419,325	0.51	97.62	C
Large-city supermarket #3	7,250	1,426,575	0.50	98.12	C
Medium-city supermarket #1	6,950	1,433,525	0.48	98.59	C
Medium-city supermarket #2	6,280	1,439,805	0.43	99.03	C
Medium-city supermarket #3	5,975	1,445,780	0.41	99.44	C
Small-town supermarket #1	4,800	1,450,580	0.33	99.77	C
Small-town supermarket #2	3,400	1,453,980	0.23	100.00	C

Leanna Fino

Retail Sales Representative
The Hershey Company

Describe your job. My official title is retail sales representative. Although most people think I just merchandise products and build cool displays, there is so much more to it. I track product delivery, everyday sales data, seasonal sales data, and work with managers and store leads to increase and maximize store sales

How did you get your job? I applied for my position on LinkedIn, and most people are surprised to hear that because they have never met anyone who has gotten a position they applied for on LinkedIn. I think it is crucial for applicants to utilize free job sites such as LinkedIn, Indeed, and Zip Recruiter, and it is even more important to have a complete profile with an updated headshot. Having a professional photo to match an impressive resume will differentiate you from other applicants and increase your chances for an interview.

What has been the most important thing in making you successful at your job? Most definitely organization. I have never been the type of person to utilize planners and calendars to remember meetings and appointments, but if I didn't set reminders or write anything down, I would 100 percent fail at my job. There is so much

Leanna Fino

to remember and so much planning and scheduling required for this position that writing everything down, planning ahead of time, and sitting down for a few minutes a day to plan a detailed schedule is required every day. And although not required, having a positive attitude and a bubbly personality makes the job a million times easier

What advice would you give soon-to-be graduates? Apply for internships! I promise you, job hunting will become so much easier. I unfortunately missed some opportunities to get an internship my last semester before graduation, therefore it was so difficult for me to get real work. Gaps in my work history and lack of work experience may have been why recruiters chose someone else for the position over me.

What do you consider your personal brand to be? SLDM, which is an acronym for say less, do more. I disconnected from social media a few years ago and instead of showing the world what I am doing, I'm keeping to myself and being more productive with my time. I am doing very positive and productive things in my life that are making me happy and making me money.

revenue—although some customers may spend more money than others, they may be more expensive to service.

3. **Lifetime value.** As discussed earlier, lifetime value is the total profit a customer brings to a company while a customer. The CRM efforts of a company, if done right, should be able to maximize the lifetime value of customers, large and small. Companies that can predict lifetime value can aim customer service efforts accordingly: They can reduce or eliminate services to customers with low LTV; by cutting back on customer service costs for those customers, the firm improves the customer equity of those customers. Similarly, the firm can maintain or even increase services to customers with high LTV, to increase sales revenue.

Understanding the criteria for measuring the effectiveness of a CRM strategy is important: Unless a firm knows the extent to which any aspect of its business is succeeding, it cannot identify and address problems that may affect its profitability. Successful CRM programs require monitoring and assessment to adequately support the firm's overall marketing efforts.

SUMMARY

John Greim/ LightRocket/Getty Images

LO 15-1 Explain the importance of effective customer service and customer satisfaction to companies.

Customer service involves all of the activities, both human and mechanical, a firm engages in to satisfy the needs and wants of its customers. A company's customer service strategy must be built around a set of common objectives for all company employees: deliver the good or service completely and in a timely manner; ensure the reliability of the process for taking and fulfilling customer orders; establish convenient communication channels between the company and its customers; and establish ease of doing business with the firm.

Some of the most common metrics companies use to track how well they are meeting these objectives include line fill rate, item fill rate, dollar fill rate, on-time delivery, perfect order rate, order cycle time, communication, and responsiveness. These metrics must be developed with customer input for customer satisfaction to be achieved.

TomBham/Alamy Stock Photo

LO 15-2 Describe methods companies use to develop good customer relationships.

Customer satisfaction is achieved when companies meet the needs and expectations customers have for their goods or services. The ultimate objective behind achieving customer satisfaction is to promote brand loyalty; if achieved in a cost-effective manner, loyalty will drive long-term profitability. Customer satisfaction does not always lead to loyalty, though. Maximizing customer satisfaction must remain in balance with profitability. Firms must seek to delight, not just satisfy, their customers.

Robinson Worldwide

LO 15-3 Discuss how companies can improve relationships with B2B and B2C customers.

Relationship marketing refers to long-term arrangements in which a firm seeks to build mutually beneficial exchanges with a customer. Its objective is to find ways to keep and build upon good relationships with current customers. Loyal customers translate to consistent profits and potential growth in sales.

The first key to building customer relationships is to establish ways in which the customer receives more value from an exchange with the company than from other firms. The second key is for the firm to deliver its goods or services in ways that meet or exceed customer expectations. If the company fails in either, the customer may have a negative experience, which can damage the relationship.

Empowerment means giving employees permission to make decisions and take action on their own to help customers who've had negative experiences. Empowered employees typically experience job satisfaction, which enables them to contribute to customer satisfaction.

Tada Images/ Shutterstock

LO 15-4 Describe how customer relationship management uses customer information to improve relations between businesses and customers.

Customer relationship management (CRM) is the process by which companies obtain new customers, keep the customers they already have, and grow the business by increasing their share of customers' purchases. CRM software gathers information about customers to understand what the customer needs and wants. The company utilizes that understanding to respond to and anticipate customer expectations in a way that delivers customer value.

The cyclical CRM process includes identifying current customers; understanding how they interact with the firm; gathering specific information about individual customer interactions with the company; analyzing the information using CRM data analysis applications and data mining techniques; and finally, using the analysis to build customer relationships. A CRM system sends information to functional areas within the company, like sales and marketing, that use it to customize their activities. The company leverages customer information to tailor customer promotions, combat buyer's remorse, and improve B2B relationships.

Sam Hodgson/Bloomberg/Getty Images

LO 15-5 Discuss the security and ethical issues involved in using customer relationship management systems.

The issue of privacy is becoming increasingly acute, and a general discomfort with invasion of privacy from companies has become widespread. Because good customer relationships are built in part on trust, any doubt about the security of personal data can prompt a customer to take his or her business elsewhere. To guard against a breach of security, CRM systems must employ protective measures to protect the privacy of customers. In addition, companies interested in ensuring the privacy of their customer information must make a concerted effort to develop such policies and to make sure they are followed every day by all employees.

Allen Creative/Steve Allen/Alamy Stock Photo

LO 15-6 Describe how companies can judge the effectiveness of their customer relationship management efforts.

There are four basic criteria a company can use to judge the effectiveness of its CRM program: (1) *Share of customer* measures purchase dollars from each customer. (2) *Customer equity* compares the financial investments a company puts into gaining and keeping customers to the financial return on those investments. (3) *Customer focus* measures how well the CRM programs prioritize customers based on the profitability of the customer. (4) *Lifetime value of the customer* measures the total profit a customer brings to a company during the time that the individual or firm is a customer.

KEY TERMS

clientelling (p. 517)
collaborative filtering (p. 514)
customer communication (p. 505)
customer communication
    metrics (p. 510)
customer equity (p. 526)
customer focus (p. 526)
customer relationship management
    (CRM) (p. 518)
customer satisfaction (p. 512)
customer segmentation
    analysis (p. 521)
customer service (p. 502)
customer value (p. 515)

data mining (p. 521)
dollar fill rate (p. 509)
ease of doing business (p. 506)
empowerment (p. 517)
fill rate (p. 509)
geofencing (p. 514)
item fill rate (p. 509)
lifetime value (p. 522)
lifetime value (LTV) analysis (p. 522)
line fill rate (p. 509)
marketing concept (p. 512)
on-time delivery (p. 510)
order cycle (p. 504)
order cycle time (p. 510)

perfect order rate (p. 509)
predictive modeling (p. 522)
recency-frequency-monetary
    analysis (p. 521)
relationship marketing (p. 515)
reliability (p. 505)
responsiveness (p. 510)
share of customer (p. 525)
social media platforms (p. 507)
timeliness (p. 504)
touch point (p. 519)
transparency (p. 516)

MARKETING PLAN EXERCISE • Marketing Yourself

This chapter focused on customer service and developing customer relationships. As you develop your personal marketing plan, ask yourself how good you are at developing relationships. We live in an age in which we text or tweet more than we write notes or have conversations. Some might think they are great at developing relationships because they have 2,000 friends on Facebook. But are those really relationships? Consider your Facebook friends: What would those people say about you and your brand if you asked them? How well do they even know you?

For the marketing plan exercise in this chapter, your assignment is to plan a strategy to improve the most important relationships in your life. Even if they are good, there are always things you can do better. Think about how you can improve your relationship with your current boss, professors, classmates, and group members. These people are likely to be important as you seek a job or apply to graduate school. (Relationship development with professors is especially important when it comes time to request letters of recommendation for graduate school.)

Next, consider how you can improve your personal customer service. Are you an ideal group member, or do you look for excuses to miss team meetings? Do you thank people who help you? Do you try to help others solve problems in a positive way? Providing great service to the people in

your life, both personally and professionally, will help you build the type of relationships that will provide a rich future in every way possible.

Your Task: Select three to five professional relationships in your life, such as a manager, professor, classmate, or group member, and then identify one or two specific actions you can take in the next three months to strengthen each of those relationships.

Next, explain in one paragraph how you have delivered excellent customer service sometime in your life, whether it was on the job, in school, or in your personal life. This will help you articulate your customer service skills in an interview.

DISCUSSION QUESTIONS

1. Discuss an experience you had as a customer in which you were either very satisfied or very dissatisfied with a company's customer service. What were the circumstances that made this particular incident stand out to you as memorable? How did this experience affect your future purchases with this company? What did you learn about customer service from this experience that you could apply to your current or future career?

2. Imagine you work as a buyer for a large consumer electronics retail company that purchases its goods mainly from Asia. Of the four factors critical to delivering customer service discussed in this chapter, select the two most important for your type of business. Why did you select those two before the others? Would your choices change if you were purchasing fresh fruit for a grocery store chain? Explain your answer.

3. Assume you are about to purchase a new television. What attributes of this particular product contribute

to your perception of customer value, and why? What attributes do not contribute to your perception of customer value, and why? In your responses, consider both the attributes of the good itself and the accompanying services the manufacturer offers in your analysis.

4. In this chapter you learned about employee empowerment as it relates to customer service. Assume that you are the director of customer service for a cell phone service provider. What types of decisions concerning customer service issues would you allow your employees to make on their own without having to check with their supervisor? What decisions would you not allow your service representatives to make on their own? Explain your answers.

5. How does the concept *share of customer* differ from the concept of market share? What types of things does a company have to do differently to increase its share of customer versus increasing its market share?

 # SOCIAL MEDIA APPLICATION

Analyze how social media affect the way that your university provides customer service to its students, using the following questions and activities as a guide:

1. If you have an issue with some part of your educational experience, such as housing, financial aid, or career services, can you get help and answers through some social media platform? If so, which platform(s) does your school use? How convenient and timely are the responses? If your school does not

use a social media platform for these issues, what platform would you suggest it use? Why?

2. Discuss two ways that your college or university can improve its efforts to communicate and respond to students via social media. Explain your answer.

3. If you were put in charge of increasing student satisfaction at your school, how would you specifically use social media to help achieve your goal?

MARKETING ANALYTICS EXERCISE

Please complete the *Connect* exercise for Chapter 15 that focuses on identifying a firm's most profitable customers.

ETHICAL CHALLENGE

Imagine that you work for a company that has had only brick-and-mortar stores but is just starting a website for customers who wish to shop online. Your CEO is concerned about some of the bad press being disseminated concerning consumer privacy. She wants to make sure that the company is not unduly intruding on the privacy of its customers through its website.

The CEO has asked you, as the chief information officer (CIO) of the company, to ensure that the firm is operating in an ethical manner. As CIO, it is your responsibility to devise a set of policies for the company to follow. Please use the ethical decision-making framework to complete the following:

1. Write a set of rules (a minimum of five) that all company employees who deal directly with customers must follow in order to protect the privacy of your online customers.
2. Next, write a set of rules (a minimum of five) that the information technology employees must follow for obtaining information, and describe how that information should be handled once it is obtained.
3. Finally, explain why you selected those particular rules.

VIDEO CASE

Please go to *Connect* to access the video case featuring Holt Cat that accompanies this chapter.

 PODCAST

Please go to Connect to access the podcast that accompanies this chapter.

Edward Craner

CAREER **TIPS**

Using Transferrable Skills

You have read in this chapter about the importance of managing customer relationships. Whatever course of study you pursue, in your career you likely will work in a variety of jobs and industries in which you will need to deal with customers in one form or another. With that in mind, Edward Craner, who was featured in the Executive Perspective at the beginning of the chapter, *shares the following career advice to help you position yourself for a career that may take you in many different directions.*

Your credentials (e.g., education, previous job experience, and industry knowledge) will help you get a job. They're easy to quantify and help employers quickly screen candidates.

But what if you lack experience or want to move into a new industry? Though they may not explicitly state it, every employer wants, even more than credentials, the unique transferrable skills a job candidate can bring to a position. Showcase your expertise and competence related to transferrable skills and provide context for how those skills can help a prospective employer. Assure the employer that you can learn the job requirements and the industry. What the employer would get by hiring you is a set of well-developed skills that may include the following:

- *Writing expertise.* Bring a customized example of what the company can expect from you in the way of written communication.
- *Oral communication.* Ask the employer for a topic (or come prepared with one) and do an ad hoc persuasive presentation (no longer than three minutes in length).
- *Creative design.* Most employers appreciate creativity in a job applicant. Describe a situation from your previous work or school experience that displays your original thinking.

- *Microsoft Office competency.* The majority of businesses consider Microsoft Office a valuable tool. Showcase an example of a data analysis, database framework, or PowerPoint presentation you've developed.
- *Organizational skills.* Don't talk about being highly organized—show it! Describe a complex project you've managed, or describe processes related to the company or industry that you've observed and how they could be improved.
- *Results-oriented outlook.* Provide specific examples of results you've achieved that the interviewer will remember.

This is only a small sampling of the things you, as a job candidate, might bring to an interview. Identify your unique transferrable skills, and then leverage them by discussing with prospective employers how they apply to the job you want.

CHAPTER NOTES

1. Help Scout, "75 Customer Service Facts, Quotes & Statistics," n.d., http://www.helpscout.net/75-customer-service-facts-quotes-statistics/.
2. Help Scout, "75 Customer Service Facts, Quotes & Statistics," n.d., http://www.helpscout.net/75-customer-service-facts-quotes-statistics/.
3. Annie Gasparro, Heather Haddon, and Sarah Nassauer, "Grocers Levy Fines for Late Deliveries," *The Wall Street Journal*, November 28, 2017, pp. A1, A7.
4. *Techopedia*, "Social Platform," n.d., https://www.techopedia.com/definition/23759/social-platform.
5. Jeremy Collins, "Top 12 Most Popular Social Media Sites in 2022," *ReviewsXP*, (n.d.), https://www.reviewsxp.com/blog/best-social-media-sites/.
6. Seth Fiegerman, "Best Customer Complaint Sites," *TheStreet,* May 25, 2010, https://www.thestreet.com/personal-finance/credit-cards/best-customer-complaint-sites-12806150.
7. Ekaterina Walter, "The Big Brand Theory: How FedEx Achieves Social Customer Service Success," *SocialMedia Today*, May 27, 2013, http://socialmediatoday.com/ekaterinawalter/1494726/big-brand-theory-how-fedex-achieves-social-customer-service-success.
8. Laura Lake, "Social Media Marketing for Non-Profits," The Balance Small Business, December 16, 2018, http://marketing.about.com/od/nonprofitmarketing/a/5-Benefits-Non-Profit-Organizations-Gain-From-Social-Media-Marketing.htm.
9. Trishia Morris, "15 Customer Service Metrics to Measure," http://www.parature.com/15-customer-service-metrics-measure.
10. Client Heartbeat, https://www.clientheartbeat.com/.
11. George Schwartz, ed., *Science in Marketing* (New York: Wiley, 1965), pp. 70–97.
12. A. Parasuraman, Valarie A. Zeithaml, and Leonard L. Berry, "A Conceptual Model of Service Quality and Its Implications for Future Research," *Journal of Marketing* 49, no. 4 (Autumn, 1985): 41–50.
13. Muhammed Saleen, "Collaborative Filtering: Lifeblood of the Social Net," ReadWrite.com, June 30, 2008, http://readwrite.com/2008/06/30/collaborative_filtering_social_web.
14. Daniel Leviton, "The Sum of Human Reasoning," *The Wall Street Journal,* September 19, 2015, pp. C5, C8.
15. Lauryn Chamberlain, "GeoMarketing 101: What Is Geofencing?" GeoMarketing, March 7, 2016, https://geomarketing.com/geomarketing-101-what-is-geofencing.
16. Harry McCracken, "Nowhere to Hide: How Retailers Can Find—and Up-Sell— You in the Aisles," *Time*, March 31, 2014, p. 20.
17. Elizabeth Dwoskin, "What Secrets Your Phone Is Sharing about You," *The Wall Street Journal*, January 14, 2014, pp. B1, B3.
18. Sam Hornblower, "Always Low Prices," *Frontline*, November 16, 2004, http://www.pbs.org/wgbh/pages/frontline/shows/walmart/secrets/pricing.html.
19. Khadeeja Safdar, "Hawking Suits Takes a High-Tech Turn," *The Wall Street Journal,* April 16, 2018, p. B4.
20. Marketing-Schools.org, "Relationship Marketing," n.d., http://www.marketing-schools.org/types-of-marketing/relationship-marketing.html.
21. Tali Yahalom, "How to Improve Your Customer Service," n.d., http://www.inc.com/jessica-stillman/coursera-s-10-most-popular-business-classes-of-2015.html.

22. John Hagel III and John Seely Brown, "How to Deepen Customer Loyalty: Be Transparent," *Fortune*, April 2, 2014. http://fortune.com/2014/04/02/. how-to-deepen-customer-loyalty-be-transparent/.

23. Medallia, "Net Promoter Score," n.d., https://www .medallia.com/net-promoter-score/.

24. Shelly Banjo, "Rampant Returns Plague E-Retailers," *The Wall Street Journal,* December 21, 2013, pp. B1, B2.

25. Shelly Banjo, "Rampant Returns Plague E-Retailers," *The Wall Street Journal,* December 21, 2013, pp. B1, B2.

26. Retail Info Systems, "Clientelling: What It Really Is," n.d., http://risnews.edgl.com/getattachment/43497b81-4729-49ff-b7b2-58061a879c19/?maxsidesize=100.

27. GreatBrook, http://www.greatbrook.com/service_ recovery.htm.

28. Micah Solomon, "4 Steps from Customer Anger to Customer Loyalty: The Expert Customer Service Recovery Method," *Forbes*, July 16, 2014, http://www.forbes.com/ sites/micahsolomon/2014/07/16/customer-service-recovery/.

29. Elizabeth Holmes, "Dark Art of Store Emails," *The Wall Street Journal*, December 19, 2012, http://online.wsj. com/article/SB1000142412788732372310457818745 0253813668.html.

30. Software Advice, https://www.softwareadvice.com/crm/.

31. Software Advice, https://www.softwareadvice.com/crm/.

32. Rejoiner, "The Amazon Recommendations Secret to Selling More Online," (n.d.), www.rejoiner.com/resources/ amazon-recommendations-secret-selling-online.

33. Alternativeto.net, "ProClarity Alternatives," (n.d), alternativeto.net/software/proclarity/.

34. Khadeeja Safdar, "Secret Scores Shape Customer Service," *The New Your Times*, November 2, 2018, pp. A1, A9.

35. Capterra, "Customer Loyalty Software," (n.d.), www .capterra.com/sem-compare/customer-loyalty-software/? utm_source=bing&utm_medium=cpc.

36. Jim Finkle and Mark Hosenball, "Security Breach Hits More Prominent U.S. Retailers," *Huffington Post,* January 11, 2014, http://www.huffingtonpost.com/2014/01/11/ security-breach-more-retailers_n_4583200.html.

37. Federal Trade Commission, "Protecting Consumer Privacy and Security," (n.d.), https://www.ftc.gov/news-events/media-resources/protecting-consumer-privacy.

38. Terlep, Sharon, "Please Continue to Fume," *The Wall Street Journal,* August 3, 2019, pp. B1, B6.

Chapter **16**

Social Responsibility and Sustainability

Rawpixel.com/Shutterstock

Learning Objectives

After reading this chapter, you should be able to

LO 16-1 Describe the features of a successful corporate social responsibility program.

LO 16-2 Explain how sustainable marketing contributes to a firm's corporate social responsibility efforts.

LO 16-3 Explain the impact of environmentalism on marketing success.

LO 16-4 Describe how companies can meet the challenges of environmental and sustainable marketing on a global scale.

LO 16-5 Analyze how firms use social media to support their corporate social responsibility efforts.

Executive **Perspective** ... because everyone is a marketer

Gina Gomez
Executive Director
**Hispanic Community
Services, Inc.**

Gina Gomez

Those who work for nonprofit organizations feel the impact of corporate social responsibility in a unique way. Gina Gomez is no exception. As a psychology major, she discovered how much she enjoyed working with people, trying to understand their behavior, and developing programs and activities that empower them and contribute to the improvement of their quality of life. Today, she works for Hispanic Community Services Inc., a nonprofit organization that supports the integration of the Hispanic population into their local communities by providing assistance through social, educational, legal, health, and other referral services.

As the executive director of Hispanic Community Services Inc. (HCSI), Gomez is responsible for making sure the organization functions well from the perspectives of management, public relations, and fundraising. In addition, she leads the organization's efforts to develop relationships with socially responsible firms interested in supporting their local community and its citizens. She is also responsible for establishing working relationships with organizations and community groups.

Firms increasingly recognize the positive effect a focus on corporate social responsibility can have on their business, both from an image and an economic standpoint. Such firms seek to partner with nonprofit organizations, like HCSI, that can help them make a greater impact on social and global problems. With an eye to the future, executives like Gomez seek to plug into this trend by identifying the challenges a firm faces that their nonprofit can help address.

What has been the most important thing in making you successful at your job?

I think passion for what you do is the key to success in any job. When you are passionate about what you do, you do your best and obtain the best results. I believe loving what you do is essential, not just to be a good employee but also to be satisfied with your life. I never take anything for granted. Everything has a cost. When HCSI became a nonprofit organization back in 2004, things were not easy. The struggle for funds was tough, but you know what? It gets easier with time. I stick to my principles. My motto is never give up, always keep trying.

What advice would you give soon-to-be graduates?

My first advice would be not to underestimate your studies. Books have always been a good inspiration for new and great ideas, and the knowledge and expertise provided by your professors is priceless. Then, persevere and always keep trying; never give up. Business life is not easy. It gets very competitive and complicated sometimes, but with your best effort and sacrifice, you will be able to reach the top.

How is marketing relevant to your role at Hispanic Community Services Inc.?

I spend a significant portion of my time promoting our events through our website, social media, and traditional marketing tools. I also work on developing products and programs that will help our community succeed and then presenting those ideas to our board of directors for approval. Finally, I work hard to communicate the value of HCSI to individuals, business community members, and potential supporters throughout the region.

What do you consider your personal brand to be?

I was raised in the Hispanic culture with a good education. I left home and moved to the U.S. looking for new opportunities in life and obtained my first job in the U.S. at the Hispanic Center. All this has combined with my natural talents, education, and experiences to make me a very compassionate, strong, and determined person. So I think that it would be true to say that my personal brand is defined by the work I have done motivating others and spending my life helping everyone around me improve their situation in life.

I have also tried to encourage people to take advantage of the opportunities given to them in this country. I hope I've set an example of how honesty, loyalty, hard work, and passion for what you do can bring you success in life.

CORPORATE SOCIAL RESPONSIBILITY

Describe the features of a successful corporate social responsibility program.

Have you ever bought a pair of Samuel Hubbard shoes made from recycled water bottles, or decided to spend more on an organic apple from Whole Food Grocers than you would have at the grocery store down the street? If so, you are part of an ever-growing group of consumers who make purchase decisions in part because of a firm's reputation for corporate social responsibility. Organizations today are forced to confront a new economic reality: It is no longer acceptable to experience economic prosperity in isolation from those stakeholders (customers, communities, and employees) who are affected by the organization's decisions. Companies have a number of reasons for taking environmental and social issues seriously, including attracting employees who want to work for a company that is concerned with environmental sustainability and pleasing investors and funds that buy stock in such companies.[1]

Consumers increasingly choose to buy from firms that value and support the same causes they do. As a result, firms have begun to accept responsibility for balancing profitability with social well-being when determining their success. Success begins with the quality of the relationships that a company develops with its customers and other stakeholders. These relationships are at the heart of corporate social responsibility. **Corporate social responsibility (CSR)** refers to an organization's obligation to maximize its positive impact and minimize its negative impact on society. CSR has been shown to benefit companies in many ways, including improving employee retention and enhancing the company's brand image.[2]

Within many organizations, the marketing department is primarily responsible for the ideas and strategies that comprise a CSR program, making this topic an important part of your marketing education. However, to succeed, a CSR focus must be adopted and enacted by all of the functional areas within a firm. Accountants who offer free tax preparation to low-income or older adults and managers who work with students to develop future business leaders in the community also have a CSR focus.

CSR includes economic, legal, and ethical accountability to stakeholders and society in general. **Stakeholder responsibility** focuses on the obligations an organization has to its stakeholders, those who can affect or are affected by a firm's actions. Stakeholder responsibility is the driving consideration across the four dimensions of corporate social responsibility: economic, legal, ethical, and philanthropic. Investors are increasingly putting pressure on companies to disclose the amount of greenhouse gas emissions their products and services emit. Government regulators are also increasing pressure on companies to accurately track and report such emissions.[3] Across a large section of the United States, corporations such as Amazon.com, Citigroup Inc., Ford Motor Company, and General Motors Co., are responding to such pressures by calling on congressional and executive branches of the government to work together cooperatively on climate change legislation.[4]

As you can see in Figure 16.1, economic and legal considerations form the foundation of CSR. The ethical and philanthropic aspects go farther. They encompass actions that, while not required of the firm, meet stakeholders' expectations for how the firm should act. We'll discuss each of these dimensions in more depth in the sections that follow.

corporate social responsibility (CSR)

An organization's obligation to maximize its positive impact and minimize its negative impact on society.

stakeholder responsibility

The obligations an organization has to its stakeholders, those who can affect or are affected by a firm's actions.

Organizations like Junior Achievement, which is dedicated to preparing students for the workplace, allow individuals from all organizational areas and backgrounds to participate in their firms' corporate social responsibility efforts. *ZUMA Press/ Alamy Stock Photo*

Economic Dimension

For-profit firms have a responsibility to their stakeholders to be profitable. Without profits, a business cannot survive. A failed business hurts employees, investors, and communities. In addition, it can no longer engage in any type of philanthropy, which has economic consequences for the causes the company supported.

Publicly traded firms have a unique responsibility to investors. These shareholders have invested in the firm with the expectation that they'll receive high share prices and dividends in return. Over 50 percent of Americans invest in the stock market in the United States alone, many through the 401(k) retirement-savings plans offered by their employers. That level of stock market participation makes the economic dimension critical not just to the firm's success but to the overall economic wealth of the country as well.[5]

Legal Dimension

Marketers have a responsibility to understand and obey the laws and regulations of the communities in which they do business. They must follow local, state, and federal laws. Beyond this, U.S. companies are also subject to the laws and regulations of the foreign countries in which they do business. CSR programs often begin as a way of reducing the likelihood of legal problems and public relations disasters, either at home or abroad.

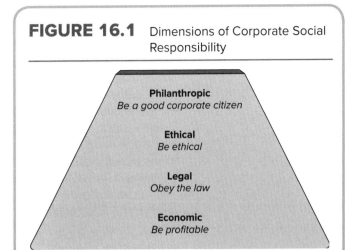

FIGURE 16.1 Dimensions of Corporate Social Responsibility

Source: Adapted from Archie B. Carroll, "The Pyramid of Corporate Social Responsibility: Toward the Moral Management of Organizational Stakeholders," *Business Horizons* 34, no. 4 (July–August 1991): 39.

The past two decades are littered with examples of firms—Enron, Arthur Andersen, and WorldCom, to name a few—whose failure to obey laws and regulations led to their demise. Such examples prove that the short-term benefits from the economic dimension will be erased if the firm eschews responsibility in the legal dimension. Despite years of economic success, the failure of these companies to obey the law hurt every stakeholder group: Thousands of employees lost their jobs; customers and suppliers lost an important business partner; and shareholders lost virtually their entire investment.

Marketers must take a broad view of the legal dimension and its relationship to ethics. In the years leading up to the recession that began in late 2007, many firms

The Dodd-Frank Wall Street Reform and Consumer Protection Act, signed into law in 2010, was passed to improve accountability and transparency in the financial system and, ultimately, to protect consumers from abusive financial service practices. *Rod Lamkey/Getty Images*

marketed products that, though legal at the time, were highly questionable ethically. This was especially the case in financial industries, ranging from banking to real estate. After the recession hit, outraged consumers demanded action. The result was new laws and regulations, such as the Dodd-Frank Wall Street Reform and Consumer Protection Act of 2010. They have altered the legal dimension for firms: Because of Dodd-Frank, real estate transactions involve more steps, stricter due diligence, and longer time frames than they did previously. These additional complexities can delay or reduce the revenue a firm might generate from the transaction. In addition, bank marketers face new pricing restrictions on debit cards and other bank services. Such new restrictions could require banks to raise fees in other areas (e.g., through the elimination of free checking accounts) to maintain revenue and profit.

Ethical Dimension

As Warren Buffett said, "It takes 20 years to build a reputation and five minutes to ruin it." One way to ruin a reputation is to do unethical things. For example, Novartis AG's Sandoz subsidiary was ordered to pay a $195 million fine for fixing prices on its generic drugs, Apple had to pay $500 million to settle a class-action lawsuit that claimed the company intentionally slowed down older model iPhones to get people to buy new ones, and the Securities and Exchange Commission looked into BMW for committing "sales punching," which is when a car company boosts sales numbers by having its dealers register cars while they are still sitting on the dealer's lot. Any of these types of unethical behaviors can turn customers away from purchasing a company's products and services.

ethics

The moral standards expected by a society.

The ethical challenges facing marketers come from many different places. Inevitably, they involve more gray areas than the legal dimension. As discussed earlier in the book, **ethics** are the moral standards expected by a society. Marketers are responsible for a number of choices with an ethical dimension and will be held accountable for making the right decision.

The ethical decision-making framework described in Chapter 1 provides a systematic tool for thinking about and making ethical decisions. Marketers who take the time to identify the ethical issue at hand and consider how their decision will affect each of the firm's stakeholders are far more likely to make the right decision and successfully resolve the problem.

An important area for companies to consider in making ethical decisions is new product development. The primary ethical consideration is the duty of a company to provide a product that lives up to the expectations of its customers. The goal should be to design and produce a new product that:

- Is safe (if used as directed).
- Has a reasonable service life.
- Can be expected to perform in a reliable manner.
- Can be maintained without excessive costs.

Most important, companies have an implied obligation to provide safe products. This obligation requires that companies:

- Design and produce a new product with due care, to ensure that the product will not injure a customer because it is defective in some way.
- Test prototypes of the product before production begins.
- Regularly test samples of the finished products for possible defects, once production starts.
- Quickly notify the public and recall the product if there is a possibility of injury or death from a product.

An example of a design defect is the 2018 Tesla Model S, which had a flawed power steering component, and Tesla was forced to recall 123,000 cars. Tesla stock dropped

22.4 percent in a single month as a result. Another example occurred in 2019, as Mattel had to perform a massive recall of its popular Rock 'n Play Sleeper. This not only hurt the company financially, there was also damage to the company's reputation—the Barbie doll maker's name became synonymous with infant deaths.[6]

Ethical issues can also arise if a company chooses not to develop important new products until an existing product has become obsolete or its patent has expired. For example, pharmaceutical companies typically put a lot of resources into developing a drug; they need many years of sales to recoup those development expenses. As a result, they may want to hold off marketing a replacement drug until they've met the revenue goals of an existing drug. Doing so maximizes profit and protects shareholders' investments. However, by waiting, the company could be holding back innovations that may improve, and possibly save, lives.

Another ethical issue related to new-product development is planned obsolescence. Planned obsolescence occurs when companies frequently launch new models of a product that make existing models obsolete. For example, companies were still producing projection TVs even as they were planning to launch flat-screen plasma and LCD TVs that they knew consumers would favor; the new TVs had better reliability and were significantly less bulky than projection TVs. Consumers who bought projection TVs quickly found that technology to be obsolete once plasma and LCD devices hit the market. Ethical issues aside, such behavior may damage a company's relationships with its business customers (the retailers who were selling the TVs) and potentially with individual consumers as well.

However, there can be a difference between planned obsolescence and products that change frequently due to changes in technology. People want the latest and greatest technology. The speed of technology change forces companies to constantly upgrade the functionality of their products, to keep up with competitors. While this may mean that the Apple iPhone you carry is two generations old, it does not mean that Apple has used planned obsolescence as a strategy. In the world of high technology, Apple is simply doing what it must to maintain or gain market share.

The most common ethical issue involves the Federal Trade Commission's definition of the term *new*. Sometimes, firms make only minor changes to a product and then claim that it is changed in a way that makes it "new and improved." Such actions raise ethical issues; they also may result in legal issues if the FTC disagrees with the company's viewpoint. The FTC's position is that the product in question must be entirely new or be "changed in a functionally significant and substantial respect." If the product fails to meet this standard, the company can be fined and required to remove the claim from the label.

corporate philanthropy
The act of organizations voluntarily donating some of their profits or resources to charitable causes.

Philanthropic Dimension

Marketers understand that giving back to the community is not only the right thing to do but also a great way to get the firm's name, product, or promotion out to consumers at a reasonable cost. **Corporate philanthropy** is the act of organizations voluntarily donating some of their profits or resources to charitable causes.

In recent years, companies have looked for innovative ways to engage in corporate philanthropy. Google is an example of such a company. The following are examples of Google's commitment to various causes:

1. **Bay Area Giving:** Google has given over $60 million to Bay Area nonprofits over the past three years.

Johnson & Johnson has a long tradition of Corporate Giving that is inspired by its "Our Credo" responsibility to communities around the world. *Noam Galai/Getty Images Entertainment/Getty Images*

2. **Code for America:** Google provides Code for America with an annual gift of $3 million to develop civic technological solutions.
3. **Programming Education Gathering:** Google donated more than 5,000 Raspberry Pi computers in order to provide a computer science education to more than 25,000 Japanese children.
4. **Raspberry Pi:** Google is giving a $1 million grant that will give Raspberry Pi computers, which are microcomputers about the size of a credit card, to 15,000 U.K. children who show exceptional enthusiasm for computer science.[7]

McGraw Hill connect Exercise **16-1**

Please complete the *Connect* exercise for Chapter 16 that focuses on the different dimensions of corporate social responsibility. By understanding the dynamics of each dimension, you should gain insight into how marketers can make strategic decisions to benefit the largest group of organizational stakeholders.

Developing a Successful Corporate Social Responsibility Program

The marketing department is typically responsible for developing an organization's corporate social responsibility program. The process begins when a firm incorporates into its marketing strategy a focus on fulfilling economic, legal, ethical, and philanthropic dimensions. This focus is often expressed through a formal corporate social responsibility statement. The CSR statement for Toyota in Table 16.1 provides an example.

The task of implementing a broad CSR focus through specific action is often difficult, but firms can use the following key elements to guide them through the process:[8]

1. *Good stakeholder management.* Marketers should seek significant interaction with the stakeholders who influence the decisions and behavior of the company. For example, Toyota might meet with investors, environmentalists, regulators, and customers to gather ideas for ensuring that the plastic resources used in manufacturing will be discarded in an environmentally friendly way. It might even implement a closed-loop supply chain for that purpose. The company could

---

TABLE 16.1   Toyota's Corporate Social Responsibility Statement

We, TOYOTA MOTOR CORPORATION and our subsidiaries, take initiative to contribute to harmonious and sustainable development of society and the earth through all business activities that we carry out in each country and region, based on our Guiding Principles.
We comply with local, national and international laws and regulations as well as the spirit thereof and we conduct our business operations with honesty and integrity.
In order to contribute to sustainable development, we believe that management interacting with its stakeholders . . . is of considerable importance, and we will endeavor to build and maintain sound relationships with our stakeholders through open and fair communication.
We expect our business partners to support this initiative and act in accordance with it.

Source: Toyota, "Toyota's CSR Concepts: CSR Policy," n.d., http://www.toyota-global.com/sustainability/csr_initiatives/csr_concepts/policy.html.

also work with the community to understand the impact of water usage by its manufacturing plant on surrounding areas.

2. *Good corporate leadership.* The firm's leaders play a vital role in guiding their organization's business practices toward social responsibility. Success requires them to demonstrate a unique array of skills and competencies. The emphasis in business thinking has shifted from process to people.[9] Today, leaders try to thoughtfully balance the four dimensions of CSR and communicate their intentions accordingly. Those who are able to do so generally succeed at implementing socially responsible behaviors.

3. *Integration of CSR into corporate policy at all levels and in all divisions of the firm.* CSR policies and procedures are most useful when they are written down, well understood, and endorsed by affected employees. These range in scope: A broad policy might be a strategic decision about the treatment of foreign workers. A smaller initiative might be procedures that require employees to shut off the lights before leaving work or installation of sensors to turn off lights when no movement is detected. Figure 16.2 illustrates how the CSR policy at Toyota guides decisions across the firm and throughout the world.

Toyota has been able to build strong connections with its stakeholders by focusing on these three key elements as it developed a CSR policy. The company's shift to a stakeholder-centric approach has brought it observable benefits, including improved customer and employee loyalty at all levels of the company.

Small businesses, too, can embrace sustainability and corporate social responsibility, while also growing and strengthening the bottom line. For example, the Stonyfield yogurt company emerged from an organic farm school that promoted family farms, a clean environment, and healthy food. To fund the farm school, the owners used milk from their cows to make pesticide-free, fertilizer-free yogurt. The product quickly became successful. It is now the focus of the company's business, which buys ingredients from hundreds of organic farms and runs on environmentally friendly principles.

Analytics for Auditing a Corporate Social Responsibility Program

Once an organization has developed a corporate social responsibility program, the focus shifts to how well it is working. This can be done by means of an audit that uses analytics to measure the success of the program. For example, UPS enlists an independent auditing firm to evaluate its progress on energy use and carbon emissions reductions; the auditing firm reports both the cost savings and the resource savings. Its sustainability report includes its total CO_2 emissions, the carbon emissions per mile driven by its fleet, the ground packages delivered per gallon of fuel used, and the number of miles driven by its alternative-fuel delivery vehicles.[10] With such data, UPS can monitor its performance from year to year and also can benchmark its performance to that of other firms.

FIGURE 16.2 The Framework for CSR-Informed Policy at Toyota

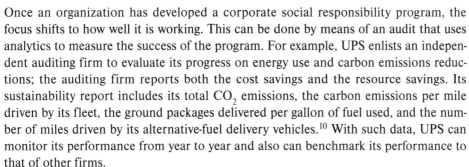

CSR policy: Contribution toward sustainable development

↓

Global vision for those we serve

↓

Medium- to long-term management plans

↓

Company policies, annual policies, regional policies, head office, and divisional policies

↓

Regular business activities

Source: Adapted from Toyota, "Toyota's CSR Concepts: CSR Policy," n.d., http://www.toyota-global.com/sustainability/csr_initiatives/csr_concepts/policy.html.

Stonyfield yogurt became successful using environmentally friendly principles to produce pesticide-free, fertilizer-free yogurt. *Michael Neelon/Alamy Stock Photo*

As part of its corporate volunteerism efforts, FedEx partners with nonprofit organization Direct Relief to deliver emergency medicine to disaster areas. *Direct Relief*

corporate volunteerism

The policy or practice of employees volunteering their time or talents for charitable, educational, or other worthwhile activities, especially in the community.

Gina Gomez

Executive Perspective . . .

because everyone is a marketer

Gina Gomez
Executive Director
Hispanic Community
Services, Inc.

What impact does corporate volunteerism have on a nonprofit organization?

We have so many great corporate volunteer partners who help us raise money and put together a number of events for the Hispanic Center. There is something very special about seeing volunteers putting in the time and effort to help nonprofit organizations in our community. I also think there is a benefit for the businesses; I know that I try to purchase from companies that I see volunteering to make our community better.

Those who are responsible for a company's CSR program should consider the following crucial points as they measure the program's effectiveness:[11]

- ***Include all significant stakeholder groups in the auditing process.*** Failure to include all stakeholder groups is perhaps the biggest misstep marketers can make when evaluating their CSR programs. The wide variety of stakeholder interests makes it challenging, but imperative, for a firm to get feedback from each stakeholder group. For example, if a CSR program is having a positive philanthropic impact in the community at the expense of stockholder return, the long-term viability of the program, and of the firm, may be at risk.
- ***Use both quantitative and qualitative measurements.*** Companies must undertake quantitative measures as part of their audit. Such measures include return on investment (ROI) and any changes in employee turnover and brand image associated with the CSR program. For example: Jain Irrigation is a global drip-irrigation-equipment supplier headquartered in India. Jain's drip-irrigation technology conserves water in a water-stressed environment and supplies it in a controlled fashion, which helps increase agricultural yields. The company offers farmers microfinance loans to help them purchase its equipment. It then provides technical advice to help farmers increase productivity and buys their output at guaranteed prices. Jain's CSR measures show that for a typical investment of $500 per hectare, farmers increased their gross income per hectare by anywhere from $500 to $6,000, depending on their crops. The added value created for its customers enabled Jain to boost its revenue while retaining its profit margins.[12]

Marketers should also do qualitative research in an attempt to measure what consumers and employees know about the organization's CSR efforts. Research involving Procter & Gamble, General Mills, Timberland, and others revealed that many of their stakeholders had only a limited understanding of the companies' corporate social responsibility initiatives.[13] Stakeholders of those companies often questioned the motivation for engaging in CSR activities. Such qualitative research highlights the necessity of communicating the firm's CSR initiatives and the rationale for those initiatives. Such communication will help make the initiatives more effective and will maximize their benefits. Companies also can use this research to refine and improve the CSR program.

Volunteerism

The Civic 50 is a scorecard of America's community-minded companies, produced by Bloomberg LP in partnership with the National Conference on Citizenship and Points of Light.[14] Firms like IBM rank near the top in this list, in part because they lead the way when it comes to promoting volunteerism.

Corporate volunteerism is the policy or practice of employees volunteering their time or talents for charitable, educational, or other worthwhile activities, especially in the community. Volunteer projects, such as FedEx delivering emergency medicine to disaster areas or Aetna tackling the health ailments of underserved communities, achieve maximum impact when they draw on a company's strengths.[15] For example, two-thirds of Raytheon's employees are engineers who use their skills to help students in local communities through programs such as Stand and Deliver and MATH Nights.[16] Retailer United by Blue has a mission: reduce the eight million tons of plastic that enter the ocean each year. It uses recycled plastic and nylon to create their clothing and accessories. The Company also organizes waterway cleanups all across the United States. For every product sold, they pledge to remove one pound of trash from the nation's rivers, ponds, streams, and coasts.[17]

SUSTAINABLE MARKETING

Today more than ever, marketers recognize that adopting sustainable strategies has become an essential element of a firm's CSR efforts. Expanding the idea of social responsibility beyond moral and ethical dimensions to sustainability contributes to long-term competitive advantage.

The concept of sustainability first came to international attention in the 1987 United Nations report "Our Common Future." The report laid the groundwork for a modern understanding of **sustainability** as a commitment to a lifestyle that meets the needs of the present without compromising the ability of future generations to meet their own needs.[18] Marketers looking to enhance the sustainability of their firm's goods and services need to form a partnership with customers, suppliers, and communities to increase the likelihood that the firm makes socially responsible marketing decisions.

Sustainable marketing is the process of creating, communicating, and delivering value to customers in a way that recognizes and incorporates the concept of sustainability. One

LO 16-2

Explain how sustainable marketing contributes to a firm's corporate social responsibility efforts.

sustainability

A commitment to a lifestyle that meets the needs of the present without compromising the ability of future generations to meet their own needs.

sustainable marketing

The process of creating, communicating, and delivering value to customers in a way that recognizes and incorporates the concept of sustainability.

General Mills collaborates to drive change from partnering with farmers to food production to feeding families. They set ambitious goals for a pathway to regeneration to do part their part as stewards of the planet. *Quiggyt4/Shutterstock*

The World Changing Ideas Awards honor products, concepts, companies, policies, and designs that are pursuing innovation for the good of society and the planet. H&M's in-store recycling system Looop, which turns old garments into new ones, was awarded within the Experimental category in 2021. *Venturelli Luca/Shutterstock*

of the easiest ways for marketers to engage in sustainable marketing is to seek ways to cut costs, using sustainable practices as a guideline. Firms can choose from a wide range of strategies and ideas, from developing different packaging to using less energy. For example, General Mills has dramatically reduced its energy consumption over the past decade.[19] The company made several sustainable business changes. It installed energy-monitoring meters on several pieces of equipment at its Covington, Georgia, plant that saved the company $600,000 in the first year.[20] At sites in California, Georgia, Illinois, Iowa, New Mexico, New York, and Ohio, the company implemented controls and technologies to improve boiler efficiency; it captured energy from exhaust flash steam, using heat exchanges to produce hot water. This saved more than 18.7 million kWh of energy on an annual basis.[21] General Mills was able to create value for investors through savings, communicate its commitment to sustainability to its stakeholders, and deliver tangible benefits for the environment.

Sustainability Vision

To get stakeholders to agree to sustainability initiatives, marketers must communicate a *sustainability vision*. That vision should highlight the importance of the organization's sustainability efforts and the potential benefits for each stakeholder. A sustainability vision begins by communicating how the company's industry and specific organization work within the larger social and natural world. It should answer important questions:

- How is the world enriched or diminished by our goods or services?
- What is our major impact on society?
- How does our overall business strategy reflect that impact?[22]

Sustainability Vision Statement   Many organizations find it useful to articulate the answers to these questions through a sustainability vision statement. For example:

- Unilever's Roadmap to Net Zero states: "Our Climate Transition Action Plan sets out the steps we'll take to reduce emissions from our own operations to zero by 2030 and to become net zero across Scope 1, 2 and 3 emissions by 2039."[23]
- DuPont's sustainability statement highlights the company's commitment to "creating shareholder and societal value, while reducing our footprint throughout the value chain."[24]
- Dow Chemical states these specific sustainability goals on its website: "Dow is committed to using resources efficiently, providing value to our customers and stakeholders, delivering solutions for customer needs, and enhancing the quality of life of current and future generations."[25]

These statements clearly articulate each company's sustainability mission. Not coincidentally, these firms are three of the leaders in sustainable marketing throughout the world.

The Benefits of a Sustainability Vision   A sustainability vision can drive innovation within an organization. For example, Unilever PLC used the lens of sustainability as a way to design and produce new products, such as a hair conditioner that uses less water.[26] Without a goal of sustainable marketing, the company's research and development efforts may not have led to the product, which has been well received by consumers and helped improve the firm's profit.

A commitment to sustainability also benefits employees. They tend to be engaged when they work for a company that expresses sustainability goals and holds itself accountable to its stakeholders. In addition, they believe they are part of something bigger than just their job or department. At Coca-Cola in Great Britain, for example, an appointed Green Team encourages employees to live more sustainably. Among other things, the group coordinates initiatives focused on reducing water usage in the workplace; it also tries to educate employees about activities that emit substantial amounts of carbon into the atmosphere, and to discourage those activities. Shortly after starting the Green Team program, Coca-Cola was ranked as one of the top-30 great places to work in Britain by the Great Place To Work Institute.[27]

Consumerism

A new generation of consumers concerned with sustainability has begun to demand more from companies and marketers than just low prices. These consumers also seek a higher meaning in the products they purchase. **Consumerism** is a movement, made up of citizens and government entities, that focuses on protecting consumers and promoting their interests.

consumerism
A movement, made up of citizens and government entities, that focuses on protecting consumers and promoting their interests.

The history of consumerism goes back more than a century. Some highlights of the movement's history are:

- The National Consumers League was founded in 1899, bringing together several state and local consumers leagues.
- The publication of Upton Sinclair's *The Jungle,* with the help of the Consumers Leagues, led to passage of the Meat Inspection Act and the Food and Drug Act in 1906.
- Ralph Nader published *Unsafe at Any Speed* in 1965, and the National Traffic Safety Act was passed the following year.
- The Consumer Product Safety Act was enacted in 1972, and much important environmental legislation has been passed beginning in the early 1970s.[28]

The movement's activities include anti-consumption campaigns, such as those against drinking carbonated soft drinks or wearing fur coats, staged as a form of resistance to a commodity culture and corporate brands.[29] Marketers should be aware of the power of these campaigns and the potential impact they can have on products and brands.

Consumerism also includes an effort on the part of consumers to avoid purchasing goods and services that have been produced in a way that is inconsistent with sustainable business practices.[30] Consumerism efforts increasingly occur both domestically and in international markets.

Despite a trend toward consumerism and sustainability, firms seeking to market sustainable products face roadblocks when it comes to reaching the larger population. Marketers face the following five barriers to encouraging sustainable consumer behavior:[31]

1. ***Lack of awareness and knowledge.*** Many consumers don't know how to reduce the social and environmental impact of their purchasing behavior. Marketers can play an important role in overcoming this barrier. Advertising, websites, social media, and other tools can educate consumers about how they can make a difference by consuming the company's products over those of competitors. In addition to traditional advertisements, for example, Pepsi used the power of social media sites to promote its "Performance with Purpose" strategy. The strategy focused on delivering sustainable products and investing in a healthy future for consumers and society as a whole.

2. *Negative perceptions.* Some consumers have negative perceptions of sustainable products. They tend to believe that, while the products might be produced in a more sustainable way, they are inferior in quality. To combat this barrier, firms must design and produce sustainable products of high quality. Equally important, they must use the various promotional tools at their disposal to communicate that quality to customers.

3. *Distrust.* Some consumers simply do not believe the sustainability claims made by marketers. Walmart has promoted its sustainability focus heavily in recent years. But it found itself in a difficult position when the government fined the company $81 million after discovery that Walmart employees improperly handled and disposed of hazardous materials at stores across the country.[32] It is essential for marketers to promote their products in an honest and ethical manner. A firm caught misleading consumers over sustainability claims could damage its reputation for years to come, reducing profit and hurting the firm's long-term viability.

4. *High prices.* Consumers also have come to believe that the cost of producing a sustainable product translates into higher prices. One of the earliest complaints customers had against hybrid and electric cars was the high cost associated with the purchase. Technological improvements and economies of scale, as well as increasingly efficient supply chains, gradually brought prices down. Beyond this, however, marketers used promotional tools to demonstrate how gas savings offset the high prices. Marketing environmentally friendly products can lead to higher prices due to the additional costs the firm incurs. In such cases, marketers must ensure that their customers understand the genesis of the high prices. If the firm can communicate the additional value the product offers, customers will be more willing to pay a high price for it.

5. *Low availability.* Consumers in small communities or developing parts of the world may have a hard time finding sustainable products to buy. The place element of the marketing mix becomes critical in overcoming this barrier. Marketing professionals must find ways to deliver products to the sustainability-minded customers who want to buy them.

A critical component of overcoming all of these barriers is communication. Marketers must effectively communicate that sustainable consumer behavior doesn't always require sacrificing current needs and wants for some distant benefit. As firms continue to develop sustainable goods and services that add value to consumers' lives, marketers must communicate this balance to consumers.

Mc Graw Hill connect Exercise **16-2**

Please complete the *Connect* exercise for Chapter 16 that focuses on marketing strategies that promote sustainable consumer behavior. By understanding the major barriers to sustainable consumer behavior and how to overcome them, you should gain insight into how marketers can most effectively influence consumer decisions and support sustainable behaviors.

LO 16-3

Explain the impact of environmentalism on marketing success.

ENVIRONMENTAL MARKETING

Historically, customers bought products solely on the bases of price, performance, and convenience. Today, customers also care about a product's origins and how it is manufactured, packaged, and disposed of. Firms sometimes mistake these emerging concerns as the domain of younger generations. In reality, over half of all Baby Boomers consider themselves environmentally conscious shoppers.[33] That's 40 million customers who choose to buy resource-conserving products from the shelves and who boycott the products of companies that pollute or engage in other activities that could damage the environment. They represent a segment of the green market. The green market is a group of sustainability-oriented customers and the businesses that serve them.

More and more, marketers face scrutiny from the green market related to whether they conduct business in an environmentally responsible way. **Environmentalism** is a movement of citizens, government agencies, and the business community that advocates the preservation, restoration, and improvement of the natural environment. Its mission affects firms large and small and cuts across numerous industries and geographic locations. For example:

- 96 percent of European consumers say that protecting the environment is important to them.[34]
- Increasingly, Chinese consumers purchase products based on concerns about climate change.[35]
- In the United States, 80 percent of customers claim to act on environmental concerns.[36]

In response to these trends, Walmart, the world's largest retailer, ran a global ad campaign designed to highlight its sustainability efforts; it sought to raise awareness about the environment and the product choices consumers could make. In addition, Walmart initiated a $30 million project, the first of its kind, focused on lifestyle and environmental improvements.[37] Walmart employees who chose to participate in the voluntary program learned in company-sponsored workshops about the benefits of carpooling to work, discontinuing cigarette smoking, and turning off the television when not watching it. They also learned about the importance of embracing environmental sustainability, reducing carbon emissions, and consuming healthy and environmentally friendly (green) food. About 50 percent of Walmart's employees worldwide opted to participate in the program.[38]

green market

A group of sustainability-oriented customers and the businesses that serve them.

environmentalism

A movement of citizens, government agencies, and the business community that advocates the preservation, restoration, and improvement of the natural environment.

American Airlines, a service company, recognizes that climate change is a pressing global challenge, and is committed to doing its part to address it. To do this, the company increased its fuel efficiency, reduced greenhouse gas emissions and has implemented plans for a low-carbon future. *Ted Hsu/Alamy Stock Photo*

The green market doesn't seek only environmentally friendly goods; its members also want environmentally friendly *services*. Service providers ranging from doctors to electricians to universities have made efforts to protect the environment as part of their service offering. Some utility companies now offer customers the opportunity to purchase their energy needs from wind, solar energy, and other renewable sources.[39]

Environmental Marketing Strategies

Environmental marketing (also called *green marketing)* activities can be divided into three levels: tactical greening, quasi-strategic greening, and strategic greening.[40]

tactical greening

A type of environmental marketing activity that involves implementing limited change within a single area of the organization.

quasi-strategic greening

A type of environmental marketing activity that involves substantive changes in marketing actions as well as broad-based coordination among nonmarketing activities.

strategic greening

A type of environmental marketing activity that integrates and coordinates all of the firm's activities on environmental issues across every functional area.

1. **Tactical greening** involves implementing limited change within a single area of the organization, such as purchasing or advertising. Tactical activities represent relatively small actions aimed at instituting environmentally friendly practices within an organization. For example, Etsy might decide to not do any business with suppliers that do not meet the company's environmental or recycling requirements.

2. **Quasi-strategic greening** usually involves more substantive changes in marketing actions as well as broad-based coordination among nonmarketing activities. For example, a firm might redesign its logo or overhaul a product's packaging to emphasize the firm's commitment to greenness. Telecommunications provider Sprint engaged in quasi-strategic greening when it began using 100 percent recycled materials in all its branded packaging. In addition, it now uses soy inks and environmentally friendly adhesives and coatings. The new packaging is also 60 percent smaller in volume and 50 percent lighter in weight than the old packaging, which has saved Sprint money.[41]

3. **Strategic greening** requires a holistic approach that integrates and coordinates all of the firm's activities on environmental issues across every functional area. It represents a fundamental shift in the way the firm markets its products. For example, SC Johnson has been reducing the impact of its products through the use of green list process (the system which ranks the environmental impact by evaluating raw materials used). The company stopped using polyvinylidene chloride in its Saran Wrap product. Additionally, it has also reduced its coal fired plants with natural gas and methane powered facilities.[42]

These three categories of marketing activities represent the various degrees to which a firm can adopt an environmental focus. The categories are governed by the overall environmental strategy a company chooses to implement. Figure 16.3 shows five types of environmental marketing strategies marketers can choose, depending on a firm's competitive advantage and the overall marketing strategy it has adopted.[43] Each of the strategies is discussed in more detail in the sections that follow.

Strategy 1: Eco-Efficiency   Marketers seeking to reduce costs and the environmental impact of their activities typically pursue an *eco-efficiency strategy*. This strategy involves identifying environmentally friendly practices that also create cost savings and drive efficiencies throughout the organization. Transportation companies like J.B. Hunt, for example, look for ways to increase fuel

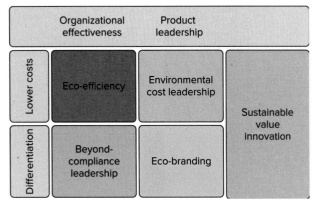

FIGURE 16.3   Environmental Marketing Strategies

Source: Renato J. Orsato, "Competitive Environmental Strategies: When Does It Pay to Be Green?" *California Management Review* 48, no. 2 (February 1, 2006): 127–144. The Regents of the University of California. Published by the University of California Press.

To increase fuel efficiency, transportation companies have reconfigured their trucks by adding extenders from the cab to the trailer and side skirts that allow for easy air flow, to decrease drag on the vehicle. *STEMCO*

efficiency. Fuel efficiency both saves the firm money and decreases the environmental impact of the company's services.

Strategy 2: Beyond-Compliance Leadership

Most marketers who adopt a *beyond-compliance leadership strategy* focus on communicating to stakeholders the company's attempts to go beyond others in adopting environmentally friendly practices. Marketers who select this strategy want to show customers that the company does more than the competition to implement an environmental strategy. Unlike an eco-efficiency strategy, companies that employ a beyond-compliance leadership strategy typically care more about differentiating themselves from competitors than about keeping costs low. For example, packaging giant Graphic Packaging Holding Co. is spending $650 million to build a new manufacturing plant in Michigan to help companies transition from such environmentally unfriendly packaging as foam cups, plastic clamshell containers, and six-pack rings to cardboard components. This is a huge financial bet for this company because the economics of customers switching from plastic to cardboard in sufficient numbers to justify this expenditure is unknown. This shows how committed the company is to the environment.[44]

Strategy 3: Eco-Branding

An *eco-branding strategy* focuses on creating a credible green brand. For this strategy to be effective, consumers must recognize a noticeable benefit from their purchase. For example, the Chevy Volt electric car provides an immediate and sizable savings on monthly gasoline purchases. The eco-branding strategy tends to succeed in industries in which significant barriers to imitation exist. To achieve differentiation as part of an eco-branding strategy, the environmental improvement, such as the technology involved in developing a desirable electric car, should be difficult to imitate.

Strategy 4: Environmental Cost Leadership

Firms seeking a price premium for their environmentally friendly products often adopt an *environmental cost leadership strategy*. Green products sometimes cost more to produce than traditional products. Thus a leadership strategy that also seeks to lower costs may be the only way for a company to pay for its ecological investments and generate a profit for its other stakeholders. Green and organic grocery stores, such as Whole

Foods, have been able to demand a price premium for their products. This, in turn, has allowed these organizations to recover the additional costs of selling only fresh, organic products to consumers.

Strategy 5: Sustainable Value Innovation   A final strategy firms can pursue is *sustainable value innovation.* This strategy entails reshaping the industry through the creation of differential value for consumers. It involves making contributions to society in the form of both reduced costs *and* reduced environmental impact. Firms that engage in this strategy do not aim to outperform the competition in an existing industry. Rather, they seek to create a new market space. In doing so, they hope to make the competition irrelevant, by giving the consumer more value per product at a lower price. Examples of this strategy in action include solar-tracking skylights designed to follow the sun and maximize daylight harvesting and walls built from straw, channel glass, and other energy-efficient materials.

Mc Graw Hill connect   Exercise **16-3**

Please complete the *Connect* exercise for Chapter 16 that focuses on environmental marketing strategies. By understanding the types of strategies that might fit best with different products and market segments, you should be able to make better marketing strategy decisions for your organization.

Benefits of Environmental Marketing

The benefits of an environmental marketing strategy extend to virtually all of a firm's stakeholders when the strategy is effectively integrated with the firm's general marketing plan. For example, the online retail and auction site eBay makes it easy for people all over the world to exchange and reuse goods rather than throwing them away, thereby lengthening the life cycle of the products. The company also introduced an eBay Classifieds section that allows individuals to buy and sell used household appliances, furniture, and other hard-to-ship items within their local community. The Classifieds section eliminates the need for shipping and packaging and keeps functional items out of landfills. Such efforts have allowed eBay to help the environment while earning a significant profit and employing thousands of workers throughout the world.

With many consumers committed to "going green," environmentally focused organizations often benefit from favorable public opinion and loyal customers. Dell has received favorable feedback in response to its commitment to use 50 percent recycled paper for printed marketing materials. Through this commitment, Dell hopes to avoid using approximately 35,000 tons of virgin fiber annually.[45] In addition, Dell's office printers now default to double-sided printing. Finally, the company has initiated a modification of its packaging policy that is designed to cut the size of its product packaging and increase the amount of recycled content inside. All of these small marketing decisions add real value in the minds of environmentally conscious consumers and, ultimately, contribute favorably to the bottom line.

Dell hopes to reap the benefits of environmental marketing by implementing new environmentally friendly policies, such as using recyclable and rapidly renewable bamboo to package and protect certain products. *Jonathan Weiss/Shutterstock*

Environmental Regulation

In addition to meeting consumer demand for green products, marketers must also consider new and changing environmental regulations. **Environmental regulations** are the laws designed to protect the natural environment against undue harm by individuals and organizations.[46] Regulations range from the 1972 Clean Water Act, which was designed to reduce industrial pollution in U.S. waters, to the Clean Air Act, which places limits on the emission of greenhouse gases.

> **environmental regulations**
> The laws designed to protect the natural environment against undue harm by individuals and organizations.

Environmental regulations, though they may limit firms in some regard, provide marketers with opportunities. For example, when the 1992 Energy Policy Act limited the amount of water showerheads could deliver, firms like Teledyne Technologies developed a new line of products, the Shower Massage showerheads. The showerheads met the new standard and captured sales and profit for the firm.[47]

Thanks to the Paris Climate Agreement, signed by nearly all countries, countries aim to substantially reduce global greenhouse gas emissions to limit the global temperature increase in this century to 2 degrees Celsius above preindustrial levels, with the further aim to limit it to 1.5 degrees Celsius.[48] Companies can take advantage of this effort by producing products that help countries achieve their goals and marketing these products as part of the companies' commitment to environmental sustainability. For example, automobile manufacturers such as GM, Ford, Honda, and Nissan are joining Tesla in converting their automobile production from gasoline and diesel to all electric models to reduce carbon-dioxide emissions, which are a leading cause of heat retention in the atmosphere.

GLOBAL ENVIRONMENTALISM AND SUSTAINABILITY

> **LO 16-4**
> Describe how companies can meet the challenges of environmental and sustainable marketing on a global scale.
>
>

As globalization brings the world closer together, marketers must develop strategies that fit with expectations in both domestic and international markets, as well as investors in the company. The strategic choice to become environmentally conscious and sustainable has proven to be profitable; it also is a good public relations decision, not just in the United States but across the globe. For example, the UK retailer Marks & Spencer spent $323 million over five years on sustainability strategies; it reported, just two years into implementing the initiatives, that its investment had already paid for itself.[49] In addition to saving on its energy costs, the company's initiative appealed to customers seeking to purchase more sustainable products. Starbucks announced that it would work to cut the amount of waste it creates in half by 2030. Part of that effort is the possible development of a more sustainable paper cup that features a liner made out of compostable materials instead of plastic.[50] Likewise, Exxon Mobil Corp. is considering pledging zero carbon emissions from its businesses by 2050. This idea is being given serious consideration due to pressure from investors, some of whom want to see a stronger effort by the company concerning climate change.[51]

Global Challenges and Opportunities

Management consulting firm McKinsey surveyed nearly 2,000 executives from around the world for their opinions about sustainability. Half of the executives considered sustainability very or extremely important in new product development, reputation building, and overall corporate strategy.[52]

However, implementing sustainability efforts on a global scale comes with its own unique set of challenges. Political barriers in some countries can limit the availability of or increase prices on sustainable goods for consumers. One political barrier, for example, is a lack of political will on the part of leaders to enact sustainability-focused

To capitalize on the interest emerging economies show in sustainability, Vodafone markets its mobile technologies to farmers in rural areas of sub-Saharan Africa who use the technology to communicate easily with prospective buyers, thus boosting their income.
Antony Njuguna/Reuters/Newscom

legislation. Elections, changes in consumer sentiment, and other external factors can increase or decrease such political barriers. On the bright side, marketers who actively scan the global environment can find foreign governments and policies that provide new opportunities for marketing sustainable products to global customers. For example, a ban on incandescent light bulbs that took effect in the European Union made compact fluorescent light bulb (CFL) and light-emitting diode (LED) technologies standard across Europe.[53] This political shift, driven by regulation and innovation, opened up new opportunities for marketers to sell green products to European consumers.

The divergence in how different geographic regions perceive sustainability also provides both challenges and opportunities for marketers. A majority of global business executives believe that sustainability is of significant importance to their business. But marketers should be aware of how the location of those executives affects their opinions: Almost two-thirds of decision makers in emerging markets, such as India and South Africa, consider sustainability critical to business.[54] Meanwhile, just under a third of decision makers in Japan and a quarter in the largest European markets (Germany, France, and the United Kingdom) feel the same.

In response to this divergence, many organizations that engage in sustainable marketing focus a disproportionate amount of their efforts on emerging economies. In these markets, they tend to find more supportive consumer and political environments.

Rationalizing Global Sustainability

The way marketers justify sustainable marketing varies in different parts of the world. For example, U.S. marketers rationalize sustainability strategies using economics or bottom-line terms and arguments. Companies owned by members of the European Union rely more heavily on language related to the idea of citizenship, corporate accountability, or moral commitment. That's not to say that European companies value sustainability to the exclusion of financial elements. Rather, they project a commitment to sustainability in addition to their commitment to financial success. Regardless of the justification, sustainable and environmental strategies tend to work best when firms can maximize the benefits for all stakeholders concerned.

Two areas in which companies can make significant contributions to global environmentalism and sustainability are new product development and supply chain management. We explore these two areas next.

Ethical and Sustainability Issues in New-Product Development and Supply Chain Management

New-Product Development
Sustainable product development is built upon the concept of **sustainable design**, which is the philosophy of building products and services in a way that eliminates negative environmental impacts.[55] Sustainable design can take various forms. A product designed for sustainability might:

sustainable design
The philosophy of building goods and services in a way that eliminates negative environmental impacts.

- Use less energy to operate (or for a service, use less energy to perform).
- Have less packaging that must be discarded when opened.
- Be able to be recycled when the consumer is finished using the product.
- Be able to be reused or refurbished.

An example of a sustainable good is the LED light bulb. Such bulbs are up to 85 percent more energy-efficient than incandescent bulbs; they can last up to 50,000 hours before being discarded. Use of LED bulbs can save hundreds of pounds of carbon dioxide emissions annually. Far fewer bulbs will end up in landfills when they are no longer usable. An example of a sustainable service is Eco Friendly Cleaning Services, which uses "organic-based and environmentally friendly products" to clean homes and businesses.

When companies want to develop and market new products in an environmentally friendly way, they need to understand the impact that such products may have on the environment. The **triple bottom line (TBL)** is one way of analyzing the sustainability of a new product. The TBL includes economic, social, and environmental impacts to a company and to the world. When companies comply with these three pillars they get such benefits as enhanced brand image, competitive advantage, and increased financial performance. An example is a reusable face mask. Economic benefits include potential profitability due to the COVID-19 pandemic due to very high demand, which must be tempered with an analysis of potential competition. Social impacts include providing health benefits for users and those they may come into contact with, as well as providing a way for businesses to stay open or reopen during the pandemic. The design of the mask can have impact on the environment, depending on whether it is disposable or reusable. Disposable masks have a negative impact because they quickly end up in a landfill. However, reusable masks that can be washed and used many times have a positive impact. By analyzing these three aspects of a new product, companies can determine the sustainability of new products and make an informed decision as to whether to market them or not.[56]

triple bottom line (TBL)
A framework for analyzing sustainability that includes economic, social, and environmental impacts of a new product.

Supply Chain Design and Management
Organizations have choices when it comes to how they design their supply chains. These choices affect their sustainability profile. Sourcing of materials and goods, transportation mode selection, facility locations, and the extent of its supply chain as a closed-loop system are examples of choices that affect sustainability.

Facility Location Where an organization locates its facilities can have a significant impact on its goal to operate a more sustainable supply chain. Near-shoring or on-shoring can be strategies for locating production facilities. Ford Motor Company, for example, moved engine production from Spain and heavy-truck production from Mexico back to the United States.[57] These moves save considerably in natural-resources consumption and emissions in transporting the products. Another strategy is to locate manufacturing facilities close to main suppliers or ask suppliers to set up operations close to the organization's facilities. An ideal setup is to have suppliers co-locate on the same grounds or share facilities with the manufacturing plant. The Diaper Genie factory, for example, shares the same facility with its main supplier. That design saves a great deal of fuel and cuts emissions by eliminating transportation between the two operations.

The Diaper Genie factory also demonstrates another environmentally friendly facility-location strategy—shipment directly from a factory to customers. Companies can reduce transportation and material handling by eliminating a distribution center and, instead, shipping directly from a producer to a consumer. This tactic, which cuts out the intermediary in a supply chain, is called **disintermediation**. The key to the environmental effectiveness of such a design is the use of *full vehicles* to transport the products. If products must be shipped in less-than-full-vehicle quantities, more shipments will be required. Those additional shipments will negate the environmental advantages of disintermediation. The more distribution facilities a company has, the more likely it will be that full vehicle loads will not always be possible. Therefore, a company may choose to reduce its number of facilities in order to reduce fuel consumption and emissions, which will help its sustainability profile.

Another environmentally friendly facility-location tactic is to locate facilities near renewable-energy power sources, such as wind and solar. Facilities can also be placed as near as possible to major highways and railroads. Such locations reduce the amount of travel for incoming and outgoing shipments. Companies can use commercially available software or consulting companies to help in selecting areas for new facilities that can help them provide a more sustainable supply chain.

Sourcing Organizations must source and purchase materials and goods in order to operate. It has become common for organizations to procure materials and goods from low-labor-cost countries. However, doing so usually means that the purchased products need to be transported over long distances, often in ways that add to air and water pollution. Additionally, the companies that produce the goods may be contributing to the pollution in their own areas through environmentally unsound practices.

The trade-off between costs and sustainability can make it difficult to source in an environmentally responsible manner. In order to overcome the natural desire to purchase goods from the lowest-cost producer, an organization must make a conscious commitment to sustainable sourcing.

Sustainable sourcing is a process of purchasing goods and services that takes into account the long-term impact on people, profits, and planet. Sustainable sourcing balances costs with other considerations: Specifically, it recognizes the trade-off between purchase and transportation costs and other costs to society.[58] Organizations involved in sustainable sourcing look not only at their own bottom line but also at the damage their way of sourcing is doing to society as a whole.

Organizations practicing sustainable sourcing have policies in place that require suppliers to comply with certain guidelines. Such policies include:

- Reducing waste and energy usage.
- Recycling and reusing materials and products.
- Eliminating hazardous materials used in production.

Purchasing managers are trained to identify and select suppliers that have a commitment to sustainability. Heinz, for example, buys only UTZ-certified cocoa that adheres to sustainable agriculture practices for the cocoa supply. Purchasing managers also

disintermediation

Elimination of intermediaries, such as distribution centers, in the delivery of products from a producer to a consumer.

sustainable sourcing

The process of purchasing goods and services that takes into account the long-term impact on people, profits, and planet.

Subway uses both internal and external audits to make sure that its corporate sustainability standards are being met. *Heorshe/Alamy Stock Photo*

monitor their suppliers to ensure that they are complying with the organization's rules. For example, Subway uses a combination of internal and external third-party audits to ensure that its sustainability standards are met.[59]

The use of ethical and environmental certifications for suppliers is increasing. Fairtrade, Rainforest Alliance, UTZ Certified, and Organic are examples of such certifications. Organizations that are interested in improving their sustainability look for such assurances of suppliers' activities. Company-specific certifications also guide the sustainability efforts of various organizations. Examples are Starbucks' CAFE practices and retailer-sponsored programs such as GlobalGAP.

Sustainable sourcing also seeks to procure goods from locations as close as possible to where they will be consumed. Efforts to source locally result in near-shoring and on-shoring:

- **Near-shoring** involves sourcing materials and finished products from countries that are close to, but not in, an organization's own country. Organizations doing near-shoring select suppliers that are closer than previous suppliers.
- **On-shoring** involves sourcing materials and finished products from suppliers in an organization's own country.

Both near-shoring and on-shoring reduce transportation costs. Also, because the goods are moved over a smaller distance, they also help avoid the environmental damage that can result from moving goods over long distances.

Transportation The choice of transportation mode, and the carriers used to transport goods, affect an organization's sustainability profile. Some transportation modes and carriers result in reduced fuel consumption, which leads to lower emissions and less environmental impact.

For international shipments, moving goods in containers on large container ships is much more efficient and environmentally friendly than air-shipping products. This is true even though container ships use the most-polluting form of diesel fuel (called "bunker fuel"). The reason is related to volume: A large container ship can move a large

near-shoring

The process of sourcing materials and finished products from countries that are close to, but not in, an organization's own country.

on-shoring

The process of sourcing materials and finished products from suppliers in an organization's own country.

A BNSF Railroad train carrying J.B. Hunt's containers. This is an environmentally friendlier way of transporting goods over long distances than by truck. *Ross Waters/agefotostock/ Alamy Stock Photo*

amount of material at one time, whereas many aircraft would be needed to move the same amount of goods. Container shipping is thus more environmentally friendly per unit of shipped product.

Domestic shipments generally involve railroads and trucking companies. Railroads can move large amounts of goods over long distances with greater fuel efficiency and emissions compared to trucks. This is why trucking companies such as J.B. Hunt and Schneider often move their trailers long distance on railcars. Railroads like BNSF use a crane to remove the container from the railcar and place it on a truck's trailer chassis. The trucking company then delivers the goods by truck to a distribution center or store. When possible, organizations can choose rail over truck to move goods, which will help them achieve their sustainability goals. Or they can choose to use trucking companies that combine rail and truck, knowing that, when possible, their goods will move by rail for much of the trip.

The "last mile" of the supply chain involves getting the product to the customer's location. Unfortunately, railroads do not generally deliver directly to the customer. (There are some exceptions: spices used by Frito-Lay in its factories, and coal used to generate electricity at power plants.) Trucks are almost always the way goods get delivered to customers, whether the customer is a retailer or an individual consumer.

With the increase in online orders that are delivered directly to consumers' homes, there is further complication to delivering the "last mile." This part of the supply chain almost always involves a truck, usually a small *pickup-and-delivery (PUD)* unit such as UPS and FedEx use. A few companies are trying to find better ways of delivering products that are also more environmentally friendly. For example, transportation-service providers UPS and FedEx are using the U.S. Postal Service (USPS) to deliver some packages to rural areas. The Postal Service is going to those areas to deliver the mail, whereas the package delivery company would need to make a special trip. Cutting out the special trip reduces the environmental impact of the last-mile delivery.

Delivery companies also are trying out other transportation modes. Amazon.com Inc. is experimenting with deliveries using bike messengers in New York City. Uber

Technologies, a service company, launched a bike-courier service called Uber Rush, which companies can use to deliver directly to consumers within cities. Efforts such as these, while not yet making a big impact, will save fuel and emissions for organizations that are interested in improving their sustainability.[60]

Closed-Loop Supply Chains Another factor in meeting sustainability objectives is the extent to which an organization has a closed-loop supply chain. A **closed-loop supply chain** is a supply chain that maximizes value creation by recovering value from product or material returns.[61] The main idea behind a closed-loop supply chain is that fewer products or product components end up in a landfill or are improperly disposed of. Products that are unwanted, damaged, defective, obsolete, or in need of recycling need to be handled in an environmentally friendly way. These products show up back at the manufacturer or distribution center as *returned goods.*

closed-loop supply chain
A supply chain that maximizes value creation by recovering value from product or material returns.

The amount of returned goods is increasing due to e-commerce. For a variety of reasons, products are finding their way back to manufacturers. Consumers return goods ordered online that did not meet their expectations. Likewise, retailers sometimes buy goods on consignment and return them to the manufacturer at the end of the season. In fact, up to 33 percent of the products sold through the Internet in the United States end up being returned. Establishing closed-loop supply chains helps reduce the environmental costs of returns.[62]

A company can set up a closed-loop supply chain using methods designed either to get the product back to the market or to be disposed of properly. Companies can do a number of things to establish a more sustainable supply chain through a closed-loop system:

- Repair returned goods and return them to the customer or sell them to another customer. Cell phones and personal computers are examples of products that make good candidates for this method.
- Break down the returned goods and reuse component parts in new products or in the repair of other returned goods. This method prevents potentially polluting raw materials (such as lead and zinc) from entering the environment.[63] For example, Best Buy takes in and recycles electronic products, regardless of where the customer purchased them. Thanks to its program, Best Buy has "collected and responsibly disposed of more than 1 billion pounds of electronics and appliances."[64]
- Find new buyers for products that are unwanted by retailers or consumers but are otherwise perfectly usable. Many products that are over-ordered by retailers are sent back to manufacturers and can be returned to the market. For example, unsold sun care products such as Banana Boat are returned after the sun care season is over; these products are returned to inventory and sold the next season (providing they have not expired).
- Use raw materials recovered from returned goods to generate power. An example is the generation of steam to run a factory by burning flammable products, such as petroleum jelly, that have been returned and cannot be recycled.
- Set up a method for consumers to return unwanted or depleted products or packaging that can then be refurbished or recycled. For example, McDonald's Corp., Burger King, and Tim Hortons are piloting a system with TerraCycle Inc's Loop, which collects, cleans, then redistributes packaging for reuse.[65]

Ideally, a supply chain is designed so that when a product has to be returned it can be recycled, reused, sold, or broken down into component parts for use in other products. Companies that establish closed-loop supply chains are doing their part to ensure sustainability in their supply chains.

Julianne Watt

Director of Research and Strategy Development
RedRover Sales & Marketing Strategy

Describe your job. As the director of research and strategy development at RedRover Sales & Marketing Strategy, I lead a team of marketing strategists and analysts to conduct a program called the Growth Optimization (GO) Plan. The GO Plan's primary goal is to provide our clients with a predictable, data-driven, and ROI-focused sales and marketing strategy.

I also play a large role in the leadership of our company. As part of the leadership team, we meet weekly to discuss the state of the company. Whether we are solving for current or future issues, or we are discussing and planning for the upcoming quarter, we're always thinking about what is the best next step for the company.

Julianne Watt

How did you get your job? My previous company went through a round of budget cuts and unfortunately my position was part of that cut. I always heard that marketing would be a "fun" career and that I would excel; however, my issue was the lack of experience.

Having never seen an agency, I took a temp job to better understand the environment. On my first day the CEO said, "We are happy you are here, but we only hire people who have a minimum of 8 years of marketing experience."

About one month later, I was offered a job. Why? Because of my work ethic, my ability to learn quickly, my intellectual curiosity, my adaptability, and my drive.

What has been the most important thing in making you successful at your job? While there are so many aspects to what makes me successful at my job—

self-awareness, accountability, courage, and work ethic—the concept that has made me successful at every job I've ever had is the willingness to be resilient and adaptable.

What advice would you give soon-to-be graduates? First, as you move through your marketing careers, or any career, understand that no matter how good you are at something, if you are unhappy, every job is going to be the wrong job. Second, never stop learning. Especially in the world of marketing, the rate of change is growing faster than the speed at which we can learn. Stop learning, and your skills will become dated. Third, you can always improve. Listen to the feedback you are provided and do something with it. If you didn't get feedback, ask for it. Even if you don't fully agree, take some aspect of the feedback and grow from it. Last, don't fear failure. You *will* fail. It's not about how hard you fall; it's about how you get up. Find a company that not only understands failure, but almost expects it.

What do you consider your personal brand to be? Authentic, driven fearless.

Mahatma Gandhi said, "Happiness is when what you think, what you say, and what you do are in harmony." I passionately believe in being the best me and that comes when I am authentic. Whether at work or in life, I know I am at my best when I am who I am.

THE IMPACT OF SOCIAL MEDIA ON CORPORATE SOCIAL RESPONSIBILITY

LO 16-5

Analyze how firms use social media to support their corporate social responsibility efforts.

In the end, corporate social responsibility, sustainability, and environmentalism, whether they are implemented domestically or globally, are about communication. Marketing professionals need to listen, consider what they hear, and respond appropriately to the widest group of stakeholders possible. Social media provide an effective means for communicating with an enthusiastic group of consumers. Social media allow people to organize, collaborate, and accomplish shared goals in ways that would have been unimaginable several decades ago.

In response, companies have evolved from a reactive state, in which they responded to customer feedback about their CSR-related strategies, to a *proactive* approach. In the proactive approach, companies make their CSR activities known to customers through the various online tools at their disposal. For example:

- Timberland branded website, www.earthkeeper.com, "allows the community to take action on sustainability through personal pledges (in areas like home, transportation, lifestyle, and food), responsible shopping, tree-planting, and involvement in events. Site visitors can also learn about Timberland's other CSR efforts by reading its sustainability report, listening to podcasts of CEO Jeff Swartz's quarterly stakeholder engagement calls, and visiting the company's Facebook, YouTube, and Twitter sites."[66]
- GE used YouTube to share a video featuring a catchy techno soundtrack for its Brilliant Machines campaign. With more than 300,000 views, GE's marketing message of industrial transportation with reduced environmental impact reached a wide audience.
- Patagonia uses Instagram where it has amassed over two million followers to feature a collection of videos, slideshows, and photographs dedicated to environmental and social responsibility focused on activism and impact with impressive finesse.

Social media play an increasingly important role in how companies shape their CSR policies and present themselves as good corporate citizens to consumers and other stakeholders.

Social Media–Based Corporate Social Responsibility Initiatives

To capitalize on the opportunity social media provide, marketers must be consistent in their social media presence. The companies leading the way in merging CSR and social media include some of the largest and most successful firms in the world:

- IBM's Smarter Planet, for example, is a website devoted to communicating the firm's sustainability initiatives. It uses compelling storytelling that showcases its work in communities and cities around the world.
- GE's Ecomagination Challenge is a $200 million experiment in which businesses, venture capital firms, entrepreneurs, innovators, and students develop clean energy ideas and submit them for funding.[67]
- Target uses social media to further its long-standing commitment to schools and education. Target partnered with Search Institute, a nonprofit organization devoted to improving the lives of children, to develop the "Turn Summer Play into Summer Learning" series on its Facebook page. The campaign provided

GE uses a number of social media tools, including a blog and a Facebook page, to list the hundreds of ideas that have been submitted as part of its Ecomagination Challenge campaign. *GSTC*

parents with fun weekly tips about how to keep their child's mind active during the summer as well as supporting research into how summer learning positively impacts child development.[68] The series illustrated Target's commitment to education and promoted the brand in a positive way to consumers. In addition, it allowed Target to connect with parents, including many current and future Target consumers.

Marketers should try to make each digital communication (tweet, Facebook post, etc.) something of value to their digital community.

Social Media and Global Sustainability

The global arena also provides a good opportunity for using social media to highlight and support CSR initiatives. In Japan, for example, over 80 percent of firms use social media and digital technology tools to engage with customers on the sustainability of their goods and services.[69]

The Global Sustainable Tourism Council (GSTC), a global coalition formed under the umbrella of the United Nations, made a significant commitment to social media in an effort to achieve its goal of promoting best practices in sustainable tourism around the world. **Sustainable tourism** is the practice of recreational traveling in a way that maximizes the social and economic benefits to the local community and minimizes the negative impact on cultural heritage and the environment. Royal Caribbean Cruise Lines set a target that by the end of 2019 all the operators of their global tour operations (shore excursions) had to be certified to meet GSTC sustainability targets.[70] The GSTC's Facebook page and Twitter feed are filled with content and conversations related to sustainable travel in a range of countries, from Greece to Mexico to Argentina.

Whether focused on the domestic or the global marketplace, the central tenets of social media—transparency, authenticity, and engagement with the community to build a strong and profitable organization—reflect the same strengths that make corporate social responsibility and sustainability such compelling business philosophies. Marketing professionals at all types of firms, from Fortune 500 companies to local small businesses, recognize that social media can serve as valuable tools in the effort to create, communicate, and deliver sustainable products and solutions to their stakeholders.

sustainable tourism

The practice of recreational traveling in a way that maximizes the social and economic benefits to the local community and minimizes the negative impact on cultural heritage and the environment.

■ connect Exercise 16-4

Social Media in Action

More and more firms turn to social media to convince potential customers that the organization operates in a socially responsible manner. This marketing action is in direct response to the growing number of consumers who say that what a company stands for affects what they buy.

Panera Bread, a national restaurant chain, used social media platforms to promote its marketing campaign "Live consciously. Eat deliciously." Panera allowed some of its fans to preview the campaign several days before the general public. By interacting with consumers and spreading its message through social media, Panera's marketers advanced their goal of being an important part of the communities in which they operate.

Well-established companies that have been in business for decades increasingly use social media to promote their CSR initiatives. For example, Bumble Bee Foods (founded in 1899) replaced much of its traditional promotional tools (e.g., television, radio, print advertising) with social media to promote its CSR theme "BeeWell for Life®." Bumble Bee Foods marketers used social media tools such as Facebook and blogs to engage consumers in their CSR activities in a more meaningful way.

The Social Media in Action Connect *exercise in Chapter 16 will let you develop specific social media strategies to promote the corporate social responsibility initiatives of an organization. By understanding the benefits and tools of different social media platforms, you will be able to spread the CSR activities of your organization and connect to consumers who pay attention to what a company stands for.*

Source: See Stuart Elliott, "Selling Products by Selling Shared Values," *The New York Times,* February 13, 2013, http://www.nytimes.com/2013/02/14/business/media/panera-to-advertise-its-social-consciousness-advertising.html?pagewanted=all&_r=0.

SUMMARY

ZUMA Press/Alamy Stock Photo

LO 16-1 Describe the features of a successful corporate social responsibility program.

Corporate social responsibility (CSR) refers to an organization's obligation to maximize its positive impact and minimize its negative impact on society. Communities, investors, employees, and other stakeholders demand that firms take a proactive stance in terms of social responsibility.

Stakeholder responsibility focuses on the obligations an organization has to those who can affect achievement of its objectives. It is the driving consideration across the four dimensions of corporate social responsibility: economic, legal, ethical, and philanthropic. There are several key elements to developing a successful CSR program, including good stakeholder management, good corporate leadership, and the integration of CSR into corporate policy at all levels of the organization.

Quiggyt4/ Shutterstock

LO 16-2 Explain how sustainable marketing contributes to a firm's corporate social responsibility efforts.

Sustainability refers to pursuing a lifestyle that meets the needs of the present without compromising the ability of future generations to meet their own needs. *Sustainable marketing* is the process of creating, communicating, and delivering value to customers in a way that recognizes and incorporates the concept of sustainability. One of the easiest ways for marketers to engage in sustainability is to use it as a guideline for cutting costs, for example, by developing different packaging or using less energy.

LO 16-3 Explain the impact of environmentalism on marketing success.

Ted Hsu/Alamy Stock Photo

Environmentalism is a movement of citizens, government agencies, and the business community that advocates the preservation, restoration, and improvement of the environment. Environmental marketing activities can be divided into three categories: tactical greening, quasi-strategic greening, and strategic greening. *Tactical greening* involves implementing limited change within a single area of the organization. *Quasi-strategic greening* usually involves more substantive changes in marketing activities by various functional areas. *Strategic greening* integrates and coordinates the environmental initiatives of a firm with all actions across every functional area.

Firms may choose which category of activities to pursue based on their environmental marketing strategy. Environmental strategies include *eco-efficiency, beyond-compliance leadership, eco-branding, environmental cost leadership,* and *sustainable value innovation.*

LO 16-4 Describe how companies can meet the challenges of environmental and sustainable marketing on a global scale.

Antony Njuguna/ Reuters/Newscom

Marketers at an increasing number of firms look to promote their sustainability efforts and to preserve and replenish the natural environment throughout the world. However, a lack of political will on the part of leaders in some countries to enact sustainability-focused legislation presents challenges to firms; the result may be reduced availability of sustainable products and high prices.

The way marketers justify sustainable marketing also varies in different parts of the world. U.S. marketers justify sustainability strategies using economic arguments; European Union companies rely more heavily on language focused on citizenship, corporate accountability, or moral commitment.

Efforts in sustainable new product development and supply chain management will bring a company closer to its global environmental and sustainability goals.

LO 16-5 Analyze how firms use social media to support their corporate social responsibility efforts.

GSTC

Corporate social responsibility, sustainability, and environmentalism are about communication. Marketers who genuinely consider the impact of their activities need to listen, consider, and respond to the widest group of stakeholders possible.

To capitalize on the opportunity social media present, marketers should be consistent in their social media presence. In addition, they should make each digital communication something of value that holds meaning for their digital community.

Regardless of the industry, the central tenets of a social media philosophy—transparency, authenticity, and engagement with the community to build a stronger and more profitable organization—are the same strengths that make corporate social responsibility and sustainability such compelling business philosophies.

KEY TERMS

closed-loop supply chain (p. 557)
consumerism (p. 545)
corporate philanthropy (p. 539)
corporate social responsibility (CSR) (p. 536)
corporate volunteerism (p. 542)
disintermediation (p. 554)
environmentalism (p. 547)

environmental regulations (p. 551)
ethics (p. 538)
green market (p. 547)
near-shoring (p. 555)
on-shoring (p. 555)
quasi-strategic greening (p. 548)
stakeholder responsibility (p. 536)
strategic greening (p. 548)

sustainability (p. 543)
sustainable design (p. 553)
sustainable marketing (p. 543)
sustainable sourcing (p. 554)
sustainable tourism (p. 560)
tactical greening (p. 548)
triple bottom line (TBL) (p. 553)

MARKETING PLAN EXERCISE • Marketing Yourself

In this chapter, we have explored the impact corporate social responsibility has on organizations and marketing decisions. As part of developing your personal marketing plan, you will consider and develop a vision of your own social responsibilities.

First you must understand whom you're responsible to. Who are the stakeholders in your career success? Your list might include those who are affected by your career path, including a current or future spouse, children, parents, or even the U.S. government that wants you to make enough money to pay back your student loans. Also think about places of worship, charitable causes, communities, and other entities your choices affect.

Next, consider whether a firm or school's corporate social responsibility policies matter to you when choosing where to work or study. If they do, you should think about how you can best market yourself as the type of socially responsible professional who would be of interest to a company or school committed to corporate social responsibility.

Being able to connect your socially responsible activities to those of a potential employer or graduate school program can be a subtle way to differentiate yourself from those competing against you for a position.

Your Task: List the stakeholders in your career success. Next, list three to five social responsibilities that you consider part of your professional career. Explain each, and discuss the specific actions you would like to take relative to each over the next 5–10 years.

DISCUSSION QUESTIONS

1. Identify a Fortune 500 company that you think is socially responsible. Why do you think this way about the company? Does your opinion influence your decision to purchase from the company? Are you willing to pay more to buy from a socially responsible firm? Why or why not?

2. Imagine that you were put in charge of marketing at a small business in your hometown. What CSR or sustainability strategies would you consider for that business? Why did you select these strategies?

3. What is the social responsibility of colleges and universities in the United States? Using the ethical decision-making framework, analyze a hypothetical decision your college or university made to raise tuition 10 percent next year. Use each of the elements of the framework in your analysis. How would you, as a marketer for your university, present the

reasons for the tuition increase to your stakeholders (students, legislators, communities, etc.)?

4. Which of the five barriers to sustainable consumer behavior discussed in this chapter most prevents you from engaging in more sustainable consumer behavior? Do you think your answer will be different in 25 years?

5. Describe how companies can approach environmental sustainability in the areas of new-product development and supply chain management.

6. Provide two examples of organizations that use social media as part of their corporate social responsibility actions. What do they do well through social media? What would you suggest they improve? Based on your experience as a consumer, what social media outlet is most effective for communicating a firm's CSR efforts (e.g., Instagram, Facebook, YouTube, etc.)? Why?

 # SOCIAL MEDIA APPLICATION

Pick (a) a for-profit firm from which you have bought something in the past month and (b) a nonprofit organization to which you might consider donating money (a charity, church, hospital, etc.). Analyze the social media presence of both organizations across all of the platforms that they employ, using the following questions and activities as a guide:

1. What does the for-profit company do on social media to promote its corporate social responsibility activities? Is it enough to influence you to become a customer of the firm? Explain your answer.

2. What does the nonprofit organization do across its social media platforms to inform potential donors about its cause? Is it enough to influence your decision to donate to the organization? Explain your answer.

3. If you were the marketing manager for both organizations, what two specific things would you recommend each do to improve their social media efforts?

  # MARKETING ANALYTICS EXERCISE

Please complete the *Connect* exercise for Chapter 16 that focuses on measuring the success of an organization's corporate social responsibility (CSR) program.

ETHICAL CHALLENGE

One of the most complex ethical challenges facing for-profit organizations today is balancing their goal of being socially responsible with their obligation to shareholders to earn a profit. Firms generally hire executives to increase profits. No matter how much good a firm does in its community, if it doesn't have a healthy bottom line, the executive may not be seen as a success. This is not unlike a college football coach who makes sure his players graduate every year, but consistently has a losing record. Odds are he won't remain the coach very long, even though he does a number of socially responsible things.

Executives at privately held companies have the right to make socially responsible decisions that might sacrifice revenue. Executives at publicly held companies have to answer to their shareholders, who expect profits and share prices to grow. Marketing executives at public companies frequently face situations that force them to choose between responsible action and the bottom line. Please use the ethical decision-making framework to answer the following questions:

1. Assume you are a shareholder in a publicly traded retail firm. Would you want that firm to raise pay rates for its employees to stay on pace with the inflation rate, even if doing so would drive product prices up and profit margins down? Explain your answer.
2. Assume you are a shareholder for a manufacturing company in a small town far from your home. Would you be willing to trade polluting the environment in that one town for an increase in the firm's profits? Explain your answer. If the CEO of the company decided not to pollute the environment and profits decreased as a result, how should the firm market that decision to you and other stakeholders?
3. Assume you are a shareholder in a publicly traded beverage company. Would you support the company's plan to advertise to children even if its beverage is unhealthy for children? Explain your answer.

VIDEO CASE

Please go to *Connect* to access the video cases featuring Williams, a Fortune 500 energy company, and the Hershey Company, a Fortune 500 chocolate manufacturer, that accompany this chapter.

PODCAST

Please go to Connect to access the podcast that accompanies this chapter.

CAREER **TIPS**

Marketing Your Future

You have read in this chapter about the important role corporate social responsibility plays in a firm's ultimate success. As you begin your career, few things will be as important as picking a successful organization to work for. Choosing an employer that stresses CSR as well as financial gain can get your career off to a great start through training, experience, and networking.

Coauthor Shane Hunt has seen too many students make poor career decisions because they decide to take

their first job out of school simply on the basis of money rather than the potential for career growth and success. In an effort to help you choose the right company to work for after graduation, he offers the following four career tips:

1. ***Research the best companies to work for.*** There are all kinds of lists out there ranking the best companies to work for in different industries. (See the Civic 50 rankings earlier in the chapter for an example.) These lists can be great resources for helping you understand how the company ranks

on corporate social responsibility, salary, benefits, advancement opportunities, and other important factors.

2. ***Talk to employees of the organization.*** This can be especially valuable if you are going to work for a small organization that may not be included in national rankings. Try to talk to current or former employees of the organization. This gives you an understanding of how your day-to-day life with the organization might be, as well as how working there can help (or possibly hurt) you in your career going forward.

3. ***Ask good questions.*** Once you get to the interview stage, almost all employers will tell you that they promote employees from within. Ask them in an interview to give an example of someone whom they have promoted from within. If they struggle to think of a specific example, they may not be as dedicated to the practice as they would have you believe.

4. ***Understand the different benefit packages.*** This is incredibly important and, unfortunately, something that many new graduates overlook. Check to see how much your health insurance benefits will cost with the organization. How does that compare to other places that you might work? If a company offers you $5,000 more per year in salary than another company, but you're going to have to pay $600 more per month (or $7,200 per year) for health benefits, the trade-off may not be worth it.

Similarly, say you are offered a job at a company that provides a 6 percent matching contribution to your 401(k). That benefit translates to an extra $3,000 per year (assuming a $50,000 yearly salary), which you should take into account as you evaluate and compare opportunities. Compare the retirement plans of organizations you might work for to make sure you are getting your financial future off to the best possible start.

CHAPTER NOTES

1. Rick Wartzman and Kelly Tang, "Companies Struggle to Stand OUT in ESG Measures," *The Wall Street Journal,* August 2, 2021, p. R10.

2. Sankar Sen and C. B. Bhattacharya, "Does Doing Good Always Lead to Doing Better? Consumer Reactions to Corporate Social Responsibility," *Journal of Marketing Research* 38, no. 2 (2001): 225–244.

3. Jean Eaglesham and Shane Shifflett, "Climate Accounting Looms for Companies," *The Wall Street Journal,* August 11, 2021, pp. A1, A8.

4. Timothy Puko, "Companies Urge Action on Climate Change," *The Wall Street Journal,* December 2, 2020, p. A4.

5. Dennis Jacobe, "In U.S., 54% Have Stock Market Investments, Lowest Since 1999," *Gallup,* April 20, 2011, http://www.gallup.com/poll/147206/stock-market-investments-lowest-1999.aspx.

6. Andrew Lisa, "25 Product Recalls That Rocked Their Company's Stock Price," *Stacker,* June 18, 2019, 25 Product Recalls that Rocked their Company's Stock Price | Stacker.

7. Adam Weinger, "5 Companies Doing Corporate Philanthropy Right," March 8, 2015, https://www.triplepundit.com/story/2015/5-companies-doing-corporate-philanthropy-right/36501.

8. R. Morimoto et al., "Corporate Social Responsibility Audit: From Theory to Practice," *Journal of Business Ethics* 62, no. 4 (2005): 315–325.

9. C. Kennedy, "The Great and the Good," *Director* 61, no. 3 (2007): 102–106.

10. V. Kasturi Rangan, Lisa Chase, and Sohel Karim, "The Truth about CSR," *Harvard Business Review,* January–February 2015, https://hbr.org/2015/01/the-truth-about-csr.

11. R. Morimoto et al., "Corporate Social Responsibility Audit: From Theory to Practice," *Journal of Business Ethics* 62, no. 4 (2005): 315–325.

12. V. Kasturi Rangan, Lisa Chase, and Sohel Karim, "The Truth about CSR," *Harvard Business Review,* January–February 2015, https://hbr.org/2015/01/the-truth-about-csr.

13. C. B. Bhattacharya, "Corporate Social Responsibility: It's All about Marketing," *Forbes,* November 20, 2009, http://www.forbes.com/2009/11/20/corporate-social-responsibility-leadership-citizenship-marketing.html.

14. "The Civic 50," *Bloomberg Businessweek,* December 7, 2012, http://www.businessweek.com/articles/2012-12-07/the-civic-50.

15. Diane Brady, "Volunteerism as a Core Competency," *Bloomberg Businessweek,* November 8, 2012, http://www.businessweek.com/articles/2012-11-08/volunteerism-as-a-core-competency.

16. https://corporatementoring.devpost.com/submissions/13695-raytheon-stand-deliver-corporate-campus-mentoring-program.

17. Brian Anderson, "5 Companies That Recognize the Value of Volunteer Work," BambooHR, August 25, 2016, 5 Companies That Recognize The Value Of Volunteer Work (bamboohr.com).

18. United Nations, "Report of the World Commission on Environment and Development: Our Common Future," 1987, p. 16, http://www.un-documents.net/our-common-future.pdf.

19. General Mills, "Environmental Sustainability: Energy," n.d., http://www.generalmills.com//media/Files/sustainability/GM_energy.ashx.

20. James Epstein Reeves, "Six Reasons Companies Should Embrace CSR," *Forbes,* February 21, 2012, http://www.forbes.com/sites/csr/2012/02/21/six-reasons-companies-should-embrace-csr/.

21. https://www.generalmills.com/how-we-make-it/healthier-planet.

22. Andrew Savitz, *The Triple Bottom Line: How Today's Best-Run Companies Are Achieving Economic, Social and Environmental Success—And How You Can Too* (San Francisco: Jossey-Bass, 2006).

23. Unilever, "Our Roadmap to Net Zero," (n.d.) https://www.unilever.com/planet-and-society/climate-action/strategy-and-goals/.

24. DuPont, "2012 Sustainability Progress Report," http://www2.dupont.com/inclusive-innovations/en-us/sites/default/files/DuPont%20Sustainability%20Report%2012%2011611612.pdf.

25. Dow, "2025 Sustainability Goal: Leading the Blueprint," n.d., https://www.dow.com/en-us/science-and-sustainability/sustainability-reporting/2015-sustainability-goals.

26. James Epstein Reeves, "Six Reasons Companies Should Embrace CSR," *Forbes,* February 21, 2012, http://www.forbes.com/sites/csr/2012/02/21/six-reasons-companies-should-embrace-csr/.

27. Coca-Cola Great Britain, "Employment: Our People," n.d., http://www.coca-cola.co.uk/about-us/employment-our-people.html.

28. John P. Tiemstra, "Theories of Regulation and the History of Consumerism," *International Journal of Social Economics* 19, no. 6 (1992): 3–27.

29. Diane Martin and John Schouten, *Sustainable Marketing* (Upper Saddle River, NJ: Pearson, 2012).

30. Diane Martin and John Schouten, *Sustainable Marketing* (Upper Saddle River, NJ: Pearson, 2012).

31. Diane Martin and John Schouten, *Sustainable Marketing* (Upper Saddle River, NJ: Pearson, 2012).

32. Tiffany Hsu, "Wal-Mart Pleads Guilty in Hazardous Waste Cases, to Pay $81 Million," *Los Angeles Times,* May 28, 2013, http://articles.latimes.com/2013/may/28/business/la-fi-mo-walmart-guilty-hazardous-waste-20130528.

33. Jacquelyn A. Ottman, *The New Rules of Green Marketing: Strategies, Tools, and Inspiration for Sustainable Branding* (Sheffield, UK: Greenleaf, 2011).

34. European Commission, "Attitudes of European Citizens towards the Environment," March 2008, p. 3, http://ec.europa.eu/environment/archives/barometer/pdf/summary2008_environment_en.pdf.

35. European Commission, "Attitudes of European Citizens towards the Environment," March 2008, p. 3, http://ec.europa.eu/environment/archives/barometer/pdf/summary2008_environment_en.pdf.

36. European Commission, "Attitudes of European Citizens towards the Environment," March 2008, p. 3, http://ec.europa.eu/environment/archives/barometer/pdf/summary2008_environment_en.pdf.

37. Jennifer Blackhurst and David Cantor, "Developing Sustainable Supply Chains: An Organizational and Supply Chain Employee View," *Center for Industrial Research and Service,* July 2012, http://www.ciras.iastate.edu/publications/Sustainable_Supply_Chains-Employee_View.pdf.

38. Michael Barbaro, "At Wal-Mart, Lessons in Self-Help," *The New York Times,* April 5, 2007, http://www.nytimes.com/2007/04/05/business/05improve.html?pagewanted=all.

39. Diane Martin and John Schouten, *Sustainable Marketing* (Upper Saddle River, NJ: Pearson, 2012).

40. M. J. Polonsky and P. J. Rosenberger III, "Reevaluating Green Marketing: Strategic Approach," *Business Horizons,* 9–10 (2001): 21–30.

41. Sprint, "White Paper: Sprint Improved Packaging Sustainability 55 Percent in Three Years," *The New York Times,* May 8, 2013, http://markets.on.nytimes.com/research/stocks/news/press_release.asp?docTag=201305081030BIZWIRE_USPRX____BW6064&feedID=600&press_symbol=109153.

42. Kelly Sampson, "10 Leading Companies That Efficiently Went 'Green'," Hummingbird International, September 30, 2015, 10 Leading Companies That Efficiently Went "Green" | (hummingbirdinternational.net).

43. Renato J. Orsato, "Competitive Environmental Strategies: When Does It Pay to Be Green?" *California Management Review* 48, no. 2 (2006): 127–144.

44. Ryan Dezember, "Packaging Giant Bets on Paper," *The Wall Street Journal,* January 3, 2022, pp. A1, A10.

45. Dell Press Release, "Dell Joins Prince's Rainforest Project," June 5, 2009, http://www.dell.com/learn/us/en/uscorp1/press-releases/DELLJOINSTHEPRINCESRAINFORESTSPROJECT?c=us&l=en&s=corp.

46. Diane Martin and John Schouten, *Sustainable Marketing* (Upper Saddle River, NJ: Pearson, 2012).

47. Diane Martin and John Schouten, *Sustainable Marketing* (Upper Saddle River, NJ: Pearson, 2012).

48. Melissa Denchak, "Paris Climate Agreement: Everything You Need to Know," NRDC, February 19, 2021, Paris Climate Agreement: Everything You Need to Know | NRDC.

49. Julian Evans, "Good Intentions," *The Wall Street Journal,* February 3, 2010, http://online.wsj.com/article/SB10001424052748704878904575031330905332468.html.

50. Heather Haddon, "Starbucks Tests a New Cup That Is Easier to Recycle," *The Wall Street Journal,* March 10, 2020, p. B2.

51. Christopher M. Matthews and Emily Glazer, "Exxon Weighs 'Net-Zero' Carbon by 2050," *The Wall Street Journal,* August 6, 2021, pp. A1–A2.

52. Michael Adams, Barry Thornton, and Mohammad Sepehri, "The Impact of the Pursuit of Sustainability on the Financial Performance of the Firm," *Journal of Sustainability and Green Business* 1 (April 2012): 1–14.

53. Eoin O'Carroll, "EU Bans Incandescent Light Bulbs," *Christian Science Monitor,* October 15, 2008, http://www.csmonitor.com/Environment/Bright-Green/2008/1015/eu-bans-incandescent-light-bulbs.

54. Accenture, "Long-Term Growth, Short-Term Differentiation and Profits from Sustainable Products and Services: A Global Survey of Business Executives," 2012, http://www.accenture.com/SiteCollectionDocuments/PDF/Accenture-Long-Term-Growth-Short-Term-Differentiation-and-Profits-from-Sustainable-Products-and-Services.pdf.

55. SCRIBD, "Ethical Dilemmas in Product Development," n.d., http://www.scribd.com/doc/16187139/Ethical-Dilemmas-in-Product-Development.

56. Omar Abdulkarem Alqudaib, "A Quick Way to Measure Sustainability," *Supply Chain Quarterly,* Fall 2021, 44–49.

57. Tim Higgins, "On the Road to Self-Driving Trucks," *The Wall Street Journal,* March 3, 2017, pp. B1, B4.

58. Jennifer Smith, "Target Tries Out New Strategy to Improve Its Supply Chain," *The Wall Street Journal,* May 15, 2018, p. B3.

59. Brian Basket, "Shippers Go Small in Strategy Shift," *The Wall Street Journal,* April 11, 2017, p. B6.

60. U.S. Department of Transportation, n.d., http://www.rita .dot.gov/bts/sites/rita.dot.gov.bts/files/publications/ freight_shipments_in_america/html/entire.html.

61. Kannan Dovinan, Hamed Soleimani, and Devika Kannan, "Reverse logistics and closed-loop supply chain: A comprehensive review to explore the future," European Journal of Operational Research, Vol. 240, Issue 3, pp. 603-626.

62. Aaron Black, "Walmart Has Room to Rise Again," *The Wall Street Journal,* September 6, 2018, p. B2.

63. Laura Stevens, "Amazon Beefs Up Its Fleet of Vans," *The Wall Street Journal,* September 6, 2018, p. B2.

64. N. Mulani, "Sustainable Sourcing: Do Good While Doing Well," *Logistics Management,* Issue 47, no. 7 (2008): 25–26.

65. Katie Deighton, "Returnable Fast-Food Cups Tested," *The Wall Street Journal,* September 23, 2021, p. B3.

66. Max Benz, "10 Corporate Social Responsibility Examples You Should Know," *Prowly,* (n.d.), 10 Corporate Social Responsibility Examples You Should Know—Prowly Magazine.

67. Martin Lamonica, "GE, VCs Offer $200 Million in Smart-Grid Challenge," *CNET,* July 13, 2010, http://news.cnet. com/8301-11128_3-20010378-54.html.

68. Tamara Gillis, ed., *The IABC Handbook of Organizational Communication* (San Francisco: Wiley, 2011), p. 77.

69. Accenture, "Long-Term Growth, Short-Term Differentiation and Profits from Sustainable Products and Services: A Global Survey of Business Executives," 2012, http:// www.accenture.com/SiteCollectionDocuments/PDF/ Accenture-Long-Term-Growth-Short-Term-Differentiation-and-Profits-from-Sustainable-Productsand-Services.pdf.

70. Global Sustainable Tourism Council, "GSTC's Role in the Marketing of Sustainable Tourism," n.d., https://www .gstcouncil.org/about/gstcs-role-marketing-sustainable-tourism/.

SAMPLE MARKETING PLAN

Personal Marketing Plan: Courtney Ewing

Throughout the chapters, you completed a personal marketing plan exercise that asked you to apply the concepts you have learned to the product you will market every day of your life: you. After going through each exercise, you have gained not only experience thinking about the various aspects of a marketing plan but also a roadmap for pursuing your professional objectives after graduation. This appendix provides a sample of what your completed personal marketing plan might look like.

MARKETING STRATEGY
   Future Objectives (Chapter 1)
SITUATION ANALYSIS
   Strengths, Weaknesses, Opportunities, and Threats (SWOT) Analysis (Chapter 2)
   Market Summary (Chapter 3)
TARGET MARKET (Chapter 4)
MARKETING RESEARCH (Chapter 5)
PRODUCT DESCRIPTION (Chapter 6)
POSITIONING MYSELF (Chapter 7)
PROMOTING MYSELF (Chapter 8)
SPIN SELLING QUESTIONS (Chapter 9)
DISTRIBUTION (Chapter 10)
PRICING (Chapter 11)
RETAILING (Chapter 12)
CONTROLS (Chapter 13)
BRANDING (Chapter 14)
RELATIONSHIP DEVELOPMENT (Chapter 15)
SOCIAL RESPONSIBILITY (Chapter 16)

MARKETING STRATEGY

Future Objectives (Chapter 1)

   1. Attend an accredited law school somewhere in the southwestern United States, preferably Oklahoma or Texas. My top three choices are the University of Oklahoma, University of Tulsa, and Texas Tech University.
   2. After law school graduation, I want to work in an established law firm, preferably in Tulsa, Oklahoma. My parents and much of my family live near Tulsa, and it would be my first choice as a home after law school graduation.

3. I want to live comfortably and have enough money to enjoy the time I have with my family. I will be 25 years old when I graduate from law school, and it is my goal to make $100,000 in annual salary by the time I am 32 years old. I arrived at that number because that is what I will need to be able to pay for the things my family would want, for example, a nice home, two cars, and an annual vacation.

SITUATION ANALYSIS

SWOT Analysis (Chapter 2)

Strengths

- I am an extremely dedicated employee. I put 110 percent into any task or assignment that I undertake.
- I possess the analytical and creative skills necessary to succeed in law school, to strategically formulate plans, to design them, and to effectively implement them.
- I am a quick learner and not afraid to operate outside my comfort zone. I am able to quickly adapt to new situations and to learn new skills.

Weaknesses

- I can be too detail-oriented, and it may take me longer to accomplish tasks or to be completely satisfied with my performance. By recognizing these weaknesses and taking on more school projects with short deadlines, I can improve the skills necessary to ensure quality work.
- I am often impatient, and a lack of patience can sometimes be a negative characteristic in an employee. However, I am working to never allow my impatience to affect my job performance or behavior.
- I do not have any real professional experience. While I have worked at a restaurant, I need more professional experience working for either a major business or a law firm. I plan to fix this by pursuing an internship this summer, even if it is unpaid, to gain experience that will build my skills and resume.

Opportunities

- My uncle is an attorney and has let me job-shadow him on several occasions. This has been a great learning opportunity and one that can help me articulate to schools why I want to be a lawyer.
- My education is both broad and versatile. With a degree in marketing and a minor in history, I have learned a unique set of skills. I believe this degree, combined with my high grades and LSAT score, will position me very well for the law schools I want to attend.

- Due to the recent state of the economy, some law firms are opting to hire less-experienced attorneys for less pay. This is a great way for companies to cut costs and allows young people like me an opportunity to prove themselves.

Threats

- While my targeted potential job market is pretty broad, the competition is extremely high. I will look to create a niche for myself by specializing in a particular area of the legal profession, perhaps oil and gas law.
- Although the economy could provide entry-level job seekers like me better opportunities, it could also be a threat. Many firms are eliminating positions and reducing the number of new associates they hire. I may have to expand my search to places outside of Tulsa. I may also have to consider working for a smaller practice when I first get out of law school.
- There could be an increase in law school applications at my targeted schools, reducing my chances for admission to my top choices for law school. I will research all of my targeted law schools to check the acceptance rates and admission requirements to make sure that I fully understand my chances of getting in.
- Personal financial issues are also a potential threat. In particular, I am concerned that national economic problems could reduce the amount of student financial aid that I can get. I plan to talk with my parents and develop a plan that sets the minimum amount of financial aid I could get and still get through law school.

Market Summary (Chapter 3)

The market for attorneys is competitive, and salaries have been generally lower in recent years. I was surprised to see that within 9 months of graduation only 55 percent of law school graduates from the most recent year had full-time, long-term jobs that required a law degree. The market is not in as good shape as I expected. It appears that more than 40,000 new law school graduates enter the job market each year, with almost half not finding jobs in the first year.

I will need to be prepared to face a difficult market upon graduation. I will need to understand the market for specific areas of specialty. For example, in recent years, law school graduates with an expertise in oil and gas, financial services, or cybercrime have been more likely to be hired by established firms.

TARGET MARKET (Chapter 4)

My preference would be to work in a B2B environment in which my clients are companies. I have seen my uncle work in this environment, and he enjoys his job very much. Since my focus is likely to be oil and gas law, I will work primarily with other businesses, rather than individuals.

There are three law firms in Tulsa that work in this B2B area that would make ideal employers when I finish law school. They are:

Hatteberg, Gonzales, and Xu
Basu, Hughes, Kieffer, and Ducham
Penn and Associates

MARKETING RESEARCH (Chapter 5)

My marketing research included online information searches and speaking with a couple of admissions counselors at potential schools. That research helped me better understand my prospects of being accepted to law school. There are over 175 law schools in the United States, but there are three that I most want to attend: the University of Oklahoma, the University of Tulsa, and Texas Tech University. I found the following data about acceptances at those schools:

- At Oklahoma, the acceptance rate is 32 percent, the median LSAT score is 158, and the average GPA is 3.48.
- At Tulsa, the acceptance rate is 40 percent, the median LSAT is 155, and the average GPA is 3.32.
- At Texas Tech, the acceptance rate is 47 percent, the median LSAT is 155, and the average GPA is 3.45.

The median starting salary for graduates from all three schools is around $55,000 per year.

My LSAT score of 156 is a little low for Oklahoma, but above the median for the other two schools. My GPA of 3.59 is ahead of the average at all of the schools. I think my chances of getting into the University of Oklahoma are a little questionable, but I feel pretty confident about the University of Tulsa and Texas Tech.

I need to improve my experience and extracurricular activities during the next year so that I can market myself as the best possible candidate to these law schools. Because my scores are close to the median at all of the schools, I also am going to apply to a couple of law schools with lower averages where I am very certain I will be accepted, just in case.

PRODUCT DESCRIPTION (Chapter 6)

I would love the opportunity to be part of your law school program. I have excelled during my undergraduate career with a GPA above 3.59 as a marketing major with a history minor. I am a hardworking person with incredible attention to detail. I am confident but personable. I follow direction very well, and I make others around me better.

I am president of the Marketing Club at my university and have been a leader in other student organizations on campus. Perhaps most importantly, I am passionate about being a lawyer and want to do great things in this profession. I have talked with and job-shadowed successful attorneys. These opportunities have given me experience and reinforced that I have what it takes to be successful as a lawyer.

I know that the job market for attorneys is challenging, but I have confidence in my ability to succeed and make a difference. I believe that I will be a great addition to your law school and a source of pride for the university after my graduation.

POSITIONING MYSELF (Chapter 7)

I am positioning myself as a candidate for law school who has a high GPA as a college of business major and who also is a leader among my peers. I received the highest grade in my business law class of 70 students. I also have taken two courses in constitutional law as part of my history minor. This has given me the opportunity, as an undergraduate, to study legal cases and write arguments for and against different rulings. I will arrive at law school on day one with a track record of academic success and a background in coursework that has prepared me to think in a legal way.

PROMOTING MYSELF (Chapter 8)

Advertising. I plan to develop a professional two-page resume that reflects my desire to work for an established law firm. I plan to join professional social networking organizations like LinkedIn and build my profile. I will eliminate or make private all of my personal social media pages, as I want employers to focus on me as a professional candidate for their law school and eventually their law firm. I also plan to use the same professional photo across all of the social media sites that I use to make me more recognizable to prospective employers, as well as to project a consistent image.

Sales promotion. Two of the firms I want to work for in Tulsa offer unpaid internships. I plan to apply to both this summer. Not only will this give me a sample of what it would be like to work for the firm, but it also will allow the firm to see my work ethic and recognize my potential. Because the internship is unpaid, I have started saving money now from my current job at a restaurant, and I will live at home with my parents during the summer to cut costs while I complete the internship. I believe these short-term sacrifices are a great long-term investment.

Personal selling. I try to always be professionally dressed and well groomed. When I was a first- or second-year student, I would often just wake up and go to class, not looking my best. Now, as I get closer to graduation and law school, I am very conscious of my appearance and what that appearance says about my personal brand. I also plan to take advantage of the mock-interview program offered at my university's career services department. The program is free and will allow me to participate in and then review a fake interview with a career services representative, which will prepare me to sell myself to future employers.

Public relations. I have always tried to be aware of how my actions may be perceived by others in my professional and personal life. When I decided I was going to go to law school, I knew that I would need recommendations from my professors. I worked very hard to do well in my classes and took the time to develop relationships with my professors. I make it a point to introduce myself during their office hours at the beginning of each semester and then to stop by several more times during the semester. I am confident that they would say very positive things about me.

I also continue to try to be a good classmate. Many of my business courses require group projects, and I have worked with some terrible group members. Through that experience, I've learned that I don't want to be a terrible group member myself, and I work hard to do my part on group projects. I will continue to be a personable, helpful member of any team.

SPIN SELLING QUESTIONS (Chapter 9)

(S) What are the major goals for your law school program over the next decade?

(P) What is the thing that is most challenging for students entering law school?

(I) How do those challenging things affect retention and placement rates following graduation?

(N) How do you think a student with my analytical skills and attention to detail would do in your law school program?

DISTRIBUTION (Chapter 10)

I plan to distribute my information through applications to five law schools, which are listed below:

1. University of Oklahoma
2. University of Tulsa
3. Texas Tech University
4. Oklahoma City University
5. University of Houston

I also plan to distribute information about myself professionally through social networking sites like LinkedIn. I will follow each of the schools that I am applying to on all of the social media platforms that they use. I will also join a networking group in Tulsa comprised of people who work in oil and gas law to start making connections that could help me in the law school application process as well with future employment.

PRICING (Chapter 11)

My goal is to make a $100,000 annual salary by the time I am 32, which is roughly 10 years after I finish my bachelor's degree. Here are the costs that I anticipate upon my law school graduation:

> Undergraduate student loans: $21,000
> Law school student loans: $47,000

When taken together, I expect to pay around $600 per month in student loan payments. In addition, I expect that my mortgage or rent payment after graduating from law school will be around $900 per month in Tulsa. When I factor in car payments, insurance, groceries, and social activities, I estimate that I will need about $3,000 per month or $36,000 after taxes to live the way I want.

Based on my research and conversations with working attorneys, I project that about one-third of my total salary will not show up in my paycheck because it will be deducted for taxes, health insurance, and 401(k) retirement plan contributions. Considering this, my total starting salary will need to be $54,000 per year or more to cover my costs and to have the chance to hit my 10-year salary goal of $100,000 per year.

Since the starting salary for graduates at my targeted law schools is $55,000, I feel good about my chances. However, I need to make sure to do well in law school and take advantage of every networking opportunity. If I make anything below the average salary, I will have to cut things out of my life (e.g., a nice home or a new car) that I would prefer to have.

RETAILING (Chapter 12)

The retail environment for attorneys is changing rapidly. All three of the firms I am targeting for employment after law school are primarily B2B firms. They are going to feel competition and price pressure from online legal advice firms such as Legal Zoom that provide an array of services for businesses including trademarks, incorporation, or forming an LLC. These online services are typically cheaper than consulting a local law firm, and they are expanding in number both in the United States and throughout the world.

I think customers are also expecting attorneys to be more flexible about when and where they meet with their clients. I expect that whatever firm I work for will spend more time in virtual meetings and less time meeting with clients at a traditional law office. I'll need to be willing to work outside "regular office hours" and be prepared with good virtual-meeting skills.

CONTROLS (Chapter 13)

Here are my objectives for the next one, three, and five years:

One year after graduation

- I plan to complete my bachelor's degree.
- I plan to be accepted at one of my top law school choices.
- I plan to apply for scholarships to reduce my student loan burden in graduate school.

Contingency plan

- I will take summer courses, if necessary, to complete my degree on time. I may have to take online classes if I am interning during the day, so I should plan ahead to see what classes are offered online and plan accordingly.
- If I do not get into one of my top law school choices, I plan to stay in school another year and get a second major (in finance) and potentially a second minor (in Spanish). I will also retake the LSAT in an effort to improve my score and chances for admission to law school.

Three years after graduation

- I plan to have a summer clerkship with an established law firm near Tulsa.
- I plan to have completed two years of law school.
- I plan to be interviewing for jobs as an associate once I finish my law degree.

Contingency plan

- If I cannot find a clerkship in Tulsa, I will try to find one in a nearby metro area, such as Oklahoma City, Dallas, or Kansas City.
- If I am unable to complete law school for any reason, I will pursue a job in marketing in Tulsa. I love marketing and think I would be successful in a career in sales or pricing.
- If I cannot find a job in Tulsa, I will pursue jobs throughout the country because I know that it is critical that I start my career with a good company where I can gain experience.

Five years after graduation

- I plan to be an attorney in Tulsa.
- I plan to be making approximately $60,000 per year.
- Between my contribution and the company contribution (which I expect to be at least 3 percent of my annual salary), I expect to be saving at least $7,000 per year through my 401(k) benefit plan.
- I plan to own a home.
- I plan to have an affordable health care policy that my firm helps to pay for and that provides my family and me with excellent care.

Contingency plan

- If I am not an attorney in Tulsa, I will evaluate how well I like the city I am living and working in. It is possible I will like that new city better, but if not, I will consider what I am willing to trade as far as money to be closer to home.
- If I am well below my targeted salary, I will consider why that is. If my performance is poor, I will look for ways to improve at what I am doing.
- If I am doing well, I will consider other opportunities at firms that might pay me better or even consider the possibility of starting my own small law firm.

Personal contingency plan There are definitely personal developments that could change my plans in the next five years:

- I may be married and my spouse will have a significant influence on where we work and live.
- I do not expect to be a parent in the next five years, but if I am, that will affect the type of law firm I choose to work for. One of my main personal goals for the rest of my life is to be a great parent, and I want to choose an employer that respects and appreciates that.

BRANDING (Chapter 14)

In the next 12 months, I plan to do the following things to build my brand:

1. Work as a summer intern for an established law firm (in the next six months). This will help me build my brand as someone who is serious about a legal career. It also will increase my knowledge and improve my chances of success in law school.
2. Become an officer of another student organization on campus (in the next eight months). I currently serve as the president of the Marketing Club, but I would like to be an officer of a different organization, probably Phi Beta

Lambda, which is for future business leaders, so that I can list that on my law school applications. I think this will help build my brand as a leader among my peers, which is an attribute that top law schools are looking for.

3. I am going to take two of my free elective classes in Spanish (starting in three months). A foreign language is a great differentiator and taking these as electives, as opposed to easier classes I could take, helps illustrate my brand of hard work and professional development.

RELATIONSHIP DEVELOPMENT (Chapter 15)

Working at a restaurant provides a large number of opportunities to deliver customer service. One of the things I pride myself on in my job is getting to know my customers and what they like. I think I am good at recognizing which customers want very attentive service and which prefer privacy. As a team lead server, I am usually brought in to talk with an unhappy customer. I have been very successful in resolving situations, mostly because I listen to what has made the customer unhappy and then find a solution. I think this skill set of providing great customer service will help me as a lawyer and throughout my life.

In the next 12 months, I plan to strengthen relationships with the following three people:

1. *Dr. Tew.* He is a finance professor at my school and also a lawyer. He is a brilliant man and potentially would be a great person to provide me with a letter of recommendation. I plan to take a course with him next semester to get to know him. I am also going to attend the next monthly meeting of our Phi Beta Lambda business organization. He serves as the faculty advisor for the organization, which would provide me with an opportunity to get to know him in a different setting.

2. *Bob Tinker.* He is an oil and gas attorney my uncle knows. He could be a great contact to have during and after law school. He has lunch with my uncle about once per month, and I am going to join them in the next two months. I also am going to ask Mr. Tinker if I can job-shadow him for a day sometime in the next year. Because he knows my uncle and is an alumnus of my university, I think he will be willing to do this.

3. *Leigh Manly.* She is the director of admissions at one of my top choices for law school. Ms. Manly is very active in organizing the local Heart Walk fundraiser for the American Heart Association. This is a great cause that I am passionate about. I plan to volunteer at the fundraiser in two months. This experience will improve my resume and also make a positive impression on Ms. Manly about how I would represent the school's law school program.

SOCIAL RESPONSIBILITY (Chapter 16)

The main stakeholders in my professional success are the following:

1. *My parents.* They have invested thousands of dollars in my education to reduce the amount of my student loans. They have been supportive and loving, and they are invested in my success. Plus, as an only child, I want to be able to assist them as they get older.
2. *My future spouse and children.* I have been dating someone seriously for more than a year. If we decide to get married and someday start a family, I want to be able to earn a good salary so that we can enjoy our lives and provide for our children.
3. *The U.S. government.* As I mentioned earlier, I expect to have $68,000 or more in student loan debt by the time I finish law school. I appreciate the great opportunities that student loans have given me, and I want to make sure I can pay them back with interest.

The main social responsibilities I feel will be part of my career and life going forward are:

1. I feel a great responsibility to help the kids in my community. Tulsa has a high percentage of children living under the poverty line. Regardless of anything else in their lives, those children deserve to have enough to eat. A great program in my area called Kans 4 Kids provides students who are on free lunch programs with food for the weekend or school breaks when they otherwise would not have enough to eat. I plan to give and raise money for this outstanding cause over the next decade.
2. As an attorney, I want to take time to offer a few hours every month of *pro bono* services to help with programs such as children's legal services, where I would represent and serve as an advocate for children in welfare and other types of cases before the court.
3. I want to support my university. I have had a lot of great opportunities here at school, and I want to give back both financially and with my time after I graduate. I am a first-generation college student whose life has been transformed by my experience, and I want to share that message with future students who are considering attending my school over the next decade.
4. I also want to help and support my local church. I have attended this church since I was seven years old, and I have developed many terrific relationships there. I want to help financially and also serve as a young leader, helping mentor the youth in our church over the next decade.

GLOSSARY

80/20 rule A theory that suggests that 20 percent of heavy users account for 80 percent of the total demand.

A/B testing Involves directly comparing two versions of a product to see which one performs better with customers. Also known as *split testing*.

accessibility (of transportation) A carrier's ability to provide service from the source of the shipment (a factory, for example) to its destination (a store or even an individual customer).

adaptive selling The altering of sales behavior during a customer interaction based on perceived information about the selling situation.

advantages In the FAB sales approach, general statements about what the features do; they may or may not be connected to an expressed or actual customer need.

advertising Nonpersonal communication about goods, services, or ideas that is paid for by an identified sponsor.

advertising campaign A collection of coordinated advertisements that share a single theme.

advertising effectiveness studies A type of research that measures how well an advertising campaign meets marketing objectives.

affective choice Process in which consumers make a choice based on how they think the product will make them feel.

affordable method A promotion-mix budgeting strategy in which firms set their promotion budget based on what they believe they can afford.

aided recall test A performance metric in which respondents are asked to recall advertisements based on clues they receive to help stimulate their memory.

allowances Trade promotions that typically involve paying retailers for financial losses associated with consumer sales promotions or reimbursing a retailer for an in-store or local expense to promote a specific product.

approach A part of the personal selling process that involves meeting the prospect and learning more about his or her needs and wants.

artificial intelligence (AI) An area of computer science that emphasizes the creation of intelligent machines that work and react like humans.

aspirational reference group The individuals a consumer would like to emulate.

assortment The selection of merchandise a retailer carries.

atmospherics Sensory-based stimuli within a retailer's environment—the sights, sounds, smells, and other attributes—that project an image and draw customers to the store.

attitude A relatively enduring organization of beliefs, feelings, and behavioral tendencies toward socially significant objects, groups, events, or symbols, typically expressed through general liking or disliking of the attitude target.

attitude-based choice Process that involves the use of general attitudes and summary impressions.

attribute-based choice Process in which consumers select a product based on attribute-by-attribute comparisons across brands.

augmented reality (AR) An interactive experience of a real-world environment where the objects that reside in the real world are "augmented" by computer-generated perceptual information.

Baby Boomers The generation born between 1946 and 1964.

behavioral segmentation Segmentation that categorizes consumers according to how they behave with or act toward products.

behavioral targeting A data-collection method that utilizes a variety of technologies to anonymously track and compile individual consumer behaviors.

belief An organized pattern of knowledge that an individual holds to be true about his or her world.

benefits In the FAB sales approach, individual values attached to the advantages offered by various product features.

Big Data A term that describes both the growth in information that inundates businesses each day and the complex tools used to analyze the data and derive meaningful insights.

blog An online journal in which people or companies post their thoughts and other content.

blog mining A research technique that uses automated tools to find and extract information on the web about a brand and then uses specialized software to analyze these large amounts of text-based data.

brand The name, term, symbol, design, or any combination of these that identifies and differentiates a firm's products.

brand community A specialized, non-geographically bound community based on a structured set of social relationships among admirers of a brand.

brand equity The value the firm derives from consumers' positive perception of its products.

brand extension The process of broadening the use of an organization's current brand to include new products.

brand image The unique set of associations target customers or stakeholders make with a brand.

brand loyalty A consumer's steadfast allegiance to a brand, as evidenced by repeated purchases.

brand marks The elements of a brand, not expressed in words, that a consumer instantly recognizes, such as a symbol, color, or design.

brand recognition The degree to which customers can identify the brand under a variety of circumstances.

brand revitalization (rebranding) A strategy to recapture lost sources of brand equity and identify and establish new sources of brand equity.

breadth of assortment The number of distinct goods or service product lines that a retailer carries.

break-even analysis The process of calculating the break-even point, which equals the sales volume needed to achieve a profit of zero.

break-even point The point at which the costs of producing a product equal the revenue made from selling the product.

business analysis The process of analyzing a new product to determine its profitability.

business format franchise Business organization in which the franchisor provides to the franchisee not just its trade name, products, and services but an entire system for operating the business.

business-to-business (B2B) marketing Marketing to organizations that acquire goods and services in the production of other goods and services that are then sold or supplied to others.

business-to-consumer (B2C) marketing Selling goods and services to end-user customers.

buyer A retail professional responsible for purchasing wholesale merchandise for retailers to sell in store or online.

buying center The group of people within an organization who are involved in a purchase decision.

cannibalization A reduction in sales volume or market share of a company's existing product due to the introduction of a new product made by the same company.

catalog marketing A retail sales technique used to group many items together in a printed piece or an online store.

category killers Specialty discount stores that are able to gain high market share within their chosen category.

category management A merchandising technique that focuses on the performance of a product category rather than individual brands.

causal research A type of marketing research used to understand the cause-and-effect relationships among variables.

channel sales representatives New-business sales representatives who focus on securing new distribution channel outlets.

clientelling A method of personalizing service by tailoring product information for individual customers, in order to provide an exceptional and personalized shopping experience.

closed-loop supply chain A supply chain that maximizes value creation by recovering value from product or material returns.

co-branding A strategy in which two or more companies issue a single product in an effort to capitalize on the equity of each company's brand.

cognitive dissonance The mental conflict that people undergo when they acquire new information that contradicts their beliefs or assumptions.

collaborative filtering A mechanism that filters large amounts of information about many consumers' previous purchases that may be related in some way in order to predict consumer preferences.

competitive advantage The superior position a product enjoys over competing products if consumers believe it has more value than other products in its category.

competitive intelligence The systematic gathering of data about strategies that direct and indirect competitors are pursuing in terms of new-product development and the marketing mix.

concept test A procedure in which marketing professionals ask consumers for their reactions to verbal descriptions and rough visual models of a potential product.

consultative sellers Sales representatives who focus on developing long-term relationships by developing a deep knowledge of the customer's industry, business issues, and needs.

consumer behavior The study of individuals, groups, or organizations and the processes they use to select, secure, use, and dispose of products, services, experiences, or ideas to satisfy needs, and the impacts that these processes have on the consumer and society.

consumer confidence A measure of how optimistic consumers are about the overall state of the economy and their own personal finances.

consumer ethnocentrism A belief by residents of a country that it is inappropriate or immoral to purchase foreign-made goods and services.

consumer tribe A consumption collective that exists when consumers identify with one another and share experiences through a variety of brands, products, activities, and services.

consumer-adoption process The process by which customers formally accept and purchase products.

consumerism A movement, made up of citizens and government entities, that focuses on protecting consumers and promoting their interests.

content marketing A marketing approach focused on creating and distributing valuable, relevant, and consistent content to attract and retain a clearly defined and profitable audience.

contests Sales promotions in which consumers compete against one another and must demonstrate skill to win.

convenience sample A research sample drawn from respondents who are easily accessible to the researcher—for example, relatives, friends, or employees.

convenience stores Small, self-service stores that are open long hours and carry a limited number of frequently purchased items.

corporate chains Two or more retail outlets that are commonly owned and controlled.

corporate philanthropy The act of organizations voluntarily donating some of their profits or resources to charitable causes.

corporate social responsibility (CSR) An organization's obligation to maximize its positive impact and minimize its negative impact on society.

corporate volunteerism The policy or practice of employees volunteering their time or talents for charitable, educational, or other worthwhile activities, especially in the community.

country-of-origin effects The beliefs and associations people in one country have about goods and services produced in another country.

coupons Documents that entitle the customers who carry them to a discount on a product.

CRM system A set of information technology tools used to help companies stay connected to customers and prospects, streamline processes, and improve profitability.

cross-merchandising A category-management technique in which a retailer carries complementary goods and services to encourage shoppers to buy more.

cross-tabulation A data analysis technique that enables someone to examine responses to one question in relation to responses from one or more other questions.

crowdsourcing The practice of getting ideas by soliciting contributions from a large, online group of people rather than the traditional way of obtaining them from employees.

culture The broad set of knowledge, beliefs, laws, morals, customs, and any other capabilities or habits acquired by humans as members of society.

currency exchange rate The price of one country's currency in terms of another country's currency.

customer communication The two-way information flow between the firm and its customer.

customer communication metrics Measurements of a firm's effectiveness in communicating with customers at the pre-transaction, transaction, and post-transaction points.

customer equity A ratio that compares the financial investments a company puts into gaining and keeping customers to the financial return on those investments.

customer focus A measure of the extent to which a company puts effort into servicing its customers' needs, based on an understanding of each customer's profitability.

customer journey map A visual representation of the process a customer or prospect goes through to achieve a goal with a company.

customer journey map A diagram that illustrates the physical and emotional steps customers go through when engaging with a company's touchpoint in order to achieve a particular goal.

customer lifetime value (CLV) The total amount a customer will spend from acquisition through the end of a relationship with a brand.

customer relationship management (CRM) The process by which companies get new customers, keep the customers they already have, and grow the business by increasing their share of customers' purchases.

customer satisfaction A state that is achieved when companies meet the needs and expectations customers have for their goods or services.

customer segmentation analysis A method of analyzing data that creates customer profiles and categorizes them.

customer service All of the activities a firm engages in to satisfy the needs and wants of its customers.

customer success manager A sales support position that is typically charged with successful onboarding of new customers, identifying account growth opportunities, and ensuring long-term client retention.

customer value The perceived benefits, both monetary and nonmonetary, that a customer receives from a product compared with the cost of obtaining it.

customer-oriented selling The adoption of the marketing concept at the level of the individual salesperson and customer.

dashboard A digital tool that provides data visualizations that enable marketing managers to assess performance over time across a range of relevant KPIs.

data mining A process that involves the computerized search for meaningful trends in a large amount of data.

data visualization The presentation of data and research results in pictorial or graphical format.

deceptive pricing An illegal practice that involves intentionally misleading customers with price promotions.

decision support system (DSS) A computer program that enables access and use of the information stored in the data warehouse.

decline stage The stage of the product life cycle characterized by decreases in sales and profits.

delivery salespeople Sales representatives whose chief role is product delivery; sometimes called *route salespeople*.

demand analysis A type of research used to estimate how much customer demand there is for a particular product and understand the factors driving that demand.

demographic segmentation Segmentation that divides markets by characteristics such as age, gender, income, education, and family size.

demographics The characteristics of human populations that can be used to identify consumer markets.

department stores Merchandise outlets that carry a wide variety of product lines, with each line operated as a separate department and managed by specialist merchandisers and buyers.

depth interview A data-collection tool in which the researcher, working with one participant at a time, asks open-ended questions about how the individual perceives and uses various products or brands.

depth of assortment The number of individual items offered within any single product line.

derived demand Demand for one product that occurs because of demand for a related product.

descriptive research A type of marketing research that seeks to understand consumer behavior by answering the questions who, what, when, where, and how.

design thinking Design thinking is a process that encourages organizations to focus on the people they're creating products for.

differentiated targeting A targeting strategy that simultaneously pursues several different market segments, usually with a different strategy for each.

diffusion The process by which a product is adopted and spreads across various types of adopters.

digital marketing The marketing of goods or services using digital media, such as e-mail, websites, search engines, and social media platforms.

direct competition A situation in which products that perform the same function compete against one another. Also called *category competition* or *brand competition*

direct marketing Advertising that communicates directly with consumers and organizations in an effort to provoke a response.

direct ownership A method of entering an international market in which a domestic firm actively manages a foreign company or overseas facilities.

direct selling Retailing in which an independent representative of a company conducts retail and sales-related activities away from a fixed retail location, most often at consumers' homes or place of business. Also known as *direct retailing*.

discount stores General merchandise outlets that offer brand-name and private-label products at low prices.

disintermediation Elimination of intermediaries, such as distribution centers, in the delivery of products from a producer to a consumer.

disintermediation Elimination of intermediaries, such as distribution centers, in the delivery of products from a producer to a consumer.

disposable income The amount of spending money available to households after paying taxes.

disruptive technology A technology that displaces an established technology and shakes up the industry, or a groundbreaking product that creates a completely new industry.

dissociative reference groups The people that the individual would *not* like to be like.

distribution center (DC) A type of warehouse used specifically to store and ship finished goods to customers.

diversification A marketing strategy that seeks to attract new customers by offering new products that are unrelated to the existing products produced by the organization.

dollar fill rate A metric that measures the value of goods shipped on time versus the total value of the order.

Dominican Republic–Central America Free Trade Agreement (DR-CAFTA) An international agreement that eliminated tariffs, reduced nontariff barriers, and facilitated investment among the United States, Costa Rica, El Salvador, Guatemala, Honduras, Nicaragua, and the Dominican Republic.

dumping A protectionist strategy in which a company sells its exports to another country at a lower price than it sells the same product in its domestic market.

dynamic pricing A pricing tactic that involves constantly updating prices to reflect changes in supply, demand, or market conditions.

e-mail marketing Highly targeted, personalized, relationship-building e-mail messages.

early adopters A category of consumers that purchase and use a product soon after it has been introduced, but not as quickly as innovators.

early majority A category of consumers that gather more information and spend more time deciding to make a purchase than innovators and early adopters.

ease of doing business The amount of effort required on the part of a customer when dealing with a firm.

elastic demand Demand for which a given percentage change in price results in an even larger percentage change in quantity demanded.

empowerment Giving employees permission to make decisions and take action on their own to help customers.

environmental regulations The laws designed to protect the natural environment against undue harm by individuals and organizations.

environmental scanning The act of monitoring developments outside the firm's control with the goal of detecting and responding to threats and opportunities.

environmentalism A movement of citizens, government agencies, and the business community that advocates the preservation, restoration, and improvement of the natural environment.

escalator clause A section in a contract that provides for price increases if certain, specified conditions occur.

esteem The need all humans have to be respected by others as well as by themselves.

ethics The moral standards expected by a society.

ethnographic research A data-collection method that sends trained observers to watch and interact with a subject population in their natural environment.

European Union (EU) An economic, political, and monetary union among 27 European nations that created a single European market by reducing barriers to the free trade of goods, services, and finances.

evaluative criteria The attributes a consumer considers important about a certain product.

even pricing Pricing tactic that sets prices at even dollar amounts.

evoked set The brands or products a person will evaluate as options for the solution of a particular consumer problem. Also known as a *consideration set*.

exchange An activity that occurs when a buyer and seller trade things of value so that each is better off as a result.

exploratory research A type of marketing research that seeks to discover new insights that will help the firm better understand the problem or consumer thoughts, needs, and behavior.

exporting Selling domestically produced products to foreign markets.

extended problem solving Consumer decisions requiring considerable cognitive activity, thought, and behavioral effort.

external information search Consumers' search for information beyond their personal knowledge and experience, to support them in their buying decision.

extreme-value retailers Stores that carry an assortment of inexpensive and popularly priced merchandise; heirs to the traditional Main Street "five-and-dime" variety stores from decades past.

facial coding The categorization of facial expressions to reveal the emotional response of an individual while processing content.

fad product A product that is very popular for a relatively short amount of time.

fashion product A product that comes in and out of favor with consumers.

fast fashion The rapid translation of high-fashion design trends by lower-cost manufacturer-retailers.

fear of missing out (FOMO) A feeling of isolation and concern about missing out on what is occurring in the world around us.

feature-advantage-benefit (FAB) approach Sales approach that conveys the product's major features, describes its advantages compared with alternatives, and details the benefits it will provide the customer.

features In the FAB sales approach, attributes or facts relating to the product being sold or demonstrated.

Federal Trade Commission (FTC) The consumer protection agency for the United States.

Federal Trade Commission Act (FTCA) A law passed in 1914 that established the Federal Trade Commission and sought to prevent practices that may cause injury to customers, that cannot be reasonably avoided by customers, and that cannot be justified by other outcomes that may benefit the consumer or the idea of free competition.

field experiment A study that examines the impact of an intervention in the real world.

fill rate A metric that measures the percentage of an order shipped on time and complete.

financial projections A bottom-line numerical estimate of the organization's profitability.

fixed costs Costs that remain constant and do not vary based on the number of units produced or sold.

focus group Data-collection tool in which a moderator engages a small group of people as they discuss a particular topic or concept with each other in a spontaneous way.

franchising A contractual arrangement in which the franchisor provides a franchisee the right to use its name and marketing and operational support in exchange for a fee and, typically, a share of the profits.

frequency A measure of how often the target market has been exposed to a promotional message during a specific time period.

full-line discount stores General merchandise outlets that carry a wide assortment of merchandise across popular categories.

gaining commitment Asking a sales prospect to move forward with the sales process, ultimately leading to a purchase.

gamification The application of typical elements of game playing (e.g., point scoring, competition with others, rules of play) to other areas of activity, typically as an online marketing technique to encourage engagement with a product or service.

geofencing A location-based technology that uses small sensors to send messages to smartphone users who enter a nearby, defined geographic area.

geographic segmentation Segmentation that divides markets into groups such as nations, regions, states, and neighborhoods.

global brand A brand that is marketed under the same name in multiple countries.

global marketing A marketing strategy that consciously addresses customers, markets, and competition throughout the world.

global segmentation Segmentation that identifies a group of consumers with common needs and wants that spans the entire globe.

gray market The sale of branded products through legal but unauthorized distribution channels.

green market A group of sustainability-oriented customers and the businesses that serve them.

gross domestic product (GDP) A measure of the market value of all officially recognized final goods and services produced within a country in a given period.

growth stage The stage of the product life cycle characterized by increases in sales, profits, and competition.

habitual decision making Consumer decisions made out of "habit," without much deliberation or product comparison.

heat map Colored regions overlaid on an image; the most frequently offered eye-tracking output.

high-involvement products Significant purchases that carry a greater risk to consumers if they fail.

high-learning products Products that take longer for consumers to see the benefits of or that do not have a good infrastructure in place to support them.

hybrid (push-pull) strategy A supply chain strategy in which the initial stages of the supply chain operate on a push system, but completion of the product is based on a pull system.

idea generation The stage of new-product development in which a set of product concepts is generated from which to identify potentially viable new products.

idea screening The stage of new-product development in which the firm evaluates ideas to determine their fit within the new-product strategy.

impulse purchases Purchases that occur when a consumer sees an item in-store and purchases it, with little or no deliberation, as the result of a sudden, powerful urge to have it.

indirect competition A process in which products provide alternative solutions to the same market.

inelastic demand Demand for which a given percentage change in price results in a smaller percentage change in quantity demanded.

inflation An increase in the general level of prices of products in an economy over a period of time.

informative advertising A type of advertising that attempts to develop initial demand for a product.

informed consent Permission granted in the knowledge of the possible consequences.

innovators A category of consumers that adopt a product almost immediately after it is launched.

integrated marketing communications (IMC) A promotional strategy that involves coordinating the various promotion-mix elements to provide consumers with a clear and consistent message about a firm's products.

intermodal transport Using multiple types of transportation for the same shipment.

internal information search Consumers' use of past experiences with items from the same brand or product class as sources of information.

International Monetary Fund (IMF) An international organization that works to foster international monetary cooperation, secure financial stability, facilitate international trade, promote high employment and sustainable economic growth, and reduce poverty around the world.

introduction stage The stage of the product life cycle that occurs after the firm launches the product into the marketplace and innovators begin to buy it.

inventory carrying costs The costs required to make or buy a product, including risk of obsolescence, taxes, insurance, and warehousing space used to store the goods.

involvement The personal, financial, and social significance of the decision being made.

isolated store A freestanding retail outlet located on either a highway or major road.

item fill rate A metric that measures the percentage of the total number of items on the order that the firm shipped on time.

joint venture An arrangement in which a domestic firm partners with a foreign company to create a new entity, thus allowing the domestic firm to enter the foreign company's market.

key-account sellers Sales representatives who focus on establishing and maintaining partnership relationships with a small set of three to five named accounts.

laggards A category of consumers that do not like change and may remain loyal to a product until it is no longer available for sale.

late majority A category of consumers that rely on others for information, buying a good or service because others have already done so.

lead scoring Analytics-based sales approach in which a company numerically rates its best prospective customers.

leased department A section within a retail store that is rented to an outside party.

licensing A legal process in which one firm pays to use or distribute another firm's resources, including products, trademarks, patents, intellectual property, or other proprietary knowledge.

lifestyle A person's typical way of life as expressed by their activities, interests, and opinions.

lifestyle segmentation Segmentation that divides people into groups based on their opinions and the interests and activities they pursue.

lifetime value The net present value of a customer's business over the span of his or her relationship with an organization.

lifetime value (LTV) analysis A comparison of the costs of retaining customers and the costs of acquiring new customers, to determine how much money each type of customer requires.

limited problem solving Refers to situations in which the consumer has established basic criteria for evaluating the product category, but is unfamiliar with suppliers, product options, prices, and so on.

line fill rate A metric that measures the percentage of item types (SKUs) on the order shipped on time and complete.

location-based marketing (LBM) The use of GPS data transmitted from a mobile device to adapt content, messaging, or service delivery to a target's location.

logistics That part of supply chain management that plans, implements, and controls the flow of goods, services, and information between the point of origin and the final customer.

logistics operations The functional areas of a supply chain that sources materials and finished goods, warehouses and manages inventories of those products, moves those products within stages of a supply chain, and handles the distribution of products to business customers or consumers.

loss-leader pricing A pricing tactic that involves selling a product at a price that causes the firm a financial loss.

low-involvement products Inexpensive products that can be purchased without much forethought and that are purchased with some frequency.

low-learning products Products with benefits customers can easily see.

loyalty programs Sales promotions that allow consumers to accumulate points or other benefits for doing business with the same company.

manufacturer brands Brands that are managed and owned by the manufacturer.

marginal cost The change in total cost that results from producing one additional unit of product.

marginal revenue The change in total revenue that results from selling one additional unit of product.

market development A marketing strategy that focuses on selling existing goods and services to new customers.

market penetration A marketing strategy that emphasizes selling more of existing goods and services to existing customers.

market segmentation The process of dividing a larger market into smaller groups, or market segments, based on meaningfully shared characteristics.

market segments The groups of consumers who have shared characteristics and similar product needs.

market share analysis Marketing analytics tool that measures the percentage of total market sales captured by a brand, product, or firm.

market summary A description of the current state of the market.

market-related knowledge An understanding of the goods, services, and processes within one's firm and of key business issues that affect the customer's success.

marketing The activity, set of institutions, and processes for creating, communicating, delivering, and exchanging offerings that have value for customers, clients, partners, and society at large.

marketing analytics The practice of measuring, managing, and analyzing market performance.

marketing concept The idea that a firm's long-term success must include a companywide effort to satisfy customer needs and wants.

marketing environment The outside factors and forces that affect a company's ability to meet its marketing goals. Those forces include political, economic, demographic, sociocultural, technological, and legal factors.

marketing information system The people, technologies, and procedures aimed at supplying an organization's marketing information needs. Such a system assesses those needs, develops the needed information, and helps decision makers use information to create and validate actionable customer insights.

marketing information system Consists of the people, technologies, and procedures aimed at supplying an organization's marketing information needs.

marketing mix A combination of activities that represent everything a firm can do to influence demand for its good, service, or idea; often referred to as the four Ps of marketing (product, price, place, and promotion).

marketing plan An action-oriented document or playbook that guides the analysis, implementation, and control of the firm's marketing strategy.

marketing research Organizational activity that links the consumer, customer, and public to the marketer through information. The organization uses that information to identify and define marketing opportunities and problems; generate, refine, and evaluate marketing actions; monitor marketing performance; and improve understanding of marketing as a process.

markup pricing A pricing method in which a certain amount is added to the cost of the product, to set the final price; also called *cost-plus pricing*.

materials management The inbound movement and storage of materials in preparation for those materials to enter and flow through the manufacturing process.

maturity stage The stage of the product life cycle during which the firm focuses on profitability and maintaining the firm's market share for as long as possible.

membership reference group The group to which a consumer actually belongs.

merchandise planner Retail management position responsible for planning, controlling, and monitoring the purchase, intake, and distribution of merchandise to stores.

merchandising The activities involved in acquiring particular goods and services and making them available at the places, times, prices, and quantities that enable a retailer to achieve its goals.

micro-merchandising A category-management technique in which a retailer adjusts its shelf-space allocations in response to overall consumer demand as well as differences in local markets.

microexpressi on A brief, involuntary facial expression that appears on a person's face according to the emotions being experienced.

Millennials The generation born between 1978 and the late twentieth century. Also known as *Generation Y*.

mission statement A concise affirmation of the firm's long-term purpose.

missionary salespeople Sales representatives who generate sales by promoting the firm and encouraging demand for its products.

mobile advertising Advertising that is communicated to the consumer via a handheld device.

mobile commerce Refers to consumers use of Internet-enabled mobile devices to conduct business or shop online.

mobile marketing research Research that involves participants taking part in marketing research via mobile devices.

mobile payment Payment services performed from or via a mobile device, and operated under financial regulation. Also called *digital wallets*.

modified rebuy A buying situation in which the customer's needs change slightly or they are not completely satisfied with the product they purchased.

moment of truth A critical touchpoint within a customer journey when a key event occurs and a lasting impression about the brand is formed.

motivation The inward drive we have to get what we need or want.

mystery shoppers Trained researchers hired to pose as customers in order to gather information about the physical appearance or customer service attributes of a store.

name-your-own-price (NYOP) auction A pricing tactic in which the consumer submits a bid at the price he or she is willing to pay for a product or service, and the auction site conducts a search to find matches with prices set by participating suppliers.

narrowcasting The dissemination of information to a fairly small, select audience that is defined by its shared values, preferences, or demographic attributes.

near-shoring Sourcing materials and finished products from countries that are close to, but not in, an organization's own country.

near-shoring The process of sourcing materials and finished products from countries that are close to, but not in, an organization's own country.

needs States of felt deprivation. Consumers feel that deprivation when they lack something useful or desirable like food, clothing, shelter, transportation, or safety.

neuromarketing The use of insights and tools from neuroscience to better understand consumer responses to different kinds of marketing stimuli.

new buy A buying situation in which a business customer is purchasing a product for the very first time.

new-business salespeople Sales representatives who are responsible primarily for finding new customers and securing their business.

new-category entries Products that are new to a company but not new to the marketplace.

new-product development (NPD) The process of conceiving, testing, and launching a new product in the marketplace.

new-product strategy development The stage of new-product development in which the company determines the direction it will take when it develops a new product.

new-to-the-market products Inventions that have never before been seen and create a new market.

niche marketing A targeting strategy that involves pursuing a large share of a small market segment.

nonprobability sampling A type of sampling that does not attempt to ensure that every member of the target population has a chance of being selected.

norms Formal or informal societal rules that specify or prohibit certain behaviors in specific situations.

North American Free Trade Agreement (NAFTA) An international agreement that established a free-trade zone among the United States, Canada, and Mexico.

North American Industry Classification System (NAICS) An industry-classification system used by the members of NAFTA (the United States, Canada, and Mexico) to generate comparable statistics for businesses and industries across the three countries.

objections The concerns or reasons customers offer for not buying a product.

objective-and-task method A promotion-mix budgeting strategy in which a firm defines specific objectives, determines the tasks required to achieve those objectives, and then estimates how much each task will cost.

observation research A data-collection tool that involves watching how people behave and recording anything about that behavior that might be relevant to the research objective.

odd pricing A pricing tactic in which a firm prices products a few cents below the next dollar amount.

off-price retail stores Stores that feature brand-name (sometimes designer) merchandise bought at less-than-regular wholesale prices and sold at less-than-retail prices.

offshore An organization that is located or based in a foreign country.

omnichannel A type of retail that offers different methods of shopping and delivery of products to consumers (e.g., online or in a physical store).

omnichannel retailing The retailing practice of integrating customer experiences across the physical and online channels.

on-shoring The process of sourcing materials and finished products from suppliers in an organization's own country.

on-time delivery A metric that measures how many shipments are delivered per the requested delivery date.

online retailing B2C electronic commerce in which individual consumers directly buy goods or services over the Internet; also known as *e-retailing*.

open innovation A way of generating new-product ideas by gathering both external ideas and internal ideas.

opinion leaders Individuals who exert an unequal amount of influence on the decisions of others because they are considered knowledgeable about particular products.

opportunities (in SWOT analysis) External factors that the firm may be able to capitalize on to meet or exceed its stated objectives.

order cycle The total amount of time that elapses from the time a customer places an order until the time the product is delivered to the customer.

order cycle time A metric that measures the length of the order cycle, or the ability of the order system to react to customer orders.

order-taker salespeople Sales representatives who primarily process orders that a customer initiates.

original equipment manufacturer (OEM) A producer whose products are used as components or subsystems in another firm's products.

outsource To procure goods, services, or ideas from a third-party supplier rather than from an internal source.

packaging All of the activities of designing and producing the container for a product.

paid listings Purchased links that typically appear either at the very top or upper right of a search results page.

panel data Information collected from a group (or panel) of consumers over a period of time.

percentage-of-sales method A promotion-mix budgeting strategy in which firms allocate a specific percentage of a period's sales to the promotion budget for that period.

perception The psychological process by which people select, organize, and interpret sensory information to form a meaningful picture of the world.

perceptual map A competitive analysis tool that creates a visual picture of product locations in consumers' minds.

perfect order rate A metric that measures how many orders have been filled, delivered, and billed without error.

persona A semi-fictional profile representing the key traits and motivations of a key segment of a brand's customer base.

personal selling The two-way flow of communication between a salesperson and a customer that is paid for by the firm and seeks to influence the customer's purchase decision.

personal selling process A sequence of seven steps that salespeople follow to acquire new customers and obtain orders: prospecting and qualifying, pre-approach, approach, presentation, handling objections, gaining commitment, and follow-up.

personality The set of distinctive characteristics that lead an individual to respond in a consistent way to certain situations.

persuasive advertising A type of advertising that attempts to increase demand for an existing product.

picking Retrieving materials from storage and bringing them to manufacturing to fulfill a production order, or retrieving finished goods from storage and preparing them for shipment to fulfill a customer order.

place As one of the "four Ps," includes the activities the firm undertakes to make its product available to potential customers. Also known as *distribution*.

planned shopping center A group of architecturally unique business establishments on a site that is centrally owned or managed.

positioning The activities a firm undertakes to create a certain perception of its product in the eyes of the target market.

positioning statement A succinct description of the core target market to which a product is directed and a compelling picture of how the firm wants that core market to view the product.

posttest An evaluation of advertisements after the ad campaign is launched by a sample of targeted consumers.

pre-approach The stage in the personal selling process in which the salesperson does research and preparation before contacting the customer.

predatory pricing The practice of first setting prices low with the intention of pushing competitors out of the market or keeping new competitors from entering the market, and then raising prices to normal levels.

predictive analytics Is an umbrella term for a set of statistical tools, techniques and algorithms that enable organizations to recognize patterns in their data and make predictions about the future.

predictive modeling Analysis that uses statistical techniques and algorithms based on patterns of past behavior to predict the future unknown events, such as future buying behavior.

premium A promotional item that is given as an incentive for performing a particular act, typically buying a product.

prestige pricing A pricing tactic that involves pricing a product higher than competitors to signal that it is of higher quality.

pretest An evaluation of advertisements by a sample of targeted consumers before an ad campaign begins.

price The amount of something—money, time, or effort—that a buyer exchanges with a seller to obtain a product.

price bundling A pricing tactic in which two or more products are packaged together and sold at a single price.

price discrimination The practice of charging different customers different prices for the same product.

price elasticity of demand A measure of price sensitivity that gives the percentage change in quantity demanded in response to a percentage change in price (holding constant all the other determinants of demand, such as income).

price fixing When two or more companies collude to set a product's price.

price sensitivity The degree to which the price of a product affects consumers' purchasing behavior.

primary data Data collected specifically for the research problem at hand.

private-label brands Products developed by a retailer and sold only by that specific retailer. Also referred to as *store brands*.

probability sampling A type of sampling in which every person in the target population has a chance of being selected, and the probability of each person being selected is known.

problem recognition The stage of the buying process in which consumers recognize a gap between their current situation and a desired end-state.

product The specific combination of goods, services, or ideas that a firm offers to consumers.

product development A marketing strategy that involves creating new goods and services for existing markets.

product development stage The stage of new-product development at which a firm determines that the good can be produced or the service can be offered in a way that meets customer needs and generates profits.

product distribution franchise Business organization in which the franchisee gains preferred or exclusive access to the products manufactured or supplied by the franchisor, but not the franchisor's system of doing business.

product launch Completing all the final preparations for making the fully tested product available to the market.

product life cycle (PLC) The series of stages a product goes through from the time it is launched into the market until the time it is removed from the market.

product line A group of related products marketed by the same firm.

product mix The combination of all the products a company sells.

product placement An advertising technique in which a company promotes its products through appearances in movies or on television shows or other media.

product-line extensions Products that extend and supplement a company's established product line.

production orientation A marketing strategy in which the firm focused on efficient processes and production to create quality products and reduce unit costs.

profit margin The amount a product sells for above the total cost of the product itself.

profit maximization A pricing objective that involves setting a relatively high price for a period of time after the product launches.

profitability analysis Marketing analytics tool that measures how much profit the firm generates, as well as how much profit certain aspects of the firm, including regions, channels, and customer segments, contribute.

profits Revenue minus total costs.

promotion All the activities that communicate the value of a product and persuade customers to buy it.

promotion mix A subset of the marketing mix that includes four main elements of marketing communication: advertising, sales promotion, personal selling, and public relations.

prospect An individual (or group) capable of making the decision on a good or service a salesperson is selling.

prospecting The search for potential customers.

prototype A mock-up of a good, often created individually with the materials the firm expects to use in the final product.

psychographic segmentation Segmentation that divides markets using demographics, psychology, and personality traits.

public relations Nonpersonal communication focused on promoting positive relations between a firm and its stakeholders.

publicity Disseminating unpaid news items through some form of media (e.g., television story, newspaper article, etc.) to gain attention or support.

pull strategy A supply chain strategy in which customer orders drive manufacturing and distribution operations.

purchase order A legal obligation to buy from a supplier a certain amount of product, at a certain price, to be delivered at a specified date.

purchasing power A measure of the amount of goods and services that can be purchased for a specific amount of money.

push strategy A supply chain strategy in which a company builds goods based on a sales forecast, puts those goods into storage, and waits for a customer to order the product.

put-away Moving goods to their temporary or semipermanent storage location and updating inventory records.

qualifying Identifying potential customers within the firm's target market who have a desire for the product, the authority to purchase it, and the resources to pay for it.

qualitative research Research approaches that address business questions through techniques that permit researchers to offer detailed interpretations of market phenomena without depending on numerical measurement.

quasi-strategic greening A type of environmental marketing activity that involves substantive changes in marketing actions as well as broad-based coordination among nonmarketing activities.

reach A measure of the percentage of the target market that has been exposed to a promotional message at least once during a specific time period.

rebates Sales promotions that allow consumers to recoup a specified amount of money after making a single purchase; most rebates require consumers to mail their receipt and proof of purchase to manufacturers.

recency-frequency-monetary analysis A method of analyzing data that categorize customers by their buying patterns.

recession A period of time during which overall gross domestic product (GDP) declines for two or more consecutive quarters.

recognition test A performance metric that involves showing consumers an advertisement and asking if they recognize it.

reference group A collection of people to whom a consumer compares himself or herself.

reference prices The prices that consumers consider reasonable and fair for a product.

regional segmentation Segmentation that divides consumers into groups whose needs and wants extend across the region or several countries.

relationship marketing A marketing strategy that focuses on attracting, maintaining, and enhancing customer relationships.

relationship selling A sales approach that involves building and maintaining customer trust over a long period of time.

reliability The company's ability to ensure that customers will receive a good or service within a stated lead time and that there will be no problems with the order.

reliability (of research) The ability of a measurement instrument to produce almost identical results over repeated trials.

reminder advertising A type of advertising that seeks to keep the product before the public in an effort to reinforce previous promotional activity.

reminder purchases Purchases that occur due to retailers' prompts to consumers while consumers are in the store.

repositioning The act of reestablishing a product's position in response to changes in the marketplace.

request for proposal (RFP) Specifies what the customer is looking for and describes each evaluation criterion on which a vendor's proposal will be assessed.

resellers Retailers and wholesalers that buy finished goods and resell them for a profit.

resilience The ability of a company to anticipate, prepare for, and effectively respond to supply chain disruptions.

responsiveness A metric that measures the firm's ability and willingness to provide fast service, answer customer inquiries, and resolve problems.

retailer A company that sells goods to consumers for their use, rather than for resale to others.

retailer cooperative A group of independent retailers that band together to set up a jointly owned, central wholesale operation that also conducts joint merchandising and promotion.

retailing All of the business activities involved in the sales of goods and services to an end consumer for their personal, family, or household use.

return on marketing investment (ROMI) A measure of the firm's effectiveness in using the resources allocated to its marketing effort.

revamped product A product that has new packaging, different features, and updated designs and functions.

revenue The result of the price charged to customers multiplied by the number of units sold.

revenue analysis Marketing analytics tool that measures and evaluates revenue from specific products or regions.

revenue per ad dollar A performance metric that is calculated by comparing total revenue to the amount of money spent on advertising.

Robinson–Patman Act A law passed in 1936 that requires sellers to charge everyone the same price for a product; also called the *Anti-Price Discrimination Act.*

sales enablement The process of providing the sales organization with the information, content, and tools that help salespeople sell more effectively.

sales engineers Technical specialists who work in high-tech sectors and typically have educational backgrounds in fields like engineering, computer science, and physics.

sales force management The planning, direction, and control of personal selling activities, including recruitment, selection, training, motivating, compensation, and evaluation as they apply to the sales force.

sales forecasting A form of research that estimates how much of a product will sell over a given period of time.

sales orientation A marketing strategy in which personal selling and advertising are used to persuade consumers to buy new products and more of existing products.

sales promotion A set of nonpersonal communication tools designed to stimulate quicker and more frequent purchases of a product.

sampling The process of selecting a subset of the population that is representative of the population as a whole.

scanner data Data obtained from scanner readings of UPC codes at checkout counters.

scrambled merchandising Selling goods and services that may be unrelated to each other and to the firm's original business.

search engine marketing (SEM) The process of generating website traffic by purchasing advertisements on search engines.

search engine optimization (SEO) Adjusting or rewriting website content and site architecture to achieve a higher ranking in search engine results pages to enhance pay per click (PPC) listings.

search marketing A form of Internet marketing that promotes websites by increasing their visibility in search engine results pages.

seasonal discounts Price reductions given to customers purchasing goods or services out of season.

secondary data Information collected for alternative purposes prior to the study.

self-actualization A person's full potential and the need to realize that potential.

selling-related knowledge Sales abilities and an understanding of selling techniques.

semi-structured interview Interview technique that asks respondents for a short essay response to a series of specific open-ended questions.

sensation The physical process during which our sensory organs—those involved with hearing, smell, sight, touch, and taste—respond to external stimuli.

sensory marketing Marketing that engages consumers' senses and affects their behaviors.

sentiment analysis or opinion mining The analysis of the feelings (attitudes, emotions, and opinions) behind the words, using natural language processing tools.

share of customer A measure of the quantity of purchase dollars each customer spends on the company's products.

Sherman Antitrust Act A law passed in 1890 to eliminate monopolies and guarantee competition.

shop-at-home television networks A type of specialty television channel in which on-air presenters provide live demonstration and sales pitches for merchandise that viewers can buy online or by phone.

shrinkflation The process of items shrinking in size or quantity while their prices remain the same or increase.

simple random sampling A type of sampling in which everyone in the target population has an *equal* chance of being selected.

simulated test markets A procedure in which the firm builds a mock shopping experience for participants, in order to observe their response to marketing stimuli.

situation analysis The systematic collection of data to identify the trends, conditions, and competitive forces that have the potential to influence the performance of the firm and the choice of appropriate strategies.

situational influences Factors like time and involvement that serve as an interface between consumers and their decision-making process.

slotting allowances Payments made by manufacturers to retailers to ensure that products are preferentially displayed by the retailer.

social media Internet-based applications that enable users to create their own content and share it with others who access these sites.

social media influencer Someone who has built a loyal following through their online content creation.

social media marketing Use of social media and social networking platforms by companies in order build relationships with customers and promote their products and services.

social media monitoring (social listening) The process of identifying and assessing what is being said about a company, individual, product, or brand on the Internet.

social media platforms Web-based technologies that enable a company to build and manage social media solutions and services.

social network A set of social actors (such as individuals or organizations) along with the set of ties between each pair of actors.

social selling The use of online, mobile, and social media to engage customers, build strong customer relationships, and increase sales.

sociocultural The combination of social and cultural factors that affect individual development.

specialty discount stores General merchandise outlets that offer a wide selection of merchandise within a single category.

specialty store A store that concentrates on selling one line of goods or services and carries a narrow but deep merchandise assortment.

stakeholder responsibility The obligations an organization has to its stakeholders, those who can affect or are affected by a firm's actions.

stimulus A detectable change in the internal or external environment that can elicit or evoke a physiological response from an organism.

stock-keeping unit (SKU) A distinct item available for sale within a retail store or e-commerce website.

stockout A situation in which a company does not have enough inventory available to fill an order.

straight rebuy A buying situation in which a business customer signals its satisfaction by agreeing to purchase the same product at the same price.

strategic greening A type of environmental marketing activity that integrates and coordinates all of the firm's activities on environmental issues across every functional area.

strategic plan An organization's plans for key functional areas, such as marketing, human resources, finance, and risk management.

strategic planning The process of thoughtfully defining a firm's objectives and developing a method for achieving those objectives.

strategy The set of actions taken to accomplish organizational objectives.

strengths (in SWOT analysis) Internal capabilities that help the company achieve its objectives.

subculture A segment of a larger culture whose members share distinguishing values and patterns of behavior.

substitute products Goods and services that perform very similar functions and can be used in place of one another.

supercenter format Full-line discount store format that includes grocery, pharmacy, and services.

supermarkets Merchandise outlets that carry a wide and complex line of groceries, meat, dairy, produce, and baked goods plus a limited array of nonfood products.

supply chain The linked set of companies that perform or support the delivery of a company's goods or services to customers.

supply chain management The actions the firm takes to coordinate the various flows within a supply chain.

supply chain orientation A management philosophy that guides the actions of company members toward the goal of actively managing the upstream and downstream flows of goods, services, finances, and information across the supply chain.

supply chain process integration When companies work *collaboratively* both internally (between functions) and externally (between companies) to provide value to the final consumer.

survey A method of collecting primary data based on communication with a representative sample of individuals.

survival pricing A pricing objective that involves lowering prices to the point at which revenue just covers costs, allowing the firm to endure during a difficult time.

sustainability A commitment to a lifestyle that meets the needs of the present without compromising the ability of future generations to meet their own needs.

sustainable design The philosophy of building products and services in a way that eliminates negative environmental impacts.

sustainable design The philosophy of building goods and services in a way that eliminates negative environmental impacts.

sustainable marketing The process of creating, communicating, and delivering value to customers in a way that recognizes and incorporates the concept of sustainability.

sustainable sourcing A process of purchasing goods and services that takes into account the long-term impact on people, profits, and planet.

sustainable sourcing The process of purchasing goods and services that takes into account the long-term impact on people, profits, and planet.

sustainable tourism The practice of recreational traveling in a way that maximizes the social and economic benefits to the local community and minimizes the negative impact on cultural heritage and the environment.

sweepstakes Sales promotions based on chance such that entry is the only requirement to win.

SWOT analysis An evaluation of a firm's **s**trengths, **w**eaknesses, **o**pportunities, and **t**hreats.

tactical greening A type of environmental marketing activity that involves implementing limited change within a single area of the organization.

target market The group of customers toward which an organization has decided to direct its marketing efforts.

targeting Evaluating each market segment to determine which segments present the most attractive opportunity to maximize sales.

tariffs Taxes on imports and exports between countries.

test marketing Introducing a new product in its final form to a geographically limited market to see how well the product sells and to get reactions from potential users.

threats (in SWOT analysis) Current and potential external factors that may challenge the firm's short- and long-term performance.

time to market The speed with which a company launches a product.

timeliness The ability of a company to deliver a good or service by the time a customer expects to have it available for sale or consumption.

touch point Any point at which a customer and the company come into contact.

trade sales promotions Sales promotions directed to B2B firms, including wholesalers, retailers, and distributors, rather than individual consumers.

transparency Involves opening up the company to the outside world by making its practices, policies, and future plans available to customers.

trialability The extent to which a potential customer can examine the merits of a new product without having to spend a lot of money or time doing so.

triple bottom line (TBL) A framework for analyzing sustainability that includes economic, social, and environmental impacts of a new product.

unaided recall test A performance metric that requires consumers to recall advertisements from memory, without any clues.

unbundling Separating out the individual goods, services, or ideas that make up a product and pricing each one individually.

underpricing Charging someone less than they are willing to pay.

undifferentiated targeting A targeting strategy that approaches the marketplace as one large segment.

unique segmentation Segmentation that targets the preferences of a group of consumers with similar needs and wants only within one country.

United States–Mexico–Canada Agreement (USMCA) A trade agreement between the United States, Mexico, and Canada passed in 2018 that supports free trade among those countries.

unplanned business district A type of retail location where two or more stores are situated together or in close proximity.

unplanned purchases Purchases made in a retail outlet that are different from those the consumer planned prior to entering the store.

user-generated content Content created by a brand's fans and followers.

validity The extent to which a research instrument measures what it is intended to measure.

values A consumer's belief that specific behaviors are socially or personally preferable to other behaviors.

variable costs Costs that vary depending on the number of units produced or sold.

video marketing The posting of digital video content on brand websites or social media sites such as YouTube, Facebook, and others.

virtual reality (VR) An interactive, computer-generated experience that takes place within an immersive simulated environment, typically incorporating multisensory feedback.

virtual selling A collection of processes and technologies by which salespeople engage with their customers remotely, using both synchronous and asynchronous communications.

visual merchandiser A retail professional that develops layout plans and displays aimed at improving store sales by highlighting select items using visually appealing displays.

volume maximization A pricing objective that involves setting prices low to encourage a greater volume of purchases; also called *penetration pricing*.

wants The form that human needs take as they are shaped by personality, culture, and buying situation.

warehouse clubs Merchandise outlets that operate in warehouse-like facilities that offer merchandise in bulk quantities, at ultra-low prices, to shoppers who pay an annual fee to join; also known as *wholesale clubs* or *membership warehouses*.

weaknesses (in SWOT analysis) Internal limitations that may prevent or disrupt the firm's ability to meet its stated objectives.

Wheeler–Lea Act An amendment to the Federal Trade Commission Act passed in 1938 that removed the burden of proving that unfair and deceptive practices had to injure competition; also called the *Advertising Act*.

white paper A concise yet authoritative report or guide that seeks to inform readers about a complex issue and presents the issuing body's philosophy on the matter.

wholesaler A company that sells to other businesses, such as retailers and other industrial companies.

wholesaling The sale of goods to retailers, to industrial, commercial, institutional, or other professional business users, or to other wholesalers.

World Trade Organization (WTO) An international organization that regulates trade among participating countries and helps importers and exporters conduct their business.

yield management A strategy for maximizing revenue even when a firm has a fixed amount of something (goods, services, or capacity).

zero moment of truth (ZMOT) The moment when a customer uses a digital device to begin learning about a potential purchase.

COMPANY INDEX

NAME INDEX

SUBJECT INDEX